RICHARD J. TEWELES, Ph.D.
is Vice-President of Cambistics, Inc., one of the leading firms engaged in commodity research, training, futures trading, and consulting to several law firms and governmental organizations. Dr. Teweles is Professor of Finance, California State University at Long Beach. He has appeared daily on KWHY-TV (Los Angeles) on the various aspects of commodity trading and has authored a long list of publications on the subject.

CHARLES V. HARLOW, D.B.A.
is President of Cambistics, Inc. (see above), has lectured on commodities throughout the country for the Chicago Mercantile Exchange, authored a weekly column on commodities for the *Independent-Press Telegram* (Long Beach), and with Dr. Teweles appeared on KWHY-TV's daily commodity program (Los Angeles.) He has conducted training programs in commodities for Dean Witter, Inc., and written articles for such publications as *Financial Analysts Journal, Commodities, Journal of Commodity Trading.* Dr. Harlow is Professor of Finance, California State University at Long Beach.

HERBERT L. STONE, D.B.A.
is a well-known consultant to industry in the areas of systems analysis, cost effectiveness, and mathematical model building (for investments, estate planning, capital budgeting, etc.) He has conducted and chaired numerous meetings throughout the country on management science, accounting, and finance and, with coauthors Teweles and Harlow, is a contributor to the leading journals on commodities and finance. Dr. Stone is Professor of Management and Management Science, California State University at Long Beach.

The
Commodity
Futures
Game

The Commodity Futures Game

WHO WINS? WHO LOSES? WHY?

Richard J. Teweles

Charles V. Harlow

Herbert L. Stone

McGRAW-HILL BOOK COMPANY

New York   St. Louis   San Francisco   Düsseldorf   Johannesburg
Kuala Lumpur   London   Mexico   Montreal   New Delhi
Panama   Paris   São Paulo   Singapore
Sydney   Tokyo   Toronto

51310

Library of Congress Cataloging in Publication Data

Teweles, Richard Jack, date.
  The commodity futures game.

  Edition for 1969 published under title: The commodity
futures trading guide.
  Bibliography: pp. 611–630.
  1. Commodity exchanges. 2. Speculation.
I. Harlow, Charles Vendale, joint author. II. Stone,
Herbert L., date, joint author. III. Title.
HG6046.T45 1974   332.6′44   74–8223
ISBN 0–07–063726–1

1234567890 KPKP 7654

The editors for this book were W. Hodson Mogan, Aline Walton,
and Beatrice Carson, the designer was Naomi Auerbach,
and the production supervisor was Teresa F. Leaden.
It was set in Caledo by University Graphics, Inc.

Printed and bound by The Kingsport Press.

Dedicated to

Bill	*Jeff*	*Leslie*
Ted	*Pam*	*Brian*
	John	

Contents

EIGHTEEN   **Plywood and Lumber** **401**

NINETEEN   **Frozen Pork Bellies and Live Hogs** **423**

Preface

To prophesy is extremely difficult,
especially with respect to the future.
CHINESE PROVERB

As the quote above notes with delectable irony, the commodity futures game, like the stock-trading game, is not easy to play well. Consistent, profitable trading is a demanding exercise that requires superior knowledge, intelligently and consistently applied. Perhaps it is because we are old (over 30) and irascible, but it seems that the sun never sets on a day when there has not been an appalling volume of utter nonsense on the subject of trading stocks and commodities. The torrent of misinformation seems to be quite durable, despite occasional perceptive attacks on its flanks. Indeed, the sheer weight of ignorance reminds us of the truth of James Bryant Conant's remarks that bad theory is never overthrown merely by uncovering facts to the contrary, no matter how impressive their number; rather, bad theory is purged only by better theory.

The Commodity Futures Game: Who Wins? Who Loses? Why? attempts to organize most of what is known about commodity futures, from whatever source, mixed liberally with a total of more than forty years of trading experience, and to transmit a package in readable form to people who are, have been, or will be trading commodity futures. The idea is simply to provide the intelligent layman with a level of understanding that might take many years to acquire by his own experience.

To accomplish this, the book is divided into five sections and a bibliography. Section 1 introduces the basics of the game to the reader. The experienced trader is urged not to skip these early chapters. Chapter 4, for example, will arouse a special interest in the professional who may have explored some of its contents subjectively. The neophyte may find the concepts discussed here somewhat difficult on the first reading, but he may be assured that additional time spent in acquainting himself with the essential behavior of prices and the nature of the markets is far from wasted. Section 2 presents the most definitive treatment of actually playing the commodity futures game that has appeared to date. The trader is taken through the decision-making process in a thorough, decisive manner. He constructs his own trading curve, explores the fundamental and technical approach (including spreads and options), and is presented with a detailed discussion of the game plan, including an in-depth treatment of money management. Section 3 details the state-of-the-art in understanding why losers lose and why winners win. Satire and serious research are combined to analyze the results of the players, including the behavioral aspects of the game. Section 4 can well serve as a blueprint for broker and client awareness of a relationship that should entail more than a modicum of mutual trust. Section 5 offers a ready reference to facts and figures for 29 markets from soybeans to coconut oil, and it is hoped that the work in this section will make the volume valuable as a continuing reference for both broker and client. The bibliography is the most complete to be found in any work to date. References have been organized so that virtually all relevant material on commodity futures and related fields may be consulted.

Indebtedness for a book like this must run wide and deep, and therefore no attempt has been made to enumerate individually all those to whom we owe our thanks. However, in addition to those mentioned in *The Commodity Futures Trading Guide,* the successful sire to this work, some special notes of appreciation are in order.

The Food Research Institute of Stanford University has long been a source of consistently excellent work in the commodity futures field. Special thanks are due Holbrook Working and Roger Gray for their considerable contribution to the level of understanding of the futures markets.

The excellence of the chapter "The Technical Approach" is owed to our research partner at Cambistics, James Alphier, whose tireless efforts culminated in what we consider the definitive survey of technical analysis extant. In addition, his extensive comments and criticisms on other portions of the book were of continuing help.

Stephen Greenberg's decision to take time out from a busy schedule to review the entire manuscript resulted in several helpful suggestions and was a labor of love much appreciated. Helmut Weymar, President of Commodities Corporation, kindly supplied updated figures for the cocoa analysis in Chapter 6, and Walter Emery of the Commodity Research Bureau graciously provided us with considerable tabular material and chart data. John Howe kindly lent assistance in the early development of the Trading Profile Interview.

Mark Powers and Ron Frost of the Chicago Mercantile Exchange and B. T. Rocca and Walt Weissman of the Pacific Commodity Exchange contributed useful material for individual commodities. Jack Salmon, Keith Morgan, Warren Nelson, Lester Abbott, and Bill Bowen of the Clayton Brokerage Company, St. Louis, assisted in many continuing ways. Ted Teweles, Neal Oberg, Al Hammond, and Tom Garland spent hours gathering data for tables and figures. Special thanks go to Donna Doughty, who bravely served as translator for rough manuscript drafts, and to Margaret Buck, who helped in the final preparation. A note of thanks must go to all those who have taken Finance 488 at CSULB, where a blend of enthusiasm and intellectual curiosity has made the commodity markets exciting subjects for serious inquiry.

Finally, each of us would be remiss if we failed to express our enduring gratitude to our wives and children, who gave cheerfully of portions of the time to which they were most clearly entitled.

In spite of all the help received, implicit and explicit, errors of omission and commission inevitably will remain. These are the sole province of the undersigned, who promise to give cheerful consideration to their remedy at some time in the future.

Richard J. Teweles
Charles V. Harlow
Herbert L. Stone

**The
Commodity
Futures
Game**

Basics of the Game

*A stock and a commodity trader were good friends and com-
pared notes often on trading philosophies. When the stock
trader fell on bad times with a series of losses, he was forced
to sell his membership. Before leaving for another line of
work, he reflected with his commodity trader friend. "Your
trouble is that you weren't over here with me trading commodities," confided the friend. "But I don't know anything
about commodities," the crestfallen stock trader replied.*

*In one way or another the advice, "You've got to know the
territory," has been profered for centuries. The four chapters
in this section are an effort to introduce the reader to "the
territory" of commodity futures.*

*In Chapter 1, "Why Trade Commodity Futures?," the idea of
speculation, as well as the specific evolution of trading in commodities, is discussed. Because many potential commodity
traders have had experience in securities, specific similarities
and differences in the two areas are noted.*

*Chapter 2, "The Nature of the Commodity Futures Markets,"
places the trader in the environment in which he is to operate. The nature of contracts, the markets for those contracts,
who plays the game, and the nature of cash and futures prices
are discussed in order that the trader may appreciate the relationships involved in market and trader performance.*

*Chapter 3, "The Mechanics of Commodity Trading," helps
the trader to choose a broker and to understand clearly the
procedures of opening and maintaining a commodity trading
account. Contract information, types of order, regulatory requirements, and tax considerations are not heady stuff, but
avoiding problems in these areas is imperative.*

*Chapter 4, "The Behavior of Commodity Futures Prices,"
lays the vital groundwork for a clear understanding of the
behavior of prices, the relation between past and future price
changes, and the question of trends.*

CHAPTER ONE

Why Trade Commodity Futures?

> When asked why he continued speculating, James R.
> Keene, a famous speculator, replied, "Why does a dog
> chase his thousandth rabbit? All life is a speculation.
> The spirit of speculation is born with men."
> BERNARD BARUCH, *Baruch: My Own Story*

INTRODUCTION

This is a book about trading commodity futures. Trading is an activity that cuts across many disciplines—economics, sociology, and psychology are three of the most obvious. Futures trading is carried on by individuals involved with the cash commodity and by floor traders and speculators as well. Speculators account for more than half the dollar value of the open interest in commodity futures, yet perhaps there is no other field in which there is more interest and less knowledge among the participants.

In this first chapter the economic role of the speculator and the history of trading from Phoenician beginnings are presented. Attacks on trading as an institution are included and speculation as an activity is analyzed, as are the specific differences between commodities and securities. A final section, "Should you speculate?", leads the trader to considerations that, although personal, must include general criteria.

ECONOMIC FUNCTION OF THE SPECULATOR

The usual justification made for speculation in commodities is simple. Futures trading is beneficial to the public which ultimately consumes the goods traded in the futures markets. The benefit most often considered primary is the probability that the hedging of commodities allows the risk of price changes to be shifted; hence the cost of production, marketing, or processing is reduced. If this is true, and if the cost savings achieved are passed on to consumers, futures trading will benefit the consumers on whose behalf the economy is supposed to function. Futures markets provide other important benefits, such as continuous, accurate, well-publicized price information and continuous liquid markets. Without the speculator futures markets could not function; therefore, if the futures markets operate for the social good, the speculator who makes the operation possible must also contribute to the social good. Speculators attempt to anticipate what prices are going to do and, by taking appropriate positions in the futures markets, make a profit if their judgment proves correct. They may or may not be correct and therefore may or may not make a profit, but in their very effort to do so they do enough trading to provide the necessary base for liquid futures markets and thereby raise the efficiency of commodity marketing. Sometimes speculators are accused of making markets unstable by virtue of their speculation, but it is not necessary for them to prove that they earn their profits, if they do earn any, by stabilizing or destabilizing prices; they earn the opportunity to profit merely by being in the market, hence making the market possible. Furthermore, there is no proof that speculators destabilize prices, and at least one study has demonstrated that the speculator probably moderates rather than accentuates price volatility.[1]

Not only is the volume of business done by trade hedgers at any given time frequently too small to provide the liquidity necessary for an efficient market, but a preponderance of hedgers frequently tends to want to buy at the same time or sell at the same time, and the speculator is needed to take the other side of some of these trades.

SPECULATING OR GAMBLING?

There are many who regard "speculation" and "gambling" as synonymous terms. One hears of "investing in securities" and "gambling in commodities." Even some relatively sophisticated investors consider commodity trading to be one step removed from a Nevada casino. Others regard speculation and gambling as distinctly different activities. The usual differentiation is based on the nature of risk and the social good. Gambling involves the creation of a risk for the sole purpose of someone taking it. The horse race, poker game, and roulette wheel themselves create risks that would not be present without them. Gamblers are willing to accept these risks in return for the opportunity to win some money. No particular social good is accomplished unless one believes that gambling provides a needed outlet for the gamblers whose needs might be satisfied by something worse if they could not gamble.

---

[1] *Margins, Speculation, and Prices in Grains Futures Markets,* Economic Research Service, U.S. Department of Agriculture, 1967.

Speculation, on the contrary, deals in risks that are necessarily present in the process of marketing goods in a free capitalistic system. As a soybean crop grows and is harvested, concentrated, and dispersed, the obvious risks of price changes must be taken by those who own the soybeans or have commitments to buy them, either in their original form or as oil or meal. These risks would be present whether futures markets existed or not. If the speculator were unwilling to take them, someone else would have to do so. Unlike the gambler who causes a game to be created merely to satisfy his desire to gamble, the speculator does not inject risk into the economy merely because he is willing to speculate.

The truth of the matter seems to lie somewhere between these two points of view. If hedgers operated in the futures markets solely to reduce their risks, passed their savings on to consumers, and the speculator made this all possible, there could be little quarrel with the argument that his services had social value. Actually, hedgers operate in the futures markets primarily to increase their profits and not just to reduce their risks. If they believe that to hedge against their inventories or to make forward sale commitments is the best course of action, they will do so. If they believe that a partial hedge is adequate, they might well hedge only part of their risk. In some cases, if they are quite certain that their judgment of the future course of prices is correct, they might carry their entire risk unhedged. Such selective hedging is far more common than is implied in many standard texts, which indicate that all risks are hedged and that most hedges work perfectly or nearly so.

Furthermore, many firms are not above attempting to take advantage of apparent opportunities in the futures markets by taking positions parallel with their cash positions—which, of course, amounts to speculations that increase risk rather than hedges that reduce it. If such speculation is successful, it works for the good of the company and its owners, and insofar as the economy is benefited by the health of companies and their owners it is also benefited by the speculation. If speculation of this kind proves unsuccessful, however, and the company, its owners, and its customers are damaged, it is difficult to argue that the speculators who took the other side of the trade and made it possible benefited anybody.

The motivation of many individual speculators could well be identical with that of gamblers; that is, they are willing to take relatively large risks in return for the chance to gain large profits. In addition, they may derive some pleasure from the activity of trading, just as the gambler derives excitement from his game and not just from the monetary result of his gambling. The major difference is that the activities of commodity speculators are essential to hedging, which, on balance, is apparently beneficial to the social good.

THE EVOLUTION OF FUTURES TRADING

Trade carried on over great distances is an ancient activity of mankind. The great trade networks of the Phoenician, Greek, Roman, and Byzantine empires were primary sources of economic power for these old civilizations. Because of the great distances and the hazards of travel, trading was done only on barter and cash-and-carry bases.

The decline of the Roman Empire in Europe resulted in the rise of disorganized and hostile European feudal states. This system of self-sufficient feudal manors undermined the basic exchange of goods among peoples of widely separated lands. When the urban tradition of Rome disappeared in early medieval Europe, only a few cities in the south of France and in Italy retained their ties with distant Eastern trade depots. During the Middle Ages economic and political stability slowly returned. In the eleventh and twelfth centuries several feudal monarchs succeeded in expanding their land holdings and their authority and thereby sowed the seeds of the modern European state system.

By the twelfth century two great trading centers had begun to flourish on the European continent as a result of a general revival in trade. In northern Italy the cities of Venice, Florence, Genoa, Pisa, and Milan competed for trading rights with the Orient and also sought to expand their trade throughout Europe. At the same time northern European trade centered about the region of Flanders (now Holland and Belgium). This area, known since Roman times for its fine cloth, developed strong economic ties with England, which was then the most important wool-producing area in Europe. The Italian traders, specializing in such luxuries as fine silk, spices, rare metals, and exotic perfumes, crossed the paths of the Flemish traders of cloth, wine, salt fish, lumber, and metalware on land held by the Counts of Champagne. Evidence shows that as early as 1114 the Counts of Champagne had established trade fairs to encourage mercantile activity from which they extracted fees. It was at these markets in Champagne during the twelfth century that the first use of forward contracts in Europe probably occurred.[2]

Once established, the market fairs became the chief centers of international exchange in Europe. Traders came not only from Flanders and Italy but from Scandinavia, England, and even Russia. The Counts of Champagne provided the traders with protection, money changers, and even storage facilities. Trade fairs were eventually held on a year-round basis, rotating initially among several raw materials and manufactured goods but eventually specializing in only one or a few related commodities; for example, linen and wool at Troyes and leather and skins at Reims.[3]

Generally, the last few days of each fair were reserved for paying bills and settling the bargains struck during the fair. Because traders at the fairs often came from widely dissimilar geographical and ethnic back-

---

[2] J. K. Sowards, *Western Civilization to 1660,* St. Martin's Press, New York, 1965, pp. 10, 384, and 391; Lee Dee Belveal, *Commodity Trading Manual,* Chicago Board of Trade, 1966, p. 3-a.

[3] Henry H. Bakken, *Theory of Markets and Marketing,* Mimir Publishers, Madison, Wis., 1952, p. 317.

grounds, disputes often arose over the settling of accounts, and because of these disputes a code of commercial law, called the "law merchant," was slowly developed. Violators of the code were taken before "courts of the fair" which were manned by the merchants themselves.

This emerging medieval code of mercantile law performed much the same function as the regulations established by today's commodity exchanges. It defined contract terms, determined methods of sampling, inspecting, and grading the commodity in question, and set down the location and date for delivery of the goods. Although most transactions were of a spot nature, an innovation of the medieval fairs was the use of a document called a *lettre de faire* as a forward contract which specified the delivery of goods at a later date.[4] Although these *lettres de faire* were first issued only in the sale of cash commodities between a single buyer and seller, they later evolved into negotiable documents which might be transferred to several parties before arriving at the warehouse where the specified goods were stored. Because of the difficulties of travel, many merchants preferred to bring only samples of their merchandise to the fairs, and the *lettre de faire* helped to make trade by sample satisfactory to both buyer and seller. Its functions became similar to the bill of exchange widely used today.[5] In addition, it had some characteristics of the modern warehouse receipt. Signed by a reputable merchant in a distant city to indicate that a specified commodity was being held in his warehouse, the receipt *(lettre de faire)* could be sold to a third party who would, in turn, either sell or take possession of the purchased goods. The forward contract trading by merchants in the late Middle Ages was in many respects like the modern commodity futures contract but differed in that the forward trades were not standardized and were consummated on a more personal basis.

Following the establishment of the Champagne market fairs, and later others like them at Bruges, Antwerp, and Amsterdam, and the proved viability of the representative sample as the basis for a commodity transaction, England created year-round meeting places at which traders could buy and sell commodities and manufactured goods. These meeting places were known as exchanges, an early example being the Royal Exchange opened in London in 1570. The Royal Exchange was later divided into specialized exchanges known as a group as the London Commodity Exchange.

Dealers soon began acting in the London commodity exchanges as middlemen willing to absorb price risks that the merchants wished to avoid in return for the opportunity to profit in forward transactions. Although spot, or cash, trades remained the essential part of the market, increasingly large numbers of traders took advantage of the forward contracts.

---

[4] W. C. Labys and C. W. J. Granger, *Speculation, Hedging, and Commodity Price Forecasts,* D. C. Heath and Co., Lexington, Mass., 1970, p. 3.

[5] Belveal, *loc. cit.*

As the system evolved, sellers sold their goods to middlemen who would, in turn, seek out a prospective buyer. In this way sellers were almost certain to dispose of their goods at reasonable prices and buyers could expect standardized levels of quality from dealers who offered goods for resale. At this point in the development of the marketing process grading systems and true futures contracts had not yet been devised, but they were on the horizon.

DEVELOPMENT OF THE FUTURES CONTRACT

The first recorded case of organized futures trading occurred in Japan during the 1600s.[6] Wealthy landowners and feudal lords of Imperial Japan found themselves squeezed between an expanding money economy in the cities and their primarily agrarian-based resources. The rents that they collected from their feudal tenants were paid in the form of a share of each year's rice harvest. This income was irregular and subject to uncontrollable factors such as weather and other seasonal characteristics. Because the money economy required that the nobility have ready cash on hand at all times, income instability stimulated the practice of shipping surplus rice to the principal cities of Osaka and Edo, where it could be stored and sold as needed. In an effort to raise cash quickly, landlords soon began selling tickets (warehouse receipts) against goods stored in rural or urban warehouses. Merchants generally bought these tickets in anticipation of their projected needs (they also suffered at times from the fluctuations of uncertain harvests).[7]

Eventually "rice tickets" became generally acceptable as a form of currency to facilitate the transaction of business. At times, however, stored rice reserves were inadequate to meet the needs of the nobility, and when this happened many merchants extended credit at interest to the landlord before the actual sale of the rice tickets.

During the late seventeenth century the Japanese Dojima rice market was characterized by the fact that only trading in futures contracts was permitted. By 1730 the Tokugawa Shogunate, or Imperial government, designated and officially recognized the market as *cho-ai-mai*, or, literally, "rice trade on book." A number of rules of the *cho-ai-mai-kaisho* (the market place) were strikingly similar to the rules of modern American futures trading[8]:

1. Contract term duration was limited.
2. All contracts within any term were standardized.
3. A basic grade for any contract period was agreed on beforehand.
4. No contract could be carried over into a new contract period.

[6] Henry H. Bakken, "Futures Trading–Origin, Development and Present Economic Status," *Futures Trading Seminar*, Vol. II, Mimir Publishers, Madison, Wis., 1953, p. 9.

[7] *Ibid.*, p. 10.

[8] *Ibid.*, p.11.

5. All trades had to be cleared through a clearinghouse.

6. Every trader had to establish a line of credit with the clearinghouse of his choice.

The major difference between the *cho-ai-mai* market and today's futures market was that delivery of cash commodites was never actually permitted. This "futures trading only" concept caused the futures cash-price relationship to function improperly and resulted in erratic price fluctuations. In 1869 this discrepancy between prices in the spot (cash) market and those of the futures market prompted the Imperial government to order trading stopped. Testifying to the essential futures trading function of maintaining an orderly market, fluctuations in the cash price of rice reached chaotic proportions less than two years after the discontinuance of the *cho-ai-mai* futures market, and a disgruntled Imperial regime was forced to reopen it.[9] Significantly, physical delivery of goods was then allowed, and as a result the Japanese futures market was effectively wedded to the cash market, thus eliminating its initial instability.

It appears that the practice of tying the cash market to the futures market in Japan may have been influenced by Western trading practices on the Oriental rice-ticket market. As the economy in the United States expanded during the early part of the nineteenth century, commodity exchanges evolved from unorganized club-type associations into formalized exchanges, the first of which was the Chicago Board of Trade, established in 1848 with 82 members. Trading in Chicago was encouraged considerably by the trading standards, inspection system, and weighing system prescribed by the board.

It was on the Chicago Board of Trade on March 13, 1851, that the first time contract was recorded. This contract authorized the delivery of 3,000 bushels of corn to be made in June at a price one cent per bushel below the March 13 price.[10]

The major commodity exchanges in the United States were established and are still situated in Chicago and New York. These sites were logically chosen because of their proximity to the major transport routes. New York, with its port located on the major ocean shipping routes, was ideally suited for international trade. Chicago, situated at the hub of rail and canal routes extending into the agricultural heartlands of the United States, inherited the bulk of internal trade.

Around the mid-nineteenth century forward contracts known as "to arrive" contracts, similar in nature to the medieval *lettre de faire,* gradually made their appearance. It was the accumulation of excess supplies at some times and their shortage at others in the expanding American money economy that caused the modification of the traditional cash-and-carry

[9] Labys and Granger, *op. cit.,* p. 6.

[10] H. S. Irwin, *Evolution of Futures Trading,* Mimir Publishers, Madison, Wis., 1954.

transaction. The first of these time contracts was not much more than a verbal agreement or a simple memorandum exchanged by both parties.

Because of the increase in the volume of trading at Chicago, the risk in forward contracts became too great to be transferred to middlemen or specialized dealers, which was the common practice in the London markkets at the time, but if another kind of middleman—a third party—could be induced to assume the risk the effect would be the same, namely the assurance of a fair price for the seller and a reasonably uniform quality of product.

Although the first "to arrive" contracts were not transferable, the printed documents that were developed to specify the grade, quantity, and time of delivery of the goods soon were.[11] These alterations to the "to-arrive" contracts resulted in the creation of a futures market in this country in which a contract was readily tradeable before delivery. The middleman drawn into the newly evolved marketing structure in the United States was the speculator on whom the risk was placed.

Because of the volume of the futures contracts traded at Chicago and the replacement of the London-type dealer by the speculator, additional rules for orderly and fair futures trading had to be drawn[12]:

1. The commodity selected for trading had to be easily graded.

2. The grading of commodities had to be maintained by regular governmental inspection.

3. Payment had to be set at the time of delivery.

4. Prices had to be reported openly and be equally accessible to all traders.

5. Buyers and sellers were required to establish financial responsibility.

6. The number of buyers and sellers had to remain large enough to provide continuous opportunities for trade.

As already noted, the rules established in Chicago were much like those of the Japanese rice futures market of earlier date.

Futures trading on the Chicago Board of Trade quickly reached sizeable proportions and was rapidly adopted by other exchanges. In New York futures trading had begun on the New York Produce Exchange and on the New York Cotton Exchange by 1870. That same year futures trading was initiated on the New Orleans Cotton Exchange, and by 1885 the New York Coffee Exchange was actively trading in futures. Since the second half of the nineteenth century a number of other commodity exchanges have been founded.

During America's history of futures trading some commodities, such as wheat, have retained their popularity with the trading public. Others, such as silk, butter, and pepper, have lost favor because of insufficient trading volume for a variety of reasons. Some, such as cotton and coffee,

---

[11] Bakken, *op. cit.*, p. 104.

[12] Labys and Granger, *op. cit.*, p. 6.

failed in interest for a number of years but regained popularity later. The American commodity futures market has now developed into a vast and complex institution consisting of 10 major and about a dozen minor exchanges on which approximately 40 commodities are traded and a large clearing-house system. It is based on widely acceptable standardized futures contracts. With the exception of a short period during World War II, when the markets were closed, the growth of this institution has been continuous since about 1865 and in recent years has accelerated enormously. The history of the commodity futures trading in the United States, however, has not been problem free.

ATTACKS AGAINST FUTURES TRADING

Futures trading has been subject to varying degrees of criticism as long as it has been in existence. Opposition grew particularly severe during the 1890s, when considerable legislation was proposed to restrict loose business practices of many kinds. In Germany all futures trading in grains was actually forbidden by a law passed in 1896, although the law was repealed four years later.

In the United States commodity exchanges were widely considered to be gambling dens full of parasitic speculators who drained off money that should have gone instead to producers or consumers of products. There were, and sometimes still are, attempts by the federal and certain state governments to abolish futures trading in whole or in part. In 1867 the Illinois Legislature passed an act that provided that the parties to futures contracts, referred to in the act as gambling contracts, should be fined $1,000 and imprisoned up to one year in the Cook County Jail. Seven members of the Board of Trade in Chicago were actually arrested under this act. Although it was repealed the following year, many more than 100 other bills to abolish futures trading have been introduced in the United States Congress alone.

In 1890 one Congressman Butterworth of Ohio introduced a bill to place a prohibitive tax on dealers in futures, and, during the ensuing debate, Representative Funston of Kansas described the futures market as follows:

> Those who deal in "options" and "futures" contracts, which is mere gambling, no matter by what less offensive name such transactions be designated, neither add to the supply nor increase the demand for consumption, nor do they accomplish any useful purpose by their calling; but on the contrary, they speculate in fictitious products. The wheat they buy and sell is known as "wind wheat" and doubtless for the reason that it is invisible, intangible, and felt or realized only in the terrible force it exerts in destroying the farming industry of the country.

Although Congressman Butterworth's bill failed to pass, agitation continued, and in 1892 Senator Washburn, speaking in the United States Senate, asserted:

As near as I can learn, and from the best information I have been able to obtain on the Chicago Board of Trade, at least 95% of the sales of that Board
are of this fictitious character, where no property is actually owned, no property sold or delivered, or expected to be delivered but simply wagers or bets
as to what that property may be worth at a designated time in the future. . . .
Wheat and cotton have become as much gambling tools as chips on the faro-
bank table. The property of the wheat grower and the cotton grower is treated
as though it were a "stake" put on the gambling table at Monte Carlo. The producer of wheat is compelled to see the stocks in his barn dealt with like the
peas of a thimblerigger, or the cards of a three-card-monte man. Between the
grain-producer and loaf eater, there has stepped in a "parasite" between them
robbing them both.[13]

Another bill that would have imposed a prohibitive tax on all futures trading in farm products failed to pass Congress in 1893 only because final
action before Congress adjourned required a suspension of the rules of the
House of Representatives and the necessary two-thirds majority vote failed
by the narrow margin of 172 to 124. A similar bill considered by the next
Congress actually passed the House but this time failed to gain approval
of the Senate.[14]

Almost all the bills designed to abolish or restrict futures trading died
before reaching a vote or were defeated. After World War II, however, the
continuing demands for restrictive legislation were largely concentrated
on two unrelated markets: onions and potatoes. In both cases the futures
markets were blamed for causing wide fluctuations in prices that inflicted
severe losses on the producers, processors, and marketers of these products. In previous attacks on futures trading those engaged in the production and marketing of the products traded were among the most vocal
defenders of the futures markets. This time they were among the attackers.
In particular, trading in onions was attacked by those who were supposed
to benefit from the existence of the market as well as by the usual unsuccessful speculators. The market had few defenders other than the Chicago
Mercantile Exchange, whose members did not relish losing the futures market in one of the products traded exclusively on that exchange.

After several years of argument Congress passed a bill in 1958 to prohibit futures trading in onions. The onion crop is a minor one, grown only
in limited areas, but those engaged in the business of trading futures did
not take the prohibition lightly. The Chicago Mercantile Exchange appealed
to a United States District Court to get the prohibition set aside as uncon-
stitutional, but the attempt failed. Some believe that those engaged in the
onion trade who attacked futures trading were really concerned, as they

[13] From a speech entitled "Regulation and Supervision of Futures Trading," by Bernard P.
Carey, Chairman, Chicago Board of Trade, delivered at a futures trading seminar April 28–30,
1965, at the Chicago Board of Trade.

[14] Holbrook Working, *"Futures Markets Under Renewed Attack."* Reprinted from *Food Research Institute Studies*, 4, No. 1 (1963).

maintained, about the wide fluctuations in price. Others believe that they were actually more interested in having accurate price information somewhat less publicized in order to capitalize on the ignorance of the farmers and consumers. The truth will probably never really be known, but there is some suspicion that the latter provided at least some basis for the trade's lack of enthusiasm for the futures market.

A similar law to prohibit trading in potatoes was considered several times during the years that followed. Although it was given serious consideration, it was not passed.

Although the equating of speculation in the futures markets with gambling is somewhat illogical, there were other reasons for the hue and cry. There has always been a widespread feeling that profits from speculation are somehow immoral, compared with profits from other seemingly more productive activities, although the concept of compensation received by other risk bearers, such as insurance companies, does not seem to cause similar resentment. This is the same sort of vague opposition that many people feel toward selling a commodity or security short. Somehow they believe that a price going up is good and a price going down is bad, and, furthermore, that the short seller not only thinks that it will go down but makes it do so by selling short.

There are consistent and loud complaints by those who have lost money in commodities and who are reluctant to believe that their losses are caused by their own failings. They prefer to blame factors beyond their control, which helps to restore their faith in themselves, if not their money.

For long periods of time the United States witnessed falling commodity prices even as the prices of finished goods rose. This divergence was caused by a number of factors which were difficult to understand by many and proved even more difficult to correct by those who did understand. It was easy for the farmer, who believed that he was paying too much for his food and clothing, to blame the speculator, who appeared to be making considerable money without growing or producing anything tangible.

A common criticism of commodity speculation is that it causes violent price moves, which work considerable hardship on those engaged in more productive pursuits. Wide publicity is given to the relatively rare but highly dramatic manipulations that cause many to conclude that speculation is not only gambling but that the game is dishonest besides. Almost any public speaker talking about commodity trading can be sure that someone in the audience will ask about "that big soybean oil scandal of a few years ago" or some similar incident.[15]

Speculators can point to equally scandalous events in all types of busi-

---

[15] The Allied Crude Vegetable Oil Refining Corp., under the leadership of its president, Anthony De Angelis, went bankrupt in 1963 and caused substantial losses to a large number of prominent banks, brokers, and commodity dealers and is considered to be one of the largest business frauds in recent history. The scandal was, however, based primarily on the issuance of fraudulent warehouse receipts rather than on any failure of the commodity futures markets.

ness at all times and in all countries, but no responsible person wants to declare all types of business activity illegal. Manipulative devices, such as artificial corners, wash sales, spreading of false rumors, and the "bucketing" of orders are illegal. All such activities are an abuse of speculative practice and certainly not an integral part of it. Nor does the fact that speculators are essential to the operation of commodity futures markets mean that they dominate these markets. Major price movements are usually caused by basic changes in the supply or demand, or both, for a given product and only rarely by a group of speculators successfully creating self-fulfilling prophecies.

Considerable research has been done in an attempt to prove that speculation does or does not cause excessive price movement. No final conclusions can yet be drawn on this subject, but the weight of evidence indicates that speculation probably does more to smooth price fluctuation than to increase it. Even the demise of the much maligned onion market did something to prove this point. The fluctuations in the price of cash onions apparently were greater both before there was a futures market and after it was prohibited than while the market was functioning. There is no doubt that the presence of speculative traders results in more transactions than would take place without their activities, but to conclude that more transactions in themselves cause more price variation than there would otherwise be is unwarranted by the facts.

WHY DO SPECULATORS SPECULATE?

The specific motivation or combination of motivations of all the millions of speculators could not be discussed here in any detail even if reliable data were available. The broad incentives that attract most speculators are quite clear, however, and can be summarized briefly.

Certainly the greatest is the opportunity to make an important amount of money in relation to the capital base used. Not many speculators are naïve enough to compare their activities with those of investors. Most of them are well aware of the risks that they take in return for the large and quick profits possible, although there are some who, like gamblers, are so convinced that they will win that they are unable to admit even to themselves that they might lose. Most of them learn all too quickly that it is a rare opportunity indeed that provides an important potential profit without an attendant large risk.

Other speculators are attracted almost as much by the stimulation of the speculation itself as they are by the opportunity for profit. For some it is the sheer excitement of the game; for others, it is the dynamics of the involvement with world politics, trade, currency fluctuation, wars, and other events that come to affect their own positions rather than just provide newspaper headlines. Aside from those who receive some masochistic pleasure from losing, it seems likely that even those motivated in large part by the desire to have something to get up for in the morning find the pleasure of speculating more satisfying when they win than when they lose.

SPECULATE IN WHAT?

The desire of man to speculate has always been so strong and widespread that hundreds of examples could be mentioned. Historically, there are some that are difficult even to comprehend today. One of the more fantastic is the trading that took place in tulip bulbs in Holland in 1634 to 1637. The high regard for the tulip held by society leaders spread throughout the country and reached the point at which everybody seemed willing to part with almost anything for rare tulip bulbs. Trading became frantic, and prices rose until entire fortunes were paid for bulbs. When the mania had run its course, the economy of Holland was shattered and it was years before it recovered.

Similar effects were felt in the eighteenth century from the Mississippi land schemes of John Law in France and the South Sea Bubble that was perpetrated on the English public. The latter created a mood that fostered a rash of some of the most fantastic schemes in the history of finance and caused the ruin of thousands of people. There was the huge subscription for a company that was to manufacture a perpetual-motion wheel. A company was formed to repair and rebuild parsonage and vicarage houses, and among others were companies to supply London with sea coal, rebuild every house in England, settle the island of Blanco and Sal Tarthgus, repave the streets of London, insure horses, and transmute quicksilver into a malleable fine metal. The most preposterous of all was "A company for carrying on an undertaking of great advantage, but nobody to know what it is." Subscribers were to buy 5,000 shares at 100 pounds each, with a 2-pound deposit. An annual return of 100 pounds for each share was promised, details to be announced in a month. The issue was oversubscribed in five hours, and the promoter left for the Continent that same night and was never heard from again.[16]

In the United States the Florida land boom of the 1920s was comparable to its predecessor bubbles. The results of the worldwide 1929 stock break are well known.

Some areas of speculation have been popular for many years. These include land, precious stones and metals, natural resources such as oil, rare items such as stamps, coins, and paintings, and securities, such as stocks, bonds, warrants, and options to buy or sell stocks.

The types and degree of skill needed for success may vary among these areas, as will the amount of capital required and the mechanics of buying and selling the items. In each case, however, the attraction is the profit possible, the stimulation received from the activity, or their combination. Certain of these items have characteristics that attract some speculators and repel others. The general characteristics of the commodity futures markets are, in some respects, unique.

[16] Charles Mackay, *Extraordinary Popular Delusions and the Madness of Crowds*, London, 1841. Reprinted in 1932 by L. C. Page & Co., Boston, p. 55.

COMMODITY FUTURES VERSUS SECURITIES AND OTHER SPECULATIONS

One reason for the popularity of commodity trading is undoubtedly the ease with which it may be done. Most brokerage houses deal in commodity futures as well as in securities. Some have research departments of their own and others subscribe to various services, but in either case the speculator looking for a suggested commodity position will have little difficulty in finding one. Some individual registered representatives choose not to handle commodity trades, preferring to specialize in securities or mutual funds, but in such cases other registered representatives in the same office are likely to be available. Few are really expert in commodity trading nor do they claim to be, but most are at least able to enter or close out positions efficiently and to pass pertinent information on to the trader if he wants it. In addition to full-line wire houses, there are firms that specialize in the handling of commodity business. They usually have a considerable amount of factual information available and are especially adept at the order and clerical end of the business, but there is no reason to believe that their market opinions are any better or worse than anyone else's.

Commodity speculators who prefer to make their own decisions may be attracted by the relative ease of securing information. Important political and economic information is readily available in general and trade newspapers. Vital supply and demand information concerning specific commodities is published in large quantities by various government departments and bureaus (particularly the Department of Agriculture) and is made available at frequent intervals. In addition to being mailed at low or no cost to anybody who requests it, such information is widely publicized in financial journals and on news wires. An adequate amount of accurate information about the handful of commodities that trade actively is considerably easier to obtain than about the tens of thousands of stocks, bonds, and mutual funds that are available. The problem faced by those who gather basic information about stocks or commodities is quite similar. To date no model clearly superior to a random walk has been published to describe the behavior of stock and commodity futures prices. Stock traders, however, may be able to take advantage of some slight trend tendencies and long-run cycles and commodity traders may be able to isolate some conditioned seasonals. Traders in stocks and commodities are both faced with the results of information that becomes available while markets are closed, which means that markets are as "active" then as they are when they are open. In both securities and commodities there are significant covariances among the prices of stocks representing related industries and among interrelated commodities such as feeds or edible oils.[17]

 A basic difference between commodity and stock markets is that commodity markets are primary and stock markets are secondary. The com-

---

[17] Labys and Granger, *op. cit.*, pp. 268–270.

modity speculator in the long run must be concerned primarily with the real forces of supply and demand. The speculator in stocks must know the markets of the company in whose stock he is speculating and the market for the stock itself, in which case he must be concerned with the influence of floor specialists whose influence on price is somewhat controversial but exists to some significant degree with little doubt.

Like the stock trader, the commodity trader has an advantage in his liquidity over speculators in most other areas. There is seldom any difficulty in finding a buyer or seller at any time for even large positions, although, of course, the price may not be so favorable as desired. Positions can normally be acquired or disposed of within a minute or two when the exchanges are open, but if markets are active an actual report of the transaction might not be received that promptly. There is no need to search out a buyer or seller or wait for an auction, as there would be in trading in paintings, and no loans to arrange or escrows to close, as in trading property.

The commodity trader, unlike the stock trader, must consider the limits that restrict the amount a commodity price can rise or fall in one day and the range over which it may trade. These "limit moves" probably concern the unsophisticated trader far more than they should. For one thing the typical trader will seldom encounter them in a commodity in which he actually has a position. In addition, of course, he is hardly anxious about limit moves in a direction favorable to him. His freedom of action is also not restricted by an adverse limit move that does not carry beyond the level of risk he was prepared to assume.

What does worry him is the possibility of an adverse limit move that will prevent him from liquidating his position with a reasonable loss. It should be made clear that a limit move does not cause a market to close; it merely prohibits trades at prices beyond the limit. On reaching the maximum possible advance or decline a market may trade any number of times at that level or trade in away from the limit. The purpose of limiting a move is to prevent unreasonable price moves based on undue reaction to news. Securities markets deal with similar situations either by suspending trading until a fair and orderly market is again possible or by allowing prices to move over a large and (it may be noted) unlimited range. For a trader liquidity under the first condition is no better than in the commodity markets when a market has advanced its permissible limit.[18]

Commodity margins differ from stock margins both in concept and method of computation. Stock margins constitute a partial payment to the broker. The remainder, or debit balance, in a margin account is a debt owed to the broker on which interest is charged. The amount of the debt is limited by the Federal Reserve, the stock exchange, or the broker himself. Commodity margins are actually good-faith deposits to protect a broker

[18] C. V. Harlow and R. J. Teweles, "Commodities and Securities Compared," *Financial Analysts Journal* (September–October 1972), 65–66.

against risk in the event of adverse price moves in the interim between the establishment of a position and its limitation either by delivery or offset. Payment for the cash commodity need be made only in the highly unlikely event that delivery is actually made or taken.

Stock margins required typically fluctuate in a range of 50 to 90 percent, although both limits of this range have been exceeded for brief periods. Commodity margins are based on fixed minimums per bushel or per contract established by the commodity exchanges, but individual brokers may require larger amounts if they believe the minimum involves undue risk for themselves or their clients. Requirements amounting to 5 to 10 percent of contract value are common, although the amount may be even less than 5 percent in low-risk spread positions. The margin on 5,000 bushels of corn, for example, might typically be about 6 to 8 cents a bushel, with corn selling at $1.25 to $1.50. On a contract value of as much as $7,500 the deposit required would be only $300 to $400. If 5,000 bushels of May corn were bought against the sale of 5,000 bushels of July corn, the total margin required might be as low as $100 for the entire position. When markets become unusually volatile, margins may be raised to protect the broker from his client and, perhaps, the client from himself. Even at such times margins of as much as 20 percent of the contract value are unusual.

The low margins not only provide the opportunity to establish large positions on a small capital base but also give the commodity markets their somewhat undeserved reputation for extreme price volatility. Commodity prices frequently remain in quite narrow ranges for long periods of time and are not more volatile than typical security prices in similar price ranges. The price movements of commodities, however, relative to margin required, can create large profits or losses relative to the available trading capital. If a trader finds the moves too great for his capital or nerve, all he need do is utilize more margin than is required and trade on a more conservative basis. Too many traders take advantage of the possible potentials without accepting or recognizing the accompanying risks by fully utilizing the available leverage. This is why it is often maintained that bulls or bears can trade profitably, but not hogs.

The cost of trading commodities is low in relation to trading in other areas. Commissions paid are usually less, considering the value of the merchandise traded, than those in land, precious goods, paintings, prints, or securities. Computation is simpler because commissions are based on the number of contracts bought or sold and are unrelated to the amount of money involved in a transaction, as they are in the security markets; for example, regardless of its price, the commission on 5,000 bushels of wheat, which is equivalent to a security round lot, is a total of $30 which covers both the purchase and sale. The entire $30 is charged against the customer's account when he liquidates his position rather than $15 at the time of entry and $15 on liquidation.

The amount of record keeping required by a commodity trader is minimal unless he holds a position so large that it must be reported to the Commodity Exchange Authority. Reportable and maximum limits are so great that they are only of academic interest to most traders.

Tax rules covering profits and losses on commodity positions are quite similar to those covering securities in that both are capital items. There are fewer long-term gains in commodities because so many traders take their profits or losses more quickly than stock traders, but nothing precludes their waiting for long-term capital gains if conditions permit. In contrast to the case for securities, there are no state or federal taxes on the purchase or sale of commodity positions.

The commodity markets operate under regulations of the exchanges and in the case of regulated commodities, by the Commodity Exchange Authority, an arm of the Department of Agriculture. There is no trade association operating in a manner comparable to the NASD.

There are those who are fond of pointing out that the commodity trader who is long in a contract of a commodity in the spot month risks getting delivery of a commodity that he really does not want. They usually refer to a person, whom they invariably do not know personally, who forgot that he owned wheat and came home to find it piled on his front lawn. In reality, the commodity trader has less to worry about concerning deliveries than the security trader. If he is short, he cannot get delivery at all. If he is long, he can avoid delivery merely by selling his position before the contract month arrives. If he carries his position into the contract month, there is still no certainty that he will get delivery; but if he does he most often has the remainder of the trading session during which he will get delivery to dispose of his position. Even if he fails to do so, the cost of carrying the delivered position for short periods is small and it can usually be sold when desired. The security trader might well have far greater delivery problems if he misplaces his securities. There is considerable time and trouble involved in disposing of securities if they are misplaced, as well as the expense of paying for a bond to protect the broker if they are found and sold by somebody else. This cost may be particularly high in the case of bearer bonds.

Trading in commodities is more like trading in securities than other types of speculation, but it should be noted that although there are differences among all these fields commodity trading is almost always the simplest. This, of course, does not imply that successful results in commodity trading are more certain. The fact remains, however, that the commodity trader is not concerned with dividends, interest, rents, royalties, stock dividends, rights offerings, handling certificates, proxies, ex-dividend dates, voting, call dates, conversions, or any other of the host of factors that might burden a security trader. The commodity trader incurs lower costs of trading relative to the amount of money that he is trading because there are no direct taxes or fees on transactions. Because the money he deposits as margin is a good-faith deposit and not a down payment, he owes his broker no money, hence pays no interest. His cost of trading, of course, could become high if he trades relatively often.

SHOULD YOU SPECULATE?

It is hardly proper for the authors of a book, brokers, or financial advisers to advise individuals to speculate or not to speculate. Some speculators make important amounts of money by speculating. They would not have been served well by someone who persuaded them not to risk losing any money and thus prevented their success. Similarly, it seems improper to suggest that everybody should speculate when it is known that most speculators are unsuccessful and therefore that the odds favor any particular new speculator losing. The decision to be conservative or aggressive with his funds is best made by the person who is going to try to acquire more at the risk of losing part of what he has. The logical basis for making the decision can be discussed productively, however.

The most common advice to a would-be speculator by many advisers is that he should speculate only when all of his financial responsibilities have been met, that is, when his insurance program is adequate, when there is an adequate equity in his home, when his children's education is complete or provided for, and when some money is available for emergencies. This approach is certainly cautious enough, but it might make some wonder what the purpose of speculating would be. The reason for increasing an individual's net worth is primarily to raise his standard of living. If he has funds available to accomplish everything that is important to him, successful speculation can do little to improve his situation significantly, whereas unsuccessful speculation could leave him in a far worse condition than that from which he began. In short, he has much to lose and little to gain.

In contrast, one with relatively little capital might appear to be irresponsible if he entered a speculative venture with the little that he has; but if a loss would not leave him despondent an aggressive program might not be altogether out of the question for him. If he succeeded, he might improve his financial condition impressively, whereas if he lost, he would be little worse off than he was before.

Regardless of the amount of capital available to a trader for speculative purposes, his own nature is probably even more important than his capital. There are those who are simply unable to take a loss or allow enough time for a profitable position to grow to its full potential. Some people are able to make a logical plan and follow it with a high degree of discipline. Others prefer to take things as they come rather than follow a rigid program. There are certainly activities to which the latter are well adapted, but speculation is not one of them.

There are those who find that the tension of carrying a position is so great that it interferes with their work or other activities to a degree that any profit they might gain is not worth the anguish of realizing it. It is well and good to suggest "selling down to a sleeping point," but there are those who are so emotional that they cannot sleep if they have any position at all because they are so concerned about where the market will open in the morning. If it is necessary to trade on such a small scale that the chance for important gains is lost, it hardly seems reasonable to expend the energy needed to trade at all.

Each person must consider his own capital position along with the responsibilities he must meet and must decide whether he wishes to risk part of what he has to try to gain more. He must also take adequate stock of himself to determine whether the cost in time and energy involved in trading is worth expending for any profits that might be achieved. Speculating in commodites might prove to be an expensive mistake for some, but not speculating might prove equally or even more expensive for others in terms of opportunity lost. It is not the function of this book to convince the reader that he should or should not speculate in commodities. The purpose is rather to provide information about the nature and behavior of commodity markets, the procedures used by successful traders and the pitfalls they face, fundamental and technical considerations, and information about specific markets to help the reader make an intelligent decision for himself.

CHAPTER TWO

The Nature of the Commodity Futures Markets

> Futures markets are an anomaly to those economists who study them least, an anachronism to those who study them a little more, and an annoyance to those who study them most. . . .
>
> ROGER GRAY, "Fundamental Price Behavior Characteristics in Commodity Futures," *Futures Trading Seminar*

INTRODUCTION

Trading commodity futures is a skill, and no skill develops powerfully when one is wearing blinders. For that reason the prospective trader must understand, insofar as it is possible, the nature of the environment in which he is to pit his skill against those of others who play the same game.

This chapter, then, discusses the nature of the contract the participants hold while playing the game, the nature of the organized markets for those contracts, the nature of the open interest (i.e., the kinds of participant in the game), and the nature of cash and futures price relationships. The last includes a detailed analysis of the structure of the hedging process. Finally, a discussion of market performance contains an analysis of the many connections between futures markets and price variability.

NATURE OF THE CONTRACT[1]

Regardless of whether the user of the futures contract is a hedger or speculator, the common bond is the nature of the contract itself. That contract is a firm legal agreement between a buyer (or seller) and an established com-

---

[1] The following discussion draws on Henry B. Arthur, "The Nature of Commodity Futures as an Economic and Business Instrument," *Food Research Institute Studies in Agricultural Economics, Trade, and Development,* 11, No. 3, 257–260.

modity exchange or its clearing house in which the trader agrees to deliver or accept during a designated period a specified amount of a certain commodity that adheres to the particular quality and delivery conditions prescribed by the commodity exchange on which that commodity is traded. The contract, if allowed to run to its termination, is fulfilled by a cash payment on the delivery date based on the settlement price for that day in return for delivery of the commodity.

During the time that the contract is open the trader must agree to a series of conditions with a qualified broker (or the clearing house if he is a member) which calls for an initial margin deposit, a prescribed margin level that protects the broker from possible losses resulting from adverse price movements, and the right to close out (offset) his contract at any time simply by properly instructing his broker to do so. The last condition is a bilateral one that permits the broker to close out the trader's position if margin is seriously impaired.

This basic commitment has several ramifications. Although the contract defines the quantity, quality, and location at which the commodity will be delivered, there are, as a rule, alternatives available to the seller that will allow him to make delivery of a commodity with substantial deviations from the par specifications. The seller faces a scale of premiums or discounts in price because of such deviations, which might include different locations of delivery or variations in the unit weight of delivery or the deliverable grade. Deliveries must be made during the delivery month traded, but the actual day of the month is selected by the seller who issues a notice of his intention in the form of a warehouse receipt, shipping certificate, or a bill of lading.

The trader holding a contract will be dealing most often through a futures commission merchant (broker) who is a member of an exchange and who will charge for his services a minimum commission set by the exchange. It is the member broker who is responsible for the fulfillment of the contract if he is a clearing member of the exchange. If he is not a clearing member, he in turn must have his trades cleared by a clearing member.

The contracts themselves are subject to legal provisions and the rules of the various exchanges such as the setting of hours and trading regulations and the daily trading limits beyond which a particular commodity cannot move. These and other attributes of each commodity contract traded on all major exchanges are reviewed fully in Chapter 3.

There are, then, two major elements of the commitment assumed when a trader enters into a commodity futures contract. The first is a promise of actual delivery of the commodity at a designated date in a way that meets exchange specifications. The second is a promise to respond financially to daily price changes by payment, if necessary, of cash to a member broker who must in turn respond to a call for cash from the clearing house, the operation of which is discussed in the following section. This daily settlement process maintains the viability of the first promise of delivery, for if any trader wishes to cancel his commitment to accept or effect delivery of the actual commodity he may merely enter the market and offset his present position. More than 98 percent of all futures contracts are settled by offset rather than by deliveries.

Until actual delivery a transaction in a commodity futures contract does not involve anything beyond the daily process of generating profits or losses against a good-faith margin deposit with a broker. No purchase or sale is required, and there is no debit balance; hence no interest is charged. All net balances are on the credit side and are marked to the market after each day's trading. The act of buying or selling occurs only after an intent to deliver occurs, when a specific buyer and seller are paired at the current settlement price.

NATURE OF EXCHANGE OPERATIONS

The need for holding commodity futures contracts has grown at a rapid pace in recent years. To facilitate this growth about 40 commodities are presently trading actively on about 15 exchanges in the United States and a much larger number in the rest of the world. Table 2-1 and Figure 2-1 illustrate the growth cycle of futures contracts trading on American exchanges, in both regulated and nonregulated commodities, since 1954.

TABLE 2-1   ANNUAL VOLUME OF
CONTRACTS TRADED ON U.S.
COMMODITY EXCHANGES,
1954–1972* (MILLION CONTRACTS)

Year	CEA regulated	Nonregulated	Total
1954	4.00	0.26	4.26
1955	3.86	0.25	4.11
1956	4.27	0.26	4.53
1957	3.73	0.38	4.11
1958	3.52	0.35	3.87
1959	3.40	0.41	3.81
1960	3.52	0.36	3.88
1961	5.79	0.27	6.06
1962	4.90	0.28	5.18
1963	6.38	0.76	7.14
1964	5.63	0.80	6.43
1965	6.99	1.43	8.42
1966	8.67	1.79	10.46
1967	6.76	2.69	9.45
1968	7.72	1.61	9.33
1969	9.35	1.86	11.21
1970	11.54	2.08	13.62
1971	11.81	2.75	14.56
1972	14.34	3.99	18.33

*Contracts are counted once, not twice, for each transaction.

SOURCE: Association of Commodity Exchange Firms, New York.

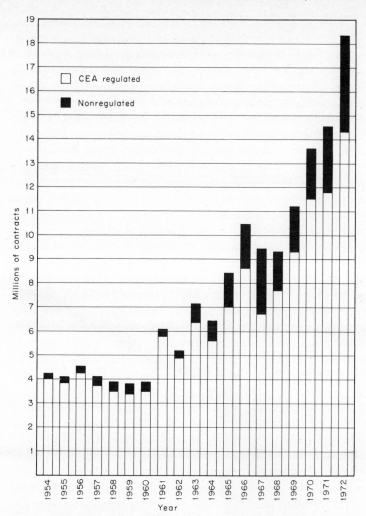

FIG. 2-1   Annual volume of trading on U.S. commodity exchanges, 1954–1972 (million contracts).

More than 18 million futures contracts at an estimated dollar value of approximately $200 billion were traded in 1972. That the volume of futures trading dominates that of physical cash trading in commodities may be seen by the fact that usually fewer than 2 percent of all those holding futures contracts take delivery and by production statistics that indicate that more than 20 times the actual crop may be traded before the expiration of the crop year. The size and value of each contract varies widely according to each commodity, as summarized in the contract facts discussion in Chapter 3.

Commodity exchanges may perform many functions, such as supplying accommodations for trading, handling, and grading cash commodities, but basically they exist to provide their members with facilities for trading commodities for future delivery. It is important to note that the exchanges themselves do not trade commodity contracts, nor do they set prices at which contracts are traded. They merely furnish a place where people in the commodity business, speculators, or their representatives can meet to buy and sell commodity futures contracts.

Most exchanges are voluntary associations of members whose primary business is the production or marketing of the commodities traded on the exchanges. The number of memberships ranges from a few dozen to the approximately 1,400 on the Chicago Board of Trade. Memberships are usually acquired from other members, subject to the approval of the exchange. In some cases an exchange may wish to expand membership and so sells memberships itself. In other cases an exchange may wish to reduce the membership and thus retires them as they become available.

Trading generally takes place in a pit or around the outside of a ring. Each exchange differs in some respects from the others, but the similarities are many. All futures orders received by member firms are transmitted to the exchange floor for execution and are filled according to bids and offers in the respective pits by open outcry to all members present at the time. Only one commodity is traded in a pit or around a ring unless the volume is too small to justify so much space. Customarily, those trading the same delivery contract of a commodity gather in the same area of the ring or on the same step of the pit so that a broker with an order can find his market as quickly as possible.

Whenever volume is high and price changes of a commodity are rapid, it is not uncommon for different prices to be bid and offered for the same delivery in different parts of the trading area at the same time. The trader must remember that these conditions might result in executions at prices that are never officially quoted or, even more difficult to understand, might cause return of an order marked "unable," even though the price on the order was well within the range of trading in that commodity. Conversely, to avoid forcing brokers to stand around the pit or ring with little to do when markets are inactive, some exchanges post orders on a blackboard. When a broker gets an order, he can find the highest bid or lowest offer on the blackboard and make his transaction against it.

Immediately after each transaction on the exchange the pit recorder, who is an employee of the exchange, writes out a record of the transaction and time-stamps it for possible future reference. The report includes the commodity traded, the month, the price, and the time of sale. The volume of each sale is not recorded as it is on stock exchanges, because it has been observed that the execution of orders in active markets would be delayed. The information from the pit recorder is transmitted to a quotations room, from which it is sent out on ticker systems for the information of those off the exchange.

Some markets start each day's trading with an open auction and continue to trade in that manner all day. Under this system all months in a particular commodity begin trading at the opening bell. Others open and close on a call basis, which means that each contract is called in turn until all orders currently on hand for that contract, except limit and stop orders away from the market, are filled.[2] After all contracts are opened, the market continues on an open auction or on the blackboard until halted by the closing call. All this makes little difference to the individual trader, except that he must remember that spread orders in call markets (e.g., silver) cannot be filled on the opening or close because only one contract at a time is being traded. The client may have a spread order limited to a given difference in price, which he has noted on the tape or a broker's board early or late in the day. When his broker tells him that he was unable to fill the order, the customer sometimes blames him unfairly for missing the market, not realizing that the order could not possibly have been filled.

At the end of each day the clearing house, which is a subsidiary of the exchange, assumes one side of all open contracts: if a broker is long, the clearing house has the other, or short, position; if a broker is short, the clearing house assumes the other, or long, side. The clearing house guarantees its members the performance of both sides of all open contracts. Each broker, therefore, who is long or short a futures contract deals only with the clearing house after initiating his position and not with the broker who actually took the other side of the trade. In effect, all obligations to receive or deliver commodities are with the clearing house and not with other brokers or individuals.

The clearing house does not care about the prices at which each trade was entered, because, as already mentioned, all profits and losses are settled daily in cash according to the latest settlement price. Because the clearing house always has a zero net position, it can operate easily without any reference to entry or exit prices for the individual trades on its books. Only the customer and his broker are interested in these matters.

The total long or short positions (which are always equal) outstanding at a given moment is called the "open interest." A broker who is long a futures contract can meet his obligation either by accepting delivery of the commodity during the delivery month or by selling his position to someone else who chooses to be long. If he sells his position to someone who replaces him, the open interest is unchanged. If he sells his position to a short who is buying in his position, the open interest is accordingly reduced. A broker who is short a futures contract can meet his obligation by making delivery of the commodity or by buying in his position either from someone else who wishes to be short or from a broker on the long side who is selling out his position. The total size of the open interest and volume indicates the degree of current liquidity in a given market and is tabulated daily by the exchanges and by the Commodity Exchange Authority (CEA). The CEA also

---

[2] These and other orders are discussed in detail in Chapter 3.

publishes monthly and annual figures. The attempt by technicians to relate changes in open interest to simultaneous, preceding, or lagging changes in volume and price is discussed in Chapter 7.

Commodities may be traded for delivery during any future month, but a few months of the year ordinarily become active, usually in accordance with trade needs or customs, such as the normal harvest time of a crop. All months in which each commodity is traded are listed with other pertinent contract facts in Chapter 3.

Some commodity exchanges, such as the Chicago Board of Trade and The Chicago Mercantile Exchange, handle long lists of commodities, whereas others, for example, the New York Cocoa Exchange, handle only one. Sometimes the same commodity is traded on more than one exchange. This is usually a matter of regional requirements, as in the case of wheat, in response to which Soft Red is traded in Chicago, Hard Red in Kansas City, and spring wheat in Minneapolis. Sometimes more than one type of a commodity can be delivered against an exchange contract; for example, Hard Red wheat is deliverable against the Soft Red contract in Chicago.

NATURE OF THE OPEN INTEREST

Although commodity exchanges differ in commodities traded, location, size, and details of their operations, the poeple who trade on them are all similarly motivated. Basically, there are floor traders of various types, outside speculators, and hedgers. Speculators and hedgers, unlike floor traders, may or may not be members of the exchanges on which they trade, but whether they are or not primarily affects their commission and margin requirements and not the manner in which they trade or their reasons for trading. Because the remainder of the book centers on the activities and techniques of the market participants, they can be introduced briefly at this point.

Speculators. A commodity speculator is interested in profiting from a price change in a commodity futures contract. He is not interested in taking delivery or making delivery of the commodity in which he trades, although he may do so sometimes in connection with his speculating. Speculators may trade from the floor of an exchange if they are members or through a broker if they are not. They differ from one another in several ways. Some trade small positions and some quite large positions, even up to the limits imposed on speculative positions by the CEA or by the exchanges, as illustrated in Chapter 3. Some prefer to trade from the long side, some from the short side, and some prefer to trade spreads rather than net positions. Spreading, like security arbitrage, is usually done by the more sophisticated traders.

One of the great differences among speculators is the length of time during which they are prepared to hold a position. A small number prefer to wait for a full move, which could take months, a year, or even more to develop, and will hold a position for as long as necessary. Position traders of this kind generally trade from the long side of the market, in order, when their trades are successful, to take advantage of the favorable long-term gain provisions of the Internal Revenue Code. Most traders hold their positions for much shorter periods, and there are some who, whenever possible, get out the day they get in. These day traders are sometimes called "scalpers." Although they are seldom able to realize large gains in so short a time, neither do they often sustain large losses. In addition, day traders receive more favorable margin requirements and, on many exchanges, benefit from a materially reduced commission rate. Unfortunately many unsophisticated day traders develop a practice of liquidating only their day trades that go in the right direction and maintaining positions that go wrong, with the inevitable eventual record of an accumulation of many small profits which are more than countered by some large losses. The number of successful day traders in relation to the number who try day trading is probably quite small.

Floor traders. Floor traders are members of the exchange who make their transactions in the pit or around the ring on the exchange floor itself, as contrasted with other members who choose to trade off the floor through member brokerage houses. A floor trader, like a nonmember speculator, can trade for his own account. He can take long-term positions, "scalp" over short periods for day trades, or even trade several times a day. He may work in one commodity or several. His advantage is the speed with which he can take positions or liquidate them, but this is in itself no assurance of a profit. A bad position quickly taken is bad nonetheless. There are some floor traders who specialize in spreads by taking opposite positions between options when the price difference appears abnormal. Floor traders have the advantage of the lower commissions available to all members of exchanges. Floor traders trading for their own accounts are sometimes referred to as "locals." Some become quite prosperous; many others do not, despite the market letters of some brokers, which leave the impression that locals almost never lose.

Some members on the floor handle orders for others but seldom or never trade for themselves. These brokers specialize in orders emanating from futures commission merchants or from customers in the trade, such as processors, exporters, and warehousers. They receive only a small part of the commissions paid by the customer to his commission house, but a broker who handles the orders for a large commission house may be involved in a substantial volume of business and his total income can be quite impressive. The orders held by this broker at any given time are referred to as his "deck." He is allowed to trade for his own account if he chooses, but must not trade in such a way that anything he does could be in conflict with his deck. As in any fiduciary business, the customers' interests are to be placed first.

Hedgers. Futures trading grew out of the needs of the manufacturers, merchants, and dealers engaged in the business of producing, merchandising, and processing commodities. Some of the earliest markets featured the grains, and most of them are important today. Their salient point was that they existed primarily for delivery and therefore were characterized by rules governing merchandising transactions, standards ensuring grade and delivery terms, and clearing arrangements. Futures contracts soon came to be viewed as temporary substitutes for cash contracts, and traders found it rewarding to be able to establish prices for a future date.

The most important role played by early futures markets was in the hedging of inventories. During the peak marketing season tradesmen often bought more than enough to fill their current orders to be sure of being able to meet the demands of their customers until new supplies became available. The merchant and dealer of those grains incurred the risk of unfavorable price changes that could easily outweigh the other risks, such as fire, theft, or windstorm, he faced as a matter of course. Grain prices, then as now, were notoriously volatile because they were subject not only to the vagaries of supply and demand but were also affected to an unusual degree by weather, unexpected political developments, and sometime illogical changes in public psychology. Merchants and dealers with heavy inventories of an unsold crop could face disastrous losses in the event of a material drop in prices. Those same participants who made forward sales based on current cash prices and who relied on purchasing inventories later to meet their commitments rather than pay storage charges for the cash grain would have a similar problem if prices rose sharply.

The hedging function, then, naturally focused on the role of transferring the risk of drastic inventory price changes to other holders in the futures markets. The other side of the transaction necessary to accomplish this might well have been taken by another hedger who was offsetting an opposite risk or was liquidating another hedge as a result of a change in his position in the cash market. More often than not it was taken by a speculator attempting to make a profit. It would appear, on the surface, as if this risk of price change would not be important in the long run because of the windfall profits that would compensate for disastrous losses. Most businessmen learned in those early years, however, that they would gladly forego large profits to avoid large losses because of the danger that they might not survive the large loss to enjoy the large profit if the loss should come first. There was also the danger that a number of losses might precede a number of profits.

The traditional risk transferral concept of hedging has evolved into a dynamic concept of risk management which accents the maximization of expected return as well as the position of merely minimizing risk. In this regard hedging is now viewed by many sophisticated users as an important management tool which can facilitate buying and selling decisions and give greater freedom for business action in markets not only dominated by the necessity of carrying inventories from one period of time to another but also in nonstorage markets. The evolution of the hedging process and an analysis of the motivation and mechanics of hedging are covered in a subsequent section.

Distribution of the open interest. It is of considerable use to the trader to examine the distribution of the value of the total open interest among the participants over a wide range of markets for a significant period of time. Table 2-2 provides such data reported semimonthly for CEA-regulated commodities over an 18-year period.[3] The analysis does not include the unregulated markets at the time of the study, such as pork bellies, sugar or cocoa, or markets that have since come into being and reflect important volume, such as cattle, plywood, lumber, orange juice, or silver. Even

[3] Charles Rockwell, "Normal Backwardation, Forecasting, and the Returns to Commodity Futures Traders," *Proceedings of a Symposium on Price Effects of Speculation in Organized Commodity Markets, Food Research Institute Studies,* Supplement, 7 (1967), 107–130. Rockwell's approach is the only published study that utilizes the commitments of reporting speculators, hedgers, spreaders, and nonreporting traders prepared by the CEA in a broad coverage of both markets and time. An earlier study by Hendrik Houthakker, "Can Speculators Forecast Prices?" *The Review of Economics and Statistics* (May 1957), reported evidence based on three markets over a shorter time period.

TABLE 2-2 VALUE OF GROUP
COMMITMENTS AS A PERCENTAGE
OF THE VALUE OF THE TOTAL OPEN
INTEREST

Trading groups*	Percentage of the value of total open interest for 25 CEA-regulated markets, 1947–1965
Nonreporting (small) traders	
Small traders, long	53
Small traders, short	39
Reporting (large) traders	
Large speculators, long	11
Large speculators, short	5
Spreaders, long	18
Spreaders, short	18
Hedgers, long	18
Hedgers, short	38

* The CEA requires that reports be filed for each day on which a trade is made, for the day before, during, and one day after a certain level of positions are held. These reportable positions, by commodity, are listed in Chapter 3.

SOURCE: Charles Rockwell, "Normal Backwardation, Forecasting, and the Returns to Commodity Futures Traders," *Proceedings of a Symposium on Price Effects of Speculation in Organized Commodity Markets, Food Research Institute Studies,* Supplement, 7 (1967), 117.

though many markets no longer viable, such as bran, middlings, shorts, onions, and butter, are included in the study, it is reasonable to assume that the three broad conclusions[4] that follow continue to be applicable.

The first conclusion is that on the average both small (nonreporting) and large (reporting) speculators are net long and that reporting hedgers are net short. Large speculators, then, tend to be on the same side of the market as the small traders and opposite that of the hedger. The implications of this distribution in regard to the effectiveness of the futures market for hedging and to the rates of return to the participants are discussed later.

Second, the data indicate the degree of balance between the long and short positions of each group. The short-to-long position ratio is 74 percent for small traders, 45 percent for large speculators, and 47 percent for hedgers. As a group, then, it would seem that large speculators and hedgers have expectations that are more unbalanced than those of small traders. Whether the greater homogeneity in large trader expectations accompanies generally superior or inferior trading results is discussed in Chapter 12.

Third, the data in Table 2-2 confirm the long-suspected notion that large speculators form an elite population. Although the percentage of the total open interest attributed to the large speculator may vary considerably from market to market, the fact is that for all markets the holdings of the large speculator's total long and short positions are less than 20 percent of the total holdings of the small traders. If it can be conservatively assumed that the average large speculator holds a position at least 10 times as large as the average small trader, then large speculators probably constitute less than 2 percent of the total futures trading population.

NATURE OF CASH AND FUTURES
PRICE RELATIONS

Introduction. There is a basic truth about commodity futures contracts. They are temporary substitutes for cash commodities. The realization that, if held to maturity, delivery of the real goods is guaranteed impresses upon the speculator, both small and large, that speculation in commodity futures is not just a numbers game which is conducted in Wonderland. Because of this, the trader should understand the relation between cash and futures prices. Perhaps this clarification can be made by indicating the complexities of the role of hedging in the futures markets.

There can be no serious exceptions to the statement that futures trading depends on hedging. Markets simply do not come into existence solely to furnish a speculative arena, nor do they persist if hedgers, the inhabitants of the land, do not find it rewarding to continue to use those markets. The

[4] *Ibid.,* 117, 118.

higher the level of hedging, the higher the level of futures business. The relation between hedging and speculation is discussed in the final section of this chapter.

The trader should be apprised that the literature on hedging in commodity futures markets is not the essence of clarity. It is often disjointed and the thoughful work is not generally available to the casual trader. In an attempt to define and develop the controversies as they have appeared, four classes of hedging theory are discussed,[5] each of which differs in the assumptions made about the attitudes of hedgers toward risk and motivation for using the futures markets.

Hedging carried out to eliminate the risks associated with price fluctuations. The risk-elimination view of hedging usually begins with a naïve illustration of the two kinds of hedge. A processor holds 100,000 bushels of cash wheat at $2.00 a bushel and is fearful of a decline in price. He immediately sells 100,000 bushels of futures contracts at $2.00 and is thereby short hedged. If the feared decline materializes and wheat drops to $1.85 a bushel, the profit on the short sale of futures exactly offsets the loss on the inventory. A long hedge is illustrated in much the same manner. A commercial business with a commitment to sell 100,000 bushels of wheat at a specific price and time in the future, which it has neither bought nor contracted to buy, can protect itself by buying a futures position equal in amount to its forward sale and thereby fix its forward costs. Thus the hedging process is said to eliminate the risk of price fluctuation.

In real life hedging decisions are neither really so simple nor mechanical. The grade of the commodity owned or sold forward by the prospective hedger may not be the same as that of the contract grade traded on the futures exchange. There might also be variations in the discounts or premiums of "off" and "on" grades which have been hedged in relation to the basic contract grade. Trade houses serving or buying from local areas might be confronted with conditions somewhat different from those affecting markets elsewhere. Sales and purchases of the cash commodities do not always correspond exactly with futures market contract units. Merchants and dealers might prefer to sell in amounts geared to contract units, but there is inevitably some variation. If elimination of risk is to be a reality, buyers in the field must report their purchases to be hedged before the market closes. Cash business can still be conducted after the futures or before they open, which means that either some hedging must be delayed until the following day or, as noted later, some must be done in *anticipation* of further cash business.

Because of the "equal but opposite" connotation implied in the naïve

[5] This approach was employed by Roger W. Gray and David J. S. Rutledge, "The Economics of Commodity Futures Markets: A Survey," *Review of Marketing and Agricultural Economics,* 39, No. 4, reported by the Food Research Institute, Stanford University, Stanford, Calif. 1972.

view of hedging, the concepts of hedging and insurance seem to be analogous. In fact, apart from the problems just discussed, the hedger is insured against price risk only if cash and futures prices move in parallel. The literature is replete with examples that indicate that cash and futures prices do *not* move in parallel.[6] The naïve view of risk elimination must, then, give way to a risk-reduction concept.

Hedging carried out to reduce the risks associated with price fluctuations. Even though it has often been found that cash and futures prices do not parallel one another, researchers have been able to muster considerable support for the proposition that a change in cash prices frequently results in a *similar* change in futures prices, particularly if some unexpected event causes a violent price change. Cash and futures prices, it has been ascertained, will not always move exactly together, but a material movement by them in opposite directions is quite unusual.

BASIS. The arithmetical difference between the cash and futures prices at any time is known as "*the* basis." The usual difference reflects a premium or discount of the cash price versus the nearby future; for example, No. 1 Soybeans in June might be quoted at 5 cents over the August future, in which case the basis would be expressed as "5 over." On the other hand, the individual hedger, concerned primarily with his own position, would be inclined to speak of "my basis." "*My* basis," refers to the difference between the price of "my" commitment in the actual product expressed as a premium or discount from the specific future contract in which the individual hedger has effected a short hedge. "My basis" remains unchanged as long as the established price relationships remain in effect. The size of the premium or discount provides a benchmark against which the closeout prices of both positions may be measured. If the spread between "my" cash commitment and the nearby future contract remains unchanged or moves to a more favorable close-out basis, "my" transactions will have been successful.[7]

Nothing, of course, precludes the basis from being quoted in distant options. Besides the current cash price being above or below that of futures options, nearby futures market prices may be above or below those more distant prices that reflect the same crop. In seasons in which supplies are normal or large the later contracts generally show a premium. Such a market is referred to as a "carrying-charge market." When supplies are tight, nearby contracts may reflect the scarcity of the cash market by selling at premiums over more distant contracts, in which case the market is said to

[6] A readily available source for the trader is *The Hedger's Handbook*, published by Merrill Lynch, Pierce, Fenner & Smith, Inc., 165 Broadway, New York, N.Y., 10006, pp. 21, 33, 37, 49.

[7] A complete discussion of "basis" is given by Henry B. Arthur, *Commodity Futures As a Business Management Tool*, Division of Research, Graduate School of Business Administration, Harvard University, Cambridge Mass., 1971, pp. 64–69.

be "inverted." Whether the current cash market is above or below prices in the futures market and whether the futures market is at carrying charges or inverted, and by how much, is vital to hedgers making price decisions. The same conditions can also influence speculators, who might attempt to make their decisions partly by considering what hedgers are likely to do.

If the risk reduction premise is accepted as the major reason for indulging in the hedging process, the usefulness of any market must depend on how closely cash and futures prices move together. The methodology employed in such a search is predictable. First changes in cash prices and then changes in the basis must be measured. If the variation in cash prices is larger than the variation in the basis, the futures market can be considered an effective tool for reducing the risks associated with price fluctuations. Studies employing this kind of analysis have confirmed that there is considerably less variation in the difference between cash and futures prices than there is in cash or futures prices alone.[8] That there is a significant positive correlation between cash and futures prices is now regarded as the first axiom of the hedging process.

At this point the usual definition of the hedger as an aloof onlooker rather than a participant in the speculative market pricing process begins to blur. Indeed, the trader begins to understand that in most circumstances hedging is merely a form of speculation—speculation on the basis. The hedger differs from the speculator only because the variation in his outcome is generally less. What the hedger accomplishes is the specialization of risk, not the elimination of it. The short hedger, for example, passes to the speculator the risks of anticipating changes in absolute prices and retains the "basis risk," that is, predicting the demand for stocks. If he can forecast the volume and timing of demand for his product for a given level of risk, a short hedger might well be able to hold a much larger volume of hedged inventory than he could hold unhedged. Such a thought raises the possibility of hedging for profit as well as reduced risk.

Hedging carried out to profit from movements in the basis. If a merchant or processor feels that he has a comparative advantage in anticipating the yield on his inventory, the important question is no longer how *closely* cash and futures prices move together (the stability of the basis) but rather whether such movement is *predictable*. Working[9] produced

---

[8] L. D. Howell authored two such studies for the USDA, *Analysis of Hedging and Other Operations in Grain Futures,* Technical Bulletin No. 971, August 1948, and *Analysis of Hedging and Other Operations in Wool and Wool Top Futures,* Technical Bulletin No. 1260, January 1962. He also coauthored, with L. J. Watson, *Relation of Spot Cotton Prices to Futures Contracts and Protection Afforded by Trading in Futures,* USDA Technical Bulletin No. 602, January 1938.

[9] Holbrook Working, "Hedging Reconsidered," *Journal of Farm Economics,* 35, No. 4 (November 1953), 544–561.

data on wheat prices that indicate that basis fluctuations are predictable. A recent study has provided supporting evidence for corn and soybeans.[10] Working's conclusions invited a significant expansion in the possible motivations of hedging:

1. It facilitates buying and selling decisions. When hedging is practiced systematically, there is need only to consider whether the price at which a particular purchase or sale can be made is favorable in relation to other current prices; there is no need to consider also whether the absolute level of the price is favorable.

2. It gives *greater freedom for business action*. The freedom most commonly gained is that of buying; for example, when a particular lot of the commodity is available at a relatively low price, regardless of its absolute level (this freedom is related to but distinct from the facilitation of decision mentioned above): often, moreover, the freedom gained is to make a sale or purchase that would not otherwise be possible at what is judged a favorable price level, as when a cotton grower sells futures in advance of harvest, or a textile mill buys futures because cotton prices are judged to be favorable, but the desired qualities of cotton cannot be bought immediately in the spot market.

3. It gives a *reliable basis for conducting storage of commodity surpluses*. The warehousing of surplus commodity stocks is a very uncertain and hazardous business when based on trying to judge when the price is favorable for storage; hedging allows operation on the basis simply of judgment that the spot price is low in relation to a futures price.

4. Hedging *reduces business risks*. There is usually reduction of risk when hedging is done for any of the previous three reasons (though often not under the second reason), but any curtailment of risk may be only an incidental advantage gained, not a primary or even a very important incentive to hedging.[11]

The enlarged concept of hedging, which emphasizes the expected returns rather than simply reducing risk, came to be called "arbitrage hedging" and stemmed from the belief that hedgers develop a sophisticated understanding of factors that determine prices in the commodities in which they deal.

Working developed the concepts of "selective" and "anticipatory" hedging to deal with actions based on expectations. Selective hedging is partial hedging which occurs when the hedger has made a subjective determination on a price rise or fall in a coming period. Because of this determination, the hedger may leave some or all of his inventory unhedged. Thus a firm would employ short hedging only when a price decline is expected and would not carry short hedges at all when a price increase is expected. Anticipatory hedging would involve the purchase or sale of futures in antici-

---

[10] R. G. Heifner, "The Gains from Basing Grain Storage Decisions on Cash-Future Spreads," *Journal of Farm Economics,* 48, No. 5 (December 1966), 1490–1495.

[11] Holbrook Working, *op. cit.,* 560–561.

pation of a formal merchandising commitment to be made later, and the operator would carry an open position in the futures market for a time without an offsetting cash commitment.

An excellent example of arbitrage hedging is reflected by soybean processors' use of the markets for soybeans, soybean meal, and soybean oil. The relation between the soybeans and their products enables processors to set hedging policies, for example, according to expectations of a large crop, short crop, processing margins, and the relative demand for meal or oil.

The major considerations of a hedger in making his decisions revolve around his particular basis and the premiums or discounts among forward future contracts. The literature developing these relationships has come to be known as the "supply of storage" theory.[12] The objective of the theory is to explain intertemporal (over time) price differences between cash and forward prices or between cash and expected future cash prices in commodities with continuous inventories. Until recently futures trading was limited to commodities that could be stored for relatively long periods; hence a significant body of knowledge was built up. Price relationships for seasonally produced commodities with discontinuous inventories, such as Maine potatoes, or for continuously produced commodities in which no inventories are held at all, such as fresh eggs or live cattle, must emphasize the forward pricing function.

The costs of holding inventory include carrying charges, such as interest and insurance, and the risk of price fluctuation. The benefits of holding inventory have been referred to broadly as the convenience yield, which arises from holding, per se, a certain level of inventory. If a processor, for example, inadvertently runs out of inventory, his sales may drop precipitously and he may not cover his overhead expenses. Insuring that inventory does not drop below a given level reduces the chance of incurring such out-of-stock costs. A processor may wish, too, to maintain a relatively stable re-

[12] M. J. Brennan, "The Supply of Storage," *American Economic Review*, 47 (March 1958), 50–72; Paul H. Cootner, "Speculation and Hedging," *Proceedings of a Symposium on Price Effects of Speculation in Organized Commodity Markets, Food Research Institute Studies,* Supplement, 7 (1967), 65–105; Nicholas Kaldor, "A Note on the Theory of the Forward Market," *Review of Economic Studies,* 7 (June 1940), 196–201; John Maynard Keynes, *The General Theory of Employment, Interest and Money,* New York, Harcourt, Brace, 1936; Lester G. Telser, "Futures Trading and the Storage of Cotton and Wheat," *Journal of Political Economy,* 66 (June 1958), 233–55; Holbrook Working, "Price Relations Between July and September Wheat Futures at Chicago Since 1885," *Wheat Studies,* 9 (March 1933), 187–238; Holbrook Working, "Price Relations Between May and New Crop Wheat Futures at Chicago Since 1885," *Wheat Studies,* 10 (February 1934), 183–228; Holbrook Working, "Theory of the Inverse Carrying Charge in Futures Markets," *Journal of Farm Economics,* 30 (February 1948), 1–28; Holbrook Working, "The Theory of the Price of Storage," *American Economic Review,* 31 (December 1949), 1254–1262.

tail price level for a product, even though raw material prices fluctuate considerably. He can accomplish this more efficiently if he has a sizable inventory base that will allow a more stable average price. The convenience yield can offset some or all of the carrying costs associated with stocks. As soon as a short hedge, for example, is placed, the processor has fixed the rate of return he will earn if he holds both the cash and the futures contract to maturity. For this reason the relation between the futures price and the cash price must be sufficient for the processor to recoup the net costs of storage from one time period to another.

If the first axiom of hedging is that cash and future prices tend to move in the same direction, the second general principle is that the price of the cash commodity and its futures price must become equal in the delivery month. If the futures price were higher than the cash price, the cash commodity would be bought, the futures sold, and delivery made. If the cash price were higher than the futures price, the processor would buy the futures and take delivery as the most desirable source of supply. Many traders notice, however, that cash prices are usually higher than the futures during the delivery month, and they wonder why they cannot buy the futures, take delivery, sell the commodity in the cash market, and pocket the difference. There are several reasons for the cash premium.[13] One is that cash and futures are not perfect substitutes until the last day of the month, which occurs after futures trading in that particular contract has ceased. Until that point, because delivery is made at the seller's option, the precise time of delivery is not known. This uncertainty can inject a premium into the cash commodity, which tends to decrease as the delivery month progresses. Factors among others that may be included are not knowing the precise quality of commodity that will be delivered and the possible inclusion of load-out or switching charges.

The trader should remember that there need be no particular incentive to deliver just because there is a gap between cash and expiring future prices. If he anticipates lower demand, the early month deliverer may reason that the recipient (most likely a speculator) will have no use for the actual commodity and will have to redeliver (perhaps many times), while relieving the deliverer of storage charges. The merchant can deliver early in the month, fully expecting to stand for delivery again later in the month.

Tactics formulated by hedgers attempting to profit from movements in the basis revolve about four basic possibilities which may accompany either the short or long hedge. A selling hedge or a buying hedge can be placed in a carrying charge market or an inverted market, and price levels may increase or decrease after the placement of the hedge. Table 2-3 summa-

---

[13] As discussed by Thomas A. Hieronymus, *Economics of Futures Trading*, Commodity Research Bureau, New York, pp. 152–53.

rizes the possible outcomes from differences in cash and futures price movements. Generally, in a carrying charge market, which is most common,
merchants and dealers will buy the cash product freely because they are
able to sell futures contracts favorably against their cash position, knowing
that the premiums on the forward futures contracts will pay part or all of
their carrying charges. The futures contract chosen will depend on the
length of time that the merchant expects to hold his cash position and on
which of the futures months traded is most favorably priced in relation to
the others at the time the hedge is placed. A dealer or merchant who is long
in the cash market and short hedged is, in effect, "long the basis"; that is,
if the basis increases because the cash price gains on the futures month in
which the hedge is placed, the hedger will make a profit by the amount of
the improvement. Similarly, a merchant who has made a forward commit-

**TABLE 2-3   VARIATIONS IN GAINS OR LOSSES RESULTING
FROM DIFFERENCES IN CASH AND FUTURE PRICE
MOVEMENTS**

Price Movements		Results			
		to one who is "long" in the cash market		to one who is "short" in the cash market	
Cash price	Future price	Unhedged	Hedged	Unhedged	Hedged
Falls	Falls by same amounts as cash	Loss	Neither profit nor loss	Profit	Neither profit nor loss
Falls	Falls by greater amount than cash	Loss	Profit	Profit	Loss
Falls	Falls by smaller amount than cash	Loss	Loss, but smaller than unhedged loss	Profit	Profit, but smaller than unhedged profit
Falls	Rises	Loss	Loss but greater than unhedged loss	Profit	Profit, but greater than unhedged profit
Rises	Rises by same amount as cash	Profit	Neither profit nor loss	Loss	Neither profit nor loss
Rises	Rises by greater amount than cash	Profit	Loss	Loss	Profit
Rises	Rises by smaller amount than cash	Profit	Profit, but smaller than unhedged profit	Loss	Loss, but smaller than unhedged loss
Rises	Falls	Profit	Profit, but greater than unhedged profit	Loss	Loss, but greater than unhedged loss

SOURCE: B. S. Yamey, "An Investigation of Hedging on an Organized Produce Exchange,"
Manchester School **19** (1951), 308.

ment to sell a cash commodity and places a long hedge by buying a futures position against his commitment is "short the basis." If cash prices drop in relation to the futures month in which the hedge is placed, he would profit; if they gained, he would lose.

When forward months are selling at discounts to nearby months, a buyer of the cash commodity has an especially difficult problem. If he places his short hedges in months selling at a discount, he does so knowing that cash and futures prices will tend to draw together as time passes and that there will not be a significant difference when the forward month becomes the cash month. This means that the basis will almost certainly become smaller, and because he is long the basis he will lose accordingly. The difficulty of hedging in such markets is even more apparent when it is noted that the degree of inversion is virtually unlimited, whereas in a carrying charge market, as already discussed, the degree of the carrying charge is limited by the possibilities of arbitrage.

Even under such conditions hedging may take place. Many hedges are placed for short periods, during which the unfavorable basis may not change or may become even more unfavorable, in which case a basis profit may even be realized. Alternatively, a cash dealer could buy "hand-to-mouth," perhaps buying only to fill orders in hand, or, if he has orders for future delivery, he can cover his commitment by buying the relatively cheap forward futures contracts rather than the presently high-priced cash commodity. This places him in the position of having a long hedge, which makes him short the basis. Later he can meet his commitment by buying in the cash market and selling his futures contract or taking delivery against his long futures position if the time, grade, and location of delivery all meet his requirements satisfactorily.

An oversimplified example illustrates the possible actions of a dealer in cash corn. Assume that in November he has bought some cash corn from the country at $1.15 a bushel. Pending its sale to a processor or exporter, the dealer decides for any of myriad reasons, to place a short hedge, assuming that he has no commitment for the sale of the corn. Perhaps corn for March delivery is then selling for $1.21 on the Chicago Board of Trade and he regards the March contract as most satisfactory for hedging purposes. The dealer therefore may decide to sell an amount of March corn approximately equal to his cash position. Having placed a short hedge, he is now long the basis. When he sells his corn, the hedge will be removed, or lifted. If the price of corn in the futures market has moved up or down by the same amount as that of cash corn, the cost of hedging to the dealer is his commissions. In practice, of course, the dealer must consider related costs, such as moving the corn into storage, holding it, and moving it out again, all of which could have been avoided by selling the corn immediately after buying it. Typically, the cash and futures prices will move in the same general direction but not in exactly the same degree. If the cash price gains on the future, the basis will have widened and there will be a basis profit on the hedge itself. If the basis narrows, there will be a basis loss by the amount that it narrowed. With so little time between November and March, a material loss resulting from the cash price losing in relation to the futures is unlikely because in March they should differ by little or nothing. A large basis loss is therefore not a great risk.

The sale of the March futures contract could be made to another hedger who is short the cash market, to a hedger long the cash market who has sold his cash position and is now lifting, or buying in, his hedge, or to a speculator who is going long or covering a short position. The short position in the March contract can ultimately be eliminated in one of two ways. The dealer can wait until March and deliver his corn against the contract, or he can sell his cash corn on the cash market and lift his hedge either by off-setting it by purchase or by transferring the position to the new holder of the cash corn, who might also choose to be hedged in the March futures month. The latter procedure is so common that the transfer of the futures position itself frequently forms the basis for determining the selling price of the cash position: for example, a sale may be made at "3 cents under March," but exactly what is March? The price of March corn might vary several cents during the course of one trading day. A determination can be made simply by the dealer buying in his own March position for the purchaser of his cash corn and setting the price from that transaction. Such deals are given different names on different exchanges, such as "ex-pit transactions" or "sales against actuals." In these transactions the brokers agree to report identical prices to the clearing house without actually executing the trades.

If, in the example, March arrived and the cash corn which had been hedged was not yet sold, the hedger still might not deliver against his futures contract. He might conclude that the cash market was too low and, noting that the premium of the May futures contract over the March was favorable, might choose to buy in his March contract (offset) and remain hedged by selling May. This is called "rolling forward." If the dealer had known in November what he came to know in March, he could, of course, have saved a commission by selling the May corn as a hedge in the first place. It is obvious that if the basis narrowed while the dealer was in a hedged position — that is, cash lost on the future — a loss on the basis would have been suffered.

Like speculators, hedgers must deposit margin against their positions, although normally their margin requirements are considerably less than those required for speculators. Sometimes margin may be handled by the hedger's bank. In such cases confirmations or statements involved in transactions will be provided to the bank as well as the hedger. Hedging involves certain costs, such as commissions and interest on margin requirements, but these may be regarded as costs of doing business. Most banks are willing lenders for hedging purposes and may be cautious about making loans to firms carrying large unhedged positions in the commodity markets. To some hedgers the ease of procuring cash loans may be the most important advantage of using the futures markets.

Because price relations are complex and the users of futures markets include producers, warehousemen, merchants, and processors, hedging carried out to profit from movements in the basis requires detailed knowledge and skill in interpretation to be successful. An excellent summary of the specific needs, practices, and behavior of the individual trade user is offered by Hieronymus[14] and Arthur.[15]

Hedging carried out to maximize expected returns for a given risk (variability of return) or minimize risk for a given expected return. Recent studies have applied portfolio theory to hedging behavior.[16] The hedger is viewed as being able to hold several assets: for example, unhedged inventory, inventory hedged by a sale of futures, or inventory hedged by a forward cash sale are all possible decisions by the hedger, depending on the probability of the rate of return on each asset. The hedger himself is considered as acting in concert with his own utility for risk and reward and the inevitable playoff between the two at any given time in much the same way as the individual trader responded, as described in Chapter 5.

The theoretical studies are an attempt to formalize a discussion of hedging behavior and are based on the Markowitz theory of portfolio selection.[17] Further discussions of the models suggested in the literature are technical and are beyond the scope of this book. The implication of portfolio theory for understanding the nature of the futures markets are clear, however. The theory emphasizes that "risk is inherent in all marketing and processing strategies, not only those in which hedging does not take place, i.e., that futures markets facilitate 'risk management' rather than 'risk transferral.'"[18]

Any business contemplating the use of the commodity futures markets as a management tool for choosing between various sets of marketing and processing strategies should answer initially several questions simply as a test of relevance.[19] These questions should include, What business are we in? What are the critical profit factors? How do price changes affect the critical factors? How do price change impacts compare with changes in the

[14] *Ibid.,* 171–240.

[15] Arthur, *op cit.,* pp. 137–314.

[16] David J. S. Rutledge, "Hedgers' Demand for Futures Contract: A Theoretical Framework with Applications to the United States Soybean Complex," *Food Research Institute Studies,* 11 (1973), 237–256.

[17] H. Markowitz, *Portfolio Selection—Efficent Diversification of Investments,* Yale University Press, New Haven, 1959.

[18] Rutledge, *op. cit.,* p. 254.

[19] Henry B. Arthur, "The Many Facets of Commodity Futures as a Tool of Management," *Workshop/72,* Coffee and Sugar Exchange, 1972, p. 36.

futures markets? Assuming that the answers to these questions indicate that risk management incorporating commodity futures can contribute to the overall business objectives, varying points of view in developing hedging policies may be considered. Exhibit 2-1 attempts to structure these views.[20] Each of the column headings relates to a business management function or interest; for example, the first column assumes total independence of cash and hedging considerations. Hedging is employed merely to offset all or some of the net inventory price risks as they occur. The second column begins building the futures contract into the business operation, columns 3 and 4 include specific procurement and marketing functions which accent decision making by those responsible for the operations, and column 5 reflects the most sophisticated use of hedging. The vertical shading of the first panel is suggestive of the degree of risk incurred which increases as the listings progress from top to bottom. The range includes an attempt at risk avoidance on the one hand to brash opportunism on the other. Real-world practices lie somewhere in between.

Critical comment. The main purpose of including a discussion of the theory and practice of hedging is to educate the trader in the singular truth that futures trading depends on hedging. Two additional purposes must share top priority, however. The first is that the treatment of the vast majority of literature with which the trader is most likely to come in contact is naïve, if not outright incorrect. The most charitable judgment one can make of these approaches is that they are exactly what they claim to be — oversimplified examples. Many commission house offerings, as well as much of the early literature, tend to perpetuate pleasant myths in the interest of obviating the need for their own understanding and that of their readership.

The second purpose of a discussion of hedging is to impress on the average trader the probable futility of attempting to relate a significant amount of this knowledge to the improvement of his own record. The differences of opinion and practices as well as the intricacies of the variables involved make it all but impossible to reduce the outcomes to general rules for the improvement of trading effectiveness. Better by far that the trader applaud the consistent use of well-traveled markets by the trade, the expansion of those markets that may have fallen into comparative disuse, and the emergence of new markets, for example, for live hogs, orange juice, and cattle, which consolidate, renew, and expand opportunities for rewarding speculation.

NATURE OF MARKET PERFORMANCE

The trader has been introduced to the nature of the futures contract and the considerable recent growth in its use. The nature of the exchanges that

---

[20] *Ibid.,* p. 42, *op. cit.,* pp. 336–337.

EXHIBIT 2-1 Points of View in Developing Hedging Policies

Primary guide or → purpose / Shading from protection to exposed position	Net position control (inventory risk)[1]	Gross position[2] (total commitment factors—"a larger market")	Procurement tool (time and cost)	Marketing tool (time and price)	Profit margins and incentives[3]
	1. Fully hedged (zero net position) Large volume "basis" operators 2. Partial hedge (constant, not zero, net position) Examples: Exclude Lifo base; hedge only seasonal accumulation 3. Variable hedge (planned or budgeted net position) Examples: Headquarters managed hedge; discretionary position within limits 4. Variable hedge (deliberate variances to profit from price swings) Examples: Cyclical position taking; leaning into the wind; special position taking situation	1. Maximize turnover without net exposure 2. Spreading and arbitrage[4] 3. Hedge excess over Lifo base 4. Hedge seasonal storage 5. Use of futures to economize cash tied up in inventories, or to shorten exposure without sacrificing current throughput 6. Disregard business needs; straight speculation	1. Take delivery on futures markets to get needed goods 2. Lock in margin through low-costing Lifo base stocks 3. Assure repurchase of temporarily liquidated Lifo base stocks 4. Anticipate storage accumulation by purchase of new crop futures 5. Use futures to attain a target exposure when actuals not available 6. Pin down attractive cost for anticipated needs 7. Reach out, speculate regardless of commercial needs	1. Deliver actuals on futures market 2. Sell futures to lock in realization on goods in inventory 3. Sell futures to assure price for anticipated production 4. Cover risks on unpriced sales, requirements contracts, or "price date of delivery" 5. Liquidate unwanted risk by selling futures when cash won't move 6. Sell futures farther ahead than actuals can be booked in the market	1. Lock in margin where actuals are bought or sold on formula price to be based on later futures quotations 2. Deal in basis (this covers a wide assortment of specialized applications) 3. Use price or margin targets to determine how much business will be done, as in deciding how much to store or process 4. Pin down other half of a cash commodity trade in futures, awaiting opportunity to fulfill with actuals 5. Buy low, sell high, wherever the opportunity presents itself—all cash, all futures, or a mix including discretionary position taking

[1] This column assumes a commercial operation in which all decisions are based on cash market considerations. The net cash positions (or portions of them) are then hedged in futures.

[2] This column assumes that added cash positions will be undertaken simply because they *can* be hedged. This is sometimes referred to as "cash and carry."

[3] The column for profit margins and incentives relates to operations in which the primary focus is not on protection from general price swings, but on earnings from residuals and differentials (basis), or even from deliberate position taking.

[4] Includes earning of storage by holding deliverable cash product against short futures.

SOURCE: Henry B. Arthur, *Commodity Futures as a Business Management Tool*, Division of Research, Graduate School of Business Administration, Harvard University, Cambridge, Mass., 1971, pp. 336–337.

trade these contracts have been discussed and a portrait of the speculator and hedger which included the impact of each on the open interest have been drawn. Cash and futures price relationships were analyzed to give the trader an appreciation of the complexities of the hedging process.

At this point it might help to ask, "How well do the markets function?" The experienced trader may retort wryly, "Too well. They're *so* tough to beat." He, of course, is referring to the behavior of futures prices which is of such importance that Chapter 4 is devoted entirely to a discussion of the characteristics of price changes. In a general sense, however, there has always been an implicit benchmark for judging whether futures markets should receive high or low performance marks. Because agricultural and raw materials commodities, which are featured in most futures markets, are subject to considerable price fluctuations (many are beyond the control of the producer or processor), markets that receive high performance marks are those in which there has been a noticeable reduction in price variability.

The question of price variability may be viewed generally from two positions — either that futures trading, in an institutional sense, tends to dampen or increase price fluctuations or that speculation itself significantly influences the variability of price changes. The various attacks on potato and onion futures trading as an institution [21] seemed to make more headway when price levels were depressed, just as similar investigations of the coffee, copper, and sugar markets were launched when prices were high. Some scholars have wondered about the pattern that exhibits concern for the *producer* of domestic commodities and the *consumer* of imported commodities. [22] Apart from such obvious bias, there is a continuing question whether the institution itself is worthy of the increasing trust that has been shown in its regard. A discussion of speculation and price variability follows later in the section.

One of the early dissatisfactions with market performance centered around the question of manipulation, which featured corners and bear raids in the finest robber baron tradition. [23] Activity by such men as Hutchinson, Leiter, and Patten in the years just before the turn of the century resulted in short-term price distortions, frequently because of inadequate supplies of a grain in the delivery position. The effectiveness of such corners gradually diminished as competitive balance appeared in the market, aided by legislation that now rewards the manipulator with five years imprisonment, a $10,000 fine, or both.

Historical evidence of the effects of futures trading on price fluctuations is not conclusive. Perhaps the most voluminous example of the divergent

[21] See Chapter 1.
[22] Gray and Rutledge, *op. cit.,* p. 32.
[23] C. H. Taylor, *History of the Board of Trade of the City of Chicago,* Robert O. Law Co., Chicago, 1917.

findings were those of the United States Federal Trade Commission,[24] which in part concluded:

> Frequently attempts have been made to deal with the question of the stabilizing effect of future trading by comparing periods prior to the practice of trading in futures with periods since there has been such trading. Such a comparison, in order to prove anything, must first prove that the other things are equal — either that there have been no other changes between the two periods or that any other changes that may have occurred had no effect on the fluctuation of grain prices. Obviously, no such proof can be offered in the case under consideration . . . (Vol. VI, p. 261).
>
> It seems to be conclusively proved by this bit of analysis that futures trading under existing conditions itself generates certain elements of risk and uncertainty. In other words, it causes some fluctuations. Its stabilizing influence must, therefore, depend upon its stilling or checking other causes of fluctuation that are more important than those it creates (Vol. VI, p. 264).

More recent studies of onions tend to support the contention that a futures market diminishes the variation in cash prices[25] as well as the seasonal range in prices.[26] In the latter study an index of seasonal price variations was computed for a period before the advent of futures trading, during the actual trading period, and for a four-year period following the ban on futures trading. The periods before and after futures trading registered similar harvest lows of about 75 and a subsequent spring high reading of about 145. During futures trading those figures were 87 and 118, respectively.

As the trader may surmise by now, there can be no single meaning in the term "price variability." A look at continuous and discontinuous inventory futures markets will illustrate the variations.[27] In continuous inventory markets the price of storage theory ensures that the level of prices for *all* months responds to change in information as it develops. Of course, the interrelations between cash prices and futures prices (the basis) change, but these changes are generally much smaller than absolute price changes, as discussed earlier. When no inventories are carried, the function of a futures market is to conduct "forward pricing" (forecasting), and the relations among prices differ from the first case. Figures 2-2, 2-3, and 2-4 present price behavior in three crops in which production decisions take place in the spring before a fall harvest — corn, soybeans, and potatoes.

---

[24] U.S. 56th Congress, 2nd Session, House, *U.S. Industrial Commission Report* (1900–1901), House Doc. 94.

[25] H. Working, "Price Effects of Futures Trading," *Food Research Institute Studies*, 1, No. 1 (1960), 3–31.

[26] Roger W. Gray, "Onions Revisited," *Journal of Farm Economics*, 45, No. 2 (May 1963), 273–276.

[27] As developed by William G. Tomek and Roger W. Gray, "Temporal Relationships Among Prices on Commodity Futures Markets: Their Allocative and Stabilizing Roles," *American Journal of Agricultural Economics*, 52, No. 3 (August 1970).

FIG. 2-2   Closing prices of December corn contract on April 30 and expiration date, 1952–1968. (W. G. Tomek and R. W. Gray, "Temporal Relationships Among Prices on Commodity Futures Markets: Their Allocative and Stabilizing Roles," *American Journal of Agricultural Economics*, vol. 52, no. 3, August 1970, pp. 374–375.)

In each case the closing prices for December corn, November soybeans, and November potatoes on April 30 are compared with expiration prices for a number of years. Corn and soybeans prices depict a tendency to move together (low variability), whereas the last day (cash) price of potatoes is clearly much more variable than the futures price throughout the years analyzed. The implications from the standpoint of the *growers'* ability through hedging to reduce price variability from year to year are interesting. Because no potato stocks are carried from May to November, the market in the spring cannot forecast any price other than the mean November

FIG. 2-3   Closing prices of November soybean contract on April 30 and expiration date, 1952–1968. (W. G. Tomek and R. W. Gray, "Temporal Relationships Among Prices on Commodity Futures Markets: Their Allocative and Stabilizing Roles," *American Journal of Agricultural Economics*, vol. 52, no. 3, August 1970, pp. 374–375.)

FIG. 2-4   Closing prices of November Maine potato contract on April 30 and expiration date, 1952–1968. (W. G. Tomek and R. W. Gray, "Temporal Relationships Among Prices on Commodity Futures Markets: Their Allocative and Stabilizing Roles," *American Journal of Agricultural Economics*, vol. 52, no. 3, August 1970, pp. 374–375.)

price until new crop information emerges. A forecast at the mean value of past observations, when coupled with a near zero variance in springtime prices, provides an excellent basis for hedging. On the other hand, as in the corn and soybean markets, routine hedging may not be helpful in reducing annual price variability because the variance in the springtime prices is about equal to the variance in the cash prices at maturity. In summation, then, as Gray and Rutledge note in their survey,

> . . . the potato grower can greatly reduce *his* price variability through hedging, as the corn and soybean grower cannot. But it is implied on the *other* sides of these coins that corn and soybean price variabilities have been reduced (through generalized production and inventory response) as potato price variability has not.[28]

The question whether speculation itself significantly influences the variability of prices is one of long standing. Many unresolved questions owe their longevity primarily to problems of measurement, and the role of speculation is no exception. An example of the data on open interest, available monthly from the CEA, is presented in Table 2-4; the reported commitments are divided into large (reporting) traders and small (nonreporting) traders. Hedgers are assumed to be numerous enough to be included in the reporting category, and small traders are considered residual, which is equal to the difference between the total open interest and that reflected by large speculators plus hedgers. All categories include the holdings of both the long and short positions. The monthly data also include the net change in the long and short positions for each group to reflect changes in the rela-

[28] Gray and Rutledge, *op. cit.*, 35.

TABLE 2-4 EXAMPLE OF MONTHLY REPORTED FUTURES COMMITMENTS

*Soybeans**

Classification	July 31, 1971 Long	Short	Net change from June 30, 1971 Long	Short
		(in thousand bushels)		
Large traders				
Speculative				
Long *or* short only	17,390	7,240	− 510	− 3,035
Long *and* short (spreading)	97,415	97,600	+16,625	+16,810
Total	114,805	104,840	+16,115	+13,775
Hedging	107,815	96,595	− 1,395	− 5,890
Total reported by large traders	222,620	201,435	+14,720	+ 7,885
Small traders				
Speculative and hedging	73,365	94,550	− 5,165	+ 1,670
Total open contracts	295,985	295,985	+ 9,555	+ 9,555
Percent held by large traders	75.2	68.1	+ 2.6	+ 0.5
small traders	24.8	31.9	− 2.6	− 0.5

Frozen Pork Bellies†

Classification	July 31, 1971 Long	Short	Net change from June 30, 1971 Long	Short
		(in contract units of 36,000 pounds)		
Large traders				
Speculative				
Long *or* short only	1,416	2,276	− 329	− 1,398
Long *and* short (spreading)	3,124	3,124	+ 230	+ 230
Total	4,540	5,400	− 99	− 1,168
Hedging	476	787	− 1,278	− 1,218
Total reported by large traders	5,016	6,187	− 1,377	− 2,386
Small traders				
Speculative and hedging	9,891	8,720	− 5,518	−4,509
Total open contracts	14,907	14,907	− 6,895	−6,895
Percent held by large traders	33.6	41.5	+ 4.3	+ 2.2
small traders	66.4	58.5	− 4.3	− 2.2

* Commitments of traders, Chicago Board of Trade, July 31, 1971.
† Commitments of traders, Chicago Mercantile Exchange, July 31, 1971.
SOURCE: Commodity Exchange Authority.

tive levels of hedging and speculative activity for the preceding period. The CEA publishes a yearly summary, *Commodity Futures Statistics,* which includes a bimonthly (1st and 15th) report of futures commitments and other useful statistical information.

Because the terms "excessive" speculation and "undue" price fluctuations are subjective and the CEA figures are the sole source of reference, the trader can appreciate the problem of assessing the impact of the speculator. Because the positions of the nonreporting traders are *not* available, the total amounts of hedging and speculating in the market cannot be accurately known. The simplest solution is to assume that all nonreporting traders are speculators. Working, however, attempted to reclassify these nonreporting traders as hedgers or speculators and preceeded to construct a "Speculative Index."[29]

The Speculative Index may be understood more easily by first referring to Table 2-2. On the average, long hedging does not equal short hedging; therefore for market balance long speculation is required to offset net short hedging. If H_L = long hedging commitments, H_S = short hedging commitments, and S_L = long speculating commitments, the degree to which short hedging is balanced by long hedging = H_L/H_S and the degree to which short hedging is balanced by long speculation = S_L/H_S. Together these ratios measure the hedging and speculative responses to short hedging.

The Speculative Index (T) isolates the amount of *net* short hedging (H_s^μ), which must be carried by long speculation (S_L),

$$T = \frac{S_L}{H_s^\mu},$$

where S_L = long speculating commitments,
$\quad H_s^\mu$ = unbalanced short hedging commitments.

In other words, long hedging (H_L) is subtracted from short hedging (H_S) to give the unbalanced short hedging commitment (H_s^μ). If a commodity has more long speculation (S_L) than needed to carry net short hedging (H_s^μ) requirements, the Speculative Index will exceed 1.

The trader must bear in mind that the Speculative Index does not distinguish between markets in which long speculating commitments are greater than short speculating commitments or vice-versa. The ratio indicates only that unneeded speculation is becoming more or less important when compared with unbalanced hedging. A more serious limitation of the Speculative Index is that it ignores spread or matching positions, which can be a significant percentage of the total open interest shown in Table 2-4 for soybeans and pork bellies. Working simply defined the problem away when

---

[29] Holbrook Working, "Speculation on Hedging Markets," *Food Research Institute Studies,* 1, No. 2 (May 1960), 199 ff.

he limited speculation to the holding of a net long or net short position for gains,[30] and Larson developed a technique for estimating the classification of the total open interest.[31] However, precise measurement of the speculative commitment and its subsequent effects on price variability will have to wait for a more detailed publishing classification of open interest.

Because of these problems in measurement, the trader would expect difficulty in reaching a consensus regarding the impact of speculation on price behavior. In one study of the grains the following was concluded for soybeans:

> Clearly, this evidence does not support the hypothesis that "excessive speculation" causes or is even associated with market periods containing "unwarranted or undesirable price fluctuation." Of the 52 separate, semi-monthly dates on which classification of total open interest indicated that the unneeded speculative fraction was high relative to hedging requirements, 39 cases were identified as markets in which prices showed little movement. However, in 36 out of the 40 cases for which the calculated Speculative Index was low, price behavior was entirely different. Prices in these particular markets moved over wide ranges, sometimes rising and falling rapidly during a relatively short period of time, and often showing wide daily price ranges over an extended period of time.[32]

A recent study of 186 monthly observations from 1950 to 1965 computed the hedging ratios and the Speculative Indexes for potatoes, cottonseed oil, soybean meal, corn, soybean oil, soybeans, rye, wheat, and oats.[33] Most of the hedging ratios (H_L/H_S) were near 0.5, which reflects a situation in which long hedging is not sufficient to cover short hedging requirements. All Speculative Indexes were greater than 1, ranging from 1.12 for oats to 1.31 for soybeans, leading to the conclusion that the market had a tendency toward imbalance, with speculation as the dominant force.

Because the futures markets are growing at such a pace, it seems reasonable to conclude that the markets of the future will require greater, not lesser, levels of speculation in order not only to survive but to thrive. The failure of some futures contracts can be traced directly to the failure of sufficient speculative activity which in turn led to the unbalanced or lopsided markets discussed in Chapter 4. The behavior of commodity futures prices is significantly affected by the levels of hedging and speculation in the markets, and it is safe to say that if no speculation marked the trading landscape the hedging interests would have to create a statistical equivalent to the speculator at great cost.

[30] Ibid., p. 187.

[31] Arnold Larson, "Estimation of Hedging and Speculative Positions in Futures Markets, Food Research Institute Studies, 2, No. 3 (November 1961).

[32] Margins, Speculation, and Price in Grain Futures Markets, Economic Research Service, U.S.D.A., Washington, D.C., 1967, p. 35.

[33] Labys and Granger, op. cit., 127.

CHAPTER THREE

The Mechanics of Commodity Futures Trading

The man who says he knows all the answers does not know all the questions.

INTRODUCTION

Many people are reluctant to trade commodities because they believe that the mechanics of trading are much more complicated than they really are. There are good reasons why some people should not trade commodities, but the complexities of taking positions or understanding the bookkeeping are not among them. Some of the mystery is probably created by individual registered representatives of brokerage firms who are loath to spend the time necessary to understand the technology themselves because of their more immediate interest in securities and mutual funds.

Perhaps if a new commodity trader making his first trade is followed, some confusion can be cleared away.

THE BROKER

Unless the trader is actually a member of the commodity exchanges himself, it will be necessary for him to deal through a member brokerage firm. Normally firms that handle public business are futures commission merchants registered as such with the Commodity Exchange Authority. Such firms are usually called brokers, commission houses, or wire houses. Brokers are of two general types, but their methods of operation are similar.

One type of broker is the mixed wire or commission house, which normally emphasizes listed securities but has other departments dealing with over-the-counter securities, bonds, puts and calls, mutual funds, and, in addition to commodities, a variety of other financial merchandise. The other is the specialized broker who deals exclusively in one, several, or all commodities. Some of these houses were originally cash commodity firms that went into the futures business to add to their incomes. Many already had sufficient investment in memberships and wire facilities to make the addition of customer brokerage relatively inexpensive. Most clients who have traded in securities and have become interested in commodities find it convenient to begin trading through the same broker through whom they trade securities if the broker is an integrated house. Others select specialty firms because they believe that they are given more varied and current information and better guidance by them.

After the firm has been chosen, the trader must select the salesman with whom he chooses to do business. This person may be a partner or stockholder of the firm or an employee variously referred to as a "solicitor," "registered representative," "customer's man," "account executive," "investment executive," or some other euphemism for "salesman." The salesmen frequently refer to themselves as "brokers" although this term technically describes their employers. Most customers spend little time or effort in their selection of this man or woman, which is probably an error. Trading may involve a significant portion of one's net worth, and the salesman is almost certain to have some effect on the results of trading in any account he handles.

In order to make his selection intelligently, the customer should give a little thought to what he wants the registered representative to do for him. If he wishes to make his own decisions and does not want to be solicited to make trades, he is primarily concerned with the service he is going to get. In this case, the customer may be satisfied with a relatively young but well-trained registered representative. Although such a man has little experience, he does have considerable time and is grateful to have his few clients. Therefore his services can be relatively good. A little time should be spent with this representative before beginning to trade to determine whether a good personal relationship will develop. There is no need to trade with a man simply because it happens to be his "floor day" in the office or because he is next in line to open a new account when the customer happens in.

If the client is going to rely on his registered representative to guide his trading, the care given to his selection is even more important. In addition to his ability to render good service, the broker will need good judgment and some personal knowledge about commodity trading. This is not easy to evaluate, but neither is it impossible. One can choose one's broker as one would choose a lawyer or physician; that is, by referral from people who have been satisfied with his performance. Another criterion is the broker's success with his own trading. If he has had good results, he may not necessarily continue to have them, but this is better than having to account for continuously poor performance over a significant period of time. If the broker does not trade his own account, one might wonder why. Presumably he is economically motivated or he would not be in the brokerage business. If he is not allowed to trade because of the rules of his firm or because of his own conservative financial objectives, of course, these are mitigating circumstances.

If a customer decides to deal with a firm with which he has had no experience, he might also ask some questions about its research department. It is not enough to know that there are some people in New York or Chicago who send out wires or prepare attractive-looking market letters and special reports. It is also important to learn that they know what they are talking about, as indicated by their results.

OPENING THE ACCOUNT

Once the brokerage house and registered representative have been selected, the opening of the individual brokerage account is a simple procedure. Various papers need to be signed, which will vary somewhat from broker to broker, but the following are typical.

The basic form is the customer's margin agreement, in which the client agrees to be responsible for any losses in his trading, just as he is in a securities account. The form may be signed by an individual client or by more than one, in which case the clients must specify whether they wish to be joint tenants or tenants-in-common. If they choose to act as joint tenants with right of survivorship, the broker will accept instructions from all joint tenants. In the event of the death of any of them, the equity in the account belongs to the survivors. If the customers act as tenants-in-common, they own the account in specified shares. Typically, a husband and wife will be joint tenants, whereas unrelated customers, such as business partners, will open their accounts as tenants-in-common.

The other form usually required is the authority to transfer funds, sometimes called the "CEA letter." When the broker opens an account for a commodity client, he is in reality opening two accounts. One is for trading in commodities regulated by the Commodity Exchange Authority (CEA) and the other for trading in unregulated commodities. Both accounts will have the same basic account number but will be differentiated in some minor way, such as "Type 1" and "Type 2" or "Type A" and "Type B." As trading takes place in various commodities, the broker will transfer the necessary funds from one account to the other as needed. It is these transfers that necessitate the CEA letter.

Commodities may also be traded by partnerships and corporations. In a partnership all partners must agree to allow the account to be opened and must designate which partners can act for all. Corporate charters must allow commodity trading, and the broker must be told which officers of the corporation are to be allowed to trade the account. Minors may be prohibited from trading by some brokers, but others permit accounts in the name of a minor if guaranteed by an adult.

Some brokers require that a minimum deposit of funds which ranges between $1,000 and about $2,500 be made available for margin. Other brokers require only the margin specified by the commodity exchanges for a particular position, which can be as low as $100. Customers who deposit bare minimums to cover only the required initial margin would have to be concerned with the regulations covering the required deposit of additional funds in case of adversity. Some brokerage firms allow somewhat more impairment than others and some are inclined to press for additional deposits more aggressively than others. Exchanges specify the maximum impairment possible and the maximum time allowed to collect additional funds, but some brokers have house rules more stringent than those of the various exchanges. A small number of wire houses require a statement of net worth and/or much higher than the usual initial minimum margins from commodity clients to make certain that they can afford to take the necessary risks inherent in commodity trading.

If an account is to be managed by someone other than the client investing the capital, the broker will require a limited power of attorney, or trading authority, which allows him to take orders from that other person. A general power of attorney permits the account manager to withdraw money as well as to trade the account. There is seldom any reason to use this kind of document for trading purposes. Managed accounts are subject by some exchanges to minimum capital requirements somewhat in excess of those required of accounts not so managed. The client is responsible for all losses in his account, even though in a managed account the positions are taken by someone else, and he should be cautious before he signs a trading authority, particularly if his account manager has any conflict of interest in the trading, such as an interest in the commissions generated. Those who wish to have their accounts managed or who wish to manage the accounts of others should take the time to note the latest exchange, state, and Commodity Exchange Authority rules applicable to such accounts.

CONTRACT INFORMATION

The decision-making processes by which a trader chooses the commodity in which to trade and how he selects the particular contract month best for his purposes are discussed at length in subsequent chapters of this book, but a summary of basic information can be indicated profitably at this point. The list in Table 3-1 is not complete, but it does indicate the major commodity exchanges in the United States, typical commodities most actively traded on them, and pertinent contract and commission data concerning these commodities. From time to time changes occur in commissions, delivery months, opening times, closing times, and, of course, the list of commodities popularly traded. Most brokers will have updated information available which is designated as "Contract Facts" or "Contract Informa-

TABLE 3-1   CONTRACT INFORMATION

Commodity	Name of exchange	Exchange hours CST	Usual par contract grade(s)*	Delivery months*	Contract size	Prices quoted in	Minimum fluctuation	Dollar value of one tick	Dollar value of a 1¢ move	Maximum daily limits above or below previous day's close (Cents)	(\$)	Round turn commissions (Regular)	(Day trade)	Spread
Wheat	Chicago Board of Trade	9:30 1:15	#2 Soft Red winter #2 Hard Red winter #1, 2 north spring	NUZHK	5,000 bu	¢/bu	$\frac{1}{4}$¢/bu	\$12.50	\$ 50	20¢/bu	1,000	\$30.00	\$20.00	\$36.00
Corn	Chicago Board of Trade	9:30 1:15	#2 yellow	ZHKNU	5,000 bu	¢/bu	$\frac{1}{4}$¢/bu	12.50	50	10¢/bu	500	30.00	20.00	36.00
Oats	Chicago Board of Trade	9:30 1:15	#1 white #1, 2 heavy white #3 extra heavy white	ZHKNU	5,000 bu	¢/bu	$\frac{1}{4}$¢/bu	12.50	50	6¢/bu	300	25.00	17.00	36.00
Soybeans	Chicago Board of Trade	9:30 1:15	#2 yellow	XFHKNQU	5,000 bu	¢/bu	$\frac{1}{4}$¢/bu	12.50	50	20¢/bu	1,000	30.00	20.00	36.00
Soybean meal	Chicago Board of Trade	9:30 1:15	44% protein	VZFHKNQU	100 tons (2,000 lb/ton)	\$/ton	10¢/ton	10.00	1	1,000¢/ton	1,000	33.00	22.00	44.00
Soybean oil	Chicago Board of Trade	9:30 1:15	Regular—one grade	VZFHKNQU	60,000 lb (one tank car)	¢/lb	$\frac{1}{100}$ ¢/lb	6.00	600	1¢/lb	600	33.00	22.00	44.00
Broilers, iced	Chicago Board of Trade	9:15 1:05	USDA Grade A whole eviscerated	FHKMNQUX	28,000 lb (60- to 65-lb boxes)	¢/lb	$\frac{2.5}{100}$ ¢/lb	7.00	280	2¢/lb	560	30.00	20.00	36.00
Silver	Chicago Board of Trade	9:00 1:25	0.999 fine	GJMQVZ	5,000 troy oz (5 bars)	¢/oz	$\frac{1}{10}$ ¢/oz	5.00	50	20¢/oz	1,000	30.00	15.00	32.00
Plywood	Chicago Board of Trade	10:00 1:00	½" CDX—standard exterior 4-5 ply 4x8s group 1	FHKNUX	69,120 sq ft 36(60-piece units) (one boxcar load)	\$/M sq ft	10¢/M sq ft	6.91	0.691	700¢/M sq ft	484	30.00	20.00	40.00
Stud lumber	Chicago Board of Trade	10:00 1:00	10/15% utility	FHKNUX	100,000 bd ft (two boxcar loads)	\$/M bd ft	10¢/M bd ft	10.00	1	500¢/M bd ft	500	33.00	22.00	44.00
Pork bellies	Chicago Mercantile Exchange	9:30 1:00	USDA seedless Green—square Cut—standard	GHKNQ	36,000 lb (12- to 14-lb bellies)	¢/lb	$\frac{2.5}{100}$ ¢/lb	9.00	360	1.5¢/lb	540	45.00	27.00	48.00
Feeder cattle	Chicago Mercantile Exchange	9:05 12:40	USDA—minimum 80% choice and maximum 20% good	HJKQUVZ	42,000 lb (650-lb average)	¢/lb	$\frac{2.5}{100}$ ¢/lb	10.50	420	1¢/lb	420	40.00	25.00	43.00
Cattle, live	Chicago Mercantile Exchange	9:05 12:40	USDA choice Live steers	GJMQVZ	40,000 lb (1050-lb average)	¢/lb	$\frac{2.5}{100}$ ¢/lb	10.00	400	1¢/lb	400	40.00	25.00	43.00
Hogs, live	Chicago Mercantile Exchange	9:20 12:50	USDA 1, 2, 3, 4 Barrows and gilts	GJMNQVZ	30,000 lb (220-lb average)	¢/lb	$\frac{2.5}{100}$ ¢/lb	7.50	300	1.5¢/lb	450	35.00	22.00	38.00
Eggs, shell (fresh)	Chicago Mercantile Exchange	9:15 12:45	USDA extras 90% Grade A Large white	All	22,500 doz (750 cases; one carload)	¢/doz	$\frac{5}{100}$ ¢/doz	11.25	225	2¢/doz	450	40.00	25.00	43.00
Milo	Chicago Mercantile Exchange	9:30 1:15	#2 yellow	NUZHK	400,000 lb (7142.8 bu)	¢/cwt	$\frac{1}{4}$ ¢/cwt	10.00	40	15¢/cwt	600	30.00	20.00	33.00
Copper	New York Commodity Exchange (Comex)	8:45 1:10	Electrolytic ASTM standards	FHKNUVZ	25,000 lb	¢/lb	$\frac{5}{100}$ ¢/lb	12.50	250	5¢/lb	1,250	36.00	18.00	50.40
Potatoes (Idaho Russett)	Chicago Mercantile Exchange	9:00 12:50	USDA No. 1 Size A 2" diameter	FHJKX	50,000 lb (500 sacks)	¢/cwt	1¢/cwt	5.00	5	35¢/cwt	175	30.00	20.00	33.00
Lumber	Chicago Mercantile Exchange	9:00 1:05	Kiln or air dried Random 2x4s Hem—fir construction	FGHKNUX	100,000 bd ft	\$/M bd ft	10¢/M bd ft	10.00	1	500¢/M bd ft	500	40.00	25.00	43.00
Mercury	Comex	8:50 1:30	99.9% pure	HKNUZ	10 flasks (76 lb each)	\$/flask	\$1/flask	10.00	0.10	500¢/flask	50	40.50	20.00	56.00
Silver	Comex	9:00 1:15	0.999 fine	FHKNUZ	10,000 troy oz (10 bars)	¢/oz	$\frac{1}{10}$ ¢/oz	10.00	100	20¢/oz	2,000	45.50	23.00	64.00

Commodity	Exchange	Hours	Grade	Symbols	Contract unit	Price							
Potatoes (Maine or Idaho)	New York Mercantile Exchange	9:00 / 12:30	USDA No. 1 Size A 2" diameter	FHJKX	50,000 lb (1000–50-lb sacks)	$/cwt	5.00	1¢/cwt	5	50¢/cwt	250	30.00	15.00	32.00
Platinum	New York Mercantile Exchange	8:45 / 12:30	99.8% pure sheet or bar	FJNV	50 troy oz (1 sheet or bar)	$/oz	5.00	10¢/oz	0.50	1,000¢/oz	500	45.00	22.50	45.00
Silver coins	New York Mercantile Exchange	8:50 / 1:20	Dimes, halves, quarters pre-1965 United States	FJNV	$10,000 (10 bags)	$/bag	10.00	$1/bag	0.10	15,000¢/bag	1,500	35.00	17.50	35.00
Palladium	New York Mercantile Exchange	9:20 / 11:55	99.8% pure	HKMQUXZ	100 troy oz (4 sheets or ingots)	$/oz	5.00	5¢/oz	1	400¢/oz	400	{40.00 / 52.00}	{20.00 / 26.00}	{40.00 / 54.00}†
Cotton #2	New York Cotton Exchange	9:30 / 2:00	U.S. Midding 1-1/16" white	FHKNVZ	50,000 lb (100 bales)	¢/lb	5.00	$\frac{1}{100}$ ¢/lb	500	2¢/lb	1,000	{45.00 / 55.00}	{22.50 / 27.50}	{54.00 / 66.00}†
Frozen Concentrated orange juice	New York Cotton Exchange	9:15 / 1:45	USDA Grade A Brix –51° 3% solids	FHKNUX	15,000 lb 44(55 gallon drums)	¢/lb	7.50	$\frac{5}{100}$ ¢/lb	150	3¢/lb	450	45.00	25.00	54.00
Wool	New York Cotton Exchange	9:00 / 1:30	64's 2¾"	HKNVZ	6,000 lb (clean weight)	¢/lb	6.00	$\frac{1}{10}$ ¢/lb	60	10¢/lb	600	50.00	27.00	60.00
Liquified propane gas	New York Cotton Exchange	9:05 / 2:10	NGPA-HD-5	FKNUZ	100,000 gal (pipe line bulk)	¢/gal	10.00	$\frac{1}{100}$ ¢/gal	1,000	1¢/gal	1,000	40.50	20.00	45.00
Cocoa	New York Cocoa Exchange	9:00 / 2:00	Standard (beans)	HKNUZ	30,000 lb (200 bags)	¢/lb	3.00	$\frac{1}{100}$ ¢/lb	300	4¢/lb	1,200	60.00	30.00	70.00
Coffee (C)	New York Coffee and Sugar Exchange	9:30 / 1:45	Columbian (beans)	HKNUXZ	37,500 lb (250 bags)	¢/lb	3.75	$\frac{1}{100}$ ¢/lb	375	2¢/lb	750	{25.00 / 80.00}	{15.00 / 42.75}	{30.00 / 96.00}†
World sugar #11	New York Coffee and Sugar Exchange	9:00 / 2:00	Raw Bulk 96% average polarization	FHKNUV	50 long tons (112,000 lb)	¢/lb	11.20	$\frac{1}{100}$ ¢/lb	1,120	1¢/lb	1,120	{42.00 / 62.00}	{21.00 / 31.00}	{42.00 / 62.00}†
Wheat	Kansas City Board of Trade	9:30 / 1:15	#2 Hard Red or Hard Yellow winter	NUZHK	5,000 bu	¢/bu	6.25	$\frac{1}{8}$ ¢/bu	50	25¢/bu	1,250	22.00	22.00	30.00
Rye	Winnipeg Commodity Exchange	9:30 / 1:15	#1, 2 Western Canadian	VZKN	1,000 bu / 5,000 bu	¢/bu	1.25 / 6.25	$\frac{1}{8}$ ¢/bu	10 / 50	10¢/bu	100 / 500	4.50 / 22.50	4.50 / 22.50	9.00 / 45.00
Flaxseed	Winnipeg Commodity Exchange	9:30 / 1:15	#1, Western Canadian	VXZKN	1,000 bu / 5,000 bu	¢/bu	1.25 / 6.25	$\frac{1}{8}$ ¢/bu	10 / 50	30¢/bu	300 / 1,500	5.50 / 25.00	5.50 / 25.00	11.00 / 50.00
Rapeseed	Winnipeg Commodity Exchange	9:30 / 1:15	#1 Canadian	UXFHM Vancouver / VXZKN Thunder Bay	1,000 bu / 5,000 bu	¢/bu	1.25 / 6.25	$\frac{1}{8}$ ¢/bu	10 / 50	20¢/bu	200 / 1,000	5.50 / 25.00	5.50 / 25.00	11.00 / 50.00
Wheat	Minneapolis Grain Exchange	9:30 / 1:15	#2 Northern Spring U.S. 13.5% protein	NUZHK	5,000 bu	¢/bu	6.25	$\frac{1}{8}$ ¢/bu	50	20¢/bu	1,000	30.00	15.00	36.00

* Chicago Board of Trade commodity month symbols for the current year listed in crop-year order when applicable:

January F	March H	May K	July N	September U	November X
February G	April J	June M	August Q	October V	December Z

Chicago Board of Trade commodity months symbols for subsequent years when needed:

January A	March C	May E	July L	September P	November S
February B	April D	June I	August O	October R	December T

† There are different commissions for different price levels.

SOURCE: Clayton Brokerage Company.

NOTE: Similar information is available for all other futures not shown here, such as those traded on the International Money Market (IMM) and the London and other foreign exchanges.

tion." There is no need for a customer to memorize the exact contract size of all commodities traded or the times at which the various exchanges open and close. He can refer to his copy of "Contract Information" and keep pertinent information in mind only for the positions in which he is currently interested.

Commodity prices appear on broker's quote equipment and on the financial pages of newspapers much as common stock prices appear in the same places. In stock trading the unit of trading is usually 100 shares; and in bond trading it is five bonds. Commodities, however, trade in terms of contract units specified by the exchanges. For most grains and soybeans the unit of trading is 5,000 bushels. Traditionally, traders do not speak in terms of being long two contracts of corn, but rather 10,000 bushels. The broker's board, quote machines, and newspapers indicate the value of grains and soybeans in terms of dollars, cents, and eights. Corn at $1.12½, for example, merely means that corn is valued at that price per bushel. It can be ascertained from "Contract Information" that a change of 1 cent per bushel on the standard contract of 5,000 bushels would represent a profit or loss to a corn trader of $50 on each contract. A change of ¼ cent is $12.50 on a 5,000-bushel contract.

DAILY TRADING LIMITS

To prevent extreme price changes in one day all exchanges limit the amount that prices are allowed to move daily. Basically there are two limitations. One restricts the amount that a price may move above or below the settlement price of the preceding day. This is usually called the "daily limit." The other is a restriction on the maximum range over which the price may move during one day. This is sometimes called the maximum permissible "daily range." Sometimes the daily limit and daily range are the same and sometimes the daily range is twice the limit; for example, in cattle the daily limit is 1 cent per pound and the daily range is 2 cents. If cattle closed at 33.55 cents on one day, then 34.55 cents would be "limit up" and 32.55 cents "limit down." However, if the price moved up to 34.55 cents, it could trade all the way down to 32.55 cents because its permissible range is twice its limit. For orange juice, however, the daily limit and range are both 3 cents per pound; therefore, if May orange juice closed at 44.70 cents and then traded up to 46.20 cents the next day it could not then trade below 43.20 cents. Any amount of trading can take place at the limit or the market can move down from limit up or up from limit down. Despite widespread misconception on this point, a market does not close because a daily price limit is reached; it merely cannot trade past that point. In the current month restrictions on limits may be modified to allow more flexibility, and directors of an exchange can change limits under conditions deemed to be an emergency. Daily trading limits and ranges are indicated in Table 3-2. As in "Contract Information," there may be changes from time to time and the trader is well advised to maintain current data which are available from his broker.

Many traders who began by trading stocks are quite concerned about the possibility of being "frozen in" by an adverse limit move. It should be noted, however, that the alternative is an *unlimited* adverse move which may provide far less comfort.

TABLE 3-2   DAILY TRADING LIMITS

Price limitations are imposed by the various exchanges to prevent extreme price changes in any one day. When prices reach the trading limit, trading beyond that limit is stopped for that day. In nearly all markets the Board of Directors or Governors has the power to change the limits in emergencies.

In the current month the limitations are broadened in certain future contracts by permitting wider price changes and in others, by removing limitations entirely.

	Usual range above or below previous close	Usual range between high and low
Grains		
Oats (CBT)	6¢ per bu.	12¢ per bu.
Corn	10¢ per bu.	20¢ per bu.
Rye, Winnipeg	10¢ per bu.	20¢ per bu.
Grain sorghum, Milo	15¢ per bu.	30¢ per bu.
Rapeseed, Winnipeg	20¢ per bu.	40¢ per bu.
Soybeans	20¢ per bu.	40¢ per bu.
Wheat (CBT, MGE)	20¢ per bu.	40¢ per bu.
Wheat (KC)	25¢ per bu.	50¢ per bu.
Flaxseed, Winnipeg	30¢ per bu.	60¢ per bu.
Metals		
Copper (NY)	5¢ per lb.[a]	10¢ per lb.[a]
Mercury	$5 per flask[b]	$10 per flask[b]
Palladium	$4 per oz.[c,d]	$8 per oz.[c,d]
Platinum (NY)	$10 per oz.[d]	$20 per oz.[d]
Silver (CBT)	20¢ per oz.[a]	40¢ per oz.[a]
Silver (NY)	20¢ per oz.[a]	40¢ per oz.[a]
Silver Coins (CME)	$120 per bag[d]	$240 per bag[d]
Silver Coins (NY)	$150 per bag[d]	$300 per bag[d]
Others		
Propane	1¢ per gal.[d]	2¢ per gal.[d]
Cattle	1¢ per lb	2¢ per lb
Soybean oil	1¢ per lb[a]	2¢ per lb.[a]
Sugar #11	1¢ per lb.[e]	2¢ per lb.[e]
Sugar (London)	10 £ per long ton[a]	20 £ per long ton[a]
Hogs	1.5¢ per lb.	3¢ per lb.
Pork bellies	1.5¢ per lb.	3¢ per lb.

TABLE 3-2   (Continued)

	Usual range above or below previous close	Usual range between high and low
Broilers	2¢ per lb.^{a}	4¢ per lb.^{a}
Cocoa (NY)	2¢ per lb.^{a}	4¢ per lb.^{a}
Coffee (C)	2¢ per lb.^{a}	4¢ per lb.^{a}
Cotton #2	2¢ per lb.^{a}	4¢ per lb.^{a}
Eggs (shell)	2¢ per dz.	4¢ per dz.
Orange juice	3¢ per lb.^{f}	3¢ per lb.^{f}
Lumber	$5 per M bd. ft.^{a}	$10 per M bd. ft.^{a}
Wool	10¢ per lb.^{f}	20¢ per lb.^{f}
Potatoes (Maine)	50¢ per cwt.^{d}	$1.00 per cwt.^{d}
Soybean meal	$10 per ton^a	$20 per ton^a
Plywood (CBT)	$7 per M sq. ft.^{a}	$14 per M sq. ft.^{a}

^{a}Limit is removed from spot month on first notice day.

^{b}Limit is removed from spot month on first day of delivery month.

^{c}$5.00 and $10.00 per ounce above or below preceding close during spot month.

^{d}Limit is removed from spot month on last trading day.

^{e}Limit is removed from calendar month prior to delivery month.

^{f}Limit is removed from spot month on eighth day of delivery month.

TAKING A POSITION

When the account has been opened, the customer can take a position in one of the approximately 40 commodities traded in futures markets.

The procedure, as far as he is concerned, is almost exactly like trading a security. He gives his order to his registered representative, who transmits it to his firm's wire room, from which it is sent to the exchange on which the selected commodity is traded. The report of the trade is then sent back to the office from which it originated and given to the customer. Orders may be placed by customers personally or by telephone, letter, or wire. Most of them are placed by telephone.

The broker is required to mail the customer a confirmation of the trade as promptly as possible. This is usually done on the same day the trade is made. A confirmation of a new position indicates the exchange on which it was made, the date, the price, and the size of the position. The confirmation of a position being liquidated contains the same information but in addition indicates the amount of profit or loss on the transaction and the total commission charged for entering and liquidating the position. This differs somewhat from a security confirmation of a closing transaction. Such confirmations do not indicate the profit or loss because the broker may not have access to this information. A stock can be bought at one brokerage house, held for years, and then sold at another. Commodity positions are held for relatively brief periods and may not be readily transferred from one brokerage house to another. Commodity transactions indicate the entire round-turn commissions on the liquidating side, whereas security confirmations indicate one commission on the entry and another on the liquidation.

LIQUIDATING A POSITION

A speculator who has established a long position may liquidate it in one of two ways; he may offset it with a sale or he may accept delivery of the commodity. One who has established a short position also has two possible routes to follow; he may cover his short position by buying or make delivery of the cash commodity if he has it in deliverable form and location or can acquire it. For virtually all speculators offset is the liquidation route chosen. Most do not want the cash commodity nor have it available for delivery. Their purpose in being in the markets is rather an attempt to take advantage of price change, not to deal in cash products.

If delivery is to become a factor, it is usually of more concern to the speculator with a long position than for one with a short position because it is the latter who has the choice of whether to make delivery and when. Sometimes the holder of a long position holds his position into the delivery month, hoping that the amount of deliverable cash product is too small or too tightly held to make his risk of receipt of any great concern. In such a case he should familiarize himself with the rules of the exchange on which he is trading to appraise his odds of receiving early deliveries if any are made. Notices of delivery are posted on dates and at times specified by exchange rules. These notices are sometimes given to the long with the oldest position in terms of the date on which it was established and sometimes to the brokerage house with the oldest net long position. The latter might well mean that a trader with a long position held with a brokerage house which itself was net short could not get delivery at all. Considering the cost and trouble that an unwanted delivery can cause, a trader who is not highly sophisticated in commodity market operations might do well to liquidate his long positions routinely before the first date that notice of delivery is possible. These dates are available from any well-informed brokerage firm.

The trader who does choose to hold his position into a delivery month must also be aware of the last day of futures trading after which offset is impossible and delivery is the only route open. Some typical rules covering notice days and the last day of trading are indicated in Tables 3-3 and 3-4, respectively.

TYPES OF ORDERS

A commodity may be bought or sold at the market, which means that the floor broker on the exchange must execute the order promptly at the most favorable price possible.

A limit may be imposed by the customer, which precludes the floor broker

TABLE 3-3 NOTICE DAYS

Commodity	Notice or first notice day
Sugar #11 (NY)	14th calendar day of month preceding the delivery month[1]
Sugar (London)	15th calendar day before 1st day of the delivery month[1]
Cocoa (NY)	7 business days before 1st day of the delivery month
Cotton #2 Propane Wool	5 business days before 1st day of the delivery month[2]
Coffee (C)(NY)	3 business days before 1st day of the delivery month
Copper Mercury } (Comex) Silver	2 business days before 1st day of the delivery month
Broilers Corn Oats (CBT) Plywood (CBT) Silver (CBT) Soybeans Soybean meal Soybean oil Stud lumber (CBT) Wheat (CBT, KC, MGE)	Last business day before 1st business day of the delivery month
Cocoa (London) Coffee (London) Eggs (shell) Grain sorghum, Milo Pork bellies Silver coins (CME) Winnipeg grains	1st business day of the delivery month
Cattle Hogs	M, Tu, W, Th, business day on or after the 6th calendar day of the delivery month[3]
Lumber (CME) Orange juice[2] Palladium Platinum Potatoes (Maine) Silver coins (NY)	1st business day after the last trading day of the delivery month

[1–4] See footnotes of Table 3-4.
SOURCE: Clayton Brokerage Company.

from paying more on a buy order or selling for less on a sell order. This limit assures the trader that he will get at least the price he wants if the order is executed but means that he will run the risk of not getting the order executed at all if the floor broker finds it impossible to fill it at the specified limit. Unlike the trader of listed security round lots, the commodity trader who sees the correct price of a commodity "sell through his limit" on the tape, board, or quote machine cannot assume that his order has been filled.

TABLE 3-4 LAST DAY OF TRADING

Commodity	Last day of trading
Coffee (C)	5th calendar day before 1st day of the delivery month[1]
Sugar #11 (NY) Sugar (London) }	Last business day before 1st day of the delivery month
Potatoes (Maine)	5th business day of the delivery month
Wool	11th last business day of the delivery month
Cotton #2	17th last business day of the delivery month
Palladium Platinum Silver coins (NY) }	14th calendar day of the delivery month[1]
Lumber (CME) Propane }	15th calendar day of the delivery month[1]
Orange juice	10th last business day of the delivery month
Cattle[1] Copper (NY)[4] Hogs[1] Mercury[4] }	20th calendar day of the delivery month
Cocoa (NY) Corn Eggs (shell) Grain sorghum, Milo Oats (CBT) Plywood (CBT) Soybeans Soybean meal Soybean oil Stud lumber (CBT) Wheat (KC, CBT, MGE) }	8th last business day of the delivery month
Pork bellies Silver coins (CME) }	6th last business day of the delivery month
Broilers Silver (CBT) (NY) }	4th last business day of the delivery month
Cocoa (London) Coffee (London) Winnipeg grains }	Last business day of the delivery month
London metals	Last business day prior to prompt date for delivery

[1] Or business day immediately preceding.
[2] At least 5 business days prior to day of delivery.
[3] No holiday or business day prior thereto.
[4] Or the full business day immediately thereafter.
SOURCE: Clayton Brokerage Company.

Because there are no floor specialists on the commodity exchanges, it is possible and often reasonable for a transaction to take place too far away from a floor broker to allow him to complete it. This is not considered "missing the market" unless there is some evidence of carelessness.

Stop orders are often confused with limit orders but are actually quite different. A "buy stop" instructs a broker to execute an order when the price of a commodity rises to a specified level above the current market. The difference between a buy limit order and a buy stop order is exemplified as follows. A customer is inclined to buy December sugar, which is then selling at a price of 5.43 cents per pound. He tells his broker to buy him a contract at a price not to exceed 5.35 cents. This is a "buy limit." Another customer under the same circumstances tells his broker to buy a contract of December sugar but not until the price rises to at least 5.55 cents, at which point the order will be executed at the market. The buy limit order is usually placed below the current market and must be executed at the limit or better. The buy stop order is placed above the current market and may be executed at the price specified on the stop, above it, or below it, because it is executed at the market after the stop price is touched, at which point the stop is said to be "elected."

A "sell stop" instructs a broker to execute an order when the price falls to a given level, at which point it is to be executed at the market. Unlike a typical sell limit order, it is below the current market level and may be executed at a price at, above, or below the specified stop when it is elected.[1]

A sell limit order may be used to establish a new position or to liquidate an old one. A buy limit may be used to establish a new long position or to liquidate an old short.

A stop order may be used to limit a loss, protect a profit, or establish a new position. In the first case a client may have bought his sugar at 5.45 cents per pound and has instructed his broker to sell it if it falls to 5.37 cents in order to limit his loss to eight points. In the second case the sugar may already have risen from 5.45 to 5.65 cents and the customer places his sell stop at 5.53 cents because he wants to keep his position if the price continues to rise but does not want to lose back all his paper profit if the price declines. Some clients will raise their stops as the price advances in an effort to gain as much as possible from a major move, while making certain that they can probably lose back only a little of the gain. This device, frequently called a "trailing stop," has great appeal to new traders but works considerably better in theory than in practice for reasons discussed in Chapter 4. Many major price moves seem to have an uncanny tendency to elect all the trailing stops just before going into their accelerating phase. In the third case a client with no position believes that if the current price declines from 5.45 to 5.36 cents it will continue to decline

[1] Some exchanges prohibit stop orders from time to time or allow only stop limit orders when they fear stops might aggravate unusually volatile markets.

substantially and he would like to take a short position, although not until it declines to that point. He thereupon tells his broker to sell his contract of sugar at 5.36 cents stop. Buy stops are used for similar reasons; that is, to limit a loss, protect a profit on a short position, or establish a new long position but only after the price begins to rise.

A somewhat more complex order is the stop limit. The client might instruct his broker not to buy sugar until it rises to 5.53 cents per pound and not to pay more than 5.55 cents. This is unlike the unlimited stop, which becomes a market order when the stop price has been touched. The limit price may be the same or different from the specified stop.

A "market-if-touched (M.I.T.) order" is used somewhat like a limit order but with a minor difference. The limit order must be executed at the limit price or one more favorable to the client. The M.I.T. order is executed at the market when the market has traded at the price specified on the order, and so it may be filled either at that price, above it, or below it. This order is often used by chartists who believe that a particular price is at the extreme of a trading range and who want to take a position immediately if that price level is reached with no risk of missing the market. M.I.T. orders are sometimes called "board orders"; for example, a client long pork bellies at 45.60 cents per pound who preferred to take his profit on a limit order might say, "Sell my July pork bellies at 48.50 cents." This instructs the brokerage firm to sell the contract at 48.50 cents or more. The order may be entered for one day, a specified period, or open (good until canceled). Another client with a similar position who preferred M.I.T. orders would instruct his broker to sell his position at the market whenever a transaction took place at 48.50 cents or higher.

Sometimes a customer may wish to take a position within a short time but would like the broker on the floor of the exchange to use some of his personal judgment in the timing of the fill. The broker will do this if the order indicates that he is to fill it at the market but is to take his time and will not be responsible if by waiting too long or not waiting long enough the price is unsatisfactory to the customer. Such orders are marked "Take your time" (T.Y.T.), "Not held" or both. Customers may also specify the time at which they wish their orders filled; that is, "on opening," "on close," or at a particular specified time.

"Alternative orders" provide for one of two possible executions: a customer may order 5,000 bushels of corn at $1.45 a bushel and 5,000 bushels of wheat at $2.56 a bushel, but not want both. A far more common example of the alternative order is the placing of an objective and a stop, with instructions to cancel one if the other is filled; for example, having bought one contract of soybean oil at 14.50 cents a pound, a customer may order his broker to sell the oil either at 14.95 or 14.25 cents stop, whichever occurs first, and then immediately cancel the remainder of the order to avoid inadvertently reversing his position. This second kind of alternative order is popular with the trader who has carefully determined his objective and maximum loss point for a position and prefers to enter the order rather than watch the market and have to hurry to place one order or another as the market approaches one of the two points. Such an order also helps overcome the temptation to overstay positions.

"Scale orders" are used to establish or liquidate positions as the market moves up or down. The sugar trader may instruct his broker to buy a contract of sugar at 5.45 cents and another contract each time the price drops five points from that level until he has accumulated six contracts. When he sells out his position, he may order the broker to sell one contract at 5.70 cents and another contract each time the price rises five points until his six contracts have been sold.

"Contingent orders" are filled by the broker after the price of another contract or even another commodity reaches a specified level; for example, "Sell one July pork bellies at the market when August bellies have sold at 32.60." This order is used when the customer believes that August bellies will set the tone of the market but that profits will be maximized in the July contract.

"Spreads" may be established at a fixed difference rather than at specified prices because the spreader is concerned only with the difference rather than the level. He may therefore order his broker to "buy one July pork bellies and sell one February bellies at 80 points difference or more, premium February." Such an order could be used to establish a new spread position, which the trader believes will narrow, or to take the profit in a position at a narrower difference and be satisfied with the profit at 80 points difference.

DAILY OPERATING STATEMENT

It is essential that a trader be completely aware at all times of the status of his account. He must realize that it is the equity that is most important, not the closed profits and losses to date. Failure to accept this allows the trader to convince himself that he is ahead when he has taken some small profits but is keeping positions with large open losses in the hope that the markets will reverse and his losses will be recovered.

To avoid overextending an account the trader should distinguish his gross power from his net power. "Gross power" is the capital (credit balance or ledger credit) in a commodity account increased or decreased by adjustments from all trades open at a particular time. The adjustments consist of margin requirements, commissions, and open profits or losses. Gross power can be used to margin new positions or can be withdrawn from the account. It is sometimes called "buying power" or "free credit."

"Net power" is gross power adjusted by the risk in open trades. This risk may be measured by the loss that would be suffered if all trades open were stopped out.

A trader, for example, has an account with $5,000 and no open positions. For the moment, $5,000 is his gross power. Let us assume that he has bought two contracts of cotton at 31.25 cents a pound, which require a margin of $900 per contract or $1,800 for the entire position. The commission expense for the transaction is $90. His gross power is therefore reduced to $3,110. If cotton moves up 20 points a contract to 31.45 cents, the open profit of $200 can be added to gross power, which would then be $3,310. As far as the broker is concerned, this amount can be used for new positions or withdrawn from the account. It a stop loss order has been entered at 30.80 cents, it would be possible for each cotton contract to drop at least 65 points before it is sold. If the drop occurs, the value of the account would decline by $650. A cautious trader, therefore, would regard only $2,660 as really available for use. This is his net power.

Traders use different devices to make certain that they are always aware of their equity. Some go to the length each day of withdrawing any excess

EXHIBIT 3-1   Daily Operating Statement
(Five weeks from _____ to _____)

	M	Tu	W	Th	F
Capital (includes unrealized gains and losses)					
Margin on open trades					
Gross power					
Risk on open trades					
Net power					
Additions and withdrawals					
	M	Tu	W	Th	F
Capital (includes unrealized gains and losses)					
Margin on open trades					
Gross power					
Risk on open trades					
Net power					
Additions and withdrawals					
	M	Tu	W	Th	F
Capital (includes unrealized gains and losses)					
Margin on open trades					
Gross power					
Risk on open trades					
Net power					
Additions and withdrawals					
	M	Tu	W	Th	F
Capital (includes unrealized gains and losses)					
Margin on open trades					
Gross power					
Risk on open trades					
Net power					
Additions and withdrawals					

created by improvement in their equity and depositing a check for the amount of the equity loss at the end of any day during which they suffer adversity. This makes them constantly aware that they are dealing in real money and not merely debits and credits.

A somewhat simpler method, and one calculated to make the trader more popular with his broker, is to maintain a simple ledger sheet (see Exhibit 3-1). If the fluctuations in an account are alarmingly large, or if the trader is overextended, this statement will make the danger clear before, rather than after, a margin call or sell-out notice is received.

BUYING POWER

Sometimes a client may wish to know how much is available for new trades or how much cash can be withdrawn from his account. This amount is called "buying power," "excess," "excess margin," or "gross power," and in either case would be the same at any given moment. To arrive at the figure it is necessary to subtract margin requirements on open positions from the equity in the account. This is just a way of saying that what is not being used is free to be utilized or withdrawn. The figure is computed by taking the credit balance, adjusting it by the open profit or loss, including commissions, on open positions to arrive at equity and then subtracting margin requirements to arrive at the buying power or free balance. A well-run brokerage firm should be able to provide its clients with his buying power, equity, and open profit or loss almost immediately on request.

THE MONTHLY STATEMENT

The monthly statement sent by the broker to his customer lists the changes that took place in the account during the month. Such changes may result from the deposit or withdrawal of funds, the establishment or liquidation of positions, or the changes in the prices of commodity positions held during the month and still held when the statement is mailed. The client must be familiar with the following terms to have a reasonably good understanding of his statement.

Credit or cash balance represents the funds deposited into the account, modified by the realized profits or losses from positions that have been closed out. The credit balance is not affected by open positions even though they may represent paper profits or losses. The only way the original credit balance represented by the customer's deposit of margin may be affected is by an additional deposit, a withdrawal, or closing out a position at a profit or loss. The margin requirements established by the broker to support open positions do not appear on the statement but merely reduce the amount of the credit balance left free to take other positions.

Equity is the amount of money the account would be worth if all open positions were liquidated. If there were no open positions in an account, credit balance and equity would be identical. If there were positions, equity would be determined by adding open profits less commissions to the credit balance and subtracting open losses plus commissions. A few firms indicate the net open profit or loss on statements to show their clients exactly where they stand. This plays havoc with the common practice of ignoring open losses in the hope that they will go away but is a desirable way to make certain that the client knows what he has. A statement that indicates the net open profit or loss is frequently called an "equity statement.

Transfers of funds made between the customer's regulated and unregulated commodity accounts are also shown on the monthly statement. Most brokers keep funds in the regulated account until the customer trades in a commodity not regulated by the CEA. A transfer will be indicated by a debit to the regulated account balanced by a credit in the unregulated account. The statement will show credit and open positions separately in the two types of account. Most firms give both on different parts of the same statement form. A few use separate statements. Transfers of funds within the accounts do not change the overall credit balance or equity but are just routine accounting entries to comply with federal regulations.

REGULATORY REQUIREMENTS

In addition to the rules of the various exchanges, a trader may be concerned with some of the regulations imposed by the CEA, which has many of the same functions relating to commodity exchanges and trading as the SEC has to security exchanges and trading. Most of these regulations, some of which require certain capital and bookkeeping procedures, apply to brokerage houses, but sometimes an individual trader may be directly concerned. One of the most common is that transactions in commodities regulated by the CEA, as opposed to the unregulated, be accounted for separately. This is the reason why two monthly statements may be necessary and why most brokers encourage their clients to sign the "CEA Letter" or "Authority to Transfer Funds." Unregulated commodities include those that trade on foreign exchanges not regulated by the CEA, such as Winnipeg, and a few commodities of foreign origin, such as cocoa, silver, platinum, sugar, and coffee.

To provide accurate information on the activities of large and small traders, the CEA requires large traders to file reports that can be compared with the number of open positions available from clearing houses to arrive at a total of small positions. These reports are easily prepared and need be of no concern to the trader who chooses to comply. Some brokerage houses will help to prepare the forms or even perform the entire task if assured that a client is not trading elsewhere, which could lead to an inaccurate report. Current CEA reportable positions are listed in Table 3-5. These reports are made on forms supplied by the Authority's regional offices. The CEA has also set maximum limits, well above the specified reportable positions, that may be held by one person directly or indirectly through his control of other accounts. These limits are indicated in Table 3-6.

TABLE 3-5   CEA REPORTABLE PORTIONS

The Commodity Exchange Authority requires that reports be filed for each day on which a trade is made, for the day before, during and one day after the following positions are reached by a person in the aggregate of all accounts which that person owns or controls:

Regulated commodities	Reportable position
Eggs (shell or frozen) Pork bellies Cattle Hogs Lumber Orange juice Potatoes Soybean meal Soybean oil Wool	25 contracts
Corn Grain sorghum, Milo Oats Soybeans Wheat	40 contracts
Cotton	50 contracts

SOURCE: Clayton Brokerage Company.

TAX CONSIDERATIONS

A commodity position in the futures market represents a contract to buy or sell and does not represent ownership of a commodity, as discussed in Chapter 2. The margin required by a broker may be viewed as a performance deposit and not as a payment in the usual sense of the word. When the contract is liquidated, the profit or loss merely represents the price difference from the level at which the contract was made, less the commission. There are those who quarrel with designations of commodity positions as "property," but they have been generally accepted as such and are considered to be capital assets. Although they are not regarded as securities (chiefly because they are seen as primary rather than secondary investments, hence do not depend on the performance of others), commodity contracts are subject in general to the same tax treatment as other capital assets, including securities.

Commodity trading does not create the deductible interest expense that stock trading on margin does because no interest is charged on commodity accounts unless they are in deficit or undermargined to the degree that the broker must deposit his own funds with the clearinghouse, pending receiving adequate funds from the client, in which case he may charge interest.

No state or federal taxes are charged directly on transactions. The cost of a trade for tax purposes includes the commissions charged.

TABLE 3-6 CEA POSITION LIMITS

The Commodity Exchange Authority has established the following limits on the positions that may be held or the daily trades made by a person in the aggregate of all accounts he owns or controls in any one contract month or in all contracts combined.

Commodity	Position limit	Daily position limit if different
Eggs (shell)	150 contracts[a]	
Pork bellies	250 contracts[b]	375 contracts[c]
Broilers		
Cattle		450 contracts
Cotton	300 contracts	
Plywood		
Stud lumber (BOT)		
Potatoes	350 contracts[d]	
Oats	400 contracts[e]	
Wheat	400 contracts[e]	
Soybean oil	540 contracts	
Grain sorghum	550 contracts[f]	
Corn	600 contracts	
Soybeans		
Soybean meal	720 contracts	
Hogs	750 contracts[g]	1,125 contracts[h]
Lumber (CME)	1,000 contracts[g]	2,000 contracts[i]
Silver		
Copper (Comex)	2,000 contracts[j]	
Mercury		

[a] In addition to the limitations of 150 carlots on total net long or short position, no person shall hold a net long or short position in excess of 100 carlots in the October egg future, 75 carlots in the November egg future, 50 carlots in the December egg future, or 50 carlots in the January egg future.

[b] 150 contracts in February, March, July, August, 200 contracts in May.

[c] 225 contracts in February, March, July, August, 300 contracts in May.

[d] 150 carlots in March, April, May—300 carlots in others.

[e] To the extent that the net position held or controlled by any one person in all futures in any one grain on any one market is shown to represent spreading in the same grain between markets, the limit on net position in all futures may be exceeded on such contract market, but in no case shall the excess result in a net position of more than 3,000,000 bushels in all futures combined nor more than 2,000,000 bushels in any one future.

[f] 825 net contracts in all months combined.

[g] 300 contracts in any one contract month.

[h] 450 contracts in any one contract month.

[i] 600 contracts in any one contract month.

[j] 4000 net contracts in all months combined.

In addition to the above CEA limits, certain limits are imposed by some of the commodity exchanges.

SOURCE: Clayton Brokerage Company.

Holding period rules are similar to those for securities; that is, transactions are considered to be first-in, first-out, unless a different choice is specified on the orders given to the broker: for example, if a trader buys one contract of May potatoes at 4.52 cents a pound in January, a second contract at 5.53 cents in March, and then instructs his broker to sell one contract in April when the price is 5.80 cents, the transaction will be closed on the earlier purchase at 4.52 cents. If the client prefers to close the transaction against his later purchase at 5.53 cents, he may do so, but he must ask the broker specifically to use the later purchase before the sale is made. Reasons for such requests usually involve tax or morale motives. There is no problem with physical delivery of certificates because there are none. There is no provision in the commodity markets for short sales against the box.

Capital gains treatment. The tax treatment of a commodity position depends on whether it was speculative or a hedge. Hedging carried on in day-to-day dealings of a business results in current operating expenses or credits and therefore in fully taxable operating profits and losses rather than capital gains or losses.[2]

Just where hedging ends and speculation begins is most difficult to determine. There appears to be little question that bona fide hedges are benefited by lower margin requirements and that losses resulting from them are fully deductible and gains fully taxable as ordinary income. It is less clear, however, just what is "bona fide" and even what is a "hedge." The definitions used by the CEA and IRS differ materially.[3]

Speculative profits and losses have consistently been held to be long-term or short-term capital gains, depending on whether the positions were held for more or less than six months and whether they were long or short positions. The holding period of a commodity futures position begins on the day after acquisition and ends on the day it is liquidated. There is no settlement period of several days, as there is in securities, which may be important to the trader who liquidates his position during the last few trading days of the calendar year. If delivery of a cash commodity is taken, the holding period consists of the time that the futures contract was held added to the time that the cash commodity is held, because a commodity futures contract and the commodity delivered against it are usually considered to be substantially identical.

As in securities, all profits on speculative short positions are regarded, with only rare exceptions, as short-term gains, regardless of how long the positions are held, in that short positions can hardly be considered to be

[2] Henry B. Arthur, *Commodity Futures as a Business Management Tool*, Division of Research; Graduate School of Business Administration, Harvard University, Boston, 1971, p. 41.
[3] Thorough discussions can be found in the Commodity Exchange Act As Amended, Section 4a, and in the Internal Revenue Code of 1954. The latter is summarized in *Standard Federal Tax Reporter*, Code Volume, Commerce Clearing House, New York, Chicago, and Washington, D.C., 1969. See especially Code sections 1221 and 1233.

capital assets. Of course, a long position is usually taken to liquidate the short position, but it is considered to be instantaneously liquidated.

In a closed-out loss reinstated by a similar position within 30 days of the date on which the loss was realized the law is not so obvious as it is in securities, where such a loss is clearly not deductible. One Circuit Court of Appeals has ruled that wash-sale rules apply and another has ruled that they do not. The decisions have not been clearly reconciled. In practice, many commodity traders apparently assume that the rule does not apply because most commodity trades are quite short-term and the government's revenue is unlikely to be materially affected in the long run.

Substantially identical nature of different commodity contract months. Although a commodity futures contract and the commodity it represents are substantially identical, with little doubt, it should be noted that there is some difference in court decisions concerning whether different contract months of the same commodity are substantially identical. This has important implications for those who trade spreads, whether motivated by speculation or tax considerations. Ultimate settlement of this point, along with others, such as whether commodity futures and options (puts and calls) are securities, could have a drastic effect on the conduct of the commodity business. These questions are difficult to resolve but will undoubtedly be settled by the courts sooner or later.[4]

If different delivery months of the same commodity are not considered to be substantially identical, as is usually presumed by most traders and their tax consultants, then a trader who is long March cotton and short May cotton is able at the same time to realize a long-term gain on the March cotton if he holds the position more than six months. If a trader is long with a substantial profit, which he is inclined to take, but needs only a short time more to be eligible for long-term capital gain treatment, he can sell another futures contract against his position without jeopardizing his holding period. There is no certainty, of course, that this procedure will ensure complete success. If the market should decline drastically, the profit on the long position would be replaced by a profit on the short side. Furthermore, the spread position itself involves the possibility of a loss on the difference and the certainty of greater commission expense. A spread of exactly the same commodity in the same delivery month on two different exchanges would certainly be considered substantially identical and therefore obviously offers no tax advantage.

Tax spreads. Much has been written about the possibility of using commodity spreads to convert short-term gains from any source into long-term gains, postponing one year's short-term gains to the next year, either in whole or in part, converting one year's short-term gain into a long-term gain the following year, or, possibly, transferring a gain from one entity to

---

[4] Laurence Goldfein and Lester Hochberg, "Use of Commodity Straddles Can Effect Impressive Tax Savings," *The Journal of Taxation* (December 1968), 342.

another. Such spreads are not easy to manage, and the United States Internal Revenue Service has a long, often successful, record of attacking transactions whose obvious purpose is to secure a tax advantage rather than a profit. A trade may yield a tax advantage and no profit, but at least a profit should have been a reasonable possibility. Spread trading for tax purposes is no area for the amateur. A poor choice of spread positions or mismanagement of the positions chosen can result in losses to a client well beyond any possible tax savings. Many clients in this position may be considered unsophisticated in the commodity area and the brokerage employee may be inexpert in taxes (and perhaps in commodities), with distinct adverse legal implications to the broker. A particular problem is caused when a short position is placed in the early month of a spread and a long position in the later month. This may result in a severe loss if a strong market in the nearby month gained substantially on the distant month. It is unlikely that an unusually strong market will cause a distant month to rise materially on the nearby.

Aside from the difficulty of selecting and timing the trades, the trader and his adviser should make certain of a high degree of probability that the commissions, interest loss on margin, and risk of loss on the trade itself are overcome by enough potential saving to justify the economic risk inherent in every trade, no matter how carefully conceived and executed.

Tax rules vary among individual speculators, among businesses that deal primarily or partly in commodities, and among dealers in commodities. Important changes are made in the rules as new court decisions are handed down. The investor or trader would do well to consult his tax adviser before making any important assumptions about his tax exposure.

CHAPTER FOUR

The Behavior
of Commodity Futures Prices

Truth is allowed only a brief interval of victory
between the two long periods when it is condemned
as paradox or belittled as trivial.

ARTHUR SCHOPENHAUER,
From Copernicus to Einstein

INTRODUCTION

An important step toward successful commodity trading is an understanding of the behavior of commodity futures prices. This chapter promotes
such an understanding by describing and analyzing some of the important
facts that are known about short- and long-run characteristics of futures
prices.

Initially a review will be presented of the statistical evidence that supports or denies the random walk theory, which suggests that short-run price
changes in speculative markets like commodity futures are difficult to forecast with only past prices as a guide.

Even if the random walk model approximates reality in the short run,
speculators can still profit from long-run changes in prices if, for example,
the average upward price change is greater than the average downward
price change. If such trends are present, do speculators profit solely and
simply for bearing the risks that hedgers transfer to them or do they profit
because they can forecast prices successfully? The "risk premium" concept
is a common point of departure in the literature of futures price behavior,
and the case for and against the existence of such a premium is analyzed.

Whether a risk premium, as such, exists, there are observable biases in
commodity futures that can lead to speculator profits, and some of these,
as well as evidence that some speculators can forecast prices, are discussed.
The process of decision making which precedes these forecasts is the subject of Chapters 6 and 7.

THE THEORY OF THE RANDOM WALK

Although the fundamental laws of supply and demand have been generally
accepted as determining the long-run price behavior of commodity futures
prices, they have certainly failed in the short run to provide a similar in-

sight. Most traders will agree that in the short run there is simply no significant correlation between "fundamentals" and prices, yet it is precisely in the short run that traders establish open profits and receive open losses.

Premises. Most discussions of short-run speculative price behavior take the "random walk hypothesis" as their point of departure. This theory suggests that successive price *changes* in commodity markets are independent and that past prices are not a reliable indicator of future prices. One of the major premises of the random walk theory is based on the concept of an "efficient" market. An efficient market is defined as one in which there are large numbers of equally informed, actively competing people attempting to maximize profits. In such a market, at any moment in time, price reflects all available information, as well as those events *expected* to transpire in the foreseeable future. Holbrook Working was the first in the commodity futures field to offer a theory of expectations that rests on the premise that futures reflect *anticipated* changes in supply and demand rather than on their immediate values.[1]

In an efficient market actual prices approximate anticipated or intrinsic value. In a world of uncertainty intrinsic value is elusive. Disagreements will cause random discrepancies between intrinsic value and actual prices. If the market is highly efficient, actual prices will move randomly about the intrinsic value.

Of course, intrinsic values change. Soybeans *do* move from $2.85 to $3.50 a bushel, and there is nothing in the random walk theory to suggest that superior intrinsic value analysis is useless in an efficient market. The trader will always do well if he can identify long-run supply-demand changes before such expectations are reflected in actual price changes. On the average, however, competition will cause most of the effects of new information regarding intrinsic values to be reflected quickly in commodity prices. It is the random quality of new information and not changes in supply or demand that is responsible for the irregular behavior of futures prices. The duration and extent of such price adjustments will be random variables that will cause prices to overadjust, underadjust, sometimes precede the information, and sometimes follow it in a manner that successive price changes are independent. Such a market has come to be known as a "random walk" market.

Behavior of traders. If price changes are formed according to anticipations of supply and demand, it is important to analyze in more depth the behavior of traders in response to news. In a *totally* efficient (hypothetical) market, when no new information is available, no new market position would be taken and there would be no price changes. A general price equilibrium would be established in which no trader who had the will to buy or sell had the power and no trader who had the power (one who held

---

[1] Holbrook Working, "A Theory of Anticipatory Prices," *American Economic Review Proceedings,* 48 (May 1958), 191.

an open position or the funds to establish one) had the will. As new information emerged, all traders would analyze it. If a change in positions were dictated, those changes would be effected rapidly and a new level of equilibrium would be established. In such a market a trader would be successful only if he were better at analyzing and interpreting the information currently available to all traders because the history of equilibrium levels would tell him nothing about tomorrow's new input of information.

Moving from such an ideal market, an analysis can be made of the after math of the input of new information on a more realistic market consisting of "insiders" and "outsiders." The first group is made up of traders who by training or position learn about new developments quickly. The second group obtains new information only after the insiders have heard about it. Such a market would be less than strongly efficient.

As new information becomes available, a double response occurs: Insiders react first and outsiders' reactions follow. The first response is clear. If the new information is bullish, insider response would push prices higher. Conversely, if the new input is bearish, prices would fall. The later outsider response cannot be disposed of so simply. If the new information is bullish, prices could rise again, remain unchanged, or drop. The first possibility could occur if the demand by the outsiders exceeded the supply offered by the insiders at the higher price established by the insiders. The second possibility could occur if outsider demand were exactly offset by insider desire to sell at the higher price. The third possibility is that outsider demand could not offset some increased insider selling at a higher price. The second case reflects the most efficient market, that is, when insiders correctly predict subsequent outsider behavior. Even if this response is not always forthcoming and the insiders do not perfectly anticipate the outsiders, the insiders are as likely to overestimate as to underestimate the outsiders' response to market news. Thus on each input of bullish news a trader could not establish a long position and expect prices to work higher, nor could he take a short position directly after the issuance of bearish news and have a high probability of profit.

The random walk theorists agree that it is unlikely that their model describes the behavior of commodity price changes exactly. Yet they assert that although successive price changes may not be strictly independent the amount of dependence is unimportant. If there is no such strategy, then a simple policy of buy and hold will equal the results from any sophisticated procedure for timing. Therefore, unless a trader can improve on the buy-and-hold policy, the independence assumption of the random walk model is an adequate description of reality.

All this does *not* mean that short-term traders will not or cannot make money trading commodity futures; it *does* mean that, on the average, those traders will not beat a buy-and-hold strategy with information they obtain from historical data.

Perhaps the clearest method of testing the random walk theory is to assume for the moment that it is *true* and that it does present an excellent "jumping off point" for the analysis of the behavior of commodity futures prices. To many traders this assertion may be heresy, yet if the theory is not backed by significant statistical evidence it can be withdrawn as a serious candidate.

EMPIRICAL STUDIES

Introduction. Those who have argued that commodity price changes are random in nature have based their assertion on the following principles: (1) price changes are such that they could have been generated by independent trials from a simple chance model such as a roulette wheel; (2) no one has been able to show that price changes exhibit a systematic pattern, even though present statistical techniques are capable of detecting data that have come from a significantly nonrandom process.

The first point is merely suggestive because it is impossible to prove the existence of randomness. Holbrook Working, writing as early as 1934 observed:

> It has several times been noted that time series commonly possess in many respects the characteristics of cumulated random numbers. The separate items in such time series are by no means random in character, but the *changes* between successive items tend to be largely random. This characteristic has been noted conspicuously in sensitive commodity prices. . . .[2]

In support of this position it has been suggested that the output of a simple roulette wheel could duplicate many of the characteristic features of commodity futures price movements. Results of this approach are illustrated in Figures 4-1 and 4-2. Although the illustration is based on price changes of a securities index, the principle is clear. Figure 4-1 represents the daily changes in closing prices of the Dow-Jones Industrial Average for the year 1956. Figure 4-2 represents changes generated by the output of a random number table. Even though the chance model demonstrated in Figure 4-2 cannot duplicate history in any sense other than one evening at a gambling casino duplicates another, the similarity of both series is striking enough to startle the would-be trader. Certainly the plotting of a series of price changes that could be generated from a random number table is not calculated to inspire confidence in the recurring "patterns" supposedly imbedded in price history.

In testing the random walk assertion, statisticians have brought to bear several kinds of tests. In the pages that follow results of runs analysis, serial correlation, filter rules and spectral analysis are presented as evidence in the controversy.

Analysis of runs. If a change in price (daily, weekly, monthly) is positive,

---

[2] Holbrook Working, "A Random-Difference Series for Use in the Analysis of Time Series," *Journal of the American Statistical Association,* 29 (1934), 11.

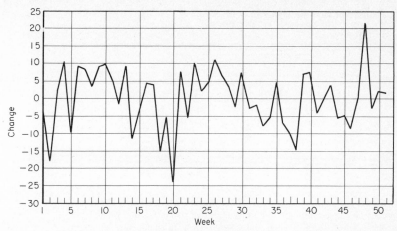

FIG. 4-1   Changes from Friday to Friday (closing), January 6, 1956, to December 28, 1956, Dow-Jones Industrial Index. (Harry Roberts, "Stock Market 'Patterns' and Financial Analysis: Methodological Suggestions," *Journal of Finance*, March 1959, p. 4.)

it can be denoted by "+." A negative change can be labeled "—." A "run" is a consecutive sequence of the same symbol. Assume the following sequence of +'s and —'s on a close-to-close basis:

— — + + — + + + + + — + — — — + + — — — + — + — .

The first four runs of this sequence are — —, + +, —, + + + +. There are 13 runs in the entire sequence.

The purpose of a runs test is to determine whether the number of consecutive days of price movement in one direction is close to that expected by pure chance. Table 4-1 summarizes the observed versus the expected runs

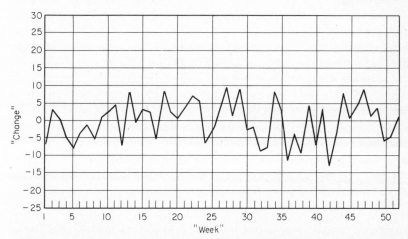

FIG. 4-2   Simulated market changes for 52 weeks. (Harry Roberts, "Stock Market 'Patterns' and Financial Analysis: Methodological Suggestions," *Journal of Finance*, March 1959, p. 5.)

TABLE 4-1   DISTRIBUTION OF LENGTHS OF RUN OF
DAILY JULY CORN AND SOYBEAN FUTURE PRICES,
SUMMARY, 1957–1968

Length of run (days)	July soybeans			July corn		
	Observed run		Expected run	Observed run		Expected run
	Up	Down	Up or down*	Up	Down	Up or down*
1	359	364	345	359	365	361
2	202	169	172	201	185	180
3	82	88	86	78	75	90
4	26	48	43	40	40	45
5	8	12	22	12	12	23
6+	10	15	22	13	7	23
Total	687	696	690	703	684	722

* Expected on the assumption of 0.5 probability of rise or fall and 2,755 close-to-close observations for July corn and 2,888 observations for July soybeans.
SOURCE: Richard Stevenson and Robert Bear, "Commodity Futures: Trends or Random Walks?" *Journal of Finance*, No. 1 (March 1970), 74.

in a recent study of daily futures prices of July soybeans and July corn over an 11-year period. Examination of these actual price changes shows that in this sample there were slightly more short (one- and two-day) runs than expected and slightly fewer long runs (five and six or more days) than would have occurred, on the average, by pure chance. The difference, however, is not significant and *could* have occurred by chance. The trader will note that these results, although slightly favoring a tendency toward reversals, in the main confirm the absence of identifiable nonrandomness in the length of runs through the 12 years observed. Also, as expected, the number of "up" runs of any given duration was about equal to the number of "down" runs of the same duration. Results of other statistical tests using runs have also been generally consistent with the hypothesis of independent price changes.[3]

Serial correlation. Serial correlation measures the correlation between a series of numbers like commodity futures prices with lagging numbers in the same series. Many different lags and many different time periods can be used to draw data for serial correlation tests. The presence of trends or reversal tendencies in commodity futures prices can be detected with this approach. The object is to find patterns in short-term price changes that can be used to trade more profitably than a naïve buy-and-hold strategy. If an up-move in price is followed more often than not by another up-move, positive serial correlation is present. If the converse is true, the trader has isolated a tendency for negative serial correlation or a reversal characteristic.

[3] See Holbrook Working, "Prices of Cash Wheat and Futures at Chicago Since 1883," *Wheat Studies,* 2, No. 3 (November 1934), 75–124, and Sidney Alexander, "Price Movements in Speculative Markets: Trends or Random Walks," reprinted in Paul Cootner, Ed., *The Random Character of Stock Market Prices,* The M.I.T. Press, Cambridge, Mass., 1964, pp. 199–218.

Following Working's discovery that fluctuations of futures prices are economically warranted responses to new information, itself unpredictable, came a study that showed a slight nonrandom characteristic in price movements. Brinegar,[4] using a new statistic, found a weak but statistically significant tendency toward "continuity" of a trend (positive serial correlation) in the prices of wheat, corn, and rye, ranging from 4 to 16 weeks. The amount of continuity varied from commodity to commodity and from time period to time period and was especially associated with periods of large price movements. A second important conclusion from Brinegar's study is the evidence of a slight "reaction tendency" (negative serial correlation) for short intervals of apparently one to two weeks.

Larson[5] expanded these findings by studying the day-to-day changes in corn prices for two 10-year periods, 1922–1931 and 1949–1958. His contribution was to measure the pattern followed by prices after inputs of new information. Larson found that on the average about 81 percent of the price effect of new demand and supply information occurs on a single day, presumably the day of changes in news. There is then a reaction, averaging about 8 percent dispersed over four days, away from the initial price movement, even though the first movement is not sufficient to discount all the news. Finally, an additional 27 percent dispersed over 45 days results in a total price movement that is just appropriate. Many markets may operate as Larson's study suggests, differing from an ideal random walk market principally in that traders react with varying skills to varying sources of information. For that reason some of the response to price making may be delayed, even though the delay is a small fraction of the total response and is dispersed over a considerable number of days in an unpredictable pattern.

Larson's evidence was important because, as Working later indicated,

> Economic reasoning suggests that the larger hedging orders should be expected to produce fairly large dips and bulges, of considerable duration. Experience of hedgers seems to bear out that reasoning. But Larson's evidence was the first to indicate clearly, from the behavior of prices, that these larger dips and bulges occurred frequently, in a large range of sizes and durations, their durations extending often to three or four days.[6]

Houthakker[7] has made a study that deals with the relative profitability of varying stop-loss order percentages as an indicator of serial correlation. Theoretically, if price changes were random, a trader who tried to limit

[4] Claude Brinegar, "A Statistical Analysis of Speculative Price Behavior," *Food Research Institute Studies,* Supplement, 9 (1970).

[5] Arnold Larson, "Measurement of a Random Process in Futures Prices," *Food Research Institute Studies,* 1, No. 3 (November 1960).

[6] Holbrook Working, "Tests of a Theory Concerning Floor Trading on Commodity Exchanges," *Food Research Institute Studies,* Supplement, 7 (1967), 16.

[7] Hendrik Houthakker, "Systematic and Random Elements in Short-Term Price Movements," *American Economic Review,* 51 (1961), 164–172.

his losses by selling (buying) whenever the price of a commodity falls (rises) by a fixed percentage below (above) his initial price would not find his average results better over a number of years than if he used no stops at all. If successive price changes were independent, a price decline (rise) of, say, 5 percent, which might be necessary to trigger a stop-loss, would not affect subsequent price changes. On the other hand, if a particular stop-loss percentage can be discovered, the use of which increases average net profit, then an instance of persistence in price trends will have been indicated. If the use of stop orders can lead to nonrandom outcomes for the trader, the problem becomes one of discovering what stop percentage is relevant. Stops placed too close to the entry price are activated by "noise," whereas if stops are placed too far away from the market losses may be too great to be adequately offset by profits.

For his analysis Houthakker chose wheat and corn futures during the periods October 1, 1921, to October 1, 1939, and February 1, 1947, to October 1, 1956. It was assumed that a trader bought or sold May wheat or corn on October 1, the September contract on February 1, and the December futures on June 1, liquidating each trade after four months unless stopped out beforehand. Commissions were not calculated.

Tables 4-2 and 4-3 summarize trading results for varying stop-loss percentages. A stop percentage of 5 means that the trader sells out at 95 percent of his purchase price, and a stop percentage of 0 means that any adversity below (above) a given entry point resulted in liquidation. A consistent long position in all three contracts of both wheat and corn was profitable, which implies a possible positive expected value over the periods covered.

In analyzing the stop percentages between 0 and 100, Houthakker cites

TABLE 4-2   TRADING RESULTS IN WHEAT FUTURES (1921–1939, 1947-1956) FOR VARIOUS STOP PERCENTAGES, IN CENTS PER BUSHEL

Stop percentage	Long positions				Short positions			
	May	Sept.	Dec.	Combined	May	Sept.	Dec.	Combined
100	+127	− 99	+ 59	+ 87	−127	+ 99	−59	− 87
20	+104	−126	+ 55	+ 33	−100	+112	−16	− 4
15	+ 96	−130	+ 69	+ 35	− 83	+ 73	−24	− 34
10	+132	−123	+ 90	+ 99	− 68	+ 90	+10	+ 32
7½	+135	− 74	+126	+187	− 55	+ 57	+27	+ 29
5	+122	− 47	+140	+215	− 34	+ 83	+79	+128
4	+133	− 15	+ 65	+183	− 19	+ 94	+53	+128
3	+116	− 5	+ 78	+189	− 19	+ 94	+70	+146
2	+ 42	− 4	+ 84	+122	− 24	+ 71	+30	+ 77
1	− 2	− 27	+ 73	+ 44	− 27	+ 60	−11	+ 22
0	+ 18	0	+ 27	+ 45	0	0	0	0

SOURCE: Hendrik Houthakker, "Systematic and Random Elements in Short Term Price Movements," *American Economic Review*, 51 (1961), 166.

TABLE 4-3   TRADING RESULTS IN CORN FUTURES (1922-1939,
1947-56) FOR VARIOUS STOP PERCENTAGES IN CENTS PER
BUSHEL

Stop percentage	Long positions				Short positions			
	May	Sept.	Dec.	Combined	May	Sept.	Dec.	Combined
100	+79	− 83	+112	+108	− 79	+ 83	−112	−108
20	+75	−114	+108	+ 69	−111	+ 94	− 36	− 64
15	+95	− 94	+119	+120	− 80	+ 91	− 48	− 37
10	+83	− 73	+141	+151	− 37	+107	− 47	+ 23
7½	+57	− 97	+151	+111	− 45	+103	− 27	+ 31
5	+21	− 47	+127	+101	− 23	+104	− 19	+ 62
4	+35	− 34	+125	+126	− 28	+117	− 56	+ 33
3	+36	− 11	+139	+164	− 12	+115	− 68	+ 35
2	+ 9	− 17	+156	+148	− 10	+105	− 53	+ 42
1	+29	− 24	+170	+175	− 9	+ 66	− 27	+ 32
0	+29	+ 2	+ 70	+100	0	0	0	0

SOURCE: Hendrik Houthakker, "Systematic and Random Elements in Short Term Price
Movements," *American Economic Review*, 51 (1961), 166.

some evidence of nonrandomness, even though the improvement is not
always large.[8] The study notes that long positions in May corn give better
results when stop percentages are relatively large but that the opposite is
true for December corn. Results for being long May and December wheat
and short September corn also favor a moderate stop percentage. Stop-
losses, of course, tend to reduce losses rather than increase profits. The
trader could not expect a stop-loss policy, no matter how efficiently formulated, to furnish him with a profitable trading record.

The best published evidence to date of attempting to scalp at least the
larger dips and bulges of prices is presented in a study by Smidt, whose
analysis of daily soybean prices produces interesting evidence of the presence of positive or negative serial correlation over a 10-year period.[9] The
data used were the daily high, low, and closing prices for May soybeans
for the 10 consecutive contracts expiring May 1952 through May 1961.
Each trading period was terminated 10 days before the contract expired,
and the length of the period available for trading varied from 137 to 188
days a year.

Table 4-4 represents some characteristics of the data and indicates that
prices at the beginning of the first trading period at 289.500 were only
21.5 cents a bushel less than the 311.000 price in May 1961. The portion

[8] Roger Gray and S. T. Nielsen, "Rediscovery of Some Fundamental Price Behavior Characteristics" (paper presented at a meeting of the Econometric Society, Cleveland, Ohio, September 7, 1963). The authors supplied additional data, using the same "stop-loss" technique,
which indicated that Houthakker's results were not necessarily typical of the markets analyzed. The tendency for trends was attributed by Gray and Nielsen to the influence of the
government price support program and Houthakker's use of distant contracts.

[9] Seymour Smidt, "A Test of the Serial Independence of Price Changes in Soybean Futures,"
Food Research Institute Studies, 5, No. 2 (1965).

TABLE 4-4   SOME CHARACTERISTICS OF THE MAY SOYBEANS
FUTURES CONTRACT PRICE SERIES USED TO TEST TRADING
RULES (CENTS PER BUSHEL, EXCEPT AS OTHERWISE
INDICATED)

Year ending	Length of time series,* trading days	Closing prices			Within trading period			
		10 days from			Maximum		Minimum	
		beginning	end	Change	Price	Day	Price	Day
1952	192	289.500	296.500	+ 7.000	309.750	50	281.500	166
1953	157	299.500	301.000	+ 1.500	311.000	41	280.000	91
1954	157	270.250	393.500	+123.250	422.000	141	268.750	11
1955	161	282.250	252.250	− 30.000	299.000	24	247.250	134
1956	161	236.750	321.500	+ 84.750	340.000	148	234.000	40
1957	161	248.250	240.375	− 7.875	269.500	43	238.000	142
1958	204	250.500	226.625	− 23.875	251.750	13	222.625	148
1959	208	233.250	229.625	− 3.625	233.500	28	217.375	110
1960	203	222.000	213.875	− 8.125	233.500	70	211.000	185
1961	201	225.750	311.000	+ 85.250	334.500	174	220.500	76
Total	...	......	......	+228.250				

* Exceeds "trading period" by 10 days at the beginning and 10 days at the end.

of the year that was arbitrarily chosen exhibits a strong trend upward. Indeed, without regard for the capital necessary to carry intrayear adverse price movement, a trader could have earned $2 a bushel if he had instituted the simple strategy of buying May soybeans at the beginning of each year's trading period and selling them 10 days before the contract expired in May of each year.

POSITIVE SERIAL CORRELATION. Traders often remark that they want to buy strength and sell weakness on the theory that strength or weakness in a given price structure tends to perpetuate itself. To check this viewpoint Smidt formulated and tested two rules, using May soybeans data from 1952 to 1961. Twenty examples of each of these tests are summarized in Tables 4-5 and 4-6. The study is designed so that the trader can utilize only two market positions, long one contract or short one contract. The only time a cash position is allowed is before the initial commitment. For both rules a moving average of N daily closing prices is computed in which N takes on values $1, 2, 3, 5, 10$; that is, the rules are tried by using moving averages of $1, 2, 3, 5$, and 10 days, respectively.

The first rule of action specifies that the trader buy (sell) soybeans if the N-day moving average should move up (down) by K cents or more in any given day; for example, if the trader selected an $N = 3$-day moving average and a $K = 2$ cents required price change before taking a position, he would follow the decision rule, "Buy (sell) one contract of May soybeans whenever the 3-day moving average advances (declines) by 2 cents or more on any day." In the study described the required change K was given the values shown in Section A of Table 4-5. The prices at which the buys (sells) were executed were statistically determined by defining a random price variable

TABLE 4-5   RESULTS OF SOYBEAN RULES TESTING POSITIVE CORRELATION, WITH ACTION SIGNALS BASED ON ABSOLUTE SIZE OF CHANGE IN THE MOVING AVERAGE

A. Summary

Total profits or losses* (cents per bushel)

Action signals		1952–1961		After commission, in year with		After commission, number of years†		Commission, cents per bushel	Total number of moves
Length of moving average N, days	Change required, K, cents per bushel	After commission	Before commission	best profits	worst losses	with profits	with losses		
1	1.0	−476	−338	1	−112	1	9	138	384
1	2.0	−176	−112	18	−108	3	7	64	117
1	3.0	− 59	− 29	100	− 66	4	5	30	83
1	4.0	146	163	91	− 19	7	2	17	46
2	1.0	− 12	52	104	− 40	4	6	64	178
2	2.0	3	28	83	− 46	4	5	25	69
2	3.0	71	84	93	− 44	5	3	13	37
2	4.0	36	44	51	− 19	3	4	8	21
3	1.0	112	154	142	− 27	4	5	42	116
3	2.0	75	89	108	− 50	7	3	14	40
3	3.0	67	73	61	− 42	4	3	6	18
3	4.0	20	23	41	− 16	1	2	3	9
5	0.5	9	57	52	− 53	3	7	48	133
5	1.0	110	131	72	− 54	7	2	21	57
5	1.5	102	112	43	− 20	6	2	10	28
5	2.0	149	155	77	− 22	6	1	6	18
10	0.5	25	47	65	− 50	5	5	22	61
10	1.0	197	203	100	− 14	7	1	6	17
10	1.5	124	127	113	− 45	3	2	3	7
10	2.0	58	60	54	− 29	2	1	2	5

*Profits and losses rounded to the nearest cent.

†Total does not always equal 10 because of years in which profits or losses were less than half a cent per bushel, or in which no trading occurred.

such that any value between the high and low price on the day following the signal was equally likely. For illustrative purposes the midrange price, or the price midway between the daily high and low, will suffice. Results using the described decision rule for $N = 1, 2, 3, 5, 10$ and for K as shown are summarized in sections A and B of Table 4-5.

Reading from section A of Table 4-5 and continuing the preceding example with $N = 3$ and $K = 2$, it can be seen that during the entire period from 1952 to 1961 the trader made 75 cents a bushel profit after commissions, the highest profit being $1.08 a bushel and the largest loss being 50 cents a bushel. The decision rule was profitable in 7 of the 10 years, commission costs were 14 cents a bushel, and 40 positions were taken by the trader. A breakdown by years is listed in section B of Table 4-5.

TABLE 4-5   (Continued)

B. Annual profits and losses‡ after commissions, cents per bushel

Action signals N	K	1951–1952	1952–1953	1953–1954	1954–1955	1955–1956	1956–1957	1957–1958	1958–1959	1959–1960	1960–1961	Total
	1.0	−86	−60	− 42	−110	− 1	−29	−16	1	−21	−112	−476
1	2.0	−41	−15	18	− 48	− 1	11	− 5	− 4	17	−108	−176
1	3.0	−35	−24	100	8	−39	3	−14	0	8	− 66	− 59
1	4.0	4	−19	91	− 17	25	12	20	0	1	29	146
2	1.0	−17	−37	104	2	46	−26	−25	−21	2	− 40	− 12
2	2.0	−46	−31	83	7	−10	12	18	0	− 2	− 28	3
2	3.0	−20	−44	93	− 3	19	6	18	0	2	0	71
2	4.0	− 9	−19	28	− 16	51	13	0	0	0	− 12	36
3	1.0	−22	5	142	0	53	−27	5	− 6	−21	− 17	112
3	2.0	−11	4	108	14	− 4	1	11	0	2	− 50	75
3	3.0	−19	19	45	− 42	61	13	0	0	0	28	67
3	4.0	0	0	−16	0	− 5	0	0	0	0	41	20
5	0.5	−18	−11	46	− 53	52	−14	−13	− 4	− 3	27	9
5	1.0	−26	−54	61	5	15	12	17	0	8	72	110
5	1.5	−20	12	43	− 15	35	9	0	0	3	35	102
5	2.0	−22	2	77	16	35	14	0	0	0	27	149
10	0.5	−50	10	55	− 37	65	−31	−10	− 4	7	20	25
10	1.0	−14	1	100	34	35	16	0	0	1	24	197
10	1.5	−10	0	113	− 45	37	0	0	0	0	29	124
10	2.0	0	0	54	0	33	0	0	0	0	− 29	59
Average per year		−23	−15	65	− 15	25	0	0	− 2	0	− 6	29

‡ Profits and losses rounded to the nearest cent.

The second rule of action is the same as the first, except that the required change is now a proportion P of the largest of the 10 past daily price ranges. This innovation is based on the hypothesis that the price volatility, as measured by the daily price range, might be an indication of the variability of future price changes. For the study P took on the values indicated in section A of Table 4-6, in which the results of trading by this rule are shown. Section B of Table 4-6, the counterpart of section B of Table 4-5, lists results year by year.

The data summarized in Tables 4-5 and 4-6 show that for the period and commodity tested a large number of the trading-decision rules (i.e., for various values of N and K or of N and P) lead to significant returns after commissions. For any given length N of moving average, gain (or loss) is a function of K (or P). The trader can immediately see that this is so; for example, a small value for K will generate more trades and therefore more commissions.

If the microscope rather than the telescope is applied to the results of soybean trading rules, interesting insights develop. Even for the most profit-

TABLE 4-6 RESULTS OF SOYBEAN RULES TESTING POSITIVE
CORRELATION, WITH ACTION SIGNALS BASED ON RELATION
OF CHANGE IN MOVING AVERAGE TO LARGEST PAST 10
DAILY PRICE RANGES

A. Summary
Total profits or losses* (cents per bushel)

Action signals		1952–1961							
Length of moving average N, days	Change required, P (fraction of maximum range)	After commission	Before commission	After commission, in year with		After commission, number of years†		Commission, cents per bushel	Total number of moves
				best profits	worst profits	with profits	with losses		
1	0.2	−460	−264	26	−105	1	9	196	544
1	0.5	−114	− 41	15	− 58	4	5	73	204
1	0.7	128	161	90	− 32	6	4	33	93
1	1.0	153	161	114	− 22	4	5	8	23
2	0.2	− 7	88	129	− 44	4	6	95	265
2	0.5	162	184	110	− 27	5	5	22	62
2	0.7	93	101	110	− 44	5	4	8	23
2	1.0	− 14	− 13	12	− 26	1	1	1	2
3	0.2	110	172	104	− 27	3	6	62	173
3	0.5	173	183	119	− 30	5	5	10	27
3	0.7	107	110	81	− 11	5	3	3	9
3	1.0	0	0	0	0	0	0	0	0
5	0.2	134	167	101	− 28	5	5	33	92
5	0.5	57	60	80	− 28	4	4	3	8
5	0.7	0	0	0	0	0	0	0	0
5	1.0	0	0	0	0	0	0	0	0
10	0.05	125	161	58	− 32	7	3	36	99
10	0.10	108	136	84	− 43	5	5	28	77
10	0.15	181	199	122	− 26	7	3	18	50
10	0.20	227	237	122	− 33	7	3	10	29

* Profits and losses rounded to the nearest cent.
† Total does not always equal 10 because of years in which profits or losses were less than
half a cent per bushel, or in which no trading occurred.

able decision rules most of the individual years generate losses or small
profits, and it is left to a few years to produce extraordinary profits. In fact,
even the highly profitable rules would not attract a trader if the one most
profitable year were deleted. Large profits are concentrated in the major
bull market years of 1954, 1956, and 1961.

From Table 4-4 it can be seen that only in 1953–1954, 1955–1956, and
1960–1961 was the intracontract range in May soybeans $1 a bushel or
more. Each of these years produced unique supply and demand factors.
In 1953 insufficient rains severely damaged the soybean crop and prices
leaped up in response to an acute shortage. The 1955–1956 soybean price
move did not originate from drought or reduced production but rather

TABLE 4-6   (Continued)

B. Annual profits and losses‡ after commissions, cents per bushel

Action signals N	P	1951–1952	1952–1953	1953–1954	1954–1955	1955–1956	1956–1957	1957–1958	1958–1959	1959–1960	1960–1961	Total
1	0.2	−73	−70	26	−105	− 2	−50	−19	−21	−69	−77	−460
1	0.5	−36	1	15	− 36	21	0	4	− 5	−20	−58	−114
1	0.7	−32	−18	90	− 10	53	23	−26	4	5	39	128
1	1.0	0	− 8	114	− 26	48	12	−22	−17	−11	63	153
2	0.2	−34	−43	129	− 14	30	−38	17	0	−10	−44	− 7
2	0.5	−27	− 8	110	− 16	56	− 2	− 8	4	5	48	162
2	0.7	−19	−44	110	0	61	13	− 6	−11	−22	11	93
2	1.0	0	0	12	− 26	0	0	0	0	0	0	− 14
3	0.2	−28	−25	104	− 21	62	−27	− 3	0	−12	60	110
3	0.5	−17	−24	119	15	61	−30	− 3	2	−26	76	173
3	0.7	− 2	0	12	17	− 8	0	11	−11	7	81	107
3	1.0	0	0	0	0	0	0	0	0	0	0	0
5	0.2	−14	− 8	101	− 21	52	3	−28	4	− 3	48	134
5	0.5	− 5	− 2	12	− 28	− 8	2	0	0	6	80	57
5	0.7	0	0	0	0	0	0	0	0	0	0	0
5	1.0	0	0	0	0	0	0	0	0	0	0	0
10	0.05	−32	2	54	3	58	−10	−10	4	0	56	125
10	0.10	−44	3	84	− 13	65	−13	−21	3	− 1	45	108
10	0.15	−15	4	122	− 22	78	−26	4	8	3	25	181
10	0.20	− 7	11	122	− 33	68	−32	6	14	5	73	227
Average per year		−19	−11	67	− 17	35	− 9	− 5	− 1	− 7	26	58

‡ Profits and losses rounded to the nearest cent.

from a heavy foreign demand for edible oil that almost completely absorbed a tremendous crop. A major bull move also occurred in soybeans during the 1960–1961 season because it was the year of a second consecutive short crop. Beginning stocks were much smaller in 1960–1961 than they were in 1959–1960, and so a limited crop had a significantly bullish effect on prices.

The supply and demand factors peculiar to these years are mentioned to underline the possibility that the distribution of price changes for those three bull-market years had a positive expected value, and therefore the gains shown for those years do not necessarily support a hypothesis of positive serial correlation. One might argue that a fundamentalist, in erecting a supply-demand model, might have good reason to project higher soybean prices in each of these three years and that he might have predicted the positive expected value.

On the other hand, nothing is quite so certain as hindsight, and the assumption could be advanced that fundamental factors are known with varying degrees of uncertainty before the fact. Could a trader take a responsible position based on a certain demand situation that he hopes will materialize or could he depend on crop damage to provide the impetus for a major bull move? Building a reliable model of expected future value is extremely difficult at best. If one rejects the assumption that it is possible to identify in advance those years in which there will be a positive expected value in soybean prices, one might argue that the profits that resulted from the application of the described rules are bona fide evidence in support of the existence of positive serial correlation in soybean prices over the period covered by the data.

NEGATIVE SERIAL CORRELATION.   It remains to examine the possibility that a rewarding futures price strategy might be to sell rallies and buy declines rather than to bank on the continuation of price strength or weakness. Smidt reversed the previously described trading rules so that the trader was to buy on price dips and sell on price rises.

Table 4-7 summarizes the results of countertrend trading by using the two most profitable countertrend rules. Interestingly enough, both rules are characterized by the fact that small price changes are required to switch the trader from long to short. Profits before commissions are higher than those generated following any rule considered earlier, and profits are distributed much more evenly over time than they were following their counterparts. Results would not be altered significantly, even if the most profitable year were eliminated. After showing that the observed profits would have been statistically unlikely if the price changes were not nega-

TABLE 4-7 ANNUAL PROFITS OR LOSSES, BEFORE AND AFTER
COMMISSIONS OF TWO MODIFIED TRADING RULES TESTING
NEGATIVE CORRELATION (CENTS PER BUSHEL, EXCEPT AS
OTHERWISE INDICATED)

	$N = 1, P = 0.2$			$N = 1, K = 1$		
		Profits or losses*			Profits or losses*	
Year	Number of moves	before commission	after commission	Number of moves	before commission	after commission
1951–52	64	50	27	59	64	43
1952–53	49	52	34	39	46	32
1953–54	44	−42	−58	52	23	4
1954–55	54	86	66	54	91	71
1955–56	38	−11	−25	28	−10	−20
1956–57	53	31	12	35	16	4
1957–58	62	− 3	−25	32	4	− 7
1958–59	62	− 1	−23	13	− 5	−10
1959–60	65	46	22	23	13	5
1960–61	53	58	39	49	94	76
Total	544	266	69	384	336	198

* Profits and losses rounded to the nearest cent.

tively correlated, Smidt concludes that the evidence supports the hypothesis that May soybean futures can profitably be traded on the basis of selling strength and buying weakness under selected conditions.

The most successful strategy summarized in Table 4-7 which produced 336 cents a bushel gross return was simple: sell following any price advance, close-to-close, of more than 1 cent a bushel; buy following any close-to-close price decline of more than 1 cent a bushel. If the initial purchase or sale was to be x bushels, each purchase or sale following the initial one would have been $2x$ bushels, thus keeping the trader continuously long or short x bushels. This rule would have resulted in gains of nearly $\frac{9}{10}$ cent a bushel before commissions for the 10-year period.

Characteristic	Five effective years*	Five ineffective years
Number of transactions	253	131
Aggregate net gain in cents per bushel of continuous holding (alternately long and short)	318	18
Gain per bushel, cents	1.26	0.014

* Classed by the criterion that the trading rule produced an average holding interval of less than four days. The years were 1952 to 1955, inclusive, and 1961.

SOURCE: Holbrook Working, "Tests of a Theory Concerning Floor Trading on Commodity Exchanges," *Food Research Institute Studies,* Supplement, 7 (1967), 16.

Working selected Smidt's results showing negative serial correlation for a pertinent comment.[10] He tabulated them according to the average length of each trade rather than by financial return and found that Smidt's rule worked well in 5 of the 10 years with the result that the average gain for those years was 1.26 cents a bushel. In the other five years, as noted later, gains and losses were almost equal. Those years in which the rule worked well and which led to an average trading period of less than four days reflected generally higher prices and wilder fluctuations than usual.

Because very short-run rules similar to those tested by Smidt become popular from time to time, the trader is cautioned that consistent profits utilizing such negative serial correlation are not easy to amass for the following reasons. First, few traders execute trades physically on the floors of the exchanges. Orders must be written to buy or sell on a market-on-close basis, leading to significant execution costs for local traders willing to execute them. These costs are generally seriously underestimated (see Chapter 10). Working alludes to the problem by indicating that the profes-

---

[10] Holbrook Working, "Tests of a Theory Concerning Floor Trading on Commodity Exchanges," *Food Research Institute Studies,* Supplement, 7 (1967), 16, 17.

sional scalper must buy or sell when a "dip" or "bulge" is *actually* forming, for it is only at that time that favorable prices can be obtained.[11] Such a consideration is paramount when it is realized that Smidt's best rule, after commissions, results in approximately ½ cent a bushel average profit per trade. Any effort to buy *after* a dip or bulge has formed could seriously impair the already minuscule profit margin.

Second, because of the small margin of profit expected on the average, a trader may be tempted to increase the number of bushels he trades, thereby substantially increasing his risks on any one trade. Unless the trader has considerable financial means, several losses on balance could do irreparable harm, both financially and psychologically. The question, then, not only of average profits but of average losses to be sustained deserves serious consideration in the setting of stop-losses.

Filter rules. It remains to inquire into the possibility of applying filter techniques to commodity futures prices. A major reason for examining filters develops from the concern that any dependence in the form of recognizable and usable price patterns will be so complicated that standard statistical analyses such as runs tests or short-run serial correlation tests will fail to uncover them. If prices exhibit patterns that persist over long periods of time, it can be concluded that the markets *have* a memory, that past price movements can help to forecast future price changes, and therefore that price changes are not independent. Such trend-following strategies, if successful, may eliminate or reduce the problems of commission costs, execution costs, and small average profits that have plagued the trader in results examined to date.

Most of the early work in trying to simulate technical trading rules centered on security prices. Alexander[12] developed a filter technique in order to apply a criterion similar to that used by some traders. The filter was defined as follows: as soon as the closing price moves up x percent from some initial point, the security is bought and held until its price moves down x percent from a high subsequent to the first purchase, at which time the long position is abandoned and a short position instituted; the short position is maintained until the closing price again rises x percent above a low subsequent to the previous sell, at which time the short position is covered and a long position is entered. Alexander used filters with varying values of x between one and 50 percent and applied the technique to American industrial stock price averages from 1897 to 1959. He concluded that his filter rule yields positive results for filters ranging from $x = 5$ to $x = 30$ percent. In other words, he finds a tendency for a price change in a stock price average to be followed by a subsequent price change in the same direction. The

[11] *Ibid.*

[12] Sidney Alexander, "Price Movements in Speculative Markets: Trends or Random Walks," No. 2, reprinted in Paul Cootner, Ed., *The Random Character of Stock Market Prices,* The M.I.T. Press, Cambridge, Mass., 1964, pp. 338–372.

profitability of this filter technique may imply similar results for other trend-following techniques, but, because the data consisted of changes in stock price *averages* and because changes in price *averages* have behavioral characteristics that differ from those of changes in the price of an individual stock, Alexander's results would not necessarily be meaningful in a pragmatic trading situation.

Cootner[13] examined the results of a rule that permitted much more rapid response to changes of direction than Alexander's strategy. The decision rule was stated as follows: buy the stock when the price exceeds a 40-week moving average by more than a given percentage (threshold amount) and sell the stock whenever the price dips below the moving average by *any* amount; sell the stock short whenever it falls below the moving average by more than the threshold amount and cover the short sale whenever the price rises above the moving average by *any* amount. This rule was applied to the weekly closing prices of a sample of 45 stocks listed on the New York Stock Exchange over a period that generally included the years 1956 to 1960.

Rates of return using a zero and 5 percent threshold rate were provided, the latter rate lowering the excessive transactions that tend to occur when the stock price remains in a narrow range. Both strategies were superior to buy-and-hold *only* if gross profits were considered. After commissions neither strategy outperformed the simple investment rule.

In a careful analysis covering all the individual stocks of the Dow-Jones Industrial Average Fama and Blume[14] tested 24 filters ranging from ½ to 50 percent over daily data for approximately five years ending in 1962. When commissions are included, the largest profits under the filter technique are those of the broker. When commissions are omitted, the returns from the filter technique are improved but are *still* inferior to buy-and-hold for all except two securities of the 30 — Alcoa and Union Carbide. In addition, empirical evidence is presented which indicates Alexander's results tended to overstate the actual profitability of the filter technique versus buy-and-hold. Such bias, it is believed, appears because the use of indices overstates the profitability of short sales. Because short sellers must incur the cost of paying all dividends, the index is reduced by dividend payments, and therefore the time spent in being short will introduce a bias estimated at about 2 percentage points in favor of the filter technique.

A recent study by Stevenson and Bear[15] reveals some success in applying

[13] Paul Cootner, "Stock Prices: Random vs. Systematic Changes," reprinted in Paul Cootner, Ed., *The Random Character of Stock Market Prices*, The M.I.T. Press, Cambridge, Mass., 1964, pp. 231–252.

[14] Eugene Fama and Marshall Blume, "Filter Rules and Stock-Market Trading," *Journal of Business*, 39 (Supplement 1966), 226–241.

[15] Richard Stevenson and Robert Bear, "Commodity Futures: Trends or Random Walks?", *Journal of Finance*, 21, No. 1 (March 1970), 65–81.

varying filters in July corn and July soybeans over the 12-year period, 1957–1968. Three trading techniques are simulated. Trading technique 1 assumes that the trader buys the future at the opening on the first day of trading and enters a stop-loss order x percent below the purchase price. If the stop-loss is not executed, the future is sold on the last day of the contract. If the stop-loss is executed, no further position is taken until the following July contract begins trading. The reader will recognize this rule as similar to the one tested earlier by Houthakker.

Trading technique 2 is divided into Plan A and Plan B. Plan A waits for the closing price to move up or down x percent and then establishes a position in the *direction of the market move.* A stop-loss order is placed x percent below (above) the established position. If price moves in favor of the trader, the stop is moved each day so that the trader never risks more than x percent from the high closing price. If prices move against the trader, the stop-loss order is not moved. When a trade is closed out, the trader repeats the process. Plan A, then, to be successful requires a tendency toward a move of x percent to be followed more often than not by another move of *more* than x percent. Plan B uses the same procedure, except that it establishes a position *against* the market rather than *with* the market. This rule should help indicate whether the tendency in the markets tested is toward price reversals.

Trading technique 3 establishes a position *with* the market when price moves up (down) x percent and holds the position until a move occurs, either up or down, of x percent. Profits are not allowed to run.

For each of the trading techniques 1½, 3, and 5 percent filters were tested. Commissions were charged on all transactions, and the dollar returns in Tables 4-8 and 4-9 reflect a commitment of 10,000 bushels or two contracts. A buy-and-hold policy over the 12-year period resulted in a profit in soybeans of $8,545 or about an average of 3.5 cents annually. However, if it were not for the large profit of $10,654 realized in 1966 (about 53 cents a bushel), there would have been a sizable loss. Buy-and-hold results for corn over the same period produced a $5,328 loss.

Trading technique 1 with a 5 percent filter worked well in soybeans but did not result in a profitable corn trading rule, even though all filters reduced the loss accruing to the buy-and-hold strategy.

Trading technique 2 (Plan A) provided the best results for both corn and soybeans. As the size of the filter increased, profitability increased when positions were established *with* the market, until results were optimized with a 5 percent filter. Eight of 12 years were profitable with the largest filter in soybeans, and 7 of 12 years yielded profits in corn. Plan B produced nearly inverse results when compared with Plan A, yet confirmed some tendency toward reversals in the shorter run price movements.

Trading technique 3 did not perform so well as the other strategies. After commissions, only a 5 percent filter in soybeans did well.

TABLE 4-8 RETURNS FROM TRADING TECHNIQUES USING VARIOUS SIZED FILTERS, JULY CORN FUTURES, SUMMARY TABLE FOR 1957–1968

	1½% Filter				3% Filter				5% Filter			
	Profit	Loss	Net	Years profit	Profit	Loss	Net	Years profit	Profit	Loss	Net	Years profit
Buy and hold	$2,955	$8,283	$(5,328)	.5	$2,955	$8,283	$(5,328)	5	$2,955	$8,283	$(5,328)	5
Trading technique 1	1,187	1,940	(753)	2	1,187	3,440	(2,253)	2	2,849	4,277	(1,428)	4
Trading technique 2 (Plan A)	460	9,397	(8,937)	1	2,915	2,381	584	7	3,990	1,577	2,413	7
Trading technique 2 (Plan B)	2,978	5,358	(2,380)	5	5,259	4,332	927	6	2,422	3,241	(819)	4
Trading technique 3	203	8,833	(8,630)	1	2,728	4,235	(1,507)	6	2,527	3,178	(651)	6

SOURCE: Richard Stevenson and Robert Bear, "Commodity Futures: Trends or Random Walks?", *Journal of Finance*, 21, No. 1 (March 1970), 77.

TABLE 4-9 RETURNS FROM TRADING TECHNIQUES USING VARIOUS SIZED FILTERS, JULY SOYBEAN FUTURES, SUMMARY TABLE FOR 1957–1968

	1½% Filter				3% Filter				5% Filter			
	Profit	Loss	Net	Years profit	Profit	Loss	Net	Years profit	Profit	Loss	Net	Years profit
Buy and hold	$21,210	$12,663	$ 8,547	4	$21,210	$12,663	$ 8,547	4	$21,210	$12,663	$ 8,547	4
Trading technique 1	10.556	3,132	7,424	3	10,556	5,832	4,724	3	21,210	6,784	14,426	4
Trading technique 2 (Plan A)	4,502	11,159	(6,657)	3	15,744	3,428	12,316	7	19,241	2,140	17,101	8
Trading technique 2 (Plan B)	9,098	8,942	156	5	4,676	13,550	(8,874)	3	5,635	16,107	(10,472)	2
Trading technique 3	3,589	15,858	(12,269)	3	2,380	11,518	(9,138)	3	16,462	4,130	12,332	8

SOURCE: Richard Stevenson and Robert Bear, "Commodity Futures: Trends or Random Walks?", *Journal of Finance*, 21, No. 1 (March 1970), 78.

Spectral analysis. Spectral analysis is a modern statistical technique for decomposing a time series like commodity futures prices.[16] This idea itself is not a new one because breaking down a time-series into a "trend," plus a "cycle," plus a "seasonal" component, plus the unexplained remainder has been studied by standard economic procedures for many years. The trend is a very smooth, slow-moving component, corresponding to a very low frequency, and therefore seldom occurs. The cyclical component, which corresponds to the next lowest frequency, is followed by the seasonal (12-month) component and finally by all other shorter term frequencies.

Spectral analysis can be compared with the swinging of the dial of a radio across a waveband. The signals received, however, are not words or music. At any particular frequency only the total *power* of the signal is measured. The static between "stations" would correspond to a purely random signal and would register as a small, constant amount. The "stations" themselves correspond to the frequencies of the transmission as well as the *strength* of each signal. Spectral analysis shows the size of the amplitude of each frequency found in a time series.

Monthly futures prices for a number of commodities for January 1950 through July 1965 were examined by Labys and Granger by spectral analysis.[17] In general, the series was flat and exhibited the behavior expected from a random walk market. The only commodity that showed a slightly significant seasonal tendency which the authors would confirm was wheat. Cotton oil, potatoes, eggs, cocoa, corn, flax, lard, soybeans, soybean meal, soybean oil, cotton, rye, and oats generated the type of spectra that would generally confirm the random walk model. Similar analysis was applied to weekly and daily futures prices. Fifteen years of weekly prices for corn, oats, rye, wheat, and soybeans were examined and the shape of the spectra of these futures also confirmed the random walk model. One year of daily prices for coffee, corn, oats, rye, rubber, soybeans, sugar, wheat, cocoa, and cotton was tested and all but the last two indicated that the random walk model provides a good explanation of price behavior. A small amount of negative serial correlation existed for cocoa and cotton.

THE QUESTION OF TREND

Even if the random walk model results in a crude approximation of the truth when it comes to explaining price changes in commodity futures, a trader can still profit. He can isolate, quantify, and trade those short-run, nonrandom changes that he can validate as offering, after commissions, a profit. This approach is discussed in detail in Chapter 7. A trader can still profit even if successive price changes are independent if their expected

[16] An excellent summary of spectral analysis is given in Walter C. Labys and C. W. J. Granger, *Speculation, Hedging and Commodity Price Forecasts*, D. C. Heath and Co., Lexington, Mass., 1970, Chapter 2.

[17] *Ibid.*, p. 66–70.

value is not zero. In other words, traders can make money in commodity futures even if they cannot predict short-term price changes consistently. A trader can simply follow a trend.

Risk premium concept. The first explanation advanced to indicate how the idea of an efficient market and a trend might coexist centered around a risk premium concept. Keynes first advanced the hypothesis in an essay in the Manchester Guardian Commercial in 1923 in which he suggested that anyone could reap handsome profits by simply holding long positions in cotton futures throughout the crop year, year in and year out.[18] This affirmation came to be regarded as the "Keynesian theory of normal backwardation."[19]

Though for years severe problems in semantics were to persist in the literature, the theory in essence stated that, although markets sometimes reflect carrying charges and sometimes are inverted, in either case a risk premium is a normal and continuing part of the difference between cash prices and futures prices. In other words, the theory required that the futures price be lower (biased downward) than the price expected to prevail at the later delivery period by an amount representing the speculators reward for bearing the risk of price change in the interim. The implication here is that short hedging will predominate, thereby leaving the speculator net long.

In its simplest form the theory predicted that under certain conditions it was necessary, *on the average,* for the price of futures contracts to rise. Early in the development of the theory there were three necessary conditions:

1. Speculators are net long.

2. Speculators are risk avoiders; that is, they require a history of profits if they are to continue to trade.

3. Speculators are unable to forecast prices.

It is clear that all these assumptions can be met if there is a rise, on the average, in futures prices during the life of each contract. It is equally clear that if speculators are net long, require a history of profits to continue the game, and have no ability to forecast the direction or extent of future price changes then obviously all profits that accrue to them must unambiguously be considered as a reward for the bearing of risk, not unlike the flow of insurance premiums between an insurance company and the insured. The speculator is guaranteed an expectation of gain, on the average, by making it possible for the hedger to hedge. The size of his speculative gain, under

[18] Quoted in Roger W. Gray and David J. S. Rutledge, "The Economics of Commodity Futures Markets: A Survey," *Review of Marketing and Agricultural Economics,* **39,** No. 4, 9.

[19] "Backwardation" is a British trade term which in American usage refers to the premium present in an inverted market or a situation in which cash prices exceed futures prices. "Contango," the opposite word, refers to a carrying charge market in which futures prices exceed cash prices. Thus Keynes considered that risk cost (backwardation) was to be considered "normal" in both kinds of markets, inverse or carry.

these assumptions, hinges *only* on the size of his position and not on his competence.

STATISTICAL EVIDENCE. Stone stated as early as 1901[20] in a report for the U.S. Congress that, among several commodities, an analysis of the cotton markets did not sustain the contention that the futures price is always less than the spot price:

> . . . if, for example, we compare October futures in July with the spot price realized in October. Out of fifty-seven different futures . . . compared with spot prices realized . . . in the N.Y. cotton market from 1881–82 to 1899, in twenty-nine cases the futures proved to be higher than the spots realized 3 months hence, and in twenty-eight cases the futures prices were lower than the spots at maturity—that is, the speculative judgment anticipated the realized value of cotton a little too favorably in half of the cases and not quite favorably enough in the other half . . . in the long run the speculative quotations for future delivery are neither uniformly above nor below the level of the proper cash value of cotton as determined at the future date, but . . . they are tentative anticipations of such realizable value as the conditions of the supply and demand are most likely to determine at the time when the future contract matures.

In the same report results for 15 years (1883–1898) of Chicago wheat prices confirmed that if the speculator were to rely on the Keynesian postulate of earning substantial profits by merely running risk and allowing one season's results to be averaged against the others he would not have fared well.[21]

A later report by the Federal Trade Commission[22] introduced evidence on which Working was later to comment:[23]

> One of the most critical and painstaking inquiries into the subject was that made by the Federal Trade Commission. It attacked the problem in several different ways. All the methods produced evidence, in price data subsequent to 1896, of some 'downward bias' in futures prices of wheat and corn but not of oats; but for the 10-year period prior to 1896, the indicated bias was in the opposite direction for all grains. The method which the Federal Trade Commission appeared to regard as quantitatively most trustworthy . . . yielded for wheat, 1906–16, the estimate that it amounted to −2.39 cents (about 2.4 percent) for a twelve-month interval.

Early in the controversy considerable doubt was raised that a speculator could amass consistent and substantial profits by merely being net long. In spite of the evidence, it does not seem that the theoretical discussion ever turned to the statistics of the organized markets for confirmation. When

[20] U.S. 56th Congress, 2nd Session, House, *U.S. Industrial Commission Report* (1900–1901), House Doc. 94, reviewed in Gray and Rutledge, *op. cit.,* 14–15.

[21] *Ibid.*

[22] U.S. Federal Trade Commission, *Report on the Grain Trade,* 7 volumes, Washington, D.C., 1920–1926.

[23] Holbrook Working, "Theory of the Inverse Carrying Charge in Futures Markets," *Journal of Future Economics,* **30**, No. 1 (February 1948), 9.

other commodities were examined in due course, it became evident that hedgers could be net long for considerable periods of time. The implication that net short hedging would predominate was not always realized. Because the level of the net short positions of hedgers may vary considerably, so will the size of offsetting speculative long positions. Therefore speculators may possibly have a history of profits *without* prices rising on the average: for example, prices rise 5 cents in the first period and fall 5 cents in the second period; speculators are long 20 contracts in the first period and only 10 contracts in the second period. Such action is still consistent with the assumed inability of speculators to forecast price changes. The opposite situation may be true also; that is, a rise in prices may not result in profits for traders who are long. Speculators may be long 10 contracts during a price rise of 5 cents and long 30 contracts during a decline of 3 cents.

The arena became packed with clamoring voices, and the ensuing controversy was instructive because it led the academic community to test what traders commonly refer to today as "seasonals." Indeed, if the presence of a trend in a commodity is to be related to the risks of carrying an inventory in that commodity, then any such trend *must* be related to the pattern of hedging.

Cootner has presented several examples[24] in support of the contention

[24] Paul Cootner, "Speculation and Hedging," *Food Research Institute Studies,* Supplement, 7 (1967), 84–103.

TABLE 4-10   WHEAT AVERAGE GAIN PER YEAR
1947–1965 UNDER INDICATED STRATEGIES

Specifications	Strategy I	Strategy II	Strategy III
Cents per bushel			
Short only	7.8*	8.5*	6.2
Long only	8.6*	9.4*	8.6
Long and short	15.9*	17.9†	14.8
Per cent of price			
Long and short	7.7	8.7	7.3

Strategy I. Go short at bimonthly point when reported short hedging first drops below 3,000 contracts. Cover short sales and go long at bimonthly point when reported short hedging first rises above 3,000 contracts. Sell long positions when you go short. All positions are taken in the nearest future in which the position can be held for the entire period.
Strategy II. Same as Strategy I except that all positions are liquidated at the point prior to the change in the balance of hedging.
Strategy III. Same as Strategy I except that all short positions are initially taken in May and are switched to the July future (if necessary) on April 30. Long positions are initially taken in March and switched to May if necessary. Not tested for significance.
  * Significant at the 5 per cent level.
  † Significant at the 1 per cent level.
  SOURCE: Paul Cootner, "Speculation and Hedging," *Proceedings of a Symposium on Price Effects of Speculation in Organized Commodity Markets, Food Research Institute Studies,* Supplement, 7 (1967), 89.

that risk premiums can exist in commodity futures. From 1946 to the present, bimonthly hedging and speculative positions are available for "large traders" as defined by the CEA. Table 4-10 provides the results of three strategies of initiating long and short positions in wheat futures based on short hedging levels. All strategies are profitable for both long and short positions for the 19-year period. These results indicate that it was possible for speculators to profit merely by being long after the peak of net short hedging and short after the peak of net long hedging.

Table 4-11 presents some evidence for a seasonal in soybeans. The period covered is from the autumn of 1949 to the autumn of 1960. Details of the strategies are given in the notes to Table 4-11. The long and short strategy keeps the trader long for six months and short for almost the same period of time. This strategy offsets what otherwise might be considered an inflationary bias. The average gains for the years 1949 to 1960 are impres-

TABLE 4-11   SOYBEANS: AVERAGE GAINS PER
YEAR, 1949–1960*

Positions	Autumn 1949 to autumn 1960†
(cents per bushel)	
Long positions	
From peak in visible supply to April 30	18.2
From peak in hedging to April 30	21.3
Short positions	
From April 30 to September 20	14.7
Long and short positions	
Long from October 20 to April 30 and short from April 30 to September 20	38.7

* Since soybeans have been in shorter supply than wheat during this period, long hedging has tended to predominate earlier in the crop year than was the case for wheat even though it is earlier in the soybean crop than in the wheat crop year.

Long positions were always taken in the May future.

Short positions were taken in the September future except in 1949–1950 and 1950–1951, when the September future was not used. In those years the position was taken in the November future.

The September 20 terminal date was near the last day of trading in the September future. The last day was chosen because the long hedging positions in that month are usually taken to protect against late or poor harvests. The harvest usually begins late in September and the hedging position is generally liquidated very late. It is the late September results which truly indicate the outcome. A smaller but still significant profit is obtained by terminating the short position on August 30.

† All results are significant at the 0.1 per cent level.

SOURCE: Paul Cootner, "Speculation and Hedging," *Proceedings of a Symposium on Price Effects of Speculation in Organized Commodity Markets, Food Research Institute Studies,* Supplement, 7 (1967), 97.

sive, even though they *omit* the 1960–1961 crop year which provided about 100 cents profit on the long side and 80 cents profit on the short. It is interesting to note that the peak in visible supplies is a good proxy for the peak in hedging.

Traders have long considered the possibilities of trading "intermarket" spreads, that is, being simultaneously long and short in different markets in which the impact of hedging comes at different periods of time. One spread is the relation between oats and corn reflected in Table 4-12. The domestic oats crop harvest is started in the spring and frequently lasts through the summer. The corn harvest, on the other hand, begins in September and is usually completed by the onset of winter. For corn, then, short hedging generally increases in the period just before the December contract goes off the board. Oats, during the same period, is a market in which the customary activity is one of hedge lifting. Again, details of the strategies are indicated in the notes to Table 4-12.

TABLE 4-12   OATS—CORN: CHANGE
IN PRICE DIFFERENTIALS OF
DECEMBER CONTRACTS, 1947–1964

| Strategy* | Mean annual change (cents per bushel) | |
	To December 15	To November 30
1	4.79†	2.67
2	5.62†	3.45‡
3	3.84†	1.67
4§	2.37	—1.20
5§	— .54	—1.72

* Hedging-oriented strategies: buy two bushels of December oats and sell one bushel of December corn on bimonthly date when

(1) reported oats net short hedging first exceeds reported corn net short hedging.

(2) reported oats net short hedging exceeds 2,000 contracts,

(3) reported oats net short hedging minus reported corn net short hedging reaches peak. When oats short hedging always meets the conditions, trades are initiated on April 15.

Calendar strategies: buy two bushels December oats and sell one bushel December corn on

(4) July 30,

(5) April 15.

† Significant at the 5 percent level.

‡ Significant at the 10 percent level. All other numbers are not statistically different from zero.

§ The figures are not significant at the 10 percent level.

SOURCE: Paul Cootner, "Speculation and Hedging," *Proceedings of a Symposium on Price Effects of Speculation in Organized Commodity Markets, Food Research Institute Studies,* Supplement, 7 (1967), 100.

The trader should note that strategies 4 and 5 show a much smaller tendency for the price differential to rise because they are computed on a calendar rather than a hedging basis. Thus, although buying two contracts of December oats and selling one contract of December corn on a hedging pattern resulted in an average rise of about 5 cents a bushel from 1947–1964, a similar strategy on a calendar basis yielded only about 2 cents a bushel. These results tend to support the existence of a risk premium.

Houthakker found, based on monthly price observations, that his sample of speculators actually made money trading commodity futures.[25] These findings required additional changes in the risk premium theory. The trader will remember that the original risk premium concept required that speculators

(a) be net long,
(b) refuse to trade if they lost money in the long run,
(c) be unable to forecast price changes.

The only price behavior that apparently would tolerate all three conditions was one of rising prices on the average. The first breach in this concept occurred when it was discovered that short hedging did *not* predominate at all times for all commodities and that speculators *could still* obtain a risk premium even if prices did not rise on the average. A speculator could simply be net long when hedgers were net short and net short when the hedgers were net long. Houthakker not only indicated that speculators earned profits but he devised a method of estimating the share of profits that should be attributed to actual forecasting skill versus the premium that would be received for merely bearing risk. The insurance premium analogy was no longer adequate in itself to explain speculators' profits. Of course, not everyone accepted these findings. Telser,[26] for one, rejected Houthakker's evidence of the ability to forecast on the basis that commissions were not charged against speculator income, the study was limited to only nine years (1937–1939 and 1946–1952), and the method of estimating profits and losses was hampered by not including the changes in prices that were available to speculators in each month.

Rockwell recently enlarged on Houthakker's study in an important analysis covering 7,900 semimonthly observations over 25 markets for the 18-year period, 1947 to 1965.[27] Among other pertinent inquiries, Rockwell attempted to define the proportion of dollars flowing to speculators that could be attributed to the presence of a risk premium. In other words, how much money would accrue to a naïve trader who is long when hedgers are net short and short when hedgers are net long? Two important conclusions emerged. First, prices rose consistently when speculators were net short,

[25] H. S. Houthakker, "Can Speculators Forecast Prices?", *Review of Economics and Statistics,* 39, No. 2 (May 1959), 143–151.

[26] L. G. Telser, "Futures Trading and the Storage of Cotton and Wheat," *Journal of Political Economy,* 66, No. 3 (June 1958), 233–255.

[27] Charles Rockwell, "Normal Backwardation, Forecasting and the Returns to Commodity Futures Traders," *Food Research Institute Studies,* Supplement, 7 (1967), 107–130.

causing them considerable losses. Second, the profits that accrue to the naïve speculator when he is net long are so small that no significant tendency toward normal backwardation is observed. Rockwell pointed out, however, that these conclusions do not imply that there can never be strong upward or downward price tendencies in different markets or in different periods within a market. In other words, even though the overall generalization might be that the futures price is an unbiased estimate of the ultimate spot price, such a statement is critically dependent on the markets which are selected.

Rockwell's study is critically important for another reason, however. If his study indicated rather conclusively that the risk premium theory is not viable for traders in a general way, his findings clearly promise a flow of profits to some traders solely on the basis of their forecasting skill. It is possible to define two levels of forecasting skill. First, a basic skill can measure the ability to be long in markets in which prices generally rise over the period examined and short when prices fall. Second, a special forecasting skill measures a trader's ability to forecast price movements that are shorter than the total period observed. The trader can see that these two definitions loosely parallel what might be called the fundamental and technical approaches to market forecasting. After developing these two approaches to decision making in greater detail in Chapters 6 and 7, the trading results of the players in the game—hedgers, large speculators, and small speculators—are fully analyzed to answer to the all important question of who wins, who loses, and why? It is of interest to note at this point that traders might participate, without the prerequisite of any basic or forecasting skill, in biases that may be present without heavy reliance on whether or not there is a risk premium.

Other causes of bias. That there might be fruitful excursions into the question whether price action could be lopsided for reasons other than the existence of a risk premium being paid to speculators has been stressed by such scholars as Gray. Gray has measured statistically the general tendency for futures prices to rise over extended periods of time for which the beginning and ending cash prices are generally unchanged.[28] If a trader holds a long position in a future, routinely rolls his position forward on maturity, and is able to generate consistent profits or losses when the cash price stays virtually unchanged, then that market may be said to be unbalanced, lopsided, or biased. Gray finds that corn, wheat, oats, beans (post-1955), and cocoa (post-1955) are examples of markets that do *not* offer the speculator a profitable bias. Soybeans (pre-1955), cocoa (pre-1955), wheat (Minneapolis), and coffee are examples of markets that *do* offer a significant bias over a considerable period of time. Markets that offer these biases are referred to as "thin" markets or markets in which the amount of speculation

[28] Roger Gray, "The Characteristic Bias in Some Thin Future Markets," *Food Research Institute Studies*, 1, No. 3 (November 1960).

does not keep pace with hedging requirements. Some markets outgrow their biases, such as soybeans and cocoa, and others do not. The latter, such as the markets for bran and shorts, fall into disuse and die. The futures market in coffee underlines the kind of pattern that characterizes a thin market. For many years after World War II coffee prices were high by historical standards, and prices for the near future were highest, followed by lower quotations for deferred contracts. This kind of pattern produces rather routine profits for the longs and losses for the shorts. It is interesting to note that in Rockwell's work, cited earlier, the markets with the smallest open interest displayed the largest bias, thus reinforcing Gray's analysis.

Another predictable bias can enter into the futures markets under the influence of a government loan program. Futures prices in wheat, for example, have regularly risen toward the guaranteed loan price, and even though that movement is predictable it cannot take place until the movement into government hands has occurred. As Gray and Rutledge observe: "So long as the movement into loan is *anticipated,* it would be an irrational price which reflected it, for such a price, incorporating the anticipation, would prevent the event."[29] It is perhaps fitting that the chapter should close as it began, with a description by Working which illustrates the underlying premise of a futures market:

> The idea that a futures market *should* quote different prices for different future dates in accordance with developments anticipated between them cannot be valid when stocks must be carried from one date to another. It involves supposing that the market should act as a *forecasting* agency rather than as a *medium* for rational price formation when it cannot do both. The business of a futures market, so far as it may differ from that of any other, is to anticipate future developments as best it may and to give them due expression in present prices, spot and near futures as well as distant futures.[30]

NOTES FROM A TRADER

The random walk hypothesis is really a simple theory. It merely says price changes are unpredictable when only previous price changes, not *all* available information, are used. Those holding that the random walk model describes reality better than any other model do *not* say that the trader cannot make money—they merely promise him the fight of his life to beat the naive strategy of buy-and-hold after paying for the privilege of trying.

The tests that have been published so far lend a great deal of credence to the theory as an excellent "jumping off point" to explain the short-run behavior of commodity futures prices. This is not to say that all possible strategies have been tested and have failed to provide consistent profits.

[29] Gray and Rutledge, *op. cit.,* 22.

[30] Holbrook Working, "Theory of the Inverse Carrying Charge in Futures Markets," *Journal of Farm Economics,* **30**, No. 1 (February 1948), 14.

The ingenuity of traders in this regard has barely been scratched. Most of them feel they have 25 trading rules that will bring them riches beyond the dreams of avarice. But the present state of the statistical art warns— "Don't look around. Something's gaining on you. It's the random-walk theory, the new 'King of the Hill.'"

A stand such as this at the *beginning* of a section devoted to *successful* trading may be considered by many as unadulterated heresy. Men make markets, and men do not release cherished falsehoods any more easily in the area of markets than they do in the area of science or philosophy. The fact that "patterns," usually described in an invincibly vague fashion, lead to profits about one-half the time they are traded does not dissuade the user. Instead, the capacity for definition is affirmed, and a new term "false breakout" is coined. Indeed, the collection of empirical contradictions to any theory, albeit impressive, never succeed solely by their presence in overturning the theory they contradict. Rather, it is a better theory that must be advanced, or error simply becomes institutionalized by the collection of reams of "exceptions to the rule."

If short-run price behavior is described crudely by the random walk hypothesis, then the theory itself becomes fair game. That it sets the tone for the game makes beating it a delicacy, never expected with certainty, yet always savored. The assumption of its tenets sharpens the trader for the battle. He *can* win, but only if he discovers the truth of the biblical injunction, "Broad is the path that leadeth to destruction." Financial salvation is a narrow gate through which pass only those traders who believe very little in luck as the cornerstone of their success. Sooner or later each trader affirms with Damon Runyon that "the race doesn't always go to the swift or the battle to the strong, but that's the way to bet." Indeed, one of the greatest contributions to traders' welfare made by advocates of the random walk hypothesis is the presentation of objective evidence that shows how difficult it is to make money consistently in the markets.

In moving from trading the markets in the short-run to taking positions to profit from expected trends, the trader should realize that the work in this area affirms that, generally speaking, the market does not habitually shower loose dollars on the casual trader who plays the game. As someone remarked, a trader will have to leave his mouth open a long time before a roast pigeon falls in. That there are trends is undeniable. That these trends are easily forecast from factors known at any point in time is an assertion grounded in naïveté. To rely on a bias upward or downward for merely playing the game is to make a risk premium or a characteristic bias the raison d'être of trading. Unfortunately, there is no universal truth about such an assertion. Each trade made with such an assumption must be examined on its own merits and validated meticulously.

The foregoing points up what is perhaps the most important lesson to be learned from the behavior of futures prices. There *has* been serious work done in the field. A bibliography *does* exist, and familiarity with it will pay the trader definable dividends. One of the most rewarding is the ability to think critically about the methodology employed by any one person or institution selling positions in this or that commodity. The methodology at times has a great deal to do with affirming or disclaiming a particular conclusion. The trader should bring a healthy skepticism to the marketplace in the realization that well-trained scholars with a deep and abiding interest in the field do not find it incredibly difficult to disagree with one another. Somehow the vision on the one hand of pockets bulging with easy money and on the other the tip sheet which glibly asserts that sugar is most assuredly on its way up to a 500-point upswing will seem more and more mutually exclusive. To such affirmations the trader aware of the behavior of commodity futures prices will remember to add that even a broken clock is right twice a day and that the capacity of the human mind to resist the intrusion of new knowledge seems close to infinite.

Playing the Game (Trading)

Armed with an understanding of the basics of the game, the trader is ready to become familiar with the decision-making processes. The six chapters in this section attempt to isolate, describe, and analyze several elements of successful trading. Successful traders have discovered the importance of sound money management which is often the least understood and most neglected aspect of trading. For that reason the section begins and ends with considerations that involve the management of funds committed to the commodity futures game.

Chapter 5, "Risk, Reward, and You," supplies the trader with a profile of his own attitudes toward risk and profit at different levels of capital and leads him step by step in constructing his own trading curve. Understanding his personal graph can help fit the trader's personality and value judgments about money with the type of trading he does.

Chapter 6, "The Fundamental Approach," analyzes those factors that constitute what traders call the fundamental approach. Conceptual supply-demand considerations and applied price-quantity relationships are studied. The often blurred distinction between explaining price changes and forecasting them is presented, as are examples of successful explanatory and forecasting models.

Chapter 7, "The Technical Approach," provides a panorama of technical tracking and forecasting methods in a format that underlines the advantages and disadvantages of each approach. Generous footnoting guides the trader to areas of further market research which may be of interest. From the simple arithmetic bar chart the trader is led through various systems of price tracking and forecasting, which include trend-following methods, character of the market approaches, and, finally, strategies that focus on market structure and more esoteric systems such as the Elliott wave theory.

Chapter 8, "Spreads and Options," may be considered by some to represent only a choice of commodity positions, but the subject is far broader than that and deserves separate and more elaborate treatment. Opportunities in these vehicles are flanked by different risks that must be carefully evaluated.

Chapter 9, "The Game Plan," attacks the problem of the trading plan directly by discussing its elements in some detail. The accent in this chapter is on gathering and organizing specific information in a format that is useful, regardless of whether the plan accents a fundamental or technical approach. The roles of stops and objectives as well as mistakes in plan formulation are analyzed.

Chapter 10, "Money Management," concludes the section by wrestling with the critical problem of money management which commodity traders ignore to their enormous peril. Even if the essential behavior of prices is understood and a rational strategy based on fundamental or technical considerations is formulated and the elements of a successful plan are followed, disaster will still strike if basic skills are not developed in the area of capital management.

CHAPTER FIVE

Risk, Reward, and You

> Sometimes the most incredible thing
> in the world is the answer to an
> unasked question . . .
>> REINHOLD NIEBUHR, *The Nature and Destiny*
>> *of Man*

INTRODUCTION

At this point the reader possesses more information about the basics of the commodity futures game than the majority of the participants now playing. A three-minute interview with a boardroom sample of traders (randomly selected, of course) will confirm that the information imparted in the first four chapters is not the subject of everyday brokerage office banter.

If such information is to be used intelligently, however, the reader must apply it to the decision-making process that leads to taking a position in the markets. Among the first decisions to be made are how to utilize one's capital and how much capital to risk. Treatment of these issues involves personal analysis and the concept of money management.

Money management is concerned essentially with four elements:

1. Objectives or preferences of the individual, including his present attitude toward money.

2. Initial and subsequent dollar capital to be utilized or risked in trading.

3. The expected value of the game.

4. The probability of ruin.

These elements are the fascinating subjects of this chapter and Chapter

10. Those playing the game are reminded that the issues of money management should share top billing with trade selection in the decision process. The first sections of this chapter discuss the concepts of probability as a numerical measure of optimism and of utility as a numerical measure of preference or satisfaction. The *relationship* of probability to utility is used to construct the trader's personal trading curve and to make some useful analysis and interpretations of it.

OPTIMISM AND PROBABILITY

The commodity trader operates in an atmosphere of uncertainty due to randomness. He cannot know with certainty what the outcome of any trade will be, but he can, and usually will, assign probabilities to the various outcomes, based on his relative optimism or pessimism. A probability is merely a number assigned to an outcome to reflect the strength of the assigner's opinion (on a scale from 0 to 1) of the possibility that the outcome will occur; for example, he may feel that the probability of reaching his objective in a trade is .4, whereas the probability of losing is .6. A probability in such a situation can be considered an index of optimism or pessimism. If the probability of reaching his objective were changed to .5 instead of .4, it could be said that he became more optimistic. It does not matter whether his probability came from objective evidence, newsletters, hot tips, brokers' research, or personal intuition. Whatever the source, the numerical probability does measure *his assessment* of the likelihood of various outcomes, and it does help to determine his action and therefore the market price. Analysts and traders often attempt to estimate this probability, or optimism index, for large groups of traders. They may, for example, analyze the actions of large traders or insiders or they may count the proportions of brokers and newsletters that recommend particular positions. These points are discussed in connection with contrary opinion in Chapter 7. If properly interpreted, such collective estimates can be useful. Even more useful and more easily measured, however, are the personal probabilities of the trader himself. Merely asking the right questions often provides useful insight.

PREFERENCES AND UTILITY

Suppose a commodity trader does assign probabilities to the various possible outcomes of a prospective trade. What principles does he use to make the decision whether or not to trade? How much is it worth to him to participate in a particular trade? Some will say that "worth" is the mathematical expectation of the gain or *expected value* or *average payoff* in money.[1] The rationale generally given for using the expected value of money involves

---

[1] The expected value, average payoff, or mathematical expectation is merely the sum of the possible *outcomes*, where each outcome is weighted by its probability; for example, in a trade in which there is a possible gain of $500 with probability .4 versus a possible loss of $200 with probability .6 the *expected value* or *average payoff* is $500 · (.4) − $200 · (.60) = $80.

an argument about what will happen in the long run, that is, when the trade is repeated many times. It is easy to see the merit of such a decision criterion for a gambling house but not for an individual trader. In the first place he trades relatively few times. Even more important, an approach that *would* give him maximum profit in the *long run* will do him no good if it leads to his economic ruin (treated in Chapter 10) in the short run. Some difficulties of choosing a simple criterion with which to make decisions are illustrated in the following examples:

The trader should put himself into each of the following four hypothetical situations and decide for each whether he would accept the bet.

1. He is offered a wager in which he will gain $200 if a (well-balanced) coin falls heads or lose $100 if it falls tails.

2. His entire fortune (which took 50 years to amass) has a cash value of $5 million. He is now offered the opportunity to gain $10 million if a coin falls heads or lose his entire irreplaceable fortune of $5 million if it falls tails.

3. He has been planning a vacation this month in Florida and intends to spend all the cash he has available during that month. Assume that he now has $5,000 available, which is more than ample for that purpose. He is offered a bet that will yield a profit of $5,000 (which he would use for *additional* spending on his vacation) if the coin falls heads or a loss of $5,000 (which would deprive him entirely of his long-planned vacation) if it falls tails.

4. He is desperate to see the next Olympic Games. He has $5,000 available in cash but the total expenses for him and his family will amount to $8,000. He is offered a chance for a profit of $5,000 if the coin falls heads or a loss of $5,000 if it falls tails.

The authors would accept the positions or bets in situations (1) and (4) but would say "no" in situations (2) and (3). What causes them to have different responses in situations (1) and (2)? The two situations are similar in that favorable 2-to-1 money payoffs were offered when it seemed appropriate to offer only even 1-to-1 money. What causes the difference in the authors' preferences? In situation 1, with equal probabilities, twice as much money can be gained as lost. In situation 2, with equal probabilities, it is also true that twice as much money can be gained as lost, but the gain of $10 million would not increase the satisfaction gained compared with the considerable dissatisfaction that would result from the loss of the entire $5 million fortune. Similarly, in situations (3) and (4), even though the money payoffs and probabilities are the same, the responses are different. These reflect the differences in the satisfaction to be gained from the money in the two different circumstances.

This indicates that if such a trade were made many times it sometimes would result in a gain of $500 and sometimes in a loss of $200, but in the *long run* the average gain would be $80 *per trade*.

Apparently, in uncertain situations people do *not* act consistently with respect to their average monetary gain. They do, however, act consistently to maximize their own satisfaction. Much theoretical and experimental work has been done in this area, and useful models have been developed to measure the preferences or satisfaction that individuals exhibit for various bets and outcomes. Just as probability is merely a number (on a scale from 0 to 1) assigned to reflect the degree of optimism, so the *utility* of a bet or of an event is merely a number assigned (on *any* scale) to reflect the degree of preference or satisfaction.

The following material includes a brief discussion of these utilities along with some examples and a step-by-step procedure by which the reader can find his own utilities and construct his own utility curve for commodity trading (subsequently called his trading curve). The construction and interpretation of his personal trading curve will serve as a useful tool in his money management and trading activities.

This chapter should be read with pencil in hand. The reader should make notes or calculations to make sure that the examples are clear to him.

UTILITY PROPERTIES

It can be shown that if a person is "rational" in the sense that he can express his preference between any two events and if he shows some measure of consistency in his preferences, then a numerical value or utility can be assigned to each event that will measure his satisfaction for that event; that is, of any two events, the one preferred will have a larger number (utility) assigned to it. In other words, if a person is guided entirely by his utility values, he will be acting in accord with his own true preferences. Therefore once a person's utility values are found they can be used to help him make rational decisions. In this chapter personal utilities are calculated and graphed in the personal trading curve. It is important to note here that each utility value reflects the preference for the particular event in the particular situation [e.g., see situations (3) and (4)] at the particular time. Attitudes and preferences do change. It should also be pointed out that different people have different tastes and therefore different utility values.

It can also be shown [2] that the utility of any bet or venture to an individual will be equal to the average or expected value of his utilities for the different possible outcomes of that bet. The average or expected value is computed by adding the utilities of the various outcomes, with each utility weighted (multiplied) by the probability of the particular outcome. (As indicated earlier, these probabilities may be personal and reflect one's degree of optimism.) It is interesting to note that for a "rational" individual the utility of a bet is shown to be equal to the expected value of the utilities of the outcomes, without any assumptions or discussion of long run effects

[2] John Von Neumann and Oskar Morgenstern, *The Theory of Games and Economic Behavior*, Princeton University Press, Princeton, N.J., 2nd ed., 1947.

or repeated trials. In other words, the relationship holds even if the prospect is to be faced *only once*. Utility, then, can always be computed by using ordinary probabilities and expected values.

COMPUTING PERSONAL UTILITIES

The computation of utilities, or measures of preference, is illustrated in the four examples that follow. Understanding these examples will make it possible for the reader to construct his own trading curve.

Example 5-1 Suppose Mr. Glassford, a famous soybean speculator, has taken a position in the commodity market and has set his objective so that, if it is reached, he will gain $1,500. He also has a stop set so that if the worst happens he will lose $900. Suppose that for Mr. Glassford the utility of $1,500 is 10 (the 10 is arbitrarily chosen) and the utility of −$900 is (arbitrarily) −6, that is, $u(\$1,500) = 10$ and $u(-\$900) = -6$. Assume further that Mr. Glassford believes his probability of success is $\frac{1}{2}$. The utility of the trade, therefore, would merely be the average (expected value) of the utilities of the possible outcomes, that is, the sum of the utilities of the outcomes with each utility multiplied by the probability of the particular outcome.

$$u(\text{trade}) = \tfrac{1}{2} \cdot (10) + \tfrac{1}{2} \cdot (-6) = 2,$$

which would be halfway between −6 and 10, the utilities of the outcomes.

If Mr. Glassford's judgment of the probability of success were $\frac{2}{3}$, his utility would become

$$u(\text{trade}) = \tfrac{2}{3} \cdot (10) + \tfrac{1}{3} \cdot (-6) = \tfrac{14}{3} = 4.7,$$

which would be exactly $\frac{2}{3}$ of the distance from −6 to 10.

Similarly, with a probability of success judged to be $\frac{9}{10}$, the utility of the trade would become

$$u(\text{trade}) = \tfrac{9}{10} \cdot (10) + \tfrac{1}{10} \cdot (16) = 8.4,$$

which is $\frac{9}{10}$ of the distance from −6 to 10. Obviously, as the probability of success increases from 0 to 1, the utility increases from −6 (the utility of the worst outcome) to 10 (the utility of the best outcome).

In order to illustrate the difference between the expected *utility* (average of the utilities of the gains and losses) and the *expected gain* (average of the gains and losses themselves), the following example may be used.

Example 5-2 Consider a trade that, if successful, would yield a gain of $600 and, if unsuccessful, a loss of $500, where the probability of gain is .8. If the utility of $600 gain is arbitrarily called 20, and the utility of $500 loss, 10, the *expected utility* (or utility of the trade) is given by

$$u(\text{trade}) = .8 \cdot (20) + .2 \cdot (10) = 18,$$

whereas the expected gain (in money) is given by

$$.8 \cdot (\$600) + .2 \cdot (-\$500) = \$380.$$

Note that the amounts differ and, as illustrated in the four cases in the preference and utility section of this chapter, that expected gains do not necessarily reflect personal preferences as expected utilities do.

Example 5-3 In Example 5-2 the utilities of the best and worst outcomes were arbitrarily chosen to be 20 and 10, respectively. If, instead, other values had been chosen, the computed expected utilities would be just as useful and would reflect the same relative preferences for different bets;[3] for example, if the utilities of the best and worst outcomes had been chosen to be 1 and 0, respectively, the expected utility of the preceding example would have been

$u(\text{trade}) = .8 \cdot (1) + .2 \cdot (0) = .8.$

Note that when the highest and lowest utilities chosen are 1 and 0, respectively, the expected utility will always be equal to the probability of the best outcome. Such a choice of values is often made because it simplifies the computation of utility values.

Example 5-4 Utilities are similarly computed in situations in which there are *more* than two outcomes; for example, assume that a certain commodity trade could result in payoffs of $1,000, $800, $500, or $200. Assume that the estimates of probabilities for the respective outcomes are .2, .1, .4, and .3. To calculate the utility of the trade, assuming that the utilities of the outcomes are as follows,

$$u(1000) = 22, \qquad u(800) = 15, \qquad u(500) = 7, \qquad u(200) = 3,$$

one merely calculates the average of the utilities; that is,

$$u(\text{trade}) = .2 \cdot (22) + .1 \cdot (15) + .4 \cdot (7) + .3 \cdot (3) = 9.6.$$

In the following section the computational methods used in examples 5-1 and 5-3 are applied to find the reader's personal trading curve.

THE PERSONAL TRADING CURVE

For the next 60 minutes the prospective trader should pick a spot in which he is unlikely to be interrupted. During that time he is going to construct his own trading curve from questions he will answer during a self-administered trading profile interview (TPI). There are some ground rules that should be clear at the outset of the self-interview:

1. The TPI is *not* a test. One answer is no more correct than another. Rather the TPI *measures* the reader's attitudes about gains and losses and about money at this point in time. The same TPI taken at a later date, especially after a large gain or loss or after a significant change in the trader's capital or income tax bracket, could well reveal a significant change in attitude. Trading curves derived from the TPI can easily measure such changes.

2. The dollar amounts risked, gained, or lost during the interview should be considered by the reader as *real* dollars with *real* purchasing power, which if lost would represent some varying degree of pain. Lost dollars can be replaced by the reader only from his savings or checking accounts, new earnings, or other sources. The pain of replacing $100 is obviously less than that of replacing $1,000, and the reader's feelings should reflect that difference to *him*, in consideration of his total current situation.

---

[3] Two utility values (any two, e.g., for the best and worst outcomes) can be chosen arbitrarily. After they are chosen, however, all the other utility values are determined by the method of computation illustrated.

3. The rewards to the reader should also be considered to be immediate and in cash, so that there will be virtually no lag between the time dollars are risked successfully and the ensuing payoff.

4. Many readers will be content to answer the questions in the TPI subjectively. Others will prefer to have paper and pencil handy. Either approach is satisfactory if the decisions reflect the reader's personal preferences and are not merely the result of some mechanistic computation. The reader should consider each trade and each level of risk capital separately and not relate them to preceding or subsequent questions. Each question should be considered independently and answered carefully.

The personal trading curve is constructed by first choosing two possible outcomes of a trade. These outcomes are called the "best" and "worst" outcomes, and utility values of 1 and 0, respectively, are assigned to them. Then, using trades involving only those best and worst outcomes, other utilities are computed in Table 5-1 and the results plotted as a preliminary personal trading curve in Figure 5-1. For purposes of verification and improved accuracy, and to measure the consistency of the trader's decisions, additional utility values are computed in Tables 5-2 and 5-3. These values use trades with new best and worst outcomes. The results, along with those in Table 5-1, are plotted in Figure 5-2. Then, in the next section of this

TABLE 5-1 COMPUTATION OF FIRST SET OF UTILITIES FOR TRADING CURVE

Utilities of		Probabilities of			Reader's cash
best outcome (col. 1)	worst outcome (col. 2)	best outcome (col. 3)	worst outcome (col. 4)	Computed utility of trade (col. 5)	equivalent of trade (in dollars) (col. 6)
1	0	1.0	0	1.00	2,000 } best outcome
1	0	.95	.05	.95	1,500
1	0	.9	.1	.90	1,250
1	0	.8	.2	.80	1,100
1	0	.7	.3	.70	1,000
1	0	.6	.4	.60	800 personal choices
1	0	.5	.5	.50	450 from TPI
1	0	.4	.6	.40	0
1	0	.3	.7	.30	−400
1	0	.2	.8	.20	−600
1	0	.1	.9	.10	−800
1	0	0	1.0	0	−1,000 } worst outcome

chapter, the trading curve is extended to include gains and losses that are larger than the initial best and worst outcomes.

Construction of a personal trading curve now proceeds in the form of a trading profile interview:

INTERVIEWER: What are the *largest* amounts you have had regular experience winning and losing on trades or investments?

TRADER: I've often had experience winning as much as $2,000 on a single venture and I've risked as much as $1,000 on single trades.

The interviewer now fills out the first five of the six columns in Table 5-1. He enters $2,000 and —$1,000 as the best and worst outcomes on the top and bottom lines of Table 5-1 in column 6. He assigns a utility of 1 to the best outcome and enters it on every line of column 1. He also assigns 0 to the worst outcome and enters it on every line of column 2. He then fills out column 3 with a fairly uniformly spaced set of probabilities. These represent the respective probabilities of winning $2,000 (the best outcome) for each of the different trades to be considered. Each line of Table 5-1 represents a separate and distinct trade. Column 4 is merely the complement of column 3. It shows the probability of *losing* $1,000 (the worst outcome) for each of the trades. In column 5 the interviewer computes the utility of each trade by taking the average of the utilities (1 and 0 in each case); each utility is weighted (multiplied) by its own probability as in Example 5-3. To illustrate the computation of the utility of .70 on the fifth line of Table 5-1, column 5, the following computation is made

$$1 \cdot (.7) + 0 \cdot (.3) = .70,$$

which yields the computed utility of the trade.

All that remains to be filled out is column 6, but doing that properly is the essence of the trading profile interview. The trader must consider each line (trade) separately and carefully, always remaining cognizant of the four ground rules stated at the beginning of this section.

INTERVIEWER: (describing the trade indicated by line 2 of Table 5-1): If you have a trading opportunity wherein you would either gain $2,000 (best outcome) or lose $1,000 (worst outcome) with probabilities .95 and .05, respectively, would you take that trade?

TRADER: Certainly! Who wouldn't?

INTERVIEWER: Obviously the trade has some worth to you. Would you pay me $800 cash for the opportunity to make that trade?

TRADER: What's going on here? You want me to hand you $800 in cash, right now, just for the opportunity to make that trade?

INTERVIEWER: If the trade ($2,000 possible gain with probability .95 or $1,000 possible loss with probability .05) is not worth $800 to you, forget it. If you think it is, then pay me the $800 now and enter the trade. Remember, whether you win or lose the trade you don't get the $800 back. It's mine, once you give it to me.

TRADER: The trade is good. I'm *almost* (.95) certain to win the $2,000. I'll pay the $800 and take the trade.

INTERVIEWER: In other words you feel that the cash value of the trade is *more* than $800?

TRADER: Right.

INTERVIEWER: I'm glad that's settled. Now, instead of $800 would you pay me $1,200 to enter the same trade?

TRADER: (after some painful introspection and colorful rhetoric): Yes.

INTERVIEWER: Then you feel that the trade is worth *more* than $1,200 to you. Now, instead of $1,200, would you pay $1,400?

TRADER: That's a tough question; $1,400 is a lot of cash to pay for that opportunity. On the other hand, that trade would yield $2,000 with a very high probability (.95) and *almost* no chance (.05) of the $1,000 loss. O.K. I'll pay $1,400, but not much more.

INTERVIEWER: You have just told me that the trade is worth *more* than $1,400 to you. Would you pay $1,600?

TRADER: Definitely not!

INTERVIEWER: Obviously the trade is worth *less* than $1,600 to you, and in your preceding statement we decided it was worth *more* than $1,400. How about $1,500?

TRADER: (after much introspection): That's difficult to decide. Maybe I would pay $1,500 and maybe not. I'm sort of indifferent at that price.

INTERVIEWER: That's fine. Then the value of that trade to you is approximately the same as the value of $1,500 to you. Therefore your utility for the $1,500 cash is the same as your utility for that trade, already computed on line 2 column 5 as .95.

At this point the interviewer enters $1,500 in column 6 of line 2 in Table 5-1. Note that the $1,500 in column 6 is entered next to its utility .95 in column 5.

By a similar careful and thoughtful process each line of column 6 is filled in. Each line represents a separate and distinct trade, with its own unique probability (column 3) of success. For each distinct trade in the table the best ($2,000) and worst (−$1,000) outcomes remain the same.

To illustrate the computation of utility for a negative amount of money, that portion of the trading profile interview (TPI) applicable to line 9 is also shown.

INTERVIEWER: (now describing the trade indicated by line 9 of Table 5-1): Assume that you have a trading opportunity in which you would gain $2,000 (best outcome) or lose $1,000 (worst outcome) with probabilities .3 and .7, respectively. Would you take that trade?

TRADER: You mean the probability of winning $2,000 is only .3? Why I have more than twice the chance (.7) of losing $1,000. That's not an opportunity. What do you take me for?

INTERVIEWER: Some people might welcome that opportunity. Obviously you have different preferences. For you that trade has a negative cash value. Would you take the trade if I handed you $100 right now? You keep the $100 win or lose, but if you accept the $100 then you must go through with the trade.

TRADER: Keep your $100.

INTERVIEWER: How about $300?

TRADER: That's better but still not enough to induce me to take that risky trade.

INTERVIEWER: Would you take the trade if I give you $400 to keep, whether you win or lose the trade?

TRADER: That's tempting. Maybe I would, but not a penny less than $400.

INTERVIEWER: That's fine. Then you would require a cash payment of at least $400 as inducement to take the trade. That trade has a negative value for you, —$400 cash. Therefore your utility for —$400 cash is the same as your utility for that trade, previously computed on line 9, column 5, as .30.

At this point the interviewer enters the —$400 on line 9 of column 6 in Table 5-1. Note that the —$400 in column 6 is entered next to its utility .30 in column 5.

With the completion of Table 5-1, a preliminary trading curve is constructed by plotting the numbers in column 6 on the horizontal axis versus the numbers in column 5 on the vertical axis. Such a plot from Table 5-1 is shown in Figure 5-1. If a smooth curve were drawn through the points in that figure, it would show some interesting preliminary results. For values of $1,000 to $2,000 the curve is concave downward. The reader can examine Figure 5-1 in that region to see that each added $100 increment of cash adds successively less utility value to the total.

For values of $0 to $1000, on the other hand, the trading curve is concave upward, and in that region, each additional $100 increment adds successively more utility value to the total. The trader has quite different attitudes toward gains and losses in these two regions.

For values of —$400 to —$1,000 the trading curve seems to be linear. In that region successively larger losses decrease the utility proportionately; for example, the decrease in utility going from —$400 to —$600 is the same as the decrease in utility going from —$600 to —$800 or from —$800 to —$1,000. The trader's reactions to possible gains and losses in this region, where the trading curve is linear, will be quite different from his reactions in regions where the trading curve is concave upward or downward. Analysis of these differences are made in the following sections of this chapter.

For purposes of verification and improved accuracy and to measure the consistency of the trader's decisions additional utility values for some of the same dollar amounts are again computed and the results shown in Tables 5-2 and 5-3. The computations are made from trades using new "best" and "worst" outcomes. The new results, along with the prior information from Table 5-1, are plotted in Figure 5-2.

FIG. 5-1   Preliminary trading curve.

To proceed with Table 5-2 the interviewer must first choose new "best" and "worst" outcomes for which the utility is known. Any two values from Column 6 of Table 5-1 will do. Assume he chooses $800 as the new "best" outcome, and —$800 as the "worst." The utility of $800 is shown as .60 in column 5 of Table 5-1. The utility of —$800 is shown as .10. These amounts are then entered in Table 5-2. The utility .60 of the new best outcome is entered in column 1 and the utility .10 of the new worst outcome, in column 2. The outcomes themselves, $800 and —$800, are entered on the first and last lines, respectively, of column 6 in Table 5-2. Then, as before,

TABLE 5-2 COMPUTATION OF SECOND SET OF UTILITIES FOR TRADING CURVE

Utilities* of		Probabilities† of		Computed	Reader's cash equivalent	
best outcome (col. 1)	worst outcome (col. 2)	best outcome (col. 3)	worst outcome (col. 4)	utility of trade (col. 5)	of trade (in dollars) (col. 6)	
.60	.10	1.0	0	.60	800	} best outcome
.60	.10	.95	.05	.575	650	
.60	.10	.9	.1	.55	550	
.60	.10	.8	.2	.50	400	
.60	.10	.7	.3	.45	250	
.60	.10	.6	.4	.40	150	personal choices
.60	.10	.5	.5	.35	−100	from TPI
.60	.10	.4	.6	.30	−400	
.60	.10	.3	.7	.25	−450	
.60	.10	.2	.8	.20	−500	
.60	.10	.1	.9	.15	−600	
.60	.10	0	1.0	.10	−800	} worst outcome

* From Table 5-1.
† Same as in Table 5-1.

columns 3 and 4 are filled in with a set (it may be the same as before) of fairly uniformly spaced probabilities. Again, as before, in column 5 the interviewer computes the utility of each trade by taking the average of the utilities (this time .60 and .10 in each case), where each utility is weighted by its respective probability. To illustrate the computation of the utility .55 in the third line of Table 5-2, column 5, the following calculation is made:

$$.60 \cdot (.9) + .10 \cdot (.1) = .55,$$

which yields the computed utility of the trade.

All that remains to be completed is column 6, and this is done by using the trader's profile interview, as before, in which the trader must again separately and carefully consider each line (trade) while remaining cognizant of the four ground rules stated at the beginning of this section. When Table 5-2 is completed in this manner, the results are plotted (column 6 on the horizontal axis versus column 5 on the vertical axis) as "2's" in the trading curve (Figure 5-2). (The results of Table 5-1, which were plotted in Figure 5-1, are plotted as "1's" in Figure 5-2.)

Further verification is achieved by completing Table 5-3 in a similar manner. New best and worst outcomes of $1,500 and −$400 are chosen, again from Table 5-1, with their respective utilities, .95 and .30. [Note that this range of values ($1,500 to −$400) is in the upper part of the original range ($2,000 to −$1,000), whereas the previous range of outcomes

**TABLE 5-3 COMPUTATION OF THIRD SET OF UTILITIES
FOR TRADING CURVE**

| Utilities* of | | Probabilities† of | | Computed | Reader's cash equivalent |
best outcome (col. 1)	worst outcome (col. 2)	best outcome (col. 3)	worst outcome (col. 4)	utility of trade (col. 5)	of trade (in dollars) (col. 6)	
						best outcome
.95	.30	1.0	0	.95	1,500	
.95	.30	.95	.05	.9175	1,200	
.95	.30	.9	.1	.885	1,150	
.95	.30	.8	.2	.82	1,100	
.95	.30	.7	.3	.755	800	
.95	.30	.6	.4	.69	600	personal choices
.95	.30	.5	.5	.625	500	from TPI
.95	.30	.4	.6	.56	400	
.95	.30	.3	.7	.495	100	
.95	.30	.2	.8	.43	−100	
.95	.30	.1	.9	.365	−200	
.95	.30	0	1.0	.30	−400	worst outcome

*From Table 5-1.
† Same as in Table 5-1.

($800 to −$800) was in the lower portion of the original range.] Table 5-3 is then completed, as were the preceding tables, and the results are entered as "3's" in the trading curve (Figure 5-2).

Figure 5-2 represents the completed personal trading curve of the trader for gains and losses between $2,000 and −$1,000. The general shape can be more readily seen by drawing a freehand *smooth* curve, passing "near" most of the points. The next sections include comments on this curve and some analysis and interpretation of personal trading curves in general.

Tables 5-4, 5-5, and 5-6 are provided so that the reader can complete them during his self-administered trading profile interview (TPI). He should be sure to follow the ground rules discussed at the beginning of this section. He should feel free, however, to change the best and worst outcomes to those that represent the relatively large gains and losses that *he* experiences regularly. Whatever his best and worst outcomes are should be entered in Table 5-4 and Figure 5-3. After the tables are completed the results (from all three tables) should be plotted in Figure 5-3 which is provided for that purpose. A smooth curve can then be drawn to pass near most of the points.

In the next section the boundaries of the trading curve are extended beyond the original best and worst outcomes so that the reader can also get a graphic interpretation of his attitudes toward the gains and losses that are larger than those with which he has had regular experience.

FIG. 5-2   Trading curve.

EXTENDING THE TRADING CURVE FOR
LARGER GAINS AND LOSSES

In this section the trading curve is completed. It not only includes that portion of the curve illustrated in Figure 5-2 but is extended to include gains larger than $2,000 and losses larger than $1,000. The interpretation of the shape and scatter of points for these larger values will yield significant information concerning the sizes and kinds of trades that should be accepted or avoided. Such information can be invaluable to the trader as well as to his broker or adviser.

As a first step in extending the curve, Figure 5-4 is prepared with gains

TABLE 5-4   COMPUTATION OF FIRST SET OF UTILITIES
FOR TRADING CURVE TO BE COMPLETED BY READER

Utilities of		Probabilities of		Computed utility of trade (col. 5)	Reader's cash equivalent of trade (in dollars) (col. 6)	
best outcome (col. 1)	worst outcome (col. 2)	best outcome (col. 3)	worst outcome (col. 4)			
						best outcome
1	0	1.0	0	1.00	2,000	
1	0	.95	.05	.95		
1	0	.9	.1	.90		
1	0	.8	.2	.80		
1	0	.7	.3	.70		
1	0	.6	.4	.60		personal choices from TPI
1	0	.5	.5	.50		
1	0	.4	.6	.40		
1	0	.3	.7	.30		
1	0	.2	.8	.20		
1	0	.1	.9	.10		
1	0	0	1.0	0	−1,000	worst outcome

and losses ranging from −$3,000 to $5,000 and with the utility scale ranging from −3 to 2. The next step is to plot all of the points from Figure 5-2 (or from Tables 5-1, 5-2, and 5-3 if it is easier) on this new scale of Figure 5-4. Then computations are made in Tables 5-7 and 5-8 to determine utilities for larger gains and losses, also to be plotted in Figure 5-4.

Utilities for larger gains. In Table 5-7 utilities are computed for

TABLE 5-5   COMPUTATION OF SECOND SET OF UTILITIES FOR
TRADING CURVE TO BE COMPLETED BY READER

Utilities of		Probabilities of		Computed utility of trade (col. 5)	Reader's cash equivalent of trade (in dollars) (col. 6)	
best outcome (col. 1)	worst outcome (col. 2)	best outcome (col. 3)	worst outcome (col. 4)			
						best outcome
		1.0	0			
		.95	.05			
		.9	.1			
		.8	.2			
		.7	.3			
		.6	.4			personal choices from TPI
		.5	.5			
		.4	.6			
		.3	.7			
		.2	.8			
		.1	.9			
		0	1.0			worst outcome

TABLE 5-6 COMPUTATION OF THIRD SET OF UTILITIES FOR TRADING CURVE TO BE COMPLETED BY READER

| Utilities of | | Probabilities of | | Computed | Reader's cash equivalent |
best outcome (col. 1)	worst outcome (col. 2)	best outcome (col. 3)	worst outcome (col. 4)	utility of trade (col. 5)	of trade (in dollars) (col. 6)
		1.0	0		} best outcome
		.95	.05		
		.9	.1		
		.8	.2		
		.7	.3		
		.6	.4		personal choices
		.5	.5		from TPI
		.4	.6		
		.3	.7		
		.2	.8		
		.1	.9		
		0	1.0		} worst outcome

TABLE 5-7 COMPUTATION OF UTILITIES FOR LARGER GAINS

| | Trade | | | | Reader's cash equivalent of trade | |
Gain (in dollars) G	Computed* utility $u(G)$	Loss (in dollars) L	Utility from Fig. 5-2 $u(L)$	Probability of winning p	Cash (in dollars) C	Utility from Fig. 5-2 $u(C)$
	$\dfrac{u(C) - .4(1 - p)^*}{p}$					
2,500	.97	0	.40	.70	1,000	.80
3,500	1.08	0	.40	.50	900	.74
5,000	1.15	0	.40	.40	800†	.70
	$\dfrac{u(C) - .3(1 - p)^*}{p}$					
2,500	1.10	−400	.30	.50	800	.70
3,600	1.30	−400	.30	.50	1,000	.80
5,000	1.75	−400	.30	.40	1,200†	.88
	$\dfrac{u(C)^*}{p}$					
2,500	1.00	−1,000	0	.40	0	.40
3,500	1.40	−1,000	0	.40	500	.56
5,000	1.33	−1,000	0	.30	0	.40

* Utility of gain $= u(G) = \dfrac{u(C) - u(L) \cdot (1 - p)}{p}$, where G, L, p, and C are as indicated in the table headings.

† Example of obviously inconsistent decisions (most inconsistencies are much less obvious).

FIG. 5-3   Reader's trading curve.

large *gains* of $2,500, $3,500, and $5,000. Each of these utilities is computed three times in order to give some information about the trader's consistency in making decisions. As in the preceding trader's profile interview (TPI), each of the nine trades in Table 5-7 is to be separately considered by the trader. He must consider the possible GAIN G, the possible LOSS L, and the PROBABILITY p of a winning trade. After sufficient introspection of this information, the trader, as before, decides on an amount of CASH C which for him, at this moment, is the equivalent of the trade; for example, in considering the second trade (GAIN $3,500, LOSS $0, PROBABILITY .50) in Table 5-7 the TPI could proceed as follows:

INTERVIEWER: Would you accept a trade in which you would gain $3,500 with probability .50 or lose $0 with probability .50?

TRADER: Certainly I would. There's no risk in that one.

INTERVIEWER: Would you pay me $500 for that trading opportunity?

TRADER: Yes.

INTERVIEWER: Would you pay me $1,000 for that opportunity?

TRADER: Probably not, but maybe a little less.

INTERVIEWER: How about $900?

TRADER: I think I would be indifferent about paying $900 for that trading opportunity. I would not pay $1,000 and I would be willing to pay $800, but I don't know about $900.

The amount of $900 is then recorded in the CASH C column of Table 5-7 for that trade. The utility .74 of $900 is then taken (approximated) from Figure 5-2 and written in the Column $u(C)$ next to the $900. Similarly, the utility .40 of the $0 LOSS is taken from Figure 5-2. The desired utility 1.08 of the $3,500 GAIN is then computed by using the formula in Table 5-7 and its footnote.

The interview and computation should proceed in this manner through each of the other trades in Table 5-7; for example, in the sixth trade the interviewer would begin as always by first asking the trader if he would accept the trade ($5,000 possible GAIN with PROBABILITY .40 versus $400 possible LOSS with probability .60). If the trader accepts, the interviewer proceeds as before to find the largest amount he would be willing to *pay* for that trading opportunity. That amount is then entered in the CASH column and the utilities of the CASH C column and the LOSS L column are estimated from Figure 5-2. The desired utility 1.75 is computed from the formula in Table 5-7.

After all nine utility values $u(G)$ of the large gains are computed in Table 5-7, they are plotted in Figure 5-4 as X's. The trading curve can now be extended to the right to $5,000, and a *smooth* curve can be drawn through the points in Figure 5-4.

Note how these points are spread out at $3,500 and even more at $5,000, especially compared with the small spread at any particular dollar value between the original boundaries ($2,000 and $-$$1,000). This spread indicates inconsistencies in the trader's decisions. Most of them are not readily apparent, but two in Table 5-7 are. Pointing these out will give the reasons for large differences in some of the computed utility values. The first inconsistency occurs between the third and sixth trades in Table 5-7. Both offer the same gain of $5,000 with the same probability .4 of winning. The third trade is better than the sixth, however, because the loss is $0 rather than $400, yet the trader has indicated that he is willing to pay more ($1,200) for the sixth trade than ($800) for the third. A similar inconsistency exists between the decisions on the second and fifth trades. Because of his tendency toward inconsistent decisions in trades involving potential gains greater than $2,500, this trader should plan such trades with great care.

Utilities for larger losses. In Table 5-8 utilities are computed for large *losses* of $1,500, $2,000, and $3,000. Each of these losses is computed four times and then plotted in Figure 5-4. As before, each of the 16 trades is treated separately by considering its GAIN G, its LOSS L, and its PROBABILITY p of success. Using that information, the trader (perhaps with the help of an interviewer) decides on an amount of CASH C which, for him, is equivalent to the trade.

Consideration of the ninth trade (GAIN, $1,000, LOSS, $3,000, PROBABILITY, .8) in Table 5-8 begins with the interviewer asking the trader if he will accept the trade. If the trader answers "no," then the interviewer may ask if he will accept the trade if given an inducement of say $500. An affirmative answer would bring forth a lesser offer. The interviewer

TABLE 5-8 COMPUTATION OF UTILITIES FOR LARGER LOSSES

		Trade			Reader's cash equivalent of trade	
Gain (in dollars) G	Utility from Figs. 5-2 and 5-4 u(G)	Loss (in dollars) L	Computed* utility u(L)	Probability of winning p	Cash (in dollars) C	Utility from Fig. 5-2 u(C)
		$-\dfrac{1.25p - u(C)^*}{1 - p}$				
3,500	1.25	−1,500	− .13	.50	500	.56
3,500	1.25	−2,000	− .37	.50	100	.44
3,500	1.25	−3,000	−1.87	.60	−1,000	0
		$-\dfrac{p - u(C)^*}{1 - p}$				
2,000	1	−1,500	− .47	.70	500	.56
2,000	1	−2,000	−1.00	.70	0	.40
2,000	1	−3,000	−1.65	.80	200	.47
		$-\dfrac{.75p - u(C)^*}{1 - p}$				
1,000	.80	−1,500	− .53	.70	0	.40
1,000	.80	−2,000	−1.20	.80	0	.40
1,000	.80	−3,000	−1.60	.80	−200	.32
		$-\dfrac{.56p - u(C)^*}{1 - p}$				
500	.56	−1,500	− .37	.70	−400	.28
500	.56	−2,000	−1.09	.80	−500	.23
500	.56	−3,000	−2.74	.90	−500	.23

*Utility of loss $= u(L) = -\dfrac{u(G) \cdot p - u(C)}{1 - p}$, where G, L, p, and C are as indicated in the table headings.

will proceed in this manner until he finds the smallest amount the trader will accept as an inducement for him to proceed with the trade. In Table 5-8 for the *ninth* trade that amount is −$200. It is then recorded in the CASH C column of Table 5-8 for that trade. The utility .32 of −$200 is taken from Figure 5-2 and written in the column $u(C)$ next to the −$200. Similarly, the utility .75 of the $1,000 gain is taken from Figure 5-2. (For the first three trades in Table 5-8 the utility of the $3,500 gain is approximated from Figure 5-4.) The desired utility −1.40 of the $3,000 LOSS is then computed by using the formula in Table 5-8 and its footnote.

After all 12 utility values $u(L)$ of the large losses are computed in Table 5-8, they are plotted in Figure 5-4 as X's. This extends the trading curve

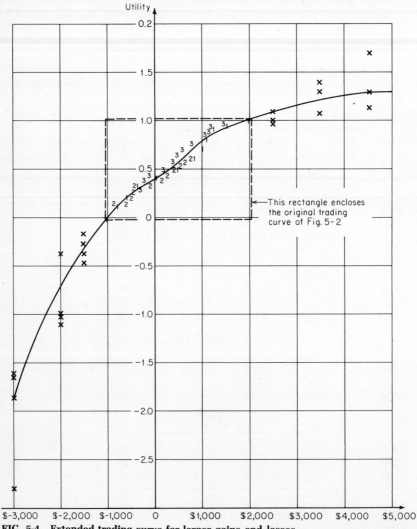

FIG. 5-4   Extended trading curve for larger gains and losses.

to the left to $-\$3,000$, and the smooth curve of Figure 5-4 can also be extended to the left and downward.

Note that the points in Figure 5-4 are slightly spread out at $-\$1,500$, much more spread out at $-\$2,000$, and considerably more at $-\$3,000$. This shows the growing inconsistencies in the trader's decisions as his losses grow large. He would do well to plan carefully when considering trades in which he will risk more than $\$1,500$.

Comments on the extended trading curve. An analysis and interpretation of trading curves follows in the next section of this chapter and in the notes from a trader. It would be useful, however, to comment on the completed trading curve shown in Figure 5-4.

From the aforementioned discussion of inconsistencies and the spread of points on the curve, it can be seen from Figure 5-4 that the trader makes uniformly consistent decisions on trades involving gains as high as $\$2,500$ and losses as large as $\$1,500$. Beyond those values extra care in planning is necessary. As experience is acquired, these boundaries could be expanded considerably. Periodic construction of trading curves will note such expansion.

The general shape of the curve is also of great interest. From small losses of $\$200$ to gains as high as $\$1,000$ the curve is slightly concave upward. This indicates that the trader's utility for gains of those amounts increases at an increasing rate. He therefore has a slight tendency to accept even an unfavorable (negative expected value) trade in those amounts. Those with such tendencies are sometimes called "risk lovers." Many traders act as risk lovers for small gains and losses.

TABLE 5-9 COMPUTATION OF UTILITIES FOR LARGER GAINS
TO BE COMPLETED BY READER

Trade					Reader's cash equivalent of trade	
Gain (in dollars) G	Computed* utility $u(G)$	Loss (in dollars) L	Utility from Fig. 5-3 $u(L)$	Probability of winning p	Cash (in dollars) C	Utility from Fig. 5-3 $u(C)$
2,500		0		.70		
3,500		0		.50		
5,000		0		.40		
2,500		−400		.50		
3,500		−400		.50		
5,000		−400		.40		
2,500		−1,000		.40		
3,500		−1,000		.40		
5,000		−1,000		.30		

*Utility of gain $= u(G) = \dfrac{u(C) - u(L) \cdot (1 - p)}{p}$, where G, L, p, and C are as indicated in the table headings.

As our trader's *gains* increase beyond $1,000, the shape of his trading curve becomes concave downward, which indicates a decreasing utility for incremental gains. His decisions in regard to larger trades will be more conservative, and he will have a tendency to take only favorable (positive expected value) trades. Such are the actions of a "risk averter." Many traders act that way for large gains and losses.

For *losses* greater than $200 our trader's curve is also concave downward, indicating that, as losses grow, his pain (dissatisfaction) increases at an increasing rate. He abhors large losses and has a tendency to avoid risking much capital on any one trade. If he is convinced that a trade is going badly, he will quickly close the position and take his loss to avoid a larger loss.

Tables 5-9, 5-10, and Figure 5-5 are provided so that the reader can complete his personal trading curve and, by using the information in this and the next section, analyze the results.

ANALYSIS AND INTERPRETATION OF
THE TRADING CURVE

Scatter of points and choice of best and worst outcomes. Widely scattered points within the original boundaries of his trading curve reflect inconsistencies in the trader's decisions. These inconsistencies result typically from one of two causes. The first is usually easy to rectify. It comes about

**TABLE 5-10   COMPUTATION OF UTILITIES FOR LARGER LOSSES
TO BE COMPLETED BY READER**

	Trade				Reader's cash equivalent of trade	
Gain (in dollars) G	Utility from Figs. 5-3 and 5-5 $u(G)$	Loss (in dollars) L	Computed* utility $u(L)$	Probability of winning p	Cash (in dollars) C	Utility from Fig. 5-3 $u(C)$
3,500		−1,500		.50		
3,500		−2,000		.50		
3,500		−3,000		.60		
2,000		−1,500		.70		
2,000		−2,000		.70		
2,000		−3,000		.80		
1,000		−1,500		.70		
1,000		−2,000		.80		
1,000		−3,000		.80		
500		−1,500		.70		
500		−2,000		.80		
500		−3,000		.90		

*Utility of loss $= u(L) = -\dfrac{u(G) \cdot p - u(C)}{1 - p}$, where G, L, p, and C are as indicated in the table headings.

A curve that is concave upward indicates that successive constant amounts of gain add larger and larger increments to the trader's utility (satisfaction). For the amounts of money for which his trading curve has that configuration (a) the trader will prefer fair (or favorable) bets to keeping his money, and (b) he will prefer larger fair bets to smaller ones. A person with this attitude toward gains and losses is a risk lover. Many traders are risk lovers, especially for small amounts of money. The risk lover will take fair or favorable trades and, in fact, will prefer large positions. He may even take them in slightly unfavorable trades. Of course, if a trade is sufficiently unfavorable, the risk lover will keep his cash and not trade. Those two situations express his preferences—all or nothing. He prefers not to diversify and would prefer large positions. A risk lover who trades often and follows his preferences has a high probability of ruin because he will often take large and sometimes unfavorable positions. He should be careful to enter only favorable trades, and the size of his positions should be consistent with a low probability of ultimate ruin. The principles of money management, as discussed in Chapter 10, are most important to the risk lover.

A trading curve that is linear indicates that successive constant amounts of gain add proportional increments to the trader's utility (satisfaction). For the region in which his curve has that configuration the trader will accept favorable trades, decline unfavorable trades, and be indifferent to the size of fair bets. In summary, the person with this trading curve will always prefer to maximize the mathematical expectation of *gain* (because doing so will also maximize his utility). Maximizing the average gain is good in the long run, but even this trader must be aware of the probability of ruin to give him a better chance of reaching the "long run."

Figure 5-6 represents five different risk attitudes in the continuum from one extreme to the other. From left to right the curves are characterized by an increasing preference for risk.

It is important to note that the risk attitudes, and therefore the trading curve, of an individual can change for a number of reasons, including additional experience, gains or losses, changes in capital, changes in personal income tax rate bracket, and loss of income source. This can be shown

FIG. 5-6   Trading curves representing different risk attitudes.

dramatically by comparing trading curves prepared both before and after a large gain or loss or a series of gains and losses. The trader would do well to prepare new trading curves at regular intervals so that they can be compared with previous ones and interpreted. Preparation and interpretation of a trading curve, after the first one, takes little time, and can be an important step toward successful money management in the commodity futures game.

NOTES FROM A TRADER

The concept of utility may appear academic to some, but it actually explains much of what makes one person act differently from others under similar circumstances. Two people may react completely differently, yet each is acting in a manner that is right for him. One may risk an important amount of money trying for an even greater amount, whereas another would not even consider risking what he has. The first is not necessarily bold or irresponsible (depending on whether he wins or loses his big bet) nor is the other wisely cautious or cowardly; they merely have different utilities for gaining or losing money. There are other utilities, not discussed in detail here, that also account for trading decisions. There is utility for time, for example. One person may wish to devote many of his waking hours to making more money, whereas another may feel that his time should better be spent for other activities more important to him. There are different utilities for avoiding pressure, so there are those who would forego making more money because they do not wish to pay the price in sleepless nights and spoiled weekends waiting breathlessly for markets to open.

It is a wise man who makes an honest effort to understand himself well enough to give proper credit for his accomplishments where due and proper blame for his failures as well. Students in school almost invariably say "I got an A" and "He gave me an F." Such a student, later in life, might say "I called that corn market perfectly," and "My broker sure touted me a miserable egg position" or "I wanted to get out and my broker wouldn't let me." Such foolishness may be a little soothing for a trader's morale in the short run, but, unfortunately, it does not help him understand himself, which is the first step to improved trading.

The trader's personal trading curve can give insights to possible biases which, if not overcome, can lead to poor decision making. The trader with biases is not unique. However, the trader who recognizes his biases and controls them with a well-conceived plan to avoid impairing his trading results is a member of a select group.

Some predispositions that the authors have noted following some experience with administering the TPI are:

1. An exceptionally large scatter of points at any dollar level for gains or losses may indicate enough inconsistency to suggest that complete trading plans should be made during periods when the markets are closed to avoid

FIG. 5-7

accepting levels of risk and reward incompatible with the trader's feelings (assuming that he understands the game).

2. The trading curve may bend sharply and flatten at an extremely low dollar level. This indicates that increased dollar gains beyond that point do not occupy a high priority in the trader's value system. A person with such a curve might first question whether he should be a trader at all. If he concludes that the curve is shaped as it is because of his own inexperience and he still wants to try his hand at trading, he could begin by trading spread positions or commodities with less than average volatility until his confidence grows enough to change his attitude and his curve so that it does not turn downward so sharply.

3. The shape of the trading curve in the "loss" region is extremely important. In Figure 5-7 the *solid* line showing the curve in the loss area reveals that the person described suffers acute pain even from relatively small losses. He would find it easy to decide on a stop-loss point, enter an order at that point, and feel little or no temptation to change it. On the other hand, the person with the curve indicated by the *dotted* line would feel little pain from even relatively large losses. This might sound good, but pain in trading is like most pain in that it is nature's way of warning that all is not well. Such a person is likely to let losses run, either ignoring them or rationalizing them; he will suffer disaster sooner or later. A broker who notes these tendencies in a client should encourage use of a stop-loss procedure or recommend that the client not make his own trading decisions.

4. The trading curves in Figure 5-8 denote a quality that can best be described as greed. The owner of such a curve may be a rational risk averter or a mild risk lover in the lower dollar values, but he reaches a point (of sharp upward curvature) at which he is seized by a consuming desire to

FIG. 5-8

"shoot the works." His type is frequently seen at the casino, where up to a point, say $250, he plays by risking small increments of his total capital. Above that point he is suddenly possessed by a fever that demands higher and higher risks, regardless of the probabilities of success. His counterpart is the trader who chortles happily as he talks about pyramiding his profits into amounts beyond the dreams of avarice. A sensible alternative for a trader so predisposed is to have a managed account (preferably by someone who has studied this book thoroughly) or to trade so lightly that the fun involved in the activity is greater than the cost of playing the game.

CHAPTER SIX

The Fundamental Approach

> . . . There's nothing *wrong* with a technician. You
> just wouldn't want your sister to marry one.
>
> A. FUNDAMENTALIST

CONCEPTUAL SUPPLY-DEMAND ANALYSIS

INTRODUCTION

In the long run conventional economic wisdom would conclude that the price of a commodity must ultimately reflect the equilibrium point of all the combined forces of supply and demand. Isolating, quantifying, and evaluating in some reasonable way the respective weight of each supply-and-demand factor is the job of the fundamentalist.

To grasp the magnitude of such a task the trader must grapple with some elementary economic theory. At this point the inevitable question arises, "Why is theory important? Give me the facts!" There are three problems with facts. First, it is not always easy to say exactly what a fact is. A court of law provides an excellent illustration of the effort that must be expended to isolate "facts," especially when two witnesses contradict each other. A second trouble with facts is that we are simply overwhelmed with them; for example, the number of facts about soybeans available to the trader is far beyond his ability to digest them. When the number of unknown facts about soybeans which can affect price are listed, the result becomes totally unmanageable. Simplification of "reality" becomes a necessity. The third trouble with facts is that the individual trader seldom can know in advance the degree to which a particular set of emerging facts has been expected (discounted). Many traders have puzzled over markets that opened lower following news that they believed was bullish and higher following news that they considered bearish.

The proper contrast, then, is not between theory and facts. The successful trader must understand and give meaning to the relevant facts about a commodity. In doing so he theorizes. The proper contrast is between good theory and bad theory, between useful theory and irrelevant theory. Good theory should lead to good practice. If theory does not do this, it is simply not good theory.

It is important for the trader to become familiar with the historical efforts to explain intelligently the supply-demand forces at work in speculative markets like commodity futures.

DEMAND ANALYSIS

A demand schedule like the one presented in Table 6-1, is a list of prices and quantities. At each price the corresponding quantity is the amount of the commodity that would be bought at that price; for example, if the price were $2.45, the quantity bought would be 10,000 bushels. The demand schedule does not indicate what the price is but only what amounts would be bought at different prices. The "law of demand" in economics reflects the fact that the lower the price, the larger the quantity bought.

A demand schedule may be transformed into a demand curve (D_1D_1), as in Figure 6-1. With unimportant exceptions, a demand curve is negatively sloped; that is, it goes downward from left to right. The "slope" of the demand curve refers, roughly speaking, to the degree of its steepness. It is examined in greater detail when the concept of elasticity is analyzed in a subsequent section.

A change in demand is a shift in the entire demand curve, represented by D_2D_2 in Figure 6-1. The quantity opposite each price becomes larger. Such action is not to be confused with an increase in quantity brought about because of a fall in price, illustrated by a given demand schedule in Table 6-1.

A demand curve is an extremely useful tool that may be used to illustrate

TABLE 6-1 A DEMAND
SCHEDULE

Price	Quantity in thousands of bushels
$2.50	5,000
2.45	10,000
2.40	15,000
2.35	20,000
2.30	25,000

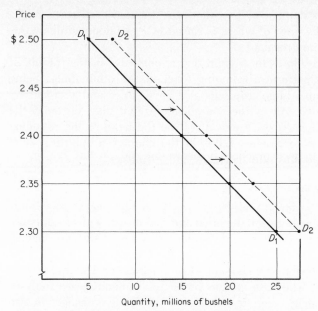

FIG. 6-1   A demand curve and a change in demand.

the meaning of commodity shortages or surpluses, both of which the trader must understand. If wheat is being analyzed in any given crop year, a demand curve may be constructed as in Figure 6-2. Assume that the total supply of wheat available for consumption is OB and the present price for wheat is P_1. At price P_1, however, the demand for wheat is only OA, which is the information transmitted by the demand curve DD. The amount AB, then, is surplus, and unless demand increases so that OB is bought the sellers must store the surplus or lower the price to P_2. On the other hand, suppose that OA is the amount of wheat offered for sale and that the price

FIG. 6-2   Using a demand curve to illustrate surpluses and shortages.

is P_2. Wheat buyers demand OB, with the result that a shortage AB is generated. Unless the price of wheat is raised to P_1 or demand decreases to OB, a disequilibrium results.

The demand curve illustrates a point that is pervasive in the trading of commodities; prices perform a rationing function. All other things being equal, in the long run a large crop sells at a lower price and a small crop sells at a higher price. All of the complications that may surround the building of a sophisticated price model rest on the truth of the rationing function which price represents. Later in the chapter a specific model will be constructed to illustrate shortages and surpluses.

ELASTICITY OF DEMAND

It is one thing for a trader to understand that a demand curve represents the inverse relationship between the price and quantity of a given commodity. It is quite another to understand the degree of responsiveness that an increase or decrease in the quantity demanded brings about in price. At lower prices more wheat may be bought. How much more? The trader must be aware of the term "elasticity" and its broad application to price analysis.

In economics elasticity refers to the ratio of the relative changes in two quantities. There is substantial literature in the field of economics devoted to the conceptual analysis of elasticity. For trading or forecasting purposes an important concept is the relative change in market demand as the price changes, that is, in the elasticity of demand E_D with respect to price.

$$E_D = \frac{\text{relative (or \%) change in demand}}{\text{relative (or \%) change in price}}$$

Because an increase in market demand will theoretically occur with a decrease in price (and vice versa), the elasticity E_D of demand is negative; for example, suppose the relative change in quantity is $+2$ percent and the relative change in price is -1 percent and that price falls. $E_D = 2\%/ -1\% = -2$. If, instead, the price goes up, then quantity demanded by definition, goes down. If the absolute value $|E_D|$ of the elasticity is greater than 1, demand is said to be elastic. If $|E_D|$ is less than 1.00 but more than 0, demand is inelastic. If $|E_D|$ equals 0, demand is considered to be perfectly inelastic.

Elasticity of demand may be understood clearly by referring to Figure 6-3, which portrays demand curves of differing elasticities. The elastic curves are relatively flat; the inelastic curves are relatively steep. The trader can quickly become aware of the important principle of elasticity by considering the changes in quantity that may be brought forth by a decrease in price from P_1 to P_2.

An elastic demand curve exhibits a greater change in quantity in response to a given price change, whereas an inelastic demand curve brings forth a smaller quantity response for a given downward price adjustment. When demand is unit-elastic at all prices, the change in quantity is identical

FIG. 6-3   Different elasticities of demand.

to the change in price. Perfect elasticity results when a change in quantity
does not affect price at all. The demand for the wheat crop of any one
wheat farmer could be considered perfectly elastic. When a demand curve
is perfectly inelastic, a price cut does not bring out any increase in demand.
Conversely, a price rise does not cut into the quantity demanded. The
demand curve for eggs is inelastic over a fairly wide price range. Because
eggs are a cheap source of protein, consumers buy them whether they are
35 cents a dozen or 70 cents a dozen. If the price of eggs drops from 70
to 35 cents a dozen, the consumer does not eat four eggs rather than two.
Therefore lowering the price in a market that faces a highly inelastic
demand curve is not a rewarding strategy for increasing total demand.

The trader should understand that to portray elastic demand curves
as relatively flat and inelastic demand curves as relatively steep is accurate enough for most purposes. For some cases, however, the concept of
varying elasticities on the same demand curve is relevant; that is, a demand
curve may be elastic at high prices and inelastic at low prices. Elasticity
of demand also varies with the length of time and the substitutability of one
commodity for another. Generally, demand becomes more elastic the longer
the period of time because of the substitution factor. The automobile industry might grumble at a substantial rise in copper prices over a two-month
period, but it would probably continue to use copper in the short run. If,
however, a long strike in the copper industry reduces output significantly
so that the long-run price outlook for copper is much higher for an indefinite

period of time, the auto industry would in all probability turn to aluminum or other substitutes.

The concept of substitutability is relevant in other areas as well. The retail demand for meat is slightly inelastic in the short run, that is, the year-to-year demand. The long-run retail demand for meat is elastic. If the meat supply were curtailed for longer than one year, prices would first rise, then fall, and consumers would spend less on meat. Generally, the closer the substitutes, the more elastic a commodity's demand curve will be. The importance of substitutability is stressed as the chapter progresses.

SUPPLY ANALYSIS

Supply, like demand, implies a schedule of prices and amounts that would be sold at each price at a given time. However, the analysis of supply is more complex than that of demand because there are so many variables that affect the quantity offered at any point in time. Among these factors are the prices of closely related commodities, the seller's expectation of future prices, weather, and strikes, ad infinitum.

Table 6-2 presents a supply schedule similar in form to the demand schedule shown earlier. At each price the corresponding quantity is the amount of the commodity that would be supplied at that price. The higher the price, the larger the quantity. Figure 6-4 illustrates the supply schedule in Table 6-2 with the curve $S_1 S_1$. Generally speaking, supply curves are positively sloped. A change in supply is a shift in the entire supply curve, as is illustrated by $S_2 S_2$, and results in the quantities opposite each price becoming larger.

ELASTICITY OF SUPPLY

Elasticity E_S of supply has a meaning comparable to elasticity of demand and may be defined as the relative change in market supply divided by the relative change in price, or

$$E_S = \frac{\text{relative change in supply}}{\text{relative change in price}}$$

Because price and quantity theoretically rise and fall together, elasticity E_S of supply is positive.

TABLE 6-2   A SUPPLY
SCHEDULE

Price	Quantity in thousands of bushels
$2.50	25,000
2.45	20,000
2.40	15,000
2.35	10,000
2.30	5,000

FIG. 6-4 A supply curve and a change in supply.

When supply is elastic, producers should respond to small price changes with significantly greater offerings. A small quantity response by sellers to price changes may signify an inelastic supply curve. Time is more important to elasticity of supply than it is to elasticity of demand. The longer the time period, the more elastic a supply curve is likely to be. The metals are a good illustration of this principle. If the short-run prices for silver or mercury, for example, should rise to high levels, producers might not undertake the production costs of opening new mines unless they were reasonably sure that prices would stay high over the long run. In other words, producers might insist on a shift in the demand curve as the price of increased production, not just a slide upward on the same demand curve.

EQUILIBRIUM ANALYSIS

Figure 6-5 helps the trader to visualize the equilibrium price of the demand and supply schedules discussed so far. The two curves intersect at A, which corresponds to 15 million bushels and $2.40, the equilibrium price. At $2.45 demand is 10 million bushels and supply is 20 million bushels. Excess supply forces prices down. Similarly, at $2.35 the 20-million-bushel demand forces prices up toward A.

It should be noted that this theoretical model of long run equilibrium is as elemental as it is elementary and may be cautiously applied to all but extremely long run situations.

One short run illustration will suffice. Assume that the closing market

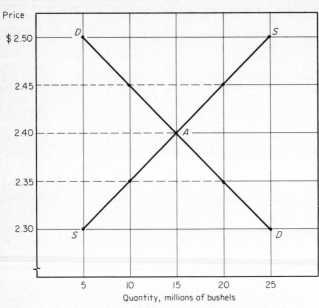

FIG. 6-5   Market price equilibrium of supply and demand.

price of a given nearby soybean option is $2.50 a bushel and a trader has a long position. Such a situation is described in Figure 6-6 by point A, where the demand curve $D_1 D_1$ intersects the supply curve $S_1 S_1$. If a sudden shift in the demand for beans occurred, the equilibrium price would tend to shift to B, or $2.55 a bushel. If the free supply of deliverable beans in Chicago was at a historically low level, because of a farmer holding movement, in the short run the trader might face a supply curve like $S_2 S_2$. If demand by crushers or exporters increased suddenly to $D_2 D_2$, the relative inelasticity of the supply curve $S_2 S_2$ means that the equilibrium point might shift to C, or $2.73 a bushel, quite a significant increase. The implications to the trader of the relative elasticities of supply curves $S_1 S_1$ and $S_2 S_2$ are enormous. He may wish to pyramid a long position established at $2.50 and follow the upward move with a trailing stop. He may wish to sell a new-crop position against his long old-crop position, thereby spreading soybeans and lowering his margin and risk requirements while not seriously impairing his potential. The important fact to realize is that, regardless of the intricacies involved, the trader's estimate of future price action is based on an explicit or implicit theoretical base. Such a base must include the dynamics of price equilibrium, which in turn features the various elasticities of both supply and demand curves and the response of each factor to changes in the others.

DISEQUILIBRIUM

It remains to discuss the implication for the trader of those conditions in which disequilibrium exists. Disequilibrium, in fact, is the normal condition

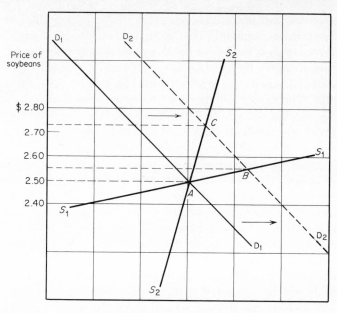

Quantity of soybeans, millions of bushels

FIG. 6-6 **An increase in demand with differing elasticities of supply.**

of a trading market. This realization does not render the theory of equilibrium useless because equilibrium is a meaningful way of referring to the direction of the long-term forces working on price and quantity changes.

Disequilibrium can easily occur; for example, assume that demand for a particular commodity can change much more quickly than supply. The fact that silver coins can be melted profitably when the price of silver exceeds $1.38 an ounce does not mean that silver futures cannot go higher than that price. Demand for silver may become so pervasive that prices may skyrocket before the supply of silver can be increased effectively in response to the higher prices or before melting in any quantity can take place. Disequilibrium would be the order of the day, in silver especially, because present reserves of the white metal are contained in ores mined chiefly for other metals. Therefore a dramatic immediate increase in production is an improbable response to higher prices.

In many commodities prices and quantities have shown pronounced cyclical movements over long periods of time; for example, much of the cocoa crop is grown by small farmers in Ghana and Nigeria. The price of cocoa for a period of two or three years affects the quantity of beans supplied in the following period. If cocoa prices are high during one period, the farmer will be financially able to expand planting or, equally important, afford insecticides and fertilizers to ensure greater yield of the trees he has. As greater yields come on line, prices drop, expenses are cut, and the cycle is slowly reversed.

A general explanation for some of the cycles that result in disequilibrium is furnished by the "cobweb theorem." This theorem is useful also because it presents one of the simplest models of the dynamics of demand, supply, and price. The model shows the relation between supply, demand, and price in a commodity like cocoa, for which output lags behind price for a given period of time. The supply and demand curves are stationary.

The cobweb theorem has been presented in many models. For simplicity and illustration Figure 6-7 presents the model in which price perpetually oscillates from high to low and output from low to high. In this model equilibrium is never attained. Assume that the average price of cocoa for the first two-year period is 40 cents a pound. During the following two-year period 1,200,000 tons is produced. The demand curve indicates that this production can be sold only at the low price of 20 cents a pound. The price for years 3 and 4 becomes 20 cents a pound. In years 5 and 6 the supply curve and lag assumption indicate that 800,000 tons will be produced. Such a quantity, however, sells at 40 cents a pound. The arrows indicate the perpetual oscillation that the cocoa market would make under such assumptions. It will be noticed that the requirement for such even oscillations is that the elasticities of demand and supply be equal and that buyers of cocoa and producers make the same kind of responses to price changes. If the supply of cocoa in the illustration is less elastic than demand, the result would be that the cocoa farmer in Ghana would respond less to changes in price than the buyers for the Hershey Chocolate Company. This lesser response would cause equilibrium to be reached eventually by the successive diminution of price fluctuation from one 2-year period to the next. The trader can verify the outcomes of different "cobwebs" by varying

FIG. 6-7 The cobweb theorem: perpetual oscillation.

the slope (elasticity) of the supply curve while leaving the demand curve constant.

APPLIED SUPPLY-DEMAND ANALYSIS

INTRODUCTION

In the real trading world good theory must lead to good practice. Good practice begins with the trader's familiarizing himself with the basic market factors underlying the price movement of any commodity. After isolating and quantifying these factors, a model or simplification of the dynamics of these basic factors must be formulated so that the trader can *explain* satisfactorily a significant amount of the *past* price movements in any commodity. In moving from *explaining* past prices to *forecasting* future commodity prices, what seem to be insuperable difficulties frequently appear. Examples of both explanatory and forecasting models are analyzed. The limits of traditional supply-demand analysis are recognized and additional price-quantity relationships such as price-volume, price-open interest and price-speculation, and hedging are referred to as possible clues in the forecasting process.

BASIC MARKET FACTORS

Total supply and demand balances for most commodities are analyzed on a crop-year, not a calendar-year, basis; for example, the season for wheat and oats begins July 1 and ends the following June 30. Comparable dates for corn and cocoa are October 1 to September 30. In Section 5 crop seasons are given for each commodity when applicable.

Generally total supply includes the old-crop carry-over, new crop production, and imports. Carry-over includes all unused stocks from all earlier seasons. Total demand is domestic consumption plus exports. Domestic usage may be broken down further, as in soybeans, for example, into the demand for the meal and oil, which result from the bean-crushing operation, and seed requirements. In addition, supply and demand factors will include the levels of inventory and various external influences on production and consumption.

If substantial amounts of any commodity are owned by the government, under government loan, or desired by the government, allowance must be made for the possibility of increased or decreased supply or demand at some point in the future. If a substantial amount of any commodity is placed under loan, it is no longer, for practical purposes, part of the "free" supply. Similarly, if the strategic level of stocks of a given commodity by government standards is low, allowance must be made for a possible non-recurring increase in demand.

For the typical trader the planning horizon is such that most of the variables affecting supply are irrelevant. For some commodities, in some instances, therefore, analysis of supply may be much easier than that of demand. If the dominant short run supply factors are "set in concrete," the number of variables involved in any analysis will be reduced, along with the probability of wrong analysis. The use of many variables enables the trader to explain past data but at the same time increases the probability of error in future analysis.

Basic market factors may result during a given crop year in total-supply shortage, total-supply surplus, free-supply shortage, or free-supply surplus. There are innumerable combinations possible within the components that make up the basic market factors; for example, the trader may well examine the timing and extent of price moves in seasons in which a large crop follows a large crop, a large crop follows a small crop, a small crop follows a large crop, or a small crop follows a small crop. Of no small interest may be the size of the carry-over at the beginning of each season when associated with any of these combinations.

To all these basic factors must be added the critical component of *expectation*. The fundamentalist finds that he is confronted not only with the factual relationships discussed above but with the compound relationships described by the demanding yet gossamer prefix "expected." Hence the multiplicity of relationships increases dramatically. Supply factors double from carry-over, new crop production, and imports to *expected* carry-over, *expected* new crop production, and *expected* imports. Where the fundamentalist was once required to reason as best he could concerning the combinational change that could occur among three dominant variables, there are now six variables, with the ensuing proliferation of possible outcomes. Demand for soybeans explodes from an analysis that includes the demand for oil and meal, the amount of beans crushed, and exports into the *expected* demand for oil, the *expected* demand for meal, the *expected* crush of beans, and the *expected* export figure.

To ensure that the trader will capture the full import of these mind-boggling variations, it is necessary only to add the concept of expectation to the rather simple analysis suggested earlier. The timing and extent of price moves in any season may be visualized by considering the following combinations;

A large crop follows a large crop when either, both, or neither was expected.

A large crop follows a small crop when either, both, or neither was expected.

A small crop follows a large crop when either, both, or neither was expected.

A small crop follows a small crop when either, both, or neither was expected.

A small carry-over or large carry-over precedes any of the foregoing combinations.

It should not be necessary to elaborate on the importance of general basic market factors. In Section 5, many of these historical supply-demand relationships for individual commodities are suggested and may be isolated, quantified, and evaluated at the individual trader's leisure.

MODEL BUILDING

Figure 6-8 is a flow graph of the cocoa industry which illustrates the magnitude of the forces that affect the price of a particular commodity at any

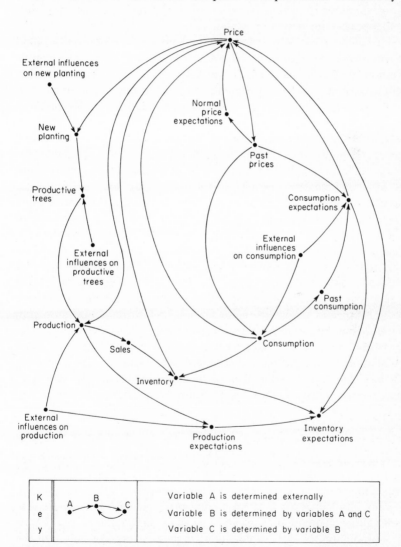

FIG. 6-8 Flow graph of cocoa industry structure. (F. Helmut Weymar, *The Dynamics of the World Cocoa Market*, The M.I.T. Press, Cambridge, Mass., 1968, p. 2.)

point in time. These relationships include hundreds of variables, some of which are quantifiable to some degree. Theoretically, if the flow chart is correct and all the factors that affect the price of cocoa have been included and weighted according to their dominance, a mathematical formula might be produced to explain the average price of cocoa for each crop year.

Because such an exercise would require many years to prepare if it could be done at all, simplification of these relationships appears to be a necessity. This simplification, referred to as model building, attempts to reduce the number of variables from that approaching the infinite to a few dominant factors that retain the power of explanation.

As a simplification of reality, models have limitations recognized by good theory. A serious one is that many factors affecting the price structure must, by definition, be eliminated from consideration. The trader must develop sufficient insight into the supply-demand factors of a given commodity to be able to identify the *dominant* price-making influences at any point in the crop year; for example, with reference to Figure 6-8, the planting of new cocoa trees will certainly have the effect of increasing the production of cocoa in the long run. The lag in such incremental supply, however, is approximately five years. The most sanguine fundamentalist would admit that the price of cocoa futures will reflect many other shorter term influences in the meantime, such as figures that may indicate that cocoa users face a second year of reduced carry-over inventory levels. Therefore caution must be used in the selection of individual elements when models are constructed.

In eliminating so many factors from consideration in the interest of simplification, care should be exercised to ensure that such simplification should not give way to contradiction of reality; for example, a case for sharply higher prices might be made for wheat futures if new-crop production fell below total estimated usage and if a simple two-variable model were constructed. However, assume that wheat futures have fallen. If a less casual study indicated that old crop carry-over had been at a 20-year high, the model for supply would have to be expanded to include carry-over as well as new-crop production to avoid future contradictions.

EXPLAINING VERSUS FORECASTING

Before proceeding to specific examples of explanatory and forecasting models, the trader should be aware of the significant differences between the terms. One of the most insistent myths surrounding fundamental analysis in commodity futures is that explaining price changes is equivalent to *forecasting* price changes. On the contrary, an explanation is seldom equivalent to a prediction. In fact, explanation frequently requires only that the trader be equipped with 20/20 hindsight.

In an explanatory model the variables used to explain a price at a particular time are also measured at the same time and thus must be currently available with the prices they seek to explain; for example, assume that the trader has found that the price of hogs is a function of the quantity of hogs available, the prices of substitutes (beef and veal, lamb and mutton, fish, and poultry), the income position of buyers, and consumer preference and that there are no further variables necessary to explain past prices. Assume further that the proper quantities for all past years are absolutely known for all four of these variables and that they have been weighted properly. As magnificent as such a model of price behavior would be, it would enable the trader only to *understand* past hog prices, not to *predict* future hog prices. The problem of turning explanatory variables into forecasting variables would still remain; for example, one determinant of the price for hogs, the quantity of hogs available, is reported quarterly in December, March, June, and September. Unfortunately no one has yet been able to forecast consistently the quantity of hogs before these reports are issued. If, as already discussed, the behavior of commodity futures prices is based partly on *expectations* and *changes* in expectations, it becomes a formidable task to predict price changes even if the trader were given a perfect preview of the figures to be reported. Unless the trader were also privy to accurate estimates of what figures were *expected,* he might still be unable to forecast the price changes that might follow the input of new information.

On the other hand, there are really only two general ways in which a *forecasting* model can be built. The first approach, using the preceding example, is to forecast the *next* hog quantity from a knowledge of past hog quantities. This simple extrapolative technique would have proven worth only if the explanatory variable, lagged for one 3-month period, were found to have predictive value when estimating the quantity of hogs in the next report; for example, assume for a moment that the trader had access to 10 years of figures reflecting the quantity of hogs available as evidenced by the annual December report. It is now March and the trader wishes to forecast accurately the March quantity-of-hogs figure soon to be released. If his only source of information is the December hog quantity figure, he has an *explanatory* variable lagged by three months. If the pattern of December figures offers a significant clue over the years to the upcoming March figures, the trader can use this lagged explanatory variable to *predict* future variables. The published material to date, however, does not give the trader much encouragement in this regard.

The second method of forecasting isolates a variable that is predictive of hog quantities apart from past hog quantity figures; for example, the trader may find that quarterly changes in hog quantities are related to changes in the price of beef. However, for this information to be of forecasting, rather than explanatory value, the prices of beef in the *present* period would have to correlate highly with the quantity of hogs available in a *future* period. Again research indicates that this approach to forecasting does not easily yield significant results.

BUILDING AN EXPLANATORY MODEL

To date the trader has been exposed to conceptual supply-demand analysis from which he gained an insight into basic economic relationships that can affect the pricing of commodities. The basic market factors intrinsic to each crop year were discussed, and the myriad possibilities that revolve around the factors themselves, as well as the expectations of those factors, were considered. The need to formulate a model that simplifies real-life complications while recognizing the limitations of such simplification leads the trader to recognize the difference between explaining commodity futures prices and forecasting them.

The ability to explain prices in any commodity necessarily precedes the ability to forecast prices. Perhaps the most rewarding way for the fundamentalist to try to explain supply-demand factors is not only to simplify the countless variables into the more dominant factors, as discussed earlier, but to shorten the span of concentration from the entire crop year into segments more easily analyzed.

A particularly interesting area of concentration might be a discussion of the effect of inventory and inventory expectations on the price of cocoa (see Figure 6-8). Many analysts agree that cocoa price levels are highly correlated with carry-over inventory levels.[1]

Table 6-3, Miscellaneous Cocoa Data, provides basic information on supply, demand, and inventory and average price levels for a number of years. Figure 6-9 graphs the yearly relation between the actual carry-over stocks (inventory) as a percentage of the world grind (consumption) and the average price of spot cocoa in New York.

Before examining this specific relationship, the trader should understand why, in general, commodity price levels should show a strong inverse relation to the ratio of carry-over inventories to the recent consumption rate. There are two basic reasons for this phenomenon: (a) the need for prices to ration existing inventories if present levels are low and (b) the need to strike an equilibrium in the longer run between supply and demand.

Inventory rationing. Inventory levels have an immediate impact on the relations between near and deferred contracts of the same commodity. An inverted market, in which the near futures are selling for premiums above deferred contracts, reflects the presence of relatively low levels of inventory. In a situation in which a manufacturer's cocoa bean inventories are

---

[1] For an excellent comprehensive analysis of the economics of cocoa see F. H. Weymar, *The Dynamics of the World Cocoa Market,* The M.I.T. Press, Cambridge, Mass., 1968. In the following discussion the authors draw as well on Dr. Weymar's article "Cocoa, the Effect of Inventories on Price Forecasting," *Commodity Yearbook,* Commodity Research Bureau, 1969, pp. 15–22. The latter was updated through private correspondence.

low he faces real business risks. He may have to change his production mix because he does not have on hand the amount or variety of cocoa beans he needs. His vulnerability to strikes or transportation difficulties increases, and he may not be able to honor his shipping commitments. For these and other reasons there is a convenience yield that attaches to the holding of a minimum cocoa inventory in and of itself. This minimum inventory will be held even though a manufacturer may expect a decline in cash cocoa prices. On the other hand, if the cocoa bean inventory being carried is large in relation to the user's historical needs, any additional inventory will not only have no added value but will not be tolerated unless the costs of carrying excess inventory can be recovered. This recovery can take place either in an increase in the price of cocoa or by short hedging in the futures market at a premium sufficient to cover carrying costs.

Throughout this process it is price that is the rationing instrument. As inventory carry-over levels decrease, all other things remaining constant, nearby contracts increase their premiums over more distant futures, thereby forcing those who hold the inventory to bear an increasing penalty for not selling it in the cash market for a high price and replacing it with a lower

TABLE 6-3   MISCELLANEOUS COCOA DATA

Crop year	World production (before 1% weight loss)	World grind during crop year	World stocks, end of crop year	Ratio, actual carry-over stocks to grind	Crop year average price New York spot Accra
	Thousands of long tons			Years	c/lb
1952/53	798	787	168	0.214	33.6
1953/54	776	770	166	0.216	55.4
1954/55	802	690	269	0.390	43.0
1955/56	843	785	319	0.406	29.3
1956/57	896	895	310	0.346	26.6
1957/58	771	890	183	0.206	42.9
1958/59	908	842	240	0.285	38.4
1959/60	1039	897	371	0.414	30.7
1960/61	1173	999	533	0.534	24.2
1961/62	1124	1089	556	0.511	21.9
1962/63	1158	1149	553	0.481	23.4
1963/64	1216	1158	598	0.516	24.3
1964/65	1482	1274	791	0.620	19.0
1965/66	1205	1378	605	0.439	22.5
1966/67	1333	1364	561	0.411	26.9
1967/68	1333	1387	492	0.354	30.4
1968/69	1225	1348	356	0.264	44.5
1969/70	1413	1335	420	0.315	37.9
1970/71	1479	1372	512	0.373	30.1
1971/72	1548	1499	545	0.364	28.2

SOURCE: As modified from F. H. Weymar, "Cocoa, the Effect of Inventories on Price Forecasting," *Commodity Yearbook,* Commodity Research Bureau, 1969, p. 16.

priced contract for delivery some months later. Conversely, when inventories are excessive, nearby prices will be battered when compared with future contract prices, for potential storers of cocoa must be induced to carry substantial inventories.

Long run equilibrium. Obviously there are many long-term fluctuations in production and consumption that influence massive price changes in the price structure of cocoa. As always, expectations about these changes, both in their timing and impact, play an important part in generating a realistic price level. Yet a glance at Figure 6-9 will confirm that whatever long-term price assessment is made in terms of production and consumption generally appears to be consistent with known current inventory levels. The

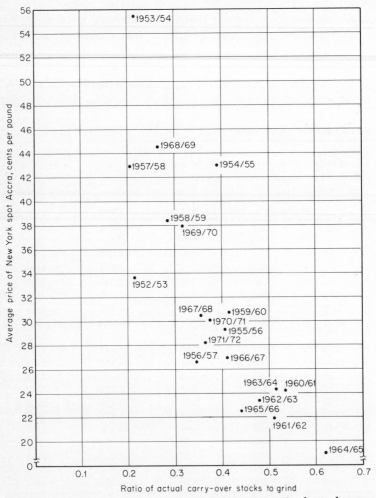

FIG. 6-9   **Average price of New York spot Accra versus ratio of actual carry-over stocks to grind (years).**

reason for this seems to lie in the fact that following a prolonged period of production surplus current inventories tend to be high, whereas subsequent to a series of short crops inventories fall to quite low levels. Thus, as Weymar notes, "The carry-over ratio alone explains major price movements reasonably well, both because it provides a measure of the near term need to ration or encourage inventory holding, and because it provides a good proxy for the market's assessment of the longer term supply-demand balance."[2]

Inventory expectations. Figure 6-9 confirms the general tendency for cocoa prices to vary in line with the ratio of carry-over inventories to the recent consumption rate. The trader must remember, however, that the price scale is quite large and that each grid on that scale represents 2 cents a pound or $600 a contract. A miss of this dimension can represent as much as a 60 percent loss of a $1,000 margin requirement; for example, the carry-over inventory ratios for the years 1952–1953, 1953–1954, and 1957–1958 crop years were almost the same, and, hypothetically, the trader would have reason to expect that prices would ration supplies in a similar fashion. Yet average price levels for those years were 34, 57, and 44 cents, respectively. Clearly, such excessive scatter is disturbing to the trader trying to explain these price levels.

This result has not been unanticipated. The reader will remember that model building presents disadvantages as well as advantages. The search for simplicity often eliminates factors that turn out to be dominant and that demand recognition if a good explanatory model is to be built. As promising as the explanation is for cocoa prices given in Figure 6-8, a dominant factor is missing. That factor, as might be surmised by now, is the variation in inventory *expectations* which have in many years differed significantly from the *actual* inventory carry-over figures eventually included in statistical records. The market never knows what world production and consumption will be for a given year until that reality is close to fulfillment.

The effect of including the expected carry-over ratio is illustrated in Figure 6-10. The basis of computation is complex[3] but it can be summarized briefly. At the beginning of each crop year estimates of the new crop production and consumption of cocoa are issued by Gill & Duffus, Ltd., in London. Because the carry-over stocks from the preceding year are known, a computation of the expected new crop carry-over ratios can be made at that time. A year later, when the actual carry-over ratio is known, there are frequent mismatches between the expected and actual amounts. Figure 6-10 plots yearly average cocoa prices against the average for each year of the initial expected and *final* actual carry-over ratios. Justification for an averaging process is based on the fact that expectations tend to trend rela-

[2] F. H. Weymar, "Cocoa—The Effect of Inventories on Price Forecasting," *Commodity Year Book,* Commodity Research Bureau, 1969, p. 21.

[3] See Appendix 4A in F. H. Weymar, *The Dynamics of the World Cocoa Market,* The M.I.T. Pres, Cambridge, Mass., 1968, pp. 195–217.

tively smoothly to their actuality at the end of a given crop year. Certainly the trader can appreciate that there is less scatter in Figure 6-10 than in Figure 6-9, which indicates a better fit and therefore a more satisfactory explanation of yearly average cocoa prices.

Toward a general model of prices. Of course, not all commodities are similar to cocoa in that the trader is able to isolate and quantify inventory adjustments as a promising approach to an explanation of price changes. There are futures markets for commodities without continuous inventories. Potatoes, for example, are produced seasonally, but most stocks are disposed of before June 1 each year. Other commodities such as live beef cattle and fresh eggs have no inventories at all in the usual sense. The

FIG. 6-10   Average price of New York spot Accra versus average of expected carry-over ratio and final carry-over ratio.

trader must approach the basic market factors in these commodities without the help of carry-over analysis.[4]

Lately interest has increased in the attempt to isolate and quantify factors that have a general explanatory effect, no matter what individual commodity is studied. The feasibility of an approach toward constructing a general model is gaining impetus because of the availability of the computer. A recent study, which utilized spectral analysis, of six commodities (soybean oil, cottonseed oil, soybean meal, soybeans, rye, and wheat), used to monthly price changes over a nine-year period concluded that in the long run prices were determined mainly by the prices of substitutable commodities, followed in importance by hedging and speculative activity, supply and demand components, and the business cycle.[5]

BUILDING A FORECASTING MODEL

The bridge from explaining past price changes to forecasting future price changes is not easily crossed. Many traders are sure that someone, somewhere, knows everything, in that this person is knowledgeable enough to list all the sets of supply and demand conditions that would cause *all* bull or bear markets. In reality, traders do extremely well to isolate, quantify, and evaluate any set of conditions *sufficient* to cause a particular bull or bear market, even if viewed retrospectively. The development of a forecasting model requires even more rigor.

There is no requirement that the trader be omniscient in order to make money. It is enough that he isolate and quantify any set of sufficient conditions for bull and bear markets in the commodities he is trading. The trader following this strategy will simply not trade a commodity (regardless of its price fluctuations, all of which are caused by sufficient conditions of which he is unaware) until he sees the sufficient conditions he has previously validated materialize. Then, and only then, will that trader take a position in the market.

Such a strategy is similar to that which might be followed by someone paid to predict fires. He might miss a great many fires caused by, say, chemical combinations of which he was completely unaware, but the specific knowledge that rags soaked with flammable fluids usually combust might be enough to earn him a generous living.

The purpose of the following discussion is to develop a basic understanding of some of the requirements for the construction of a successful forecasting model. To accomplish this the informal process with which the ex-

---

[4] The recent emergence of futures markets for noninventory commodities is discussed by William G. Tomek and Roger W. Gray, "Temporal Relationships Among Prices on Commodity Futures Markets: Their Allocative and Stabilizing Roles," *American Journal of Agricultural Economics,* 52, No. 3 (August 1970), 372–380, and the ensuing "reply," 53, No. 2 (May 1971), 362–66.

[5] Walter Labys and C. W. J. Granger, *Speculation, Hedging, and Commodity Price Forecasts,* D. C. Heath and Co., Lexington, Mass., 1970, Chapter 8.

planatory model dealt must give way to an actual step-by-step statistical process; for example, assume that a commodity analyst is attempting to isolate and quantify a supply-demand relationship in the soybean market which will have predictive value. Because inventory stocks were found to be an integral part in explaining cocoa price changes, the analyst similarly will decide to use the quantity of soybeans crushed and exported as a measure of the demand for a given period and the stocks of soybeans in all positions as an indicator of supply. Stocks in all positions are reported quarterly during the soybean crop year, which, for the purpose of this historical analysis, begins October 1. Crush figures are available monthly and export figures weekly. The earliest practical period, therefore, on which a meaningful comparison of usage and supply may be made is in January of each calendar year. Historically, the date of the "stocks-in-all-positions" report for soybeans has not varied significantly from January 24. At that time annual comparisons may be made between the size of the October–December crush plus exports and the stocks of beans in all positions.

In Figure 6-11 the X axis represents the annual ratio of January 1 stocks of soybeans in all positions, divided by the previous quarter's usage. Since 1952 that ratio has been as low as 2.22 and as high as 3.38. The lower the figure, the higher the October–December usage of soybeans relative to the present supply. Plotted on the Y axis is the highest price reached by the July soybeans future between March 1 and the end of the July contract, measured against the Chicago equivalent of the loan price each year; for example, if the average farm loan price for soybeans in 1966 was $2.50 a bushel, approximately 20 cents would be added to it to equal the Chicago equivalent. If the actual high reached by July soybeans on the Chicago Board of Trade from March 1 to the end of the contract was 3.77\frac{1}{4}$, it may be said that July soybeans sold as high as 1.07\frac{1}{4}$ above the Chicago equivalent of the loan price.

If there were a perfect linear relation between the variables X and Y, as shown in Figure 6-11, the yearly dots would fall exactly on the regression line that serves to measure the historical average relation between the variables. The scatter about that regression line measures the "goodness of fit." Given the value of the January supply-demand factors that constitute the variable X, the "best" estimate of the high price in July beans is given by the Y' value of the regression line. This step may be accomplished graphically or by using the predictive equation $Y = 3.99 - 1.213X$,[6] which was computed by using the data from 1952 to 1972. As X becomes available on January 24 each year, the trader has only to solve for Y' to estimate the July high. The coefficient of determination r^2 is .55. This measures the proportion of change in Y that can be attributed to changes in X. The standard deviation $S_{y \cdot x}$ of Y for any given X is 26.7 cents a bushel, which indicates that for any value X that becomes available on January

---

[6] This equation was determined by using the least-squares method, which is illustrated in any elementary statistics text.

24 the July high price will be within 26.7 cents of the Y' value, as shown on the regression line approximately 68 percent of the time.

To date Figure 6-11 has been constructed as a simple two-variable explanatory model that illustrates a principle with which the trader is now familiar: prices tend to vary inversely to the ratio of inventories to the recent consumption rate. However, to achieve a *predictive* value from such a relationship a significant amount of the price rise in July soybeans in any given year must occur *after* January 24.

Certain conclusions are evident in a study of the relationships in Figure 6-11. First, research indicates that the profit potential is poor when X is greater than 2.60. For most of these years the closing price of July soybeans

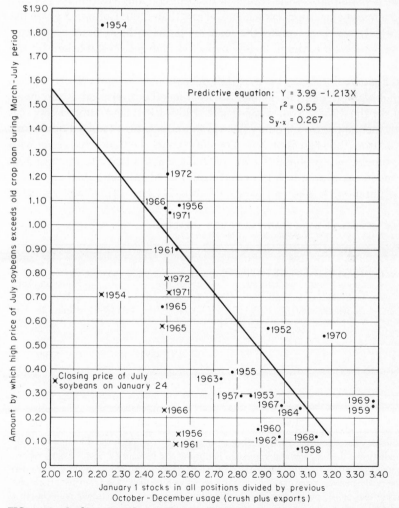

FIG. 6-11 Soybean supply (stocks in all positions, January 1) and demand (October-December crush plus exports (X) versus price highs (Y) in March-July for July soybeans, 1952–1972.

on January 24 was not significantly below the high price reached in the subsequent March–July periods. There is no significant forecasting value to the model in these years. Second, when X is less than 2.60, the probability of a major bull market in soybeans in that crop year becomes high. The years 1954, 1956, 1961, 1965, 1966, 1971, and 1972 produced such a ratio. The trader in these years was faced with the possibility of sufficient conditions for a price rise of extraordinary amplitude. Because the "stocks-in-all-positions" report issued quarterly does not become available until about three weeks after the effective date, January 24 thus becomes the earliest practical date on which the trader may take the position dictated by the predictive equation in Figure 6-11.

Table 6-4 summarizes the results of instituting a long position on January 24 of each soybean crop year when X is less than 2.60. Column 2 gives the price of July soybeans versus the loan on January 24 of each crop year. Column 3 shows the March-to-July expected high price established by the predictive equation. The potential profit is entered in column 4. By referring to Figure 6-11 it may be seen that in each year except 1964–1965 the expected high price in July soybeans was equaled or exceeded in the given period. In the 1953–1954, 1955–1956, 1960–1961, and 1965–1966 seasons, the actual price on January 24 was more than two standard deviations removed from the regression line. For these years the trader could say with an extremely high probability (.95) of being correct that the price of July soybeans in the March-to-July period would be significantly higher than it was on January 24. The crop years 1970–1971, and 1971–1972 reflected

TABLE 6-4   RESULTS OF LONG POSITIONS IN JULY SOYBEANS
INSTITUTED ON JANUARY 24 WHEN X IS LESS THAN 2.60

(1)	(2)	(3)	(4)
Crop year	Premium of January 24 price of July soybeans over Chicago equivalent of loan price (to nearest cent)	Predictive equation price $(Y = 3.99 - 1.213X)$	Equation profit potential (3) minus (2)
1953–54	$0.71	$1.30	$0.59
1955–56	0.13	0.90	0.77
1960–61	0.09	0.91	0.82
1964–65	0.58	0.98	0.40
1965–66	0.23	0.97	0.74
1970–71	0.72	0.94	0.22
1971–72	0.78	0.96	0.18
1972–73*	1.98	1.09	− 0.89

* Preliminary data for 1972–1973 present an interesting example of the dilemma faced by every trader using the fundamental approach. Following the January 24, 1973, stocks report, the premium of the price of July soybeans over the Chicago equivalent of the loan price was $0.89 *above* the average price expected by the predictive equation. Clearly, expectations of a bull market had pulled prices very high early in the crop year, and a trader believing that prices could go even higher was faced with establishing a long position over $4.00 a bushel, a level rarely attained historically. The fact that July soybeans exceeded $6.00 a bushel in early March is one more illustration that historical relationships, although of immense help, do not guarantee the trader a clear outline of Camelot.

a ratio of less than 2.60 on January 24, which called for $0.22 and $0.18 increases, respectively, in prices sometime between March and the end of the July contract. These expectations were exceeded in 1971 by $0.10 and in 1972 by $0.25.

LIMITS OF SUPPLY-DEMAND ANALYSIS

Because intrinsic value at any point in time is elusive, disequilibrium can well be the normal condition of commodity futures markets. For this reason the trader must go slowly in applying conventional supply-demand theory to the markets, especially in the short-run. Many traders begin to feel comfortable with traditional supply-demand analysis just in time to lose 85 percent of their capital in one trade because cocoa or soybeans simply "cannot go down." Such traders find out too late that the supply coming into the market does not always decrease when the price falls. In fact, the fear of a further fall in price may be an inducement to offer an even greater supply on the market, thus causing prices to weaken beyond the point indicated by traditional equilibrium analysis. The same possibility exists on the demand side, where the fear of a further price rise may induce tremendous demand in the short-run which can outstrip all economic projections and account for many a tragic tale of getting short "too soon." The inapplicability to the trader of "equilibrium" prices in the short run is reflected by rather substantial totals in the loss column each year.

The implicit possibilities of such a trap were discussed in an early study which argued that, even though a price run, up or down, could not continue indefinitely without regard to basic supply-demand considerations, rather large price movements could occur within broad limits. The area between these limits was defined as the "penumbra."[7] Figure 6-12 illustrates an attempt to explain the relation between bar-charts and supply-demand curves by using this concept.[8]

Instead of assuming that supply and demand can be represented by single lines that intersect to give a single equilibrium price, as in Figure 6-5, the penumbra concept assumes a series of lines that oscillate about an intrinsic value to form price bands. These bands serve as a proxy for the penumbra under conditions of fixed supply-demand (Part A) and fixed supply-increased demand (Part B). In Part A prices reflect a trading range within a broad equilibrium state, whereas Part B illustrates the same trading range with an upward drift that reflects an increase in demand. Unfortunately, for the trader, the concept of a single equilibrium price or a band within which prices move is difficult to test on a rigorous basis.

The analysis of the behavior of commodity futures prices has emphasized that price changes are formed according to *expectations* of changes in supply and demand rather than their known values. Because the behavior of

[7] F. W. Taussig, "Is Market Price Determinate?" *Quarterly Journal of Economics,* 35 (May 1929), 394–411.

[8] L. A. Bernstein. "How Commodity Price Charts Disclose Supply-Demand Shifts," *Commodity Yearbook,* 1958, pp. 33–42, as modified by Labys and Granger, *op. cit.,* p. 113.

traders provides price changes, it is the constant search for significant new information that produces the key to future changes. This new information and its impact is, itself, unpredictable. Therefore the random quality of new information, not actual changes in supply and demand, is responsible for the disequilibrium that is too often the norm in futures prices. The implications of these concepts for the trader include the avoidance of his relying exclusively on conventional supply-demand estimates as the cornerstone of successful trading.

ADDITIONAL PRICE-QUANTITY RELATIONSHIPS

Traditional supply-demand analysis does not generally include price-quantity relations apart from the basic market factors discussed earlier in the chapter. Yet there is merit in the suggestion that prices might be related to quantities other than carry-over, production, imports, exports, and usage. Price-volume, price-open interest, and price-speculation and hedging are examples of intermarket speculative relationships that might be considered in the search for explanatory and predictive variables. These and many other indicators have long been the province of what is known as technical analysis, or the attempt to construct a model of future price changes using past trading statistics as a guide. Chapter 7 discusses the specific advantages and disadvantages of trading utilizing this approach.

NOTES FROM A TRADER

There is little argument against the proposition that, competently and ·consistently performed, fundamental analysis provides the trader with a powerful tool in his quest for profits in the commodity futures markets. Those who are aware early of changes taking place in dominant factors may initiate positions that ultimately yield handsome profits. Yet there can be several rocky detours along the way.

BASIC DATA

Errors in basic data will obviously lead to errors in forecasts. The trader must realize that every statistic, whether generated by government or private sources, has a band of error about it. There are many problems in specifying what, how, and when to measure the factors that influence prices. Masses of data are meaningless unless they are grouped in some manner; however, there is the problem of the most representative totals or averages for various markets, seasons, or time periods.

No matter how accurate the estimate of a crop size, for example, may be, that estimate is based on a sample. Samples are less than perfect reflections of reality for many reasons, the most important of which is cost. At some point the return in the form of increased accuracy is not so great as the increased cost. The trader should remember that accuracy is also impaired because of revisions to data that are constantly being made. The words "preliminary" and "estimate" liberally dot most factual summaries.

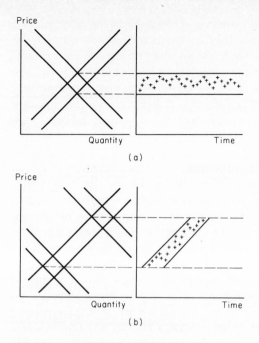

Price

Quantity   Time

(a)

Price

Quantity   Time

(b)

FIG. 6-12 Influence of supply
and demand on futures price
movements. (a) Fixed supply-
fixed demand; (b) fixed supply-
increased demand. (W. C. Labys
and C. W. J. Granger, *Speculation, Hedging and Commodity
Price Forecasts*, D. C. Heath and
Company, Lexington, Mass.,
1970, p. 113, as modified from
L. A. Bernstein, "How Commodity Price Charts Disclose Supply-
Demand Shifts," *Commodity
Year Book*, Commodity Research
Bureau, New York, 1958, pp.
35–36.)

THE ANALYTICAL FRAMEWORK

Even though there are no substitutes for competent statistical tools in the
process of appraising the outlook for prices, the trader must bear in mind
that such tools are not reliable substitutes for judgment. Because judgment
is present continually, it can be extremely difficult to reproduce, on a
quantifiable basis, fundamental sutdies performed at a particular point in
time. As one study concluded, when referring to the estimation of certain
variables in the pork bellies market, the procedure used "was not systematic, was not documented, and could not be duplicated."[9]

An important source of error is in the construction of the model itself.
Explanatory models attempt to specify historical price responses to supply-
demand forces which involve a complicated set of varying leads and lags.
Forecasting models bear the additional burden of having to lead actual
price response. Because models are but a simplification of reality, no model
can include all of the relevant factors. A second source of error may be the
choice of equation form. Some relationships are linear, whereas others are
curvilinear and may be more difficult to identify. Some relationships may
best be studied in terms of changes rather than levels. Finally, estimates of
elasticity are subject to a range of error which may arise from inaccurate
basic data or a poorly constructed model.

OPPORTUNITY COST OF CAPITAL

The trader employing the fundamental approach is not concerned so
much with the question *when* prices will move significantly up or down as

---

[9] Vance L. Nimrod and Richard S. Bower, "Commodities and Computers." *Journal of Financial and Quantitative Analysis*, 2, No. 1 (March 1967), 64.

he is with the probability *whether* prices will move in a given direction and the possible extent of such a move. If prices move immediately through the objective indicated by his study, the trade presents no hazard. However, if prices move opposite to the trader's expectation, he is confronted with the vexing problem of losses or, at least, foregone alternative opportunities. If such action persists for months and other trades are rejected because capital has been unavailable for commitment, the cost of capital becomes a real consideration.

INCREASED MARKET EFFICIENCY

Implicit in the fundamental approach is the search for the discrepancy between the actual price of a commodity and its intrinsic value, as indicated by the price model formulated. As information systems become more complex and computer capability becomes more accessible, it seems logical to predict a damping effect on the quantity and degree of discrepancy that a given market will allow to remain unexploited.

It will be remembered that the concept of an efficient market is implicit in the random walk model developed in Chapter 4. The implications of this model for the fundamentalist are clear. The closing price of a commodity for any one day or month is generally as good a clue as any fundamental factor to the closing price on the following day, week, or month. If the full import of such a truth dawns on the trader with something less than instant clarity, he may be comforted to learn that a sage observer of futures markets for many years has wryly observed:

> It is remarkable how long a known fact can in effect remain unknown, for lack of sufficient thoughtful attention to it; the near randomness of speculative price movements has long been widely recognized, in the limited form of recognition that no simple method was known for reliable prediction of speculative price movements.[10]

At least one study has documented the fact that commodity futures prices are almost as active when markets are closed as they are during formal market hours[11]; that is, prices vary almost as much overnight and over any weekend as they do during the actual trading period. Such continuation of activity underscores the never-ending search by traders for new information. It seems that expectations never sleep, and prices are pulled inexorably toward events unknown but about to transpire. Indeed, on those plains of expectation bleach the bones of countless traders who insist that in the short run there must be a continual significant correlation between basic market factors and prices.

[10] Holbrook Working, "Tests of a Theory Concerning Floor Trading on Commodity Exchanges," *Proceedings of a Symposium on Price Effects of Speculation in Organized Commodity Markets, Food Research Institute Studies,* Supplement, 7 (1967), 14.

[11] Labys and Granger, *op. cit.,* pp. 81–82.

CHAPTER 7

The Technical Approach

> . . . There's nothing *wrong* with a fundamentalist. You
> just wouldn't want your sister to marry one.
>
> A. TECHNICIAN

INTRODUCTION

"Technical analysis" refers to a study of the market itself rather than of the external factors that affect the supply of and demand for a given commodity. The basic assumption underlying all technical analysis is that by studying statistics generated by the market it is possible to come to meaningful conclusions about future prices; that is, the way the market behaved yesterday may indicate how prices will behave today. The technician does not believe that price fluctuations are random and unpredictable. He believes that if he studies the transactions taking place impending price movements will tip their hands.

The fundamentalist reasons inductively, seeking to isolate and quantify dominant factors. By taking into consideration the expected supply and expected usage of a commodity, which includes such factors as carry-in, carry-out, production, exports, free supplies, substitutability, and a host of others, the fundamentalist tries to deduce the intrinsic value of the commodity. If the current price is substantially above or below this appraisal, appropriate action is taken in the futures market.

The technician contends that this is a futile procedure. The factors the fundamentalist is examining are in many cases estimates subject to important revision. Furthermore, the technician asserts that there are so many fundamental elements in play at any time that an important one can often be overlooked or those being analyzed may be weighted improperly. Even if all relevant supply/demand factors can be estimated with total accuracy, the technical analyst still believes that the result would be of only limited value in appraising prices. As two advocates of the technical school declare:[1]

> Of course, the statistics which the fundamentalists study play a part in the supply/demand equation—that is freely admitted. But there are many other factors affecting it. The marketplace reflects not only the differing value opinions of many orthodox (commodity) appraisers, but also all of the hopes and fears and guesses and moods, rational and irrational, of hundreds of potential buyers and sellers, as well as their needs and resources—in total, factors which defy analysis and for which no statistics are obtainable—In brief, the going price as established by the market itself comprehends all the fundamental information which the statistical analysts can hope to learn (plus some which is perhaps secret from him, known only to a few insiders) and much else besides of equal or even greater importance.

Even a cursory look explains why the technical approach to commodity trading has had little trouble gathering followers. Only three series of data are required: price, volume, and open interest. These data are easy to get and to store and are available with almost no time lag. The models that the technician constructs with this statistical information are relatively simple and straightforward, applicable to anything that can be traded on a free market, anywhere, at any time. One noted technical analyst has stated, "The technician of 1900 would be completely at home in the markets today."[2] The same certainly could not be said of the turn-of-the-century fundamentalist.

These considerations have appeared to be especially attractive to many traders searching for a better and easier way to make decisions. In the last several decades a vast amount of work has been done to erect a maze of technical tools—all with the aim of anticipating future prices from trading statistics.

Every technical approach, from the simplest to the most complex and esoteric, falls into one of four board areas of technical analysis: patterns on price charts, trend-following methods, character of market analysis, and structural theories. Volumes could be—and have been—written about many of the methods contained in these four basic areas. To go into great detail on any one method would be beyond the scope of this book, but a comprehensive survey is presented, with ample references for further study of the key methods within each area.

[1] Robert D. Edwards and John Magee, *Technical Analysis of Stock Trends,* John Magee, Inc., Springfield, Mass., 1948.

[2] John Magee, *The Stock Advisory Service,* John Magee, Inc., Springfield, Mass., 1964.

PATTERNS ON PRICE CHARTS

The use of patterns of movement on price charts is one of the oldest methods of market analysis known. The approach is said to have gained great popularity in 1901 when William Peter Hamilton, then editor of *The Wall Street Journal*, stunned his readers by recounting in detail precisely what James R. Keene was doing when he successfully promoted the first public offering of stock in U.S. Steel. Hamilton was said to have had an informant in Keene's inner circle, and Keene himself believed this. *The Wall Street Journal* readers were amazed to learn that all of Hamilton's deductions were made by simply tabulating—and shrewdly analyzing—the price and volume action of U.S. Steel stock on the market.[3]

Although Hamilton used only common sense in analyzing the price movement of U.S. Steel, it was not long before many other researchers attempted to catalog and codify any number of price patterns with supposed forecasting value. At first it was said that the "pools" (secret groups of wealthy speculators who manipulated stock prices) revealed their actions to the trader who charted prices and volume. In later years, when the pools were banished by legislative fiat, the charts were supposed to show "changes in psychology." Whatever one believes is being measured, this entire approach rests on the assumption that certain repetitive patterns of price and volume action will often occur before significant price movement.

BAR CHARTS

The most popular method of storing price and volume history in searching for these repetitive patterns is the bar chart. In standard procedure each day (week, month, or year) is represented by one vertical bar on a graph. The bar is drawn to cover the range between the extreme high and low price of the day and a "tick mark" indicates the close. This is illustrated in Figure 7-1, which shows three consecutive days of price action for wheat. Each day is plotted to the right of all preceding days until a record of prices is compiled. Below each price plot on the graph another bar could be drawn to indicate volume of trading for that day.

A number of variations are possible on this standard procedure. Some technicians will graph the close only. A "midrange" price can be entered on the graph, which consists of the high plus the low divided by 2. The opening price can be shown as well. All of these procedures have advantages and disadvantages and each technician must decide which he considers most useful.

As a trader records daily (or weekly) price action, he will begin to observe those patterns that the chartists assume are of a recurring vari-

---

[3] William Peter Hamilton, *The Stock Market Barometer*, Harper & Brothers, New York, 1922. Hamilton explained in some detail the kind of reasoning he used in his deductions. Hamilton's exposition of the basic premises employed in technical analysis remains one of the best available, even after more than half a century.

Price data for wheat, March 1965

	28	29	30
High	$151\frac{3}{8}$	$150\frac{1}{8}$	$149\frac{7}{8}$
Low	150	$148\frac{5}{8}$	$148\frac{1}{2}$
Close	$150\frac{1}{8}$	$148\frac{5}{8}$	$149\frac{5}{8}$

December 1964

FIG. 7-1 Constructing a bar chart. (*Guide to Commodity Price Forecasting,* Commodity Research Bureau, New York, 1965.)

FIG. 7-2 Typical chart patterns. The mirror image of most of these patterns has an opposite implication.

ety.[4,5] Figure 7-2 illustrates a number of patterns that have been well publicized. The price action of May soybeans in Figure 7-3 reveals how these and other popular patterns may be noted and used by a trader. A, B, and C may be said to form a "head-and-shoulders" top, which is completed during the first week of December. Following classical lore, measuring from the head B to D on the "neckline" indicates a minimum objective of 10 cents below the "breakout" at E, or $2.14. F illustrates an "exhaustion gap" and H shows the "resistance" met by the 10-cent rally from G as prices "pull back" into the "left shoulder" (A) area. I represents a "double bottom" which takes 11 weeks to form before supporting a 7-cent rally to J. Throughout this entire time "trendline" T1/T2 is drawn across three important tops and is used as a benchmark to indicate the development of the downtrend, as well as possibly helping to time its ending.[6]

It should be clear from this brief discussion that the field of bar charting could be discussed in great detail. Because of a multitude of alleged patterns, quite an extensive vocabulary has been developed to describe all manner of price-action phenomena.

POINT AND FIGURE CHARTS

The point and figure chartist makes two assumptions that the bar chartist does not. First, he views the volume of trading as unimportant, a mere side-effect of price action with no predictive significance. Second, he dismisses the importance of how much time has elapsed as price moves from one level to another. Only one thing matters and that is the direction of price change. Point and figure charts are constructed to show the direction of price change and nothing else.

Figure 7-4 illustrates a typical point and figure chart for cocoa. The chartist had decided in advance that he wants to characterize every fluctuation of 20 points or more and has scaled the chart accordingly. Each box on the graph equals 20 points.

If the price of cocoa rises by 20 points, an "X" is used to indicate the price change. As long as the price of cocoa continues to rise, new "Xs" will

[4] Edwards and Magee, loc cit. This work is the definitive source of information on chart patterns and their analysis. Another work is William Jiler, How Charts Can Help You in the Stock Market, Commodity Research Publications Corp., New York, 1961.

[5] Two out-of-print works which detail methods of technical analysis using price charts are Richard W. Schabacker, Technical Analysis and Stock Market Profits, B. C. Forbes Publishing Co., New York, 1934, and Robert Rhea, The Dow Theory, Vail-Ballou Press, Binghamton, N.Y., 1932. Both books can be found in many big-city libraries. More modern publications will overlap all or most of their content, but these books are based on original research.

[6] A strong exponent of using charts to trade commodities, and one who believes in paying special attention to "measuring implications" of price patterns, is Houston Cox, A Common Sense Approach to Commodity Trading, Reynolds & Co., New York, 1968. A slightly revised edition of this book, Concepts on Profits in Commodities, was published in 1972.

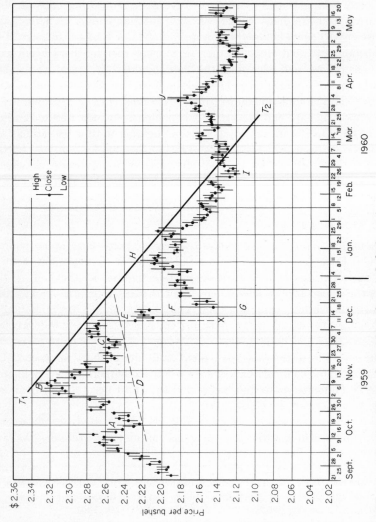

FIG. 7-3   1959–1960 May soybeans: high, low, and closing prices.

be entered on top of those preceding, one for each 20 points of rise. If the price of cocoa rises 3 cents (300 points) with no interruption of as many as 20 points, 15 "Xs" would be placed on top of one another in the same column. This would continue until the price drops by the minimum amount decided on previously, in this case 20 points. Once this happens, an "O"[7] is placed in the column to the right. Each additional 20-point drop causes an "O" to be placed below the preceding "O" as long as the price continues down with no 20-point interruption. When a 20-point rise finally occurs, an "X" is placed in the next column to the right, and the sequence continues as changes in the prices dictate.

The P & F chart is a record of price reversals with no reference to time. For comparison purposes a weekly chart of cocoa for the same period is shown in the lower half of Figure 7-4. The closing price each week is blacked in on the chart to make the comparison easier. Clearly, the more often cocoa reverses direction by 20 points, the more vertical columns are used up.[8]

Any amount of price fluctuation can be shown on a point and figure chart. A chartist with an extremely short-term orientation could, if he had access to successive prices during the day, construct a chart to show reversals of the minimum fluctuation of 1 point. A single day's action might use up scores of columns. On the other hand, another trader interested in a long-run view of cocoa, might construct a chart to show reversals of no less than 300 points. With such a large unit of reversal, a considerable history of price fluctuation could be compacted onto a small chart.

Despite their unique construction, point and figure charts are used much like bar charts.[9,10] Figure 7-5 illustrates many of the popular bar-chart patterns in a point and figure format. The most important difference in claims made for these two methods of charting, and perhaps the only substantive difference, is that many chartists believe that the *extent* of future price moves can be predicted by using point and figure charts. This is accomplished by a consideration of what is known as "the count."

In its simplest form the count is the number of squares across an area of lateral movement on a point and figure chart. Chartists who use the count believe that a direct relation exists between how many squares are used up during a lateral movement and the size of a subsequent rise or fall out of

---

[7] Some technicians will use an "X" in both up and down columns of price movement.

[8] The two standard works on the interpretation of point and figure charts are Alexander Wheelan, *Study Helps in Point and Figure Technique,* Morgan, Rogers and Roberts, New York, 1962, and A. W. Cohen, *The Chartcraft Method of Point & Figure Trading,* Chartcraft, Larchmont, N.Y., 1960.

[9] The first published work on point and figure charts is Victor DeVillers, *The Point & Figure Method of Anticipating Stock Price Movements,* printed by Traders Press, New York, 1972. This book shows how importantly DeVillers was influenced by the Dow theory and other classical technical concepts.

[10] An exceptionally intricate theoretical rationale of the use of point and figure charting is presented in John W. Schulz, *The Intelligent Chartist,* WRSM Financial Service Corp., New York, 1962.

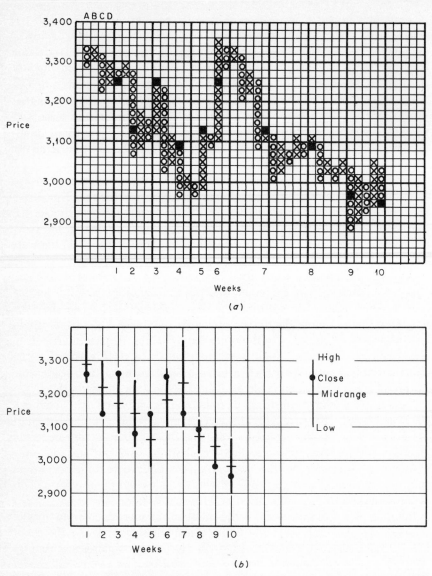

FIG. 7-4   Point-and-figure chart versus bar chart. (a) Point-and-figure chart for a 10-week period in cocoa: each X or O represents a change of 20 points; (b) bar chart for cocoa covering the same 10 weeks as (a).

this congestion area. There are several variations on precisely how to use the count to project the extent of the future move.[11]

[11] Wheelan, *loc. cit.,* Cohen, *loc. cit.,* and Schulz, *loc. cit.,* all present several variations of "the count" in point and figure charts. An ardent point and figure chartist who believes the projection of price targets to be a worthless pastime is James Dines, *How the Average Investor Can Use Technical Analysis for Stock Profits,* Dines Chart Corp., New York, 1972. Dine's book contains several variations on basic point and figure techniques.

FIG. 7-5 Examples of patterns of point-and-figure charts. (*Guide to Commodity Price Forecasting*, Commodity Research Bureau, New York, 1965.)

OLD-TIME PRICE PATTERNS

In many old books and courses considerable space is devoted to the observations of "veteran traders" who have detailed simple price patterns that allegedly have predictive significance. Although these principles of chart reading fell into obscurity for many years, a recent flood of reprints of these old works has led to renewed interest.[12] Possibly the reason these patterns are largely ignored in modern publications is that invariably they are presented with no accompanying rationale and are described as being short-term in nature.

An example will illustrate one bit of market folklore: the "stair-step" principle. To put this principle into operation the following elements must be present:

1. A rise in price of at least three upward waves and two downward waves, working steadily higher.

2. The bottom of each downward wave is below the top of the preceding upward wave.

3. When the bottom of the last downward wave is penetrated, the principle says, "when the last step is broken, all will be broken."

Figure 7-6, which shows a daily chart of May soybeans, is a real-world example.

It is worth noting that many of these old-time patterns are described in far more objective and explicit terms than their modern counterparts.

STRIKING THE BALANCE—ADVANTAGES AND DISADVANTAGES OF USING PRICE PATTERNS IN TRADING

The advantages. (a) The trader does not even have to prepare charts. Many services sell up-to-date charts for modest prices, and some brokerage houses will even supply them gratis. (b) It cannot be denied that successful analysts, past and present, have used price-pattern concepts successfully. Although studies[13] on the accuracy of chartists' forecasting have yielded disappointing results, they have also unearthed the occasional practitioner who has achieved substantially nonrandom results over a long period of time. Individuals making successful forecasts from this kind of analysis are not unknown, though they are, admittedly, few. (c) Even if the use of any specific price patterns for forecasting purposes is considered unacceptable, it is nevertheless true that a study of price charts can reveal information about market action that may assist the trader in making a decision; for instance, a trader contemplating purchase of two different commodities might well use a different operating plan in a commodity whose chart showed a steady descent to ever lower levels, as opposed to another whose chart showed prices soaring to record highs.

The disadvantages. (a) The use of most chart patterns has been widely publicized in the last several years. Many traders are quite familiar with these patterns and often act on them in concert. This creates a "self-ful-

---

[12] Some extensive and detailed old works with interesting technical methods are the several courses written by Mark and Jared Pickell, Ralph Ainsworth, Burton Pugh, and W. D. Gann. These courses have long been out of print and can be picked up only occasionally through such specialty dealers as Allan C. Davis, 1617 Linner Road, Wayzata, Minn. 55391, and James Fraser, 283 S. Union Street, Burlington, Vt., who maintain sizable inventories of books and courses on speculation.

[13] Alfred W. Cowles, "Can Stock Market Forecasters Forecast?," *Econometrica,* 1 (1933), 309–324, and Daniel Seligman, "The Mystique of Point & Figure," *Fortune* (March 1962). These studies do not increase the prestige of chartists or price forecasters in general.

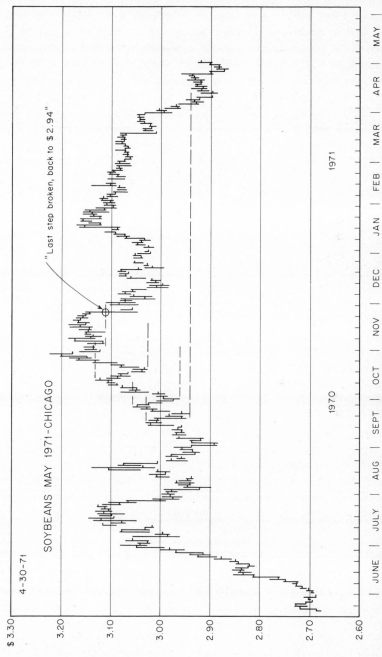

FIG. 7-6 **Daily May 1971 soybean bar chart illustrating the stair-step principle.** (*Commodity Chart Service*, Commodity Research Bureau, New York.)

filling prophecy," as waves of buying or selling are created in response to "bullish" or "bearish" patterns. After this chartist buying or selling is exhausted prices will very often reverse direction to create vicious "chart traps." Just as positive or negative fundamental information can be discounted in the prices, so can positive or negative technical information be discounted. (b) Chart patterns are almost completely subjective. No study has yet succeeded in mathematically quantifying any of them. They are literally in the mind of the beholder. This subjective element makes it impossible to put any of them to an objective test to see how they have worked in the past. (c) The few analyses done to date of the records of the chartists themselves have not been encouraging. Chart-oriented advisers have, in almost all cases, given advice that was no better than random. Even with the few who have distinguished themselves, there is no evidence their success rests solely in chart reading. It is safe to assume that whatever predictive value there may be in price patterns is not easily comprehended.[14]

TREND-FOLLOWING METHODS

Isaac Newton can be given credit for probably the best-known assumption on which most technicians operate: "A price trend once established is more likely to continue than to reverse." This is simply a restatement of Newton's first law of motion, applied to price action. If this concept is accepted as true, then a successful trading strategy can be built on the simple principle of buying strength and selling weakness. The only problem remaining is the optimum way in which to carry it out.

MOVING AVERAGES

An average is defined as "the quotient of any sum divided by the number of its terms." Thus a 10-day average of soybean closing prices is the sum of the last 10 days' closings divided by 10. A moving average of prices is a progressive average in which the divisor number of items remains the same, but at periodic intervals (usually daily or weekly) a new item is added to the end of the series as, simultaneously, an item is dropped from the beginning.

If one is constructing a 10-day moving average of soybean closes, the average on the tenth day is the sum of days 1 through 10 divided by 10. On the eleventh day the eleventh day's close is added to the total and the close of day 1 is subtracted. This new sum is then divided by 10. On day 12 the close of that day is added to the total and the close of day 2 is subtracted. This total is divided by 10 and so on. Table 7-1 illustrates the com-

---

[14] *Ibid.* Seligman's study unearthed one point and figure chartist whose results over a long period were exceptionally good and much better than chance alone would indicate. Nonetheless, it was obvious that this chartist used many other factors than charts in achieving this result. For a cynical view of any successful trader see Fred Schwed, Jr., *Where Are the Customers' Yachts,* John Magee, Inc., Springfield, Mass., 1955, Space Age Edition, in the chapter entitled, "A Brief Excursion into Probabilities."

TABLE 7-1 COMPUTATION OF A 10-DAY
MOVING AVERAGE FOR A TYPICAL MAY
SOYBEANS CONTRACT

Date	Close (in cents)	10-day net change*	10-day total†	10-day average‡
3/15	290.000			
16	291.500			
17	294.000			
3/20	290.500			
21	291.500			
22	300.500			
23	304.000			
24	204.500			
3/27	301.250			
28	305.250	. . . .	2973.000	297.30
29	297.750	+7.750	2980.750	298.08
30	300.250	+8.750	2989.500	298.95
4/3	300.500	+6.500	2996.000	299.60
4	299.750	+9.250	3005.250	300.53
5	302.250	+10.750	3016.000	301.60

* Difference (plus or minus) between latest close and the tenth close, counting back.

† Sum of 10 latest closes.

‡ The 10-day-total column divided by 10. These figures in sequence make up the moving average.

putation of a 10-day moving average based on the closing prices of May 1961 soybeans.

Figure 7-7 shows a 10-week moving average of soybean closes. An examination of this chart will point out the important properties of moving averages. The 10-week moving average smooths out the erratic week-to-week changes in actual prices and thereby indicates the underlying trend. Further, the moving average lags behind prices and crosses the current price only when a new direction is established. These same properties are characteristic of moving averages calculated for any time span.

Shown on the chart are "buy" and "sell" signals, given when price penetrates the 10-week moving average. The technician acting on this signal is following the strategy of buying strength and selling weakness. He hopes that the prevailing trend, like the buy signal of late 1953, will continue long enough—and powerfully enough—to compensate adequately for the kind of whipsaw losses that resulted from the first two signals of 1952.

There are countless systems that use moving averages,[15,16] but all are based on variations of just two factors:

[15] A number of moving average systems are presented in the following works: C. W. Keltner, *How to Make Money In Commodities,* Keltner Statistical Service, Kansas City, Mo., 1960; Garfield Drew, *New Methods for Profit In The Stock Market,* Metcalf Press, Boston, Mass., 1955; Curtiss Dahl, *Consistent Profits In The Commodity Futures Market,* Tri-State Offset Co., Cincinnati, Ohio, 1960, with 1961 addendum; Irving Levine, *Successful Commodity Speculation,* Levro Press, Newark, N.J., 1965; Robert Joel Taylor, "The Major Price Trend Directional Indicator," *Commodities Magazine* (April 1972). Dunn & Hargitt, P.O. Box

FIG. 7-7 Weekly May and November soybeans, weekly closing price versus 10-week moving average. Prices of contracts adjusted to each other for continuity. (*Guide to Commodity Price Forecasting*, Commodity Research Bureau, New York, 1965.)

1. The length of time used in computing the moving average. It is here that an important trade-off is involved. The shorter the length of time, the more sensitive the moving average will be to any change in trend. New trends will be acted on earlier and do not need much time to establish themselves. The trader pays for this sensitivity because the shorter the moving average's length, the greater the number of trades that will be made. This means greater commissions and a larger number of whipsaw losses. A longer period of time used to calculate the moving average will

101, Lafayette, Ind., 47902, sell a computerized study of hypothetical trading in several commodities for a number of years in which most of the best-known moving average trading systems are used.

[16] An increasingly popular form of moving average is one that has been "exponentially smoothed." It is doubtful if exponential smoothing is an important improvement on the standard calculation of moving averages. One source on this as well as other smoothing methods is Robert Brown, *Smoothing, Forecasting & Prediction of Discrete Time Series,* Prentice-Hall, Englewood Cliffs, N.J., 1963. Brown's book particularly stresses the "how-to" aspect of smoothing procedures.

reduce the number of trades and the number of whipsaw losses but will signal new trends much later—often so late that the trend will be closer to completion than initiation.

2. The kind and amount of penetration required. In an effort to reduce false signals, many technicians demand more than just a simple penetration of the moving average; for instance, having the price in Figure 7-7 penetrate the moving average by 5 cents before acting on any signal would eliminate several whipsaws. This strategy, however, is subject to the same limitations described above. Too small an amount of penetration does little to reduce whipsaws and excess trades. Too large a penetration has the effect of cutting down profits on successful signals. The trader is referred to Chapter 4, in which many competent academic studies using several moving-average decision rules are discussed in some detail.

SWING CHARTS

Swing charts provide many of the trend-following properties of moving averages but they are usually easier to calculate. Swing charts are similar to point and figure charts because the trader is interested in price movements of a certain minimum amount. Figure 7-8 is a chart of July 1971 platinum constructed by drawing in only those swings of 300 points or more. The key difference between the swing chart and a point and figure chart covering the same time period is that the swing chart shows the precise highs and lows and a point and figure chart is likely to show them to the nearest 20 or 50 points.

To carry out the basic trend-following strategy of buying strength and selling weakness the trader buys when the top of a previous swing is penetrated on the upside and sells when the bottom of a previous swing is penetrated on the downside. These signals are shown on the chart.

The theory behind swing charting is that tops and bottoms in price become "important" if they are terminations of swings of some minimum amount. If they are later penetrated, a new trend is presumed to be in force. The trader who employs swing charts is following the age-old dictum to "take positions along the line of least resistance."

Any swing-charting method[17] is composed of just two elements: (a) The amount of the minimum swing to be charted and (b) The amount and type of penetration required when price penetrates a previous top or bottom. The same trade-off occurs here that occurs with moving average methods. The smaller the amount of penetration required, the more quickly new trends are signaled and the more whipsaws that result. A larger required price penetration reduces whipsaws, but also puts the trader in later on the more successful signals. The choice of the amount of minimum price

---

[17]Keltner, *loc. cit.*; Wm. Dunnigan, *New Blueprints For Gains In Stocks and Grains,* privately published, San Francisco, Calif., 1956 (out-of-print but available from various specialty dealers), and Richard Donchian, "Trend Following Methods in Commodity Price Analysis" in *Guide To Commodity Price Forecasting,* Commodity Research Bureau, New York, 1965, are comprehensive sources of information on swing charting, as well as moving average and other trend following techniques.

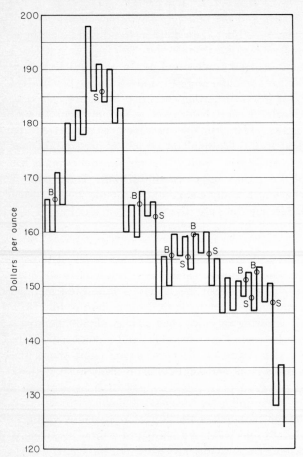

FIG. 7-8   July 1971 platinum, 300-point swing chart. Buy and sell signals shown for February–October 1971.

swing charted is analogous to the choice of the number of days used for a moving average.

Some technicians have constructed swing charts based not on price but on time.[18] Tops or bottoms that hold for some arbitrary number of days (or weeks) are defined as important. When they are penetrated, "buy" or "sell" signals are generated. The choice of the length of time during which a top or bottom must stand, and the amount and type of penetration required, makes this kind of chart subject to the same limitations of standard swing charts.

[18] W. D. Gann, *How To Make Profits Trading In Commodities*, Lambert-Gann Publishing Co., Miami, Fla., 1951, revised edition (out-of-print but found in many big-city libraries) was probably the originator of this kind of swing chart. Gann covers the subject in more detail in many of his commodity trading courses cited elsewhere. A time factor is also used by many moving average devotees; instead of requiring price to penetrate the moving average by a certain amount, the trader requires price to penetrate and then stay beyond the moving average by a certain number of days.

A mathematical technique highly analogous to swing charting is the use of "filters." This approach was discussed in detail in Chapter 4, where the results of several studies based on various filter rules were presented.

STRIKING THE BALANCE—ADVANTAGES AND DISADVANTAGES OF USING TREND-FOLLOWING METHODS

The advantages. (a) A trend-following technique is, by definition, objective. All the elements must be clearly defined before it can be put into practice. This means that a trader can, if he has the facilities, determine how well any technique has worked in the past and define its important characteristics. Any number of variations can be back-checked in an attempt to optimize results. (b) Any trend-following method provides the trader with a sizable part of his operating plan, with all of the attendant benefits in terms of results and peace of mind. Because his action points are so clearly defined, the trader is not so likely to be beset by uncertainties. (c) The trend follower believes, along with many famous traders, that "the big swing makes the big money." By employing any trend-following method it is impossible for a big move to occur without his participating in it.

The disadvantages. (a) The trader who uses a trend-following method begins with two counts against him. First, whipsaws are inevitable. One technician, himself an ardent trend-following advocate, indicates that 50 percent of all trades entered into by any such method will result in whipsaw losses.[19] Second, all signals acted on are late by definition. To compensate for these two liabilities, the trader must realize substantial profits on the successful signals, and even during a normally active market this may be difficult to achieve. (b) A commodity moving within a trading range will provide the trend follower with seemingly endless losses until a major trend is initiated. As long as there is no pronounced bias to the up or the down side, long positions will be taken on strength near the top of the range and short positions will be assumed on weakness near the bottom. Some cursory studies have indicated that commodity prices are without important trending characteristics as much as 85 percent of the time.[20] If true, this consideration may present a formidable obstacle. (c) Optimum rules established for a trend-following method during one period of time may result in a poor performance during another; for example, appropriate rules for a moving average system for trading 1960 world sugar, which had a range for the entire year of less than 100 points, would certainly not have been appropriate for that same commodity three years

---

[19] Donchian, *loc. cit.*

[20] This statement is made by John R. Hill in his course *Technical and Mathematical Analysis of the Commodity and Stock Markets*, Commodity Research Institute, 141 West Jackson, Room 855, Chicago, Ill. 60604, 1971. Most of the course is concerned with the presentation of graphical trading methods which assume that futures prices are usually without important trending characteristics. Such methods are antithetical to those used by a trend follower.

later. In 1963 world sugar had a range of more than 900 points, and often had a two-day range exceeding 100 points. To be used at all successfully, the elements of any trend-following method must be adjusted to both current and predicted volatility. The trader must be certain that his rules are not out of date for each commodity he is following.[21]

CHARACTER-OF-MARKET ANALYSIS

The trader using character-of-market methods operates on premises completely different from those of the chartist or trend follower, both of whom have constructed a number of techniques based on the interpretation of price action. Those technicians who employ a character-of-market approach believe that a deceptive veneer has been painted over the true picture of supply and demand.

The character-of-market analyst seeks statistical measurements of supply and demand that are independent of price or at least uses price information much more subtly than the chartist or trend follower. The important question asked by those traders who use this approach to technical analysis is, "What is the *quality* of a given move in price?" The trader then tries to commit his capital in line with price movements of good quality and to avoid, or even take an opposite position to, movements of poor quality.

As noted before, the technician has only three series of trading data to work with: price, volume, and open interest. Nevertheless, so many combinations and permutations of these data have been employed in character-of-market methods that it is possible here to touch only on the most illustrative and basic.

OSCILLATORS

The term "oscillator" is given to a family of technical indicators based on measurement of price changes rather than price levels. The simplest type of oscillator is based upon the distance the price of a commodity has traveled over a given period of time; for example, a 10-day oscillator is constructed by taking the price on the latest day and subtracting the price of the tenth trading day previous. The number obtained is either positive or negative, depending on whether the commodity has risen or fallen in the last 10 days. The same procedure is followed during subsequent trading days.

The calculation of oscillators has often been carried to surprising complexity.[22] Some oscillators are specially smoothed, some are weighted,

---

[21] Cox, *loc. cit.*, presents a moving average method that to some extent does adjust to current price volatility. A simpler, but similar, procedure is presented by Levine, *loc. cit.* Taylor, *loc. cit.*, adjusts the length of the moving average in relation to current volatility.

[22] A potpourri of oscillator calculation and interpretation is to be found in the following: many special studies in the "Indicator Digest" Advisory Service, Palisades Park, N.J. 07650, have appeared over the last several years; Drew, *loc. cit.*; Carl W. Floss, *Market Rhythm*, In-

and some are modified in conjunction with one or more additional factors (such as volume). Sometimes all of these options are used. Time periods employed for constructing oscillators can range from two or three days (or even less if the trader has access to intraday data) to several weeks or longer. The use of *any* oscillator, however, rests on one or both of these contentions:

1. A price rise or price decline can become overextended if it gathers too much velocity. If the price of any commodity enjoys an unusual gain that is compacted into a short time span, the presumption is that buying is temporarily exhausted and part of all of the gain will be retraced. Such a market is said to be "overbought." The opposite kind of price action would lead to an "oversold" market. By constructing an oscillator the technician seeks to monitor excessive rates of price change that could lead to exhaustion and subsequent price reversals.

2. A price trend can simply peter out as it steadily loses momentum. In this case a price trend continues but generates less and less energy until it dies. A top is signaled when, for instance, the price continues to make new highs for the move but the oscillator moves from large positive numbers to small positive numbers. The reverse is true for a bottom. Used in this way, an oscillator is a tool for measuring the exhaustion of a price trend.

These two concepts are not mutually exclusive. Figure 7-9 shows the daily action of November 1970 eggs against a 20-day price change oscillator. For this period levels in the oscillator above +300 (meaning that price had advanced more than 300 points in the preceding 20 days) spotlighted markets that were overextended on the upside. Similarly, levels in the oscillator below −300 indicated that price had become oversold.

During this period the penetration of "trendlines," drawn across key tops or bottoms in the oscillator, indicated, exhaustion in the current price trend. In line with this concept of exhaustion, it will also be noted that the oscillator can peak or bottom ahead of price in many instances, thus signaling possible reversal.

STRIKING THE BALANCE—ADVANTAGES AND DISADVANTAGES OF USING THE OSCILLATOR

The advantages. (a) Overbought/oversold signals generated from oscillators will usually work well in trading markets, which occur more frequently then trending markets. If there is no dominant trend, points of upside and downside exhaustion can, in theory at least, be identified with a fair degree of accuracy. (b) Signals of an overbought or oversold market can act as a valuable check on a trader's emotions. No matter how bullish

---

vestors Publishing Co., Detroit, 1955 (out-of-print but available from specialty dealers); James Waters and Larry Williams, "Measuring Market Momentum", *Commodities Magazine* (October 1972), H. M. Gartley, *Profits in the Stock Market,* H. M. Gartley, Inc., New York, 1935 (out-of-print but available from specialty dealers), gives highly detailed instructions on trading with price oscillators and discusses a number of possible predictive relationships mentioned by no other source.

FIG. 7-9   November 1970 shell eggs daily close versus 20-day net change oscillator for May–October 1970.

a situation may appear, a high positive reading on the oscillator at the same time could be a sobering influence. The reverse is also true. (c) History is replete with examples of price trends that peaked or troughed, whereas accompanying rate-of-change oscillators showed a clear loss of momentum well in advance.

The disadvantages. (a) Acting on overbought/oversold oscillator signals will lead to financial disaster in any market with a dominant price trend. During a powerful bull or bear swing an oscillator will repeatedly move into "overextended" territory and will often stay there for a long time. This danger cannot be avoided because a trader who could consistently anticipate dominant price trends in advance would not be using an oscillator as a trading device. (b) Zones that represent overbought or oversold markets must be decided on the basis of history. If the commodity being followed suddenly becomes either more or less volatile, whether still in a trading range or not, previously determined zones will be worthless. All commodities do change their volatility over time. (c) Loss of momentum before key tops and bottoms are reached is well documented, but this phenomenon is much easier to see in retrospect. In Figure 7-9 trendlines are drawn on the oscillator itself to determine loss of momentum. These trendlines could have been drawn in many other ways, and several of them would not have yielded satisfactory results. In practice, declining momentum will indicate a pause in the price trend or a reversal, and there is no way to tell which. Using this technique, the analyst can often explain past price action, but he cannot easily predict future price changes.

TRADITIONAL VOLUME AND OPEN-INTEREST METHODS

"Volume" refers simply to the aggregate number of contracts or bushels of commodity futures traded in a given period; it is a measure of the combined futures market supply and demand for that period. "Open interest" is the total purchase or sale commitments outstanding. At any time, the purchase commitments or number of contracts "long" are equal to the sale commitments or number of contracts "short." The different types of trades and their effects on the open interest are listed below. "Old" buyers are those who have outstanding long positions, whereas "old" sellers have outstanding short positions in the market. "New" buyers or sellers are those who are just entering the market to take a long or short position.

Transaction	Effect on open interest
Purchases by old sellers from old buyers	Reduced
Purchases by old sellers from new sellers	Unchanged
Purchases by new buyers from old buyers	Unchanged
Purchases by new buyers from new sellers	Increased
Sales by old buyers to new buyers	Unchanged
Sales by old buyers to old sellers	Reduced
Sales by new sellers to old sellers	Unchanged
Sales by new sellers to new buyers	Increased

The open interest increases only when new purchases are offset by new sales. Decreases in open interest occur only when previous purchases are sold and are offset by the buying in of previously sold contracts. Since it is the effect on open interest that is reported and not the type of transaction, the technician interested in this aspect of market behavior must infer the latter from the former.

Volume and open-interest data are reported daily in newspapers and wire services. They are also printed and distributed at different intervals by the CEA and by various advisory services.[23] Most technicians use the totals for both the volume and open interest of a given commodity rather than the figures for individual contract months.

Significant changes in volume and open interest generally last over a period of a few days to a month. These changes must be related to their respective seasonal patterns before a meaningful analysis may be undertaken. The seasonal changes are substantial for open interest, whereas seasonal changes in volume are not so wide or significant. Illustrations of the seasonal changes in both volume and open interest are presented in Section 5 for several specific commodities.

To illustrate the relevance of seasonal adjustments consider the following example. Suppose the total open interest in all soybean contracts amounts to 125 million bushels on October 15, when the May contract is selling at $2.75 a bushel. By November 15 May soybeans have risen to $2.86 and the open interest for all soybean contracts has increased to 137,500,000 bushels. A quick judgment may conclude that prices have risen 4 percent in the same period that open interest has increased 10 percent. Inspection of the soybean seasonal open interest and volume chart on page 356 indicates that the seasonal rise from October 15 to November 15 is 14 percent (from 118 to 132 percent). Although actual open interest increased 10 percent, on a seasonally adjusted basis it has really *decreased* for the period being examined. In order for a net increase of 10 percent to occur, open interest would have had to increase to 155 million bushels by November 15.

Because there is no measurable seasonal pattern for volume, technicians generally compare it to that of the immediate past; for example, if total soybean volume has hovered around 50 million bushels a day and suddenly increases over a period of a week to 75 million bushels, a significant change may be occurring in the psychology of the market.

General rules have been formulated to indicate how significant net changes in open-interest and volume figures may be analyzed in conjunction with price analysis.[24]

The tendencies for volume alone may be summarized as follows:

1. When a major price advance is under way, volume tends to increase on rallies and to decrease on reactions.

2. Conversely, during a major price decline, volume tends to increase on down moves and decrease on rallies.

[23] Edward B. Gotthelf, *The Commodex System*, Commodity Futures Forecast, 90 West Broadway, New York, N. Y. 10007, presents a completely mechanized system that converts traditional price/volume/open interest relationships into daily index numbers interpreted with objective rules. Hamilton, *loc. cit.*; Rhea, *loc. cit.*; Edwards and Magee, *loc. cit.*; Hill, *loc. cit.*, are all sources of interpretation of price/volume relations and generally follow the "Classical" rules of divination. Two more involved procedures for using volume data are "Quinn's Moving Volume Curve", found in Drew, *loc. cit.*, and the *Relative Volume Index* published by Trend Way Advisory Service, P. O. Box 7184, Louisville, Ky. 40207. All but one of these sources refer to analysis of stocks, but the identical principles can be applied to commodities.

[24] An advisory service that places much stress on analysis of open interest and presents rules of interpretation to its readers is John K. Hart, *Commodity Trend Service*, 518 Empire Building, Columbus, Ga. 31901.

3. Volume expands sharply as bottoms and tops are approached.

Open interest, when compared with price action, tends to act in the following ways:

1. If prices advance and open interest advances more sharply than a seasonal analysis would suggest, aggressive new buying would seem to have taken place.

2. If prices advance and seasonally adjusted open interest declines, the advance has been fueled by short covering and might be regarded as technically weak.

3. If prices decline and aggressive new selling is taking place, the market may be considered to be technically weak.

4. If prices decline and open interest decreases beyond seasonal expectations, the decline has been fed by discouraged longs who have liquidated their unprofitable positions, leaving the market relatively strong technically.

A perhaps oversimplified form of some of the relations among volume, open interest and price is sometimes given as follows:

If prices are up and   (a) volume and open interest are up—the market is strong;

                     (b) volume and open interest are down—the market is weak.

If prices are down and (a) volume and open interest are up—the market is weak;

                     (b) volume and open interest are down—the market is strong.

The confidence level of such observations has not been statistically measured. One cursory study[24a] found the following:

1. There was some forecasting value in blow-off action at major tops where prices advance sharply on high volume and a sharp drop in open interest.

2. Similarly, after a long decline when prices drop sharply on heavy volume and a sharp drop in open interest, a major bottom is possible.

3. Price moves away from consolidations tend to be greater if the consolidations period was marked by a sharply higher than seasonal buildup in open interest.

STRIKING THE BALANCE—ADVANTAGES AND DISADVANTAGES OF USING TRADITIONAL VOLUME AND OPEN-INTEREST METHODS

The advantages. (a) The basic principles of interpreting volume and open interest appear quite logical. It seems reasonable that the expansion and contraction of volume and open interest compared with price action should yield worthwhile clues to the balance of supply and demand in the market.

[24a] William Jiler, "Volume and Open Interest Analysis as an Aid to Price Forecasting," *Guide to Commodity Price Forecasting,* Commodity Research Bureau, Inc., New York, 1965, pp. 63–64.

(b) The trader following volume and open-interest principles uses a three-dimensional model rather than one of single dimension found in other technical approaches. There are many other ways in which price action can be viewed, and many more shadings can be used to describe bullish or bearish behavior. (c) If the forecasting ability of volume and open interest is denied, there is still a significant amount of information to be obtained by simply monitoring such data. The trader knows which contracts are most active, the size of the market in which he is dealing, and any important properties of trading activity.

The disadvantages. (a) This type of analysis is replete with a number of ill-defined terms: "low volume," "increase in open interest," "decline of greater than seasonal expectation," and several others. To make use of this approach the technician must quantify his terms to avoid meaningless generalities. (b) General rules for volume and open-interest interpretation are well publicized. Application of these classical principles leads to the problem of the "self-fulfilling prophecy" discussed among the disadvantages of using price patterns. Volume and open-interest behavior which is clearly bullish or bearish can be discounted in the present price level as easily as other more familiar supply-demand factors. (c) The validity of these standard principles rests on unproved assertion. No publicly available studies that use volume and open-interest decision rules confirm their value in actual trading.

ON BALANCE VOLUME

The bulk of character-of-market analysis originates from the belief that "big-moneyed" traders consistently take positions prior to substantial price moves in any commodity. The "big money" is seen, for instance, as surreptitiously acquiring sizable long positions before price advances, well ahead of the "ignorant masses." This quiet buying is known as "accumulation." When these same interests are selling their longs and going short at the top of a rise, before a large decline, their activity is called "distribution." Tracking the supposed clandestine flow of accumulation and distribution has led to the growth of countless technical methods over the years.

An old approach to measuring accumulation and distribution by the action of price and volume, which has enjoyed a popular renaissance since the early 1960s[25] is currently known as "on balance volume," or OBV. Easily calculated and graphed, OBV attempts to provide information on the quality of price movements by yielding a volume curve that can be compared directly with the price curve.

Table 7-2 illustrates a hypothetical OBV calculation. Each day's closing price is compared with the closing price of the preceding day. If the latest day has a higher closing price, *all* the volume of trading that day is assigned

---

[25] Joseph Granville, *Granville's New Key to Stock Market Profits*, Prentice-Hall, Englewood Cliffs, N.J., 1963, has popularized this approach in recent years.

TABLE 7-2   COMPUTATION OF ON-BALANCE VOLUME

Date	May cocoa daily closing price	Volume (number of contracts)	OBV (cumulative volume)
March 1	27.09	—	—
2	27.15	+3,000	+3,000
3	27.22	+2,500	+5,500
4	27.07	− 800	+4,700
5	26.85	−1,200	+3,500
8	27.01	+2,500	+6,000

a plus sign. If the latest day's close is lower than that of the preceding day, all the volume is added to a cumulative running total. This cumulative total is the OBV. The absolute level of the OBV curve is of no significance; the technician is interested only in the contour of this curve when it is compared with the contour of price, either graphically or in tabulated form.

The dominant theory behind OBV, as previously noted, assumes that large-scale accumulation or distribution can take place in the market. Because this activity would have to be done quietly, it is further assumed that worthwhile accumulation or distribution is carried out under cover of small net or deceptive price changes. The OBV curve is believed to illustrate the true state of affairs by showing whether volume of trading is highest during periods of rising or falling prices. When the bias in volume deviates significantly from the price curve, unusual activity is presumed to be taking place.

Under normal circumstances the OBV curve will move parallel to the price of the commodity under surveillance. As long as this relationship remains the trader using OBV will have no particular interest. However, when the OBV curve begins to diverge from price, notice is taken because many analysts believe that such divergence indicates accumulation or distribution. In Table 7-2, for instance, the price of cocoa dropped a nominal eight points between March 1 and March 8. Yet the OBV record shows that 6,000 more contracts changed hands on days of rising price than of falling price. If this kind of behavior continued for a significant period of time, the technician would conclude that cocoa was being intensively accumulated. Moneyed interests would be presumed to be buying heavily, putting prices up for a day or so before quietly allowing them to drop on low activity until they moved again into a satisfactory buying area. In theory, this process would continue until accumulation was completed. Prices would then move much higher as the "big money's" analysis was proved correct and the "crowd" began to act on the now favorable news developments affecting cocoa.

Figure 7-10 illustrates an actual example in which a daily OBV analysis spotlighted an impending break in pork bellies. During the period labeled "1" in late May 1967 prices moved to their final high above 43 cents while several thousand more contracts changed hands at lower prices than changed hands at higher prices. The OBV curve peaked 16 days before the price. Again in late June during the period labeled "2" a 300-point rally hoisted prices well above the early June highs but left the OBV seriously lagging. These two marked divergences, presumably showing strong distribution, were followed by a sharp and sustained break in the market.

There are more sophisticated, and complicated, ways to calculate and use OBV,[26] but the basic principle of interpretation remains the same.

STRIKING THE BALANCE—ADVANTAGES AND DISADVANTAGES OF USING OBV

The advantages. (a) If there is, in fact, important money from intelligent sources that quietly assumes positions in advance of large price moves or if such substantial buying or selling takes place for any reason, it cannot help but leave a record in daily transactions. OBV pinpoints periods in which a substantial excess of volume takes place at higher or lower prices, thus giving the technician a "lead" for further study. (b) Whatever interpretation is used, OBV gives the analyst information with which to quantify the volume of any price move. Even if the trader is not looking for "signals" per se, the knowledge that the largest volume occurs on rising or falling prices, and how it compares with price, can be helpful in appraising market action.

The disadvantages. (a) Research to date indicates that the profit-making ability of the large trader is impressive.[27] These studies have shown that large traders succeed mainly by trading *short-run* price fluctuations. Such conclusions do not support the relatively longer term accumulation/distribution thesis on which much of OBV analysis rests. (b) No objective rules of interpretation have ever been presented by advocates of OBV,[28] thus ensuring the impossibility of performing any tests that would determine whether the use of OBV would lead to nonrandom trading results. (c) On theoretical grounds the calculation of the most commonly used form of OBV is open to serious question. Each day's price change is determined by transactions on both the buying and selling side, and it does not seem reasonable to assign *all* the volume to the plus or minus side simply because the close one day is higher or lower than the close of the preceding day. If pork bellies, for example, were up 130 points during the day but closed down 5 points,

---

[26] David L. Markstein, *How To Chart Your Way to Stock Market Profits,* Parker Publishing Co., West Nyack, N.Y., 1966, advocates multiplying the amount of price change by the volume of trading. R. F. Martel, *Charting Supply and Demand for Stock Analysis,* Martel & Co., 1505 Old Mill Road, Reading, Pa. 19610, presented a system in 1972 that also attempts to quantify price/volume activity by means of a highly modified OBV curve.

[27] C. S. Rockwell, "Normal Backwardation, Forecasting, and the Returns to Speculators," *Food Research Institute Studies,* Supplement, 7 (1967), 107–130.

[28] Granville, *loc. cit.,* presented many objective collateral OBV calculations but failed to present a completely quantifiable set of decision-making rules.

FIG. 7-10   August 1967 pork bellies daily close versus daily on-balance volume (OBV) for May–July 1967.

it would not seem proper to assign all of the volume that day to the minus side. Calculation of basic OBV may be too simplistic.[29]

[29] Two attempts to weight OBV more precisely in accordance with intraday price activity are David Bostian, *Intra-Day Intensity Index,* privately printed, Fort Benjamin Harrison, Indiana, 1967, and Larry Williams, *The Secret of Selecting Stocks for Immediate and Substantial Gains,* Conceptual Management, Carmel Valley, Calif., 1973. These two variations are also open to criticism on theoretical grounds.

ARMCHAIR TAPE READING

In the late 19th century, when "pools" manipulated the stock and commodity markets, tape readers attempted to monitor the flow of "inside money." They would watch every transaction on the tape and note the price and volume. If the tape reader were shrewd enough, he might be able to deduce the action being taken by the pool and follow its lead.[30]

An important element of tape reading consisted of paying special attention to large blocks that appeared on the tape, as these were presumed to be the actual transactions of the pool. In later years, with the pools but a memory, the analysis of large transactions is still an integral part of tape reading. The tape-reading technician believes that large transactions, by their very nature, represent important and far-seeing money.

Some years ago a method was published[31] that enables a trader to "read the tape by proxy." It was designed solely to indicate when large transactions are appearing on the tape and thereby to provide a lead for further study. It is not presented here as a complete or proved indicator.

Each day the trader calculates a "resistance index" in the following way:

$$\frac{\text{(number of contracts traded)}}{\text{(high price)}-\text{(low price)}}$$

This ratio measures the number of contracts that changed hands in relation to the range for the day. When the ratio is unusually large, it may be presumed that unusually large transactions are crossing the tape. High ratios do not occur often, but they do stand out as "spikes" on the chart.

Figure 7-11 shows the daily closing prices of June 1971 live hogs graphed with a daily resistance index. The three figures greater than 60 (meaning that 60 or more contracts changed hands per point of range in price) are numbered 1, 2, and 3. All three of these high index days came close to advantageous buying or selling areas. Whether these days with unusually large tape transactions actually saw informed money taking a position in the market before a price reversal is an open question.

There is no question, however, that this technique can only be subjective and could not be used effectively without information from other sources or methods. Furthermore, price action and volume varies greatly over time. A large resistance index during one period may not be significant in another span of time, thus adding yet another interpretative problem.

[30] Humphrey Neill, *Tape Reading and Market Tactics*, reprinted by Fraser Publishing Co., Wells, Vt., 1960, and Richard Wyckoff, *Studies in Tape Reading*, reprinted by Traders Press, New York, 1972, are sources of detailed instruction on tape reading. Edwin LeFevre, *Reminiscences of a Stock Operator*, reprinted by the American Research Council, New York, 1964, provides a number of absorbing insights into tape reading from the legendary Jesse Livermore.

[31] Edwin H. Tomkins, *Systematic Stock Trading*, The Moore Guide, P. O. Box 42, Riverside, Ill. 60546, contains a complete discussion of his "resistance index." The author also discusses tape reading and short-term trading techniques.

FIG. 7-11   June 1971 live hogs daily close versus daily resistance index for December 1970–January 1971.

ANALYSIS OF OPEN INTEREST TO DETERMINE ACTIVITIES OF LARGE AND SMALL TRADERS

Another way to measure accumulation and distribution is the proposal made by many technical analysts to differentiate between "smart money" and "stupid money." Those making this differentiation believe that there are, essentially, two categories of traders: winners and losers; for example, in the stock market, exchange specialists have often been identified as a winning group and odd-lotters as a losing group. Techniques long in use with these and other series can be applied to commodities as well.[32] This approach attempts to focus on data showing the activities of winning and losing groups of traders and then suggests the following action:

1. Initiate positions opposite those of the losing group when it shows a strong preference for one side of the market.

2. Initiate positions in line with those of the winning group when it shows a strong preference for one side of the market.

Twice monthly the U.S. Government[33] provides a breakdown of the open interest in all regulated commodities. Both long and short positions are tabulated for three groups: bona fide hedgers, large traders with legally reportable positions, and the remaining portion of open interest which consists of small traders with less than a reportable position. If it can be assumed that generally large traders are winners and small traders are losers over a reasonable period of time, it is possible to construct a number of technical indicators that might delineate the actions of these groups.[34]

Figure 7-12 illustrates one of many gauges that could be constructed to measure the activity of large traders. The closing prices of December 1969 cattle are plotted at two-week intervals against a ratio that measures large trader short positions as a percentage of the total open interest. When large trader short positions are "low," on this chart below 6 percent, it might be assumed that they are strongly biased to the bullish side of the market and prices therefore should rise. When they are "high," 9 percent or higher on this chart, an important degree of pessimism would be indicated and lower prices expected to follow.

It is surprising that although similar procedures have long been used to analyze stock prices and regular breakdowns of open interest have been supplied since 1923 this area of technical analysis has attracted almost no attention in the commodity field.

Because the total open interest is divided into six constituent parts, a great number of ratios and/or oscillators can be derived between these

---

[32] In-depth discussions of techniques for handling odd-lot trading data are found in Drew, *loc. cit.*; Garfield Drew, "A Clarification of the Odd-Lot Theory," *Financial Analysts Journal* (September–October 1967); Thomas J. Kewley and R. A. Stevenson, "The Odd-Lot Theory-A Reply," *Financial Analysts Journal* (January–February 1969); Stanley Kaish, "Odd Lot Profit and Loss Performance," *Financial Analysts Journal* (September–October 1969). Expositions of techniques for handling both specialist and odd-lot data are found in Indicator Digest, *loc. cit.*; Walter Heiby, *Stock Market Profits Through Dynamic Synthesis,* Institute of Dynamic Synthesis, Chicago, Ill., 1965 (a supplement to this book, explaining new techniques, "The New Dynamic Synthesis," was published in 1967); William X. Scheinman, *Why Most Investors Are Mostly Wrong Most of The Time,* Lancer Books, New York, 1970.

[33] Periodic reports on open interest are available from the Commodity Exchange Authority. Different regional offices publish separate reports for commodities directly under their supervision. The CEA, Washington, D.C. 20250, will furnish information on all reports available and how to obtain them.

[34] Chapter 13 discusses in detail estimated rates of return for the large speculator, small trader, and hedger.

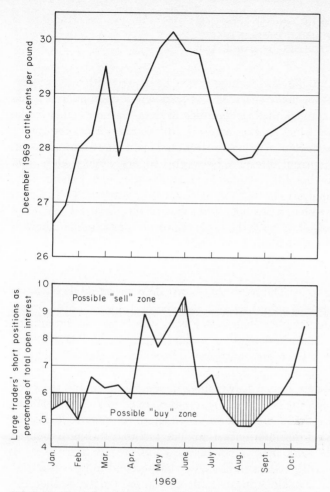

FIG. 7-12   December 1969 live beef cattle bimonthly closing price versus bimonthly large traders' short positions as percentage of total open interest for January–October 1969.

available series. It is also possible to play the large traders off against the small traders and isolate marked dichotomies of opinion; for example, a ratio of various large trader positions to comparable small trader positions would clearly pinpoint times of sharp disagreement between the two groups.[35]

[35] Roy E. Christian, *New Methods for Long Term Stock Market Forecasting*, Physician's Market Letter, 1691 Wilshire Drive, Aptos, Calif. 95003, 1966 (there is also a supplement, *Long Term Study*, and several back letters) has discussed numerous means of using odd-lot, specialist, and other data that specifically employ the technique of measuring marked divergences of opinion between two groups of traders. The Physicians Market Letter is defunct but many of these studies are still available.

**STRIKING THE BALANCE—ADVANTAGES AND
DISADVANTAGES OF USING OPEN INTEREST
TO REVEAL THE ACTIVITIES OF LARGE AND
SMALL TRADERS**

The advantages. (a) Similar techniques have been used with some success in the stock market for many years. The breakdown of open interest available on regulated commodities yields series of data that are highly analogous to those used in stock market analysis. (b) Whether or not the trader constructs operative technical indicators from the open-interest breakdown, knowledge of the current interplay between hedgers, large traders, and small traders can be helpful in explaining market action in any commodity. (c) This kind of analysis can become exceptionally intriguing when it is realized that little research has been published in this area. The six series of data available regularly have the potential of yielding large numbers of permutations and combinations in the form of ratios, rate-of-change oscillators, and other indices. Interesting new territory is offered the inquiring technical analyst.

The disadvantages. (a) The work that has been done on the behavior of large and small traders argues against the value of open-interest breakdowns. Small traders, rather than acting consistently on the wrong side of the market, are better described as trading haphazardly. Large traders are consistent winners but are short-term oriented as a group.[36] It might be concluded that there is no available information on "stupid money," and that "smart money" data are available but come too late and too infrequently to be helpful. (b) The biweekly report on open interest is available to the public with a time lag of two weeks or more, thereby reducing the effectiveness of using this information. (c) The fact that technical analysts have done so little work here is not because this area is obscure. Most commodity traders with even a rudimentary background in the stock market would see the possible relevance of open-interest data. Rather this neglect might well indicate how arid the field is.

CONTRARY OPINION

> . . . the supposedly stolid Dutch were overcome by the Tulip Craze, the volatile French had their Mississippi Bubble, while the sturdy English had their South Sea Bubble.
>
> As I read the account of these madnesses, I was tempted to shout, 'This cannot have happened'. Yet within my own lifetime I have seen similar deliriums in the Florida land boom of the 1920's and the stock market speculation that led to the 1929 crash. Something of the same crowd madness may have been at least partially responsible for Hitler's rise to power in Germany.
>
> These crowd madnesses recur so frequently in human history that they must reflect some deeply rooted trait of human nature . . . if his book showed how baseless are man's moods of wild hope, it also showed that man's moods of

---

[36] Rockwell, *loc. cit.*

black despair are equally unfounded. Always in the past, no matter how black the outlook, things got better . . . Whatever men attempt, they seem driven to try to overdo.[37]

With these words, Bernard Baruch explained how he related an account of the "madness of crowds"[38] written in 1841 with the extremes of psychology that he had observed in his own experience. His astute decision to sell his holdings in 1929 has been credited to his reading this book at an opportune time. Baruch apparently never attempted to utilize the lessons of history contained in McKay's book in any systematic way, but a stock market analyst named Humphrey Neill did ponder on the implications of swings in mass psychology. The result was a new way of thinking called "contrary opinion."[39]

Neill's contention was that crowd madness did not have to go to the point of making history before it could be detected and used to advantage. His belief was that any crowd, such as stock or commodity traders, could frequently be carried to extremes of action and opinion. The astute observer could recognize these extremes and act opposite to the prevailing psychology to his own advantage. In other words, he would adopt a "contrary opinion." Neill attempted in his book to demonstrate that this phenomenon extends far beyond trading stocks or commodities.[40] However, only its use in practical commodity trading is considered here.

In market letters and boardroom talk the term "contrary opinion" appears frequently. Apparently most traders have come to believe that the contrarian takes positions opposite the prevailing opinion almost as a reflex action. This popular notion is far too simple; the true contrarian does more than merely lean against the current state of thinking.[41]

Before money is committed to a trade the contrarian insists that certain basic elements be present. First there must be a strong consensus about the

[37] Bernard Baruch, *Baruch: My Own Story,* Henry Holt & Co., New York, 1957, p. 219.

[38] Charles Mackay, *Extraordinary Popular Delusions and the Madness of Crowds,* L. C. Page & Co., London, 1932, reprinted from the 1841 edition. Several reprints of this book have since been published; it documents scores of historical occurrences in which people lost all semblance of reason and were dominated by mass psychology.

[39] Humphrey Neill, *The Art of Contrary Thinking,* The Caxton Printers, Caldwell, Ohio, 1960, is the definitive source of information on contrary opinion. Transcripts of various "Contrary Opinion Foliage Forums" held over the years are also available from Fraser Publishing Co., *loc. cit.*

[40] Neill, *loc. cit.,* contains an addendum in which he notes that popular expectations at the time of major world events were directly opposite of what actually occurred.

[41] Other excellent sources of information on singular aspects that might be related to contrary opinion are Gustave Le Bon, *The Crowd,* The Viking Press, New York, 1960, which delineates the difference between a solitary individual and an individual in a crowd; James Dines, *loc. cit.,* discusses myriad psychological aspects related to trading and is a prolific source of still more highly specialized references on subjects relating to psychology and contrary opinion; Hadley Cantril, *The Invasion From Mars,* reprinted by Harper & Row, New York, 1966, contains one section of interest to traders that centers on *how* a fantastic rumor (in this case, the celebrated 1938 radio broadcast by Orson Welles) can gain wide acceptance.

future price or behavior of a commodity. This opinion must be almost unanimous — virtually taken for granted — before there is any chance that mass psychology has been carried to extremes. Examples of widely held opinions that would interest a contrarian would be: "Beans are going much higher", "July cotton will go off the board weak", "February bellies will gain on the May", "Cocoa will take its lead from next month's purchase figures and not do much until then", and so on. Any of these opinions unfulfilled could represent a trading opportunity. Note that the opinion need not be only one of price direction. A normally popular commodity that has been unusually neglected is one example of a consensus that could provide a contrarian with much food for thought.

A second and equally important prerequisite is that the strong bias of opinion be supported by "weak" reasons. In determining how strong or weak these supporting reasons are, the contrarian differs sharply from the fundamentalist. The trader using contrary opinion is not interested in how important the facts are or even if they are true. The reasons behind an opinion are judged strong or weak only according to the manner in which they have been disseminated and the reaction they have produced.

To the contrarian supporting reasons are weak if they have one or both of these characteristics:

1. The facts have been widely publicized and well known for some time.

The presumption here is that any such facts are already discounted in the current price; for example, suppose that the great majority of traders are bearish on wheat. If such a position is popular because a coming bumper crop has been apparent for several weeks and prices have already dropped substantially, the question how much risk remains on the downside may well be raised. If news of the impending record crop has generated most of the selling it warrants, any favorable developments will be a surprise to most traders.

This kind of well-publicized fact is especially weak if its realization is far in the future. If, for example, the expected bumper crop is many months away from being harvested, a great many things could happen in the meantime (including the discovery that the crop is not nearly so large as the earlier estimates) to change the present bearish psychology sharply.

2. The facts of the situation are not known but only supposed.

This sort of situation can occur anywhere but is more common in those international commodities that are unregulated, such as sugar, cocoa, copper, silver, and coffee. Opinion is formed on the basis of preliminary indications that have all been in agreement but for which no hard evidence is yet available. Cocoa may be regarded as an exceptionally bullish situation on the basis of preliminary crop estimates long before any solid facts are in on the crop size. Even if the crop is small, such expectations may already have been discounted in the current price. Other than extravagantly bullish news could find the market vulnerable to decline following the first factual reports.

If the trader who uses contrary opinion can find a situation in which there is a near-unanimous opinion supported by weak reasons, he has, at least in theory, found a trade with high potential and low risk. The low risk comes from the probability that the factors that caused the consensus have been discounted. The high potential comes from the element of surprise that can be a dominating influence when mass psychology carries to extremes and only one-sided news is expected. If the reason behind the crowd's opinion turns out to be entirely invalid, which has happened frequently in the past, the contrarian gains a bonus.

STRIKING THE BALANCE—ADVANTAGES AND DISADVANTAGES OF USING CONTRARY OPINION

The advantages. (a) More than almost any other technical approach, the premises behind contrary opinion are solidly logical. When strong feelings prevail toward a particular commodity, it is indisputable that conditions in that market are abnormal. Most known facts are likely to have been discounted completely or partly, offering little potential to the trader who is following the lead of the majority. Of equal importance, such a market is extremely vulnerable to unexpected developments not in line with current thinking. (b) Even if a contrary opinion approach is not used to signal trades, it can be valuable to the trader who wants to keep emotions in check. Watching for weak reasons behind strongly held opinions will keep the trader from being carried away by the arguments of the moment and losing his perspective. (c) A contrary approach can often turn up important facts for both technician and fundamentalist. Contrary opinion is more than a means of generating signals. It is a way of thinking that can be conceptually and practically useful. In the final analysis the success of contrary opinion depends completely on neglected facts coming to the fore. By directing attention away from popular thought patterns contrary opinion is one method whose primary purpose is to enable the trader to think for himself and possibly to unearth key factors on which trades may be based.

The disadvantages. (a) Collecting an accurate sample of opinions can be most difficult. Myriad sources must be consulted to determine whether there is a strong consensus toward any commodity. Newspapers, brokerage house letters, private advisory letters, brokers themselves, their clients, and the "signals" currently being given by popular trading methods are only a few of the inputs needed to monitor a consensus situation that may be shaping up. It can be an arduous sometimes almost impossible task to uncover the prevailing psychology, even given a strong consensus. (b) Even if the state of prevailing opinion is known, the depth of that opinion may be hard to evaluate. One group of traders expecting plywood to "consolidate and retrace recent large gains during the next few weeks" is certainly not so bearish as others who expect a major collapse. Weighting these and other shades of opinion can be a perplexing problem.[42] (c) Although contrary opinion can provide the trader with numerous psychological advantages, it can spawn at least one large psychological disadvantage. Used heavily, it can breed arrogance. (d) Points of extreme mass psychology in any commodity are quite infrequent. Even the most adept contrarian may have to wait a long time between trades. (e) The approach is not as precisely quantitative as is generally believed. Because of this, contrary opinion has not yet been put to an objective historical test to determine its validity and characteristics, as some other technical methods have. (f) It is much easier to initiate trades by following a contrary opinion method than to know when or where to close them. In closing a trade, the contrarian must rely heavily on other methods or personal judgment.

STRUCTURAL THEORIES

The final quadrant of technical analysis is as controversial as it is varied. Structural theories include one eminently respectable approach (seasonals) that is possibly the most widely accepted of any technical method used to trade commodities. Another approach in the same category, also well known, is an excursion into the bizarre and the occult. Some structural theories require an exotic brand of thinking; others are far more mundane.

The technician who uses structural theories does not construct indices for predictive purposes as is the case in character of market analysis, nor does he rely on trend following to assist in making decisions. The structural theorist believes, rather, that an intense study of historical performance will reveal understandable and repeating price patterns in the market itself.

This approach is radically different from that discussed earlier of looking for price patterns on charts. Price patterns are expected to occur at irregular intervals, consume a limited amount of time, and predict prices for a limited time in the future. Their form is only general and can assume many variations. The use of structual theories is generally far more comprehensively based. Prices are seen as "following a blueprint" that can provide guidance at all times. When this "blueprint" is understood, the trader should know where prices stand within the structure and what is going to happen next.

SEASONAL PRICE MOVEMENTS

The most respected structural blueprint attempts to define times of the year when commodity prices have a high probability of moving in one direction or the other. These seasonal price trends are usually due to the particular way a commodity is produced and/or distributed. In grains, for instance, the sudden increase in supply at harvest time should lead to lower

---

[42] One advisory service, Market Vane Commodity Letter, 431 E. Green Street, Pasadena, Calif. 91101, attempts to weight the composite opinion of a number of brokerage house letters and to apply the results of this tabulated sample by suggesting positions opposite strong consensuses.

prices. Later in the season, as supplies are used, prices could be expected to rise. Indeed, the desire to stabilize seasonal price fluctuations was one of the most important reasons leading to the birth of the Chicago Board of Trade.[43] It was believed, and subsequently confirmed, that a futures market could at least moderate the violent seasonal price tendencies in grains.[44]

The trader using seasonals believes that although futures trading has moderated formerly marked price tendencies they have not been entirely eliminated. He contends that there are specific times in various commodities that remain significant each year and during which opportune sales or purchases can be made.

Because, ultimately, any seasonal price pattern is produced by the interplay, however subtle, of production and/or consumption factors in a commodity, it is clear that this approach can be classed as fundamental rather than technical. Chapter 4 discusses seasonal price patterns in detail that are of a fundamental nature. For the purposes of this chapter seasonals are defined as repeating patterns of price action that can be discovered and measured from observations alone, with no thought to the factors underlying production or consumption. There will, of course, be considerable overlap in these two "types" of seasonals.

Table 7-3 is a good example of a seasonal tendency that a technician might be interested in exploiting. It was uncovered solely from studies of

[43] See Chapters 1 and 2.
[44] See Chapter 4.

TABLE 7-3   A SEASONAL TENDENCY IN MARCH SOYBEAN MEAL

Years	Long Oct. 5	Close Out Feb. 5	Net Change in Points
1957–58	45.50	45.10	−40
1958–59	48.90	56.40	+750
1959–60	54.70	58.15	+345
1960–61	53.90	61.25	+735
1961–62	50.55	53.85	+330
1962–63	61.95	68.95	+700
1963–64	73.90	71.15	−275
1964–65	68.60	69.20	+60
1965–66	61.10	68.80	+770
1966–67	74.40	75.25	+85
1967–68	72.35	74.35	+200
1968–69	73.75	72.20	−155
1969–70	69.90	78.50	+860
1970–71	79.60	77.80	−180
1971–72	81.40	85.50	+410

SUMMARY: 11 years profitable = 74% of all years.
4 years unprofitable = 26% of all years
Total points gained =   5,245.
Total points lost = 650.
Average points gained in all 15 periods = + 306
SOURCE: Commodity Research Bureau's Futures Market Service Publication.

past price action.[45] A trader interested in this approach would attempt to develop a "calendar portfolio" of seasonals which would indicate the action to take in a number of different commodities at various times of the year.[46]

Table 7-4 presents a summary of allegedly important seasonal tendencies in a variety of commodities. There are many other sources of seasonal patterns in commodity prices.[47]

Seasonal "blueprints" of price action can be expressed in several ways. The two most common forms are in Tables 7-3 and 7-4. Either a particular period during the year is selected as likely to see rising or falling prices or a

[45] This example, and several others, is taken from various publications of The Commodity Research Bureau, 140 Broadway, New York, N.Y. 10005, an organization that has performed research into seasonal price action of futures. Their weekly "Futures Market Service" and their "Commodity Yearbook" are sources of information on seasonal price action.

[46] The trader interested in developing such a "portfolio" is referred to the "X-11 Procedure" used by the Bureau of the Census, Washington, D.C. 20233, which not only mathematically identifies seasonal tendencies in data but also generates a "stability factor" that measures the consistency of such tendencies.

[47] Gann, *loc. cit.*; Hill, *loc. cit.*; Pickell, *loc. cit.* All sources also mention the famous "Voice from the Tomb" grain seasonals.

TABLE 7-4   SEASONAL PATTERN OF SPOT COMMODITY PRICES *

Commodity	High	Low
Barley	May	June
Cocoa	January–March	June, December (double bottom)
Coffee†	January–February	April, November (double bottom)
Corn	August	November–December
Cotton	July	October–December
Cottonseed meal†	March	December
Cottonseed oil†	June	October
Eggs	November	March–April
Flaxseed	May	October–November
Hides	August, October	March
Oats	(January) May‡	August
Potatoes	June–July	October
Rubber	September	March
Rye	February	July–August
Soybeans	(January) May‡	October
Soybean oil	July	October
Soybean meal†	April	December
Sugar (world)†	September	March
Wheat	(January) May‡	August–September
Wool	December	June

* Some commodities such as the metals do not have clearly defined seasonal price patterns.

† More than the usual number of exceptions to the seasonal pattern.

‡ These grains have often been subject to sharp reactions in February (known as the February break) after which a good rally sometimes has occurred.

SOURCE: Commodity Research Bureau.

particular month is selected as most likely to encompass a key high or low for the entire year.

Another form of seasonal analysis widely used could be called a "conditional seasonal."[48] This concept suggests that a price move will occur provided that some previous condition has been met. Examples of well-known allegations of this kind include, "Potatoes can advance into January if they make a new high in November"; "Eggs can decline sharply in August if cash prices are flat or soft"; "January soybeans can gain on deferreds if Chicago stocks are low in November."

Data on seasonals were presented in Chapter 4, and additional information on alleged seasonal tendencies is included in the later chapters on individual commodities.

STRIKING THE BALANCE—ADVANTAGES AND DISADVANTAGES OF USING SEASONALS

The advantages. (a) If any clear, repeating seasonal tendency has been isolated,[49] the trader can usually then determine the dominant reason for its existence. As long as that reason exists in succeeding years, the presumption is that prices will probably repeat their performance. (b) Seasonal information can be used to argue for or against trades accepted in any other form of analysis. The trader who wishes, for example, to short orange juice during the last half of October is made aware of a strong tendency for prices to rise at that time of year. When any commitment is made, seasonal information may help in appraising the risks. (c) If nothing else, careful analysis of seasonals can help the trader to achieve a better understanding of the basic forces affecting the balance of supply and demand in any single commodity.

The disadvantages. (a) The means by which commodities are produced and consumed are always in a state of flux. For this reason the life-span of the best validated seasonal tendency can prove to be quite limited. (b) Any seasonal tendency that becomes well known is almost certain to be totally smoothed out as more and more traders act on it. Chapter 17 describes how this has occurred in corn, to note just one instance. Seasonal forces can be discounted in the price, as can other fundamental and technical facts previously discussed. (c) Although seasonal trading is unique in that both an entry and exit date are usually indicated in advance, little is said about what can be termed "interim risk." In holding a commitment for one, two, or more months, the trader is exposed to the chance of considerable loss while waiting for the presumed gain. Referring to Table 7-3, for example, the average seasonal profit on March soybean meal is approximately 300 points. Yet between the starting and ending date of this trade meal often showed

---

[48] This approach is particularly favored by many brokerage houses that deal exclusively in commodities.

[49] The tendency should be validated by sound statistical techniques.

300 points or more adversity before the ultimate profit occurred. How is the trader to control losses in this or any other seasonal trade? The answer is not clear. Seasonal analysis, as usually presented, provides little information on "interim risk." Much judgment must be employed to determine if a seasonal trade is on course and how to deal with real and possible interim losses.

TIME CYCLES

Seasonals, no matter how derived, deal with repeating annual phenomena. For at least the last century, however, a great many investigators have concluded that there is a longer term structure in commodity prices.[50] Even longer term cycles have been isolated and documented. In 1875 Samuel Benner wrote a short book[51] wherein, among other things, the prices of pig iron and corn were predicted for the next several decades. Had a hypothetical trader, with the required money, warehouses, and other resources, bought and sold pig iron during the years indicated, dollar gains would have exceeded losses by a ratio of 31 to 1.[52] Benner's predictions on corn were less spectacular, but gains still shaded losses by a margin of $3\frac{1}{4}$ to 1, and the average annual gain trading in cash corn would have exceeded 7 percent compounded.[53] Results like these, achieved over a span of more than 80 years, strongly suggest that Benner's success might have been correlated with underlying cyclical phenomena.

The technician who uses time cycles to forecast prices employs a unique *modus operandi*. He believes that back records of prices contain evidence within themselves of at least one and usually several time cycles during which prices are carried up or down. Whether a computer or a paper and pencil is used, the trader attempts to isolate and quantify the important cycles in any commodity. These cycles are then combined to yield a prediction of the dates of future high and low prices. The trader then takes action accordingly.

Although the concept of time cycles can be spun into elaborate complexity, most cycles fall into three categories, no matter how sophisticated the mathematics.

1. Important highs and lows are spaced by distinct, repeating intervals. Table 7-5 shows a regular $67\frac{1}{3}$-month cycle in cash corn prices. The pre-

[50] Perhaps the first person to investigate time cycles in a scholarly way was Hyde Clark, who alleged an 11-year cycle in speculation and famine in 1838. Influenced by Clark, William Stanley Jevons published, *The Periodicity of Commercial Crises and Its Physical Explanation* and *The Solar Period and the Price of Corn* at the University of Manchester in 1875. Jevon's thesis was that repetitive cycles in sunspots affected crop yields, and therefore prices, on a predictable basis.

[51] Samuel Benner, *Benner's Prophecies of Ups and Downs in Prices,* privately printed, Cincinnati, Ohio, 1875 (reprinted by The Foundation for the Study of Cycles, 124 South Highland Avenue, Pittsburgh, Pa. 15206).

[52] Edward R. Dewey, "The $5\frac{1}{2}$ year Cycle in Corn Prices" and "Samuel Turner Benner" in *Cycles Magazine* (February and March, 1955).

[53] *Ibid.*

TABLE 7-5   IMAGINARY PURCHASE AND SALE OF CORN ON
THE BASIS OF A 67⅓-MONTH CYCLE (CASH NO. 3 YELLOW
AT CHICAGO)

Date	Buy	Sell	Short	Cover	Gain in cents		Percent gain	
					Long	Short	Long	Short
May 1899	33							
Mar. 1902		59	59		26		78.8	
Jan. 1905	42			42		17		28.8
Oct. 1907		65	65		23		54.8	
Aug. 1910	64			64		1		1.5
Jun. 1913		60	60		—4		—6.3	
Mar. 1916	73			73		—13		—21.7
Jan. 1919		143	143		70		95.9	
Nov. 1921	47.4			47.4		95.6		66.9
Aug. 1924		117.3	117.3		69.9		147.5	
Jun. 1927	98.9			98.9		18.4		15.7
Apr. 1930		82.0	82.0		—16.9		—17.1	
Jan. 1933	23.6			23.6		58.4		71.2
Nov. 1935		62.1	62.1		38.5		163.1	
Sep. 1938	52.7			52.7		9.4		15.1
Jun. 1941		73.7	73.7		21.0		39.8	
Apr. 1944	114.5			114.5		—40.8		55.4
Feb. 1947		141.9	141.9		27.4		23.9	
Nov. 1949	116			116		25.9		18.3
Sep. 1952		176	176		60		51.7	
Jun. 1955	147			147		29		—16.5
Apr. 1958		129	129		—18		—12.2	
Feb. 1961	113			113		16		12.4
Dec. 1963		119	119		6		5.3	
Sep. 1966	144			144		—25		—21.0
Jun. 1969		130	130		—14		—9.7	
Mar. 1972	118			118		12		9.2

Total cents gained long	=	341.8		% Gained long	=	660.8
Total cents lost long	=	52.9		% Lost long	=	45.3
Net cents gained long	=	288.9		Net % gained long	=	615.5
Total cents gained short	=	282.7		% gained short	=	294.5
Total cents lost short	=	78.8		% lost short	=	59.2
Net cents gained short	=	203.9		Net gained short	=	235.3

SOURCE: Cycles Magazine (February 1955).

dicted highs are 67⅓ months apart from one another, as are the lows. This
cyclical analysis is common among technicians who use time cycles to predict commodity prices.[54]

2. "Kick in the pants" cycles. A certain span of time carries prices
strongly up or down and this action repeats at regular intervals. Figure 7-13
shows a monthly chart of world sugar prices in which a brief but powerful

[54] Gann, loc. cit., is a typical exponent of this analysis. His book contains extensive historical
price tables for a wide variety of commodities.

FIG. 7-13 **Starting in 1939, powerful "kicks" at 6-year intervals.** (*Commodity Chart Service. Commodity Research Bureau, New York.*)

upward "kick" is seen at roughly six-year intervals. This form of analysis is also common.[55]

3. Complex and sophisticated mathematical models. Many organizations have developed models of considerable depth which are designed to define precisely the timing, shape, amplitude, and other characteristics of time cycles being investigated.[56]

Although virtually any trader can do research by using a record of commodity prices[57] in an effort to discover profitable time cycles, this approach has never been popular.[58] Occasional waves of interest in cyclical forecasting have always subsided, leaving those using these techniques in the backwater of technical analysis.

STRIKING THE BALANCE—ADVANTAGES AND DISADVANTAGES OF USING TIME CYCLES

The advantages. (a) Hard evidence has been presented that time cycles are probably a real phenomenon, not a statistical fantasy. A mathematical test has been developed to calculate the probabilities that any observed cycle is due to chance.[59] Because commodity prices possess a structure that is at least partly ordered by time, trading on the basis of cycles is theoretically possible. (b) Even if time cycles are not used to signal commitments, such research can be valuable in helping to appraise the risks behind any trade. The trader becomes aware if his contemplated actions agree or disagree with the underlying cyclical background.

The disadvantages. (a) Not all the evidence indicates that cycles are a real phenomenon. Extremely sophisticated mathematical techniques[60] have not

[55] Again the best source is Gann, loc. cit. A short interesting article on the subject is Edward R. Dewey, "Kick In the Pants Cycles", Cycles Magazine (August 1961). An imaginative use of cycle types 1 and 2 is George Lindsay, "A Timing Method For Traders", in The Encyclopaedia of Stock Market Techniques published by Investor's Intelligence, 1965 rev. ed.

[56] One organization that appears to be heavily influenced by members interested in investment and speculation is The Society for Investigation of Recurring Events, P.O. Box 174, Bowling Green Station, New York, N.Y. 10004. The pre-eminent force in this field is the Foundation for the Study of Cycles, 124 South Highland Ave., Pittsburgh, Pa. 15206. A not-for-profit, tax-exempt foundation, it has carried on research into cyclical phenomena found in virtually every available time series. Cycles Magazine and the now defunct Journal of Cycle Research, both published by the Foundation, can be found in many big-city libraries. Written on a scientific level, these publications are an extensive repository of facts and theories on cyclical phenomena.

[57] This can be done by hand or on a grander scale. The Foundation for the Study of Cycles has published several computer programs for isolating and measuring cycles in statistical data.

[58] Only two books that attempt a comprehensive discussion and evaluation of repetitive time cycles in statistical data have been written: Edwin R. Dewey, Cycles, The Science of Prediction, Henry Holt & Co., New York, 1949, and Edwin R. Dewey and Og Mandino, Cycles: Mysterious Forces that Trigger Events, Hawthorne Books, New York, 1971.

[59] This is the Bartels Test of Significance. See Charles E. Armstrong, "Testing Cycles for Statistical Significance", Journal of Cycle Research (October 1961).

[60] See Walter C. Labys and C. W. J. Granger, Speculation, Hedging and Commodity Price Forecasts, Chapter 3, D. C. Heath & Co., Lexington, Mass., 1970. Paul Cootner, Ed., The Ran-

supported the contention that repeating time cycles of any length are present in commodity prices. (b) Even if cycles are accepted as a real phenomenon, there is still a great deal about them that is not known. It is impossible to know for any particular commodity what causes observed cycles, how many cycles are currently operating, or even the curvature of a cycle. That there is nothing approaching a complete cycle model is a major obstacle to the technician attempting to use cyclical data. Any time cycle the trader has isolated may prove to be useless as hidden properties of the cycle become apparent or other undetected cycles nullify or override it. (c) Almost all published serious work in commodity price cycles has been conducted with cash prices, not futures prices. The corn forecast in Table 7-5, although accurate for several years, would have been of little value to the futures trader at that time. The cash and futures markets do not always move in tandem. Also, the fact that futures have a limited life and can represent different crops makes it far more difficult to analyze prices in any meaningful way. (d) Even with complete cycle knowledge the trader has only part of the picture. Important current developments can ruin the clearest cyclical indications, with prices getting back "on track" too late to help the trader.

THE ELLIOTT WAVE THEORY

As must be common to all who publish investment services, I received frequent letters from individuals who had developed "infallible" methods or systems for forecasting the stock market. My usual reply was that the individual go on record with me over a market cycle after which I would determine whether I cared to investigate the matter in detail. In most instances, at some point in the cycle the system went haywire and correspondence died on the vine.

Elliott was one of three notable exceptions. He wrote me from California in late 1934 that a bull market had begun and would carry for some distance. . . . In March 1935 the Dow Rail average crashed under its 1934 low, accompanied by an eleven percent break in the industrial average. Having recent memories of 1929–32, this development scared the lights out of the investing public. On the bottom day for the industrial average, the Rails having leveled off four days previously, I received a late evening telegram from Elliott in which, as was always his way, he *dogmatically* affirmed that the break was over and that another leg of the bull market was beginning. This break, looking back, was Primary Wave No. 2 of the Cycle movement then under way under Elliott's Wave Principle although, at the time, I had no idea as to his method."[61]

It was in this way that the Elliott wave principle, possibly the most unusual technical theory ever conceived, first became known to Mr. Charles Collins and then to an ever-wider audience. If Elliott's forecasts were spec-

---

dom Character of Stock Market Prices, The M.I.T. Press, Cambridge, Mass., 1964, discusses periodic time cycles related to stock prices in Chapters 6, 8, and 9.

[61] Hamilton Bolton and Charles Collins, "The Elliott Wave Principle—1966 Supplement", *The Bank Credit Analyst,* 1245 Sherbrooke Street West, Montreal 109, Quebec, Canada.

tacular, so were the basic tenets underlying his theory. In brief, Elliott believed in "counting" waves of advance or decline in stock prices. These waves, he felt, fell into patterns so complete and so comprehensive that one could know at any time where prices stood in their development, how much potential they had on the upside or downside, and roughly how much longer a trend would persist.

Elliott's basic theory was that prices move in a five-wave sequence in line with the direction of the main trend and in a three-wave sequence during "corrective" movements against the main trend. Figure 7-14 illustrates how these main trend and corrective movements are formed. One of many fascinating aspects of Elliott's theory is that each wave is broken up into subwaves of its own (either three or five waves) and that these waves, in turn, break down into smaller subwaves, and so on. In principle, Elliott waves can be carried down to the level of each individual trade. The theory can also be extended to a larger scale, in which each wave is a subwave of a larger wave which in turn is part of a still larger wave. Elliott actually believed that some waves in prices were centuries long. His system of labeling waves is extremely complicated, and references should be consulted to study Elliott in proper detail.[62]

Given this all-inclusive system of categorization, it is theoretically possible for the trader to know where prices stand at all times. Figure 7-15 shows an Elliott wave analysis of Chicago rye, plotted on a monthly scale. The major bull market that began in 1942 may be visualized as a sequence of five waves which carried prices up into 1948. The trader who thought Elliott would pinpoint the top would begin counting after wave 4[63] was clearly over, expecting the fifth and final wave to break down into five subwaves (not shown on the chart). Once the "fifth wave of the fifth wave" became apparent, possibly on a weekly chart, the trader would use more detailed data to determine the fifth wave of *that* fifth wave.

Following the major bull move, a three-wave, or "A-B-C," correction

[62] The most comprehensive single work on the wave principle is Hamilton Bolton, *The Elliott Wave Principle—A Critical Appraisal*, Bolton, Tremblay & Co., Montreal, 1960. Bolton, Tremblay & Co.'s *Bank Credit Analyst* has also published a number of supplements for irregular years, starting with 1961, that seek to up-date Bolton's original work and provide current interpretations. Cox, *loc. cit.,* is a strong advocate of using Elliott's principles for commodity trading. William O'Connor, *Stocks, Wheat & Pharaohs*, Weiner Books Co., New York, 1961, is an offbeat source of information on Elliott applied to futures prices. The book is out of print but available in many big-city libraries. O'Connor not only uses unique principles of interpretation but is the only source that places great stress on daily charts for identifying Elliott waves in the very short run. Elliott's two monographs are long out of print and almost impossible to obtain, as are past issues of his advisory letters. R. N. Elliott, "The Wave Principle", *Financial World* (1939), reprented by BCA Distributors, Ltd., Montreal, 1963, consisting of a series of articles that appeared in *Financial World Magazine*, is his only work still readily available.

[63] Bolton, Collins, and O'Connor are the *only* practicioners of the Elliott wave theory who adhere to the vital rule laid down by Elliott that wave 4 must not, under any circumstances, overlap wave 1. Every other Elliott theorist in print at the time of this writing has ignored this rule with no word of explanation.

I   The main trend

Up

breaks down into

4th wave may be a "triangle" of 5 instead of 3 waves broken into 3 subwaves

Down

II   The correction

Up

Zigzag

Flat

Triangles

Down

Inverted zigzag

Inverted flat

(4th waves only) Made up always of 5 waves, each of 3 subwaves Contracting

Inverted triangles

Horizontal

(a)

FIG. 7-14   (a) Basic Elliott wave sequences. (Hamilton Bolton, **The Elliott Wave Principle**—A Critical Appraisal, Bolton, Tremblay and Co., Montreal, 1960. **(b) Corrective patterns and triangles.** (*Financial World*, 1939.)

would be expected, and this broke into the "zig-zag" 3-3-5 corrective pattern shown in Figure 7-14. Following the final wave of the A-B-C correction in 1954, no new Elliott pattern appears to have taken place.

This approach, which is increasingly popular in technical analysis of commodity prices, certainly is most unusual, and results in some bizarre considerations when the advantages and disadvantages of using this method are discussed.

(b)

STRIKING THE BALANCE—ADVANTAGES AND DISADVANTAGES OF USING THE ELLIOTT WAVE THEORY

The advantages. (a) During the time that Elliott was using his method he compiled a spectacular record of forecasting stock prices. Following in his footsteps, both Collins and Bolton continued to make surprisingly

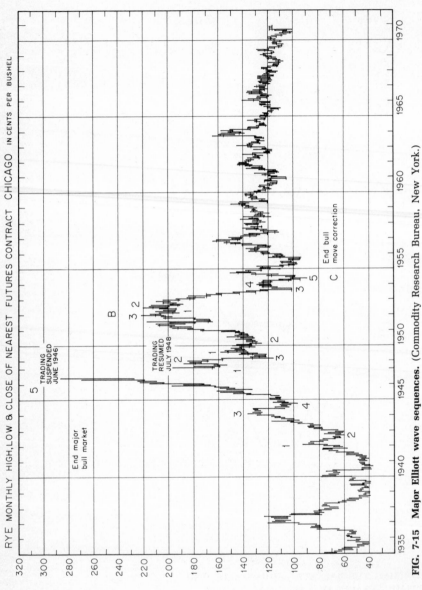

FIG. 7-15   Major Elliott wave sequences. (Commodity Research Bureau, New York.)

accurate predictions of the stock market averages.[64] Using a "side-effect" of Elliott's concepts, Bolton was able to forecast the level of a key stock market top with an accuracy of 99.6 percent.[65] These accomplishments argue strongly for some viability in the wave principle. (b) Elliott's wave counts are based on the "Fibonacci Summation Series," a number series with interesting properties. It has been affirmed that both living and inanimate objects obey a number of laws that revolve around the mathematical properties of this series. Using a Fibonacci summation (1-2-3-5-8-13-21-34-55-89-144-233-etc.) it is possible for scientists to predict how populations of animals will multiply, how plants will grow, how crystalline structures will form naturally, and a great many other things.[66] This series also yields the "golden mean" that is used in architecture. Although detailed discussion of Fibonacci is beyond the scope of this book, it is evident that study of this series discloses mathematical relationships that hold in real-life situations. It has been hypothesized that these relationships are so all-inclusive that they extend into the psychological arena as well, with price fluctuations reflecting their subtle but all-pervasive influence.

The disadvantages. (a) Elliott never hinted that his "law" might apply to commodity prices. His forecasting work centered almost exclusively on the Dow Jones Averages. Even in individual stocks research performed indicates that application of Elliott's principle is quite intricate and possible only in selected instances.[67] (b) The entire concept of the Elliott wave theory rests on counting "waves." Yet it is impossible to answer objectively the question, "What *is* a wave?" Elliott himself gave no answer to this question.[68] This means that the technician is forced to use highly subjective judgment to label a wave on the chart and also to identify the time scale which the wave fits. Figure 7-15 illustrates the problem. The last wave of the major bull move seems to break up into many more than five subwaves. Either the theory is wrong or some of the subwaves should not be counted for some unknown reason. This problem occurs quite frequently in Elliott's

[64] The Bank Credit Analysts' annual Elliott Supplements, *loc. cit.*, especially those written by Bolton, give explicit forecasts of general stock market action. Several important major bull and bear markets were correctly forecasted. Charles Collins, "Market Ebb Tide," *Barrons* (March 1970), contains an accurate prediction relating to the Dow Jones Averages.

[65] Bolton, "The Elliott Wave Principle—A Critical Appraisal," predicted in 1960 that the "super cycle" high for the Dow Jones Industrial Average would theoretically be 999. The actual level of Elliott's "super cycle" peak was 995, reached in January 1966.

[66] *Ibid.* Bolton, discusses several mathematical properties of the Fibonacci Summation Series. The "1968 Elliott Supplement", *loc. cit.*, presents a technical analysis of the Fibonacci Series by W. E. White. A brief article for the layman is "The Fibonacci Numbers", *Time* (April 1969), which also contains further references.

[67] In Elliott's series of articles in *Financial World* in 1939, *loc. cit.*, he gave brief examples of forecasting prices for individual stocks. The "1964 Elliott Supplement" devoted some space to the problem of adapting Elliott waves to individual stock prices and came to disappointing conclusions.

[68] The "1967 Elliott Supplement," written by A. J. Frost, posed the question. Though a devoted Elliott practitioner, Frost stated the question could not be answered.

analysis. (c) The theory is so flexible that it is possible to get several radically different wave counts by using the same price data, and leading Elliott interpreters are in almost constant disagreement.[69] A particularly disturbing corollary to all of this is that the more back data the trader has accumulated, the greater the number of possible counts. In most endeavors additional information usually clarifies; with Elliott, additional information can just as easily add to the confusion. (d) One flexible aspect of the theory is the fluid concept of "extensions"; for example, a five-wave move can, under Elliott's rules, extend itself without warning into nine-waves. These and other features of the theory make it difficult to come to any decisions at any given moment and easy to see the correct count (and decision) after the fact. (e) Elliott, beyond question, intended that his wave principle mold current prices into a comprehensive structure that would provide guidance at all times, but virtually any commodity chart will show long "blank" spots in which it is impossible to get any sort of wave count. Because one of the fundamental tenets of the theory is that *all* waves can be categorized, the existence of these blank spots means either that the premise is invalid or that the count at these times is subtle enough to escape all observers. (f) It is not generally realized that Elliott was a mystic who also believed in numerology. In his monograph,[70] published in 1948, he discussed how mathematical relationships in the Great Pyramid of Gizeh not only predicted future world events but tied in with his own wave theory as well! Although the trader should keep an open mind in regard to the claims of technical analysis, a trading method that is in agreement with pyramid numerology should, indeed, be cautiously evaluated.

NOTES FROM A TRADER

Isolating, quantifying, and successfully trading nonrandom elements in commodity futures trading data requires unusual determination and discipline. The efficient market is a worthy adversary and, in attempting to forecast, the technician must beware of trying to get more out of an experience than is in it to begin with. As Mark Twain warned, "The cat, having sat upon a hot stove lid, will not sit upon a hot stove lid again. Nor upon a cold stove lid." Consistent profits are earned only when commitments are made on the basis of analysis which is far from obvious to the majority of other traders at a given point in time.

There seems to be an overwhelming urge among most technicians to develop a simple, totally mechanical system that works with near-perfect accuracy. The professional trader quickly becomes aware that the search for a

[69] The "1963 Elliott Supplement" gives several different interpretations from various analysts and includes a discussion on this problem.

[70] R. N. Elliott, *Nature's Law—The Secret Of The Universe*, privately published, New York, 1946. Long out of print. The title perhaps indicates Elliott's view of the importance of his methodology.

foolproof trading system in which all observations promptly find their pre-ordained place has the same large challenge and the same small promise as any all-encompassing system in any other discipline, be it medicine, philosophy or law. The mature trader recognizes that although judgment can be reduced it can never be eliminated and that many losing trades will mar even the best trading results.

At least two important lessons can be retrieved from technical analysis. First, almost all methods generate useful *information*, which if used for nothing more than uncovering and organizing facts about market behavior will increase the trader's understanding of the markets. Second, the trader is made painfully aware that technical competence does not ensure competent trading. Speculators who lose money do so not always because of bad analysis but because of the inability to transform their analysis into sound practice. Bridging the vital gap between analysis and action requires overcoming the threat of greed, hope, and fear. It means controlling impatience and the desire to stray away from a sound method to "something new" during times of temporary adversity. It means having the discipline to "believe what you see" and to follow the indications from sound methods, even though they contradict what everyone else is saying or what "seems" to be the correct course of action.

The rewards are great and they are attainable. As one astute observer of the markets remarked,

> . . . commodity price developments are watched by relatively few traders, most of them quite set in their ways; even in the most active futures markets, the volume of serious research by participants seems to be quite small. It is therefore possible that systematic patterns will remain largely unknown for a very long time.[71]

---

[71] Hendrick Houthakker, "Systematic and Random Elements in Short Term Price Movements," *American Economic Review,* 51 (1961).

CHAPTER EIGHT

Spreads and Options

> Why worry about realized losses?
> They are more than overcome by potential profits.

INTRODUCTION

Spreads and options may be considered by some to represent only a choice in a type of commodity position, but the subject is far broader than that and deserves separate and more elaborate treatment.

Most unsophisticated commodity traders are converted security traders who bring their habits with them. They are much more likely to be long the market than short and know little or nothing about spreads and options. The professional trader is at least as conversant with the short as the long side of the market and knows considerably more about spreads and the concept of option trading.

SPREADS

Spreads may represent a significant percentage of the open interest of a commodity and may be entered for reasons that may be either technical or fundamental in nature. The word "spread" has several meanings to commodity traders but all imply a price difference. The word in its most general sense applies to the difference between the cash and futures price of the same commodity. In a more restricted sense it refers to the difference in the prices of two contract months.

A spread also describes the actual position taken by a trader who is simultaneously long one commodity contract and short another. He may hold equal but opposite positions in two different contracts of the same commodity, such as long 10,000 bushels of March wheat and short 10,000 bushels of May wheat. He might also have equal but opposite positions in two different but related commodities and still hold a spread position; for example, he could be long 10,000 bushels of corn and short 10,000 bushels of wheat or long 25,000 bushels of oats and short 25,000 bushels of corn. Opposite positions in unrelated commodities are not considered spreads. A trader may be long copper and short sugar, but these would merely be considered separate positions because there is little or no basic price relation between copper and sugar.

Historically, the terms "spread" and "straddle" had some shades of difference, but they have since become interchangeable among commodity traders, and in practice the word "spread" is now more commonly used in the futures markets. There was once some tendency for traders to speak of spreads in connection with grain positions and straddles in connection with other commodities, such as cotton. The terms "spread position" and "hedge" are used interchangeably but incorrectly by some traders. A hedge refers to the concurrent holding of two opposite commodity positions, one in the cash, or spot, market and the other in the futures market. A spread position also refers to two concurrent and opposite positions, but both are in the futures markets. In its more general sense spread describes the price difference between the cash and futures markets in a hedged position. "Arbitrage" is a word related broadly to the others described herein, but it generally suggests two positions entered simultaneously, or virtually so, one long and the other short, "locking in" a price difference so great that a profit is virtually assured. In the commodity markets this condition exists when a distant contract exceeds the price of the nearby by an amount exceeding the carrying charge, as in the example on page 218. Such opportunities also exist in the security markets by trading the same security on two different markets at two different prices or the same security in two forms such as common stock against bonds or preferred stock convertible into the same common. Some also are able to take advantage of the price discrepancies that exist in foreign exchange.

SIGNIFICANCE OF PRICE DIFFERENCES

Most of the following discussion centers about the taking of a spread position, but it is worth noting how important the spread differences among the prices of various contract months are to the intelligent establishment of a position. Suppose that it is August and that a trader believes that the price of wheat is likely to go up. He decides to establish a position of 10,000 bushels to take advantage of the expected price rise. He is aware that wheat is then trading for delivery in September, December, March, May, and July. How does he decide which to buy?

There are several factors to consider. One is the crop year which he believes presents the greater opportunity. The crop year for wheat begins on July 1. If he wants to take his position in the forthcoming new crop, he has little choice because the only new-crop contract trading in August is the July of the following year. If he believes the greater opportunity is offered in the current, or old, crop, he must choose among the September, December, March, and May contracts. One factor affecting this decision is the amount of time believed needed for the expected upward price move to develop and when it is expected to begin. If he expects something to happen within a few days because of some near-term development, such as important export business, he could buy any of the old-crop contracts. He would probably lean toward the September delivery because there is less time available for the tightness in wheat to be alleviated and it would best reflect a tight cash market.

If he expects to retain his position for some months, there is no point in considering September and no great attraction in the December contract. He can gain considerably more time by acquiring the March or May contracts. He has also gained the advantage of a possible long-term capital gain on his tax return if he should happen to hold the position more than six months, which would not have been possible had he bought the September or December contracts. In addition, he saves the commission that would be incurred if he bought an early contract and later "rolled forward" into a later one.

The choice between the March and May contracts must still be made. Too many traders make this decision with little or no thought at all or, worse, for the wrong reasons. They may choose the March merely because they or their brokers have been keeping a chart of that contract and they have not followed the May, or they may buy the May because that contract happens to be on the quote boards in the broker's office and the action on the March contract has not been followed. The decision would better be made logically on the current price difference, or spread, between the March and May prices.

To clarify this point assume that the carrying charge on a bushel of wheat is $2\frac{1}{4}$ cents a month. That would be the actual cost of handling, storing, insuring, and financing one bushel for one month. The cost of carrying a bushel of wheat from the March contract into the May delivery would therefore be $4\frac{1}{2}$ cents for the two-month period. It would be virtually impossible for May wheat to sell for significantly more than $4\frac{1}{2}$ cents over the March delivery for any length of time. If it were to do so, it would become profitable for somebody to buy the March and sell the May at the unusually wide price difference. This activity is sometimes called "arbitrage" and anyone engaged in it an "arbitrager." He would be prepared, if necessary, to take delivery of his March wheat, hold his short May position as a hedge, and then deliver his cash wheat against the May contract during the month of

May. More likely, the abnormal spread difference would dissolve sooner or later, and the arbitrager would take off both sides of his spread position and realize his profit. In either case he would be certain of a gain approximating at least the difference between the 4½-cent normal carrying charge and the wider spread difference at which he had taken his position, unless there was a material short-run change in the carrying charge.

Because opportunities like this are so obvious to professional traders and profits in the real world are not so easily attained, the spread difference between March and May would almost certainly stop short of the 4½-cent full carrying-charge difference. Yet if the spread difference was near the full carrying charge it would be of considerable help to a net position trader trying to make an intelligent decision. At near the full carrying charge he would probably place his long position in the March rather than the May contract. Both contracts might go up equally and he would realize the same gain in either one. Both might go down equally and he would suffer the same loss in either one. If the spread difference changed, however, it would almost certainly do so either because March went up more than May or down less, and in both cases the trader would find the March contract the better alternative. March could not lose materially on May, but there is no limit to the amount it could gain on May in a strong market. It could not only sell for more than May, but there is no 4½-cent barrier to its premium. Because clocks run only one way, nobody has yet found a way to buy the May contract of a commodity, take delivery, and then redeliver it against the previous March contract. Premiums of nearby contracts over distant ones can get quite large in strong markets. When nearby contracts sell for more than distant contracts, the market is called "inverted." Traders must remember that risks in carrying-charge market spreads are limited; inverted market spreads are not.

If, with wheat at near a full carrying charge, the trader believed that wheat was going to go down rather than up and he wanted to go short either March or May, his decision would be just as obvious. He would certainly go short the May contract rather than the March. Here again, the only way the spread difference would change materially would be for May to lose on March because March could not lose on May. With May providing the added attraction of two additional months for the trade to work profitably, the choice of March would be a poor one indeed.

There is a third type of trader who is alert to these price differences and who hopes to take advantage of them. This is the position spreader.

SPREAD POSITIONS

A position spreader is less interested in the direction of price than in the difference between two prices. Rather than decide that a given contract price is too high or too low, he is interested in taking advantage of price differences that he considers abnormal. The possible positions open to this trader are intracommodity (or intercontract or interdelivery spreads), inter-commodity spreads, intermarket spreads, or a combination of them. The logic of those taking such positions is best made clear by example.

INTRACOMMODITY SPREADS

An intracommodity spreader tries to take advantage of price differences that he believes are too wide or too narrow in the same commodity in the same market at the same time. He might note that May corn is selling for 4 cents over March and expect a strong market in corn to develop soon. If this should happen, he believes that not only would the general price level of corn go up but that the March contract would gain on the May. If he is right, there is no limit to the amount that March could gain because it could not only close the prevailing discount but could sell for more than May by a substantial amount. If he is wrong, there is little to lose because here, again, March cannot sell below the May for long by much more than the full carry-ing charge. The spread trader would take advantage of this opportunity by buying the March contract and selling an equal amount of the May against it. The position could be entered either by putting on both sides at the same time or by entering one at a time in order to try to establish a still more favorable difference. The latter takes unusual skill and sometimes results in losing the opportunity observed in the first place.

When the spread has been established, the spreader merely has to wait for March to gain on May as much as he thinks it is going to and then take off (lift) his position. He does this by selling out his March contract and buy-ing in his May. The removal of a spread position is often called "unwinding" or "backspreading." Here, again, he can take off both sides simultaneously by instructing his broker to remove the spread at the current market differ-ence or at a difference of a fixed number of cents. He could also take off (lift) one side (leg) at a time and hope to improve his total profit by doing so. Like entering a spread one side at a time, removing it by lifting one leg at a time is not a good practice. Most traders seem to develop a peculiar knack for taking off the wrong side of their spreads first and then watching a profit achieved over a period of weeks dissolve in a few days or hours.

One of the most frequent questions asked by inexperienced traders is, "Why spread in the first place?" If a trader like the one described above thinks corn is going to go up, why not just buy the March? If the spreader is correct in his analysis, he will make a profit on his March contract, lose on his May, and show a net profit on the difference because the March profit will exceed the May loss. It is obvious that he would have had a greater profit per contract if he had just bought the March. His action in taking the spread, however, is not quite so foolish as it may appear. By taking the spread position he has reduced his investment. The margin on one contract, 5,000 bushels of March corn long against a short position of 5,000 May, may be only $500 for the entire position, compared with a margin requirement of $1,500 required for long March corn alone. If the price of March corn rises 15 cents and that of May, 9 cents, the return on investment is greater on the spread than it would have been on the net position. The profit on the net March would have been $750 on a $1,500 investment, or 50 percent. The spread position results in a profit of $750 on the March and a loss of $450 on the May, but this represents a net gain of $300 on a $500 investment, or 60 percent. If he chooses to be more aggressive, he can carry 15,000 bushels in a spread position for the same margin as a net position of 5,000 bushels.

It should also be noted that the analysis of the corn situation may have been wrong in the first place and that corn might go down and not up. In this case a net position in March corn could have been costly or even ruinous, whereas the spread position could hardly prove painful at all because March could not lose significantly on May. The cost of this insurance is not great because the commission on a 5,000-bushel spread position is only $36 versus $30 for a 5,000-bushel net position and, as it has been seen, the funds needed to margin the position are much less. The spread trader has therefore increased his potential profit and reduced both his risk and his investment. It is even possible that the spreader could be completely wrong in his analysis and still make money just because he spread. The price of corn could fall drastically, and the price level of May could lose on March simply because more net traders choose to sell it or have to sell it because of pressure to liquidate. March, of course, still could not lose significantly on May because of the ever-present watchfulness of the arbitrager.

There is hardly any limit to the number of combinations open to the intracommodity spreader, but certain spreads do tend to be relatively popular, such as May potatoes against November, July soybeans against November, July cocoa against December, July flax against October, May wheat against July, and July sugar against October.

INTERCOMMODITY SPREADS

Some commodities are used for the same general purposes as others and therefore are interchangeable to a degree. The easier it is to substitute one for the other, the closer the relationship of their prices. Oats and corn are a case in point, as are hogs and cattle. If a spreader believes that the price relation between two commodities is unrealistic, he can sell the higher priced, buy the lower priced, wait for the relative price levels to approach normality, and then take his profit. The advantages of trading in this manner are similar to intracommodity spreads. The margin on cattle against hogs is usually about the same as it would be for either hogs or cattle taken alone. This is greater than in the case of the intracommodity spread, in which the margin on the spread is considerably less than it would be on one side alone. Unlike the intracommodity spread, however, there is seldom a commission reduction for spreads involving more than one commodity.

Because drastic changes in the price levels of both commodities are likely to be similar, the risk of ruinous losses is considerably reduced at the cost of the opportunity to achieve windfall profits.

Among the more popular spreads of this kind are those involving soybeans and the products produced from the soybeans, namely, soybean oil and soybean meal. A spreader usually assumes that a crusher will find either oil or meal more profitable at a given time and that one of the product prices will be the stronger. If the current prices do not reflect the strength of one of the products adequately, the spreader can buy the product that he feels should be the stronger and sell the other against it. If he believes that the value of the two products combined is too low relative to the beans, he can sell one contract of beans and buy one contract each of soybean oil and soybean meal. This position is usually called a "reverse crush" because it is opposite to the position taken by the soybean crusher, who is typically long beans, which he crushes in order to be able to sell the products. A contract of oil plus one of meal does not exactly equal the amount of oil and meal that could actually be produced from the contract of 5,000 bushels of beans, but it is usually close enough to yield a profit if the beans prove to be selling too high on the products. If the trader thinks that beans will gain on the combined products, he can buy the beans and sell the products, just as a crusher does. The establishment of such a position is sometimes called "putting on running time."

Popular intercommodity spreads include wheat versus corn, hogs versus bellies, domestic versus foreign sugar contracts, and oats versus corn. In the latter case, traders frequently spread one contract of corn against two contracts of oats because they consider a contract of oats to be worth only about 56 percent of a contract of corn.

INTERMARKET SPREADS

Many commodities are traded on more than one market. Wheat is traded on the Chicago Board of Trade, the Kansas City Board of Trade, and the Minneapolis Grain Exchange. Chicago trades basically Soft Red winter wheat, Kansas City, Hard Red winter wheat, and Minneapolis, spring wheat. There is, however, a close relation among all these types, which are interchangeable for many purposes. In some cases the type trading on one exchange is actually deliverable against the type trading on another. All three basic types of wheat are deliverable on the Chicago Board of Trade. In this case the important limiting factors include the cost of transportation between cities, as well as differences in the characteristics of the different types of wheat. If a speculator believes that price differences are out of line between commodities trading in two cities, he sells the higher priced contract and buys the lower priced. In spreads of this kind there is no commission advantage and seldom much, if any, margin advantage.

Popular positions include Winnipeg oats versus Chicago oats, New York cocoa or sugar against London cocoa or sugar, and Chicago versus Kansas City or Minneapolis wheat.

COMBINATIONS

The fact that a trader decides that Winnipeg oats are low on Chicago oats does not mean that he should be long December Winnipeg oats and short December Chicago oats. If he thinks that oats are too high on corn, it does not mean that he should be long March corn and short March oats. The fact that he chose both contracts in the same delivery month may indicate that he has not thought enough about his spread position. More often than not the nearby contract will gain on the distant in strong markets because of the influence of strong cash markets on the nearby futures contracts, and carrying charges will decrease or inversion will increase. In weak markets nearby contracts tend to lose on the distant, and carrying charges will increase or inversion will decrease. The long side of a spread trade should probably be the contract that is lowest priced in terms of the prevailing spread differences in the commodity, and the short side should probably be the contract that appears highest priced at that time. For the best logical choice of both sides to be in the same delivery month would be sheer coincidence, yet this is the choice all too often made by spreaders who have given their positions only superficial thought.

LOW-RISK SPREADS

Many traders contemplating speculation in commodity futures markets are in great fear of the risk involved. In order to reduce fear, many writers and speakers interested in attracting new commodity speculators are fond of discussing the "no-risk spread." The usual example given is an intracommodity spread trading at full carrying charge so that a trader could buy the nearby contract and sell the distant with virtually no risk at all except for a material change in the carrying charges. Actually, attractive opportunities of this kind are quite rare. Other traders will take spread positions before the contracts reach full carrying-charge difference, with the result that the spreads may never get there. The closer the actual prices approach the apparent ideal, the more likely it is that there is such extreme weakness in the nearby lower priced contract that there is no reason for it to gain on the distant contract. The low-risk trade, therefore, may involve little risk but will have little potential. Traders who wait for full carrying-charge situations involving real potential may spend a long time waiting for a trade that will never be made successfully.

TAX SPREADS

There are some who advocate entering spread positions to achieve some tax advantage rather than to realize a profit. Purported advantages include the postponement of gains to another year or the conversion of short-term to long-term gains. The possibility is even advanced of converting a short-term gain in one year to a long-term gain in another.

Trading for tax advantages is a complex process and probably should not be attempted by traders acting without skilled professional advice. It is not only quite difficult to accomplish the objective economically, but there is always the uncertainty that the government will allow the trade to be used for the purpose for which it was intended. Taxes were discussed briefly in Chapter 3, but a really detailed coverage of the subject is beyond the scope of this book and probably beyond that of some brokers and others who are sometimes too generous with advice in this complex and hazardous field.

MISTAKES

The most frequent mistake made by those who trade spread positions is establishing them for all the wrong reasons. A common example is the net position trader who has an open loss that continues to get worse until he receives a margin call. He could, of course, solve his immediate problem by reducing or eliminating his position, but for some reason he regards a real-ized loss as something so much worse than an equity loss that he will do anything to avoid it. This error is so widespread and usually so disastrous that it is worth examining in some detail.

Presume that a cocoa trader is convinced that the price of May cocoa at 31 cents a pound is such a bargain that it is worth the full use of his available trading capital of $5,000. The margin requirement for a contract of 30,000 pounds of cocoa at the brokerage house of his choice is $1,200. He there-upon buys four contracts of May cocoa at 31 cents a pound and waits for great wealth to come his way. Unfortunately the news items concerning cocoa become unfavorable. Ghana announces that its crop looks better than had been expected. Holland and Germany speak of decreased consumption, and suddenly May cocoa is 29 cents and "not acting well." The trader is convinced that this adversity is temporary, that the forthcoming rise will be bigger than ever, and wishes that he could buy the cocoa now instead of when he did. Nevertheless, his broker's margin clerk, concerned only with numbers, points out that the open loss is $2,400 and that there is insuffi-cient margin remaining to support four cocoa contracts.

The trader now has several choices. First, he could deposit additional funds, but he has none available for this purpose. Second, he could sell two cocoa contracts and keep the other two, but he does not like the prospect of having to make 400 points on each of two contracts to compensate for the 200 points he lost on each of the four. Third, he could admit that he was wrong about the cocoa market and get out of all four. This he finds impos-sible to do because he would now have a realized loss of about $2,000 in addition to the necessity of admitting to himself, his wife, his broker, and his accountant that he is not a particularly good trader. So he seeks a way to postpone the inevitable by buying time. Accordingly, he orders his broker to sell four contracts of July cocoa at its present price of 29.30 cents a pound.

The margin requirement on a cocoa spread is only $400 compared with the $1,200 on a net long or short position, so his total margin requirement is reduced from $4,800 to $1,600. The equity in the account was reduced from $5,000 to $2,600 by the decline in May cocoa and so the margin call is satisfied.

On close examination it should be apparent that the trader has not really improved his position and may have made it worse. He has reduced his margin requirement from $4,800 to $1,600 but would have had no requirement at all if he had simply sold his May cocoa. His new plan, if he has one, is probably to cover his short July position after cocoa stops going down and take his "profit." It should be clear, however, that his position will be no better than if he had just taken off his May cocoa and reinstated it. It is probable that the May will drop just as much as July if July goes down, and therefore his July closed profit will be equaled by an additional May open loss. The commission expense of trading the four July contracts is just the same as that incurred in taking off the four May. The moment the July short position is lifted, the margin requirement reverts to $4,800 and the trader has the same problem he had before because there has been no equity improvement. A common procedure for such people would be to take off July early one day and hope that May would rise enough by the close to overcome the margin call—which, of course, might happen. Because the trend of cocoa has been down, however, it is at least as likely that cocoa will go down during the day and make matters worse. In the end he might trade his July cocoa several times, paying commissions of about $200 every time he does until he has a margin call even on the spread position and his situation has become hopeless. At this point he will probably blame the cocoa exchange, his broker, or his bad luck, when actually he was guilty of over-trading, failing to take a loss quickly, and spreading for the wrong reasons. Aside from a rally in the May futures on the day he covers his July position, the only other way out of his predicament is an improvement in the spread itself resulting from May gaining materially on July, but in a bear market the reverse is more likely. The chances of spreading a bad position and then recovering by day trading one side of the spread or by improvement of the spread itself are extremely slim ones.

A second serious error common among spreaders is choosing a spread in preference to a net position primarily to reduce margin and then putting on such a large spread position, just because the margin is low, that they ultimately take more risk and pay more in commissions than they would have paid with a net position. Such traders fail to realize that a spread provides some but not complete protection. A spreader might consider a price difference warped and thereby offering an opportunity, but it might well become even more warped and result in a loss before it returns to normal, that is, assuming it was warped in the first place and did not merely reflect some condition overlooked by the spreader.

A corn trader, for example, may consider May corn cheap at $1.22 and consider the purchase of 5,000 bushels for an anticipated 6-cent gain, for which he would risk a 2-cent loss. The gain would give him a profit of $300 at the risk of a $100 loss. The required margin might be $400 and the round-turn commission $30. The $300 profit would be almost 75 percent of the margin deposited, but the trader concludes that he would do even better spreading because his broker will carry 5,000 May corn long against 5,000 December corn short for only $100. He believes that the expected 6-cent gain in May corn will result in its gaining 3 cents on December corn during the same time, which would represent a potential profit of $150 on the $100 margin, or a rate twice the 75 percent on the net position. The commission on the spread position would be $36 a contract compared with $30 on the net position, so the rate of net profit would still be materially higher.

This seems so attractive to the trader that he is reluctant to leave idle the remainder of the $400 margin that the net corn position would have required. He thereupon decides to utilize the same capital for the spread and puts on four of the spreads, or 20,000 long May corn against 20,000 short December. If his trade succeeds, he will realize a gross profit of $600 less the total commission of $144 or $456 on his $400 margin. What he fails to consider is the possible adversity. It is unrealistic to assume that one could be prepared for a possible loss of less than 1 cent on a spread of this kind, which means that an unplanned loss caused by some unexpected event like a change in the corn loan could easily cause a loss of 2 cents or even more. A 2-cent loss on the spread would be $400 plus the $144 commission, which would more than wipe out the trader's capital. This is a far greater loss than could reasonably have been suffered on a net position. As a result the apparently safer position with a smaller investment has become a far greater risk with an equal investment and a larger commission.

There is sometimes a temptation to establish a spread one leg at a time or to remove it one leg at a time. This has at least one clear disadvantage and usually two. The spread commission is lost. Instead of a corn spread, for example, costing the spread commission of $36, the customer must pay the full $30 for each side, or $60. Second, most traders have an uncanny ability to put on the wrong leg first or take off the wrong one first. This is so probably because most of them try to choose the exact moment that a market will turn, which is almost impossible to do; for example, suppose that the corn spread previously discussed has worked favorably and that May corn has gained the planned 3 cents on December. The trader could take off the spread at the prevailing difference and realize his profit. He could also cover his December short and allow the May to continue to rise. Instead, he will more often yield to the temptation to take off the May because it is the profitable side and stay short December, hoping that it will go down, overcome its paper loss, and allow him to show a profit on both legs of the spread. Actually, what seems to happen all too often is that the May side is taken off on a day when corn is strong, which very strength caused the spread to succeed. It is also taken off early in the day because the trader wants as much time as possible for December to react. So corn continues strong and the 3-cent profit that was realized over a period of months is lost in hours.

A mistake that is not quite so serious, but quite common, is the haphazard choosing of contract months. The trader could have timed his transaction by watching a chart indicating the difference between May and December corn, but at the moment of entry July might be a better choice than May or March better than December. The choice should be based on all pertinent factors, not on the casual choice of contracts on a spread chart or a broker's quotation board.

OPTIONS

Like so many words in the financial field, "option" is used in more than one way in the commodity futures area. One, really a popular misnomer, applies to a designated futures month such as "the July option" for soybeans. Another, and more nearly correct form, has to do with the purchase of the right to buy or sell a commodity at a designated price during a designated future period. This is similar to the same procedure used in stock, real estate, and personal services.

There are three basic forms of option applicable to the commodity markets. One is a "call," which is an option to buy a specified commodity at a specified price (the "striking price") for a designated period of time. The payment for this call is determined by market conditions such as the price level of the commodity, its expected price volatility, and the supply and demand conditions for the calls themselves. The payment is designated as the "premium." To profit by a position the price of the commodity must move up enough to cover the cost of the premium rather than merely the round-turn commission. The option trader nevertheless gains some advantages. His loss is absolutely limited to the cost of his premium. The trader in the futures markets could enter a stop to limit his possible loss, but there is no assurance that the market will not sell through his stop or that he will not remove the stop as is so often the case. More important, the option trader need not fear interim adversity. Regardless of adversity, he receives no margin calls and need only hope that he will achieve a satisfactory profit sooner or later during the period he has bought with his option.

A second popular form of option is the "put," which operates much as the call, with the same advantages and similar costs, except that the buyer of a put has the right to sell a commodity contract at a set price over a specified period of time. He expects and hopes that the price will decline.

The third type is a "straddle" or "double option." This gives the buyer the right to buy or sell the commodity at a fixed price over a specified period of time or even both if the price moves over a range wide enough to yield him a profit on the upside and downside. The straddle amounts to nothing more than a combination of a call and a put and, logically enough, costs approximately the same as a call and put combined would cost.

Usually the only options available are those that are written by underwriters in the London markets on sugar, copper, silver, or rubber. Intermittently, however, options written in the United States have been popular.

Trading in options (often called "privileges" in the past) was carried on from time to time between the early 1860s and middle 1930s. There were many efforts by the exchanges and the state and Federal governments to stop trading but early rules and laws were largely ignored by those who were supposed to obey them and by those who should have enforced them largely because the violations were so widespread that enforcement would have disrupted the entire commodity business.

The Commodity Exchange Authority finally stopped trading in options on regulated commodities after 1936. The government was concerned about many aspects of options trading but especially by the artificial price movements caused by option traders attempting to protect the options they had bought or sold. The volume of options traded became so large that it disrupted regular commodity trading on the exchanges, especially at the close of the markets, and was uncomfortably closer to a gambling practice rather than a speculative activity.[1]

One flaw in the law prohibiting options proved to be its limitation to regulated commodities. About 1970 several firms took advantage of this loophole to begin trading in popular unregulated commodities such as silver, platinum, copper, silver coins, cocoa, sugar, and plywood. About the same time the prices of many of these commodities became extremely volatile which permitted option buyers to recover their premiums in unusually short times. Buyers of straddles could hardly lose and found themselves making important amounts of money within a few weeks or even days. Bernard Baruch's two and two still made four, however, and with everyone winning losers had to be found. As long as new buyers of options entered the field faster than old ones left it there was no problem. In fact, the old ones were more anxious to reinvest in new options than they were to withdraw even their profits, much less their capital. From a short-term cash-flow point of view there was no immediate problem, but in 1973, as throughout history, the piper had to be paid. When regulatory bodies stopped trading "temporarily" and most of the public lost their confidence, liquidations equaled and finally exceeded new purchases of options, and the option companies could raise sufficient capital only by speculating successfully with the cash received for options quickly enough to pay off their underwriting obligations. The amount needed to be earned proved too great and

[1] Paul Mehl, *Trading in Privileges on the Chicago Board of Trade,* U.S. Department of Agriculture Circular No. 323, Washington, D.C., December 1934, pp. 75–78.

the time available to earn it proved too short, and widespread failures of commodity option firms resulted.

The London options, which are written against actual cash commodities, underwritten by substantially capitalized companies, and realistically priced, remain popular among a small group of sophisticated traders. From time to time some American exchanges, particularly those in New York, move toward initiating option trading similar to that available in London. The Chicago Board of Trade began trading in stock options in April 1973, but theirs was more of an effort to attract business from the over-the-counter dealer's market in such options than an emulation of the old and largely discredited privilege markets.

NOTES FROM A TRADER

Spread trading is not so simple as taking net long or net short positions in a commodity. The advantages are sometimes so great, however, that it is well worth the necessary time and energy needed to master them. Most spread positions involve less risk than net positions and frequently less investment. The extra commissions incurred are usually a small consideration compared with the advantages. The avoidance of catastrophic losses is one of the greatest advantages of spread trading. Commodity markets sometimes have sudden violent price movements. When one of these movements is in favor of a trader, he realizes a welcome windfall profit, but when one is against him he is no longer a commodity trader. Many speculators with experience in trading are happy to forgo the opportunity for such windfall profits if the equal chance for a disastrous loss can be avoided. Spreads accomplish this reduction of risk because what is lost on one side in an unusually large adverse move is frequently matched by an approximately equal gain on the other side. The cost of this insurance against disaster is quite low. For a new trader spreads provide an opportunity to enter the commodity markets with minimum capital and risk.

If unregulated option trading revives, buyers should be as concerned with the financial integrity of the underwriters as with the volatility of the underlying commodities relative to their price.

CHAPTER NINE

The Game Plan

"Would you tell me, please,
which way I ought to go from
here?"
"That depends a good deal on
where you want to get to."
LEWIS CARROLL, *Alice in Wonderland*

INTRODUCTION

Many traders find themselves in a position similar to that of the German High Command as it faced its adversary across the Channel during World War II. The invasion of Britain was planned but never executed, whereas the Battle of Britain was executed but never planned. Similarly, many commodity futures traders seem to go through life planning trades they never execute and executing trades they never plan. The preceding chapters in this section have dealt with various elements of the decision-making process of futures trading. The objectives of the individual trader and the size of his initial capital commitment were analyzed in Chapter 5 which deals with risk and rewards, and the trade selection process was thoroughly discussed from the fundamental and technical approaches. The tasks that remain are to synthesize specific information into a game plan that will provide for any eventuality in a trade and to complete the consideration of the elements of money management begun in Chapter 5.

Bernard Baruch, who was no mean trader in his own right, knew the danger of arguing with numbers. He was fond of pointing out that two and two equal four. Once he said that "two and two make four and no one has ever invented a way of getting something for nothing."

Many speculators less intelligent than Baruch, and much less prosperous, seem to go through life unaware of this simple truth. They take positions based on impulse instead of reason and then wait to get lucky. They have not learned that even the best speculators consider themselves fortunate to be right on most trades or even to make significant profits during most years. Some traders find that their trading has resulted in more losses than profits, that the size of their average loss exceeds the size of their average profit, and execution costs and commissions must be added to their losses and subtracted from their profits. Such traders eventually learn that two and two equal four.

The speculator has no more hope of winning on every trade than the gambler has of winning on every roll of the dice or every turn of the cards. The gambler learns to use words like "maybe," "usually," and "perhaps," and the speculator should learn the same. He can no more know all the contingencies of determining price change than a card player can know the makeup of every hand before the cards are dealt.

If the speculator will plan his trades properly, he can possibly have the odds on his side in the long run, which is something few gamblers can achieve. Over a long period of time the skilled speculator who follows a carefully thought out plan in a disciplined manner should expect to have favorable results. The gambler can win in the short run, but in the long run the odds prevail and most will lose. No reasonable person would expect good luck to prevail forever or expect skill to fail forever. At least, not so long as two and two still make four.

If there is one consistency among successful traders, it is the disciplined use of a good plan. In the following pages the manner of developing a plan and the elements it should contain will receive careful consideration. Mistakes in formulating as well as implementing such a plan will be noted so that losing tactics may be avoided. It should be evident, however, that no chapter in this book or any other, no tract, nor any lecture can make successful commodity traders out of everyone. There is a considerable amount of art, and perhaps luck, that affects results so that no simple set of rules can ever guarantee profits. Furthermore, if every trader became successful, there would be no losers to provide the profits acquired by the winners.

THE BROAD PLAN

Reduced to its most basic elements, the trading plan provides the reasons for logically entering and getting out of any position, whether or not it proves ultimately profitable. Once a position is taken in the markets a price level can do nothing but rise, fall, or remain unchanged, and a trading plan must provide a blueprint for entering a trade and establishing the action to be taken by the trader in *any* of the *three* eventualities.

Although there are several key elements of a game plan to be considered, the core of a plan must indicate, unequivocally, how the trader is to exit from trades that have been entered. Such an approach consists of not one exit plan but three. There must be a plan for accepting losses if a position shows adversity, a plan for accepting profits, and a plan for getting out of a trade if the price change over a significant period of time is negligible.

There is usually only one valid procedure for exiting from a trade that shows a loss, and that is by means of a stop-loss order. Before entering any trade the trader must decide how much adversity — for whatever reason — he is willing to accept and then place a stop-loss order at that point. An exit plan that does not involve the use of stops to close out losing positions will almost certainly be a disaster.

If a trade shows a profit, the guidelines to the trader who is composing a game plan are not nearly so clear-cut. Several possibilities exist, and a case can be made for all of them. Depending on the method of trade selection used, one obvious procedure is to decide, on entering a trade, at what price profits will be taken. Trading by price objectives may not, however, suit a trader who uses other methods of trade selection. A trader need not be a trend follower to believe in letting profits run until some gauge, technical or fundamental, gives a "signal" for opposite action. In this case the exit plan might read, "sell at the stop-loss point or when Indicator X gives a sell signal, whichever comes first."

Other methods of trading may call for holding a position until a certain amount of time has passed and then accepting whatever profit (or loss) exists. Whatever plan for accepting profits is used, the important thing is that the trader recognize that accepting profits is ultimately the name of the game. Unless he plans to rely on luck, he should have in mind one or more clear conditions that will tell him to close out his trade and take whatever profits there are. Many successful traders have found that "It is easier to make money than to keep it," and the trader who ignores the part of his plan that calls for realizing profits will ultimately learn the painful truth behind this saying.

The problem caused by a trade that does virtually nothing after it is entered is not nearly so serious. If it happens often, the trader may find that he is not trading the proper commodities; thinly traded commodities may trade at approximately the same price for years. For the occasional trade that "goes dead" there are two possible solutions. Either an arbitrary time limit can be placed on the trade (closing it out if little net change has occurred at the end of this alloted time) or it can be held until the delivery month approaches. The method of trade selection will determine which concept is followed.

The trader with well-conceived exit plans not only has completed a large part of his total trading plan but will find that in the heat of actual trading he now has important peace of mind. Knowing exactly where and why to exit a trade is the best medicine for maintaining calm nerves in the commodity futures trading game. The alternative to such planning probably causes a trader to make his greatest mistake, namely "watching the market" and making decisions based on impulsive reactions to random price moves or to margin calls. Watching the market does not alter the basic price directions that are possible once a position has been entered, that is, up, down, and sideways. The dangers of watching a market include the often overwhelming temptations to cut profits quickly, ride losses, or overstay positions going nowhere which tend to tie up capital, waste energy, and confuse and demoralize the trader.

KEY ELEMENTS OF THE PLAN

CAPITAL

Basically, any plan worthy of the name contains certain key elements. One of the first decisions to be made by any speculator who has decided to trade commodities is the amount of capital that he is willing to devote to this trading. The extremes that limit this decision are clearly definable. The minimum is the margin on the books of the broker offering the most liberal terms. The maximum is the net worth of the trader plus all he can borrow. In practical terms, neither of these extremes would be considered by a reasonable person, although there is little doubt that both routes have been followed more than once.

The actual amount of the trader's net worth to be utilized for commodity trading depends on many considerations. These were discussed at length in Chapter 5, but some should be noted here because they influence construction of the trading plan. One is the motivation of the trader. If commodity trading is to be only a stimulating avocation, it might serve its purpose just as well if done on a small scale. Another consideration is the personal aggressiveness of the trader expressed by his desire to make money in relation to his willingness to risk losing what he already has. Some traders might be willing to risk a substantial proportion of their net worth in an effort to increase the total by an important amount. Others might be willing to risk only a comparatively small amount of capital because of fear of loss, the difficulty of replacing what might be lost, or personal responsibilities. These considerations in turn may be based on the age of the trader, the effort that was expended to accumulate the capital that must be risked, the size of his family, his health, the type of job he holds, the attitude of his family toward his trading, and his nerve. Basically, a trader should not take a risk disproportionate to the importance to himself of the potential profit. Traders vary in their reactions to different types of trade which helps explain why one trader will enter a trade rejected by others and reject others that somebody else may find appealing. Sooner or later each trader should become familiar with his own trading curve and select trades partly in accordance with it.

In formulating a plan, a trader is faced with a major question of the types of technical and/or fundamental data on which to base his trade selections. Before he embarks on the all-important trade-selection process, however, he should probably consider the related problems of learning where the data are to be found and how to obtain them regularly with the expenditure of reasonable time, effort, and cost; for example, one might use a point and figure chart based on a ¼-cent reversal in an active soybean market only to learn that the difficulty of scanning miles of ticker tape searching for the ¼-cent reversals is impracticable and that buying such data might cost too much or take too long to be of any use.

If a trader must study data to make intelligent decisions, he must have a place to do his studying and the time in which to do it. Part-time trading is difficult, and haphazard preparation under adverse conditions makes satisfactory results highly unlikely. The trader must know what types of order he prefers, hopefully for carefully considered reasons, and how to communicate his instructions to his broker without missing markets. These last items may seem mechanical and routine, but they may prove more difficult to resolve satisfactorily than they first appear, and they *must* be resolved satisfactorily.

TRADE SELECTION AND EVALUATION

No rational person would undertake trading in commodities unless he felt that he possessed some method of selecting profitable trades. Recommending any single trade-selection method is not the province of this book. In-depth surveys have been presented of technical and fundamental trading methods so that the reader will be aware of many lines of inquiry. These possibilities are expanded in Section 5 for 29 active commodities. The purpose of this discussion is to illuminate some of the vital factors that must be considered when a trader chooses a particular method of trade selection and to present some general guidelines on how the method chosen may be evaluated.

Choosing a trade-selection method. The would-be trader is bombarded constantly with advertisements and claims. He is informed of methods by private advisory services, brokerage houses, and acquaintances. Few of these methods are worth serious study and some can produce dangerous errors in thinking. Because most methods are alleged to be wildly profitable, choosing a method by the sole criterion of having produced the largest past profits is probably an exercise in futility. Instead careful consideration should be given to other important characteristics that should mark any method of trade selection.

At some point in time the trader must make a general determination of the factors that will cause him to enter into a market position. He may follow the guidance of some other person or a service or he may gather sufficient fundamental and technical data of his own to justify a position. Some traders engage primarily in technical research. Others rely on basic fundamental research and seek out situations they believe to be undervalued or overvalued. Still others rely on their own feelings which may be designated a "judgment," "the touch," or "a hunch," depending on how much dignity one wishes to lend to this usually fatal approach. The type of research preceding the trade entry will help to determine a trader's strategy; that is, whether he will lean toward short-term trades or positions held for extended periods, prefer the long or short side of the market, or search out net positions, spreads, or options. If he considers being against the speculative crowd as of great importance, he might have to prefer the short side. If small margins and the elimination of drastic adverse moves are sought, spread positions may be preferred.

A popular opinion holds that "fundamentals will give the main direction of prices, and technical factors will provide the timing." Although it is true that most fundamental methods are concerned with long-term factors, one has only to consult a commodity calendar to realize that daily fundamental factors are available for a number of commodities, and there is no logical base for assuming that short-term methods of trade selections based on such information could not be devised. Moreover, a valid technical method can easily be long-term as well as short-term oriented. The authors cannot conceive of a technical method that indicates when to take action but gives no clue to the anticipated direction of price. The trader should realize that fundamental and technical methods are probably independent means of analyzing markets and as such are not necessarily complementary or contradictory.

Apart from the basic approach, other factors may be considered. Does the trader wish to follow a well-publicized method or a more obscure method which has been purchased or is based on the trader's own research? Advantages and disadvantages may be noted for both approaches. In the first instance the trader may feel that one or more popular methods of trade selection embody valuable truths and that discipline is the one missing element needed to trade them profitably. An analogy has been made that there are hundreds of thousands of pianos in the United States but only a handful of virtuosos. A disadvantage in trading many popular methods, however, is that large numbers of traders may act on such signals. This may result in poor executions because signals from these methods may be efficiently discounted. Even worse, such methods have often caught the public fancy because they rely on axioms of market behavior that appear to be logical but have no basis in fact. They are testimony to a saying often attributed to Jesse Livermore, "With ease, human beings believe what it pleases them to believe."

Perhaps scores of obscure trading methods, some mechanically complicated, are privately printed and sold to limited numbers of people for prices ranging from $10 to several thousand. An advantage to procuring one of these methods may be that the approach to markets may be viable but the seller may not have the discipline or the desire to trade himself. If this is the case, the quality of the seller's research is not necessarily low. Another reason for buying a method may be that the method of trade selection is sound but that the trading plan is incomplete, with no allowance made, for example, for money management considerations. In this case both the inventor and his clients may have experienced losses due to poor planning and not because trade selection was inherently poor. Because the importance of a complete plan is usually overlooked, the chances are that any valid private method of trade selection that the trader does locate will become available to him because of this reason. The disadvantages of securing private methods are clear and are probably applicable most of the time. That these methods are available calls into question their efficacy. Assuming that their originators are economically motivated, if the trading methods were successful, there would be little need to broadcast their availability to others.

It is possible that the trader may conclude that most, if not all, methods of trade selection available to him are of little use and may wish to do research of his own. If this is the case, he must overcome the almost insuperable obstacle of fooling himself. To avoid self-deceit the trader should vow to be as conservative as possible in validating his method and even then to add an extra margin for error. Results in the real world are seldom as good as they look on paper, using hindsight. Worse than this, frequently some overlooked problem in the method of trade selection is apparent only after the trader's capital has been lost. The number of handwritten worksheets and computer printouts detailing methods of trade selection, all with "excellent" results, must approach infinity.

The frequency of trades should be considered. Some traders may feel comfortable trading every day, whereas others may prefer only a handful of trades every year. Two factors will have an influence on how many trades are made over any time span. The first is the number of commodities followed. If a trader follows many commodities, he will trade more actively over a significant period of time. The second depends on whether the method used is designed to select trades for long-term or short-term price changes. As a general rule a long-term method will select fewer trades than a short-term method.

Whatever method of trade selection is chosen, the trader must have enough confidence in it and be comfortable enough with it to build it into his trading plan. Once a method of trade selection has been integrated into the total plan it should not be changed or substituted while trades are being contemplated or made. If, after unhurried consideration, a better method of trade selection appears or an improvement on the existing method seems feasible the entire trading plan should be redrawn, with the new method of trade selection inserted.

Because of the time factor, the trader may feel that he prefers to use the trade selection method of a broker, an advisory service, or some other organization. If so, he has saved himself considerable work in this area, but a crucial problem remains. Whether a trade selection procedure is based on his own or someone else's work, it *must* be validated by the trader himself.

Evaluating a trade-selection method. Trading commodities with a trade-selection method that has not been validated makes a mockery of the rest of the trading plan. There are few methods of trade selection available to the trader that will not bear the claim that they have been exhaustively validated. The trader is best advised to ignore such claims and validate the method himself. If he does so, two important advantages will accrue. First, he will have certain knowledge of how the method has performed to date without having to rely on the claims of others who are more likely to have a vested interest in displaying impressive results. Second, validating a method of trade selection makes the trader more aware of its properties in a way that cannot be duplicated. This information can lead to valuable peace of mind during the periods of adversity inevitably encountered by even the most successful traders.

A number of considerations must distinguish all worthwhile trade-selection methods or the generation of "buy" and "sell" signals. These are:

1. The method must rest on a solid, logical theory. If the basic concept doesn't make a modicum of sense, the trader would do well to leave the pioneering stages to others.

2. The method must have a back record with the following properties: (a) The back record must be in real time, not hypothetical time. If a trader is employing a signaling method and "tests" the signals over some period *in the past,* such a test is in hypothetical time. If a trader compiles a record of signals *before the fact,* the test is in real time. Although considerable back testing must be done, a significant portion of the back record must be in real time. Almost any literate person can invent a system that will produce vast hypothetical profits over any past period. Few methods will work under real-time conditions when interpretative principles cannot be modified by hindsight. (b) The real-time record of signals must include many different types of markets. Some methods work quite well when prices are in a relatively narrow trading range; others succeed in dynamic trending markets. Still other methods are most profitable when price action is somewhere between these two extremes. It may require a considerable amount of time to produce a back record that is extensive enough for purposes of evaluation. If the trader is too impatient to obtain a back record or is falsely persuaded by others that his requirements are not reasonable, he runs a serious risk of evaluating the method by using what is known as a "biased sample." This approach would be equivalent to a poll taker determining national attitudes toward taxation by polling only those people who work on Wall Street.

3. The signals themselves must have the following properties: (a) The entry and exit prices at which the method suggests action should be realistic. Wheat, for example, might give a buy signal at $2.40, calculated

on Tuesday night. If it opens on Wednesday at $2.45 and then rises from there, the entry price must be considered as $2.45 or the trade must be abandoned. It is surprising how many back signal records use the closing price of the signal day rather than a realistic price on the day the trader would act. The same point can be made about exit prices. If the method suggested a stop-loss price of 38.50 cents a pound on a short pork bellies trade and the price rallied 100 points in the last minute of trading to close at 39.00, the exit price should be figured at 39.00. Not only must the most conservative entry and exit prices be used in compiling the record of any method, but it is sound practice to make an extra allowance for "execution costs" in compiling a back record. Adding an extra commission on each trade is one possible procedure. Almost all professional traders will insist that they have never seen a method that made adequate allowance for execution costs. (b) Results should be consistent; a number of methods will fail badly when tested in this way. The question the trader should ask is, "To what extent does *each* profitable trade support the overall result?" A method that "would have" transformed $10,000 into $20,000 over a span of 100 trades is not deserving of confidence if the entire gain was achieved by five spectacular winning trades plus 48 nominal losses. A method that made less cumulative profit but had its gains evenly distributed among the successful signals might be much more deserving of confidence. (c) The signals must be validated by using sound statistical principles. It can then be determined how worthwhile any signaling method is likely to be and what the probability is that observed results could have been duplicated by chance alone. Chapter 10, Money Management, covers this important point in more detail.

A hypothetical method with a logical theory behind it, a three-year back record that includes 20 active commodities with 600 real-time signals, of which 450 were profitable, does not require lengthy calculations to suggest that it may be worth trying for the next several months. Hopefully, a great deal of realistic research on the trader's part will simplify this evaluative step. Nonetheless, it must be done. Jumping to false conclusions about the validity of a method from a sample of observed trades that is too small is probably one of the most common errors of the speculating public.

4. The method must provide for a realistic stop-loss order on every trade. Stops must not be placed at obvious points suggested by books that explain how to get rich in the commodity markets. But stops must be entered. Without them, the question is not *whether* the trader will lose all of his trading capital but only *when* that event will occur.

NUMBER OF COMMODITIES TO FOLLOW

An important element of the game plan mentioned briefly to date has to do with the number of commodities to be followed and, of that number, how many to trade actively at a given time. The trader who speculates only as an avocation and who relies on detailed analysis of fundamental information or elaborate technical analysis may find it difficult to follow all active commodities without making significant errors. The margin of difference between success and failure in commodity speculation is narrow enough without having to deal with opportunities that were inadvertently overlooked or losses that were taken on trades that should not have been entered in the first place. Concentrating on only a few markets permits the accumulation of a larger amount of valuable fundamental knowledge and gives a better feel for the technical action of a particular market. The limitation of such concentration is that many markets may present opportunities for a time but then trade within narrow limits for extended periods while new or previously inactive markets become active. Willingness to trade in any market that becomes active provides an adequate number of opportunities, but it is possible to be tempted into too many positions or to know too little about a situation to justify taking the necessary risks. Because concentration in selected areas provides fewer opportunities, there may be a tendency to compensate by plunging heavily into riskier positions that will result in large profits if right and large losses if wrong.

TIME HORIZON

The expected life-span of a trade deserves some thought. The overall objective is to realize the greatest possible return on the capital commensurate with risk which has been made available for commodity trading. As in any risk venture, "return" is a function of the time required, not just the number of dollars returned. A small profit attained in two or three days may justify the time expended and the capital risked, whereas a small profit that takes months to realize may be worth little even if the chance of attaining it is quite high because of the unavailability of the capital tied up in margin while the trade is open. The trader who makes a quick paper interim profit on the way to what may be a significantly greater objective must give considerable thought to his wisest course of action. Exhibit 9-1 may help to clarify this problem.

EXHIBIT 9-1   Alternative Price Objectives.

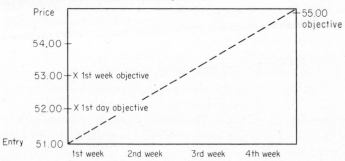

If a trader has bought pork bellies for a 4-cent (400 points) gain over a one-month period, he may be willing to accept a 100-point profit the first day or a 200-point profit during the remainder of the first week. Any point significantly over the line connecting the entry price with the price objective may be considered attractive at any time. Some traders may even wish to enter orders each day to liquidate their positions at a point significantly over the line but within a reasonable day's range. Any order taken alone is unlikely to be filled, but over a lifetime of trading a large number will be.

Considering such alternative price objectives allows the trader to avoid the problem of casting aside a well-conceived plan to take a small profit impulsively which may be as sure a road to ultimate ruin as any. Most traders willing to seize the opportunity to realize a quick small profit are much less willing to liquidate a position when faced with a quick small loss. Replacing possible large profits with small ones but leaving large losses because stop-loss points are considered inflexible produces a series of small profits and large losses and this requires a ratio of gains to losses far too favorable for most traders to achieve.

ADDING TO POSITIONS

The simplest type of plan might provide only for entering a position and liquidating it, but some traders prefer something more elaborate. A trader might intend, for example, to add to an initial position after the price has moved in a direction favorable to him. He is averaging *with the market.* Having bought a contract of sugar at 5.65 cents a pound, he could average by buying an additional contract at 5.80 cents, or, having sold short a contract of copper at 55.50 cents a pound, he could average by selling another at 53.50 cents. The logic of this procedure is that the new price level offers the opportunity to increase the potential profit but that the open profit already achieved allows the possible loss on the expanded position to be little or no greater than it was on the original position. It might even be less if the paper profit was large enough when the new units were added. The sugar trader was willing to risk 15 points from the current price, so that when he bought his first contract of sugar at 5.65 cents his 15-point risk would have come out of his working capital if the market had gone against him. When he added his second unit at 5.80, the market continued to rise, but if it had reacted 15 points and he got out he would have lost 15 points on the second unit but nothing on the first except his paper profit. If he had added a third unit, or line, at 5.95 cents, he would no longer have lost any of his capital on a 15-point reaction because he already had a 45-point open profit to act as a buffer. The disadvantage of trading in this manner is that each new unit offers less potential and more risk than those previously added because the market is closer to its ultimate objective by the amount of the price change that has already taken place. The result of poorly timed additions might well be the loss of profits already achieved in order to try to gain

even larger profits. The trader who regards equity as the ultimate measure
of his financial strength does not consider the loss of paper profit very
different from the loss of any other kind of capital, and this might well be
the most logical attitude.

Averaging *against the market* is the alternative to averaging with it,
which provides for the addition of new lines after the initial position shows
a loss. Use of this averaging technique against the market assures the trader
of making more money than the trader who averages with the market when
he proves to be right in his selection of a position and his timing. It also
means that his worst positions will be his largest because so much adversity
has provided him with the "opportunity" to add so much. His best positions
will be his smallest because they provide no opportunity to add to the original line. Eventually the averager against the market is likely to find himself in a position that deteriorates so far that he can no longer support it,
much less add to it. It has been said that sooner or later all that an averager
will have left is averages.

Both types of averager face the problem of how many units to add to their
initial position and when to add them. Adding a number of units at the new
level greater than the number originally established is a technique too
aggressive for most traders to accept. The trader, for example, who buys
one contract of cotton, adds two more on strength, three more on still more
strength, and continues to add in this way eventually risks buying such a
large number of units near the top of the price move that even a relatively
slight reversal quickly eliminates all of the paper profit that was gained
on the smaller number of units acquired at lower price levels.

STOPS

The trader must estimate the amount of loss that might have to be suffered in the event that the trade proves unsuccessful. This amount may be
determined from a price level indicated by chart analysis or a percentage
of some dollar figure deemed to provide a valid guide, such as a percentage
of the margin or of the current price level of the commodity. It may also be
nothing more elaborate than the monetary loss the trader is willing to take
before abandoning the trade. The potential proft may then be compared
with the potential loss. Many traders erroneously believe that the potential
profit must be at least twice the potential loss before a position is justified,
whereas others are willing to vary the ratio according to what they regard
as the *probability* of achieving the profit. They may feel, for example, that a
potential profit of a given amount is worth seeking even at the risk of a loss
of an equal or even greater amount if the chance of achieving the gain is
materially greater than that of suffering the loss. The opportunity for even
a small profit can be quite attractive if the risk of losing a small amount is
minimal. This concept is discussed in detail in Chapter 10. Regardless of
the favorability of the ratio of expected profit to expected loss, some trades

must be passed just because the dollar amount of loss that must be risked is too great for the trader's capital to bear. Erosion of his capital by the attrition of one bad (or unlucky) trade after another is a hazard that no trader can eliminate, but to risk consistently so much of his capital in trades that "can't miss" that recovery is not reasonably likely is a certain road to ruin. For some perverse reason the trades that cannot miss are always the ones that seem to.

There is some difference of opinion concerning the relative wisdom of actually placing orders to liquidate a position at predetermined points and liquidating when the market touches one of them. Generally it is difficult to justify failure to enter an order when the objectives and stop points have been determined. Actually entering the orders assures that a carefully prepared plan will not be replaced by impulse during the heat of a trading session. A satisfactory profit that was expected, achieved, and then lost in the effort to try for more can be completely demoralizing. A reasonably small planned loss that is replaced by an unreasonably large unplanned loss can be more than demoralizing; it can be ruinous. To spend an important amount of time watching short-term ripples in a market in order to avoid entering orders in advance is usually a useless expenditure of time and energy.

Some traders are reluctant to enter stop-loss orders because of some vague feeling that somebody will force the price toward their stop price until their position is lost, after which the market will promptly go the other way. As often as not, this is an excuse to avoid putting in the stop.

A trader who decides not to use stops should at least consider their use carefully before he rejects them. If the market does not move to the stop point, no harm has been done. If the stop is elected and the price moves well beyond that point, the trader may have been saved from complete disaster. If the price moves just a little beyond the stop point, the trader often has time to reconsider without the bias of having to defend a position he is presently holding. If he wants to reinstate, he may do so, and the only cost to him is the added commission which the market may have saved for him anyhow by going far enough past his stop.[1] The only really painful course that the market could take would be to elect the stop and reverse almost immediately. If this happens to a trader often, he is probably placing stops at rather obvious points, such as just below recent lows or above recent highs. Moving markets have a tendency to reverse temporarily and clean out stops before continuing their moves, and traders should take this into consideration before using stops. Difficulties in this area result not from the use of stops but from their improper use.

Few traders are sufficiently well disciplined to be able to dispose of a position showing a loss quickly. Those who are might not be able to reach

---

[1] Some exchanges grant reduced commissions for day trades, which make the total cost of liquidating and then reinstating a position quite minor.

their brokers quickly enough to act before a small loss becomes large. Even those who have both the necessary discipline and good communications with their brokers seldom gain by not having the orders entered in advance.

THE PLAN IN ACTION

FORM OF THE PLAN

Plans may be mental or written, but written plans are preferable for most traders because they are more likely to be complete and to be followed conscientiously. Each trader may develop a plan form of his own to complement his own style of trading. Exhibit 9-2, although not exhaustive, probably contains most elements that most traders will wish to consider for each position entered but it is best for the trader to devise the form that he finds most useful. Some may wish to add or delete items or leave more or less room than is provided in the illustration for specific items. Errors are more likely to result from a plan that is too sparse than one that is too elaborate. The time and energy spent in thinking through a plan is doubtless worth the money saved through trading haphazardly. A brief explanation of the purpose and use of most items in the plan exhibited follows.

The first item, "commodity position," can be completed by indicating the commodity chosen and the contract month after either "long" or "short." If a spread position is to be entered, both blanks could be filled in or a third blank marked "spread" could be added. If a trader keeps his plan forms filed together, he will be kept aware of his overall position. Considering each trade on its own merits may result in the trader's having a number of positions all long or all short. Certain events, such as war or currency devaluation, may cause many seemingly unrelated commodities to move sharply in the same direction and leave the trader with a greater loss than he was prepared to take. This should be considered when adding new positions.

The margin for any new position, whether long, short, or spread, should be considered before a trade is entered, not after. Margins can be changed by exchanges or individual brokers and sometimes by considerable amounts. If the trader had expected to be called for an amount materially smaller than is actually required, he may find himself faced with an unexpected shortage of margin immediately after a trade is entered.

The commission per contract must be considered in order to make certain that the possible profit compared with the possible loss is adequate to justify the trade. The trader who decides to scalp 25 points in cocoa only to realize that this would represent a $75 gross profit, which must be reduced by a commission of perhaps $60, finds that he is trading for the benefit of a cocoa broker rather than for himself.

The "type of plan" may depend on the nature of the opportunity or the personality of the trader. Some people prefer to trade in one consistent

EXHIBIT 9-2   Trading Plan Summary.

1. Commodity position: Long _____ Short _____   Per contract or per spread: Margin ____ Commission ____   Trade # _____

2. Type of plan: ☐ Scalp ☐ Full move ☐ Averaging with position ☐ Averaging against position ☐ Other

3. Entry plan:

| Line number | Conditions necessary for entry of lines | | | Quantity | Cumulative quantity | Average price |
	Date	Price	Other			

4. Actual entries:

Line number	Date	Quantity	Price	Cumulative quantity	Average price

5. Liquidation plan:

| Line number | Conditions for liquidation of line | | | Quantity | Remaining quantity | Final objective | Interim objective | Initial stop | Adjusted stop | Final date |
	Date	Price	Conditions							

(A) Net dollar gain to final objective _____ X Probability of achieving objective _____ = $ _____

(B) Maximum dollar risk _____ X Probability of reaching stop point _____ = $ _____

(C) Expected dollar value,(A) minus (B)   = $ _____

6. Actual liquidation:

| Line number | Reason for liquidation (check one) | | | | Other | Date | Quantity | Price | Gross dollar gain or loss | Commission | Net gain | Net loss |
	Planned date	Final date	Objective reached	Stop elected								

Summary: Actual dollars gained _____   Actual dollars lost _____

7. Other factors (where applicable)

Technical comments _____

_____

Seasonal _____

Historical price level _____ High _____ Neutral _____ Low _____ Consensus _____ Government loan equivalent _____

Price nearest option month _____ Carrying charge _____ Cash price _____

Crop year supply-demand comments _____

_____

Near term supply-demand comments _____

_____

Landmarks necessary to indicate trade on course (include dates where applicable) _____

_____

Perils (include dates where applicable) _____

_____

Comparable years

Year	Results	Comments
19__		
19__		
19__		

_____
_____
_____
_____
_____
_____

8. Trade evaluation:

Entry plan versus actual entry   Liquidation plan versus actual liquidation
☐ Good   ☐ Fair   ☐ Poor   ☐ Good   ☐ Fair   ☐ Poor

Mistakes committed:
Entry _____

Liquidation _____

manner, whereas others believe themselves flexible enough to trade in different ways at different times or at the same time in different trades. If additional lines are not to be added to the initial position, a quick profit, or scalp, may be expected or perhaps a major change in price level over a relatively long period of time would be possible, in which case the trader may hold his position for a full move. If additional lines are to be added, they may be made when the market has moved favorably for or against the trader. In either case he must determine what factors, if any, will cause him to add a second, third, or more lines. Additions may be made at fixed intervals, as predetermined price levels are reached, or based on some other factor that seems important to the trader, such as a reaction after a rise in price. Adding new lines by utilizing paper profits is called "pyramiding."

The "actual entries" may differ from the "entry plans" because of the manner in which orders are filled; for example, a trader may have planned to enter a position in platinum on the opening of the market at a price of about $139 an ounce only to be surprised by an opening at $145 because of some unexpected news. If differences between the planned entries and actual entries are so great and so material that they affect trading results to any great degree, a change in the method used to enter trades is indicated.

The "liquidation plan" is the heart of any plan form. In providing for an exit from a trade that covers any eventuality, the trader avoids the demoralizing experience of riding losses or taking profits impulsively. It is also important that such a plan forces a trader to think through the expected dollar value of a trade before he enters, not afterward. The "expected value" concept is covered in detail in Chapters 5 and 10, but the computational aspects are not difficult and may be introduced at this time.

Assume that the trader believes he has isolated, quantified, and validated a nonrandom technical device that results in profits in 65 percent of the indicated trades over a reasonable period of time. Further assume that the technical device has signaled a particular trade that, if successful, should result in a profit of $780, whereas the execution of a stop would mean a $600 loss. Multiplying the profit $780 by the probability .65 of achieving the profit gives $507. Similarly, if the dollar risk on the trade $600 is multiplied by the probability .35 of losing, the result is $210. The expected dollar value of the trade, $297, is computed by subtracting $210 from $507. Obviously the expected value of a trade should be positive or the trade should be rejected.

The summary following the section "actual liquidation" refers to the *actual* dollars gained or lost on the trade. The trader should check his record of closed profits and losses frequently to ensure that results generally parallel expectations, both in the number of profits and losses and the average dollar amount of profits and losses.

The section headed "Other Factors" can be adapted by each trader to summarize the factors he considers important. "Technical comments" may include chart formations, volume, open interest, or response to news.

The "seasonal" item is noted because some traders think that many commodities have seasonal trends. There is nothing wrong with sometimes attempting to take advantage of a contraseasonal move, but the trader should at least be aware that he is doing it.[2]

Noting the "historical price level" makes certain that the trader knows whether he is trading at prices that have been proved unusually high or low in the past. This might not dissuade him from buying at historically high prices or selling at historically low prices, but it guarantees that he is doing it knowingly rather than inadvertently.

The "consensus," particularly of brokers and services that influence a number of traders, helps to determine whether a contemplated position is with or against the crowd. This factor, again, may not be considered critical, but it does help one to avoid being the last to buy or sell.

The "government loan equivalent" (where it applies) should be considered with the historical price level to help determine whether the current price of a future is too high or too low. If the price seems historically high but the loan level has been increased drastically, the market price may appear to be not nearly high enough rather than too high.

The relation of the cash price to the near-term option often is a clear indicator of near-term strength or weakness. A change in the relationship may provide an early indication of a change in price direction of the futures market.

"Landmarks" point out events that can reasonably be expected to happen if the trade is to be considered on course; for example, the results of a government report which is scheduled to be released on a given date should generally be in line with expectations of what the report will indicate.

"Perils" are closely related to landmarks because a report that contains statistics unfavorable to the trader's position may prove to be a peril instead of a landmark. Some perils, of course, such as a late freeze in Florida when a trader is short orange juice or a large unexpected release from the government stockpile of copper when he is long copper futures, cannot be definitely dated.

The "comparable years" section simply indicates past years in which conditions were similar to those in the current year. If the direction of price or timing in those years is not consistent with the trader's intended position, he should have some reason to believe that there are conditions existing in the present year different enough from the past to justify his position. Because the list of "other factors" may be wide and deep, additional space should be provided for their notation.

---

[2] Seasonal movements, like most apparent consistencies in the commodity markets, have a natural tendency to disappear or become distorted when they become well known. If a trader believes he has discovered a consistency, he would do well to keep it to himself.

The "trade evaluation" section of the plan is a control of the trader's discipline. Sooner or later price movement must have elected a stop or an objective or time must have run out. In any case, the result of most trades should be in accordance with the objectives and risks covered in the plan. The trader should eventually have a plan form complete enough and a discipline strong enough so that there is seldom a significant variation within his control between the possible results, good or bad, and the actual results.

A SPECIFIC PLAN

A plan is so basic to successful trading that it is worth pausing to explore in depth some of the thought that goes into its construction. Assume that a speculator has decided to enter the commodity markets and will risk $10,000 for this purpose. He has selected a brokerage house and a registered representative, opened an account, and deposited his money. He has also decided to limit his trading to wheat on the Chicago Board of Trade until he becomes knowledgeable enough to enter other markets.

It is October, the recently harvested wheat crop was a large one, and current prices are low. The trader has decided that the current price level adequately reflects the size of the crop and that there is no logical reason for it to go much lower. He also concludes that potential foreign and domestic demand, as well as anticipated commercial hedge lifting, should result in a price rise. The chart he keeps also indicates that the decline in price has stopped, and he interprets this as a signal that bullish forces are about to become dominant and that a rise is probable. He therefore decides to enter a long wheat position.

Having decided to buy wheat, a rational choice must be made among the various markets where wheat trades. This decision will be based on the estimated location and time of the greatest demand for wheat and the type of wheat that will be in the shortest supply. If the trader decides that the anticipated demand will reflect in Soft Red more than Hard Red and in winter more than in spring wheat, he will probably take his position on the Chicago Board of Trade rather than on the Kansas City or Minneapolis exchanges. He will then have to determine which contract will best reflect the expected tightness. He can do this either by making a fundamental judgment or by looking at wheat charts from other years with similar fundamentals and noting what happened then. He may also consult charts of other commodities in an effort to find similar patterns. It appears to the trader that the December contract does not provide him with enough time before having to risk taking delivery, but believing that a rising market will cause inversion he prefers nearby contracts to those more distant. He therefore compromises by selecting the March contract. He notes that in recent years during which wheat prices have risen, March gains on May, and May gains on July. Therefore a spread position in which March is bought against a short position in July might be profitable. Because the trader has adequate capital available for margin and because he believes that the risk of a net long position is reasonable, he decides merely to buy the March wheat, which is selling at $2.54½ a bushel.

Analysis of the recent market, as well as of those in years with similar characteristics, indicates that a gross profit of 8 cents a bushel has a .55 probability of being achieved by December 15, whereas a decline to $2.47 a bushel would indicate that the market is not "acting right" and that the trade should be abandoned. The probability of the latter is judged to be .45. If the price were to rise 18 cents, the gross profit on a contract of 5,000 bushels would be $900, which would leave a net profit of $870 after deduction of the round-turn commission of $30. If the trade had to be closed out unfavorably at $2.47, the decline of 7½ cents a bushel would represent a loss of $375, plus the $30 commission, or a total of $405. Considering that the expected value of a profit is worth $478.50 ($870 times .55) and the possible loss estimated at only $168.75 ($375 times .45), the trader decides to enter the trade.

Because he thinks the ratio of profit to loss is small and because so much time may be needed for the position to reach its potential, he decides not to tie up much available capital in this trade. The modest objective and close stop-loss level preclude any additions to the original position on either strength or weakness. The speculator decides that the most he is willing to lose on this trade if it proves to be unsuccessful is 5 percent of his trading capital, or $500. Note that he is concerned more with the amount of his trading capital he might lose than with the percentage of his margin or the change in the price of the wheat itself. Accordingly, he buys 5,000 bushels of wheat at $2.54½ and immediately enters another order to sell the 5,000 bushels at $2.72½ or at $2.47 stop O.C.O. (one cancels the other). A reminder is written on the trading plan to liquidate the position at the close of the market on December 15 if neither the objective nor the stop-loss points have been reached by that time. The amount of thinking and planning represented by a plan even as simple as this is probably considerably more than is done by many traders, which may be why so many people lose money trading.

A refinement of the plan outlined here is a provision for accepting something less than an 18-cent profit before December 15 in order to consider the time needed to make a profit as well as its amount. As an extreme example, a rise of 17 cents on the very same day that the position was taken would leave the trader in the position of possibly waiting for at least two months or more to make one more cent at the risk of losing back the 17 cents plus the other 7½ cents to the stop point. It may appear to be logical to accept the 17 cents because the additional gain is too small to justify the possible loss from the new price level. By the same token, it is never possible to make 18 cents in a position if a profit is always taken at 17 cents. One possible solution is to wait for the other cent in accordance with the plan. Another is to have the plan provide for such possibilities by allowing partial profits to be taken if achieved quickly; for example, it may provide a profit of 14 cents be taken during the first week, 16 cents during the next two weeks, and 18 cents thereafter. It is important, however, to work these possibilities into the plan rather than to modify the plan in accordance with impulses.

MISTAKES

As in most activities requiring skill, success or failure in trading commodities is largely a matter of how many mistakes are made. Most of them occur in the area of planning, but the greatest is not having a plan at all because no plan, no matter how poorly constructed, will allow for the loss of a trader's entire trading capital. A plan should give him a chance to try again. The alternative to planning is "watching the market," which usually results in trades being made in response to haphazard impulses triggered by random news items or hunches. It also results in considerable time being wasted watching a tape or a quotation board, time that could be used more productively by doing almost anything else. Boardroom traders too often take a small profit as quickly as possible and then rationalize by saying, "You never go broke taking a profit," or they ride a loss and say "I'm locked in."

It should be remembered that the primary advantages of planned trading include the limitation of losses in relation to available capital and a formula for getting out of a trade, regardless of the direction taken by price. If a trader devises a plan that permits him to risk all of his trading capital or does not allow him to get out of a trade unless it goes in only one direction, he had better spend some time thinking about plans before he does much trading.

Aside from not having a plan at all, the greatest possible mistake probably is to have one and not follow it. The temptations to make errors when a plan is not followed may be overwhelming. When the profit objective has been reached, the market has obviously been "acting well," and the trader must beware of "waiting for a while" to see what happens next. If still more profit is made, he can put in a new stop at the level of his original objective and make more money. The danger, however, is a reaction just after the initial objective is reached and before a stop can be inserted at a favorable point. If reasonable profits are attained and then lost back, the chance of success in the long run becomes remote. Even worse is making excuses not to take a loss when the stop point is reached. Every trader is able to rationalize riding losses by convincing himself that recovery is virtually certain from the new level, that if he were not already in the trade he would certainly enter it now, that further adversity is simply impossible, or that it is the wrong day or wrong time of the day to take the loss. The fact remains that the risk level influenced the size of the position being carried, and this in turn influenced the amount of capital being risked, which was the maximum considered reasonable. Any further loss therefore becomes unreasonable by definition. The solution to this problem is to remove temptation by putting in the stop order to liquidate the position immediately after the position is taken and leaving it in regardless of current news, time of the day, or anything else. Unfortunately the alternative to a planned loss is an unplanned loss, and the trader who habitually receipts for unplanned losses is firmly embarked on the road to ruin.

Perhaps the most stultifying mistake that can befall a trader is the assumption that success is virtually certain if he adopts a rational trade selection strategy and intelligently follows the elements of a successful plan as developed in this chapter. Unfortunately there is a final obstacle to success—money management—which is the proper concern of the closing chapter of this section for those who play the game.

NOTES FROM A TRADER

The most important aspect of planning is to *have* a plan. The second most important point is to follow it. A plan not followed is like an automobile seat belt not buckled. A plan should be kept to oneself. When other people are looking over the trader's shoulder, things start to go wrong, because he begins to attach some importance to their reactions to what he does, when they really should not affect what he does at all.

There is always some apparent reason for trying for still more profit or not taking a loss. If the trader lacks the discipline to set objectives and risk limits and to act when either is reached, he should not trade commodities.

The trailing stop seems to be an infallible method of taking advantage of big moves with modest risk. For reasons developed thoroughly in Chapter 4, this device rarely works.

Plans may be difficult to devise and adapt to one's own trading preferences and even a carefully conceived plan may not work. Markets may act in a way in which they have never acted before, and all the work that went into a plan's preparation may appear to have been wasted. Discouragement from time to time is part of the game and famines have a way of following feasts. Despite any apparent disadvantages, there can be no doubt that trading with a game plan is far better than trading without one.

CHAPTER TEN

Money Management

It is remarkable that a science which
began with the consideration of games
of chance should become the most
important object of human knowledge. . . .
The most important questions of life
are, for the most part, really only
problems of probability.

PIERRE SIMON DE LAPLACE, *Théorie Analytique
des Probabilités, 1812*

INTRODUCTION

Games of speculation are different from gambling games in both the
economic and legal senses, but to the typical speculator the similarities of
the two activities greatly exceed the differences. His reasons for engaging
in either one are the same; profit, excitement, diversion, compulsion, or
some of their combinations. Most important, many of the rules are quite
similar, and therefore the extensive thought applied to gambling games is
quite applicable to the commodity trading game as well.

The trader, like the gambler, will find it far more difficult to handle his
money in a logical and disciplined manner than to learn the rules of the
game. Anyone, for example, can learn to play draw poker—the ranking of
possible hands and local interpretations of the rules and procedures—in an
hour or so. Many people, however, have played the game for years and have
lost consistently because of poor money management. Most of these losers
bemoan their bad luck, just as losing commodity traders tend to blame their
brokers, unexpected events, or bad luck for their own errors in money
management.

It is impossible to develop a set of rules in this chapter to serve as a guide
for all traders under all conditions. Trading is an individual decision-making
process and each trader brings his own unique intellectual and behavioral

background to bear on the problem of approaching commodity trading most profitably. Traders have different goals in the markets, different attitudes toward their profits and losses, and different preferences in their styles of trading, to say nothing of a host of other differences such as time available, tax considerations, and financial and psychological strength. The trader who hopes to succeed in the long run must be able to recognize and develop his behavioral skills in order to determine a set of objectives most logical for his concept of maximum advantage. To employ a money management system effectively a trader must consider its four basic elements:

1. Initial capital.
2. Objectives.
3. The expectation of the game being played.
4. The probability of ruin.

The first two were discussed in preceding chapters. The remaining two are considered in the pages that follow. The discussion here does not consider subjective motivations in great detail because it would require an extensive foray into psychology involving a wide range of personal drives such as a guilt-ridden risk-lover's desire to lose his money.

EXPECTATION OF THE GAME PLAYED

Probability. A game, as discussed here, may consist of one or more trials which a gambler would call bets and a speculator would call trades. The expectation, or average payoff, of the game being played indicates whether it consisted primarily of fair bets (those with zero expectation), good bets (those with a positive expectation), or bad bets (those with a negative expectation). If the game consisted of only one trial, the expectation of the game and the trial would be the same. A basic element of expectation is the long run relative frequency of an event occurring. This element is probability, expressed as a number ranging from a low of zero to a high of one.

An example is provided by a game centering on the flipping of a coin. The probability of "heads" is .5 and the probability of "tails" is .5. Another example is provided by the draw poker player who is holding four spades and draws one card to his hand hoping to find a fifth spade to make a flush and, hopefully, winning the pot. The probability of drawing that fifth spade from a deck of cards without a joker is .191; the probability of not drawing it is .809.

It should be noted that the gambler or player of a social card game has a decided advantage over the speculator in the commodity or stock market in that the gambler is able to determine the precise probabilities inherent in his game and to act accordingly. (This is not to say, of course, that the player will actually use his advantage or that knowing his probabilities will enable him to profit from playing the game.) A roulette player may be interested in betting on red versus black or odd versus even. He can readily determine that the wheel has 36 numbers, half odd, half even, half on a red background, and half on black. In addition, most American roulette wheels have a "0" and "00" on a green background, on both of which the casino wins all red, black, odd, and even bets. The player knows, therefore, that he has 18 chances to win and 20 chances to lose, regardless of how he bets. The probability of winning is .4737 ($\frac{18}{38}$) and the probability of losing is .5263 ($\frac{20}{38}$).

Unlike the coin flipper who knows that after many flips approximately half will have resulted in heads, the commodity trader who concludes that sugar is going to increase in price is far less certain of measuring the probability of this event occurring before an unreasonably large adverse move. He may believe that the chance of an adequate rise in price before a substantial drop is .7, but this probability is subjective. Regardless of the thoroughness of his fundamental or technical research, the commodity trader is applying his knowledge of the past to make his evaluation of the future. But in an area as dynamic as the commodity futures markets conditions as well as probabilities change frequently. Even a huge number of samples to serve as a guide cannot lead to certain determination of the probabilities of success or failure because of the complex and fluid nature of the game and the rules under which it must be played.

Payoff. One who plays a game or trades a market normally hopes to get more out of it than he puts into it. The emphasis here is placed on money payoff rather than psychic costs and income (most people seem to get more satisfaction out of winning than losing, anyway). The money payoff of a game (gambling or trading) can be used to measure what may be won versus what may be lost, modified sometimes by an admission charge to a casino or a commission charged by a broker. A player may be in a position, for example, to win $1,000 if he wins or to lose $500 if he loses. In this case his "money odds" may be said to be 2 to 1 of winning.

It should be clear that the mathematical *expectation* of a game depends on the probabilities and payoffs. Specifically, it is the sum of the possible payoffs with each payoff weighted (multiplied) by its respective probability. The player who stands to win $1,000 or lose $500 with a probability of winning of .5 has a mathematical expectation or average payoff of $1,000 $\times$ .5 — $500 $\times$ .5 = $250, and obviously might consider playing the game because in the long run he will average $250 gain per play of the game. Suppose, however, that a player stands to win only $500 if he wins or lose $1,000 if he loses. He might be tempted to reject the game out of hand, but what if the probability of winning were .9 and the probability of losing only .1? The expectation of the game would be $500 $\times$ .9 — $1,000 $\times$ .1 = $350, still a positive value. On the basis of monetary expectation, the second game is even more favorable than the first, for which reason the often-given advice to take a position in the stock or commodity markets only if the trader will make two or three times or more what he may lose is ordinarily so foolish. Those giving such advice rarely speak of the *probability* of winning or losing, and without it the expected monetary value of taking the position cannot be determined. A game in which the player may win twice as many dollars as he stands to lose is no different in expectation from a game in which he may lose twice as many dollars as he may win if his probability of winning the first game is .33 and the second game, .67. Expectation, in short, is nothing more than the average payoff which is derived by modifying the payoff of an event by its probability of occurring.

Depending on the combination of probability and payoff, a game may be said to be favorable if its expectation is more than zero or unfavorable, if less. Returning to the roulette player discussed above, it will be recalled that the probability of his winning was .4737 and of losing, .5263. In the usual casino the player will be offered a money return equal to the money that he risks; that is, a player who bets a dollar on red, black, odd, or even will lose the dollar if he loses and win a dollar if wins. Usually there is no admission charge to a casino, so the payoff to the player is even (or the odds may be said to be 50-50). The mathematical expectation of the game to the player betting on one of the four items listed would therefore be 47.37 cents of each dollar bet and the expectation of the casino would be the other 52.63 cents. The house "take" or "advantage" is the difference of 5.26 cents on a one-dollar bet or 5.26 percent of all bets. The player may be said to be making a bad bet, and because the house has the other side of all players' bets it may be said to be making all good bets, each by the same margin.

The commodity trader who tries to discover whether he is in a better or worse position than the roulette player finds his analysis difficult. He is aware precisely of only one aspect of his expectation of winning and that is some part of his payoff. He can probably determine the commission that he will have to pay and estimate the opportunity cost on the capital that he utilizes for margin. The remaining element of the payoff, that is, how much he will win or lose because of market action, is far more difficult to determine accurately. A disciplined trader can, of course, determine the points at which he intends to liquidate his position, win or lose. He may even be sufficiently disciplined to enter orders at the two points he has determined —one intended to take his profit at the objective and the other to stop his loss when he has all the adversity he cares to suffer on a trade. If he sets his objective at a definite limit and leaves an open order in at that point, the chance of his getting exactly his price on a *successful* trade is quite high. He obviously cannot get less and only infrequently will a market act so favorably for him that he will be filled at a price even better than he has asked. On a losing trade, however, the outcome is far less certain. If he enters a stop-loss order which is elected, that order can be filled at his stop price, but also at better or worse. A fill at a better price than the stop specified is even rarer than a fill at a price better than a limit on the order at a trader's objective, but a fill at a price worse than that specified on a stop-loss order is quite common and sometimes the fill is *much* worse. On balance, therefore, if he wins, the trader's objective will usually be exactly as planned, but if he loses the loss will frequently be greater than expected. (This is one of the major reasons why trading in the real world seldom turns out to be so profitable as one's paper trading has indicated that it should be). The sophisticated trader must learn eventually to take this into consideration and plan in advance for the "execution costs" of his trades to include not only commissions but also some extra adversity on his losing trades. He may well have learned that the cost of extra adversity over a long period of trading may approach the far more obvious cost of commissions.

Despite his problems of probability and payoff, the trader must reach a conclusion concerning his chance of being ahead after making one or a series of trades, determine how much he expects to be ahead if he wins, how much he expects to lose if he loses, and use this knowledge to help plan how to play the game. He may, of course, also decide not to play at all after completing an evaluation of his expectation.

Fair bets. It is obvious that if a game consisted of one or more fair bets it would involve a zero expectation and be an even game. It might be concluded that participants in such a game must be playing basically for fun and that no one has the right to expect to win in the long run. This, however, is not the case. Although the amount of money a person has does not affect the expectation on a single play of the game (whether the flip of a coin or a trade in plywood), the capital available to the players can be of tremendous importance in determining their eventual financial outcome.

If two players are betting on coin flips and one has significantly more capital than the other, that player's chance of eventually winning all the other's money, hence ruining him, is considerable. The greater the difference in relative capital and the more of his capital the poorer of the two players bets, the greater the probability that the richer will ruin the poorer and the faster it will happen. Even though the coins will work toward 50 percent heads and 50 percent tails, the probability of "runs" of heads or tails also increases as the game progresses. The probability, for example, of a series of 10 heads being flipped consecutively in 10 trials is not great, but if one continued to flip a coin for days at a time the probability of 10 heads appearing in a row *sooner or later* actually will become rather high. If this event should be favorable to the poorer player, he will increase his capital and the richer player will be somewhat impaired, but if the series favors the richer player, the poorer can well be ruined. The richer player can expect to have his run sooner or later. That is why a gambling casino competing against small players does not even need its favorable probability to win on balance from a high proportion of its small opponents. This also helps the large commodity trader to win even more from smaller traders as time goes on. In commodity trading, as in so many other areas of financial endeavor, the nature of the game favors the rich getting richer.

Good bets. The player making a good bet, which may be referred to as favorable or positive, has in his favor a mathematical expectation of winning money each time he makes it. A game consisting of one such bet or a preponderance of them is a favorable game. (Some consider each bet a game and a series of bets would then be a series of favorable games, but the difference in semantics is of more interest to game theorists than to commodity traders.) Positive expectation merely requires some combinations of probability and payoff (including cost of playing the game) that makes the bet or game financially favorable to the player. The coin flipper, for example, may be betting even money that he can flip one head before his opponent flips two, or he may be betting that he will flip a head before his opponent flips a tail, but he will win a dollar if he wins and lose 50 cents if he loses. He may need to flip one head to win a dollar at the risk of losing one dollar if his opponent flips a tail, but he gets paid a dime for playing the game. Better still for the fortunate player such as a racetrack which has a positive expectation of winning a high proportion of wagers placed but still charges its patrons for the opportunity of entering the premises, to say nothing of collecting fees for allowing them to park their cars outside, is some combination of these favorable terms.

Bad bets. One might ask why a person would make a bad bet, that is, one in which he has a negative expectation when probability and payoffs are considered. One reason, of course, is that some players do not realize that their bets are bad or how bad they are. Others choose to play in negative games, knowing they are unfavorable, because they have motivations explained by psychological drives rather than logically based financial factors. Presumably some people find a masochistic pleasure in losing or pride themselves on their courage in playing David to the bookmaker's Goliath. Some maintain that they enjoy playing the game enough to warrant the inevitable cost of playing, but here again the subjective world of individual psychological makeup (or mixup) would have to be examined. This chapter assumes that the reader is interested in making good bets and playing favorable games.

In passing, it might be noted that there can be a high probability of eventually winning a game by ruining your opponent, even in a game in which each bet is bad, provided that it is not *too* bad and that the player making the bad bets has capital materially exceeding that of his opponent and that bets are large. This happy circumstance, however, can never accrue to a commodity trader who is trading badly because he is always small in relation to the combined size of his opponents. The large trader who tried to overcome an unfavorable approach to commodity trading would almost certainly find himself among the small traders within a reasonably short time.

Strategy for a favorable game. The commodity trader typically has, or thinks he has, a positive expected payoff, and it is that kind of game that is examined in more detail for a logical approach to ultimate victory. The reader should not treat this subject lightly. The *manner* in which he plays the commodity futures trading game is far more likely to cause his ultimate success or failure than is any other aspect of his trading, including his method of selecting trades.

It would be of considerable value if a money-management strategy applicable to all traders could be offered here. This is impossible, however. The number of possible variables in the solution of all possible trading strategy problems would extend this book into at least a five-foot shelf. Factors that would have to be considered include not only differences in personal attitudes toward profits and losses but also the specific probabilities that traders believe are inherent in the trades they select. The varying differences in probabilities of success and various ratios of profit to loss, differences in commissions, and different possible combinations of "good trades," "better trades," and "best trades" make for a huge number of possible variations. A single trader with an elaborate system of selecting trades may enter positions with wide variations in probabilities, payoffs, temporary adversity possibilities, commissions, required capital commitments, and time requirements. Too, there may be times when certain completely unexpected events create biases that were not taken into consideration and unexpectedly cause many simultaneous positions to have good or bad results at the same time. A trader, for example, may have long positions in four commodities presumed to be reacting to different forces, with all four trade entries based on apparently independent technical signals. An event may occur that will prove to be bearish on *all* commodities, and the trader will suffer four losses. Had he been short, he would have had four profits.

An individual trader facing this problem must consider the data he has available that apply to his own methods of trade selection and, even recognizing some of the subjectivity in money management and determination of probabilities, at least do his best to solve his problem logically. This is considerably better than making decisions haphazardly and hoping that everything will turn out well. The numbers that might apply to a mythical trader and what they mean to him should be a useful subject for detailed examination.

Assume that a trader has initial trading capital of $10,000. He has developed a technical trading method he believes will indicate trade opportunities that will offer a profit opportunity equal in dollars to the risk of loss when commissions and other execution costs are considered. Based on his research or experience, the trader believes that his chance for a profit on any given trade is .55 and his chance for a loss, therefore, .45. His mathematical advantage on each trade is .10. (He may feel that some trades will give him more advantage than that, but he has learned to temporize optimism and always take the conservative approach to any of his trading decisions.) It is also assumed that the trader plans to trade indefinitely rather than aim for some specific objective, no change is expected in his presumed probabilities based on his continuing research, and that his attitudes toward his gains and losses will remain unchanged as his fortunes ebb and flow. If he is successful, his gains could range between reasonably satisfactory and huge, depending on the frequency of his trades. As he proceeds from his research into real-time trading, the trader should be alert to bench marks to make sure that he is on course.

Real-time validation. As has been indicated, life in the real world has a way of being more difficult than paper trading has shown it should be. The trader implementing his untested plans should make some effort to be sure that he is "on course." The statistics will vary with the plan being used, results expected, and degrees of variation from the expected acceptable to the trader, but at some point a method counted on to yield a given number of profits should begin yielding them.

The trader who anticipates a 10 percent advantage could make use of the figures in Table 10-1. This table can help to show him how many losses he should have suffered in a given number of trades. Suppose, for example, that he has taken three losses in his first five trades and is concerned because he believes he should have had only two. The first line of Table 10-1 indicates that he has a probability of .9497 of more than zero loses, .7438 of more than one, .4069 of more than 2, .1312 of more than three, and .0185 of losing on all five. Three losses in five trades represent more than 40 percent, and in the column headed by "40" he will note that the chance of three or more losses was .4069. Three losses in five trades, there-

TABLE 10-1   PROBABILITY OR MORE THAN p PERCENT
UNSUCCESSFUL TRADES WITH A PROBABILITY .55 OF
WINNING (10 PERCENT ADVANTAGE)*

No. of trades \ P—>	0	10	20	30	40	50	60	70	80	90	100
5	.9497		.7438		.4069		.1312		.0185		.0000
10	.9975	.9767	.9004	.7340	.4956	.2616	.1020	.0274	.0045	.0003	.0000
20	1.0000	.9991	.9811	.8701	.5857	.2493	.0580	.0064	.0003	.0000	.0000
30	1.0000	1.0000	.9960	.9306	.6408	.2309	.0334	.0016	.0000	.0000	.0000
40	1.0000	1.0000	.9993	.9717	.7376	.2624	.0283	.0007	.0000	.0000	.0000
50	1.0000	1.0000	.9998	.9835	.7615	.2385	.0165	.0002	.0000	.0000	.0000
60	1.0000	1.0000	.9999	.9903	.7820	.2180	.0097	.0001	.0000	.0000	.0000
70	1.0000	1.0000	1.0000	.9942	.7998	.2002	.0058	.0000	.0000	.0000	.0000
80	1.0000	1.0000	1.0000	.9965	.8156	.1844	.0035	.0000	.0000	.0000	.0000
90	1.0000	1.0000	1.0000	.9979	.8294	.1706	.0021	.0000	.0000	.0000	.0000
100	1.0000	1.0000	1.0000	.9987	.8426	.1574	.0013	.0000	.0000	.0000	.0000
150	1.0000	1.0000	1.0000	.9999	.8909	.1091	.0001	.0000	.0000	.0000	.0000
200	1.0000	1.0000	1.0000	1.0000	.9209	.0791	.0000	.0000	.0000	.0000	.0000
250	1.0000	1.0000	1.0000	1.0000	.9440	.0560	.0000	.0000	.0000	.0000	.0000
300	1.0000	1.0000	1.0000	1.0000	.9592	.0408	.0000	.0000	.0000	.0000	.0000
400	1.0000	1.0000	1.0000	1.0000	.9778	.0222	.0000	.0000	.0000	.0000	.0000
500	1.0000	1.0000	1.0000	1.0000	.9877	.0123	.0000	.0000	.0000	.0000	.0000

* In this table and in Tables 10-2 and 10-3 probabilities shown for trades 5 through 30 were derived from binomial distributions; for 40 through 500 they were derived from normal distributions that approximate binomial distributions.

fore, should come as no great shock. By the same token, if he had lost on all five of his first five trades he should also note carefully that there was a chance of only .0185 of this happening if in fact his probability of winning had been .55. Some traders might go back to their paper trading for a while, even at this early juncture, but others might go on trading despite the uncomfortable odds of more than 50–1 that the real world is not doing what their paper worlds said it should. If after 30 trades such a trader has had more than 18 losses (more than .60, hence $P = 60$) he will know that he is still in an unpleasant area with only a .0334 chance of being right, and if he has had more than 21 losses the chance of his being on a satisfactory course is an almost ridiculous .0016. As he approaches his hundredth trade, his percentage of losses should be clearly closing in on the expected .45. The chance of anything over .50 losses at this level is only .1574, over .60, only .0013, and over .70, statistically approaches the impossible.

Tables 10-2 and 10-3 provide the same information for traders who believe that they have probability advantages of .20 (.60–.40) or .30 (.65–.35). Traders with greater advantages have an inkling much sooner than those with smaller advantages whether they are on course, and at each level the chance of their judging correctly whether they are on course is higher than those with smaller advantages at the same level. A trader with a .30 advantage, for example, who has traded 100 times and who has had more than 50 losses knows that there are only eight chances in 1,000 that his real-world trading is in line with his researched expectations.

A trader following his program has two tasks in the area of validation.

TABLE 10-2   PROBABILITY OF MORE THAN p PERCENT
UNSUCCESSFUL TRADES WITH A PROBABILITY .60 OF
WINNING (20 PERCENT ADVANTAGE)

No. of trades	$P \longrightarrow$ 0	10	20	30	40	50	60	70	80	90	100
5	.9222		.6630		.3174		.0870		.0102		.0000
10	.9940	.9537	.8328	.6178	.3670	.1663	.0548	.0123	.0017	.0001	.0000
20	1.0000	.9964	.9491	.7501	.4045	.1277	.0222	.0017	.0001	.0000	.0000
30	1.0000	.9997	.9829	.8238	.4216	.0972	.0083	.0002	.0000	.0000	.0000
40	1.0000	.9999	.9951	.9017	.5000	.0983	.0049	.0001	.0000	.0000	.0000
50	1.0000	1.0000	.9981	.9256	.5000	.0744	.0019	.0000	.0000	.0000	.0000
60	1.0000	1.0000	.9992	.9430	.5000	.0570	.0008	.0000	.0000	.0000	.0000
70	1.0000	1.0000	.9997	.9561	.5000	.0439	.0003	.0000	.0000	.0000	.0000
80	1.0000	1.0000	.9999	.9661	.5000	.0339	.0001	.0000	.0000	.0000	.0000
90	1.0000	1.0000	.9999	.9736	.5000	.0264	.0001	.0000	.0000	.0000	.0000
100	1.0000	1.0000	1.0000	.9794	.5000	.0206	.0000	.0000	.0000	.0000	.0000
150	1.0000	1.0000	1.0000	.9938	.5000	.0062	.0000	.0000	.0000	.0000	.0000
200	1.0000	1.0000	1.0000	.9981	.5000	.0019	.0000	.0000	.0000	.0000	.0000
250	1.0000	1.0000	1.0000	.9994	.5000	.0006	.0000	.0000	.0000	.0000	.0000
300	1.0000	1.0000	1.0000	.9998	.5000	.0002	.0000	.0000	.0000	.0000	.0000
400	1.0000	1.0000	1.0000	1.0000	.5000	.0000	.0000	.0000	.0000	.0000	.0000
500	1.0000	1.0000	1.0000	1.0000	.5000	.0000	.0000	.0000	.0000	.0000	.0000

TABLE 10-3   PROBABILITY OF MORE THAN p PERCENT
UNSUCCESSFUL TRADES WITH A PROBABILITY .65 OF
WINNING (30 PERCENT ADVANTAGE)

No. of trades \ P →	0	10	20	30	40	50	60	70	80	90	100
5	.8840		.5716		.2352		.0540		.0053		.0000
10	.9865	.9140	.7384	.4862	.2485	.0949	.0262	.0048	.0005	.0000	.0000
20	.9998	.9879	.8818	.5834	.2376	.0532	.0060	.0031	.0000	.0000	.0000
30	1.0000	.9981	.9414	.6425	.2198	.0301	.0014	.0000	.0000	.0000	.0000
40	1.0000	.9995	.9766	.7463	.2537	.0234	.0005	.0000	.0000	.0000	.0000
50	1.0000	.9999	.9869	.7707	.2293	.0131	.0001	.0000	.0000	.0000	.0000
60	1.0000	1.0000	.9926	.7938	.2062	.0074	.0000	.0000	.0000	.0000	.0000
70	1.0000	1.0000	.9957	.8098	.1902	.0043	.0000	.0000	.0000	.0000	.0000
80	1.0000	1.0000	.9975	.8258	.1742	.0025	.0000	.0000	.0000	.0000	.0000
90	1.0000	1.0000	.9986	.8401	.1599	.0014	.0000	.0000	.0000	.0000	.0000
100	1.0000	1.0000	.9992	.8527	.1473	.0008	.0000	.0000	.0000	.0000	.0000
150	1.0000	1.0000	.9999	.9003	.0997	.0001	.0000	.0000	.0000	.0000	.0000
200	1.0000	1.0000	1.0000	.9309	.0691	.0000	.0000	.0000	.0000	.0000	.0000
250	1.0000	1.0000	1.0000	.9512	.0488	.0000	.0000	.0000	.0000	.0000	.0000
300	1.0000	1.0000	1.0000	.9653	.0347	.0000	.0000	.0000	.0000	.0000	.0000
400	1.0000	1.0000	1.0000	.9819	.0181	.0000	.0000	.0000	.0000	.0000	.0000
500	1.0000	1.0000	1.0000	.9905	.0095	.0000	.0000	.0000	.0000	.0000	.0000

One is determining statistically or by excellent judgment whether his results are approaching his expectations at various levels of real-time trading. The other is deciding on the level that will cause him to abandon this method if results are less than favorable. One trader with losses indicating only a .20 chance of his being right may continue trading, whereas a second may go back and do more research, and a third may throw up his hands in disgust and buy U.S. Treasury bills.

PROBABILITY OF RUIN

Conceptual foundation. Success presents few problems to most traders; it is the loss of trading capital, or ruin, that must be considered primary. Consideration of ruin demands an early and one of the most critical decisions in the area of money management. The risk of ruin in favorable games increases directly as more of the available trading capital is utilized for each trade. Increasingly conservative approaches also result in less profit potential, either because less will be gained on each winning trade or because there will be fewer trades. An intelligent median must be chosen.

Assume that the trader decides to use $2,500, or one-fourth of his $10,000 capital, for each trade and plans to continue making $2,500 commitments indefinitely. His risk of ruin is heavily concentrated in the early stages of his trading program. If he loses on his first two or three trades, he is in serious trouble, and if he loses on his first four trades he is out of the trading business. The chance of his losing on his first trade is .45. His chance of losing on all four of his first four trades is only $(.45)^4$, or .04.

If he is ahead after the first four trades and finds himself with trading capital five or six times the size of his $2,500 commitments, four losses (consecutive or net) can no longer ruin him, but then he also faces an increasingly high probability of more than four net losses as he continues his trading over time. The probability R of his eventual ruin is given by the formula

$$R = \left(\frac{1 - A}{1 + A}\right)^C,$$

where A is the trader's advantage in his trades expressed in decimal form and C is the number of trading units with which he begins.[1] If a trader is willing to risk one-third of his capital in a trade, he has three initial trading units. If he risks $\frac{1}{20}$, he has 20 trading units. The trader being considered here will risk $2,500 of his $10,000 on each trade and so has four trading units when his trading begins. His chance of eventual ruin is $[(1 - .1)/(1 + .1)]^4$, or .45. He may find this number uncomfortably high and may examine his chance of succeeding if he risked only one-tenth of his capital on each trade rather than one-fourth. The trader may consider survival more important than maximizing expected profits as fast as possible but having to accept more risk to do so. Some traders, of course, may choose maximization and accept the added risk that goes with it. The risk of only $1,000 of the trader's $10,000 capital on each trade provides a dramatic example of the virtue of taking small risks if survival is the major motivation. The chance of losing all of the $10,000 capital in the first 10 trades drops to $(.45)^{10}$, or less than one chance in 3,000. Even if he continued to trade indefinitely, risking $1,000 on every trade in order to gain $1,000, his chance of ruin would be only .1341. The probability of success on any given trade has remained unchanged, but the trader's chance of survival has increased from .55 to .87 merely by his trading on a more conservative scale.

One of the most difficult and important decisions to be made by the trader is what to do if his account grows on schedule, thereby further indicating that his favorable research projections were correct. If his original capital of $10,000 has grown to $20,000, his chance of being ruined if he continues trading on a scale of $1,000 has become much smaller than the original .1341 because it would now take 20 net losses rather than 10 to ruin him. The probability of this happening is only .018. The chance of his continuing to add to his capital over time becomes more and more certain as it builds in size if he does not greatly increase his scale of trading. Having reached $20,000, the chance of reaching $30,000 is even greater, and having reached $70,000, say, the chance of then reaching $80,000

---

[1] William Feller, *An Introduction to Probability Theory and its Applications*, John Wiley & Sons, New York, 1957. A good source of basic probability theory is Samuel Goldberg, *Probability: An Introduction*, Prentice-Hall, Englewood Cliffs, N.J., 1960.

is even greater still. On the other hand, when the trader reached $20,000, he could have become more aggressive. He could have begun trading $20,000 with the same degree of probability of reaching $40,000 as he originally had of reaching $20,000 from $10,000. The chance R of being ruined before reaching a higher specified level from any given starting point is provided by the formula

$$R = \frac{\left[(1 + A)/(1 - A)\right]^{W} - 1}{\left[(1 + A)/(1 - A)\right]^{C + W} - 1},$$

where A is the trader's advantage, C is the original trading capital expressed in trading units, and W is the number of those same sized units he hopes to accumulate.[2] In the case of the trader being considered in detail here, his original capital is $10,000, which represents 10 trading units. With his .10 advantage his chance of getting to $20,000 successfully is .8815. If he arrives at the $20,000 level and chooses to try for $40,000 by using $2,000 units of trading, his chance of arriving at $40,000 is again .8815. Each time he doubles his money, he will have the same chance of doubling it again by doubling his trading units. This assumes that he will not eventually find himself trading on a scale that will raise market liquidity problems, thereby decreasing his assumed .10 advantage, or that he will pass his "stress point" and damage his judgment. Such a program may seem quite exciting because a trader has to double his original $10,000 only seven times to accumulate $1,280,000. Before he is too quick to give up his virtual certainty of continuing to accumulate money (if he never raises his scale of trading) he should realize that if he doubles his scale of trading his overall risk of ruin will increase considerably. The chance of success in seven successive series with a chance of .8815 of winning each series is $(.8815)^7$ and the chance of ruin is $1 - (.8815)^7$ or an uncomfortable .5866. Even this may be exaggerating the real chance of success because (a) the presumed .10 advantage may have some high hopes mixed in with the research; (b) independence of results often does not exist, which makes runs of "bad luck" more likely than the computed probabilities would indicate; and (c) the growth of execution costs and market liquidity problems, as capital grows, becomes increasingly likely.

A trader must work out his own probabilities, given his own facts, judgments, and attitudes, but it may be of interest to note in Table 10-4 the probabilities faced by traders with advantages of 10, 20, and 30 percent in their favor on each trade, including all costs, with payoffs equaling losses. The effects of different sizes of commitments and the length of time during which trading is planned to continue become quite clear; for example, if a trader has an assumed 10 percent advantage, capital of $10,000, and a plan to risk $2,000 (one-fifth of his capital; hence his capital represents five original trading units), with payoff and dollar risk also $2,000, and expects

[2] *Ibid.*

TABLE 10-4   TRADER'S CHANCE OF RUIN WHEN HE HAS A
.10, .20, OR .30 ADVANTAGE ATTEMPTING EITHER TO
DOUBLE HIS INITIAL CAPITAL OR TRADE INDEFINITELY

C	W	.10 advantage probability of		.20 advantage probability of		.30 advantage probability of	
		success	ruin	success	ruin	success	ruin
1	1	55	45	60	40	65	35
1	∞	18.2	81.8	33.3	66.7	46.2	53.8
2	2	59.9	40.1	69.2	30.8	77.5	22.5
2	∞	33.1	66.9	55.6	44.4	71.0	29.0
3	3	64.6	35.4	77.1	22.9	86.5	13.5
3	∞	45.2	54.8	70.4	29.6	84.4	15.6
4	4	69.1	30.9	83.5	16.5	92.2	7.8
4	∞	55.2	44.8	80.2	19.8	91.6	8.4
5	5	73.2	26.8	88.4	11.6	95.7	4.3
5	∞	63.3	36.7	86.8	13.2	95.5	4.5
6	6	76.9	23.1	91.9	8.1	97.6	2.4
6	∞	70.0	30.0	91.2	8.8	97.6	2.4
7	7	80.3	19.7	94.5	5.5	98.7	1.3
7	∞	75.5	24.5	94.2	5.8	98.7	1.3
8	8	83.3	16.7	96.2	3.8	99.3	.7
8	∞	79.9	20.1	96.1	3.9	99.3	.7
9	9	85.9	14.1	97.5	2.5	99.6	.4
9	∞	83.6	16.4	97.4	2.6	99.6	.4
10	10	88.1	11.9	98.3	1.7	99.8	.2
10	∞	86.6	13.4	98.3	1.7	99.8	.2
11	11	90.1	9.9	98.9	1.1	99.9	.1
11	∞	89.0	11.0	98.9	1.1	99.9	.1
12	12	91.7	8.3	99.2	.8	99.9	.1
12	∞	91.0	9.0	99.2	.8	99.9	.1

Key: C, trader's initial capital in units; W, the number of additional units the trader is attempting to gain; the symbol "∞" indicates that the trader expects to trade indefinitely. Format of this table was derived from Edward O. Thorp, *Beat the Dealer*, Random House, 1962, p. 63.

to trade indefinitely, his chance of success would be .633 and his chance of ruin .367. If he reduced his exposure and objective on each trade to $1,000, his chance of long-term success would increase to .866 and his chance of ruin would drop to .134. If a trader thought that his advantage was .30 (.65 − .35) his chance of ruin, risking only one-tenth of this capital and trading indefinitely without increasing his scale of trading, if successful, would be a minuscule .002. It should be obvious that a greater advantage vastly increases the chance of success in trading, just as it does in gambling, but it should now also be obvious that a trader with less probability of success but trading conservatively can actually have a better chance of long-term success (winning the game) than a trader with a higher probability of success who chooses to trade more aggressively. The trader with .30 advantage, using one-fourth of his initial capital on each trade, faces a chance of ruin of a little more than .08. The trader with only a .10 advantage, however, can achieve about the same low risk merely by trading in units of one-twelfth of his capital. The outlook for the time that it would take for each to make important profits, assuming success, would vary considerably.

Multiple positions. The problem of how much of a trader's available capital should be committed to one trade is compounded when he decides to add lines to an original position. This may occur when he follows a program of averaging or when he believes that he has a new reason for taking a position beyond that already existing. This might happen, for example, when a chartist is following various signals and notes a second signal which indicates that he should enter a position when he already has a similar one based on a previous chart signal. He might conclude that these signals should be treated separately and distinctly or even that the second signal will reinforce the first and make its favorable outcome more certain. This situation deserves some thoughtful consideration before it is carried too far. No reason for adding units to an open trade makes a favorable outcome certain. A large number of signals all followed will eventually cause a trader to hold a position so large that an unfavorable outcome will ruin him.

To deal with this situation, which results in great opportunity accompanied as usual by great risk, the trader should consider a protective policy. One such policy might be a limitation on the number of multiple lines to be accepted. This, in turn, will depend on how large his trading capital is and how great a risk he thinks each unit entails. A trader who risks only 2 percent of his capital on each line will still be risking only about 8 percent on four lines of the same commodity. An 8 percent loss is painful but not disastrous. A trader who risks 15 percent on a line, however, would find himself with a loss of about 60 percent if all four lines failed.

Stop-loss points. When the trader has determined how much risk he is willing to face in a trade, he has a starting point from which he will determine his stop-loss level and, hopefully, place an actual stop-loss order. If he believes that a logical stop loss can be placed at a point involving less than his acceptable maximum risk, the closer stop, is, of course, to be preferred. Placing stops may involve many criteria, some of which are regarded as important by some traders but not by others. It would appear that there are two considerations that cannot be ignored by any trader. First is the amount of money that would be lost if the stop were violated. Second is the current price volatility of the commodity being traded. In regard to the first of these points, whether the stop points themselves are based on the current market price of a commodity, the margin required, a chart point, or the day of the month multiplied by the phase of the moon, the number of dollars of loss, including execution costs, can easily be expressed as a percentage of the trader's capital. The trader should also have an informed idea of the maximum number of net losses he may reasonably have to suffer, based on his experience or research. If he risks so much that reasonable adversity will ruin him, his route is suicidal. It should be reiterated that ruin does not consist of a series of losses but rather a series in which the number of losses exceeds the number of profits by enough to cause ruin, regardless of their order; for example, if a trader with $4,000 risks a total of $1,000 on each trade, he will be ruined if he loses four times in a row. He will be just as ruined, however, by a bad period during which he has four patterns of one profit followed by two losses. He will have four profits, eight losses, and no money, even though he never had more than two losses in a row. Because an adverse series becomes increasingly likely as trading is carried on over time, it is obvious why trading too large a position is so deadly.

The second point that must be considered by any trader determining his stop points is the degree of volatility in the markets he is trading. Traders who base their stops on current prices or chart patterns must take into consideration how logical stop-loss points may change drastically as commodities trade at higher or lower levels or current volatility becomes greater or less. Stop-loss levels should be adjusted to recent volatility, but even this must be defined by the trader on a logical and validated basis. Is "current" defined as the range of prices for the last week, month, six months, or something else? Of course, next week may prove to be greatly different from last week, but this is an unavoidable risk that always accompanies speculation. Volatility, like most of the vital data in commodity trading, is fluid and nonstationary, unlike the more stable mass of data to be considered by coin flippers, poker players, and dice shooters. The importance of stop-loss strategy cannot be overestimated. This element of strategy will affect the trader's mathematical expectation in the following manner. If the stop loss is placed far from the current price, the probability of losing will be small but the amount of the loss may be large. If the stop loss is placed close to the current price, the probability of losing will be greater but the amount of the loss will be small. Consistently placing stops too close and getting stopped out in "noise" areas or placing stops so far away that the inevitable losses will be unreasonably large will lead to almost certain ruin.

Strategy following significant success. When an account has grown impressively, a trader has a difficult decision to make, but it cannot be avoided. If a $10,000 account has grown, on schedule, to $20,000, which was the objective hoped for when trading in commodity futures was started, the action to be taken is obvious. A check is requested, deposited in a convenient Savings and Loan institution, and the commodity account is closed. If, however, the trader is thinking in terms of acquiring a chateau in France, a chauffeured limousine, and a cellar of Rothschild wines, he must prepare for the next phase of his trading. Again, no definitive course of action acceptable by all traders can be marked out here, but the alternatives are clear. The trader can leave well enough alone and continue trading in the same way and on the same scale as he had before. Now that he has

$20,000, however, he may be concerned that if he trades on the same scale as he did when he had only $10,000 half of his new level of capital will appear to be idle. If he chooses instead to double his scale of trading, he can achieve his ultimate goals faster, if he reaches them at all, but with the usual added risk and stress. If he doubles his commitments to each trade in his effort to reach $40,000 from $20,000 as rapidly as he reached $20,000 from $10,000, he risks finding himself back at $10,000 in only half that time. After all, it took 10 net successful trades, each yielding a $1,000 gain to reach $20,000, but it would take only five net trades, each resulting in a $2,000 loss, to bring his trading capital back down to $10,000. A delicate balance of probabilities and personal feelings must be considered by each trader at critical points such as these and decisions made according to his own mix of knowledge and emotions.

Strategy following significant adversity. Even presuming that a trader's basic method is viable, if adversity precedes success, he would find his position difficult. The fact that failure came first does not ensure that success is inevitable after that point. All that is completely certain is that his capital is impaired. If he continues to take risks similar to those he has already taken, the chance of ruin becomes ever greater. Most traders would choose to employ a defensive strategy, but here again there is a price to pay.

A defensive strategy can consist basically of one of two courses of action. One is the elimination of trades, for the time being, that have the least chance of success. The other is the elimination of any trades that require the risk of too many dollars in relation to the lower level of the account. Of the two the second would appear to be the better. Regardless of the quality of a trade, the probability of success is never 1 and therefore there is always some chance of loss. Furthermore, trades with knowingly poor ratios of success to failure would never be utilized, regardless of the condition of the account. The range between the most acceptable and least acceptable trades for the typical trader is not wide, considering all the uncertainties of trading. It is unlikely that any trade can ever have much more than a .8 probability of success, and it is also unlikely that a trader would be willing to accept knowingly a trade below about .65 (assuming in both cases an even money payoff). This practical range of only about .15 does not provide much room to maneuver.

If there is a limit on dollar risk in relation to the total number of dollars in the account in a given trade, then trades exceeding this risk can of course be eliminated, but this will reduce the number of trades available to recover the dollars lost, and recovering money lost may take longer than losing it in the first place. If the trades with smaller risks also have smaller profit potentials, as is likely, the trader must again face an ugly statistic. He might have lost half his money by having a series of trades yield 10 net losses and have followed with a new series yielding 10 net profits only to find that he was only halfway back to his original level of capital because his profits were smaller than his losses. A loss of 60 percent from a given level requires a profit of 150 percent merely to get even. Profits of 150 percent are not easy to achieve, getting even is not the most exciting goal, and, of course, the trades entered to attempt recovery would themselves entail the risk of further loss.

Systems. The trader, like the gambler, should learn early the fruitlessness of wasting his time and money trying to profit from a game with a negative expectation by the use of some clever strategy. It is to be hoped that a trader's research has resulted in some method of selecting trades that will yield better results than random selections. The mathematical expectation of a game is not affected by the strategy of varying the size of individual bets. If a trader has a valid method that yields on the average 65 wins for 35 losses in a series of independent trials, he will have the same ratio of wins to losses, regardless of his betting strategy, and no system of risking more or less, depending on the result of his recent trades, will change the ratio. If a game is fair, it will remain fair; if it has a positive expectation, it will remain positive, and, if negative, it will remain negative, and the latter two will maintain their biases with no change in degree.[3] No mechanical system can change probabilities one iota.

Money management "systems" designed to overcome a negative expectation in any game, whether trading or gambling, are usually based on some common misconceptions about the statistical law of large numbers, itself frequently incorrectly called the "law of averages." The designers of systems almost invariably depend on some theory that numbers will average out in time to yield profits. A coin having fallen tails a number of times owes some heads, and so one should bet on heads to take advantage of the certainty that the average number of heads flipped will approach 50 percent of all flips sooner or later. A coin, however, has neither a memory nor a conscience, and one may overlook the significance of the difference between percentages and absolute numbers. Certainly, as the coin is flipped longer and longer, the percentage of heads or tails flipped will inevitably approach 50, but not because a short-term series of tails will be immediately followed by a series of heads. Rather, in the long run, the law of large numbers declares that a large number of subsequent trials will overwhelm any apparent aberrations in any part of the series. In a word, as a game is played longer and longer, the *percentage* of wins and losses will inevitably approach the statistical expectation, but seemingly unusual differences will occur just as inevitably. A pattern of 100 flips of a coin alternating precisely from heads to tails would be almost as miraculous as a consecutive series of 100 heads or 100 tails. This means that streaks of luck (both good and bad) are expectations, not aberrations.

Although variation in the sizes of bets will not change the statistical chance of ultimately winning or losing the game (if the size of bets is varied),

[3] Richard A. Epstein, *The Theory of Gambling and Statistical Logic,* Academic Press, 1967, p. VII. Some of the conclusions that follow were drawn in part from this same scholarly reference, especially in its section entitled, "The Basic Theorems," pp. 58–93.

the ultimate amount of money won or lost and the time it will take to win or lose could be affected. This, however, results entirely from the different average level of capital involved in the game, not a change in the probability of winning or losing on each game or trade. A betting system intended to overcome the disadvantage of a basically bad bet is sometimes called the "gambler's fallacy," and it could be called the "commodity trader's fallacy" just as well. The number of commodity traders who have spent good money for systems and who have lost money following them is legion, as is the number of gamblers who have followed the same ruinous path.

Betting and trading systems are sought with more zeal than are quests for perpetual motion machines and sources of everlasting youth. The chance of finding a reasonably simple system that will consistently "beat the odds" is no greater than satisfying a craving for any other delusion, but the idea refuses to be laid peacefully to rest. There will probably always be men who believe that the coin being flipped, having yielded a series of heads, is due for tails, the clear fallacy of the "maturity of the chances" notwithstanding.[4] A series of bad trades having been suffered just as clearly will indicate to many that a series of good trades is due. Bad luck indicates that good luck is coming and vice versa as surely as a pendulum will retrace its path. This idea of retribution or symmetry permeates philosophical thinking throughout history, back to the ancient Chinese, and will probably influence the actions of gamblers and traders as long as dice roll and people trade in securities and commodities.

All systems, regardless of their complexity, are based on wagering or trading that depends on the outcome of previous trials. Some of these systems, which involve multiplicative, additive, or linear betting, can become extremely complex, but the basic premise remains the same. Linear systems have a fixed additive constant. Additive systems increase stakes at an arithmetic rate. Multiplicative systems increase bets geometrically, depending on the immediately preceding result. One of the best known geometric systems is the "Martingale." The Martingale system has many proponents because many people who have used the system have won games and credit the system with the win, whereas actually all it has done is offer a high probability of small gains and a small probability of a large loss. If the system is used for a long period of time, however, the chance of suffering a large loss becomes greater. If the game is continued indefinitely, the large loss becomes certain. The basic idea behind Martingale (or any other progression system) is that bet sizes will be increased each

---

[4] The "maturity of the chances" is a doctrine that, in effect, attempts to assign dependence to basically independent events by attributing to them a memory that they lack by definition. A roulette player may, for example, bet on black after four consecutive reds have come up because a black "is due." The poker player, having failed to complete the last few straights and flushes that he tried for, believes that the next one will be achieved almost with certainty. The horse player may play the favorite each time three favorites in a row have lost because, after all, most of them should win each afternoon.

time a bet is lost until a win covers the most recent string of losses and leaves the player even or ahead; for example, a player who loses one unit can follow by betting two. Therefore, if he wins, he is ahead one unit, and if he loses he will be behind three. If he wins, he will bet one unit and start a new series. If he loses he will bet four units. If he wins, he will be ahead a total of one unit and start a new series. If he loses, he will be behind seven units and will bet eight. Sooner or later he will win, and when he does, he will be ahead one unit for his series. He therefore figures to win one unit for each series, although some series will be longer than others.

The Martingale player soon finds out, however, that he is caught between two bet (or trade) limitations; the lower and the upper. If the least he can bet or use as margin is reasonably close to the upper limit, it will not take many progressive increases of his bets following losses to equal or exceed the upper limit. In gambling the lower and upper limits are determined by the casino. In trading the lower limit is determined by the margin requirement and the upper by the capital or stress point of the trader or liquidity problems in markets; hence good results as bets become larger become increasingly unlikely. The time required for a progression to become unreasonable in trading is undoubtedly shorter than in gambling and the time available even in gambling is too short in itself for long-term success to be expected. The gambler forced to double his $1 bet in a series of 20 losses would have to risk more than a million dollars to have the opportunity of winning his series on the twenty-first bet. This is ludicrous enough even without considering that minimum bets must often exceed $1 and that a house limit often restricts the maximum to about $500. The ninth loss of a geometrically increased $2 bet would carry the player past a $500 house limit. The player might argue that nine losses in a row are highly unlikely. This is true for any particular series of nine bets, but the player who continues playing for a long period will almost certainly have nine losses in a row sooner or later, as will the commodity trader.

The system player would do well to test his system against a random number table. If ostensibly it can, say, double his capital before he loses it with a high degree of probability in a game involving many independent events, merely by "betting smart" he should be able to beat the random number table in a paper game by doubling his capital three or four times in long games before he is ruined. (A person who did this and published his results would have the first such publication in history.[5])

Size of commitments. Despite the fact that varying the size of commitments will not change probabilities, it could well change an outcome by ending the game sooner or later than might otherwise be the case. The trader, as well as the gambler, must be vitally concerned with loss of the

---

[5] An elaborate discussion of systems may be found in Allen N. Wilson, *The Casino Gambler's Guide,* Harper and Row, 1970, pp. 234–258. The mathematics of system fallacies is covered in Epstein, *loc. cit.*

money he has available for trading because its loss eliminates any chance of winning or even trading unless he can later replace his capital. In a word, ruin precludes success and must be avoided if at all possible. Sizing of commitments according to the nature of the game has a vital effect on the possibility of ruin. The correct guiding principles may surprise many traders and gamblers. For fair or unfavorable games, the strategy of betting should be aggressive, and for favorable games the approach should be conservative.

If a commodity trader who regarded commodity trading as a basically losing game intended to take only one position and had a specific money objective in mind, his best strategy would be precisely the same as that of a gambler facing the same problem. If the expectation of a profit is negative or zero, but the game is still to be played for some reason, the best chance available to reach the objective is obtained by making a large commitment and playing the game only once. Of course, the capital might be lost and the objective not reached, but the probability of reaching the objective is less for any other strategy. As one decreases the size of one's commitments in an unfavorable game, the chance of eventually reaching one's objective becomes ever smaller and the chance of ruin greater.

The informed commodity trader, unlike the gambler who competes against a casino's odds, is presumed to be playing a favorable game against a far better capitalized adversary (the market) and should wager accordingly. His wisest policy is simple. *He should trade on a small scale.* The specific amounts risked, of course, depend on the size of his capital, his objectives, and how long he expects to continue his trading. If he intends to trade indefinitely, his positions should be modest in relation to his capital, and errors should be made on the conservative side. Because the probabilities favor his winning in the long run, his primary objective in the management of his capital is to make every effort to *reach* the long run. The best way to defeat himself is to risk so much that he cannot realistically recover from adversity on one trade or a series of bad trades. Regardless of how good the odds are, there is some chance of losing, and there is a certainty of periods of severe adversity even when the system used is valid and the expectation favorable. The longer a game is played, the more inevitable such periods of adversity become. Adverse runs should not be surprising. They are to be expected and should be planned for. The best way is to expose so little capital that ruin will not be the result when nothing seems to go right.

The trader who maintains that his research is valid and that he has a positive expectation on every trade may argue that he could afford to risk one-fourth of his capital on every trade because the chance of his losing four times in a row is quite small. He would be correct in making this assertion, but he should think further before engaging in such an aggressive course. The chance of losing four times in a row, even with favorable probabilities, becomes quite high after several series and after a long series is virtually certain. Even worse is the fact that the trader does not need four losses in a row to be ruined, but only one point in his series of trades at which he has lost on four trades *on balance*. Even with a high expectation of success on any given trade, his chance of surviving a long game without being net loser by four trades at any given time would be poor. If the capital risked were reduced from one-fourth to one-tenth, the chance of being ruined on any series of 10 trades would be infinitesimal and his chance of surviving a long series of trades would become high. In any case, the trader must determine the size of his commitments by his probability estimates, the payoffs, and his own degree of optimism of what his trading talent is worth.

In summary, frequent small commitments in a favorable game will almost certainly yield an ultimate profit, whereas continued large percentage commitments will almost certainly cause ruin. In an unfavorable game large commitments made over a short duration provide the only chance of winning and the best expectation (or rather the least bad expectation) results from playing once. One who is ahead in a game with a negative expectation may be said to be losing at a negative rate. If one with a dollar to risk insists on playing a slot machine, his best strategy is to bet his entire dollar in a one-dollar machine and then quit, win or lose, rather than put 20 nickels in a nickel machine.

The inviting, but usually fatal, temptation to bet too heavily in favorable games is probably what leads so often to the most usual type of overtrading; that is, risking too much of one's capital on any one trade. The other types of overtrading, which include trading too many positions at the same time or trading too often, may also cause severe damage, but trading on too large a scale is probably worst of all.

NOTES FROM A TRADER

If money management now appears to be an area that requires considerable thought, full of dilemmas and contradiction, and generally quite frustrating to the reader, he has made real progress. The first step in solving this problem, like most others, is to recognize its existence and face up to it. Ignoring it merely because its solution is difficult and indefinite and relying instead on blind luck is hardly an intelligent alternative.

Money management principles contain so many decisions that must be determined by each trader for himself that no specific program adequate for all traders can ever be devised. This does not mean, however, that some basic principles that are useful for all cannot be suggested. Some poker players like to bluff frequently and others seldom or never. There are winners to be found among those belonging to either school, most of whom think that those who do not agree do not know how to play poker. Those holding either conviction, however, cannot possibly make money by consistently drawing to bad hands and paying more for the privilege than the hand is worth. There are rules that must be followed by all traders and gamblers if they are to live long enough in the world of games to reach the long run while still solvent. Most of these rules for basic survival are to be found in the area of money management, in which few traders are especially interested, rather than in the area of trade selection, which is the basic interest of most of them.

A wise principle of money management is to make mistakes on the side of the too conservative. It is better to accumulate money too slowly than to lose one's trading capital quickly. If debating whether to buy one unit or two, buy one. If debating whether to take a position, pass it by. As an account grows, consider withdrawing some or all of the profits. If aggressiveness is desired, the number of dollars risked can increase as the account grows, but the percentage risk can be held unchanged or even reduced at the same time. The unexpected always seems to be costly rather than profitable. A trader who assumes that he will be right 65 times out of every 100 trades he makes each year assumes that he can look forward to about 30 winning trades net in the next year (65—35). Somehow a considerable number of things will go wrong. If he has a hundred trades and the number of net wins is not 30, it will almost certainly be smaller. He might find himself with only 20 net profitable trades instead of 30. Execution costs will be higher than expected, especially because bad trades will go further through his stops that he thought reasonable, but the less frequent windfall profits that should logically compensate seem rarely to arrive on time, and then they are smaller or more infrequent than had been anticipated. Errors will almost always impair results and rarely improve them. Oversleeping and missing the opening of the market will not cause one to miss a position that opens unfavorably, but a market that opens within a satisfactory range and then moves toward the trader's objective without any retracement is likely to result in an opportunity lost forever. If the market opens sharply in the anticipated direction, even the trader who wakes up on time may be inclined to wait and try to enter it at a more favorable level. If the market provides the hoped-for adversity, the trader will enter some trades that will work and some that will not. If adversity never comes, however, only the good trades can be missed, not the bad ones. With all this the trader might consider himself lucky to find himself with only about 10 net good trades remaining to make his year profitable. Even the most favorable "trading system" will depend for its ultimate favorable results on a surprisingly few net good trades. It does not take many errors (bad luck) to miss them. Furthermore, 65 correct decisions in a hundred was probably an overly optimistic estimate in the first place.

It is interesting to observe the way most commodity traders play the commodity trading game in relation to the possible ways that money games can be played:

1. The most effective approach to the objective of maximizing results is to play a favorable game on a small scale.

2. Less desirable, but still providing a reasonable chance of success, is playing a favorable game on a large scale with enough profits coming early in the game to avoid ruin.

3. A basically unfavorable game may yield profitable results (presuming that one insists on playing unfavorable games) if one plays seldom and bets heavily.

4. The only road that leads inevitably to disaster is playing an unfavorable game continuously.

The trader who trades on impulse or some other invalid method of making trading decisions is following the fourth route—which is crowded with bumper-to-bumper traffic.

Some of Finagle's laws as applied to speculators and market researchers are especially valuable to traders concerned with money management[6]:

1. If anything can go wrong with a research project, it will.

2. No matter what the result, there is always someone willing to fake a better one.

3. No matter what the result, there is always someone eager to misinterpret it.

4. No matter what occurs, there is always someone who believes it happened according to his pet theory.

5. In any collection of data the figure that is most obviously correct—beyond all need of checking—is the mistake.

6. Even if it is impossible to derive a wrong number, still a way will be found to do it.

In the area of money management, as in no other, the trader should beware of self-deceit. The successful trader does not lie to himself. He does not substitute hope for facts. Fagin's cynical comment in the musical production of "Oliver" is quite appropriate for consideration by an economically motivated trader attempting to evaluate the money management program he has been using. "In this world, one thing counts; in the bank, large amounts."

---

[6] Compiled in the original form by John W. Campbell, Jr., late editor of *Analog Science Fiction Magazine*.

Losers and Winners

In every game there are winners and losers. The scorecard in the commodity futures game, which is brutally simple, consists merely of a credit or debit in a trading account over a period of time long enough to exclude luck, either good or bad, from playing a prominent role. Because more speculators lose than win, the section title makes allowance for that sobering fact by reversing the consideration of the outcomes.

Chapter 11, "The Commodity School for Losers," creates satirical composites of the classic losers. Habits that reinforce unsuccessful trading results are examined with tongue in cheek in the hope that familiarity will breed a determination to avoid the losers' line-up.

Chapter 12, "Maxims: Good and Bad," subjects the conventional wisdom of market lore to critical analysis. That there are platitudes to reinforce any position the trader desires to take should not surprise the reader. Rather, the study of market maxims underlines the innate desire of many traders to avoid coming to grips with the actual behavior of commodity futures prices and the implications of that behavior for their own.

Chapter 13 "Who Wins? Who Loses? Why?" concludes the section by focusing for careful study on the returns to the players of the commodity futures game. Hedgers, large speculators, and small traders reflect varying trading results in the long run. Studies are examined to shed light on the question of the distribution of profits and losses and the skills employed by the winners. These skills involve behavioral as well as analytical competence, and one systematic approach to understanding the role of feelings and thoughts is presented.

The Commodity School for Losers

The capacity of the human mind to resist the intrusion of new knowledge is infinite.

INTRODUCTION

Some commodity traders learn their lessons at the School of Experience early and well. They go on to realize profits and enjoy the exciting dynamics to be found in the world of commodities. Others never learn much of anything and spend their lives at the Commodity School for Losers repeating the same mistakes or happily discovering minor variations. This school has campuses in most areas of the world and traces its beginnings to the seekers of lodestones and to Dutch traders of tulip bulbs. It might help future commodity traders who wish to avoid attending the school to interview members of the present student body who have been attempting to graduate, unsuccessfully, for many years.

THE STUDENT BODY

Herbert Hoyle has had more friends, relatives, and counterparts at the school than anyone else. Herbert himself enrolled as a student more than 40 years ago just after averaging up his security holdings on a 20 percent margin, starting in August 1929. He has spent all the years since trying to develop a simple set of mechanical rules (secret, of course) that will help him to achieve a substantial profit each year at a constant rate while using a small amount of capital and entailing virtually no risk. Herbert became seriously interested in his project some years ago when he noticed

277

that his rules worked spectacularly, particularly when applied carefully
to the body of historical data from which the rules had been developed.

"I noticed," says Herbert, his eyes narrowed, "that December Wheat
sold at a significantly higher price on September 8 than it had on July 20
throughout the entire period covered by my records at the time (four years).
On the July 20 following the completion of my research, I quietly bought
all the December Wheat that I could afford (5,000 bushels) but unfortunately a recent reduction in the government loan price had not been
fully discounted, and I lost 14 cents a bushel. I decided that henceforth
wheat should be bought only in years when there was no adjustment in the
loan price, and I changed my rules accordingly.

"The following year I bought wheat again on July 20 but lost 19 cents
a bushel by September 8. I noticed too late that the difference in price
between wheat and corn was wider than it had been for the last five years
and I had failed to consider the importance of this in my earlier conclusions. There was no point in abandoning my work because, of the six observations I now had, four had worked successfully and the other two could
be easily filtered out. The following year I was a little unlucky. There was
no change in the loan price, but the spread between wheat and corn prices
was even wider than it had been the year before, so I naturally did not buy
the wheat. In fact, utilizing the information I had gained, I sold it short
instead. When it rose 47 cents a bushel by September 8 with no reaction
greater than $\frac{1}{4}$ cent a bushel, I was a little disappointed, of course, but then
I suddenly realized the significance of the late Lenten season which obviously cancels out the effect of the wheat-corn spread. Of my seven observations, actually five had worked, although I did not benefit by the latest
one and two were filtered out. The eighth year was really quite upsetting.
I again bought the wheat on July 20 and it was 4 cents higher on September
8, just as I had expected in light of the narrow wheat-corn spread and early
Lent. Because of some rumor of heavy French exports in August, wheat
prices dropped more than 50 cents and before they could rally back my
margin was gone and my broker sold me out $\frac{3}{8}$ cent off the bottom. My
record, however, really is six wins in eight years with the other two years
filtered out. Now I am sure that I have all the important factors, and if I
can get $500 together before July 20 I expect to make some really important
money in the wheat market from now on, unless my creditors attach my
account again before the realizing move takes place."

Herbert's rules, including the filters and exceptions, now fill 37 type-
written pages (single-spaced) which Herbert keeps in a padlocked drawer
for security reasons along with instructions to pass the notes along to his
children in the event of his passing or being committed to an institution.

Gary Gullible finds Herbert Hoyle's scholarly fundamental approach
far too complicated and believes the soundest approach to trading is a basically simple one. Gary initially tried to achieve wealth at the horse races
after buying a book suggesting that the proper approach was to bet on the

favorites to show on the last race each day early in the season. The theory held that the winning betters would all have gone home by the last race and that the handicappers had not yet had time to evaluate sufficient data to weight the horses properly. Gary became discouraged when he realized that his profits did not equal the cost of his racetrack admissions, his parking, hotdogs, and cleaning bills for his checked sportcoat. Neither did they exceed his losses.

Gary next tried to make some money playing blackjack at Nevada gaming palaces after reading a book suggesting that it was necessary only to keep track of picture cards and fives and always double down on two nines. Unfortunately, when Gary finally screwed up enough courage to take a bus to Las Vegas, his results were not nearly so good as they had been when he dealt himself several thousand hands on his dining room table. He encountered a flinty-eyed dealer who worked with five decks of cards and dealt them from a card shoe so rapidly that Gary could not keep count. It was then that Gary turned to commodity trading.

"There is no point examining the fundamentals," Gary tells us, "because everything is reflected in prices anyhow. The most important thing is to trade only consistently with the basic trend. Never trade against the trend! When it is up, only be long. When it is down, only be short. The basic trend may be easily determined in many ways, but one of the best is with a line chart. Just draw a line along recent bottoms in a rising market or recent tops in a falling market and you have a clear picture of a market's direction and its rate of movement.

"The best way of all, though, involves the proper use of moving averages which requires some intelligence (I.Q. exceeding 55) and some knowledge of mathematics (addition and subtraction). I have discovered something really remarkable," continues Gary in a confidential tone of voice. "When you use moving averages of different time spans, like 3 days and 10 days, in markets that are moving around at all and plot these averages as lines on a chart, the 3-day line will cross the 10-day line from time to time, although I am not certain what causes this." Gary leans back in his chair to give the listener time to absorb the implications of his revelations. "In order to make the lines clear during periods of narrow price fluctuations I find it best to use colored pencils. It is wise to use chartreuse for the 3-day average and turquoise for the 10-day average. When the chartreuse line is below the turquoise line, I sell short and when it goes above I cover and go long. Of course, I get whipsawed once in a while, but at least when there is a major trend I am in the market the right way and I stay with the move until it has run its course." Unfortunately, while Gary was trading there proved to be more narrow trading markets than trending markets (which was also true before Gary began trading as well as after) so Gary has been whipped and sawed rather thoroughly. He is currently working to improve his system either by requiring sharper crossing of the lines (as measured by a plastic protractor) or by waiting for some period of time to elapse after a crossing before considering a position to be worth taking. So far the ideal period to wait has proved historically to vary from one to 254 days, but Gary believes that the key is on the chart somewhere and needs merely to be discovered. Currently he is unable to trade anyhow because he has lost two-thirds of his capital trading unsuccessfully and spent the other third on chart paper, colored pencils, and the protractor.

Fred Fantasy turned to commodity trading many years ago after suffering grievous losses trading Czarist bonds. He has become a recognized expert in the art of spreading positions to avoid realizing losses. Fred is especially pleased with his results so far this year during which he has not had a single closed loss. He believes that he is finally about to overcome the misfortunes he has borne during the last 26 years, having lost money in 25 of them. (He broke even one year when he was too busy dealing with his divorce and bankruptcy proceedings to trade). Fred has told everyone who will listen of his market successes this year during which he has had six consecutive profits. He has taken particular pains to keep three board-room acquaintances informed because he is currently trying to induce them to allow him to trade their accounts in return for 3 percent a month of their invested capital plus one-half of all closed profits unadjusted by open losses.

"In January I bought December silver," relates Fred, "because of the continuing imbalance of supply and demand, the outlook for more use of film because of the recent invention of a new type of camera, and substantial sales of a series of medals portraying famous Indian chiefs by a private mint. I was a little early, and December silver dropped 600 points, and I thought I had better buy time, so I sold March against my long December. The market dropped another 300 points, just as I thought it would, so I took my profit in the March. To take advantage of the short-term irrational weakness in the market and to protect my December position I sold a May contract. Sure enough, the market continued down and I was able to take a $200 profit in the May and managed to sell July after a further drop of only 50 points. This market has been like a money machine. I have now taken six straight profits on the short side, and now I have a no-risk position short September and still long that original December which will probably yield the greatest profit of all."

Fred proudly displays his six confirmations showing the $1,470 profits on the short-side transactions which he carries with him at all times to help him sell his managed-account program which he has recently had copyrighted as "The Fred Fantasy Infallo Program." Unfortunately the market rallied a little after Fred's seventh short sale and he now has a $150 open loss on the short September silver as well as the open loss of $2,375 on the original purchase of the December silver, but this does not dishearten Fred. He has a plan. "When the market takes its next dip, I'll cover September and stay with the December. This will give me seven profits in a row, so even if December doesn't recover I'll still have seven profits out of eight, and the random walk boys can't laugh that off." A visitor has some questions to ask Fred about some aspects of his logic as well as how he will provide the margin required to support his December position after he liquidates the September, but Fred has been led away for his daily tranquilizer injection.

William Wilde really wanted to be a gladiator but was born in the wrong place at the wrong time. Unable to realize his primary ambition, he turned to commodity trading. "This whole business is kill or be killed," says William, holding up his clenched fist and facing the emperor. "The way to beat this thing is to probe for the big one and then milk it dry." William accomplishes this by waiting until he sees what he believes to be a great opportunity and then moving in with all his resources. "The way to determine the size of an initial position is to divide your credit balance by the margin deposit required and buy all you can. When the market goes your way even a little, your base is big enough so that even the small move will create enough additional capital to pyramid quickly, and then you keep on pyramiding until you have all the money that you can carry home."

William is quite confident at the moment that he is about to achieve a great victory because he has just succeeded in replacing the $2,000 he lost by holding seven pork bellies two days too long with money he borrowed from the Credit Union and is hoping that the 25,000 bushels of wheat he intends to buy in the morning will rise quickly enough for him to repay the loan before his wife learns of it and orders him out of the house again. William's ultraconservative friend, Long E. Bonds, asks what he is going to do if wheat goes down and he finds himself in debt to the Credit Union without the means to pay back the obligation. "When the going gets tough" replies William, "the tough get going." "But," Long persists, "isn't it true that in any game in which probabilities are involved the longer you play the more certain it becomes that a series of losses will occur? And isn't it also true that you are never even prepared for the first loss, much less a series of them?" Utilizing all of his keen reasoning power, William replies, "If you can't stand the heat, stay out of the kitchen."

Marcus Mule once read in a booklet that cash and futures prices have a tendency to meet during the delivery month sooner or later. This made a tremendous impression on Marcus who ranks the importance of this bit of information somewhat above the Bill of Rights. He is currently long one contract of October live cattle which is selling 4 cents a pound below the cash price of cattle as quoted on the newswire in the brokerage office. "Someone is going to make that 4-cent difference," brays Marcus, "and it might as well be me." When Marcus placed the order with his broker, his registered representative volunteered to check with the research department in Chicago for an opinion on the potential in Marcus' trade. Although the research department was about to leave for a hamburger and a milk shake for lunch, he did take the time to reply and the broker, Tradum Offen, called Marcus back with the bad news. "In order to be sure of making the 4-cent difference," Tradum said, "You must have considered such things as location of the cattle, differences in grade, and possible problems with certification for delivery by the exchange. Also, presuming that the 4-cent difference is made up before futures trading stops in October and not after, it could be met just as well by the cash price dropping to meet the futures prices as by the futures price rising to meet the cash, in which case, you would make no money. As a matter of fact, the cash price could drop 8 cents and the futures 4 cents and you could lose." His sharp mind functioning in its usual manner, Marcus replied, "Have you a late quote on November potatoes?" "The futures business is one thing and the cash is another" continued Tradum after telling Marcus that November potatoes are limit up (Marcus is short), "It is not wise to play another man's game." "I have to move my car", replied Marcus shrewdly, "It's in a loading zone."

By the time he returned from moving his car, he had received delivery of the contract of cattle. Only then did he learn that it was the last day of trading and the cattle cannot be redelivered. Shortly thereafter one of Marcus' cattle died and two others are not looking well. Marcus still has the remainder of his contract of cattle and has spent a busy morning writing letters to the Commodity Exchange Authority, the Chicago Mercantile Exchange, Dow-Jones, and the State Consumer Frauds Division bitterly complaining of the false and misleading cash prices reported on the newswires by an incompetent wire operator and questioning how any honest trader could possibly beat a game with such unfair rules. Nothing worse has happened to Marcus since he took delivery of a carload of onions only to learn that trading had ended in that commodity forever and his onions were sprouting through the bags in which they were delivered. He did succeed in selling some of the bags to a dealer in secondhand burlap for almost as much as it cost him to have the bags deodorized. Marcus would like to tell of some other of his experiences, but he has to leave for court to fight the ticket unjustifiably placed on his car for parking in the loading zone.

Ivan Bentaken has had trouble all his life with unreasonable people. In school, whenever he was prepared for "Show and Tell" he never got called on, but when unprepared his name was invariably called. In the Little League he was called out on every play. Policemen herd him out of traffic to give him tickets, although everyone else is clearly going faster. Now he trades commodities. He recently opened his third commodity account to replace the one he has just closed with another broker whom he is suing for recommending the purchase of corn which went down 9 cents a bushel following a surprisingly bearish crop report issued two weeks after the purchase. "My broker obviously knew of the report and got me to buy the corn so he or his firm's partners could bail out," declares Ivan, his eyes blazing. "Even if he did not know it, he is derelict in his fiduciary relationship to me because he should have known it. After all, his firm claims to have a Research Department in Chicago right in the Board of Trade Building."

Having calmed down enough to discuss his trading philosophy, Ivan talks of objectives. "A $1,000 account really ought to provide an average return of several hundred dollars each month and sometimes $1,000 or more. After all, it would yield 5 percent in a Savings and Loan with no risk at all (to say nothing of the use of a notary public at no charge). If you don't get a chance for greater reward, it's foolish to take the extra risk.

"You have to be especially careful of brokers," he continues. "They are always foisting advice on you like urging you to use stops and objectives to make sure that you are always getting out of your position one way or the other. I had a big profit a few months ago, took the profit and went into another position which also resulted in a profit, but I would have made more just staying with the first position. My broker did not make a single move to stop me from switching the position. I am still waiting for the CEA to do something about it, but they won't answer my letters anymore. Three or four years ago I doubled my money in the first six months of the year, and my broker thought that was a big deal, but I had a friend who tripled his money during the same period across the street. My friend's broker is quite conservative and told me that he really only expected an annual yield of 80 percent. I figured if he only did half that well, I was certain of 40 percent so I opened an account. In spite of his virtual guarantee, I lost my money on my first two trades in only a week, so I am having my lawyer file a suit based on material misrepresentation, lack of suitability, and churning."

Eric Von Director believes acting is everything, so he bases all his trading decisions on the manner in which markets are acting during the infrequent periods when he knows what is happening. When his broker calls him with a trading suggestion, Eric checks his charts and then follows the suggestions that have acted well recently (gone in the direction of the broker's suggestion for a least one day). When he is advised to take a loss, Eric usually replies that "the market is acting as if a reversal is about to occur." When advised to take a profit, Eric studies his charts and proclaims that "it is premature to liquidate the position because the market is acting well." Because any position that shows a profit has had to act well, Eric has great difficulty in liquidating positions at a profit. Eric once read in a book that prices tend to act best just before they collapse and worst just before they rally so Eric sold the book.

A friend once suggested that Eric determine objectives and stops in advance and place orders at those points in the market, but Eric prefers to use his judgment and make decisions at points at which market action indicates he should take action. He is not disturbed by the fact that the moment he usually takes action is always one during which he happens to be in the brokerage office or on the telephone to his registered representative. "You should never place stops," intones Eric, "because they will invariably drive the market just to your stop, knock you out of your position, and then run the market just to where you thought it would go in the first place!" When asked whether his problem might not be the placement of his stops, and just who buys or sells the hundreds of contracts necessary to touch off his stops on his one or two contracts, Eric says "You just don't understand the Commodity Futures Markets." He says this with the same haughty air that his ancient ancestor, a Carthaginian general, assumed when explaining the strategy he planned to use against the approaching Romans.

Deposit N. Withdrawal believes in following a strategy of observing statistical runs. Knowing his own trading limitations, which are legion, Deposit follows the advice of his broker who is always sincere and occasionally lucky. Whenever Deposit has a series of successes with small positions, he adds money to his account and takes large positions just in time for the inevitable series of losses. Following this, he withdraws most of his capital in order to trade a minimum amount until his broker recovers his touch. "I couldn't believe it," sobs Deposit. "I no sooner withdrew part of my remaining funds than he was right nine times in a row. I had to pass up four of his suggestions and take positions in the other five only about half as big as I had taken on the way down. On one of those five, I couldn't take the adversity necessary to achieve the profit so I had a loss. The broker claims to be ahead for the year but it certainly doesn't show in my account. He claims it has something to do with money management, but I think he is misrepresenting his results." Following the advice of Ivan Bentaken, Deposit is about to make a claim against the broker for the difference between the results in his account and those he believes he should have had according to the broker's record.

Oscar Ostrich believes that all adversity is temporary. When all is going his way, Oscar can be found telling of his successes to the small group of gray men in gray suits with gravy on their ties who spend all day in the boardroom because their wives drive them from their homes. When markets go against him, however, Oscar is not there. Sometimes he can be seen walking slowly around the block, his lips moving in silent prayer, hoping to find a miraculous recovery in his positions by the time he completes the circuit. More frequently he cannot be found at all.

"If I didn't have bad luck, I would have no luck at all," he tells all who will listen. "I was doing all right until I got into those 12 contracts of May potatoes. I am usually in the boardroom or keep in constant touch with my broker so I know at all times where I am. However, I got busy and I had no time to call or even read a paper for nine days. By the time I was informed, news that the crop was 72 percent greater than expected had become known to everyone but me, and the market sold down so far that I got sold out." Someone suggests that if Oscar had placed a stop in the market, he would have suffered little, but he is busily digging a hole in the school's sandbox in order to plunge his head into it.

Wheeler Bandini is known to every registered representative in the brokerage business except the youngest and least experienced, and they will undoubtedly meet him soon. He can always be recognized by the nature of his proposals which involve unorthodox transactions, huge amounts, and considerable time, effort, and cost to the broker (all wasted). "I have

access to 8,000,000 pounds of Mexican coffee which I can place anywhere
you want within twenty-four hours" he confides, "if there is some way we
can place a hedge against it and cinch the big difference between the present futures market and my cash coffee. Of course, I would expect no margin
on the short futures position because this is a bona fide hedge." Or, "I am
in touch with a shipload of nonquota sugar being brought in by some Cuban
refugees and if we can dispose of it through your cash department I would
be glad to split the profit with you." Or, "I handle the financial affairs
of a group of 220 brain surgeons who won't make a move without my say-so.
If I open a commodity account with $3,000,000, how might we both benefit
a little from it?"

Wheeler is not a major menace except to himself when attempting to
cross the street unaided and to unsophisticated brokers so anxious to build
a profitable clientele that they accept his hallucinations at face value. This
has happened twice. In each case an account was opened and an order actually placed against Wheeler's cash positions only to have him disappear
into the night leaving behind a disconnected telephone and an "address
unknown." A fellow student attempts to ask Wheeler why he does what he
does, but Wheeler is furtively slinking down the corridor, eating strange-
looking mushrooms, and muttering something about getting the exclusive
right to market the entire Russian output of platinum through a holding
company he is about to form.

Barry Brass is known to every broker in the country, although he invariably does business elsewhere. He is always the first to mail in the coupon
that appears with a firm's advertisement. When the registered representative begins calling prospective clients, he always reaches Barry first. "Put
me on your market letter list for a few months," demands Barry, "and send
me daily charts on price, open interest, and volume covering mercury,
broilers, and rapeseed for the last few years. Also, would you have your
research department take a look at the spread relationship between April
potatoes and February propane during the third quarter of leap years and
let me know what they have to say? I can be reached evenings after 10:30."

Once this initial contact has been made, the broker need have no concern
about Barry remaining in touch, especially when reports are due. "When
is the cold storage report on bellies coming out and what does the floor expect it to say?" asks Barry on line one while the broker's best client is waiting on hold on line two to place an order for 400 shares of stock at the
market. Within one minute after the report is issued Barry will be certain
to call back to learn the figures and ask for the reaction on the floor and
some estimate of where the market will open in the morning. He would call
his own broker, of course, but does not wish to disturb him, especially because Barry has no position in bellies anyhow.

Barry is most in evidence at workshops and seminars presented as
business-building devices by brokerage firms. He can be easily recognized
by the dogeared notebook and charts he is carrying and by the holes in his

shoes. Just as the broker pauses for breath before making his major point about the enormous opportunity in the cocoa market because Ghana and Nigeria have invaded one another, Barry raises his hand and asks, "How much wheat is transported into Kansas City by barge relative to rail and how much does each barge hold? Also, when does it get too cold for barge traffic and what historical implications has this had for the Chicago-Kansas City wheat spread?" While the speaker tries to answer Barry's questions without admitting that he has no knowledge whatever of the Kansas City freight structure, the well-dressed man sitting near the door who was about to ask how to open a $10,000 account looks at his watch, puts his checkbook back into his pocket, and leaves.

During the refreshment period following the speech, Barry has the speaker backed into a corner asking him why the tomato paste market did not have more volume, considering all the pizzas that are sold in the United States. By the time the broker escapes from the corner and cleans the coffee off his suitcoat that Barry has spilled on it, the entire audience has left. Barry picks up four copies each of all the literature, takes all of the remaining cookies and doughnuts, gets his parking ticket validated, and leaves muttering something about the unproductivity of the evening.

Benjamin Franklin Bartlett believes that there is a wisdom in maxims that covers any contingency likely to be faced by a trader. Benjamin has had two articles published, one of which attempts to reconcile "Absence makes the heart grow fonder" with "Out of sight, out of mind" and the other explaining why "Birds of a feather flock together" is completely compatible with "Eagles don't flock." His "Thoughts on Maxims as Applied to Trading" is the definitive work on the subject and has formed the basis for the chapter that follows.

CHAPTER TWELVE

Maxims: Good and Bad

> If, could, should, might;
> Weasel words are always right.　　CANDY TREAT

INTRODUCTION

Although the bulk of the work done by Benjamin Franklin Bartlett is presented in this chapter, the reader should be aware that some of Bartlett's conclusions have been attacked by an unfriendly reviewer whose work should be noted, partly because it is quite stimulating and partly because he has made a considerable fortune trading commodities, unlike Bartlett who is currently in charge of french fried potatoes at a small hamburger stand. The reviewer, Orin Thevault, believes that success in trading commodities requires more than the judicious choice and observation of old saws. Some may present a real danger to novices or undisciplined traders, in some cases because they accept them and in others because they do not. There is some old saying that will justify almost any action or lack of action. Many people are not disturbed by the fact that equally plausible maxims might appear to justify diametrically opposed actions. They just blithely choose the one that encourages their doing what they want to do anyhow. Sociologists have named this phenomenon "selective perception." The most favored alibis comfort the trader when he has taken a loss or a smaller profit than he should have. There is real danger in confusing alibis with wisdom, and it might help to provide a small part of Orin Thevault's master list of alibis at this point:

1. I should have entered a stop.
2. I should have taken the profit.
3. I should have let the profit run.
4. I should have had a bigger position.
5. I should have had a smaller position.
6. I should have entered a stop.
7. I should have averaged up.
8. I should not have averaged up.
9. I should have averaged down.
10. I should not have averaged down.
11. I should have bought time by spreading against my position.
12. I should have just got out—the first loss is the best loss.
13. I should have entered a stop.
14. I should have listened to my broker.
15. I should know better than to listen to my broker.
16. I should never trade on the close.
17. I should never trade on the opening.
18. I should have got out before the report.
19. I should just ignore the report and stay in the market.
20. I should have entered a stop.
21. I should have taken the seasonal into consideration.
22. I should know that seasonals are too simplistic an approach.
23. I should have met the margin call and gone just two days more.
24. I should never meet a margin call.
25. I should have entered a stop.

Orin concludes that no list of maxims can replace the time and effort that must go into a carefully prepared trading plan. In fact he derides maxims as conventional wisdom that are overly general, have no predictive value, and belong more in an explanation of the random walk theory than in a trading plan. It is best left to the reader to study some of Bartlett's work on maxims and judge for himself whether they are a consistent and adequate tool for skilled, experienced traders. The following summary of Bartlett's work on maxims has been rather thoroughly edited by Orin Thevault who could not resist editorializing from time to time. In fact, he has even taken the liberty of inserting maxims of his own choosing from time to time which lead to conclusions sharply contrasting with those of Bartlett's. The first group of maxims deals with the selection of a trade.

SELECTION

One of the first decisions to be made by any trader is whether the wiser policy is concentration or diversification of positions. The trader who chooses diversification has widely quoted the maxim. "Don't put all your eggs in one basket," to justify his choice. The more aggressive speculator who chooses to concentrate in order to achieve more potential in a given position can retort with, "It is much easier to watch a few than many," or "Put all your eggs in one basket and watch the basket."

In reality, either of these two broad policies may be correct for people with different objectives or different styles of trading, or for the degree of aggressiveness they might choose to select in their pursuit of profit. The relatively conservative traders can always say, "Patience is a virtue," whereas another who is willing to accept greater risks might answer, "There are two ways to get to the top of an oak tree: climb it, or sit on an acorn."

The choice of specific trades may be made even more difficult by trying to reconcile such conflicting popular advice as "Never sell after a big decline" with the equally popular "Never buy after a long decline." Under given conditions either of these may prove correct; but if both are correct a commodity cannot logically be either bought or sold after a long decline.

A trader may not be too badly injured by heeding the advice to "Buy what will not go down in a bear market." The implication is that such a choice will probably lead the next rise, which is possible, but it also may be out of favor with many traders because it is not considered to have much potential and, although it might not go down, it might not go up either. Similarly, one might heed the advice "never buy something that won't go up in a bull market," only to discover that he has been persuaded not to buy something that merely has not gone up yet and is just about to do so.

The potential buyer who wants a rule that will allow him to do anything that he really wants to can turn to "When a bear market turns to bull, buy what has gone down the most and also what has gone down the least." This sounds plausible, but the security buyer who buys a high-grade preferred stock because it has gone down the least might also find that it will also go up the least. If he hedges by buying what has gone down most, he may find that he has bought stock in a company whose stock is discounting its impending bankruptcy, at which point it will continue down to zero. He learns the truth of the warning, "Many a healthy reaction has proved fatal."

Whatever the reason for which the choice of a purchase is made, it should be because of the opportunity inherent in the trade, not because the buyer wants to acquire a given amount of money for an automobile, a trip, or a new suit. There is considerable validity in the warning, "Never speculate for a specific need," as any poker player can attest if he has played for his supper and subsequently gone hungry. The potential in a trade is proved by the trade itself and not by the desires of the buyer or seller.

The potential seller of a position finds his choices no easier than those of the buyers. He is told on the one hand, "Sell what has gone up the most because it will react the most," but at the same time, "Sell what has gone up the least because what could not go up must come down." If he observes the former, he could find himself short in a market rising most rapidly; if he chooses the second alternative, he might find himself short in a market so completely demoralized that the only real possibility is an ultimate move higher or little move at all for a long period of time. One of the near certainties in speculation is that when everyone is bearish a market must go up because there are no sellers left, just as when everyone is bullish a market must go down because there are no buyers left. The reasons to justify these seemingly unlikely moves will appear after the moves have taken place.

There are those who argue, with considerable logic, that it is best to sell something before it goes down rather than after. Those who warn "Never sell something because it seems high priced" leave the trader in a position of selling positions only if they seem to be low priced. This is difficult to reconcile with the successful trader's ability to buy low and sell high, which appears to be an infallible route to success.

Both a trader who prefers selling on rallies and another who would rather sell something that could not go up might prove to be correct at one time or another. The first can maintain that "The warrior who is first to weaken in battle is often seen as the leader of a retreat," whereas the other can insist that it is wise to "Sell short what will not go up in a bull market."

OPINIONS

The trader who finds it difficult to select positions for himself might choose the seemingly easy course of accepting the advice of others whom he considers to have superior judgment or better sources of information. To do so, of course, he must ignore the admonition, "Don't rely on the advice of insiders." He must also disregard the comment of a highly regarded successful trader who said, "Given time, I believe that inside information can break the Bank of England or the United States Treasury."[1] For some reason he has discounted the elaborate survey that indicated that people who work in the grain trade have managed to lose their own money about as fast as anyone else and that farmers frequently manage to lose even faster than most.[2]

It would appear that brokers would be interested in giving traders good advice in the interest of keeping their business, building their capital, and receiving referral business, but the results obtained by those who slavishly follow the suggestions of registered representatives of brokerage houses have been something less than outstanding. Many customers eventually come to accept the remark of a cynical trader to the effect that "The only sure tip from your broker is a margin call." Another said, "Few people ever make money on tips. Beware of inside information. If there was any easy money lying around, no one would be forcing it into your pocket." One would probably be well advised to "Beware of one who has nothing to lose," because "Markets are never wrong; opinons often are" and "Opinions are worthless; facts are priceless."

If a trader does have enough faith in someone else to accept his judg-

[1] Bernard Baruch, *Baruch: My Own Story*, Holt, Rinehart and Winston, New York, 1957, p. 123.

[2] Blair Stewart, *An Analysis of Speculative Trading in Grain Futures*, Technical Bulletin No. 1001, U.S. Department of Agriculture, Commodity Exchange Authority, October, 1949, pp. 67 and 68.

ment, he would probably be well advised to follow it through to the conclusion of the trade. There are many speculators who have suffered a large
loss in a position suggested by someone else only to find that his adviser
had seen the error of his selection quickly and liquidated with a much
smaller loss or even a profit. This is why one successful speculator advised
a friend, "If you get in on Smith's tip, get out on Smith's tip."

Contrary-opinion advocates suggest that one ascertain the prevalent
opinion of the trading public in some way and then take the opposite
position on the basis that "The public is always wrong." At least, it tends to
be wrong at critical junctures. This assumes, of course, that the trader can
take note of the same facts available to the remainder of the trading public
and be able to accept an opposite position. It is well and good to advise
sagely, "Buy when others sell and sell when others buy," but how could
everybody follow the advice without making it meaningless?

TIMING

Most successful traders are convinced that timing represents the ultimate
difference between profit and loss in trading. "When to buy and sell is more
important than what to buy and sell" would be accepted as sound advice by
virtually all experienced traders. Most would also agree that "A bull can
make money, and a bear can make money, but a hog never can," including
Baron Rothschild, who gave as a major reason for his success his rule, "I
never buy at the bottom and I always sell too soon."

When to take profits can cause endless problems if one chooses not to
develop and follow a plan. Hardly anyone would quarrel with the basic
admonition to "Cut losses and let profits run." Just when to cut the losses
or how far to let the profits run is difficult to determine. One might agree
with such thoughts as "The real money made in speculation has been in
commitments showing a profit right from the start." Those who follow this
advice probably provide the fuel for the relatively common phenomenon
of the false breakout.

"Sell when the good news is out" probably has a better reputation for
validity than it deserves. Some markets discount news to a far greater degree than others. Accordingly, the first response to news might reflect all
the change in price that there is going to be, but in other cases it might be
only the beginning of a major change in the price level. In the latter case
buying when the good news is out rather than selling might prove to be far
the better alternative. "Never sell on strike news" is in the same category.
Some strikes are anticipated and some are not. Some end quickly and present a welcome opportunity to work off surplus inventory, whereas others
last for extended periods and result in temporary or even permanent loss
of markets, in which case selling on strike news might prove wise.

"Sell on the first margin call" appears to be valid because it really suggests that a position be abandoned before all of the trader's capital has
been lost. Much would depend, of course, on the amount of loss that took

place before the margin call was received. In most cases considerable attrition must already have taken place, which might imply that a well-constructed plan would not have allowed the position to have been held long enough for the margin call to have been received at all. Margin calls usually indicate that a speculator has either been overtrading or has not cut losses soon enough.

It is debatable whether an attractive trading opportunity always exists. Accordingly, some traders maintain that "There is no need to be always in the market" because they are convinced that money cannot consistently be made by trading every day or even every week. Most speculators agree that overtrading is one of the worst possible errors that can be made and accordingly they advise, "Trade too often and be the broker's good friend, trade less often to be your own true friend."

Others, however, may be going too far when they say, "When in doubt, do nothing." This might lead to considerable trouble. If one is out of the market and in doubt, he might do nothing and miss a profitable opportunity. Even worse, he might be in a market with a losing position and be in doubt. Accordingly, he might do nothing but watch his small loss become a large one. A trader could take the opposite course and listen to those who suggest, "When in doubt do something" and "If you would not buy, sell." Most experienced traders find themselves consistently beset by doubts, and they could hardly react by consistently doing nothing or always doing something. If their doubts become too disturbing when they have an important position, they might well observe the old adage to "Sell down to a sleeping point."

The best way to resolve such problems is to have a carefully prepared trading plan and do one's best to suppress doubts while the plan has time to work. This probably would provide more profitable results than a program based on impulse. Impulse usually results in entering positions at high prices and selling them at low prices because commodities and stocks "Look best at the top of a bull market and worst at the bottom of a bear market." It is only human to want to buy when the market looks good and to sell when it looks bad, which is why it has been said that "The human side of every person is the greatest enemy of the average investor or speculator." The trader might be well advised when he is told, "Trust your own opinion and back your judgments only when the action of the market itself confirms your opinion."

Even when a plan has been devised, it is not always easy to follow it logically if any credence is given to popular maxims; for example, it is often said, "Don't try to get the last eighth." On the same point it has been written that "One of the most helpful things that anybody can learn is to give up trying to catch the last eighth—or the first. These two are the most expensive eighths in the world. They have cost stock traders, in the aggregate, enough millions of dollars to build a concrete highway across the continent."[3] These sound quite logical but if one never tries to reach the last eighth of the entry point or objective specified in his trading plan, how does he ever reach either? A trader might bid 71⅜ for 10,000 bushels of oats when the market is 72½. If the market hesitates at 71¾, he might be tempted to raise his bid to be sure not to miss the market. If his objective was 73 and the price met resistance at 72½, he might sell at the market in order to be sure to get out. If his order is filled at 72¼, he has barely covered his commissions. Those last eighths he failed to gain represented his entire potential profit. When the market turns just short of an entry or liquidation point, it can be highly annoying, but if more flexibility is needed, the plan should provide for it. There are times when a market order is the best way to take or liquidate a position, but there are other times when a limit order is wiser. In the latter case the trader has little choice but to wait for the last eighth.

CHARACTER OF THE MARKET

Some maxims provide some general advice to traders concerning the nature of the market itself. As in the other areas, however, some of them sound logical, but there is frequently a maxim that sounds just as logical but suggests an opposing course of action. One might hear one sage maintain that "The market has no past," only to hear another say that "Nothing new ever occurs in the business of speculation or investing in securities or commodities," which implies that much can be learned from the past. Most traders and all technicians would agree with the latter, although in trading, as in most ventures, there are any number of people who will not or cannot learn from history, as well as some who cannot learn from anything.

There are those who believe, often with good reason, that one should "Never quarrel with the tape." They believe that the current price of something is all that really counts, and if it is not in line with what was expected the wise course is to "Quit while the quitting is good." They feel that it is not productive to be too curious about all the reasons behind all the price movements because so much time might be spent learning about the factors that could influence a trade no trade would ever be made; or that so much effort might be used to justify retaining a position when the tape says it should not be retained severe losses would result. That is why "Wishful thinking must be banished."

Those who believe that inactive markets should be avoided are fond of asserting, "If money cannot be made out of leaders, it will not be made out of the market as a whole." They must contend with the equally popular and probably more accurate assertion that "the leaders of today may not be the

---

[3] Edwin Lefevre, *Reminiscences of a Stock Operator,* George H. Doran Co., New York, 1923, p. 65.

leaders of tomorrow." Trading in today's leaders may result only in trading where there is no longer any opportunity and not trading where there is. Those who are unable to agree with either view can take the middle road by accepting the proposition, "All stocks and commodities move more or less with the general market, but value will tell in the long run." Just how much move indicates a genuine move toward economic value is not so easy to determine. One must remember that "value has little to do with temporary fluctuations in prices" and that this problem will always be with us because "The market will continue to fluctuate."

Some traders even personify a market. They believe that you can "Plot the pattern of a bull market and you will have also plotted the pattern followed by nature for most living things; a slow start and gradual acceleration in growth that terminates at maturity." Most bull markets actually do appear to follow this sort of pattern.

NOTES FROM A TRADER

There is hardly a maxim that someone could not find fault with. There are one or two, however, that most traders believe sooner or later. Many of those who believe them later would have done better to believe them sooner. One of these is, "Put half your profits in a safety deposit box." Although it should be possible to find an investment wiser than cash in a safety deposit box, it hardly seems necessary to utilize any profits gained to take larger and larger positions with the ever-increasing risks that accompany them. Although it may not seem logical, it is probably true that money is easier to make than it is to keep.

Adversity is part and parcel of trading. The only benefits that come from adversity are the knowledge and strength gained. It detracts nothing from the truth to acknowledge it with such seemingly inane statements as, "Winners never quit and quitters never win," or one more profound like "God grant me the serenity to accept the things I cannot change, the courage to change the things I can, and the wisdom to know the difference." The point of both is equally valid. The simple truth is that most successful speculators have been bloodied at least once before achieving success, but all have tried again. Hopefully, one need not accept the cynical proposition that "A speculator who dies rich has died before his time."

CHAPTER THIRTEEN

Who Wins? Who Loses? Why?

Who Wins?

The race is not always to the swift nor the battle to
the strong—but that's the way to bet.

DAMON RUNYON

Who Loses?

The greatest tragedy in all history is the murder of a
beautiful theory by a gang of brutal facts.

ANONYMOUS

Why?

I contradict myself. I am large, I contain multitudes.

WALT WHITMAN

INTRODUCTION

The purpose of this concluding chapter of the trading section is to focus on
the results, however limited, of those who play the commodity futures trading game and to suggest reasons for the outcomes. A discerning trader might
take the position that such an inquiry should *precede* the trading section,
not succeed it, for if commodity futures trading is a zero sum game in which
total profits and losses must be equal it is possible, theoretically at least, for
the participants to cannibalize in a kind of suicidal rotation in which no one
wins in the long run. In such a dismal activity a continual advantage could
be held only by the broker who charged each participant an entry fee in the
form of a commission. Under these conditions the potential trader might
conclude that the game is suited only to those hardy souls who might be
characterized as gladiators who look on each trade as an exercise in "kill
or be killed." Unless the shape of his trading curve indicates an exceptionally active greed factor, the potential trader may find such a game totally
unsuitable. Fortunately there are some facts about the outcomes of futures
trading that square well with hypotheses that are not quite so bleak.

DISTRIBUTION OF PROFITS AND LOSSES

THE BLAIR STEWART STUDY

Probably the best known analysis of the trading record of speculators is that by Blair Stewart, as a consulting economist for the Commodity Exchange Authority.[1] The complete trading records of 8,922 customers of a Chicago commission firm which went bankrupt in the 1930s were turned over to the CEA for analysis. The study is restricted to results in grain futures (wheat, corn, oats, and rye) for a nine-year period from 1924 to 1932.

Futures market participants were divided into two broad classifications—hedgers and speculators. Three broad groups were distinguished among the speculators: scalpers, who were defined as buying and selling on small fluctuations in prices and closing the day with near even positions; spreaders, who were long and short positions of equal amounts; other speculators, who represented all remaining traders. The Stewart study focused on the results of the last group:

		Profit traders			Loss traders	
Commodity	Number	Total net profits	Average profit per trader	Number	Total net losses	Average loss per trader
Wheat	2,045	$1,508,407	$738	5,496	$ 9,411,620	$1,712
Corn	1,525	$1,183,993	$776	2,403	$ 2,222,602	$ 925
Oats	589	$ 124,038	$211	997	$ 772,132	$ 774
Rye	497	$ 293,042	$590	816	$ 825,838	$1,012
All grains*	2,184	$2,064,800	$945	6,598	$11,958,200	$1,812

* The "all grains" figures are not equal to the totals of the figures for the individual grains because some traders made profits in one or more grains but lost on their futures transactions in one or more of the other grains.

The overwhelming conclusion from the general summary is that the vast majority (75 percent) of the speculators (other than scalpers and spreaders) lost money. There were 6,598 speculators in the sample with net losses compared with 2,184 with net profits, or three times as many loss traders as profit traders. Net dollar speculator losses of approximately $12,000,000 overwhelmed net dollar profits of nearly $2,000,000 by sixfold. Speculators were not discriminating—they lost in every commodity, consistently and impressively.

The distribution of profits and losses indicated that for most traders the results indicated that the game was not played for high stakes. Eighty-four percent of the winners during the nine-year period won less than $1,000. Stewart's sample of traders who held reportable positions did not indicate that large speculators were any more successful than small traders, although the sample was too small to warrant any such generalization.

[1] Blair Stewart, "An Analysis of Speculative Trading in Grain Futures," USDA, Technical Bulletin No. 1001, October 1949, p. 57.

Other significant points included the following:

1. Speculators showed a clear tendency to cut their profits short while letting their losses run.

2. The speculator is more likely to be long than short.

3. The entire period was one in which prices declined, and speculators receipted for a disproportionate share of the total losses during the last three years when the price decline accelerated.

4. No occupational group was able to claim results that differed from the general conclusion in regard to aggregate profits and losses. Managers in the grain business were somewhat more successful than other groups, yet they could produce aggregate profits in dollars that were only 28 percent of aggregate losses.

5. There was a clear tendency of long speculators to buy on days of price declines and for shorts to sell on price rises. This action indicates that traders were predominantly price level rather than price movement traders.

The study also presented two case studies which isolated in detail the trades of the largest winner and loser. The loser traded virtually throughout the nine-year period and his losses were more than $400,000 in wheat futures. In the spring of 1928 he had amassed a moderate profit, which he was to give back and follow with heavy losses resulting from a seasonal strategy, beginning in 1928, of buying wheat heavily at harvest time and selling it in the subsequent spring. The most successful trader struck quickly in 1924 by being long corn, wheat, and rye, staying with his position until October of that year, and then fading away with profits of almost $300,000. He did not trade again during the nine-year period.

THE HIERONYMUS STUDY [2]

Hieronymus was able to secure the summary records of closed trades for a commission house for the calendar year 1969. Even though conclusions derived from a one-year inquiry must of necessity be tentative, it is instructive to compare recent results, however selective, against Stewart's observations 35 years earlier. The aggregate results for three major metropolitan offices of the firm are as follows:

Number of accounts	462
Number of accounts with profits	164
Total profits (dollars)	$462,413
Profit per account (dollars)	$2,819
Number of accounts with losses	298
Total losses (dollars)	$1,127,355
Losses per account (dollars)	$3,783
Average result (loss) (dollars)	$1,439
Net loss, all accounts (dollars)	$664,942
Commissions paid (dollars)	$406,344
Put to clearing house (dollars)	$258,598

[2] Thomas A. Hieronymus, *Economics of Futures Trading*, Commodity Research Bureau, New York, 1971, pp. 252–258.

Thirty-five percent of the firm's customers (versus 25 percent in the Stewart study) closed 1969 with a profit. A total of $1,589,768 changing hands between winners and losers and involving 462 people is an *average* of $3,441, a game that cannot qualify as representing staggering sums. This is confirmed by a frequency distribution which indicates that half the winners and losers won or lost less than $1,000 and 84 percent won or lost less than $5,000. Except for a few big losers (16 over $15,000) and fewer big winners (6 over $15,000), the clients of the commission house tended to pass money back and forth, paying commissions in the shuffle. It is interesting to note that a large number (170) of accounts were traded only once or a few times at most. This group, although constituting 37 percent of the total number of accounts, contributed 64 percent of the total losses. Regular traders (those who won or lost at least $500 and contributed $250 in commissions during the year) did better as a group and their net profits were nearly enough to offset their net losses. Regular traders (42 percent) paid $364,647 of the total $406,344 commissions, or almost 90 percent, which strongly suggests that the regular traders relieved the one-time traders of their money and then deposited it with the firm in the form of commissions.

ADDITIONAL EVIDENCE

The authors have been able to confirm that the average expectation of a trader making net profits in any given year will be one in four. The records of one respected brokerage firm indicated that for 10 years, beginning in 1962, the percentage of traders concluding the year with net profits ranged from a low of 14 percent to a high of 42 percent, with an average of 26 percent. In 1969, 23 percent of the accounts made money, compared with 35 percent in the Hieronymus sample of 462, which was approximately 10 percent of the size of the firm the authors examined. At any rate, the three estimates do not seem to be mutually exclusive in their implications for any given year. As the rates of return for the CEA trader classifications are examined, however, it will be seen that there is a significant difference between making profits in any *one* year and making *consistent* profits over a period of many years.

THE ROCKWELL STUDY [3]

The Rockwell Study, based on Houthakker's earlier method of analysis,[4] makes use of more than 7,900 semimonthly observations covering 25 CEA

---

[3] Charles Rockwell, "Normal Backwardation, Forecasting, and the Returns to Commodity Futures Traders," *Proceedings of a Symposium of Speculation in Organized Commodity Markets, Food Research Institute Studies,* Supplement, 7 (1967), 115. Portions of this study have been referred to in Chapters 2 and 4. Before proceeding, the trader should review the breakdown of the percentage of the value of the open interest by participant in Table 2-2.

[4] Hendrik Houthakker, "Can Speculators Forecast Prices?" *The Review of Economics and Statistics* (May 1957).

regulated markets for 18 years, beginning in 1947, as described in Table 13-1. The study does not include the markets such as pork bellies, cocoa, and sugar, which at that time were unregulated and which constitute a significant percentage of futures trading in more recent periods. Three different market aggregations were used; "All Markets," covering 25 markets, "Large Markets," including only Chicago wheat, New York cotton, and soybeans, and "Small Markets," which included the remaining 22 markets. A reasonably stable general price level occurred from the beginning of the period to the end, as shown in Table 13-1.

For the 18-year period in all markets there is a positive total return of about $750 million on the long open interest, as illustrated in Table 13-2. About 40 percent of the return to the long open interest goes to the small speculator and the remainder is divided fairly equally among the large speculator, the hedger, and spreader.

If, in all markets, those holding long positions account for about $750 million in profits, there must be an offsetting $750 million loss to those holding short positions. Again the small speculator bears approximately 40 percent of this loss.

The large speculator again makes a profit, albeit a small one ($25 million) when compared with his gains on the long side. It is important to note that the large speculators are the *only* group that has an aggregate profit on the short side for All Markets. The short hedger bears 40 percent of the short side losses in All Markets, about equal to those of the small speculator. The hedger, however, does not offset his short losses with long profits because his long side gains account for only 20 percent of the long profits.

In the Small Markets small speculators lose money on their long positions. Their long losses are offset by large speculators and long hedgers, so that the total dollar returns to those holding long positions in the Small Markets is virtually zero. On the short side only the large speculator makes money and he achieves these profits mainly at the expense of the short hedger.

In the Large Markets the small speculator makes almost 50 percent of the long side profits. On the short side the large speculators make a little money, but the short hedgers lose more than twice the amount of their gains on the long side. The total returns on the long open interest in the Large Markets ($751.4 million) contrast markedly with the insignificant returns on the long open interest in the Small Markets.

A summary follows of the significance of the net returns to each group for the 18-year period, as presented in the last three rows of Table 13-2. It should be noted that the profit flow in the three Large Markets determines to a great extent the behavior of the All Market aggregate.

1. When the short-side losses of small traders are compared with their long-side profits, the group shows a small net loss for All Markets.

2. Large speculators win consistently (though unevenly) in Small and Large Markets, and their total winnings ($178.8 million) come almost entirely at the expense of hedgers in the Large Markets.

3. In the Small Markets hedgers do much better ($6.5 million) than they

TABLE 13-1 DESCRIPTION OF DATA AND PRICE LEVELS

Commodity and markets*	Period of observation		Number of semi-monthly observations	Change in price level of nearby contract† (dollars)		Annual percentage price change	
	from	to		start	end	from start to end	between maturity years
Wheat, Chicago Board of Trade	7/47	6/65	432	2.39375	1.42250	−2.3	−2.2
Wheat, Kansas City Board of Trade	7/50	6/65	360	2.30375	1.43500	−2.3	−1.6
Wheat, Minneapolis Grain Exchange	7/50	6/65	360	2.36125	1.59750	−2.2	−2.5
Corn, Chicago Board of Trade	7/47	6/65	432	2.30375	1.32250	−2.2	+1.4
Oats, Chicago Board of Trade	7/47	6/65	432	1.02000	.67750	−1.9	−5.1
Rye, Chicago Board of Trade	7/47	6/65	432	2.52000	1.15750	−3.0	−1.6
Soybeans, Chicago Board of Trade	7/47	6/65	432	2.78000	2.96000	+0.36	−0.7
Soybean meal‡, Chicago Board of Trade	7/47	6/65	432	87.50	71.10	−1.0	−12.0
Soybean oil,§ Chicago Board of Trade	7/50	6/65	360	0.1245	0.1008	−1.3	−3.1
Cotton, New York Cotton Exchange	7/47	6/64	408	0.3898	0.3328	−0.9	−2.8
Cotton, New Orleans Cotton Exchange	7/50	6/60	240	0.3569	0.3278	−0.8	−4.3
Cottonseed meal, Memphis Merchants Exchange Clearing Association	7/47	6/60	312	79.90	54.00	−2.5	−9.4
Cottonseed oil, New York Produce Exchange	7/47	6/65	432	0.2350	0.1232	−2.6	−0.6
Lard, Chicago Board of Trade	7/47	6/62	360	0.1960	0.0870	−3.7	−1.6
Flaxseed, Minneapolis Grain Exchange	7/50	6/62	288	3.7150	3.1900	−1.2	+2.0
Shell eggs, Chicago Mercantile Exchange	7/47	6/65	432	0.5262	0.3490	−1.9	−0.1
Frozen eggs, Chicago Mercantile Exchange	7/61	6/65	96	0.2635	0.2687	+0.5	−4.6
Potatoes, New York Mercantile Exchange	7/47	6/65	432	2.96	2.58	−0.7	+5.0
Wool tops, Wool Association of the New York Cotton Exchange	7/47	6/62	360	1.570	1.666	+0.4	−4.7
Grease wool, Wool Association of the New York Cotton Exchange	5/54	6/63	257	1.413	1.190	−1.7	−0.2

Bran, Kansas City Board of Trade	7/47	6/56	216	58.50	33.20	−4.8	−7.8
Shorts, Kansas City Board of Trade	7/47	6/56	216	60.00	38.90	−3.9	−9.8
Middlings, Kansas City Board of Trade	7/55	6/56	24	37.00	35.15	−5.0	−3.4
Onions, Chicago Mercantile Exchange	9/55	6/59	91	2.10	1.30	−9.5	−1.0
Butter, Chicago Mercantile Exchange	7/47	6/53	144	0.6775	0.6120	−1.6	−2.4

* "Large markets" are wheat at Chicago, cotton at New York, and soybeans.

† The nearby contract is the first contract that expires after the first observation; generally it is July.

‡ Soybean meal is for the Memphis Merchants Exchange Association until July 1953.

§ Soybean oil is for the New York Produce Exchange until July 1950.

SOURCE: Rockwell, *op. cit.*, 115.

TABLE 13-2   AGGREGATE PROFITS BY TRADING GROUPS: LONG, SHORT, AND NET (MILLION DOLLARS)

Trading group	Large Markets		Small Markets		All Markets[*]	
	Long	Short	Long	Short	Long	Short
Small traders	369.7	−303.6	−68.1	−1.4	301.6	−305.0
Reporting speculators	114.8	3.1	38.8	22.2	153.5	25.3
Reporting spreaders[†]	159.0	−159.6	5.5	−3.4	164.5	−163.1
Reporting hedgers	108.1	−291.2	25.4	−18.8	133.5	−310.1
Total long open interest[*]	751.4		1.5		,752.9	
Small traders, net	66.1		−69.5		−3.4	
Reporting speculators, net	117.8		61.0		178.8	
Reporting hedgers, net	−183.2		6.5		−176.6	

[*] Because of rounding, totals are not necessarily exact sums of the components shown.

[†] This category is included only for balance purposes. The sum of the net positions is not zero because of its omission.

SOURCE: Rockwell, *op. cit.*, 119.

do in the large markets, and the profits of the large speculator ($61 million) are made at the expense of the small speculator.

4. The losses of hedgers in the three Large Markets provide the profits to large speculators and almost enough profits to small speculators to offset their losses in the 23 Small Markets.

Even more instructive is the yearly presentation in Table 13-3 of the an-

TABLE 13-3   ANNUAL PROFITS FOR ALL MARKETS (MILLION DOLLARS)

Year	Small traders, net	Large speculators, net	Hedgers, net	Total
1947/48	16.2	19.5	−34.2	115.9
1948/49	−13.5	− 0.5	13.8	− 48.2
1949/50	7.9	17.0	−24.9	153.3
1950/51	−47.5	28.9	−76.11	229.5
1951/52	−10.5	7.8	2.7	126.2
1952/53	−44.3	− 4.3	46.4	−171.9
1953/54	12.8	16.3	−29.7	113.4
1954/55	−17.0	5.1	12.0	− 27.7
1955/56	2.5	12.7	−15.5	73.9
1956/57	− 6.4	6.5	− 0.1	5.8
1957/58	− 9.4	0.9	8.4	− 27.4
1958/59	− 3.6	1.4	2.5	− 3.7
1959/60	−14.6	4.5	10.2	− 38.3
1960/61	63.3	35.2	−98.6	217.8
1961/62	−19.4	− 5.4	24.8	− 95.9
1962/63	− 3.6	2.1	1.6	50.5
1963/64	−24.1	10.0	14.1	− 75.0
1964/65	13.0	21.2	−34.1	155.0
Total	− 3.4	178.8	−176.6	752.9

SOURCE: Rockwell, *op. cit.*, 120.

nual profits in All Markets for all participants. The small speculator loses in 11 of the 18 years. His average loss is $15.1 million and his average profit, $23.7 million. If the largest profit years are removed (1950–1951 and 1960–1961), the average profit drops to $10.5 million, well below the average loss. There is little consolation to the small speculator in the realization that 68 percent of his profits for the 18-year period may be attributed to only two years.

The large speculator, on the other hand, shows a profit in 15 of the 18 years. His average yearly profit is almost $13 million, even though he accounts for perhaps less than 2 percent of the total value of the open interest, whereas his average annual loss is only $3.4 million. If the two largest profit years are removed, the average profit is $9.6 million, still virtually three times the average loss of $3.4 million. The consistency of the profit-making capacity of the large speculator is impressive.

The hedger, during the 18-year period, shows a $6.5 million profit in the 23 Small Markets, yet his loss in the Large Markets is so large ($183.1 million) that he suffers an All Market loss of $176.6 million. Recent research by Working[5] is consistent with these findings. Working indicated that the major proportion of hedging losses may spring from market execution costs, which can be considerably greater than the reduced member commissions paid by most large hedgers. Because hedgers' orders tend to be large, any buys and sells would tend to make price bulges and dips which scalpers would trade. Such action, if true, renders understandable why the amount of speculation in a given market is closely tied to the amount of hedging. Hedgers may be the major source of income of the large speculator. Because most hedging is short hedging, most large speculator profits should come from the long side of the Large Markets. This may be verified by referring to Table 13-2.

If the annual rates of return to the participants are defined as gross profits as a percentage of contract value, Table 13-4 can present the trader with an idea of the individual rates of return by trading groups. Even though commissions, taxes, and capital reserves are omitted, the fact that margin requirements are only 5 or 10 percent of the contract value means that the actual returns on margin money may be as much as 10 to 20 times the returns indicated here. Regardless of the level of absolute profits, the relative profits of the different trading groups may be compared.

For All Markets the rate of return on the long open interest is 4 percent annually. The hedger makes about this amount on his net long positions so that the large speculator picks up what the small trader loses on the long side in Small Markets as well as what the hedger loses in the Large Markets. On the short side the large speculator wins from the small trader and the hedger in both Small and Large Markets. Again the large speculator is the

---

[5] Holbrook Working, "Tests of a Theory Concerning Floor Trading on Commodity Exchanges," *Proceedings of a Symposium on Price Effects of Speculation in Organized Commodity Markets, Food Research Institute Studies,* Supplement, 7 (1967), 5–48.

TABLE 13-4   AGGREGATE RATES OF RETURN BY
TRADING GROUPS (PER CENT)

Groups and positions	Large markets	Small markets	All markets
Total positions			
All groups	6.1	0.0	4.0
Small traders, long	5.6	−2.0	3.0
Small traders, short	−5.8	−0.0	−4.1
Large speculators, long	10.1	4.3	7.6
Large speculators, short	0.5	5.0	2.7
Hedgers, long	5.3	1.7	3.8
Hedgers, short	−7.1	−0.6	−4.3
Net positions			
Small traders, net	0.6	−1.2	−0.0
Large speculators, net	7.2	4.6	6.1
Hedgers, net	−3.0	0.1	−1.7

SOURCE: Rockwell, *op. cit.,* 122.

standout in the Large and Small Markets. His overall return of 6.1 percent is earned because he does well in both his long and short positions and because the ratio of his long to his short positions is large during the periods that short hedgers are losing. The small trader loses so much on his short positions that the resulting profits on his long positions do not overcome the deficit. If the hedger is offsetting existing or expected positions in the cash market, the overall loss (−1.7 percent) may provide an insight into the gross cost of placing a year-long hedge.

Until recently the risk premium concept, as developed in Chapter 4, was the consistent, if overworked, springboard into any discussion of the distribution of profits and losses in futures trading. The naïve strategy (being net long when hedgers are net short and being net short when hedgers are net long) does not result in an acceptable explanation of the profit flow. The failure to isolate and measure persistent evidence that speculators are paid for merely playing the game implies that speculative profits must be explained by reference to the trader's forecasting ability. Forecasting ability however, may be defined as two broadly differing skills. The first refers to the basic ability to be long in markets when prices are going up on the average and net short in markets when prices are going down on the average. This measure of forecasting skill indicates the long-run ability of a given trading group to stay on the "right" side of a given market and is referred to as "basic skill." On the other hand, a second level of forecasting ability refers to the "special skill" that a trading group exhibits when it makes profits from price movements that are shorter in duration than the total period under observation.

Table 13-5 presents a division of the rates of return according to basic and special skills. Small traders make important money only in the Large Markets, where rising prices result in a positive figure for basic skill (R^B). Small traders exhibit a consistent negative value for special skill (R^F). Large speculators, as is obvious by now, make money on the evidence of both skills. There are no "minus" values for the large trader in the Large Markets, Small Markets, or All Markets summary. Almost 80 percent of the total profits of the large trader comes from his special skill and only 20 percent from his basic skill. The large trader, then, is not rewarded chiefly by executing the strategy of buy and hold in an extended up move or sell and hold in an extended down move but rather by trading price changes in the relative short run.

Working's recent study[6] of the detailed record of one professional trader in cotton futures for a brief period is important for several reasons. In attempting to test the theory that most floor trading is scalping and that the execution costs of hedging are perhaps the chief source of income to speculators in futures markets, the definition of "scalping" was considerably enlarged to cover not only the smallest dips and bulges that occur but those that last up to a few days. In the large, well-traveled markets professional scalping tends to specialize sometimes into three distinguishable classes — unit-change scalpers, day-trading scalpers, and day-to-day scalpers. Unit-change scalpers, who stand ready to buy one tick below the last sale or sell one tick above it, almost invariably end the trading session in a zero net

[6] *Ibid.*

TABLE 13-5   DIVISION OF RATE OF RETURN ACCORDING TO BASIC AND SPECIAL FORECASTING SKILLS BY NET TRADING GROUPS* (PERCENT)

Trading and skill groups	Large markets	Small markets	All markets
Small traders net			
Rate of return from special forecasting skill (R^F)	−0.1	−1.2	−0.4
Rate of return from basic forecasting skill (R^B)	0.7	0.0	0.4
Total rate of return (R^A)	0.6	−1.2	−0.0
Large speculators net			
Rate of return from special forecasting skill (R^F)	5.0	3.9	4.8
Rate of return from basic forecasting skill (R^B)	2.2	0.7	1.3
Total rate of return (R^A)	7.2	4.6	6.1
Hedgers net			
Rate of return from special forecasting skill (R^F)	−0.9	0.8	−0.6
Rate of return from basic forecasting skill (R^B)	−2.1	−0.7	−1.0
Total rate of return (R^A)	−3.0	0.1	−1.7

* In a given market the decomposition of the total actual rate of return (R^A) into basic forecasting skill (R^B) and special forecasting skill (R^F) is discussed in Rockwell, *op. cit.*, 127.

SOURCE: Rockwell, *op. cit.*, 127.

speculative position. Day traders tend to concentrate on dips and bulges of greater than unit size and may decide to hold some small percentage of their positions overnight. Day-to-day scalpers more often than not are prepared to carry most or all of their positions into the next trading session or for two or three successive days.

As indicated by the Stewart study, nearly all speculators, on or off the floor of the exchange, make some attempts at scalping. Price level traders may wait for price dips before getting long or for price bulges before initiating a short position. These traders, of course, run the risk of missing the market completely in those trades that, by definition, are the most successful. An alternative is to place orders "at the market," which ensures some execution costs at the hands of floor traders who are, themselves, scalping. The small trader is not on the exchange floor and cannot easily, for example, buy "on a dip" while the dip is forming.

Because the professional scalper derives profits from trading dips and bulges of varying time lengths, it seems difficult to understand why the ability to recognize price trends is asserted by floor traders to be the most important requirement for successful scalping.[7] The adage, "Cut your losses and let your profits run," heard by every trader alive, including those who came down with the last rain, has always been regarded as a basic rule of successful trading. Yet the effort to comply with the directive is successful only for the trader who can consistently anticipate the continuation of price trends. Such success is highly doubtful for reasons considered at length in Chapters 4 and 7. How, then, can the concepts of scalping and trend following coexist?

Working's thoughts, following a study of a two-month record of floor trading by a professional trader, explains why the adage, "Cut your losses and let your profits run," combines in one statement two entirely different approaches that are important for different reasons:

> (a) because a "trend" is the converse of a dip or bulge, trend recognition is a means of recognizing dips and bulges; (b) a scalper recognizes, in order to partially offset the losses that he incurs from trends whose beginnings he mistakenly regards as initial moves in a dip or bulge; and (c) the adage, "cut your losses and let your profits run," which is highly respected by floor traders, deserves such respect even if its application cannot be made a source of net gains. By letting profits run, to the best of his ability, a scalper derives such profits as he can from the emergence of unpredictable trends that happen to be in his favor, partially offsetting inevitable losses from the emergence of trends that run against him. By setting a limit on the amount of loss that he allows himself to incur, per unit of the commodity, a scalper accepts unneccessary loss to a greater extent than he avoids further loss (a consequence of the supposition that brief price trends are a source of net loss); but the practice, while slightly reducing his overall rate of profit per unit of the commodity, allows him to

[7] *Ibid.*, 44.

trade safely on a scale several times as large as would be prudent if he did not thus limit his losses per unit . . . effort to deal as successfully as possible with brief price trends is necessarily an integral part of professional scalping; and therefore, evidence that a floor trader makes such efforts does not, by itself, warrant classing him as a trend trader.[8]

SKILLS OF THE TRADER

FORECASTING SKILLS

The bald, unyielding fact is that small traders, as a group, seemingly possess no basic forecasting or special forecasting skill. They hold 46 percent of the value of all contracts and their gross profits are zero. Substantial losses occur when commissions are included. On the average, then, a small trader has the expectation of losing money—the losses over a reasonable period to equal commissions. It is evident that small traders do not require a history of profits to continue trading. The explanation of such a phenomenon may take several directions. First, the needs of some small traders may be met by merely playing the game. Having something that is dynamic and fast-paced to get up for in the morning is so exciting that the trader may be more than willing to lose money for the privilege of speculating. Second, traders may continue to trade because they believe they can forecast prices. The fact that they cannot consistently do so does not deter them because they tend to remember profits and forget losses. Third, the small trader may continue to trade because his group is amorphous and consists not of a crowd, but of a parade. The successful small trader becomes large as a result of his competence, whereas the unsuccessful small trader is eventually forced to withdraw from the market and is replaced by new blood. Fourth, the small trader may be convinced that his latest mistake is also his last mistake and, having learned, there is nothing ahead but smooth sea and blue sky.

On the other hand, small traders have years in which they post impressive profits. Referring to Table 13-3, it may be seen that in the years 1950/1951 and 1960/1961, for example, small traders show returns four and six times larger, respectively, than the average profit of the five other profitable years. This performance may well be explained by the tendency of the small trader to rely on the existence of positive serial correlation as the basis for his trading strategy; that is, small traders tend to rely on long-run trend-following methods for profits, in which they assume that the tendency of a rising market is to continue to rise and the tendency of a falling market is to continue to fall. Such trading theories result in trading strategies of buying strength and selling weakness, which may enable the small trader to reap extremely high profits in years when such trends are of

[8] *Ibid.,* 45.

long duration. Unfortunately, in the long run, more markets are trading markets than long trending markets; that is, there seems to be more of a tendency for price reversal than for price continuation.

Large traders generally tend to view markets as trading markets rather than trending markets. They may rely more heavily on the presence of negative serial correlation; therefore they may tend to sell certain rallies and buy certain declines. Such a result is consistent with an examination of the returns of large traders in their biggest profit years, again 1950/1951 and 1960/1961. In those years large traders show a return, respectively, of 3 and 3.7 times the average profit of the other 13 profitable years, considerably lower than those for the small trader.

It should be emphasized that there is a considerable difference between a winner in any given year and a consistent winner over a significant period .of time. Although the studies to date have indicated that a trader in any given year has an approximate probability of one in four of achieving a net profit, the probability of extending his supremacy consecutively drops precipitously. Of the 25 percent who win in any given year, only 2 percent manage their skills in a consistent manner that ensures their reappearance in a ratio approaching 15 of 18. For the remaining 23 percent *sic transit gloria.*

It is important to note that the dismal profitability of the small trader results in no small part as a consequence of his inability to manage money intelligently. Of the four elements of money management, the two discussed in detail in Chapter 10 are probably the chief culprits—the expectation of the game being played and the probability of ruin. The small trader seldom approaches the expectation of the game in the spirit of fair, good, and bad bets as determined by the profitability of the event occurring, the ratio of gain to loss, and the cost of playing the game. In his desire to play a speculative game to the hilt, in which results, either good or bad, occur quickly, the probability of ruin does not receive the cool reflection it deserves, and the small speculator remains generally unconvinced that he cannot change the mathematical expectation of the game by the way he plays the game.

There are quantitative and qualitative reasons for the supremacy of one trader over another. Many of the quantitative skills, which certainly may be acquired by patience and intellectual diligence, have been the subject of much of this book. Many of the skills that must be developed, however, deal with behavior and the reaction of the trader to on-going events and conditions.

BEHAVIORAL SKILLS

It is difficult to discuss the development of skills that cannot be internalized adequately except by experience. The fact that such behavioral skills exist is clearly illustrated by a neophyte who, having been sensitized to a particular behavioral skill may say, "Why didn't you tell me that before?"—

to which the professional trader replies, "I did." Men make markets. The nature and behavior of man, although not reducible to formula, is at least agreeable to analysis. The behavior of the trader should move toward the kind of behavior necessary to survive.

Past studies. Only three studies since World War II have dealt specifically with the behavior of traders. One, by Blair Stewart, has been examined. Another, by Ira Glick, deals with the professional trader, and the most recent effort by Seymour Smidt attempts to analyze the characteristics of the amateur speculator.

Glick's study[9] analyzed three styles of trading that professional traders on the Chicago Mercantile Exchange believed could lead to success:

> One successful pattern is exemplified by the scalper, and, from the trader's point of view, is probably the most difficult to realize. The typical scalper is thought of as young, relatively new in the occupation; flexible, aggressive and exhibitionistic in his behavior, and *always* minimizing losses.
>
> A second career pattern for success is the older, more mature trader, actively and in a large way engaged in some phase of the egg business. He has excellent sources of information and is regarded as intelligent, able to view and grasp the total market situation in terms of a span of time and a diversity of factors. He is thought of as being wealthy and as having many wealthy friends, probably some of whom are also in the cash egg business.
>
> A third successful career line is quite similar to the above type, but this type of successful trader does not often appear on the exchange floor. Instead, he is thought of as purposely staying away from the (physical) marketplace, developing his trading strategy and tactics on the basis of good sources of objective information and executing his purchases and sales through representatives on the trading floor. . . .[10]

Smidt's analysis[11] reported findings on many characteristics of 349 futures traders who were interviewed personally or by mail. Because of the difficulty of obtaining access to a random sample of the trading population, Smidt relied on cross tabulation of his data to identify valid relationships.

When traders were classified into chartists and norm traders, that is, technicians and fundamentalists, results indicated that chartists are (a) less likely to take long positions and more likely to close out positions before receiving a margin call, (b) less likely to put up additional margin if they do receive a margin call, and (c) more likely to trade in a larger number of commodities and to pyramid their profits.

Initial sources of trading information were furnished by personal friends and brokers, and most traders interviewed preferred commodities about

[9] Ira O. Glick, "A Social Psychological Study of Futures Trading," an unpublished Ph.D. dissertation, Department of Sociology, University of Chicago, 1957.

[10] *Ibid.*, pp. 245–246.

[11] Seymour Smidt, *Amateurs, Information and Speculation: A Study of Amateur Commodity Speculators and Speculation,* Agricultural Industries Research Program, Graduate School of Business and Public Administration, Cornell University, Ithaca, N.Y., 1962.

which they had some information. The majority indicated that they anticipated no great change in their habits, and only 12 percent considered the
possibility of discontinuing trading as the result of losing money.

An interesting comment in the study concerned the limitations in information used by the amateur speculator in commodities. For most traders
in Smidt's sample

> . . . the broker is the only source of information, available more frequently
> than once a week, which contains more detail than would be available in *The
> Wall Street Journal* or some other daily newspaper. Considering the volatility
> of commodity markets, and the degree of leverage involved in commodity trad-
> ing, this is somewhat surprising. It suggests that traders who do not rely heavily
> on their brokers can be expected to lag by as much as a week in their response
> to new information." [12]

Although interesting information is contained in these studies, they do
not provide a systematic insight into the behavior of the commodity futures
trader. A systematic approach would be useful not only to explain the
trader's present behavior but to outline useful paths for change in the
future.

Transactional analysis. One systematic approach that may serve as an
explanatory model of the role of feelings and thought and their interaction
is available in a recent popular study. [13] The model, originally developed
by Erich Berne, has been named "transactional analysis" and is based on
the premise that in every person there are at least three different people—
the Parent, the Adult, and the Child. The Parent is the recording in the
brain of the individual's first five years. The data in the Parent are not
edited and permanently record all the verbal and nonverbal admonitions
that the child heard and saw in his own parents. The replay of the Parent
is a powerful influence throughout every individual's life, and the impera-
tives given in the early years can be a burden or a blessing, depending on
whether they have been updated by the Adult. The Child is the body of data
of internal events that was recorded when the little person was dependent
and clumsy and had no vocabulary to speak of. Because of this condition,
the Child is composed of feelings and emotions. Harris maintains that the
Adult develops as soon as a person begins finding out for himself what is
different about life from the "taught concept" of life in his Parent and
"felt concept" of life in his Child. [14] The Adult relies on a "thought concept,"
which examines and updates the data from the Parent and Child to determine whether it is true and applicable.

It is important for the trader to understand the implications of the Whitman quote at the beginning of the chapter. Just as there are important

---

[12] *Ibid.*, pp. 54–56.
[13] Thomas A. Harris, *I'm OK–You're OK*, Harper & Row, 1967.
[14] *Ibid.*, p. 29.

relationships that are external to the trader, many of which may be quantified and learned, there are transactions that take place internally and may be involuntary as well. The boundaries between the Parent, Adult, and Child are fragile, and the total person may not always know which person is going to respond to a given transaction.

One of the basic reasons for understanding the identity of his Parent, Adult, and Child is illustrated in the trader's need for a plan. When a trader enters a position, but does not plan an objective and a stop, the plan is incomplete. When queried about the omissions, the trader may reply "I'll watch it." The problem with "watching it" is that it is not a statement made by the Adult in the trader. If the trade goes badly, the amount of loss taken will probably be greater than the amount that would have been taken had the Adult required the trader to take the time to make a basic decision about the value of a complete plan. Just as it is impossible to teach navigation in the middle of a storm, it is impossible to build an optimum plan in the middle of a bad loss. The Adult, functioning as a probability estimator, *knows* that losses must be planned in advance. The Child wants the feeling of assurance that everything will be all right without the plan. The Child wants no truck with unsavory consequences. The Parent might get in the act by quoting maxims appropriate to the occasion, such as "Never meet a margin call" or some other rule that will be marked by "should" or "ought."

Having a plan originated by the Adult before the trade is a vital step to success. The trader must, however, recognize that the temptation to tamper with the plan is founded in his Child and its fears and vulnerabilities. The Child is responsible for pulling out a stop-order just before it is elected or wishing to cancel an objective because the market is "acting well." Such directives from the Child may be seen in orders marked "cancel when close" or "good until executed."

The way in which the trader confronts reality gives a basic clue to his eventual success or failure. The successful trader with a well-developed Adult is good at adapting to various market and trading conditions. He learns that stop-loss orders must be placed irrevocably or the question becomes not *whether* he will be ruined but *when* he will be ruined. The successful trader has learned to cope with his feelings of fear (Child), primarily that what is wanted most — money — can be lost or denied. He has controlled his feelings (Child), for he realizes that a victim of fear cultivated by greed can be lost to the stultification of hoping for much but acting to ensure little.

The unsuccessful trader copes with unpleasant reality in a far different way. He does not depend on changing himself but rather on fantasizing or changing the way he views reality. He tends to be selectively perceptive and retentive; that is, he tends to see and remember what fits his needs and expectations. The trader in this situation is dominated by his Child; for example, most easily constructed trading systems, trend-following or otherwise, will have long-run dollar results approaching 50 percent profits and

50 percent losses. When commissions and execution costs are subtracted, the normal expected path of such a trader's capital is a gentle downward slope that terminates considerably short of his capacity for self-deception. If such a trader eliminates but one loss that a newly devised filter would not only never have permitted but would have reversed for a profit, while including a profit that was virtually certain before an unfavorable news item caused a loss, his record on the trades becomes seven profits and three losses. Only a trader stripped of all vision, he reasons, can quit on a system that is 70 percent accurate. The capacity of the dominant Child for misinterpreting reality is virtually limitless.

No matter how successful a trader becomes, he still finds it difficult to live in the real world. Where members of the animal kingdom must adjust to the external environment on its terms, man can manipulate reality over a broad range by the use of symbolism. A trader must realize that desirable qualities can be bestowed by words alone and that such words can be affixed more readily to the occasion than the occasion can be modified to fit the actual meaning of the words. A trader does not enjoy being wrong. Besides ruining his credit balance, being wrong does not build a good image of the self. Yet mistakes must be constantly perceived and remembered for no other reason than that under no other conditions can they be controlled.

Successful trading is reached, if at all, by following a series of successive approximations. Early in the process ignorance is the rule, and the trader knows that he knows nothing. Following a sometimes long apprenticeship in which the vocabulary symbols are acquired, a false sense of competence spreads like a thin veneer and serves to entertain friends with the glibness of skills not yet acquired, though seeming to be. Given enough time, patience, and perseverance, the successful trader enters into that third state in which he believes he knows something and no more. In this state he is "inner directed" and not "other directed."[15] The "other-directed" man reacts to what others believe about him. His roles and values tend to be derived from what his peers expect of him. The "inner-directed" man holds to the Adult course he has set for himself. Rather than being solely radar-equipped, as in "other-direction," the "inner-directed" man relies on a gyroscope that is not at the mercy of whim or caprice. The successful trader's gyroscope is finely tuned. He realizes that without a well-developed Adult he faces the same problem as the German High Command in World War II, in which the invasion of Britain was planned but never executed, whereas the Battle of Britain was executed but never planned. Many traders never move beyond the point of development where they tend to execute trades that are never planned or plan trades that are never executed.

The trader must understand that decisions with favorable consequences (made by the Adult) become built into a trading approach only if they are consciously reduced to principles and followed with *great effort*. Traders

[15] David Riesman. *The Lonely Crowd*, Yale University Press, New Haven, Conn., 1950.

who buy or sell on impulse find sooner or later that mere feelings about trading are 50-50; that is, there is no significant statistical correlation between good feelings and profitable trades. Therefore to avoid the results of emotional activity the successful trader must be prepared to give up trading what he finds most rewarding in interpersonal relationships — good feelings. The propensity for the trader to resist such depersonalization is high, and there is a constant temptation to spill out over the boundaries of the well-defined role of trading. Good feelings will come as a result of the successful plans that the Adult conceives and executes.

The broker is equally well advised to understand that he has three people for a client, not just one. Perhaps the "suitability" rule should include not only a financial but a behavioral match-up as well. The first rule of communication is that when stimulus and response, in the P-A-C sense, make parallel lines the transaction is complementary and can continue indefinitely.[16] In other words, a transaction between broker and client may go on indefinitely as Parent-Parent, Adult-Adult, Child-Child, Parent-Child, Child-Adult, and so on:

1. *Parent-Parent Transaction*

CLIENT: Those people you have on the floor always get the worst fills possible.
BROKER: Makes you wonder where it will all end, doesn't it?

2. *Adult-Adult Transaction*

CLIENT: I don't know whether to buy the bellies here or wait until after the report.
BROKER: I'll wire Chicago and see if they have any information on expectations.

3. *Parent-Child Transaction*

CLIENT (Parent): I see where the 3-day moving average in May cocoa crossed the 10-day moving average on the upside yesterday and so I took a long position. It's off a little today but the weekly chart is bullish and when the weekly says up, you just don't worry about any adversity in the daily signal, especially during the time when the seasonal trend is up. In fact, I think I'll scalp about 30 points on the upside today and buy it back on Thursday morning after the Wednesday break.
BROKER (Child): Right.

4. *Adult-Parent Transaction*

CLIENT (Adult): I know I have trouble leaving the stop in when the market is acting poorly. I want you to promise me you won't listen when I try to pull out the stop.
BROKER (Parent): I won't change any stop for you during market hours.

[16] Harris *op. cit.*, p. 70.

The second rule of communication in transactional analysis is that when stimulus and response cross, in the P-A-C sense, communication stops.

CLIENT (Adult): I have a long position in July platinum and have been notified of delivery. How do I handle that?

BROKER (Parent): Who put you in July platinum?

The broker and client can't talk about how the delivery is going to be handled. They first have to decide who is to blame for the trade.

CLIENT (Child): I'm short soybeans just like you said and they have been up the limit for three days. They should sell off today, shouldn't they?

BROKER (Adult): The validation on that trade called for a 5-cent stop which you did not enter.

The client in this case is asking the broker to take the responsibility for a bad trade. The broker, speaking from his Adult, points out that the recommended stop was not entered and leaves the client with a tarnished self-concept.

As might be suspected by now, brokers and clients can play roles for varying periods of time, but a solid relationship between two people cannot be built or extended without the Adult. Perhaps the most significant assistance a broker can render to a client is to take the time to help him make the big decisions about how and under what conditions the broker-client relationship is to continue. This process makes a multitude of small decisions unnecessary and encourages the good feelings made possible by a meeting of the minds before, not after, situations occur that might create stress.

EPILOGUE

The problems to which the trader has set his face have developed because his aspirations are infinitely expansible; the solutions lie in the hope that his knowledge and behavior are infinitely perfectible. In between the recognition of the problems and the acquisition of the quantitative and qualitative skills for their solutions lies a series of searches that must, many times, include the experience of failure. Indeed, no successful traders the authors have known can follow their paths backward very far without running into failure. It is not the act of failure, however, that differentiates the ultimately successful or unsuccessful trader. Rather, it is that the successful trader gets up, spends a few days healing, reaffirms what he knows, and goes about the business of adding to his store of wisdom. In such a growth process the quality of persistence looms large and is virtually irreplaceable.

The person involved responsibly, both intellectually and behaviorally, with the experience of trading may, to paraphrase Theodore Roosevelt, know at his best the triumph of high achievement or, if he fails, will have failed while daring greatly, so that his place will never be with those timid souls who know neither victory nor defeat. Perhaps, then, in the final analysis, it may be as rewarding to travel as to arrive.

The Broker in the Game

There are at least two reasons for the inclusion of Chapter 14, "Building, Maintaining, and Servicing a Commodity Clientele." The first is the obvious one of providing the commodity broker with a guide to on-going activities which show no clear beginning or ending. In that sense the chapter will have served its purpose if it proves useful as a yardstick of the broker's individual performance. The second reason, however, is as important as the first. The chapter should be studied by the trader so that as a client he may be aware of the principles on which the performance of a knowledgeable broker is based. The setting of standards does two things: first, both broker and client will more readily recognize substandard performance because good performance is defined; second, avenues to better performance are explored by which improvement in the quality of services rendered may be effected as much by client awareness as by the broker's presentation.

CHAPTER FOURTEEN

Building, Maintaining, and Servicing a Commodity Clientele

> To profit from good advice requires more wisdom than to give it.

INTRODUCTION

The registered representative who specializes in commodities is, like his counterpart in the securities area, basically a salesman. He must build a clientele by effective prospecting methods, maintain it by replacing clients lost, and serve those who deal with him efficiently. It is a truly rare person who is so skilled and knowledgeable that he can perform capably as salesman and researcher at the same time. Both research and sales are full-time jobs for most people if done competently. The primary function of a commodity salesman is to locate potential clients who, because he serves them honestly and well, will continue to do business with him over time.

BUILDING A COMMODITY CLIENTELE

Sales personality. The impression made by a registered representative on his clients is based on attitude, appearance, and ability to communicate. The attitude that any salesman should have is obviously beyond dispute. He should believe that his product is good for all concerned; his client, his firm, and himself. The client's interests must come first, but the firm and the salesman should also gain from satisfactory service. Long-term success is virtually impossible if all three do not benefit adequately and fairly. The brokerage company must make a profit from its business, the registered representative must be able to earn an adequate living handling his accounts, and the customer must be financially or psychically rewarded to justify his trading. Some salesmen believe that no client ever profits in the long run. Others are so disturbed by the high percentage of traders who lose money that they are unable to function effectively. These salesmen would help all concerned, including themselves, by selling some other product or by making a living in some other way. If the salesman can accept the fact that trading commodities is right for some people and wrong for others and tell all with whom he deals the truth about the business as he knows it, assuming that they are interested in his knowledge, then he can show enough sincerity to sell effectively. If he induces people to trade who clearly should not trade or persuades others not to trade who might enjoy it, profit from it, or both, or pretends to know what he does not know, he is helping no one. The proper sales attitude for most good salesmen is derived in large part from the enthusiasm that comes from a real understanding of what they are selling and what motivates the people who are buying.

The salesman's appearance is dictated by the same standards that apply to anyone in the investment field. He should look successful enough to avoid having his customers wonder why he is offering financial advice when he looks like a failure himself. He should not, however, dress so extravagantly that he gives the impression he has acquired all the money that his clients have lost. Extremes of dress are almost certain to prove offensive to some people who may respond by patronizing a different salesman.

The salesman communicates with his customers personally or by telephone or mail. He must know how to speak, write, and spell. If his speech, vocabulary, or writing ability is inadequate, he should recognize the deficiency and do something about it beyond hoping that the office stenographer will note and correct his errors. Effective formal courses in speech are available, and most communities have clubs dedicated to the improvement of public speaking. Group prospecting, such as addressing a luncheon meeting of a civic club, is too effective a sales device not to be utilized merely because a salesman is too inexperienced or shy to learn to speak well. Vocabulary and spelling may also be improved by taking positive steps that can be fun as well as economically rewarding. Formal courses in letter writing are part of the program of virtually all business schools.

Product knowledge. It has been said that commodity traders pass through three stages. First, they know not and know that they know not. Then they know not and know not that they know not. Then they know and know that they know. The first and third stages are relatively safe, but most traders seem to enter the dangerous second stage rather quickly and stay there. Worse, many registered representatives are there as well and are even more dangerous than individual traders because of their influence on others. Many inexperienced traders are led to believe that a registered representative knows more than he really does because of his fluency in the language of the business and his knowledge of its mechanics.

Some brokers study securities and commodities constantly in a truly professional manner and are really well informed. Others who become quite humble when they realize how little they do know approach trading with the caution it deserves. Too many, however, cover their lack with glib pretense and superficiality. It behooves the trader to ascertain the category into which his registered representative fits.

To establish himself as a professional in the area of product knowledge a registered representative need not build a reputation for enriching all his clients or selecting winning positions infallibly. A client who hopes to find such a man to service his account is hopelessly naïve, unreasonable, or both. There are, however, some constructive steps that may be taken by a salesman. He can become thoroughly informed of the services offered by his firm and by the commodity exchanges. He can master the rules, regulations, and mechanical procedures that apply to his job and learn enough about the legal, accounting, and tax aspects of commodity trading to provide his clients with general guidance, but he should never try to replace a qualified accountant or lawyer. Some of this basic knowledge is necessarily possessed by most salesmen because of the requirement of many exchanges that an examination be passed (see the appendix at the end of this chapter). Like any professional, a salesman in the commodity field should keep pace with all developments and changes and be aware of the implications they may have for his clients. Different commodity futures become popular or unpopular. Sometimes new ones appear on the futures exchanges and the old become dormant or disappear completely. Areas of activity such as trading currencies on the commodity exchanges or the periodic resurgence of trading in commodity options may offer new opportunities.

An important step toward professionalism constitutes a familiarity with the old and new literature in the industry. In addition to the obvious sources of current information available in financial magazines, newspapers, and services, there is the scholarly work done in commodities and the closely related areas of probability, money management, and utility theory with all of which the salesman should become acquainted in order to better understand his product and the customer who buys it. It is not a matter of unreasonable expense or effort for the salesman to build himself a personal library of appropriate books and government and private research publications. The rapid rate of growth of commodity trading makes it mandatory for the salesman to keep abreast of all changes for his own and his clients' benefit.

Probably the most important word to learn in the area of product knowledge is "validation." Half-truths and unsupported opinions such as "Gaps on a chart must be closed" or "When a 3-day moving average line crosses a 10-day moving average line, a trading opportunity is evident" should not be inflicted on unsuspecting clients who will almost certainly lose their trading capital. The salesman who induces his clients to make decisions based on such fragile foundations will sooner or later lose them and his reputation and will well deserve to lose both. The same applies to thought-less advice in the area of money management. One of the most popular of these high-sounding but questionable concepts is "Always keep a cash reserve." Obviously a cash reserve is useless if it is never to be put to work. Even more common is the frequently offered advice to set profit objectives at some dollar multiple of the risk; for example, if a trader is to risk 4 cents in a corn trade, his objective should be no less than 8 cents. Hence he is ostensibly taking a favorable two-to-one bet. Actually this is meaningless if no weight is given to the odds of achieving the profit or suffering the loss. Trading corn with a stop of ¼ cent and a goal of $1.25 profit a bushel hardly offers a trader odds of 500 to one, whereas a position with a risk of 4 cents and a goal of 4 cents is well worth taking if the probability of achieving the 4-cent profit is four times the probability of suffering the 4-cent loss.

Knowledge of the firm. The salesman should realize that there is no ideal firm in terms of size or specialization. Each has its advantages and limita-tions, but he should make an effort to understand the strengths and weak-nesses of his own company and capitalize on its strengths and compensate for its weaknesses. If the weaknesses prevail on balance, he would do well to make a change.

Basically, there are two types of firm in the commodity futures field. One is the full-line wire house which, in addition to commodities, offers stocks, bonds, mutual funds, and various other types of financial merchan-dise. The other is the commodity specialty house. The full-line house is usually considerably larger than the specialty house in terms of capital, offices and number of personnel. The salesman for the first can offer the client the advantage of doing more of his trading in various types of financial merchandise with one firm, thus simplifying record keeping and transfer-ring funds for his various financial ventures. The salesman with the spe-cialty firm can sometimes offer more sophisticated service in terms of speed, interpretation of news, and technical knowledge because neither he nor his back office personnel have to diversify in so many complex areas.

The salesman must thoroughly understand the structure of the firm with which he is associated. A client has the right to know whether a firm hold-ing a significant amount of his capital is financially stable. The salesman should either be fully aware of his firm's financial condition or have a good reason to explain why he is not. He should know which exchange member-ships are held by his firm and which of them are clearing memberships. If the number of memberships is relatively limited, the salesman should be prepared to deal with the questions of a client rightfully concerned about the possibility of having recommendations concentrated among the com-modities traded on the exchanges to which his firm belongs rather than among those presenting the best opportunities.

The salesman should be familiar with his own firm's market letter and its other published material as well as that of its competitors. He should be able to take advantage of other services such as charts, floor information, commodity calendars, and offers of specific trading recommendations and should know how to interpret his clients' confirmations and monthly statements.

The one area in which nearly every salesman expects more than his firm can deliver is that of providing consistently successful specific recommendations of market positions. The life of the commodity salesman would be easy indeed if all he had to do was pass on the recommendations of his firm's research department to clients who would then make a significant amount of money within a short time. Telling the client the glad news of his latest important profit is among the pleasantest experiences a salesman can have, whereas breaking the news of the latest market catastrophe is among the worst. Regardless of the size or degree of specialization of his firm, the salesman must realize that its good intentions are probably beyond question. It would like its clients to make money in the markets because it profits from commissions paid and knows that it is easier to retain a satisfied client than it is to replace him with a new one, particularly as its reputation for losing clients becomes known. Furthermore, a client who is successful in the market has an ever-growing account, and the commissions he pays grow accordingly if he does not withdraw all his profits. In addition, he is far more likely to refer new accounts to the firm than if he were a loser.

The magnitude of the problems faced by a commodity firm, regardless of the purity of its intentions, should not be underestimated by its employees or its customers. Making profits in the commodity markets is possible for the skilled, disciplined trader who is carefully managing an adequate but not unreasonably large pool of capital. If the firm recommends positions and its recommendations are followed by many of its clients, it acts much as if it were loosely managing many accounts, each influenced to some degree by its owner. If the firm is consistently successful, the amount of money it influences will grow almost geometrically as the accounts of its customers grow and new customers are attracted by tales of success. Ultimately, the firm's own clients will drive prices so high when they buy and so low when they sell that the firm's recommendations will become self-defeating. Although the commodity markets are generally sufficiently liquid to handle the business of individual traders, they cannot absorb concentrated orders of unusual size without distortion. Despite this problem, customers almost invariably demand and receive trade recommendations from the firms with which they deal in addition to the more reasonable basic data and current market information. The fact that long-term success is virtually impossible does not seem to deter many customers or their salesmen from demanding specific trading advice. It is interesting to note in passing that customers who ask for valid and specific records covering significant periods of time are far more likely to receive a reason why the records are not available than to receive the records themselves. The salesman should be aware that customers who follow a firm's recommendations precisely over a period of time are quite likely to lose money and virtually certain to blame him for their losses. If they make money, customers are likely to credit their own wisdom in selecting trades wisely. The situation for the salesman is analogous to the teacher whose successful students invariably say "I got an A", whereas the losers say "He gave me an F." Many of these students grow up and become commodity traders.

Prospect knowledge. Identification of potential commodity clients is difficult except in a most general way. The Chicago Mercantile Exchange surveyed 4,000 traders in 1971 and found that the closest approach to a profile would be a man about 45 years old who had a college background, an annual income of more than $10,000, was employed as an executive or professional, and who traded few contracts at any one time. Most of the sample had traded over a relatively short period and had security accounts. Although an effort to describe the potential clientele for a business is laudable, the wide band of characteristics attributed to the trader to date is too general to be really useful to salesmen. Pure conjecture would lead one to the conclusion that potential clients should have adequate resources which would eliminate most young people who have not yet had time to acquire speculative capital as well as the older segment of the population who are often more concerned, and properly so, with capital preservation than with growth. Even the excess number of male traders over female will probably diminish in time.

The job of any salesman is to identify the buying motives of his clients and to present selling points that will appeal to these buying motives as much as possible. In a broad sense commodity clients are motivated by some combination of the desire to make significant money and to play an exciting game for the sake of playing it. The two most common conflicting motives with which the salesman must deal are greed and fear. Most investors would be glad to realize substantial gains from commodity trading but are afraid to pay the price, namely, the risk of loss.

Registered representatives should be prepared to give honest answers, whether the questions are actually asked or only implied. Most potential clients can be expected to ask what gains can be expected from successful trading. The salesman's answer should be based on something more than pure conjecture, hope, or selective perception but must in no way offer any assurance of profit. He should realize that the fear expressed by a prospective client may not be his basic one. Many people are concerned with possible substantial deficits, endless limit moves, or physical delivery of the commodity in which they are trading, but their real doubt is most likely based on simple ignorance or the apprehension attendant on losing money. They must be made to realize that the risk of loss must be accepted in any venture in which the profit potential exceeds the interest paid on a bank savings account. The salesman should neither fan the greed nor quell the fear beyond reason but should try to contain both within reasonable bounds. Clients who expect to double their money monthly and others who are afraid that opening a small commodity account could easily result in a fore-closure on their homes are equally guilty of faulty thinking and should be corrected.

One frequent problem centers around the question, expressed or implied, of the salesman's own success in the commodity markets. In effect, if the opportunities are vast as often implied, why is he not rich himself? Handling this question is neither so difficult nor embarrassing as one might think. Basically, the good salesman deals with this question as with all others; that is, merely by telling the truth. One possibility, of course, is that he *is* rich and has accumulated his wealth by following his own advice. There are many others, however. The salesman may be too young to have accu-mulated enough capital to justify speculating. He may be conservative in nature and more concerned with not losing than with the chance of win-ning. The salesman, like any other customer of a financial firm, should adapt his financial merchandise to his own nature. It is also possible that he has a talent for guiding others, although he cannot play the game well himself. This is analogous to the athletic world in which many excellent coaches have never been good players and many good players could never succeed as coaches. Other salesmen feel that trading their own accounts would create a bias in their handling of clients' accounts and that they would have to make a choice between one direction or the other. They may conclude that in their own trading they would make important money four or five years out of six, which is true of most successful professional traders, but that by handling accounts of others they will make reasonably good money six years out of six.

The motivations and fears of his clients should be clear to the salesman. Both are described at considerable length in other chapters.

Salesmanship. In addition to natural talent, some training is necessary to develop an effective salesman. Procedures of the firm as well as the prin-ciples of salesmanship must be learned. Some of this training is the respon-sibility of the firm employing the salesman, although this responsibility is frequently abdicated by having inadequate classes conducted by people who have little more expertise in the subjects taught than the trainees themselves or by those with expertise but without the ability to teach. Re-gardless of the quality of his firm's training, a salesman should be willing to improve himself by learning what he can about the commodity area and how to present himself and his ideas effectively.

The principles of describing his product, meeting a client's objections, and closing sales in commodity positions are similar to those in selling any intangible product and are not presented here in detail. Most of them can be handled merely by knowing enough about the field to answer questions and making suggestions reasonably and honestly. Prospecting for new clients is so important and, for some, so difficult that it warrants some dis-cussion.

When the thoroughly trained salesman has passed the necessary tests and obtained the required registrations, he is ready to begin prospecting. This is not a popular activity with most salesman, but in the investment business it is never ending. Not only would most salesmen like to have the largest clientele possible but they would also prefer to improve its quality.

Some sales managers reduce the subject of prospecting to its essentials: simply walk, talk, and meet the people. Finding customers thus becomes a simple numbers game. Approach enough people enough times and the result will be a number of interviews. Conduct enough interviews and the result will be the conversion of prospects to clients. Continue the process long enough and the result will be a large clientele of high quality. Basically, this philosophy of prospecting is quite correct, but the new salesman may well question the source of all the people to whom he is supposed to walk and talk. If 10 contacts ultimately result in one interview and three interviews produce one new account, a hard-working salesman can use up a great number of names within a short time. Replenishment of a real prospect list at reasonable cost is not so simple as it may appear.

Some firms rely heavily on newspaper advertising, particularly of the kind that requires some sort of reply. Favorites include the coupon that is returned for literature, an invitation to call a salesman who will provide desired information, or an invitation to a lecture. All of these usually provide names that result in new business and so are popular with salesmen. For their employers who pay for the advertisements, however, this method is somewhat less popular. Although most people interested in trading commodities read newspapers and magazines, most people, hence most readers, do not trade commodities, and a publication's advertising rates must be large enough to cover the cost of reaching its entire unspecialized audience. A small number of publications are devoted exclusively to commodities, but most of them appeal to those already engaged in trading rather than to those who are potential traders. When the cost of preparing, inserting, and following up an advertisement is considered, the expenditure for each new name placed on a firm's prospect list may approach or even exceed the revenues reasonably expected to be gained from new accounts. Some of this may be justified by the firm's desire to engage in institutional advertising simply to keep its name before the public. When this motive is combined with the effort to gain new business, the total cost may be judged reasonable.

Lectures, often dignified by the title "seminar" are sometimes effective but are also sometimes delivered by the wrong speaker to the wrong audience. Not infrequently they are given by people new to the business who have not yet developed a clientele to an audience that has not formulated an approach to trading. Alternatively, they may be presented by more experienced salesmen. Some may have changed locations or firms, and others may be trying to replace a clientele that has been lost. There may or may not be a correlation between knowledge of trading and skill of presentation, but sometimes glibness is confused with wisdom, and some members of "seminar" audiences have been damaged by what they thought was sound advice. Even well-promoted, effectively delivered, and efficently followed up lectures often result in the opening of only rather small, low-profit accounts, for sophisticated traders with large accounts seldom feel the need to attend. Workshops held regularly once or twice a week at the same location to examine current markets in a professional manner (not merely by indicating trend lines on a chart with a pointer) have proved quite successful for some brokers at a reasonable cost. The same prospective clients may return several times, thus allowing time for confidence to build, and they may bring friends. In addition, workshops tend to appeal more than general lectures to serious students of the market.

Conducting a seminar is a skill in itself and deserves some thought. Certainly the lecture should be carefully planned in every detail. A trader who will learn sooner or later that a well-prepared plan is the key to successful trading can hardly be impressed by a meeting at which the microphone does not work, the reading material is in short supply, the slides are shown upside down, or the number of chairs provided differs substantially from the size of the audience. Some problems can be avoided by asking for reservations by coupon or telephone. Although some who make reservations will not appear and others will come without reservations, a good approximation is at least possible. Some way of obtaining names and addresses inoffensively must be arranged if the productivity of the lecture is not to be defeated. Those who attend can sign in at the door or a door prize can be offered. Names and addresses can be written on the ticket stubs to be drawn.

If the audience contains people of varying degress of sophistication, the level of the talk should be determined by the least knowledgeable but must move fast enough to hold the attention of those who are more familiar with the markets. If analogies are used, the speaker should be careful to go from the familiar to the unfamiliar and not from one unfamiliar activity to another. Slides and projections should be large enough to be seen clearly be those at the back and along the sides of the room. Questions should be answered at the end of the presentation to avoid breaking its continuity by permitting diversion into areas of interest to only small segments of the audience. When questions are allowed, answers should be concise. Long-windedness tends to stifle questions from other prospects who might open accounts if they could get just one more answer but are afraid that a question will result in another 20-minute speech and that they will never get home. Sixty seconds for each answer is usually long enough.

It is wise for a speaker to consider in advance the most frequent objections to his product. If an answer to the objection can be turned into a selling point by treating the objectionable aspect to better advantage, the salesman has nothing to fear if he knows his material and his answer is ready and well phrased. If questions that are difficult to treat favorably are expected, the speaker can do much to lessen their effect by raising them himself before the audience does and by phrasing them as favorably as possible, thus forestalling some of the adverse effect. Typical questions might involve the delivery of the cash commodity, the tremendous adversity caused by a series of limit moves against the trader's position, the Salad Oil Scandal of the early 1960s, and the instability of a small commodity firm, particularly if no financial statements are made available to its customers.

Mass mailing undoubtedly brings in leads but has most of the disadvantages of advertising in mass media; especially the high cost per lead. Because commodity traders have so few common characteristics other than speculative captial and a willingness to accept a risk, it is most difficult to define a mailing list that could prove especially useful, even presuming its availability. Lists of doctors, dentists, airline pilots, and those who have written commodity exchanges for information are especially overworked. Even salesmen who "work a list" often do so ineffectively. It is important to keep good records when contacts are made, eliminating names only when accounts are opened or when it becomes evident that they never will be. Too often a salesman is unwilling to approach prospects that would become accounts only after four, five, or even more contacts. It is usually unwise to attempt to sell commodity accounts or positions to people by mail or telephone. It is more productive to rely on interviews during which the sale of an account is easier. It is also easier to determine whether a prospect would make a suitable account at a face-to-face meeting.

Unannounced personal calls are unquestionably sometimes effectively made but are generally unpopular both with prospects and salesmen. Prospects, especially busy ones, often resent being disturbed at a time convenient only to the salesman, and many salesmen believe that the time consumed in seeking out a qualified prospect is beyond reason, especially in large cities. In addition, it places the salesman in a difficult psychological position. He is selling a trading activity that is supposed to present a handsome profit potential while he himself is walking door-to-door looking for customers. Any attempt to explain this away because one is new in the business is futile, for the customer will soon realize that he can pay his commissions to a salesman who is too well established to take the time to ring doorbells.

A more effective way to meet people is by personal radiation; that is, by joining and working in various organizations and gaining the friendship and respect of other members who might open accounts. It is important, of course, not to become an obvious "glad-hander" who is usually more avoided than patronized.

Many new salesmen believe that the difficult task of building a list of clients will take only a few months and that after a brief period a substantial clientele can be relied on to provide a good lifetime income with the commissions they will pay. This, however, is not the case. Attrition among traders, especially after a few recommendations have worked out badly, is the rule and not the exception. Referrals by satisfied clients provide less business than might be expected. Losers rarely make any. Even winners are sometimes reluctant to suggest highly speculative ventures to their friends for fear that they will be held accountable for any losses suffered and ultimately lose their friends with no hope of personal gain. (This fear is probably well founded.)

Salesmen employed by full-line wire houses are often able to convert some of their stock clients to commodity clients. Such conversions, typically constitute about 70 percent of the traders in commodities, but although speculators in the security markets provide an obvious source of clients, they are also a source of a number of problems. Sometimes the salesman becomes overenthusiastic about the opportunities in commodity trading and induces a stock client to trade commodities for whom commodity trading is unsuitable, and sometimes he overestimates the skill involved in his own or his firm's short-term success in selecting commodity positions and underestimates the risk, after which the client claims misrepresentation. Even in the case of a speculatively inclined client for whom commodity trading is suitable it frequently happens that an unsuccessful venture into commodity trading on a relatively small scale ultimately causes the loss of the larger stock account which might well have proved profitable over a period of years. It is for this reason that many executives of brokerage firms look unfavorably at such conversions. Some will separate security and commodity activities completely by having different salesmen handle the different products or even by maintaining entirely separate commodity and stock offices. Some will eliminate commodity trading from their firm's portfolio of products altogether, which might, however, have the effect of losing a stock account to another firm offering a more complete line of financial merchandise.

MAINTAINING A COMMODITY CLIENTELE

The ideal way to maintain a profitable commodity clientele would be to provide a continuous stream of highly profitable trade suggestions. If the salesman can do this, he will not need to be unduly concerned with servicing his clientele because he will have difficulty losing a customer, even intentionally. The registered representative with a trading method that has been validated in real time or who has a high degree of market judgment that permits him to select the positions of others will easily build and retain a substantial clientele. Just as surely the salesman who passes on shallow opinions based on superficial observation of a quote board, tape, or naïve chart cannot in a real sense succeed. Depending entirely on good trading results to maintain a commodity clientele will seldom lead to success. If the salesman suggests unprofitable trades, he will, of course, lose his clients because they will lose their money, faith or both. Even if his clients select their own positions, he will lose them sooner or later either because they will lose their capital or will find a way to justify blaming the salesman and his firm for the results, although neither had much to do with them. There are, however, some positive courses of action that the salesman can follow to help maintain his clientele.

A registered representative of most wire houses has a full line of merchandise. He should not induce his clients to trade in the parts of his line that he prefers either because they are most profitable to him or because they fit his personal biases, neither should he attempt to persuade them to avoid trading in areas in which he himself has not been successful. A salesman of investment and speculative vehicles would do well, in the long run, as would salesmen of anything else, to adapt his product line to the wishes and needs of his clients rather than to adapt the client to the items he prefers to sell. He should be careful neither to exaggerate nor to understate the profit potential of his security or commodity lines. A salesman who speaks convincingly of annual expectations of 100 percent or more will undoubtedly open many commodity accounts but will just as surely lose them when it becomes evident that he cannot possibly meet the standards he has set for his own performance. Understating objectives can be just as harmful to a client who has invested a small amount of money in a conservative venture yielding a small return when he might have made a greater gain in a more speculative venture. It is always best for a salesman to tell the truth about his merchandise, as far as he knows it, and not attempt to expound when he does not know the facts. He must stop short of the point at which the client makes his own decision concerning the amount of risk he chooses to take. The salesman should make every effort to provide honest guidance, but he should never try to be his brother's keeper.

As far as possible, the salesman should avoid becoming personally responsible for trades. Some may feel that the role of order taker is below their dignity and prefer to insert themselves into trades suggested by their Research Departments or by their customers, but this is seldom wise. Those who do will learn sooner or later the truth of the aphorism, "When I am right no one remembers—when I am wrong, no one forgets."

SERVICING A COMMODITY CLIENTELE

In the servicing of clientele one of the least popular but most important tasks is record keeping. If a client asks what his position is or when he established it and at what prices, he is entitled to a prompt and correct answer. The salesman who is days behind in his posting or does not do it at all does not deserve the continued patronage of his clients. Failure to maintain accurate records can result not only in the justified loss of clients because of poor service but also in costly errors. One of the most important ledgers is the holding record in which the name, account number, telephone number, and market positions, including prices and dates, as they are taken and liquidated for each client, are entered. This record book should be posted as confirmations are received or, at worst, at the end of each day. It should be available and open to the client's page while speaking to him. Relying on memory to fill an order can be a serious matter and using an erroneous account number can have surprisingly grave results. The client who places the order will not get a confirmation and will suspect that his order was neither promptly nor properly handled. Another of the firm's clients who did not place an order will get a confirmation and will wonder whether trading is being carried on in his account without authorization. The back office effort required to correct the error may cost the brokerage firm more money than it earned for its commission on the trade.

Much more serious, if a posting record is not maintained, is the possibility of allowing a client to think that he is liquidating a position previously liquidated, with the result that an unwanted position is created. A market order may be entered and an open order forgotten which, when filled later, can cause the same position to be established or liquidated twice. Misunderstandings in directions are easier if written records are not consulted. The salesman may find that he has tried to liquidate a short position by selling or a long position by buying. He will therefore have two positions instead of one. It may appear that the market will make the latter prove profitable half the time, but for some reason this seldom seems to work out. (Somehow, when someone drops a piece of toast onto the floor, it seems to have an uncanny way of landing buttered side down.) Losses incurred because of these or similar errors are almost invariably borne by the brokerage firm and, in turn, by the salesman himself, at least in part. In most cases the salesman deserves his loss.

It is also wise for the salesman to maintain a cross-file organized by commodities in order, if he wishes, to determine quickly which of his clients or prospects is interested in a given commodity. This record is especially important in the servicing of clients who rely on the advice of a brokerage firm. If a client enters a position that the firm later recommends should be liquidated and is not called promptly, he will not react happily to the news that he has suffered a loss or lost his profit because the salesman forgot that he had a position. When the salesman posts his customer's file, it takes only a few extra minutes to post the cross-file. If the newswires, financial journals, the government, or the firm itself release any information that could be of interest to clients holding positions in various commodities, it is easy for the salesman to identify them and convey the information to them by mail or telephone. For the salesman who is trying to increase the size of his clientele, it is also wise to post the positions of potential clients with whom he is in some communication in his cross-file and keep them informed of matters pertinent to them. His service may prove to be better than that offered by their present brokers who may be taking their business for granted. Eventually some or all of this business may be acquired. If a salesman ranks second on the lists of a large number of people who are determining where to place their business, he will ultimately receive a surprising number of accounts as the first choices fall out of favor. This happens frequently as customers become disenchanted with trade selections, when confirmations of trades are not received promptly or are considered to be unsatisfactory, when information is not passed on promptly or accurately, or when a check is not sent out quickly on request. Because a substantial number of commodity traders have more than one account or have traded with more than one broker, being next in line can prove to be most lucrative.

Because most accounts are opened after several contacts, it is important to maintain a lead file. This may be no more than an alphabetic filing of prospects, but it can prove to be invaluable. The best organized files also have a tickler section organized by date. If a prospect suggests calling back at a later time when he expects to have raised some capital or to have returned from a trip, the salesman can file his card under a future date to remind himself to call again at the proper time.

To service a client well, it is most important to determine what he will want when the account is opened. Some clients will prefer to follow the suggestions offered by the firm or the salesman. It is necessary to find out what kind of information they will need and when and where they wish to be called. Some of them will ask the salesman to trade for them when they cannot be reached, but if this is done the understanding between them and the salesman must be perfectly clear if problems are to be avoided when losses occur.

Other clients prefer to make their own decisions and do not care to be influenced even by comments about their own choices, much less have trades suggested to them. Presuming that such clients do not lose their money or decide to trade elsewhere for reasons beyond the control of the salesman, all that the latter need do is provide good service. This involves little more than maintaining accurate records, confirming a client's trades promptly, entering his orders properly, and making sure that the telephone is answered. A salesman who has many clients of this kind would do well to form a partnership of some sort with another registered representative to make sure that his phone is answered at once when he is away from his desk or office or on vacation.

It is in handling self-traders that brokers are really able to excel. This is especially true of young brokers who find no need to explain away their lack of experience as they would have to do with a customer who demanded more detailed direction. All that is necessary is to have a good working knowledge of the procedures of the business and to observe and pass on currently important information and facts rather than offhand opinions, glib guesses, and bluffs. The client who makes his own decisions has the right to expect really outstanding personal service in return for the often significant commissions he pays. The salesman who limits himself as much as possible to giving good service and passing on facts requested by his clients will not do so much business in the short run as his bolder counterpart who is willing to make specific suggestions, but he is quite likely to do more in the long run, build a better reputation, and sleep better at night.

Many salesmen may be dissatisfied with a role that is little more than order taker, but reflection may convince them that it can be more important than it appears. If a salesman has no reason to believe that neither his personal trade suggestions nor those of his firm will lead to long-term success, he is left with two functions that he can perform well, both of which are vital. One is the proper servicing of the customer's account. The other, and even more important, is acting as a customer's alter ego to help jog him along the right road; for example, a customer may tell his salesman that he believes every position taken should be protected immediately with a stop order, yet may omit placing such an order. The salesman who asks "Where do you want your stop?" and causes one to be entered may be performing a service far more important than that done by the salesman who calls his clients to tell them that wheat is acting well because it has been up for two days and that they should consider taking a long position.

The registered representative who guides his client toward logical money management can make a vital contribution to his success. He can avoid reinforcing his client's errors by acting as if all were well. If he does not know, he should say that he does not know. When a client shows loser's characteristics, the broker can take steps to induce him to change his ways before it is too late. "You never go broke taking a profit" warns of taking short profits. "I'm locked in" warns of a person who will not take a loss. "I'll watch it" is a clear indication of a lack of planning which is the most certain way to lose sooner or later. The salesman who learns the correct approach to trading, develops sufficient authority to warrant a hearing, and communicates well enough to deliver his message effectively can build a rewarding commodity clientele and serve and maintain it well.

APPENDIX

Preparation for the Chicago Board of Trade Commodity Solicitor Examination

The Commodity Solictor Examination is required of anyone who wishes to become registered as a commodity solicitor with the regulated commodity exchanges in the United States. The test itself consists of 125 multiple-choice and true/false questions which the examinee is given two hours to answer. A score of 70 percent is considered a passing grade.

The examinee is provided with reading material and sample test questions by the brokerage house that employs him and by the Chicago Board of Trade. Although the test is periodically up-dated, there are 10 areas of knowledge that will prove to be of substantial assistance in passing the test.

1. *Government Agencies and Commodities Exchanges.* The organization and responsibilities of many relevant government agencies and commodity exchanges, including the jurisdiction of key exchange committees, are examined.

2. *Glossary of Futures Markets Terms.* A significant amount of time should be

spent studying the general defintions of such terms as "normal," "carrying-charge," "inverted," "overbought," "oversold," and many others which describe price relationships and behavior of the futures markets.

3. *Type and Ownership of Accounts.* The examinee should be familiar with the various methods of carrying commodity futures accounts and the legal aspects of the major alternatives.

4. *Speculation, Hedging, Gambling, and Investing.* Some time should be devoted to defining these terms and comparing and contrasting their roles.

5. *Margin* and *Margin Calls.* The exam will include questions about setting margins and the responsibilities of the exchange, broker, and customer relating to margin activities.

6. *Technical versus Fundamental Analysis.* The applicant should be able to compare and contrast the elements of each approach to trade selection.

7. *Types of Orders.* Study should include orders of all types, their wording, application, and limitations.

8. *Spreading.* The exam will emphasize the theory of spreading, including the types of spreads and their application.

9. *The Soybean Complex.* The examinee should understand the relationships in the complex, including the crush, reverse crush, and conversion equivalents between soybeans, soybean meal, and soybean oil contracts.

10. *Contract Facts.* For each commodity the applicant should know

> contract size,
> reportable limit,
> position limit,
> commission,
> minimum and maximum allowable price fluctuation,
> whether regulated or unregulated,
> contract months traded,
> delivery procedure, including any special rules for retenders.

SAMPLE QUESTIONS

The following are typical questions asked on the exam. An answer key follows the questions (although there are undoubtedly those who would disagree with the answers suggested.)

1. Which of the following is *not* necessary for handling a discretionary account:
   (a) Written approval of client before entry of each order.
   (b) Written confirmation after the trade.
   (c) Original authorization from the customer.
   (d) All of the above.

2. The basis is
   (a) difference between one future price and another future price,
   (b) difference between cash and near future prices,
   (c) future price divided by cash price,
   (d) none of the above.

3. The protection of customers' funds by special handling procedures is the responsibility of
   (a) board of trade,
   (b) clearinghouse,
   (c) commission market,
   (d) Commodity Exchange Authority.

4. Every Monday figures are released on visible supplies, as compiled by the
   (a) CEA,
   (b) clearinghouse,
   (c) Chicago Board of Trade,
   (d) Department of Agriculture.

5. A soybean processor who buys beans and sells the products in the futures market would be placing a
   (a) reverse crush,
   (b) processor conversion,
   (c) crush hedge (putting on crush),
   (d) intermarket spread.

6. True or false: The major economic role of a futures market is to determine prices.

7. True or false: Speculation in commodities increases the range of price fluctuations.

8. True or false: Open interest in a given delivery month is the total long and short positions held in that month.

9. The CEA is interested in all of the following except (more than one is possible)
   (a) limits maximum positions,
   (b) prohibiting price manipulation,
   (c) testing of all commodity solicitors,
   (d) designating a futures market as a contract market,
   (e) protection of customers' funds,
   (f) commodity broker registration,
   (g) specification of commodities covered,
   (h) registration of futures commission merchant,
   (i) registration of floor brokers.

10. Regarding an account opened as tenants in common, the following are true or false:
    (a) On the death of one party all equity in the account becomes that of the survivor with no restrictions.
    (b) On the death of one party the survivor gets no additional equity and the estate of decedent is taxed on all equity in account apart from that which the estate can prove belongs to the survivor.

11. True or false. Domestic and world sugar prices move independently on occasion.

12. The daily permissable limit on cocoa is
    (a) 4 cents
    (b) 1½ cents
    (c) 1 cent

13. True or false. Fish meal is a regulated commodity.

14. True or false. The institution of insurance is a method of sharing the risk of speculative events with others.

15. True or false: Bona fide hedgers must abide by position limits.

Answer Key

1. a
2. b
3. a
4. c
5. c

6. True
7. False
8. False
9. c, f
10. a, false; b, true
11. True
12. a
13. False
14. True
15. False

It should be emphasized that there is no necessary correlation between the passing of the examination and the ability to handle commodity accounts effectively. As in many other fields, the examinee often treats the test as a barrier that must be hurdled, not as an indication of real competence or as a substitute for experience.

Choosing the Game (Markets)

*In the final analysis the decision-making process, or playing
the game, eventually extends to the individual commodity
in which a commitment is to be made. Because the factors
that affect the prices of copper and corn, for example, are
nearly independent, there is good reason to employ the term
"markets for commodities" rather than "the commodities
market." The following 15 chapters (15 through 29) describe
and analyze 29 active commodities. Basically, each is discussed within a common framework which includes contract
facts, the factors that influence prices, sources of information,
the nature of production or supply, the nature of utilization
or demand, pertinent seasonal information, and notes from a
trader. Commodities are generally grouped by the Exchanges
on which they trade. The information given, although not
exhaustive, should give the trader or broker a good grasp of
the significant elements that affect prices. It is important
to note that different techniques may be illustrated in different chapters for individual commodities; however, each is
transferable to the others; for example, the seasonal analyses
for soybeans, potatoes, and pork bellies may be applied as
well to wheat, eggs, or cattle. Similarly, the regression analyses applied to cocoa, potatoes, and eggs should not be viewed
as unique to those commodities.*

CHAPTER FIFTEEN

Soybeans, Soybean Oil, and Soybean Meal

Before World War II Manchuria was the major source of the world soybean supply. An average of 70 million bushels was shipped in the 1930s. Because of the United States' wartime need to become self-sufficient in the supply of fats and oils, its soybean production was increased from 100 million bushels in 1941 to approximately 200 million in 1946, 850 million in 1965, and more than 1 billion bushels today. The United States is by far the largest soybean exporter.

Because of the war, soybean futures were not traded during the four years 1943–44 to 1946–47. With the resumption of trading, significant bull markets occurred in the 1947–48 season as well as in 1948–49 and 1949–50. The huge profit potential increased speculative interest, as is evidenced by the large volume and open interest that developed. Subsequent bull markets, 1953–54, 1955–56, 1960–61, 1965–66, and 1972–73, maintained and extended the speculative interest in trading soybean futures.

Soybean futures are traded principally on the Chicago Board of Trade, as are futures in soybean oil and soybean meal.

Soybean contracts traded are September, November, January, March,

CHART 15-1

SOYBEANS CHICAGO – WEEKLY HIGH,LOW & CLOSE OF NEAREST FUTURES CONTRACT   IN CENTS PER BUSHEL

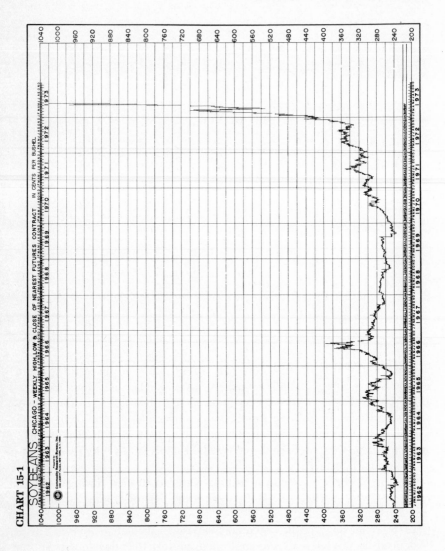

May, July, and August. Trading typically begins 11 or 12 months before the delivery month of the contract. The contract traded is 5,000 bushels, to be delivered during the months indicated. Price is quoted in cents per bushel, the minimum price fluctuation being ¼ cent, which represents $12.50 per contract (or 5,000 bushels). The maximum allowable daily range is 40 cents a bushel, with a maximum fluctuation of 20 cents, either up or down, from the settlement price of the preceding day.

The soybean oil contracts traded, and therefore the delivery months, are September, October, December, January, March, May, July, and August. Trading customarily begins 11 or 12 months before the delivery month. The contract traded is a unit of 60,000 pounds of oil. The price is quoted in cents per pound, the minimum price fluctuation being $\frac{1}{100}$ cent, or 1 point, a pound, which represents $6 a contract. The maximum allowable daily range is 2 cents a pound, with a maximum fluctuation of 1 cent, either up or down, from the preceding day's settlement price. These limits are removed from the spot month on the first notice day.

The contracts traded, the delivery months, and the commencement of trading for soybean meal are the same as those indicated for oil. The contract traded represents 100 tons of meal. Price is quoted in cents per ton, with a minimum fluctuation of 5 cents a ton, which represents $5 per contract traded. The maximum daily range and the maximum fluctuation, in either direction from the preceding day's settlement price, are $10 and $5 a ton, respectively. As with oil, these limits are not in force for the spot-month contract on and after the first notice day.

FACTORS WHICH INFLUENCE PRICES

The soybean crop, which is harvested from September to November, must fill the entire demand until the subsequent crop is available. Historically the carry-over has not been large, indicating that the supply has been well rationed over the year. However, carry-overs have recently been decreasing and are becoming a more significant price factor.

The rationing device is, of course, the fluctuating market price, which effectively regulates the utilization rate in such a manner that the total production is absorbed over the year. If the crop is small, enough users will be priced out of the market to leave some soybean inventory at the end of the crop year. If the crop is large, bargain prices bring new users into the market, and most of the supply will be utilized. Even if a substantial carry-over remains, the expanded use at the low price level makes it desirable.

Table 15-1 shows the supply and distribution of soybeans in the United States for the crop years 1960–61 to 1973–74, each crop year beginning September 1 and ending August 31. The old-crop August 31 carry-over stocks, which become the beginning September 1 stocks for the new year, plus the new-crop production, make up the total supply. The disappearance, often referred to as "utilization," when subtracted from the total

CHART 15-2

SOYBEAN OIL WEEKLY HIGH, LOW & CLOSE OF NEAREST FUTURES CONTRACT — CHICAGO BOARD OF TRADE IN CENTS PER POUND

Commodity Research Bureau, Inc.
ONE LIBERTY PLAZA, NEW YORK, N.Y. 10006

CHART 15-3

SOYBEAN MEAL WEEKLY HIGH, LOW & CLOSE OF NEAREST FUTURES CONTRACT—CHICAGO BOARD OF TRADE—IN DOLLARS PER TON

Prepared by
Commodity Research Bureau, Inc.
ONE LIBERTY PLAZA, NEW YORK, N. Y. 10006

supply, leaves the August 31 stocks, or new carry-over. Occasionally important year-to-year changes occur in the carry-over, and must be considered in the supply analysis. Most of the important year-to-year changes in disposition occur in the crushings (oil and meal principally for domestic use) and exports. Usage for seed and feed is relatively minor. The residual category merely covers unexplained differences. Because disappearance data are fairly accurate, the differences must be attributable to estimating errors in crop-size and quarterly-stocks reports.

Demand for the soybean products, oil and meal, increases with population and with the increased per capita demand for edible fats and oils. Improved livestock-feeding practices, intended to increase the protein content of livestock products, also results in greater demand for soybean meal. These trends are important in an analysis of the demand.

Each of the soybean products is part of the larger supply of edible fats and oils and protein foodstuffs. The large world trade in these commodities shows that world supply and demand must be considered for purposes of price forecasting. Since the total demand for fats, oils, and protein foodstuffs is relatively inelastic, large price changes are required in order to change the usage rate. This accounts for the high volatility in the price of soybeans and their products.

The price of soybeans depends on the price of the oil and meal made from the beans, less the cost of processing the beans and distributing the products. Changes in the processing and marketing margins often give rise to opportunities for potentially profitable spread trades. Typically, however, when forecasting changes in soybean prices, possible variations in the processing and marketing margins are ignored because they tend to be small in relation to variations in the price of soybeans.

In the short run soybean processors increase or decrease the price of oil and meal as soybean prices change. For short periods, therefore, the price of beans may dominate the prices of oil and meal. However, because almost all the oil and meal supplies are sold each crop year and because they must be sold for whatever prices the world market will allow, the product prices will determine the basic soybean price level over the crop year. Forecasts of oil prices and meal prices should be made separately and used, after adjustment for the margins, to predict soybean prices. Because the available supply for a given crop year is not subject to change, prices can be considered as essentially determined by demand.

The government price support program has generally not exerted a significant influence on soybean prices, except when prices are low, near the price support loan. If, in the future, the government establishes a large reserve of soybeans, as it did of wheat and corn, government policy will become a major determining factor of soybean prices.

Because changes in the spot or cash prices of soybeans often cause changes in the futures prices and because cash prices vary with location and other

TABLE 15-1 SUPPLY AND DISTRIBUTION OF SOYBEANS IN THE UNITED STATES (IN MILLIONS OF BUSHELS)

Crop year beginning Sept. 1	Supply						Distribution					
	Stocks, Sept. 1‡				Production	Total supply	Crushings	Exports	Seed	Feed	Residual	Total distribution
	Farms	CCC	Mills, elevators†	Total								
1960	3.4	.8	19.0	51.8	555.1	606.9	406.1	134.7	32.5	1.3	5.2	579.8
1961	1.6	0	4.4	27.1	678.6	705.7	431.4	149.4	33.3	1.3	12.0	627.4
1962	13.8	.3	43.5	78.3	669.2	747.5	472.7	180.5	34.6	1.1	12.6	701.5
1963	4.0	0	11.1	46.0	699.2	745.2	436.8	187.2	36.0	0.9	17.0	677.9
1964–65	15.2	0	16.8	67.3	700.9	768.2	479.0	212.2	40.3	0.9	6.1	738.5
1965–66	7.6	0	22.1	29.7	845.6	875.3	537.5	250.6	42.9	0.9	7.8	839.7
1966–67	4.4	0	31.2	35.6	928.5	964.1	559.4	261.6	47.1	1.0	4.9	874.0
1967–68	41.2	0	48.5	89.7	976.4	1,066.1	576.4	266.6	47.8	0.9	8.1	899.8
1968–69	60.7	—	105.6	166.3	1,107.0	1,273.3	605.9	286.8	47.7	0.8	6.6	947.8
1969–70	70.6	5.3	247.3	325.5	1,133.1	1,458.7	737.3	432.6	48.9	0.9	9.2	1,228.9
1970–71	40.6	8.7	180.5	229.8	1,127.1	1,356.9	760.1	433.8	48.3	1.0	14.9	1,258.1
1971–72°	20.6	—	78.2	98.8	1,176.0	1,274.8	720.5	416.2	51.1	1.0	14.0	1,202.8
1972–73	11.8	0	60.2	72.0	1,282.9	1,354.9	721.8	479.7	58.2	1.2	34.7	1,295.1
1973–74§	9.5	0	50.2	59.8	1,588.4	1,634.4	775	550		85		1,410

° Preliminary.
† Also warehouses.
‡ Stocks at farms, CCC and mills before 1965 are as of Oct. 1. Figures therefore will not add up to the total stocks, which are for Sept. 1.
§ Estimates.

factors, it is convenient to choose standard reference prices. That used by the USDA is No. 1 yellow soybeans loaded in boxcars beside county elevators at Track Country Station, Illinois shipping points. The price at Chicago, because of shipping charges, is typically 7 to 10 cents a bushel higher.

The soybean futures contract calls for No. 2 soybeans in storage at Chicago. Although soybeans are rarely moved from central Illinois to Chicago, the difference in the two prices is related to the transportation costs; for example, during the harvest season, the November futures price tends to remain 7 cents over the cash price of No. 1 beans at Illinois points. If the Illinois crop is small in relation to the total crop, this difference will be small; for example, in 1964 the prices were essentially equal when the Illinois crop was damaged by drought. The cash price tends to gain on the futures after the harvest. The two prices may be even by May. Abnormally large or small stocks at Chicago have a significant effect on the price of the near-futures contract.

Because oil futures prices are those for delivery of crude oil at Midwest mills, the cash and near-futures prices tend to be about equal.

SOURCES OF INFORMATION

The following U.S. Department of Agriculture publications constitute the primary sources of economic information relating to soybeans and their products.

The *Weekly Grain Market News* is perhaps the best source of current data relating to the grain markets. It lists weekly price changes, CCC sales, stocks, exports, all crop estimates, crop-loan data, domestic consumption, and export data.

The *Fats and Oils Situation Reports* are published five times a year; for example, in 1972 they were released in January, April, June, September, and November. In addition to professional comments on general economic conditions affecting the soybean yield, disappearance (crushing and exports), processors' margins, and government programs, the reports provide summaries of most of the important statistical data about soybeans, soybean oil, and other fats and oils.

The *Feed Situation Reports*, which are also released five times a year— for example, in 1972 in February, April, May, August, and November— provide similar information about soybean meal and competing animal feeds.

The *Crop Production Reports*, issued monthly on the tenth, includes the *Prospective Plantings Report*, released March 15, and the *Annual Summary*, issued during the third week of December. These publications give the planting intentions, acreage, yield, and other data relating to all crops, including soybeans.

The *Stocks of Grains in All Positions Report*, released about the third week of each month, shows stocks at the first of each month.

The following nongovernment publications are also important sources of information.

The *Reports of the Chicago Board of Trade* contain daily prices, volume, and open interest of soybean and product futures (as well as other grains) for each contract, as well as daily cash prices. The reports also provide important historical statistical information relating to supply and demand.

The *Oil World Quarterly and Weekly* publications (ISTA Mielke & Co., Langenberg, West Germany) analyze developments and make forecasts concerning the world oil markets. They also provide information on world production, consumption, stocks, weather, and crops.

The *Wall Street Journal* and especially *The New York Journal of Commerce* are valuable sources of daily information on all commodities.

SOYBEAN SUPPLY

The earliest estimates of soybean crop sizes are available in March in the form of a summarization of the results of the USDA survey of planting intentions. In most years farmers follow their intentions closely. However, significant changes in government programs relating to other crops may cause changes in intentions and reallocation of acreage to the various crops.

The U.S. Department of Agriculture *Crop Production Reports* give mid-July estimates of the planted acreage as of July 1. The aforementioned survey of planting intentions *(Prospective Plantings Report)* provides a good March estimate of this July report. The July acreage estimate is not amended until the final crop estimate is made during the third week of December.

Yield estimates appear in the crop reports from August 10 through December 10, with the final estimate in the December *Annual Summary.* Since acreage estimates are not made between the July 1 and the final December estimate, it appears that the USDA Crop Reporting Service makes adjustments in the November and December yield estimates to compensate for changes in acreage during the growing season. Thus the total production estimates are kept current.

SOYBEAN DEMAND

In general soybeans are utilized as shown in Figure 15-1. Because changes in usage of seed and feed are small, the analysis of disappearance involves analysis of crushings and exports. Exports are discussed first. Crushings are then examined in an analysis of the demand for oil and meal.

SOYBEAN EXPORTS

Soybean exports have increased significantly since the 1950-51 season, when approximately 9 percent of the soybean crop was exported. In recent years approximately 30 percent of the U.S. crop has been exported. Western Europe is the principal destination, especially The Netherlands, West Germany, Denmark, Italy, Spain, and the United Kingdom, and accounts for approximately half the total exports. Japan accounts for almost one-fourth and Canada takes about one-sixth.

The total-trend increase in exports seems to have been approximately 10 percent in recent years. This trend can be estimated with greater precision by examining the trends of individual countries; for example, exports to Japan are increasing more rapidly than those to other parts of the world. The USDA releases figures on soybean exports each month and summarizes the data in the *Fats and Oils Situation Report.* These are watched closely and are compared with those of the preceding year and with the forecasts for the current season. The latter comparison can be made on a more current basis by using the weekly inspections of soybeans for export available in the USDA's *Weekly Grain Market News.*

In European markets the domestic production of oilseeds and the readily imported peanuts, sunflower seeds, etc., are fully utilized. Soybeans are imported only to make up the deficit. Because soybeans are relatively cheap, compared with the high-value use to which they are put, importers are willing to pay high prices, relative to the other products, for the supplementary supply. Therefore the price elasticity of demand is low; that is, changes in price do not significantly alter the demand. As a practical approach, at a reasonable price level it may be assumed that price changes will not alter the quantity demanded by Western European nations. However, during periods of extremely high price levels, as during the major bull markets, exports do decrease significantly as inventories are allowed to fall in anticipation of lower prices.

In Japan soybeans are also put to high-value uses, principally as human

FIG. 15-1   Soybean utilization.

food. Therefore, as in Europe, the price elasticity of demand is very low at reasonable price levels. Statistical tests have verified that there is no significant correlation between soybean prices and exports.

DOMESTIC SOYBEAN OIL MARKET

In the United States soybean oil is used primarily for human food in salad oils, margarine, and shortening; more than 90 percent of the soybean oil produced is used for these purposes. A relatively small proportion goes into industrial uses, such as plastics and paints. Cottonseed oil, corn oil, lard, and butter compete with soybean oil in the edible-oil market. Together these four oils account for more than 90 percent of the edible production. Soybean oil alone accounts for more than half the total.

Although the price of the edible oils has varied greatly during the last decade, domestic per capita demand has been remarkably stable — approximately 45 to 50 pounds. Domestic disappearance of fats and oils is not related to price; that is, the elasticity of demand to changes in price has been close to zero. Most of the edible oils are either by-products or joint products whose supply is related to prices other than those of the oils themselves; for example, cottonseed oil is a by-product of cotton, corn oil is a by-product of cornstarch, lard, like pork bellies, is a by-product of hog production, and butter, which is losing its market to margarine, is a by-product of milk and is determined by milk-pricing and dairy-support programs. There is hardly an imaginable price of any of these by-products that could cause an increase in the supply. Thus, except for soybean oil, the supply is not altered by changes in the price of fats and oils. However, the supply of edible fats and oils can be influenced by other factors; for example, by a big hog run that would make lard plentiful and relatively cheap. This will exert downward pressure on soybean oil prices as commercial bakers switch to the lower priced shortening.

As for soybean oil, it is not a by-product but a joint product with soybean meal, but the domestic demand for meal has been increasing faster than the oil demand and the value of the meal processed from soybeans has been generally higher than that of oil. Consequently, in recent years the price of meal has generally determined the amount of soybeans crushed and therefore the domestic supply of oil as well as meal. For purposes of estimating domestic supply, oil was considered a by-product of meal for many years. There is no doubt, however, that a substantial increase in the price of soybean oil has encouraged the crushing of soybeans, thereby increasing the supply of oil.

Because neither the supply nor the demand is price-determined within a wide range, perhaps equivalent to that between 8-cent and 18-cent soybean oil, it is apparent that the market price of fats and oils is not determined by forces in the domestic market but by those in the incredibly complex world market.

SOYBEAN OIL EXPORTS

The production, exports, and domestic disappearance of oils other than soybean oil have remained almost constant in the United States during the last decade, whereas until recently soybean oil has increased in all three categories. The rising production of Russian sunflower seed oil and the low price at which it is offered have been important factors in slowing the uptrend in exports of United States soybean oil. It can be considered that the fixed supplies of cottonseed oil, corn oil, lard, and butter are made available for their regular domestic and export use. Soybean oil is used to meet the additional fixed per capita domestic demand as well as that for increases in domestic inventories. Any balance in the soybean oil supply must then be made available on the world market for fats and oils; it must be exported at the world soybean oil price. It is thus that the domestic price is related to the general world price.

The United States is by far the largest exporter of fats and oils, primarily soybean oil. Africa is an important exporter of peanut oil and palm oil, southeast Asia exports coconut oil, and Russia and Argentina are sources of sunflower seed oil.

Most of the demand for these exports comes from Europe whose needs are unfilled by its own production; demands from countries with preferential trade agreements are filled primarily by exports of soybean oil from the United States. Japan also is a major importer of fats and oils.

In addition to the commercial exports to Europe and Japan, exports of oil are determined to a large extent by special programs under Public Law 480, also called "Food for Peace." Public Law 480 was designed to enable countries without a surplus of dollars to buy United States oil. The program is administered so that no "normal" demand for oil is supplanted. Sales are made for foreign currencies and for long-term dollar credits; charitable donations are also made. Until recently exports of soybean and cottonseed oils under Public Law 480 amounted to approximately one-fourth of the total exports of those oils, including the oil content of soybeans exported. It had become politically difficult to reduce oil shipments to countries accustomed to receiving them, and it seemed that Public Law 480 shipments had become a somewhat permanent commitment, part of the fixed-demand structure that must be supplied even if the supply is short. Until 1972, however, there was a tendency for countries receiving Public Law 480 authorizations for oil to buy only a small portion of the authorization. The trade was facetiously quoted as saying, "We can't even *give* it away."

World oil supply and demand are difficult to estimate accurately. Estimates must be made and revised frequently. Over the years prices have tended to vary inversely with inventories. Because of the inelastic supply and demand, small changes in inventories can cause substantial price changes.

Table 15-2 shows the soybean oil supply and disappearance for the crop years 1960–61 to 1973–74.

SOYBEAN MEAL SUPPLY

The supply of meal in any given season depends on the quantity of soybeans available for processing; that is, the soybean carry-in plus production minus ·the exports, seed, feed, residual, and a minimum carry-out. The carry-out is the only nontrivial source of variation in this pattern; for example, if soybeans are held under government programs or in anticipation of short-ages, even these variations tend to be relatively minor so that the supply in any season can be taken as fixed in amount.

SOYBEAN MEAL DEMAND

The demand for meal is influenced by price; end users will buy only those amounts that can be utilized profitably at current prices. Therefore, if the supply is relatively large, prices will decline to increase the demand. Simi-larly, relatively small stocks with resultant increased prices will quickly decrease demand. Because the demand for soybean meal is thus more elastic in relation to price than the demand for oil, such price changes may be easier to predict in the case of meal. Because relatively small inventories of meal are held at any given time, cash prices tend to reflect the imme-diate supply-demand situation and are not much affected by the price of futures contracts; rather the lines of causation frequently run in the oppo-site direction.

Soybean meal produced in this country is utilized primarily for two pur-poses, exports and animal feed. Table 15-3 shows the total supply and dis-tribution of soybean meal in the United States for the crop years 1964–65 to 1973–74.

SOYBEAN MEAL EXPORTS

Soybean meal exports from the United States go principally to Canada and Western European countries; Japan is also an important outlet. Theoreti-cally, the world supply-and-demand structure of high-protein animal feeds (including the domestic supply and demand) should be combined and con-sidered in a single set of relationships. Because these relationships are complex and much of the data imprecise or unavailable, such analysis is difficult. All is not lost, however, because the increase in the use of high-protein animal feed has been so rapid in recent years that the other varia-tions have been overwhelmed. In computing meal exports for purposes of evaluating this trend, it would be more accurate to add the meal equivalent of the soybean exports to the meal exports and make computations based on that total. In recent years the trend increase in world demand has been filled by increases in the soybean meal supply. Supplies of competing prod-ucts have remained relatively constant. Such an assumption has led to good

TABLE 15-2 SUPPLY AND DISTRIBUTION OF SOYBEAN OIL IN THE UNITED STATES (IN MILLIONS OF POUNDS)

Year beginning October	Production	Stocks Oct. 1	Exports and shipments	Total	Food					Nonfood					
					Shortening	Margarine	Cooking and salad oils	Other edible	Total food	Paint and varnish	Resins and plastics	Other drying oil products	Other inedible‡	Foots and loss	Total non food‡
1960-61	4,420	308	721	3,329	1,097	1,073	793	26	2,989	96	64	4	36	139	340
1961-62	4,790	677	1,308	3,540	1,353	1,036	771	20	3,180	88	74	4	43	151	359
1962-63	5,091	618	1,165	3,624	1,222	1,069	933	15	3,239	90	78	6	48	163	385
1963-64	4,822	920	1,106	4,058	1,391	1,126	1,146	21	3,684	97	84	6	42	146	374
1964-65	5,146	578	1,357	4,069	1,404	1,107	1,100	32	3,643	94	105	5	57	165	426
1965-66	5,800	297	948	4,687	1,739	1,241	1,200	38	4,218	100	104	6	53	206	469
1966-67	6,076	462	1,105	4,837	1,691	1,273	1,353	58	4,375	96	97	7	61	201	462
1967-68	6,032	596	993	5,096	1,816	1,234	1,494	44	4,588	86	97	7	59	259	508
1968-69	6,531	540	899	5,756	1,978	1,290	1,967	36	5,271	87	94	7	61	236	485
1969-70	7,904	415	1,448	6,328	2,255	1,415	2,150	37	5,857	94	79	7	48	243	471
1970-71	8,265	543	1,782	6,253	2,077	1,381	2,888	34	5,780	82	65	6	52	267	472
1971-72*	7,892	773	1,430	6,449	1,992	1,412	2,591	29	6,024	81	55	4	40	249	429
1972-73†	7,509	785	1,188	6,695											
1973-74†	8,450	512	1,100	7,000											

* Preliminary.
† Forecast.
‡ Includes soap, fatty acids and other miscellaneous.
SOURCE: Economic Research Service, USDA.

results in projecting the export trend of meal, but for future projections it should be tested regularly.

Analysis in recent years shows that the export demand for meal is somewhat inelastic, much more so than the domestic demand. Soybean meal exports respond to prices below approximately $50 and above $85 per ton, but between these amounts exports do not seem to vary much with changes in price. Within the indicated price range, therefore, exports should be estimated by projecting their trend. The remaining supply should then be available to the domestic market.

SOYBEAN MEAL DOMESTIC MARKET

The high-protein feeds, oilseed meals, and animal protein (including fish meal), are generally considered part of the total supply of high-protein feeds. Except for soybean meal, however, the supply of the major high-protein feeds is not affected by price. Cottonseed meal is a by-product of cotton, and the other oilseed meals—linseed, peanut, and copra—are by-products of oil. Similarly, the animal protein feeds are by-products and depend more on livestock slaughter than on demand for feed.

In recent years, therefore, as the demand for high-protein feeds has increased, both because of increased numbers of animals and because of increased consumption per animal, only the supply of soybean meal has increased in response to the demand. Although one often sees reference to the supply of other high-protein feeds when soybean meal prices are analyzed, except for unusually large changes in their supply these competing feeds do not influence soybean prices significantly.

Although the yearly supply of cottonseed meal sometimes shows significant variation, it does not compete directly with soybean meal. Cottonseed meal is processed in a different geographical region and is mainly used to feed beef cattle and cows, whereas soybean meal is mainly consumed by hogs and poultry, although its consumption by dairy and beef cattle is increasing.

Although production of such feed grains as corn, oats, sorghum, and barley is large, they do not readily substitute for soybean meal because of the relatively low protein content of grains. Therefore, although the price of feed grains may determine an upper limit beyond which soybean meal prices will not go, the grain supplies typically do not need to be considered in forecasting meal prices. This is true even though prices of both grains and meal are regulated by livestock prices and tend to move in the same direction in the short run.

Perhaps 80 to 90 percent of the soybean meal is sold to mixed-feed manufacturers and consumed, in order of importance, by poultry, hogs, dairy cattle, and beef cattle. Lately, however, a significant increase has become apparent in the demand for soybean meal for feeding hogs and beef cattle.

The various livestock mentioned above constitute the main source of

TABLE 15-3 SUPPLY AND DISTRIBUTION OF SOYBEAN MEAL IN THE UNITED STATES
(IN THOUSANDS OF SHORT TONS)

Year beginning October	Supply			Distribution				Price (44%) dollars per ton Decatur—bulk
	Stocks Oct. 1	Production	Total	(Domestic) Feed†	Exports	Shipments to U.S. territories	Total	
1964	122	11,286	11,408	9,243	2,036	23	11,302	70.20
1965–66	106	12,901	13,007	10,219	2,604	52	12,875	81.50
1966–67	132	13,483	13,615	10,772	2,657	49	13,478	78.80
1967–68	138	13,660	13,798	10,693	2,899	60	13,652	76.90
1968–69	145	14,581	14,726	11,469	3,044	56	14,569	74.10
1969–70	157	17,596	17,753	13,514	4,035	67	17,616	78.40
1970–71*	137	18,035	18,172	13,406	4,559	61	18,126	78.50
1971–72†	146	17,024	17,170	13,110	3,805	63	16,978	90.20
1972–73‡	192	16,712	16,904	11,925	4,745	52	16,722	229.00
1973–74	182			13,000	5,700		18,700	

* Preliminary.

† Includes small quantities used for industrial purposes, estimated at 30,000 tons annually.

‡ Estimate.

SOURCE: Economic Research Service, USDA.

soybean meal demand. Forecasting this demand is somewhat simplified by using the USDA's "Protein Consuming Animal Unit," which is a weighted index of amounts consumed by the various livestock animals.

Although some livestock, broilers, laying flocks, and turkeys, are generally fed a balanced feed ration at all times, other types of livestock, notably hogs but including beef and dairy cattle and egg flocks, are fed more protein in their rations as livestock prices increase and the ratios of livestock prices to feed prices increase. In the case of hogs the price of soybean meal has a significant effect on the total demand for the meal, more so than the year-to-year change in the number of hogs. The USDA's monthly index of "Livestock and Livestock Product Prices" can be used as a measure of livestock prices.

Any meaningful analysis of soybean meal demand must include the recent trend of increased usage, especially by hogs and beef cattle.

PROCESSORS' MARGINS

Because processing capacity has increased faster than the demand for soybean products, the soybean-processing industry has become extremely competitive; processors' margins (the excess of the price of oil and meal over the cost of beans crushed to obtain those products) have decreased to a point at which they are often lower than the historical 12 cents-a-bushel operating costs. During seasons when the crush is reduced from the year before the idle crushing capacity heightens competition and drives the crushing margins below this level. During years when the crush is substantially increased margins widen. Crushing margins also exhibit certain seasonal tendencies, widening during the soybean harvest season when more capacity is utilized, reaching a low point in late spring, and increasing during the summer to reach a peak during the harvest.

Computation of the crushing margin requires calculation of the value of oil and meal obtained from a given quantity of beans—for example, a bushel—and comparison of that value with the price of the bushel of beans. One bushel (60 pounds) of soybeans yields approximately

    11 pounds of soybean oil
    48 pounds of soybean meal
     1 pound of waste

    60 pounds of soybeans per bushel

Prices are typically quoted as follows:

	Example
Beans in price per bushel	$ 2.94
Oil in price per pound	0.1106 (or 11.06 points)
Meal in price per ton	75.10

To compute the value of oil and meal per bushel of beans

(1) multiply the price of oil by 11 lb/bu; e.g., 0.1106
    dollars/lb × 11 lb/bu =   1.22 dollars/bu
(2) multiply the price of meal by

$$\frac{48 \text{ lb/bu}}{2,000 \text{ lb/ton}} = 0.24 \text{ ton/bu}$$

e.g., 75.10 dollars/ton × 0.024 ton/bu =   1.80 dollars/bu
    Using the example, the total value of products would be   3.02 dollars/bu
    Since the price of beans is shown at   2.94 dollars/bu
    the crushing margin would be   0.08 dollars/bu

THE REVERSE CRUSH SPREAD

The "reverse crush spread" is a futures trade—long soybean oil and soybean meal, short soybeans—in which the trader makes a transaction in the futures market which is opposite to processors' transactions in the cash market in which beans are bought for crushing purposes. Of course, if the processor puts on a hedge, he may also be selling the products in the futures market. In any case, the trader holding a reverse crush spread position expects the price of oil and meal to increase in relation to the price of beans; that is, he expects the processors' margin to increase.

Numerous factors influence the crushing margin. Two important ones mentioned earlier were the potential amount of the crush, which is influenced by the total beans available, and the seasonal pattern. In the short run, if the margin falls too low, processors will curtail crushing operations, simultaneously reducing the demand for beans and the supply of products; such action can improve margins, at least in the near term.

In determining the relative number of contracts of beans, oil, and meal to trade in the reverse crush spread, the following computations will prove helpful.

Expanding the previously noted product yield of a bushel of soybeans to that of a contract gives the following yield for one contract, or 5,000 bushels (300,000 pounds), of soybeans:

  55,000 pounds of oil
240,000 pounds of meal
  5,000 pounds of waste
—————
300,000 pounds of soybeans per contract

One contract of oil involves 60,000 pounds and a contract of meal involves 100 tons or 200,000 pounds, so that spreading one contract each of beans, oil, and meal will not give the correct proportions, but it is probably sufficiently close for practical purposes. A spread involving

     10 contracts of beans = 3,000,000 pounds
      9 contracts of oil   =   540,000 pounds
and 12 contracts of meal = 2,400,000 pounds

gives a closer approximation of the correct proportions.

The reverse crush spread may be used profitably by exploiting the risk premium based on hedging patterns.[1]

SEASONAL INFORMATION AND CARRYING CHARGES

Some traders profess to detect a seasonal tendency from a low price during the harvest season to a high price in the spring and summer as supplies become scarce. As shown by studies of open interest (see Figures 15-3, 15-4, and 15-5), speculators typically build up net long positions during the harvest and then gradually liquidate those positions until summer. Hedgers have opposite open positions of equal size; this accomplishes the shifting of the inventory risk from the hedger to the speculator.

Because the speculators are the highest bidders during the harvest and offer the commodity at the lowest price during the spring (else they could not buy and sell, respectively, at those times), they exert a contraseasonal effect on prices. The extent of this force is so great in the well-developed markets, such as in soybeans, that is has virtually eliminated, except for carrying charges, any seasonal characteristics.

Table 15-4 shows the monthly midrange prices of May soybeans from 1961 to 1973. It also shows each midrange as a percentage of the average price for the season. Figure 15-2 is a graph of those percentages for the last 13 years. Except for a rise equal to the cost of storage, there is no repetitive seasonal variation in soybean prices. This applies equally well to oil and meal and probably to most widely traded commodities.

Figures 15-3, 15-4, and 15-5 show the seasonal variation in open interest and volume of trading on the Chicago Board of Trade for soybeans, soybean oil, and soybean meal, respectively.

The schedule of maximum carrying charges for grains, including soybeans, is shown in the Wheat chapter. Carrying charges are approximately 18 to 20 points per pound per month for oil and 90 to 125 per ton per month for meal when interest rates are moderate.

NOTES FROM A TRADER

Soybeans are more popular than most markets among spreaders. In addition to the usual old-crop-new-crop spreads, it is possible to spread oil versus meal or both products versus beans. The September-November spread is appealing to those who expect late crops when the carry-over is small. One should remember that oil and meal need not go in opposite directions and also that one contract of beans does not equal one contract of oil plus one contract of meal. The latter position emphasizes the oil.

Long oil versus short meal has seldom worked favorably when oil has been in a carrying-charge market. Traders in the reverse crush would like

---

[1] See Paul H. Cootner, "Speculation and Hedging," *Food Research Institute Studies, Supplement*, 7, (1967), 102.

FIG. 15-2 May soybeans, seasonal: monthly midrange price of May soybeans as a percentage of average yearly price.

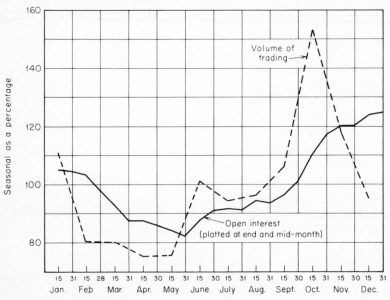

FIG. 15-3 Soybeans: monthly open interest and volume as a percentage of average monthly open interest and volume for the years 1962–1971 at the Chicago Board of Trade. (Commodity Exchange Authority, USDA.)

TABLE 15-4 MONTHLY MIDRANGE PRICE OF MAY SOYBEANS AND PERCENT OF AVERAGE YEARLY PRICE

Year of delivery	Year before delivery							Delivery year					Monthly average price and percent
	June	July	Aug	Sept	Oct	Nov	Dec	Jan	Feb	Mar	Apr	May	
1961	—	223.50	227.00	224.75	226.00	225.94	230.38	253.75	286.50	296.25	315.75	316.25	256.92
		87.00	88.36	87.49	87.97	87.94	89.68	98.77	111.52	115.32	122.91	123.10	100.00
1962	259.88	260.75	254.81	250.31	250.63	249.06	247.94	248.31	245.69	246.38	249.75	249.44	251.08
	103.50	103.84	101.48	99.68	99.81	99.19	98.74	98.89	97.85	98.12	99.46	99.34	100.00
1963	243.88	241.63	242.44	246.00	251.50	250.13	251.13	266.13	266.38	260.50	258.44	260.38	253.21
	96.32	95.43	95.75	97.15	99.33	98.79	99.18	105.10	105.20	102.88	102.07	102.83	100.00
1964	265.88	275.38	264.38	276.13	288.63	285.88	283.13	277.56	268.31	264.13	257.38	250.81	271.47
	97.93	101.43	97.38	101.70	106.31	105.30	104.28	102.23	98.82	97.28	94.80	92.38	100.00
1965	276.00	250.75	259.50	276.13	282.06	287.63	291.56	297.38	305.88	299.25	297.13	284.25	283.96
	97.18	88.29	91.37	97.23	99.32	101.28	102.66	104.71	107.70	105.37	104.62	100.09	100.00
1966	256.69	259.13	256.75	257.94	256.69	260.44	268.89	282.25	290.44	285.63	296.25	302.99	272.84
	94.09	94.99	94.12	94.55	94.09	95.47	98.57	103.46	106.47	104.70	108.60	111.07	100.00
1967	307.44	326.13	332.00	323.94	305.38	299.56	295.13	288.81	286.69	288.75	284.38	282.13	301.69
	101.90	108.10	110.04	107.37	101.22	99.29	97.82	95.73	95.03	95.71	94.26	93.51	100.00
1968	287.75	279.19	277.44	274.31	272.94	274.56	275.06	276.62	277.50	275.44	271.13	271.81	276.14
	104.22	101.12	100.49	99.35	98.86	99.44	99.62	100.19	100.51	99.76	98.20	98.45	100.00
1969	267.69	264.31	262.31	260.94	261.13	265.31	265.00	266.75	266.44	264.44	264.25	266.50	264.59
	103.84	99.89	99.13	98.62	98.69	100.27	100.15	100.81	100.70	99.94	99.87	100.72	100.00
1970	246.75	249.25	248.56	249.75	255.56	258.25	255.13	257.69	260.69	260.50	263.19	266.38	255.97
	96.39	97.36	97.09	97.56	99.83	100.88	99.66	100.66	101.83	101.76	102.81	104.05	100.00
1971	303.06	305.00	301.88	297.13	310.44	311.63	303.30	309.19	310.00	303.50	292.94	295.13	303.60
	99.82	100.46	99.43	97.87	102.25	102.64	99.90	101.84	102.11	99.97	96.49	97.21	100.00
1972	321.00	339.63	332.50	326.88	328.56	323.50	324.31	317.75	326.63	341.00	351.50	351.38	332.05
	96.66	102.27	100.12	98.43	98.93	97.41	97.65	95.68	98.35	102.68	105.84	105.80	100.00
1973	333.75	335.81	340.44	352.38	353.75	373.00	412.63	441.38	547.50	597.50	646.00	884.00	468.18
	71.29	76.64	72.71	75.27	75.56	79.67	88.13	94.28	116.94	127.62	137.98	188.82	100.00

to see carrying charges in the beans to indicate large supplies but inversion in at least one of the two products to indicate good demand.

Traders bullish on beans may prefer to go long nearby contracts versus short distant contracts rather than to establish outright long positions. Bears may wish to sell nearby and buy distant contracts. The trader should be careful about using distant contracts for spreads to reduce margin only to find that the open interest is so small that the real risk in the spread is greater than would exist in a net position if adversity developed. Oil and meal have call openings, and meal is completed before oil resumes, so that the broker should not be faulted for failing to complete spreads on openings.

Rain in July and early August is especially critical to new-crop beans; therefore the market is especially responsive to weather during the late summer. Soybean futures markets have tended to react to government reports more violently than grains, although as the size of the crop in relation to demand continues to expand this will become less obvious.

Some believe that the trade is quite interested in market closes on Fridays. Country elevators like weak closes during the harvest season because

FIG. 15-4 Soybean oil: monthly open interest and volume as a percentage of average monthly open interest and volume for the years 1962–1971 at the Chicago Board of Trade. (Commodity Exchange Authority, USDA.)

FIG. 15-5   Soybean meal: monthly open interest and volume as a percentage of average monthly open interest and volume for the years 1962–1971 at the Chicago Board of Trade. (Commodity Exchange Authority, USDA.)

they are bean buyers over the subsequent weekend, whereas oil exporters would prefer strong Friday closes to set the stage for weekend sales.

As the bean crop year wears on, especially after the December 1 crop estimate, price becomes more and more a function of demand. If there is one "moment of truth" in the bean market, it is probably the January 1 stocks in all positions.

CHAPTER SIXTEEN

Wheat

INTRODUCTION

Wheat, with no further explanation, means to most speculators Chicago wheat futures, traded on the Chicago Board of Trade. A wheat futures contract on the Chicago Board of Trade consists of 5,000 bushels of No. 2 Soft Red winter wheat, the variety commonly grown in the Chicago area. Although wheat is also traded on the Kansas City and Minneapolis exchanges, the Chicago Board of Trade is by far the leading exchange, accounting for more than 80 percent of the trading activity. Chicago wheat has high volume and open interest; it is usually one of the most active commodities traded. Chicago wheat contract months are July, September, December, March, and May. The July future is the first contract of the crop year, which begins July 1.

Knowledgeable speculators enter buy or sell orders for wheat and other grains in multiples of the contract unit of 5,000 bushels, such as "Buy 15,000 bushels" (three contracts is understood). Once the position is established, the speculator stands to gain or lose $12.50 (5,000 $\times$ $\frac{1}{4}$ cent) on each favorable or unfavorable minimum move of $\frac{1}{4}$ cent on each contract.

CHART 16-1

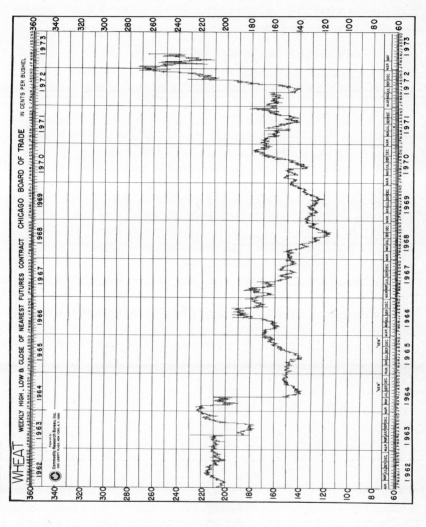

WHEAT WEEKLY HIGH, LOW & CLOSE OF NEAREST FUTURES CONTRACT CHICAGO BOARD OF TRADE IN CENTS PER BUSHEL

Because of the limit on moves established by the exchange, the speculator may gain or suffer adversity of no more than 20 cents, from the preceding day's closing price, in any given day. If the trader establishes a position in excess of 200,000 bushels, he must report his position to the Commodity Exchange Authority; in any case, he may not establish a net position in excess of 2 million bushels.

FACTORS WHICH INFLUENCE WHEAT PRICES

Wheat is harvested around the world in nearly every month of the year. In the United States wheat is harvested during the summer, winter wheat during the early summer, and spring wheat during the later summer. Harvesting begins in the south end of the wheat belt in early summer and moves northward as the summer progresses. Kansas, the largest wheat-producing state, accounts for a substantial percentage of the total crop. Figures 16-1 and 16-2 show the wheat-growing-areas in the United States and throughout the world.

Table 16-1 shows the supply and distribution data for the crop years 1960–61 to 1973–74, each beginning July 1 and ending June 30.

As is true with most commodities, wheat prices are dominated by the basic supply-demand relationship; however, many factors alter the effect that this relationship has on wheat prices.

Government action is the most important of these factors. Although some programs affect the plantings, and thus the supply, the most direct government influence on wheat prices occurs because of the price support program, which includes government loans, diversion payments, and marketing certificates. Another important government-controlled factor, although

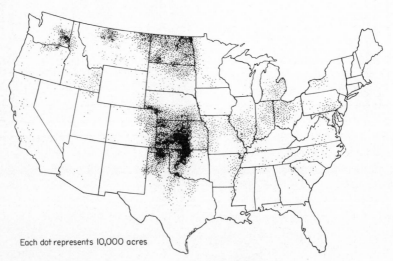

Each dot represents 10,000 acres

FIG. 16-1   Where wheat is grown in the United States.

Each dot represents 1 million bushels

FIG. 16-2   Where wheat is grown around the world.

it is related to foreign need, is the export program under Public Law 480, the Agricultural Trade Development and Assistance Act, and its various titles.

In the commercial sector a variety of factors may alter the effect of total supply on wheat prices. The availability of domestic commercial storage and freight-car facilities are important short-run factors.

The price of wheat in relation to the price of feed grains can alter the domestic demand because farmers will feed wheat to livestock if it is economically practical to do so. Because they are much more variable than domestic usage, commercial exports are important in any price analysis.

The farmers' collective attitude often represents an important price-determining factor in the short run. Farmers tend to expect prices to be good in years immediately following bull markets, and they often hold onto their crops in surplus years hoping for better prices. Not all farmers react rationally toward government support programs. Some put their crops under loan no matter what the economics of the situation perhaps because it is convenient. Others do not use the support programs no matter what their economic loss from such action. These actions by growers make it difficult to predict accurately, using customary economic analysis, the impact on prices of changes in government support programs.

Hard Red winter wheat is deliverable on the Kansas City contracts. Minneapolis contracts are settled with Hard Red spring wheat. Either of these varieties, or Soft Red winter wheat, can be delivered against Chicago contracts. The most common class of wheat tendered at Chicago is No. 2 Soft Red winter.

TABLE 16-1 SUPPLY AND DISTRIBUTION OF WHEAT IN THE UNITED STATES (IN MILLIONS OF BUSHELS)

| Year beginning July | Supply | | | | | | Domestic disappearance | | | | | | Exports | Total disappearance |
| | Stocks, July 1 | | | Total stocks | Production | Imports§ | Food | Seed | Industry | Feed | | Total domestic disappearance | | |
	On farms	Mills, elevators‡	CCC							Residual	(On farms where grown)			
1960–61	95.9	1,154.1	63.5	1,313.5	1,354.7	8.1	497.2	64.2	0.1	41.9	(24.9)	603.4	661.5	1,265
1961–62	137.1	1,203.7	70.6	1,411.3	1,232.4	5.7	501.5	56.4	0.1	50.1	(22.4)	608.0	719.4	1,327
1962–63	102.4	1,160.0	59.5	1,322.0	1,092.0	5.4	500.4	61.4	0.1	18.4	(16.1)	580.3	643.8	1,224
1963–64	95.5	1,061.4	38.3	1,195.2	1,146.8	3.9	503.3	65.0	0.1	20.2	(15.2)	588.5	856.1	1,445
1964–65	75.7	813.0	12.7	901.4	1,283.4	1.1	509.2	65.6	0.1	68.8	(31.4)	643.7	725.0	1,369
1965–66	132.5	673.7	11.0	817.3	1,315.6	0.9	515.4	61.9	0.1	153.9	(41.7)	731.3	867.4	1,599
1966–67	130.8	394.9	9.5	535.2	1,304.9	1.8	501.9	78.4	0.1	92.6	(26.1)	673.1	744.3	1,417
1967–68	144.9	278.5	1.0	424.4	1,507.6	0.9	519.2	71.5	0.1	42.6	(42.9)	633.3	761.1	1,394
1968–69	229.5	308.3	0.7	538.5	1,556.6	1.1	519.7	61.3	0.1	154.3	(60.8)	735.4	544.2	1,280
1969–70	325.9	490.0	0.8	816.7	1,442.7	3.2	520.6	56.8	0.5	193.7	(61.0)	771.6	606.1	1,378
1970–71	307.1	576.6	1.2	884.9	1,351.6	1.1	519.5	63.2	0.1	185.9	(62.0)	768.6	737.5	1,506
1971–72*	240.3	489.4	1.8	731.5	1,617.8	1.0	526.0	63.0	–	266.0	(72.0)	854.7	632.5	1,487
1972–73†	354.9	506.3	1.9	863.1	1,544.8	1.3	526.0	66.0	–	203.0	(47.0)	795.0	1,184	1,979
1973–74†	125.0	301.0	1.2	427.8	1,726.8	1.0	528.0	77.0	–	150.0	–	755.0	1,150	1,905

* Preliminary.
† Estimated.
‡ Also warehouses and all off-farm storage not otherwise designated, including flour mills.
§ Imports and exports are of wheat, including flour and other products in terms of wheat.
SOURCE: Economic Research Service, USDA.

SOURCES OF INFORMATION

The *Annual Report* of the Chicago Board of Trade is one of the most convenient sources of wheat prices; it lists the daily high, low, and closing prices during the year covered for each contract traded. It also includes monthly high and low prices, often going back as many as 12 years. The report is also a useful source of historical statistical data; carry-over, cash prices, crop in the United States and world-wide, exports by class and country of destination, exports of flour, wheat in store and afloat at Chicago, loan rates, parity prices, prices received by farmers, receipts and shipments at Chicago, stocks in all positions, stocks in Chicago monthly, and visible supply are among the most useful.

The *USDA Crop Production Report* (regular issues of which are released monthly on the tenth), including the *Prospective Plantings Report* released March 15 and the *Annual Summary* issued during the third week of December, is the accepted authoritative source of planting data such as intentions, acreage, yield, and crop size. These reports are widely distributed and quoted in the trade. Private crop estimates, although often fairly widely circulated, are given less credence than those of the USDA reports and are typically used merely to predict the USDA's next revisions. Although estimates of the winter wheat crops are made earlier, it is not until July 1 that the first actual spring wheat estimate is made. At this time the total crop estimate is available. From this "as of July 1st estimate" until the "as of December 1st estimate," there is a monthly estimate for each first of the month.

The *Wheat Situation Report* is the single most useful source of information for the trader. It is issued four times a year in March, May, August, and November and contains a valuable overview of the current wheat market. Although it is not an up-to-the-minute source of data, it furnishes an excellent base on which a more current analysis can be constructed. The analyst will find much historical data for comparative reference in this analysis. Much of what is published in the *Wheat Situation Report* consists of convenient summaries of data published elsewhere by the USDA. The *Wheat Situation Report* has excellent narrative sections that summarize wheat fundamentals in an authoritative manner. Included are the following categories: recent developments, government programs, current outlook, prospects for the future year, and the world situation. Although the report is aimed at the farmer and the trade, rather than the speculator, and although the narrative may emphasize government policy and objectives, it is written by competent professionals who have timely authoritative information with which to work.

The *Grain Market News* (both weekly and monthly summary and statistics), published by the USDA, is a convenient and relatively current source of information dealing with supply-demand data. Each week it includes a summary of the week's markets, reports (in various forms), the activities of the government programs (particularly Public Law 480), and exports of wheat and flour. Other information may include wheat supply and disposition monthly, CCC dispositions, storage capacity of elevators and warehouses, monthly exports, Canadian acreage estimates, and prospective plantings in the United States.

The *Quarterly Stock of Grains in All Positions Report,* as of January 1, April 1, July 1, and October 1, which is issued about the twenty-fourth of each month, provides the analyst with a breakdown of the stocks of wheat by size, location, and ownership. It is one of the major reports and can have dramatic effect on prices both after its release date in the short term and in the long term as its content is digested by the farmers, the trade, and the speculators.

Commitments of Traders in Commodity Futures, issued monthly by the Commodity Exchange Authority in Chicago, reports the open interest of holders of both long and short positions in the following manner:

Large traders:
  Speculative
  Long *or* short only
  Long *and* short (spreading)
  Hedging
Small traders:
  Speculative and hedging

The information is gathered from mandatory reports filed by all traders with positions of 200,000 or more bushels of wheat and is combined with information from the exchange clearinghouse. Thus the small traders' positions are computed by taking the difference between the total long or short positions and the respective holdings of the reporting large traders. A trader with a 195,000-bushel position is defined as a small trader.

As indicated in Chapter 7, many speculators profess to see certain relations between the quantity of the positions held by the large traders and the quantity held by the small traders. These speculators usually prefer a position in line with the former.

SUPPLY

Wheat can be classified in two broad ways: first, according to the time of planting, and second, according to physical characteristics. Winter wheat is planted in the fall and after lying dormant during the winter is harvested during early summer. Spring wheat is sown about as early as the ground is workable in the spring. The plant grows and develops continuously until it is harvested in the late summer.

Wheat is also classified as hard, soft, or durum. Hard Red spring and Hard Red winter wheats are especially suited for making bread flour. These two varieties of wheat contain large quantities of strong, elastic gluten—an essential element in making a bread that meets public favor in the United States. Hard wheat, which constitutes the major part of the total U.S. crop, is grown mainly in Kansas, Oklahoma, Texas, Nebraska, North Dakota and South Dakota, and Montana. Soft Red winter is usually low in protein content and is especially suited for making pastry, crackers, biscuits, cakes, and similar products. Durum wheat is used for making a semolina that is especially suited for the manufacture of macaroni, spaghetti, and similar products.

The supply of wheat consists of unused wheat from the preceding season (carry-over), production, and imports. U.S. imports of wheat, consisting of wheat used for seed, are negligible. The fact that historically the wheat supply has consistently been greater than the demand would suggest that prices would fall, increasing demand and reducing supply, until a balance in the supply-demand situation occurred. In considering the level and fluctuations of futures prices, several additional factors must be taken into account:

1. Most of the carry-over from year to year is owned and controlled by the Commodity Credit Corporation (CCC), an agency of the Department of Agriculture; CCC stocks do not directly influence prices.

2. The "loan rate" to producers, set by the government, is the level around which prices fluctuate.

3. The movement of wheat "into loan" tends to siphon off the surplus, thereby tending to bring demand and "free" supply into balance as prices move close to the "loan rate" (see Figure 16-3). Thus it is evident that government programs directly influence the price of wheat.

Wheat prices have been supported since 1938 by the federal government. The basis for determining the price support level generally has been parity prices. "Parity" is a term meaning "on par with," and its importance to wheat-price determination lies in its reflection of changes in the purchasing power of a bushel of wheat from a given base period to a later period. Over the years several different methods of measuring this purchasing power for wheat have been used.

Price support operations of the CCC consist primarily of allowing producers who comply with acreage and/or marketing quotas to obtain a specified price for wheat. Farmers utilizing price support receive money from the CCC and pledge their wheat as collateral. These loans are of a non-recourse nature. This simply means that producers do not have to repay the amount of money received and that the wheat used as collateral is considered as full payment of the loan. However, the producer may repay the loan at any time up to the maturity date of the loan and sell his wheat on the open market. Under existing law the CCC is empowered to sell wheat on the open market at a specific percentage above the support level, plus reasonable carrying charges.

The long-term effect of the loan program is to maintain prices at relatively

FIG. 16-3   Relation of Red winter wheat price with effective support-price loan plus carrying charges. (*Grain Market News,* Consumer and Marketing Service, Grain Division, USDA.)

high levels in times of low demand or large supplies and to reduce prices during times when demand is large in relation to supply. It should be noted that although the support program essentially puts a "floor" (loan rate) and a "ceiling" (CCC resale prices) around prices seasonal fluctuations sometimes carry prices beyond these "limits."

Stocks of wheat not only have a significant effect on prices but also a complex relation to prices. It is often important to know where stocks are located, who owns them, and the extent of their potential mobility (freight-car availability). Stocks in western Kansas are unlikely to have a dramatic short-run effect on Chicago prices, especially if transportation facilities are in short supply. Government-owned stocks are likewise of little importance if their sale would have an unfavorable effect on the support program or if they are not eligible for sale at current prices under current government policy. Stocks' locations and their effect on prices are often difficult to determine and thus are often subordinate in the analysis of potential price action. This is not true of the stocks under government control, which at times may be the dominant factor in price analysis.

If the price of wheat is above the level at which the government is willing to sell, the government supply of wheat under loan becomes an important aspect of the total supply and must be considered in any meaningful economic analysis. If, on the other hand, the price of wheat is below the loan price, the effective supply will be reduced as farmers place their wheat under loan. When the price is between these extremes, the free stock (not under loan) plus the crop, if applicable, will constitute the total supply to be considered.

DEMAND

Demand for wheat comes from two broad sources—exports and domestic usage. Exports break down into commercial exports and exports under government programs. Domestic usage of wheat breaks down into food, feed, seed, industrial feed, and military requirements.

Commercial exports are a major factor in analyzing prices and are heavily dependent on world crop conditions. In years when foreign crop prospects are high and world wheat prices are low the United States' commercial exports tend to be low. This is true because exporters cannot buy domestic wheat at competitive prices (primarily because of the government support program) and sell it at a profit in the world market in competition with other surplus producers, such as Canada, Australia, and Argentina.

Exports under government programs, such as Public Law 480 and Aid for International Development, usually account for more than 60 percent of the exports from the United States; thus government action is needed in that area. The programs are especially important in years of large United States crops, when commercial exports are not competitive, and in years when deficit-producing nations, particularly India and Pakistan, have poor crops.

In recent years Asian farmers, particularly those in India, Turkey, and Pakistan, have begun using a new hybrid wheat developed from strains of Mexican Semidwarf. Farmers in those countries are harvesting yields of 50 to 90 bushels an acre on which they once got as little as 10 bushels. These yields compare with the average yield in the United States of 25 bushels an acre. These Mexican hybrids would have only limited success in the United States because much of the Great Plains is too arid for their growth and because they lack the milling and baking characteristics preferred by the United States mills and processors. The new varieties, however, will be a significant price factor in the years ahead when the United States will probably need to trim its wheat aid shipments abroad.

In analyzing domestic consumption, the analyst may disregard industrial usage, which represents less than 1 percent of the total, and military procurement, which is a complement to civilian food; both factors have been reported with the food classification.

Seed usage represents 5 to 10 percent of the total disappearance of wheat and varies enough so that it can influence price. The factors that control seed usage are, of course, primarily farmer expectations based on current prices, expected carry-over, and the expected or announced intention of the USDA in regard to its proposed price support program for the following year.

Although feeding wheat to livestock occurs to some extent in all years, it can represent a substantial percentage of the usage when wheat prices are low, particularly when wheat is low in relation to other feed grains. From less than 1 percent to as high as 30 percent during and after World War II, it has recently averaged between 1 to 5 percent of usage.

The last and largest source of domestic wheat usage is food consumption, which varies little from year to year because it is primarily dependent on per capita consumption and the number of consumers. Thus, although it is the largest source of domestic disappearance, it is not necessarily the most influential domestic demand factor in forecasting price changes.

GOVERNMENTAL PROGRAMS

Governmental policies have a significant influence on wheat prices; they are second only to the basic supply-demand factors in which they also often play an important role.

The primary tool in the government wheat program is the loan. It is set by the Secretary of Agriculture and becomes the most important point of reference for the trader. This observation is illustrated in Figure 16-3, from the *Wheat Situation Report* WS-197, July 1966, 26. Note that although wheat prices may vary around the effective support-price loan, plus carrying charges, they do not vary from it dramatically at any time unless there are extreme cases of supply-demand imbalance.

Another important government tool, Public Law 480, came into being under the Agricultural Act of 1954. Under this law the government casts the shadow of its influence over more than half the country's exports. This is done under four titles, as summarized below:

Title I: Sales subject to agreement between the United States and friendly countries. Sales are made by private exporters from their stocks.

Title II: Donation by the U.S. government to a foreign government from CCC-owned commodities for relief and emergency efforts of the recipient government.

Title III: Barter—through private firms, for strategic and other commodities; or donations—through private charitable agencies to needy countries. Raw commodities usually come from CCC stocks.

Title IV: Long-term credit agreements for export of surplus United States commodities. Payment can extend to periods in excess of 20 years.[1]

Sales of CCC-owned surplus can be an important wheat price determinant. Although these sales normally occur when wheat prices are above effective support levels by a given percentage (usually 5 to 15 percent), the CCC can sell any deteriorating commodity to save it from spoilage. These sales can have a significant though short-term effect on prices; they almost always come as a surprise.

These programs and their variations, as well as farmer and speculator reaction to them, are of great importance to traders. Reading the *Wheat Situation Reports* is probably the best and most convenient method of being aware of and understanding possible government actions affecting the wheat market.

[1] For a more complete review, see *12 Years of Achievement under Public Law 480*, Economic Research Service, U.S. Department of Agriculture, 1967.

SEASONAL INFORMATION

Wheat has a normal tendency to reach its low price during harvest time, then to rise to a high price after December, when supplies become scarcer. Speculators typically build up long positions during and after the harvest, as the dealers sell short to hedge. The speculators then gradually liquidate those positions until the spring as the hedgers buy in their shorts. Speculators are the highest bidders during harvest and offer at the lowest prices during the winter. Thus they exert a contraseasonal force which tends to eliminate, except for carrying charges, any seasonal price fluctuation in the large and efficient market for wheat.[2]

One of the favorite vehicles for speculators has been the spread of long December wheat versus short December corn. This trade, when the position is put on about June 1 and taken off on November 1, has had a profit-

[2] The reader can refer to the evidence for the presence of a risk premium in wheat based on hedging patterns discussed in chapter 4, p. 98.

TABLE 16-2 RESULTS OF SPREAD,
LONG DECEMBER WHEAT—SHORT
DECEMBER CORN: POSITION
INITIATED ON JUNE 1 AND CLOSED
ON NOVEMBER 1, 1949–1973

Year	Price difference, December wheat minus December corn (in cents per bushel)		
	June 1	Nov. 1	Gain (+) or loss (−)
1949	78.625	94.625	+ 16.000
1950	83.750	71.000	− 12.750
1951	80.625	74.750	− 5.875
1952	68.250	71.500	+ 3.250
1953	67.750	48.875	− 18.875
1954	58.875	67.125	+ 8.250
1955	65.750	75.000	+ 9.250
1956	69.750	97.875	+ 28.125
1957	84.500	99.250	+ 14.750
1958	73.250	83.375	+ 10.125
1959	77.875	90.750	+ 12.875
1960	80.500	91.250	+ 10,750
1961	74.750	94.250	+ 19.250
1962	107.375	100.000	− 7.375
1963	75.875	98.125	+ 22.250
1964	39.000	32.375	− 6.625
1965	28.500	50.125	+ 21.625
1966	53.875	32.000	− 21.875
1967	42.000	36.000	− 6.000
1968	26.375	17.000	− 9.375
1969	10.875	17.500	+ 6.625
1970	19.875	28.125	+ 8.250
1971	18.000	44.875	+ 26.875
1972	26.000	80.875	+ 54.875
1973	74.500	194.250	+119.750

**TABLE 16-3 RESULTS OF SPREAD,
SHORT DECEMBER WHEAT–LONG
DECEMBER CORN: POSITION INITIATED
ON MARCH 1 AND CLOSED ON JUNE
1, 1949–1973**

Price difference, December wheat minus
December corn (in cents per bushel)

Year	March 1	June 1	Gain (+) or loss (−)
1949	81.125	78.625	+ 2.500
1950	81.125	83.750	− 2.625
1951	75.250	80.625	− 5.375
1952	77.875	68.250	+ 9.375
1953	79.000	67.750	+11.250
1954	76.000	58.875	+17.125
1955	68.625	65.750	+ 2.875
1956	71.000	69.750	+ 1.250
1957	98.625	84.500	+14.125
1958	84.250	73.250	+11.000
1959	80.125	77.875	+ 2.250
1960	80.000	80.500	− 0.500
1961	84.000	74.750	+ 9.250
1962	100.625	107.375	− 6.750
1963	83.125	75.875	+ 7.250
1964	47.125	39.000	+ 8.875
1965	31.125	28.500	+ 2.625
1966	43.750	54.000	−10.250
1967	44.000	42.000	+ 2.000
1968	30.875	26.375	+ 4.500
1969	23.375	10.875	+12.500
1970	26.000	19.875	+ 6.125
1971	8.250	18.000	− 9.750
1972	26.750	25.875	+ 0.875
1973	84.000	75.000	+ 9.000

able average in past years. This is perhaps due to the tendency for both wheat and corn prices to decline during their respective harvest periods. Because the wheat harvest occurs during the summer months and the corn harvest during the fall, the speculator putting on the spread goes long wheat during its harvest and simultaneously sells corn before its harvest. Table 16-2 shows the result of the spread trade during the last 24 years. Table 16-3 shows the results of a similar spread with opposite positions taken March 1 and held until June 1 in order to take advantage of the "harvest low" price in wheat. The graph in Figure 16-4 summarizes the results of taking both trades in each of the indicated years. The points in the first quadrant indicate the years in which both trades were profitable; in those years falling in the third quadrant both trades resulted in losses.

Figure 16-5 shows the seasonal pattern for open interest and volume for wheat futures trading on the Chicago Board of Trade.

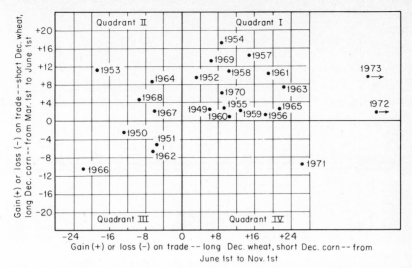

FIG. 16-4   Results of wheat-corn spreads.

CARRYING CHARGES

There is no "normal" carrying charge in grains; but if the price premium of a distant futures contract over a nearby contract exceeds the costs of carrying the commodity, speculators will buy the near futures, take delivery, and hold the grain long enough to deliver against the distant futures. The monthly carrying charges for the grains, at specified prices and interest rates, are shown in Table 16-4.

Because of variations in price and interest rates, carrying charges are not stable; what is not shown is the variation in the storage costs for the various holders; thus Table 16-4 is an average. To determine the theoretical maximum premium between two futures contracts it is necessary only to multiply the number of months between the contracts by the appropriate carrying charge; for example, if the grain supplies were adequate (no reason for the nearby to sell above the distant), the March contract, at $2.50 a bushel with 7 percent interest charges, would be expected to be 6.72 cents under the May contract. If, however, supplies of the grain were scarce, the March contract may sell at a higher price relative to the May contract.

The full carrying charges approximated in Table 16-4 are costs that the speculator would have to bear. It is well to remember that the trade can carry the commodity at substantially lower prices because trade facilities are used for storage and interest may not be so important at certain times; for example, to take delivery and carry 5,000 bushels of wheat at $2.50 a bushel for 30 days and then redeliver the speculator may pay $3-a-day storage (or $90 a contract, which is approximately 1.8 cents a bushel); 6 percent interest on $12,500, which is about $63 per month a contract

FIG. 16-5   **Wheat: monthly open interest and volume as a percentage of average monthly open interest and volume for the years 1962–1971 at the Chicago Board of Trade.** (Commodity Exchange Authority, USDA.)

TABLE 16-4   **GRAIN CARRYING CHARGES (IN CENTS PER BUSHEL)**

Price of commodity per bushel	$1.50		$2.00		$2.50		$3.00		$3.50	
Interest rate	6%	7%	6%	7%	6%	7%	6%	7%	6%	7%
Storage charge on grains (or soybeans) at elevators, cents per month per bushel	1.80	1.80	1.80	1.80	1.80	1.80	1.80	1.80	1.80	1.80
Insurance	0.05	0.05	0.06	0.06	0.08	0.08	0.10	0.10	0.12	0.12
Interest @ 6 or 7%	0.75	0.87	1.00	1.17·	1.25	1.46	1.50	1.75	1.75	2.04
Total carrying charge cents per bushel per month	2.60	2.72	2.86	3.03	3.13	3.34	3.40	3.65	3.67	3.96

or 1.25 cents a bushel; and insurance, etc., as indicated, making a total of 3.15 cents a bushel per month. The wheat market, however, as well as the other grain markets, frequently reflects a carrying charge of only 2 cents a bushel per month. Because carrying charges vary, it would be wise for a trader to verify the amounts with his broker before basing a trading decision on them.

NOTES FROM A TRADER

Fundamentalists sometimes tend to underestimate the difficulty of analyzing the wheat situation. One of the complications is the great number of areas in which wheat is grown. Weather patterns and political developments in all parts of the world and during all seasons have tremendous influence. Countries such as India and Russia may have large surpluses one year and shortages the next. Small producers, such as France, Argentina, and Australia, may influence the world market with exports to a degree far beyond what would be expected by the size of their crops. The use of wheat exports to achieve political ends does not make the analyst's job any easier.

Many traders get trapped by crop scares, which occur frequently. Of course, wheat, like all crops, is sometimes damaged, but more often than not timely rains seem to arrive just about the time that the last speculative long position is established. It then develops that some slight damage has occurred in a few scattered areas but that the crop is doing beautifully elsewhere. Traders should remember that the type of wheat grown in the United States is adapted to dry weather and can be hurt by too much rain almost as readily as by too little. An old saw among some wheat growers is, "Plant in the dust and your pockets will bust."

The yield of the important winter wheat crop can vary greatly from year to year, depending on the amount of snow cover. When snow cover is light, the danger of topsoil blowing away is a serious one.

Wheat provides more opportunities than most commodities for those who like spreads. In addition to the usual intracommodity spreads, such as old-crop May verus new-crop July, there are intermarket spreads available among Chicago, Kansas City, and Minneapolis which may prove profitable when there is unusual variation in the supply and demand for the various types of wheat or when a price adjustment is necessary to allow costs of transportation from one market to another to be overcome. Other spreaders take advantage of products that have different growing seasons, such as corn. Buying wheat during the harvest period in June versus the sale of new-crop corn is especially popular. The theory is that the hedging pressure in wheat will soon be replaced by the bullish effect of hedge lifting, whereas in the later corn crop the bearish effect of hedging is still to be felt. To assume that this spread will always work at the same time and in the same way for the same reasons is rather naïve, as are any other apparently consistent lead-lag relationships in commodity trading.

CHAPTER SEVENTEEN

Corn and Oats

CORN

INTRODUCTION

Field corn is the most valuable crop in the United States, although most of it never leaves the farm on which it is grown. The United States typically produces more corn than the total from all other countries combined. Corn was the first crop to be planted as settlers moved westward from the East. The small amount which moved commercially to the East was mostly in liquid form and became known as Bourbon whiskey.

Corn futures are traded principally on the Chicago Board of Trade, with December, March, May, July, and September being the contracts traded. Trading typically begins 11 or 12 months before the delivery month of the contract. The crop year in the United States begins on October 1.

As with other grains (and soybeans), the contract traded is 5,000 bushels and the price is quoted in cents per bushel. The minimum-price fluctuation is ¼ cent a bushel, which represents $12.50 per contract (or per 5,000 bushels). A daily range of 20 cents a bushel is the maximum allowed, as is a fluctuation of 10 cents a bushel above or below the close of the preceding day.

CHART 17-1

CORN WEEKLY HIGH, LOW & CLOSE OF NEAREST FUTURES CONTRACT CHICAGO BOARD OF TRADE IN CENTS PER BUSHEL

Prepared by
Commodity Research Bureau, Inc.
ONE LIBERTY PLAZA, NEW YORK, N. Y. 10006

FACTORS WHICH INFLUENCE PRICES

As with other commodities, the cash price of corn ultimately determines the futures prices, although in the very short run it may be the other way around because cash trading is done on the basis of futures prices. However, cash trading reflects the supply of, and the demand for, inventories held for various interests, and eventually changes in cash prices are reflected as changes in futures prices. The change in inventory pattern over a season probably has little effect on average price for the year but does affect the interim price because most of the corn bought and put into inventory must later be sold out of inventory. Because futures prices affect the willingness of trade interests to take positions in the futures market, these futures prices affect the inventory pattern, hence the price movements during a season. As with most commodities, however, corn inventories are not completely offset by futures positions. Most of the inventories are held by farmers and the government. Because government holdings are completely outside the market structure, important factors affecting futures market prices are exogenous to those markets. Therefore, when forecasting corn futures prices at the Chicago Board of Trade, the trader might first make a forecast of the cash prices. The cash prices can then be related to those of the futures markets. Predicting corn futures prices requires analysis of the supply of corn, which is treated in a later section. It also requires some analysis of the demand, which is represented mostly by livestock-feed requirements. These two factors and their relation to the government programs and price support activity are probably the most important fundamental influences of corn futures prices. The relation of cash to futures prices will also have to be examined, as will seasonal variations in the price of corn.

SOURCES OF INFORMATION

Concerning corn and other grains, the yearbook, or *Grain Trade Statistical Annual*, of the Chicago Board of Trade provides the following information for historical analysis:
 1. Daily and monthly futures and spot prices at Chicago
 2. Crop in the United States and the world
 3. Domestic disappearance and exports
 4. Harvest calendars
 5. Carry-over
 6. Corn in storage and afloat in Chicago, weekly
 7. Loan rates in the United States
 8. Corn on farms in the United States
 9. Parity prices monthly
 10. Prices received by farmers monthly
 11. Stocks of corn in Chicago monthly
 12. United States exports by ports

13. United States stocks in all positions quarterly

14. Visible supply monthly and weekly

The most important source of general background information and government activity is the *Feed Situation Report*, published five times a year in February, April, May, August, and November (the Outlook issue). Articles aimed at farmers and the trade, and crop and utilization reports on a fairly up-to-date basis are featured. Included also is the most convenient and reliable source of information about government price support programs: how they work, what changes are being made, and what goals the government is pursuing. Information about foreign trade is also readily available here. The *Report* is an excellent source of corn statistics, semi-current and historical.

The *Grain Market News* (Weekly Summary and Statistics) is perhaps the best source of current information for the corn trader. This publication provides much relevant information, including inspections for exports, crop yield and production, stocks on farms, and CCC dispositions.

The *Crop Production Reports,* issued monthly on the tenth, the *Prospective Plantings Report,* released March 15, and the *Annual Summary,* issued the third week in December, contain detailed crop estimates and production data by state, with comparisons for the preceding year.

Commitments of Traders in Commodity Futures (published monthly in Chicago) gives information on the makeup of the open interest, whether it is dominated by large or small traders, and includes commitments of the trade.

Other sources are indicated in the wheat and soybean chapters.

PRODUCTION

Although corn is grown in almost every state, more than three-fourths of the total production of commercial corn is grown in what is known as the Corn Belt—Iowa, Illinois, Minnesota, Indiana, Nebraska, Ohio, Missouri, and South Dakota, in descending order of the amount of production. Of the field corn grown in the United States, 85 to 90 percent is fed to hogs, poultry, beef and dairy cattle, and sheep. The size of the livestock and poultry inventory is a basic determinant of the demand for corn. The remaining 10 to 15 percent which is not fed to livestock amounts to 400 to 500 million bushels of the average production of more than 3.6 billion bushels and goes principally to the corn-processing industry or is exported.

The corn kernel, consisting of hard and soft starch, hull, and germ, is the basis of the corn-refining industry (wet milling), which processes corn chiefly to get starch, whose principal markets are the paper, textile, laundry, and food industries. Starch is also converted into syrup and sugar used in the candy and food industries, respectively. Corn oil, another by-product extracted from the corn germ, is in demand as a cooking oil and as a base for mayonnaise and salad dressing, although its use in margarine is expanding rapidly. Gluten feed is a further by-product and a high-protein feed concentrate. The dry-milling industry produces cereals and other such products.

Approximately 30 percent of the crop lands in this country are used to produce the food-fiber and tobacco requirements. The remaining 70 percent is used in the production of various animals feeds. Slightly more than half the total animal feed supply consists of hay and pasture. The animal feed concentrates, consisting of grains such as corn and processed feeds including soybean meal, make up most of the balance of the total feed supply.

Corn, which constitutes a major part of the feed-grain supply, makes up approximately one-fourth of the feed concentrates. Any economic analysis of corn prices must therefore take into account the total feed-grain production as well as the feed-concentrate production. Information showing details of the production and utilization of feed concentrates, as well as beginning and ending stocks and other current data, is available in the USDA *Feed Situation Reports*. Tables 17-1 and 17-2 list this information with respect to corn. The production of feed concentrates has increased greatly since 1954. Beginning at that time, acreage allotments were put into effect for wheat and cotton and substantial numbers of acres were shifted to barley and the sorghum grains. This resulted in substantial barley and grain sorghum production increases through 1959. The large corn production increase in 1959 resulted from the increased number of acres allotted to corn and from record yields per acre. The increase in acreage was associated partly with the elimination of the government-agency allotments. The government feed-grain program caused a substantial reduction in 1962 but, because of the high prices and advancing technology, corn production reached record levels in 1963. Reduced acreage and an unfavorable growing season in 1964 caused a sharp reduction in production. Other feed concentrates have increased over the years, mostly because of the large and increasing soybean meal production. Corn production had not increased much through 1970–71. The last couple of years, however, have seen higher production and yield per acre.

FEED-CONCENTRATE UTILIZATION

In order to gain a proper perspective with respect to corn utilization, it will first be necessary to examine utilization of feed concentrates in general. Nonfeed uses—for example, human and industrial consumption—have relatively high value compared with animal consumption and thus have first claim on all of the feed concentrates, which they require. However, the amounts demanded for nonfeed uses have been relatively constant and of small size compared with the demand for animal feed. Utilization of feed concentrates for nonfeed uses will not appreciably increase at lower prices.

Demand for exports from the United States are more responsive to price fluctuation. When United States supplies are short and prices are higher compared with those of other exporting countries, exports decline. On the

TABLE 17-1   ACREAGES AND SUPPLY OF CORN IN THE UNITED STATES (IN MILLIONS OF BUSHELS)

Year beginning October	All purposes Planted	All purposes Harvested	Harvested (in millions of acres) For grain	For silage	For forage	Yield, grain per harvested acre (bu.)	Carry-over, Oct. 1 Farm	Term. mkt.	CCC bins	Others[c]	Total	Production For grain	For all	Imports[b]	Total (all supply grain)
1960	81.4	80.9	71.4	7.2	2.1	54.7	452	[e]	599	736	1,787	3,097	4,353	1.2	5,695
1961	65.9	66.2	57.6	6.3	1.5	62.4	588	[e]	615	813	2,016	3,598	[e]	1.4	5,615
1962	65.0	65.4	55.7	7.2	1.5	64.7	578	[e]	484	590	1,653	3,606	[e]	1.0	5,260
1963	68.8	[e]	59.2	7.7	1.4	67.9	534	[e]	396	435	1,365	4,019	[e]	1.0	5,385
1964	65.8	[e]	55.4	8.6	1.4	62.9	681	[e]	414	441	1,537	3,484	[e]	1.0	5,022
1965–66	65.2	[e]	55.4	8.1	1.2	74.1	581	[e]	308	258	1,147	4,103	[e]	1.0	5,251
1966–67	66.3	[e]	57.0	7.9	.9	73.1	530	[e]	134	176	840	4,168	[e]	1.0	5,011
1967–68	71.2	[e]	60.7	8.4	1.0	80.1	569.2	[e]	97.6	156.5	823	4,860	[e]	1.0	5,687
1968–69	65.1	[e]	56.0	7.9	.7	79.5	781.8	[e]	103.3	277.2	1,162	4,450	[e]	1.0	5,620
1969–70	64.3	[e]	54.6	7.9	.6	85.9	728.2	[e]	143.3	241.9	1,113	4,687	[e]	1.0	5,806
1970–71	66.8	[e]	57.4	8.1	.7	72.4	575.6	[e]	111.3	318.3	1,005	4,152	[e]	4.0	5,161
1971–72	74.1	[e]	64.0	8.8	.7	88.1	426.7	[e]	24.5	215.5	667	5,641	[e]	1.0	6,309
1972–73[a]	66.8	[e]	57.3	8.2	.6	96.9	751.3	[e]	26.3	348.7	1,126	5,553	[e]	1.0	6,680
1973–74[d]	71.5	[e]	61.5			92.4						5,763			

[a] Preliminary.
[b] Includes grain equivalent of cornmeal and flour.
[c] Interior mills and elevators and terminal mkts.
[d] Estimate.
[e] Discontinued, no longer reported.
SOURCE: Statistical Reporting Service, USDA.

TABLE 17-2 DISTRIBUTION OF CORN IN THE UNITED STATES (IN MILLIONS OF BUSHELS)

Year beginning October	Breakfast foods[a]	Food and industrial products[g]	Cornmeal, etc.[b]	Wet-process products[c]	Alcohol and products	Seed	Livestock feed[d]	Exports (incl. grain equiv. of pdt's.)	Total utilization	Domestic disappearance
1960	16	284	96	154.8	32.8	11.1	3,092	292	3,679	3,387
1961	17	304	102	168.7	36.4	10.9	3,212	435	3,962	3,527
1962	18	311	105	179.4	28.2	11.6	3,157	416	3,895	3,479
1963	19	352	112	195.0	25.8	11.2	3,009	500	3,848	3,348
1964	19	358	110	201.0	28.0	11.0	2,957	570	3,875	3,305
1965–66	20	348	111	204.0	30.0	13.0	3,361	687	4,409	3,722
1966–67	21	355	117	205.0	33	14.0	3,329	487	4,185	3,698
1967–68	21	365	117	213	34	12	3,507	633	4,518	3,885
1968–69	22	374	114	221	33	12	3,580	536	4,502	3,966
1969–70	22	381	116	226	31	13	3,796	612	4,801	4,189
1970–71	22	379	119	229	24	17	3,581	517	4,494	3,977
1971–72[e]	22	394	115	242	25	15	3,978	796	5,183	4,387
1972–73[f]	23	399	116	250	26	16	4,365	1,000	5,780	4,780
1973–74										

[a] Estimated quantities used during the calendar year following the corn harvest.
[b] Estimated quantities used in producing cornmeal, flour, hominy, and grits during the calendar year following the corn harvest.
[c] Starch, sirup, sugar, etc.
[d] Feed and waste (residual, mostly feed).
[e] Preliminary.
[f] Forecast.
[g] Total quantities processed and breakdown between domestic use and exports.
SOURCE: Economic Research Service, USDA.

other hand, when domestic quantities are large and prices tend to be low, the value of feed grains in import countries, primarily those in Europe, is higher than the low value in the United States, and therefore the export market takes first claim on the supply of feed concentrates.

The increase in utilization of feed concentrates is associated with an increase in the number of animals fed and also with an increase in the amount fed to each animal. Increased production of feed concentrates preceded the increased utilization because it requires time to adjust livestock inventories. In the short run the amount of feed required depends on the number of animals. In the long run, however, the line from cause to effect runs in the opposite direction. The amount of feed concentrate available determines the number of livestock.

The inventory size of different types of livestock adjusts at different rates to the availability of feed. Because hog inventories can be adjusted relatively quickly, these inventories change rapidly in response to feeding ratios. The hog-corn ratio is discussed more fully in the chapter dealing with pork bellies and with hogs. Some types of livestock inventory change much more slowly in response to the availability of feed; for example, cattle inventories can take a long time to change. Cattle producers are reluctant to reduce cattle numbers by liquidating expensive breeding herds. Poultry inventory, on the other hand, does not seem to be directly related to feed supplies, even in the long run. Thus a primary shift, caused by availability of greater feed supplies, will first cause an increase in the number of hogs and then an increase of other types of livestock such as cattle.

In the longer run, however, a secondary change occurs which tends to increase the supply of all livestock. As the number of hogs increases and causes the price of hogs to go down in relation to the price of cattle and poultry, the hog-feeding ratio becomes less favorable compared with the feeding ratios for other livestock. This causes a shift in the economic resources from hogs to cattle and poultry. Thus the long-term effect of an increase in feed supplies produces a rather uniform increase in the livestock inventory.

Because of the relative increase in the feed concentrate supply compared with that of other animal feed and also because of the increase in the salable-product livestock animal units, requiring more feed per animal, the total amount of feed concentrate, as well as the amount per animal unit, has increased rapidly during the last 20 years.

The average prices of livestock feed in general and of corn specifically must be examined in a situation in which the basic price structure is complex. Among other things, it depends on the quantity of feed available and the consumer expenditures for the end products of the animals.

CORN UTILIZATION

Most of the corn utilization over the years has been for livestock feed. The other uses, however,—dry processing of food, wet processing of food, alcohol, seed, and exports—although in total representing a small proportion of corn production, are discussed briefly. Their relative importance is shown in Table 17-2.

Dry-processed corn is used mainly for breakfast food, cornmeal, and grits. An increase in the use of dry-processed corn for brewing and industrial purposes occurs when the price of corn goes down to a level where it can compete with barley and rice.

The wet processing of corn results in the manufacture of corn sugar and corn syrup. During periods of high sugar prices, as in the 1960s, these corn sugar products, because of their relatively low price, tend to replace sugar for some purposes. Because of this factor, their use grew rapidly during the early 1960s.

The use of corn for alcohol production, although erratic, is relatively small and has little effect on total corn utilization. Similarly, the use of corn for seed is small and has a negligible effect on the total disappearance of corn.

As shown in Table 17-3, corn exports have increased since 1955 and constitute a substantial share of the total usage. The major destination of the United States corn exports continues to be Europe, both inside and outside the Common Market. The increasing demand for meat and dairy products in Europe has caused increased feed requirements, which are filled mainly from United States supplies. Certain policies of the Common Market, however, especially attempts to make it self-sufficient, may tend to curtail these exports.

The United States is also the principal source of increasing quantities of corn exports to Japan, where consumer demand for livestock products has been increasing rapidly. Japan imports a high proportion of its animal feed-stuffs.

Because most of the corn utilization is related to livestock feed, estimation of that part of the demand becomes of primary importance. Any meaningful estimate of feed utilization must take into account the number of hogs, cattle, dairy cattle, and poultry—all corn-consuming animals. The USDA conveniently determines and publishes in its *Feed Situation Reports* the number of grain-consuming animal units to be fed. Such information constitutes an excellent starting point from which to estimate the feed requirements for the coming season.

Foote, Klein, and Clough[1] publish an excellent formula based on the total supply of corn, the number of grain-consuming animal units, and the USDA index of livestock and livestock product prices as factors with which to determine the average price of corn. This formula, however, assumes that the total supply of corn is available in the free market. Obviously the method is not effective when the government holds large quantities of corn, as it has in recent years. The supply of corn available to the free market de-

[1] R. J. Foote, J. W. Klein and M. Clough, *The Demand and Price Structure for Corn and Total Feed Concentrates*, USDA Technical Bulletin 1061, October 1952.

TABLE 17-3 DOMESTIC DISAPPEARANCE AND FOREIGN TRADE OF CORN IN THE UNITED STATES (IN MILLIONS OF BUSHELS)

Crop year	Exports—grain only					Imports—grain only					Domestic disappearance				
	Oct.–Dec.	Jan.–Mar.	Apr.–June	July–Sept.	Total	Oct.–Dec.	Jan.–Mar.	Apr.–June	July–Sept.	Total	Oct.–Dec.†	Jan.–Mar.	Apr.–June	July–Sept.	Total
1960	73.0	68.3	70.0	64.9	276.1	0.3	0.3	0.5	0.2	1.2	925.5	954.4	779.3	743.3	3,403
1961	90.4	117.7	118.1	89.1	415.3	0.3	0.3	0.6	0.2	1.4	1,032.6	984.9	788.8	741.5	3,548
1962	102.2	81.3	124.0	90.0	397.3	0.2	0.3	0.1	0.3	1.0	946.7	1,081.2	794.0	675.3	3,497
1963	143.7	114.2	105.6	114.0	477.5	0.2	0.2	0.3	0.3	1.0	896.2	952.3	796.7	726.1	3,371
1964	145.8	115.5	145.5	143.2	550.0	0.2	0.3	0.2	0.3	1.0	1,000.4	954.4	766.5	603.5	3,325
1965	197	171	177	142	687	0.2	0.3	0.2	0.2	0.9	1,001	1,012	906	803	3,722
1966–67	140	126	107	114	487	0.2	0.1	0.3	0.2	0.8	1,163	847	874	814	3,698
1967–68	183	158	129	163	633	0.2	0.3	0.3	0.2	0.9	1,184	919	913	869	3,885
1968–69	158	71	134	173	536	0.2				1	1,192	1,135	849	790	3,966
1969–70	186	139	133	154	612	0.5				1	1,243	1,206	953	787	4,189
1970–71	156	121	93	147	517					4	1,234	1,103	881	759	3,977
1971–72*	160	173	192	271	796					1	1,449	1,145	1,014	779	4,387
1972–73*	257	301	323	377	1,258						1,607	1,184	1,076	848	4,715
1973–74															

* Preliminary.

† Includes all corn fed in silage and forage or hogged off, part of which is consumed after January 1.

SOURCE: Economic Research Service, USDA.

pends in an important way on government activities. Therefore government activities have a substantial influence on price. In turn, those activities are to some extent a function of price. Because of the depletion of inventories held by the government, this influence will probably be less important in the foreseeable future.

GOVERNMENT PROGRAMS

As with wheat, the primary influence of the government over the price of corn is exerted by the loan program. Each year the government sets a farm-loan (note) price and a price at which it will sell government supplies on the open market.

These two prices may be especially influential at three important market-price levels:

1. A market price at harvest time sufficiently below the farm loan price so that farmers will be willing to place their crop under loan. This level forms a "floor," at least early in the crop year. This movement of corn into loan, by decreasing the free market supply, should cause the price to rise, frequently to the loan level.

2. A market price sufficiently in excess of the loan to cover the cost of redemption, including interest on the loan. This interest, incidentally, is due only on redemption and not if the farmer forfeits his crop to the government. If the loan has effectively reduced the free supply, the market price should rise to the redemption level.

3. The market price at which the government will sell its stocks on the open market. This level becomes a "ceiling" price, and is effective in years of short supply. Legally the government cannot sell at a price that is below the loan plus "reasonable" carrying charges except in "special" circumstances. The words "reasonable" and "special," however, are subject to a wide range of interpretation, and therefore the level at which government sales will be made may be uncertain.

Some relevant data concerning price support levels are shown in Tables 17-4 and 17-5. This summary, together with hindsight, suggests that corn should be bought at prices below the loan price and sold at or above the statutory sales price. It must be pointed out, however, that (a) such a policy will not always yield gains and (b) other actions may lead to gains with much larger potential and greater certainty than the stated policy.

Because the futures market price range of corn has been closely related[2] to the farm loan price over the years, the "futures price equivalent" of the loan is often a matter of concern. This quantity is usually estimated by adding handling charges and freight to Chicago (usually totaling 15 to 20 cents) to the country farm-loan price, but such a procedure is not reliable because of the large variation by location in the charges and loan rates.

Perhaps a more reliable forecasting procedure would be to use supply-

---

[2] See Chapter 16 for an example of this relationship.

TABLE 17-4 CORN PRICE SUPPORT DATA IN THE UNITED STATES

Year beginning Oct. 1	National average price support (¢ bu)	Per cent of parity	Placed under support			Redemptions	De-livered to CCC	Re-sealed	Total deliver-ies†	Stocks at close of market year (Sept. 30)			Support price to noncom-pliers (¢ bu)	CCC inventory as of Dec. 31	
			Loans	Purchase agree-ments	Total					Under loan or owned by CCC	"Free"	Total		Million	
							(millions of bushels)							Bushels	Dollars
1960	106	65	562.5	75.0	637.5	113.9	324.1	199.8	474.8	1,890	126	2,016	106	1,471	2,445
1961	120	74	581.3	77.3	658.6	25.5	477.9	155.2	634.8	1,535	118	1,653	0	1,412	1,783
1962	120	75	535.4	55.4	590.8	106.5	345.1	139.2	460.0	1,275	90	1,365	0	958	1,830
1963	125	79	386.1	9.2	395.3	241.5	14.6	139.2	16.0	1,300	237	1,537	0	794	1,673
1964–65	125	80	215.7	0.1	215.8	142.3	1.9	71.6	12.0	924	223	1,147	0	835	1,606
1965–66	125	80	214.9	–	214.9	152.6	0.2	62.1	7.8	437	403	842	0	530	1,135
1966–67	130	81	263.0	–	263.0	129.1	0.2	133.7	12.5	374	449	826	0	119	588
1967–68	135	83	466.7	30.3	497.0	104.8	116.7	275.5	193.0	714	448	1,169	0	138	
1968–69	135	81	403.4	0.5	403.9	262.6	11.1	130.2	36.0	736	377	1,118	0	261	
1969–70	135	78	398.1	–	398.1	289.8	2.1	106.2		543	457	1,005	0	295	
1970–71*	135	75	323.4	0.6	324.0	205.8	5.9	112.3		330	337	667	0	115	
1971–72*	135	72	955.0	–	955.0	510.0	18	417.0		718	408	1,126		145	
1972–73*	135		420.0		420.0	100.0	1.0	330.0		172	535	707		117	
1973–74*	135														

* Preliminary.

† Includes "delivered to CCC" from original program and deliveries from reseal program and over-deliveries as determined by weight of farm-stored grain when delivered to CCC.

SOURCE: Commodity Stabilization Service, USDA.

TABLE 17-5 CORN UNDER PRICE SUPPORT THROUGH THE END OF THE MONTH: CUMULATIVE TOTALS FROM CURRENT SEASON'S CROP (IN MILLIONS OF BUSHELS)

Crop year	Oct.	Nov.	Dec.	Jan.	Feb.	Mar.	Apr.	May	June	July	Aug.	Sept.	Total
1960	2.5	21.0	152.1	376.2	475.6	516.4	545.1	611.4	562.6	—	—	—	637.5
1961	2.0	11.7	82.9	287.3	412.2	498.5	548.5	625.9	580.9	581.2	—	—	658.6
1962	4.7	28.6	135.3	353.0	464.0	504.1	532.0	572.8	535.8	—	—	—	590.8
1963	2.2	41.0	156.3	319.9	357.6	376.0	382.5	387.7	386.0	—	—	—	395.3
1964	3.7	53.9	106.9	186.5	200.6	207.5	210.7	212.9	214.4	—	—	—	215.8
1965–66	2.4	32.0	102.7	181.8	196.9	205.3	209.1	211.0	213.0	—	—	—	214.9
1966–67	2.1	45.0	110.5	192.9	217.7	229.1	235.1	238.9	242.4	242.9	—	—	263.0
1967–68	5.0	52.2	193.9	347.0	386.9	410.9	420.3	427.5	438.7	—	—	—	497.0
1968–69	10.2	72.0	180.3	329.5	367.5	384.5	393.3	396.2	398.6	401.8	—	—	403.9
1969–70	9.0	51.8	166.8	336.5	365.5	381.9	389.7	392.6	395.5	397.4	—	—	398.1
1970–71	22.3	91.6	171.9	280.2	297.8	310.3	316.1	318.9	320.8	322.0	—	—	324.0
1971–72	60.2	313.2	585.9	833.9	881.8	907.6	918.9	923.5	937.2	950.4	—	—	952.0
1972–73	20.7	100.4	245.3	360.2	395.5								
1973–74													

SOURCE: USDA.

and-demand relations to estimate the country price and determine the relationships between the country price and the cash and futures prices in Chicago.

CHICAGO CASH AND FUTURES PRICES

During recent years the spot or cash price of No. 2 yellow corn at Chicago was, on the average, 15 cents a bushel above the U.S. average farm price. The difference varies significantly, however, and factors determining this variation should be examined:

1. Corn is first harvested in the Middle West Corn Belt; the harvest then moves eastward. Therefore early in the season relatively small supplies in the East and in Chicago cause increases in the Chicago price. Later in the season the Chicago premium tends to decrease.

2. Approximately one-half the harvested corn is sold for livestock feed, and a major portion of the feed processing and mixing is done in the Chicago area. Therefore, as processors buy corn during and after the harvest season, inventory stocks build up in Chicago. The rate of processing and reduction of this inventory depends on the demand for exports and for domestic (mostly Eastern) feed. Domestic feed demand depends on the number of animals and the amount of local feed production. In any case, if these demands are relatively high (low), inventories will be low (high), and the Chicago premium will be increased (decreased).

Weekly series of Chicago spot corn prices, receipts, shipments, local usage, and free stocks can be obtained from the *Grain Trade Statistical Annual* of the Chicago Board of Trade. This series can be kept current by using the weekly *Grain Market News*.

By comparing the July futures price with the Chicago spot price certain general relationships become apparent; for example, on the average, the July futures price is at a 10-cent premium at the beginning of the season (October). By March or April this premium disappears, and at the end of the July contract the futures price is at a 3-cent discount.

Cash corn sells at a discount to futures during the harvest because of the storage and other carrying charges which are not a factor in holding futures contracts. The amount of the spot price discount depends largely on the supply of and the demand for storage space; for example, in years of relatively large crops storage space is scarce and the discount is large.

During and just before the delivery month the price difference depends on the size of Chicago stocks and the rate of movement out of Chicago. At this time the level of Chicago stocks is of primary importance.

FUTURES MARKET SPREADS
AND CARRYING CHARGES

As with other grains, differences in the price relations of the various futures contracts are caused mainly by the relative level (as compared with the rate of out movement) of deliverable stocks in Chicago. If stocks are large, then distant contracts will sell at large premiums, perhaps equal to full carrying charges, when compared with nearby contracts. The Wheat chapter shows details for estimating the carrying charges for corn and other grains. If the distant contracts are selling at small premiums or at discounts compared with the nearby, then it is highly probable that a scarcity of corn exists at the current price and that prices will rise. These observations are consistent with the old proverb well known to commodity traders: buy discounts and sell carrying charges.

SEASONAL INFORMATION

The "seasonal tendency" of commodity prices is discussed in the Wheat and Soybean chapters. In corn, as in those commodities, speculators exert a contraseasonal force which has, except for carrying charges, virtually eliminated seasonal fluctuations.

The trader should realize that the corn market is large and efficient and that, even ignoring commissions, commodity trading in it is a two-person, zero-sum game. Without information, either technical or fundamental, which is, on the average, better than that of his adversary, the commodity trader will not have gains in the long run.

At any moment in time the futures market price reflects the aggregate judgement of traders of the *current* value of the commodity to be delivered as specified in the contract. It is not an estimate of what the price will be at a later time. The price is therefore a statement of the collective judgment of what the commodity contract is worth and what it is expected to continue to be worth. Only as this collective judgment changes does the price of the futures contract change. The frequent changes in price can be the result of errors in aggregate judgments, the participants in which attempt to discount all known and anticipated factors when they agree on the current price. When the individual trader takes a position, he is making a judgment that is different from that of the aggregate. He is betting that the market is wrong.

The seasonal pattern of open interest and volume for corn futures trading on the Chicago Board of Trade is shown in Figure 17-1.

OATS

INTRODUCTION

Although oats is one of the largest domestic crops in terms of bushels produced, it has no large cash value. The post-World War I high point of production was reached in the mid-1940s, when approximately 1.5 billion bushels were harvested. Production has decreased steadily since then, and in recent years it has been about 800 to 900 million bushels. Because of increased yields for oats, the acreage has been reduced continuously and substantially.

Oats futures are traded primarily on the Chicago Board of Trade, al-

FIG. 17-1   Corn: monthly open interest and volume as a percentage of average monthly open interest and volume for the years 1962–1971 at the Chicago Board of Trade. (Commodity Exchange Authority, USDA.)

though a substantial market once existed on the Winnipeg Commodity Exchange in Canada. As with other grains, a futures contract consists of 5,000 bushels and orders are typically given in bushels. The price is quoted in cents per bushel, with a minimum fluctuation of $\frac{1}{8}$ cent a bushel or $\frac{1}{8} \times$ 5,000 = \$6.25 per contract. The maximum allowable daily range for oats on the Chicago Board of Trade is 12 cents a bushel, with a maximum fluctuation of 6 cents either up or down from the preceding day's settlement price.

The crop year in the United States begins July 1. Contracts traded in Chicago include July, September, December, March, and May.

FACTORS WHICH INFLUENCE PRICES

Oats, like corn and soybean meal, are used primarily as animal feed. Economic forecasting methods therefore must take into account the total feed supply-and-demand situation. This is considered in detail in the Soybeans chapter and in the Corn section of this chapter. Table 17-6 shows the supply and distribution of oats in the United States for recent years. Table 17-7 shows some other salient statistics. The government price support program affects the oats price range much as it does that of corn and wheat. The support prices and number of bushels under price support are shown in Table 17-7.

TABLE 17-6 SUPPLY AND DISTRIBUTION OF OATS IN THE UNITED STATES (IN MILLIONS OF BUSHELS)

Year beginning July	Carry-over, July 1					Production	Imports^b	Total supply	Break-fast foods	Seed	Live-stock feed^c	Disappearance		
	Farm	Commercial	CCC bins	Other^a	Total							Exports^d	Total	Domestic^f
1960	226.7	7.6	1.1	31.6	267.0	1,153	1.3	1,421	45.0	82.9	943	29.0	1,097	1,068
1961	267.6	g	.8	56.0	324.4	1,010	1.1	1,335	46.0	75.0	919	21.0	1,059	1,038
1962	228.4	g	1.7	46.2	276.3	1,012	4.4	1,292	46.0	71.0	878	24.0	1,019	995
1963	230.3	g	2.7	39.8	272.8	966	3.7	1,243	46.0	65.0	815	6.0	931	925
1964	249.0	g	4.6	58.7	312.4	852	4.0	1,168	45	61.0	780	5.0	891	886
1965–66	213.7	g	6.5	56.3	276.5	930	3.0	1,210	45	60.0	752	37.0	893	856
1966–67	241.2	g	9.4	66.1	316.7	803	4.0	1,124	43	53.0	737	20.0	853	833
1967–68	199.3	g	6.7	64.7	270.6	794	3	1,068	44	60	681	10	794	784
1968–69	207.7	g	6.7	59.8	274.2	951	2	1,227	45	60	735	8	848	840
1969–70	278.7	g	6.7	93.3	378.6	966	2	1,347	45	62	734	5	848	843
1970–71	352.8	g	8.0	137.8	498.6	917	2	1,418	46	57	782	18	902	884
1971–72^e	316.2	g	11.3	189.5	517.1	881	4	1,402	46	54	737	24	861	837
1972–73^e	336.5	g	10.0	194.9	541.4	692	3	1,238	——98——		705	24	827	803
1973–74^e	230.7	g	6.6	176.9	412.0	664	3	1,116	——97——		649	40	786	746

^a Interior mills, elevators, and warehouses.
^b Imports include grain equivalent of oatmeal.
^c Residual; includes small quantities for other uses and waste.
^d Exports are grain only.
^e Preliminary.
^f Total disappearance minus exports of oats and grain equivalent of oatmeal.
^g Included in other.
SOURCE: Statistical Reporting Service, USDA.

TABLE 17-7 SALIENT STATISTICS OF OATS IN THE UNITED STATES AND CANADA

| | | | | | | | U.S. government price support program | | | | | | | Canada (Aug.–July) | | |
| | Acreage | | Yield per harvested‡ acre (bu) | Farm value of product (millions $) | Farm disposition (millions bu) | | Owned by CCC July 1 | Under price support (1,000 bu) | | | De-liveries to CCC | Nat. avg. sup-port rate ($ bu) | | | |
Year beginning July	Planted† (1,000 acres)	Har-vested‡			Feed and seed	Sold		Loans	Pur-chase agree-ments	Total			Aug. 1 stocks	Ex-ports§	Dom. dis-appear. (millions bu)
1960	31,419	26,588	43.4	693	813	340	14,514	18,286	1,384	19,670	500	0.50	101	3	381
1961	32,314	23,886	42.3	650	730	281	9,025	19,311	1,306	20,617	8,400	0.62	115	4	322
1962	29,500	22,377	45.2	636	720	292	16,700	29,544	2,479	32,023	19,000	0.62	79	22	401
1963	28,054	21,308	45.3	608	657	309	17,087	35,052	3,833	38,885	31,900	0.65	150	19	398
1964	25,634	19,759	43.1	541	570	282	28,254	41,200	3,700	44,900	25,100	0.65	179	16	380
1965	24,010	18,522	50.2	585	613	314	42,151	43,700	200	43,900	6,800	0.60	130	16	387
1966–67	23,301	17,877	44.9	538	526	275	50,573	22,700	–	22,700	6,500	0.60	127	5	387
1967–68	20,646	16,110	49.3	525	523	266	47,796	37,200	400	37,600	19,500	0.63	110	4	333
1968–69	23,166	17,703	53.7	569	586	353	45,206	89,200	5,700	94,900	70,000	0.63	82	3	313
1969–70	23,532	17,971	53.7	565	578	372	61,088	152,500	10,100	162,600		0.63	129	5	354
1970–71	24,469	18,638	49.2	581	558	351	104,254	108,900	4,800	113,700		0.54	141	13	371
1971–72*	21,956	15,772	55.9	546	538	338	168,910			82,000		0.54	125	9	376
1972–73*	20,296	13,612	51.1	471			178,128			50,000		0.54	146		
1973–74*	21,000														

*Preliminary.
† For all purposes.
‡ For grain.
§ Including products.
SOURCE: Statistical Reporting Service, USDA.

SOURCES OF INFORMATION

The most important sources of information are the same as those shown in the Corn section of this chapter. Comments about these sources are also applicable to oats. As with all other grains, volume and open-interest data are issued daily and are available on request from the Commodity Exchange Authority of the USDA.

PRODUCTION

U.S. production runs about a third of the total world production of approximately 3 billion bushels. Oats are grown in most countries, with heaviest production centering in North America, followed by Europe and the U.S.S.R.

White oats comprise most of the U.S. crop and are grown generally north of the Ohio River and westward to the Rocky Mountains. Red oats are raised south of the Ohio River and in Texas, Oklahoma, and Kansas, and gray oats are grown in the Pacific Northwest. Red and gray oats are planted in

CHART 17-2

TABLE 17-8 WORLD PRODUCTION OF OATS (IN THOUSANDS OF METRIC TONS)‡

Crop year	United States	Canada	Argentina	Australia	Turkey	U.S.S.R.	West Germany	Spain	Netherlands	Denmark	France	Sweden	United Kingdom	Poland	World total
1960	1,153	456	58	95	35	750	150	30	27	47	188	81	144	190	3,955
1961	1,010	284	49	69	30	600	132	34	30	47	179	93	128	203	3,410
1962	1,012	494	34	86	31	385	161	35	32	42	178	75	122	189	3,375
1963–64‡	14,014	6,988	906	1,238	475	3,700	3,444	466	424	671	3,247	1,156	1,461	2,830	47,725
1964–65	12,371	5,508	805	1,271	425	3,900	3,476	390	420	821	2,680	1,448	1,346	2,218	43,278
1965–66	13,492	6,399	480	1,102	450	4,600	3,027	370	363	780	2,898	1,340	1,232	2,476	45,315
1966–67	11,660	5,778	540	1,943	450	7,500	3,366	442	357	864	3,031	1,154	1,120	2,594	47,046
1967–68	11,522	4,691	690	719	475	9,700	3,841	492	365	904	3,411	1,396	1,386	2,768	49,348
1968–69	13,799	5,591	490	1,710	450	9,700	4,135	522	318	861	3,066	1,584	1,224	2,831	52,821
1969–70	14,020	5,728	425	1,247	468	10,700	4,250	533	322	765	2,842	1,129	1,308	3,063	53,396
1970–71	13,313	5,672	360	1,613	415	11,800	3,481	395	201	631	2,556	1,685	1,217	3,209	52,882
1971–72*	12,792	5,606	475	1,277	455	12,100	4,247	582	206	701	3,137	1,867	1,368	3,200	54,931
1972–73†	10,087	4,630	530	740	395	11,600	4,030	442	140	636	2,463	1,627	1,255	3,235	50,700
1973–74	10,194	5,141	575	1,700	375	17,500	4,129	500	115	485	2,219	1,390	1,148	2,850	54,659

* Preliminary.
† Estimated.
‡ Data before 1963–64 are in millions of bushels.
SOURCE: Foreign Agricultural Service, USDA.

TABLE 17-9 DOMESTIC DISAPPEARANCE AND FOREIGN TRADE OF OATS IN THE UNITED STATES (IN MILLIONS OF BUSHELS)

Crop year	Exports — grain only					Imports — grain only					Domestic disappearance				
	July–Sept.	Oct.–Dec.	Jan.–Mar.	Apr.–June	Total	July–Sept.	Oct.–Dec.	Jan.–Mar.	Apr.–June	Total	July–Sept.	Oct.–Dec.	Jan.–Mar.	Apr.–June	Total
1960	11.0	5.9	5.7	4.2	26.8	0.3	0.2	0.4	0.3	1.3	328.0	225.4	287.6	229.3	1,070
1961	5.8	1.9	0.2	10.8	18.6	0.2	0.2	0.5	0.2	1.1	326.6	196.2	279.7	207.4	1,041
1962	11.9	5.1	3.0	2.8	22.8	0.4	1.3	1.0	1.6	4.2	313.8	193.3	278.4	211.6	997
1963	3.4	0.5	0.1	1.0	4.9	1.2	1.0	0.9	0.5	3.5	302.7	170.9	252.3	198.7	924
1964	1.6	1.3	—	1.2	4.1	0.4	0.8	1.0	1.4	3.5	314.3	156.4	232.6	184.2	888
1965	9.2	13.2	1.5	13	37	0.7	0.9	1.0	0.6	3.1	275	144.0	226.3	207.6	856
1966–67	9	7	1	3	20	0.5	0.7	1.1	0.9	3.2	276	166	220	170	833
1967–68	5	1	2	3	10	0.4	1.3	0.7	0.5	2.8	274	130	208	172	784
1968–69	3	2	1	2	8	0.3	0.4			2	276	153	234	177	840
1969–70	2	1	1	1	5					2	303	143	210	186	843
1970–71	2	14	1	1	18					2	309	169	212	193	884
1971–72*	1	3	11	9	24					4	304	147	197	188	836
1972–73*	3	2	2	17	24						302	152	193	156	803
1973–74*	17										253				

*Preliminary.

SOURCE: Economic Research Service, USDA.

the fall; white oats are seeded in early spring. The harvest begins in May in the South and is completed by late August in the Northern states.

Table 17-8 summarizes world production data.

UTILIZATION

Except for breakfast foods (5 percent), seed (8 percent), and a small amount that is exported, domestic oats consumption centers on feed. Oats are excellent for horses, breeding animals, young stock, and poultry, and the bulk of the production is used for this purpose near where the crop is grown. The decline in the production of oats is related to the decline in the number of horses and mules employed as work animals.

The edible products of processed oats are rolled oats, steel-cut oatmeal, and ground oatmeal, plus some of the ready-to-eat cereals.

Table 17-9 shows the salient data for domestic disappearance and foreign trade for oats in recent years.

SEASONAL INFORMATION AND SPREADS

The largest movement of oats to market typically occurs about a month after the harvest. The peak of marketing occurs in August, but a substantial amount of oats is "pushed" into market as corn is harvested in October. Therefore low seasonal prices for oats frequently occur in August and October. Many oats are utilized in the fall and winter when feed requirements are heaviest because of lack of grass.

Because the corn harvest is later than that of oats, a particular type of oats-corn spread has been advocated by some traders and services. The spread, for example, "Buy December oats — sell December corn," initiated on April 1 and closed out on November 1, is based on the premise that after the summer oats harvest has passed prices will become firmer but the later corn harvest will tend to weaken corn prices. The results of a spread for the past 26 years are shown in Table 17-10.

The ratio of two bushels of oats to one bushel of corn is used because a bushel of oats weighs only 32 pounds compared with 56 pounds for a bushel of corn. It is generally considered that the value, as feed, is almost the same *per pound* for the two commodities.

Note that although the trade generally worked in the earlier years the record has been poor over the last 14 years. This is another example of the elimination of seasonal fluctuations by speculators. However, the potential for gain from exploiting the risk premium based on the hedging patterns for oats and corn can be reviewed in Chapter 4, p. 100.

Two of the factors of vital importance in any consideration of an oats-corn spread are (a) the total supply of each (related to the rate of usage) and (b) the stocks at Chicago.

Figure 17-2 shows the seasonal pattern of open interest and volume for oats futures trading on the Chicago Board of Trade.

TABLE 17-10   DECEMBER OATS–DECEMBER CORN: NET
CHANGE IN PREMIUM OF PRICE OF TWO BUSHELS OF OATS
OVER ONE BUSHEL OF CORN, APRIL 1 TO NOVEMBER 1

	Prices, April 1			Prices, November 1			Gain or loss
Year	Two bushels oats	One bushel corn	Premium, two bushels oats over one bushel corn	Two bushels oats	One bushel corn	Premium, two bushels oats over one bushel corn	Net change in premium of two bushels oats *over* one bushel corn, April 1 to November 1
1948	170½	167¼	3¼	156	137⅜	18⅝	+15⅜
1949	126½	114⅞	11⅝	146	118	28	+16⅜
1950	136¼	125⅛	11⅛	169½	154¼	15¼	+ 4⅛
1951	176½	171¼	5¼	179½	176⅞	2⅝	− 2⅝
1952	169	173⅞	−4⅞	173¼	166⅛	7⅛	+12
1953	152¾	156⅜	−3⅜	156¼	147⅞	8⅜	+12
1954	147¾	144¾	3	164¾	156¼	8½	+ 5½
1955	135¾	137⅞	−2⅛	128¾	129⅛	−0⅜	+ 1¾
1956	139¼	141	−1¾	160½	138½	22	+23¾
1957	136¼	129¼	7	135½	118⅜	17⅛	+10⅛
1958	132¼	117¾	14½	130	111¼	18¾	+ 4¼
1959	137¾	115½	22¼	153	109⅞	43⅛	+20⅞
1960	150½	110¾	39¾	127¼	108⅜	18⅞	−20⅞
1961	138½	117¼	21¼	132	108½	23½	+ 2¼
1962	149	118	31	128¾	107½	21¼	− 9¾
1963	142½	113⅞	28⅝	142¾	118⅜	24⅜	− 4¼
1964	139	120	19	135¼	119½	15½	− 3½
1965	140¾	120⅝	20⅛	134¾	114¼	20½	+ ⅜
1966	140	120½	19½	151½	137	14½	− 5
1967	154	142	12¼	143¼	114	29¼	+17
1968	149½	127	22¼	134¾	110¾	24	+ 1¾
1969	137	114½	22½	121¾	117⅞	3⅞	−18⅝
1970	132½	118	14½	158	147⅝	10⅜	− 4⅛
1971	145	143⅜	1⅝	147½	114¾	32¾	+31⅛
1972	138¼	127	11¼	176¾	137⅞	38⅛	+27⅝
1973	164	147½	16½	239	239½	−0½	−16

NOTES FROM A TRADER—CORN AND OATS

The enormous size of the corn crop and the volume of hedging in corn produce a futures market which seems to be somewhat ponderous at times. Moves are usually slow, turns are rounding, and the market can absorb relatively large orders without reacting violently. It is a popular market for the relatively new speculator because the risk of sudden great adverse moves is less than elsewhere. Furthermore, the margin requirements are generally rather low. Some, however, have called this market a "Sleeping Giant," because when it begins to move it can go farther than anyone expects and occasionally its movements are sharper than traders are used to experiencing.

When the U.S. corn crop is compared with that of other countries, its overwhelming size is evident, but that does not mean that the crops of other countries are not without influence; for example, Argentina's importance is out of proportion to the size of its crop because it sells a high percentage of its production into world trade rather than as domestic feed.

Many traders, in attempting to analyze corn, forget that it is basically a feed grain and that many substitutes other than the obvious soybean meal and oats are available. Sorghums of various types grow in great quantity but are overlooked by many traders because they do not trade heavily on domestic exchanges.

For both corn and oats weather, particularly at certains times of the year, can be extremely important. In the case of corn, for example, subsoil moisture is usually entirely exhausted by the middle of July, and rain from that time until the middle of August may be critical if there is not to be severe damage. Too much rain, however, during the same period can prevent storage because of the crop's excess moisture and the result may be crash marketing and low prices. Conversely, continuing rain can even postpone the harvest until the fields dry, another cause of short-term tightness.

FIG. 17-2   Oats: monthly open interest and volume as a percentage of average monthly open interest and volume for the years 1962–1971 at the Chicago Board of Trade. (Commodity Exchange Authority, USDA.)

Worse, the rain may be followed by an early frost, which can severely damage the wet corn and the bank accounts of those who had been selling corn because they regarded the rain as bearish. Late drought may appear bearish, but it may have a beneficial effect if it arrives after the corn crop is made and serves only to dry the corn and the fields. Oats mature earlier than wheat and are not so hardy a crop. They need adequate moisture, and they may be severely damaged by hot weather near the end of their growing season.

The oats market acts more like a thin market than one would expect from the apparently large crop. One reason is that the small size of a bushel of oats is sometimes forgotten and that the crop is not so big as it appears. Furthermore, the oats market is sometimes dominated by a few large trade houses, so that its response to small speculative activity may be more than had seemed likely.

In spreading oats against corn, most traders will regard one contract of corn as equivalent to two contracts of oats, but large traders should keep in mind the thinness of the oats market to avoid suffering a loss greater than expected. Liquidity is seldom a problem in popular corn-wheat spreads, but it may be one for those who choose to spread Chicago oats, particularly a maturing contract of oats against a more distant contract.

CHAPTER EIGHTEEN

Plywood and Lumber

PLYWOOD (SOFTWOOD)

INTRODUCTION

The ever growing demand for new homes since World War II and the increased amount of plywood used for each new building have been the major factors in the phenomenal growth of the softwood plywood industry. The year 1946 saw 33 plants produce 1.4 billion square feet of plywood. In 1971 more than 16.4 billion square feet were manufactured by approximately 180 plants. This rapid change has given rise to large profits and losses for many in the industry. The Chicago Board of Trade introduced a futures trading contract in (softwood) plywood in 1969.

Contracts currently traded on the Board of Trade are January, March, May, July, September, and November; trading typically begins 10 to 12 months before the delivery month for the contract. The contract unit traded is a boxcar of ½ inch plywood; that is, 36 banded units of 60 pieces each, or 2160 pieces of 4 x 8 plywood—69,120 square feet total per car. Price is quoted in units of 1,000 square feet, with minimum fluctuation of 10 cents per 1,000 square feet or $6.912 per contract. The daily limit on price movement is $7.00 per 1,000 square feet above or below the preced-

CHART 18-1
PLYWOOD - CHICAGO (WEEKLY HIGH, LOW & CLOSE OF NEAREST FUTURES)

DOLLARS PER 1,000 SQ. FT.

ing day's settlement price. The daily limit is suspended on the first notice day of the expiring delivery month.

FACTORS WHICH INFLUENCE PLYWOOD PRICES

Because residential construction consumes almost 60 percent of all soft-wood plywood produced and because the rate of residential construction fluctuates significantly, the influence of housing activity on the plywood market has been pronounced. Major turns in housing activity have caused major turns in the market. See Figure 18-1. A seasonally adjusted annual rate (SAAR) is announced by the federal government monthly. It represents the *total* number of units expected to be started by the end of the calendar

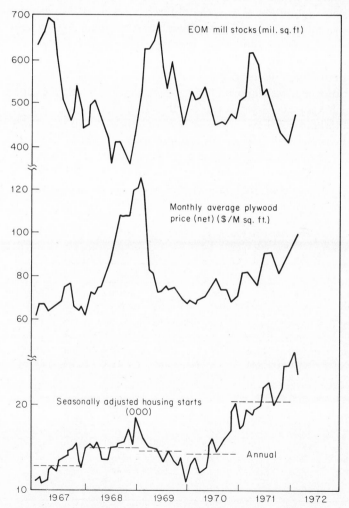

FIG. 18-1 Comparison of changes in plywood prices with those of housing starts and mill stocks.

year. Each succeeding monthly estimate is a revision of the preceding month's estimate. See Table 18-1 for monthly SAAR estimates since 1969. It also shows the actual monthly housing starts. The *totals* of the columns should be compared with *each* of the SAAR estimates.

The cost of producing plywood panel, that is, the basic mill price, is influenced greatly by stumpage costs, plywood plant capacity, and wages. Stumpage cost is the cost of buying standing timber from government lands or the cost of maintaining company-owned forests. Plywood plant capacity and level of operation are other important cost factors. Because fixed costs are high, the cost per unit of plywood produced drops sharply as the level of production increases. Wages and changes in wage rates can affect plywood prices, especially in the Northwest, where unions are strong.

Besides housing and production costs, futures market prices can be influenced in a number of other ways. Weather, particularly snow and drought, can have a significant (though perhaps short-term) influence on prices. The impact of weather conditions on lagging operations can cause shortages and sharp price increases.

Strikes constitute a most important short-term futures market factor. *Rail strikes* which keep the mills in the Northwest from shipping lumber to the various markets will have a strong bullish impact on prices. *Dock strikes* (West Coast), however, have only a minor impact in that Northwest lumber, normally shipped to California by boat, will have to take higher cost land routes. *Mill strikes,* if extensive, can be bullish. *Construction strikes,* only if extensive and long, can curtail demand enough to have a bearish effect on prices.

**TABLE 18-1 SEASONALLY ADJUSTED ANNUAL RATES (SAAR)
FOR U.S. HOUSING STARTS (PRIVATELY OWNED UNITS IN
THOUSANDS)**

Month	1969 SAAR*	1969 Actual starts	1970 SAAR*	1970 Actual starts	1971 SAAR*	1971 Actual starts	1972 SAAR*	1972 Actual starts
January	1,705	101.5	1,059	66.4	1,810	110.6	2,487	149.1
February	1,639	90.1	1,306	74.3	1,794	102.2	2,682	152.2
March	1,588	131.9	1,392	114.7	1,938	167.9	2,369	203.9
April	1,505	159.0	1,224	128.4	1,951	201.1	2,109	211.6
May	1,533	155.5	1,242	125.0	2,046	198.5	2,350	225.8
June	1,507	147.3	1,393	135.2	2,008	193.8	2,330	223.1
July	1,429	125.2	1,603	140.8	2,091	194.3	2,218	206.5
August	1,376	124.9	1,425	128.7	2,219	204.5	2,484	228.6
September	1,481	129.3	1,509	130.9	2,029	173.8	2,366p	100.4p
October	1,390	123.4	1,583	140.9	2,038	179.7	2,410p	211.7p
November	1,280	94.6	1,693	126.9	2,228	173.7	—	—
December	1,402	84.1	2,028	121.4	2,457	152.1	—	—
TOTAL		1,466.8		1,433.6		2,052.2		

* SAAR: Seasonally adjusted annual rate; p = preliminary.
SOURCE: U.S. Department of Commerce, Bureau of Census.

Boxcar shortages, when seasonal demand for plywood is high in summer, tend to slow deliveries and cause a seasonal rise in prices. Availability of mortgage funds and the level of interest rates influence the rate of construction and can result in long-term price changes. Vacation shutdowns for two weeks in July and for the Christmas and New Year holidays are sometimes overrated as price factors. These shutdowns are planned and will not affect prices, except in a situation in which they extend the period of already short supply.

Stumpage costs, mentioned earlier as a production cost factor, can also be an excellent indicator of available supply. Increasing stumpage costs can indicate decreasing availability of timber, a bullish situation. Conversely, decreasing stumpage costs can be indicative of increasing availability of saw timber, a bearish indication.

Exports generally have little effect on plywood futures prices. Japan is the major foreign source of demand for U.S. plywood, but Japan prefers Hemlock and most of the Pacific Northwest plywood in the United States is from Douglas Fir. Furthermore, because of the Morse Amendment, Japan can purchase only 350 million board feet of logs from federally owned forests. Japan, therefore, must purchase most of its timber from state-owned forests. Because the State of Oregon will not allow this, the State of Washington is the major supplier of timber to Japan.

SOURCES OF INFORMATION

The SAAR of housing starts is estimated each month and is available from the U.S. Department of Commerce, Bureau of Domestic Commerce, by subscription to *Construction Review,* their monthly publication.

Much timely information is available from the Western Wood Products Association (WWPA). Details of WWPA and other publications are shown in the lumber section of this chapter.

Information on plant capacity, production, etc., can be obtained from *Crow's Newsletter,* from *Random Lengths,* or from Reuters Wire Service each Monday.

Stumpage costs are extremely difficult to calculate in time to be useful for trading decisions. Figures are available on a quarterly basis, but such information tends to be thoroughly discounted in the futures market. Current prices can be determined only from reports issued by individual mills.

A more comprehensive list of information sources is shown in the lumber section of this chapter.

NATURE OF PRODUCTION AND DISTRIBUTION

The important producing areas for softwood plywood in the United States are as follows:

1. The Pacific Northwest region—Washington, Oregon, and northern California—has approximately 130 plants which produce 70 to 75 percent of the U.S. total.

2. The Southern Yellow Pine region, comprised of eastern Texas, south-eastern Oklahoma, and all states eastward to the Atlantic coast and south of the Ohio River, has approximately 40 plants which produce more than 20 percent of the national total.

3. The Inland region of Idaho, western Montana, southwestern Colorado, and northern Michigan has approximately 12 plants which produce less than 10 percent of the total.

Table 18-2 shows the total capacity and production for each year since 1960.

Plywood production begins when the cut logs are transported to the mills, where they are stored in water or stacked in tiers. After being cut to length (blocks) and debarked the blocks are turned on lathes to produce veneer. After being cut and dried the veneer or plys are glued, pressed, and stacked for shipment. Plywood is normally shipped by rail except in the Southern Yellow Pine region from which most shipments are made by truck. Figure 18-2 is a simplified flow chart of the distribution system.

NATURE OF UTILIZATION

Figure 18-2 shows the five major categories of final users in the distribution system. An analysis of that demand follows.

The residential construction market utilizes almost 60 percent of the softwood plywood produced. New single family homes (most of the plywood is needed in roof sheathing and floors) account for about two-thirds of the total residential construction and, with multifamily homes (another 16 percent of the total), make up the largest demand factor in price fluctuations. Additions and alterations account for 12 percent, mobile homes, 3

**TABLE 18-2   SOFTWOOD PLYWOOD
INDUSTRY CAPACITY AND
PRODUCTION**

Year	Industry capacity	Production	Percent of capacity
1960	9,200,000	7,815,600	85
1961	10,100,000	8,577,300	85
1962	11,300,000	9,513,000	84
1963	11,700,000	10,216,200	87
1964	12,400,000	11,678,600	94
1965	13,600,000	12,446,600	92
1966	15,500,000	13,056,200	84
1967	16,600,000	12,957,600	78
1968	16,600,000	14,694,500	89
1969	16,800,000	13,694,400	82
1970	17,800,000	14,300,000	80
1971*	17,300,000	16,400,000	95
1972†	18,000,000	17,200,000	95

* Preliminary.
† Estimate.
SOURCE: American Plywood Association.

FIG. 18-2   Flow chart of distribution system for softwood plywood industry.

percent, and forms for concrete, 1 percent of the total. As already noted, the SAAR of housing starts (see Table 18-1) is the best indicator of this most important demand factor.

Industrial construction accounts for approximately 20 percent of the plywood production, most of which is used for manufactured products such as furniture (30 percent), materials handling applications such as boxes, crates, and pallets (23 percent) transportation equipment such as trucks, trailers, and vans (18 percent), in-plant repairs and maintenance (8 percent), and other applications which include export, military, government, and general equipment (21 percent).

Over-the-counter sales constitute approximately 8 percent of all plywood production, mainly for do-it-yourself users (58 percent) and small builders and minor industrial use (42 percent).

Agricultural requirements account for approximately 2 percent of the plywood production for building and repairing barns, sheds, pallets, and so on.

LUMBER (SOFTWOOD)

INTRODUCTION

The growth in the demand for new homes and other construction has greatly increased the demand for forest products in general. In 1970, after

CHART 18-2

LUMBER - CHICAGO   (WEEKLY HIGH, LOW & CLOSE OF NEAREST FUTURES)   DOLLARS PER 1,000 SQ. FT.

introduction of the futures contract for plywood in 1969 by the Chicago Board of Trade, the Chicago Mercantile Exchange offered a contract for (softwood) lumber. This was followed by a (softwood) stud lumber contract which began trading on the Chicago Board of Trade in 1972.

LUMBER FUTURES CONTRACT

Lumber contracts currently traded on the Chicago Mercantile Exchange are for delivery in January, March, May, July, September, and November. Trading typically begins 10 months before the delivery date. The trading unit is 100,000 board feet of kiln or air-dryed Hem-Fir, nominal 2 x 4's, standard grade, in random lengths of 8 to 20 feet. Price is quoted in units of 1,000 board feet, with minimum fluctuation of 10 cents per 1,000 board feet or $10.00 per contract. Daily fluctuations are limited to a maximum of $5.00 per thousand board feet, upward or downward from the preceding day's settling price. This fluctuation limit is not suspended at any time.

STUD LUMBER FUTURES CONTRACT

Stud lumber contracts traded on the Chicago Board of Trade are for delivery in January, March, May, July, September, and November, the same as the lumber contracts. The trading unit, minimum price fluctuations allowed, and the maximum daily price changes are also the same as those of the lumber contract, except that the 2 x 4's are 19 percent dry Lodgepole Pine, Western White Spruce, or Engelmann Spruce studs (technically 8 feet long).

FACTORS WHICH INFLUENCE LUMBER PRICES

The principal factors that influence lumber prices are essentially the same as those discussed in the plywood section of this chapter. In broad terms these factors are the following:

1. Demand for lumber and other wood products.
2. Total production from commercial forests and its availability.
3. Government programs, especially economic and forest management.

Residential construction consumes almost 60 percent of the lumber produced. Because the rate of housing starts fluctuates significantly, the monthly SAAR estimates provide the most significant demand information.

SOURCES OF INFORMATION

Supply and demand data and forecasts concerning lumber and other forest products are readily obtainable. The U.S. Department of Agricultural Forestry Service and the U.S. Department of Commerce provide comprehensive data and excellent historical information. The most timely data are available from the WWPA and the Southern Pine Association. Current data can be obtained from commodity brokerage firms which subscribe to commodity news wires.

Following is a list of some of the more important publications:

1. *Barometer* (WWPA), weekly. Production, orders, shipments, unfilled orders and lumber inventory, compiled from sawmills currently reporting; made up every Friday for the week ending on the preceding Saturday. Covers the entire Western United States and is broken down by coast and inland mills.

2. *F.O.B. Price Summary Past Sales* (inland mills), weekly (WWPA). Covers species produced in the inland area showing breakdown by grade, footage, and average price per thousand board feet for current week, last four weeks, and year to date. Also includes the Inland Index.

3. *F.O.B. Price Summary Past Sales* (coast mills), monthly (WWPA). Covers species produced by coast mills and shows breakdown by product, grade within product, footage, and average price per thousand board feet for current month, preceding month, and year to date.

4. *Western Lumber Facts,* monthly (WWPA). Monthly industry estimates of production, orders, shipments, unfilled orders, and lumber inventory and charts of trends of average prices received, relationship of orders, unfilled orders, inventory, housing starts, and end-use markets.

5. *Lumber Price Trends* (Inland Index), monthly (WWPA). Reflects the trend of weighted prices for inland species.

6. *Destination of Lumber Shipments,* monthly (WWPA). Analysis of rail, truck, and water shipments, by species, to unknown destinations; transit cars are shown separately. Rail and truck shipments by state are shown separately for inland and coast mills.

7. *Statistical Year Book* (WWPA). Production for the 12 Western states broken down by county. Summaries of production, shipments, orders, unfilled orders, and inventory. Export and import information, charts, and tables containing various information pertaining to the lumber industry.

8. *U.S. Department of Agriculture—Forest Service. Production, Prices, Employment, and Trade in Pacific Northwest Forest Industries* (Portland, Oregon: Pacific Northwest Forest and Range Experiment Station, quarterly). Provides current information on the timber situation in Oregon and Washington, including data on log production, lumber and plywood production, and prices, employment in the forest industries, international trade in logs and lumber, volume and average prices of stumpage sold by public agencies, and other related items.

9. *Southern Pine Association. Weekly Trade Barometer* (New Orleans, La.: Southern Pine Association). Quotes and statistics on Southern Pine lumber production, shipments, new orders, stocks, and other related data.

10. *National Forest Products Association. Fingertip Facts and Figures* (Washington National Forest Products Association, monthly).

11. *U.S. Department of Agriculture—Forest Service. Timber Trends in the United States (Forest Resources Rep. 17. Washington: Superintendent of Documents, U.S. Government Printing Office, 1965).* A comprehensive appraisal of existing and prospective demands for and supplies of timber in the United States at the time of publication.

12. *U.S. Department of Commerce, Construction Activity.* (Construct, Reps. C30. Washington: Superintendent of Documents, U.S. Government Printing Office, monthly). A statistical report showing the value of new construction put in place, by type of construction.

U.S. Department of Commerce. News release from Bureau of the Census issued two to three months before publication of above document. Entitled, "Value of New Construction Put in Place."

13. *U.S. Department of Commerce, Bureau of the Census. Housing Starts.* (Construct. Reps. C20. Washington: Superintendent of Documents, U.S. Government Printing Office, monthly). Contains statistics showing new housing units started, total, and nonfarm by ownership, type of structure, and location.

U.S. Department of Commerce, Bureau of the Census. News release from Bureau of the Census issued two to three months before publication of above document. Entitled, "Housing Starts and Building Permits (months and year)."

14. *U.S. Department of Commerce, Bureau of the Census. Lumber Production and Mill Stocks* (Cur. Indus. Reps. Ser. MA24T. Washington: U.S. Department of Commerce, Bureau of the Census, annual). Contains statistics on lumber production by major species and producing regions.

15. *C40 Housing Authorized in Individual Permit—Issuing Places.* Monthly reports on the number of new housing units in single and multiple-family structures authorized by local building permits, by individual permit-issuing places. The report also presents data on new housing units in public housing projects for which construction contracts were awarded, by place. Annual subscription (including annual summary), $5.00. U.S. Department of Commerce, Bureau of the Census.

16. *Random Lengths* (weekly lumber prices), P.O. Box 867, Eugene, Oregon, 97401.

17. *Crow's Weekly Letter* (weekly lumber prices), C. C. Crow Publications, Inc., Terminal Sales Building, Portland, Oregon, 97205.

18. *F. W. Dodge Construction Bulletin* (monthly), Division of McGraw-Hill, 1040 Merchandise Mart, Chicago, Ill., 60654. Cost: $3.05 per year. Complete statistics on construction activity in the United States.

19. *Commodity Year Book*, annual. Published by Commodity Research Bureau, Inc., 140 Broadway, New York, N.Y. 10005.

Note: Much useful information included in the sections relating to sources of information and the nature of supply and demand was obtained from the Chicago Mercantile Exchange and from their publication "Fundamental Factors Affecting Lumber."

NATURE OF PRODUCTION AND DISTRIBUTION

Approximately 33 percent of the total land area in the United States is made up of forests; only 22 percent, however, or about 500-million acres, has commercial forest value. Softwood[1] lumber production is concentrated in the Southeastern United States (see Figure 18-3) and the Pacific Northwest; hardwoods are primarily in the Central and Northern U.S. forests. Approximately 40 percent of softwood production comes from the Southern Pine forests that cover the Southeastern states from East Texas to the southern coastal area of Virginia.

The other 60 percent, approximately 75 percent of which is concentrated in Washington, Oregon, and Northern California, comes from the 11 Western states.

Ownership of these commercial forest lands, that is, forests with commercial value, is divided between lumber firms, private individuals and the local, state, and federal governments. Approximately 50 percent of all commercial timber is privately owned.

Logging, an industry in itself, includes small logging outfits as well as large, integrated lumber companies. All bid competitively for stumpage on both government-owned lands and privately owned forests. The small logging outfits sell their logs on the open market to large and small lumber and plywood producers. The logging operators in the West encounter great difficulty in getting their logs to market. The rough and rugged terrain challenges the operators to the fullest. Weather and fires are hazards that directly affect log prices and normal demand.

Stumpage prices on government timber lands are an important element

---

[1] Lumber is usually divided into two broad categories according to hardness of the wood and coarseness of grain. Woods that are relatively soft with open grain are classified as softwoods, and woods that are relatively hard with closed grain are classified as hardwoods. This chapter is concerned only with softwoods.

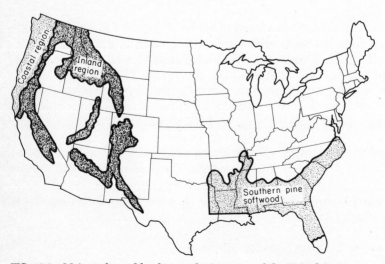

FIG. 18-3   Major softwood lumber producing areas of the United States.

in the overall supply picture. The bidding for timber rights or stumpage on government land is done on a competitive basis by sawmills and independent loggers who sell to sawmills. The minimum bids allowed are established by the Forest Service or Bureau of Land Management. They are predicated on location, accessibility, established roads, if any, and commercial lumber/plywood prices for the preceding quarter. Transportation costs, which play an important part, affect the various levels of bids at or above the minimum allowed. These past prices are corrected and weighted to fit into the equations that establish the base bid price. Generally the winning bidder must log within three years, and if he fails to do so penalties are imposed.

Average softwood stumpage prices since 1960 are presented in Table 18-3. When prices are high, they can depress the logging level in future years if the economic-cycle forecast shows that a low level of activity could prevail. This is just the opposite of what usually occurs in other commodi-

TABLE 18-3   AVERAGE STUMPAGE PRICES FOR SOFTWOOD
SAWTIMBER SOLD FROM NATIONAL FORESTS, BY SELECTED
SPECIES, 1960–1970 (DOLLARS PER THOUSANDS OF BOARD
FEET)

	Softwoods							
	Douglas-Fir		Southern Pine*		Ponderosa Pine†		Western Hemlock‡	
Year and quarter	Current dollars	1957–59 dollars§	Current dollars	1957–59 dollars§	Current dollars	1957–59 dollars§	Current dollars	1957–59 dollars§
1960	32.00	31.80	34.50	34.30	19.10	19.00	10.50	10.40
1961	27.60	27.50	26.80	26.70	12.10	12.10	9.70	9.70
1962	24.80	24.70	26.00	25.80	16.10	16.00	8.90	8.80
1963	27.90	27.80	25.10	25.00	15.80	15.80	10.40	10.40
1964	38.10	37.90	27.80	27.70	19.00	18.90	13.30	13.20
1965	42.60	41.60	31.70	30.90	19.80	19.30	19.10	18.60
1966	50.00	47.20	38.60	36.40	19.80	18.70	20.50	19.40
1967	41.70	39.30	38.30	36.10	22.20	20.90	21.80	20.50
1968	61.20	56.30	42.20	38.80	30.20	27.80	35.60	32.70
1969	82.20	72.70	51.70	45.80	71.00	62.80	45.10	39.90
1st quarter	120.90	108.70	53.40	48.00	93.60	84.20	69.90	62.90
2d quarter	93.20	82.80	57.40	51.00	73.40	65.20	48.30	42.90
3d quarter	66.10	58.30	45.00	39.70	36.70	32.40	39.70	35.00
4th quarter	64.60	56.40	47.30	41.30	60.40	52.70	30.30	26.40
1970								
1st quarter	59.50	51.20	42.10	36.20	41.00	35.30	29.70	25.50
2d quarter	34.40	29.50	45.50	39.00	30.00	25.70	17.30	14.80
3d quarter	45.70	38.90	43.80	37.20	36.40	31.00	20.20	17.20

* Southern region.
† California region.
‡ Western Washington and Western Oregon.
§ Derived by dividing the price in current dollars by the Bureau of Labor Statistics wholesale price index of all commodities (1957–59 = 100).
SOURCE: U.S. Department of Agriculture, Forest Service.

ties, which, when prices are high, experience production increases until a glut occurs and prices retreat to marginal profit levels or losses are incurred.

Weather, which also plays an important part in overall production, can have a critical influence three times a year: in late summer when hot, dry days and nights create a fire hazard, in winter when snow and rain slow logging to a standstill at lower elevations, and in spring—if late—when loggers cannot get into high country to begin logging operations and the length of the harvest season is reduced.

The trends in domestic production, imports, exports, apparent consumption, and per capita consumption since 1960 are presented in Table 18-4. It is interesting to note that since 1960 domestic production has somewhat decreased, whereas imports of softwoods have increased to offset relatively constant consumption.

By good land-use management, along with technological advancements, the timber supply is expected to keep pace with the demands of a growing population. Gains and losses of commercial forest land most likely will balance out over the next 30 years. Improvements in seeding, growing, and developing higher yield trees will ensure an adequate supply of lumber. In addition, progress in fire control will manifest itself to reduce losses of valuable timberland. Technologically, advances in manufacturing and in end-use will improve the yield from a log, thus reducing the number of logs required to produce the same amount of product.

Even though total softwood production appears adequate to meet anticipated domestic demands, the supply of specific species of lumber can vary from time to time and become in short supply, at least temporarily. This variation is based on the availability of the timber in question on either private or government forest lands and whether the particular species stands have been properly scheduled for bidding and logging. Consequently, fluctuations in price are common over the short term. It is during such times of distorted prices that substitute products appear and bring prices back into balance. It should be kept in mind, therefore, that an overall increase in production does not necessarily mean an increase in the supply of a particular species.

Lumber, like almost everything else, has a problem with substitutes. Competitive materials exist whether lumber prices are high or not. If the competition can do the job, it wins. Substitutes for lumber vary, depending on the specific application. The biggest competitors are metal studs (either steel or aluminum) and plywood ("sheeted lumber"). Plastics and hybrids are also coming into use but currently have more of a decorative than structural or functional nature. Plastics are replacing lumber in such areas as shutters, millwork, and furniture. Competitive materials will make inroads if cost trade-offs justify substituting; consequently, the price of lumber versus substitute materials is important to keep in mind.

Estimating lumber production is difficult because of the fragmentation of the industry and the resulting inexact reporting of production. The U.S.

TABLE 18-4 LUMBER PRODUCTION, IMPORTS, EXPORTS, AND CONSUMPTION, BY SOFTWOODS AND HARDWOODS, 1960–1970*

Year	Domestic production (billion board feet)			Imports (billion board feet)			Exports (billion board feet)			Apparent consumption (billion board feet)			Per capita consump. (board feet)		
	Total	Softwoods	Hardwoods	Total	Softwoods†	Hardwoods	Total	Softwoods†	Hardwoods	Total	Softwoods	Hardwoods	Total	Softwoods	Hardwoods
1960	32.9	26.7	6.3	3.9	3.6	0.3	0.9	0.7	0.2	36.0	29.6	6.4	199	164	35
1961	32.0	26.1	6.0	4.3	4.0	0.2	0.8	0.6	0.2	35.5	29.5	6.0	193	160	33
1962	33.2	26.8	6.4	4.9	4.6	0.3	0.8	0.6	0.1	37.3	30.8	6.5	200	165	35
1963	34.7	27.6	7.2	5.3	5.0	0.3	0.9	0.7	0.1	39.2	31.8	7.3	207	168	39
1964	36.6	29.3	7.3	5.2	4.9	0.3	1.0	0.8	0.1	40.8	33.4	7.4	213	174	39
1965	36.8	29.3	7.5	5.2	4.9	0.3	0.9	0.8	0.1	41.1	33.4	7.7	211	172	39
1966	36.6	28.8	7.7	5.2	4.8	0.4	1.0	0.9	0.2	40.8	32.8	8.0	207	166	41
1967	34.7	27.3	7.4	5.1	4.8	0.3	1.1	1.0	0.2	38.8	31.1	7.6	195	156	38
1968	36.5	29.3	7.2	6.2	5.8	0.3	1.2	1.0	0.1	41.5	34.0	7.4	206	169	37
1969†	35.6	28.3	7.3	6.3	5.9	0.4	1.1	1.0	0.1	40.8	33.1	7.6	201	163	38
1970‡	34.0	27.0	7.0	6.1	5.8	0.3	1.3	1.2	0.1	38.8	31.6	7.2	189	154	35

* Data may not add to totals because of rounding.

† Includes small volumes of mixed species (not classified as softwoods or hardwoods).

‡ Preliminary estimates.

NOTE: Estimates of lumber production for 1970 are based in part upon data published by the National Forest Products Association and related associations.

SOURCES: U.S. Department of Commerce, Bureau of the Census, U.S. Department of Agriculture, Forest Service.

Government compiles statistics that are important in defining trends. Because delays are frequent between the gathering of these data and their publication by the governmental agency, they are not too useful in analyses of short-run price changes. One of the best sources of anticipated western softwood production and supply is the Western Wood Products Association, which compiles member data frequently and publishes estimates in usable form soon after collection.

There are approximately 1,200 sawmills in the western sector of the United States, and from those in the California, Oregon, and Washington markets more than 60 percent of production moves through wholesalers.

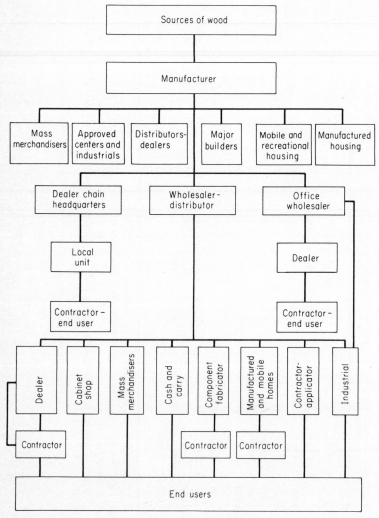

FIG. 18-4   Major distribution flow pattern of wood construction products.
(National Building Materials Distributors Association.)

TABLE 18-5   ESTIMATED SOFTWOOD CONSUMPTION (IN MILLIONS OF BOARD FEET)

Markets	1964	1965	1966	1967	1968	1969	1970
Residential construction	14,055	13,953	11,330	12,434	14,184	13,377	12,848
Other new construction	6,306	6,933	7,312	7,051	7,225	7,070	6,972
Repair and remodeling	5,378	5,354	5,513	5,385	5,608	5,687	6,001
Materials handling	2,090	2,435	2,895	2,563	2,717	2,829	2,255
All others	4,228	3,816	4,517	3,589	4,161	3,728	4,145
U.S. consumption	32,057	32,491	31,567	31,022	33,895	32,691	32,228

There are approximately 600 wholesalers nationally. Other lesser avenues of distribution are direct to user, direct to retailer, company-owned distribution yards, and to other factories for remanufacture. See Figure 18-4 for a diagramatic depiction of the marketing channels for lumber.

NATURE OF UTILIZATION

The major demand for softwood lumber comes from five broad categories: residential construction, other new construction, repair and remodeling, materials handling, and, other uses such as furniture, manufactured products, railroads, and mobile home construction. Table 18-5 shows the demand for lumber in these categories for the last several years. It is important to note that the trend in new construction is a good indicator of the long-term demand for lumber.

As the population grows, so will new households, which are projected to increase from approximately 1 million a year in 1970 to 1.3 million a year by 1980. It is estimated that more than 40 percent of western softwood production goes into residential construction and approximately 20 percent into other new construction. Consequently, it can readily be seen that general economic conditions have a direct bearing on the demand for and price of softwood lumber.

New residential buildings consume more lumber than any other form of lumber usage. This construction constitutes single and multiple units up to high-rise housing. Single and duplex structures, however, use the most lumber, as revealed by the following WWPA statistics:

Demand for Lumber in Housing—1970

Units	Board feet
Single	10,600
Multiple low-rise	5,500
Multiple high-rise	1,000

The reason for the smaller amount of lumber in multiple high-rise housing is that steel or metal studs are substituted for lumber.

Generally, housing statistics are examined in light of

(a)   actual units started,

(b)   actual permits,

(c)   seasonally adjusted annual rates of units started,

(d)   seasonally adjusted annual rates of permits.

SAAR of housing starts are the values forecast for the ensuing 12-month period, based on current actual starts. Table 18-1 in the plywood section of this chapter illustrates housing starts since 1969 in seasonally adjusted annual rates. It can readily be seen how the recent economic downturn and tight money situation affected the housing industry and the demand for lumber. However, 1971 witnessed a resurgence in housing. Housing starts increased during 1971 to an annual rate of more than 2.0 million units, a significant increase over the 1.4 million units of 1970. The trend continued in 1972. Therefore, even with per capita consumption of lumber reduced to 189 board feet in 1970 from 279 board feet in 1950, the total demand for forest products should grow. The major elements that could disturb the picture are the price structure and competing substitute materials.

Other items that influence housing starts in addition to population growth are mortgage interest rates, government programs (Federal Housing Authority, Federal National Mortgage Association policy, and Federal Reserve Board monetary policies and rules), the general economy of the country and resulting "tight" or "easy" money, attitudes of the population toward spending (savings inflow to outflow), income growth, and general business expansion.

Interest rates have some effect on the buying of new homes but are generally not so influential as one would expect when coupled with inflation and the Gross National Product (GNP). A ½ of 1 percent reduction in interest rates over a period of time does not necessarily result in a lower total cost. There is a trade-off, for the $1,000 or so that might be saved in interest can be more than offset by increased labor and material costs. Interest rates seem to be important psychologically in buying a home.

Most mortgage money for new housing comes from savings and loan institutions. Consequently, when people are spending freely rather than saving, mortgage funds may not be readily available; conversely, if the public increases its saving activity, more funds for mortgages may exist. Savings and loan money flows are important indicators to follow.

As business gets better and manufacturing companies begin to expand, they develop a demand for funds, which could serve as a depressant to the housing industry because these companies are frequently willing to pay a higher price for short-term borrowings. As a result, lenders are more inclined toward them because such investments turn the money over faster and at a higher return than long-term home mortgages.

As income increases, bigger homes and second houses for vacation purposes are desired. Another factor to consider is that affluence often brings earlier retirement and, combined with longer life-expectancy, creates a corresponding demand for retirement communities.

An increase in government-backed housing, particularly low-cost, will also be a part of the increase in housing starts in the future. Such government programs, however, have some instability associated with them because, to a certain degree, they are political in nature.

As the population grows, it also needs schools, office buildings, medical and shopping centers, churches, public buildings and facilities, and highways and other transportation facilities. Again, as in housing, the statistics to be alert to are the actual monies invested and their seasonally adjusted annual rates.

New construction, in current dollars, has grown from an annual total of $66,200 million in 1964 to $91,266 million in 1970. In September 1971 total new construction activity had a seasonally adjusted annual rate in current dollars of $112 billion.

Demand for lumber for this activity has increased steadily. In 1964 approximately 5,400 million board feet were used, and in 1970 the level had risen to 6 billion board feet. Housing and commercial buildings are continually in need of repair and upgrading, especially in the inner cities. A federal home replacement law requires local housing authorities to replace dwelling units destroyed in urban renewal programs with new or remodeled units on a one-to-one basis.

Lumber is used extensively in materials handling, all the way from wooden pallets to containers. The combination of softwoods with other materials is increasing rapidly, and even though it is moderate at this stage it still imposes a demand on the total lumber supply.

This area of demand takes into account miscellaneous lumber requirements; for example, demand by the railroads for lumber and timber has been on the decline for quite some time but now seems to be stabilized. Even though total trackage has been reduced, capital spending to replace ties continues. In addition, new and rebuilt car construction requires a moderate amount of lumber. Other uses to which softwood lumber is put on a moderate scale include the manufacture of furniture, mobile homes, and other wood products.

Softwood lumber exports are increasing but still remain relatively small in relation to domestic demand. These exports, which grew from 0.4 billion board feet in 1950 to 1.2 billion feet in 1970, represent approximately five percent of the softwood production in that year. However, the demand for *logs* reached the equivalent of 2,460 million board feet; shipments to Japan accounted for 96.2 percent of that total (Table 18-6). Japan has always been the principal user of our exported logs and is an important factor in the total demand for U.S. forest products.

Imports of lumber are primarily from the forests of Western Canada and are mostly softwood. They have not been a significant factor in the total supply.

In any useful economic analysis of lumber (or plywood) futures prices the overall demand for wood products must be considered. Fluctuations in this demand are often dominated by the national economic picture and therefore should be an important factor in the analysis.

TABLE 18-6 1970 SOFTWOOD LOG EXPORTS FROM PACIFIC
COAST PORTS (IN MILLIONS OF BOARD FEET)

From (Customs Districts)	Washington	Oregon	Northern California	Alaska	Total
To All Countries					
1961	148	188	28	—	364
1962	164	147	38	2	351
1963	412	297	38	9	756
1964	464	371	13	4	825
1965	618	283	15	11	927
1966	720	389	22	16	1,147
1967	1,069	502	43	40	1,654
1968	1,321	653	212	47	2,233
1969	1,309	561	207	32	2,109
1970	1,579	637	192	52	2,460
To Japan					
1961	141	187	27	—	355
1962	140	146	37	2	325
1963	343	295	38	9	685
1964	384	355	13	4	756
1965	495	280	13	11	799
1966	651	372	22	16	1,061
1967	1,006	489	43	37	1,575
1968	1,222	638	199	46	2,105
1969	1,239	551	201	31	2,022
1970	1,515	630	175	47	2,367
Percent of total exported to Japan 1970	95.9	98.9	91.1	90.4	96.2

SOURCE: "Production Prices, Employment, and Trade in Northwest Forest Industries," John W. Austin, Pacific Northwest Forest and Range Experiment Station Forest Service, USDA.

GOVERNMENT PROGRAMS

Federal programs that affect supply and demand are constantly changing. As Congress initiates or amends legislation from time to time, supply and demand and resulting price levels are affected.

Changes in monetary policy in general and legislation designed specifically to stimulate housing starts have a great impact on demand. Timber management programs instituted and controlled by the government also have a significant effect on supply.

Current programs that have a bearing on supply and demand and could be amended include the National Housing Act, Operation Breakthrough, and Timber Management.

National housing act. Within this act are the FHA Title I and Title II sections. Title I deals with property improvement and mobile home loans. Title II is concerned with single and multifamily loan insurance programs. Within the scope of Title II are the following sections:

FIG. 18-5   FOB prices of kiln-dried random length 2 × 4s. 1968–1970, white fir; 1971, hem fir (inland). (*Random Lengths*, Eugene, Oreg.)

Single Dwelling

Section 203(b)	Home mortgage insurance
Section 220	Urban renewal mortgage insurance
Section 221(d) (2)	Home mortgage insurance, low and moderate income
Section 235(j)	Low-income home ownership

Multiple Dwelling

Section 235(j)	Mortgage insurance for low-income family rehabilitation housing
Section 236	Rental and cooperative housing for lower income families

Several other housing programs are administered by the U.S. Department of Housing and Urban Development. The complete program covers all facets of national housing—from high income to low income and from single dwellings to condominiums and land development. Policies within sections can change or new legislation can be enacted. Consequently, one should keep abreast of important federal housing programs.

Operation breakthrough. This program is oriented toward combining factory-built housing, advanced fabricating technology, and large land areas to accelerate housing production.

Timber management. Timber management of national forest lands comes under the Forest Service—U.S. Department of Agriculture. Management is governed in part by the Multiple Use—Sustained Yield Act of June 12, 1960, which defines the division between commercial and recreational use of national forest areas, including the maintenance of production on the land. Within the Forest Service policies are established to optimize forest land use to achieve maximum utilization. These policies include such considerations as recreation, roads, bridges, clear cutting, shelter wood (which leaves some growth to assist regeneration in areas in which growth would be inhibited if clear cut), and processing and cutting of timber tracts. Again all policies and legislation can be up-dated and/or changed with minor or major impact on the timber supply.

SEASONAL INFORMATION

Lumber and other forest products exhibit seasonal changes in both supply (harvesting of logs) and demand (construction, especially residential building). It is doubtful, however, that a price seasonal would occur that could be profitably utilized by the futures trader. Figure 18-5 shows cash prices for four recent years. If any significant price seasonal did exist in the past, it will, as usual, tend to be eliminated by the futures trader as he tries to take advantage of it.

NOTES FROM A TRADER—
PLYWOOD AND LUMBER

Both plywood and lumber appear to be affected by the short-term direction of the stock market to a greater degree than most other commodities. Prices also appear to react inversely to changes in interest rates because of the effect of such rates on new housing starts, as well as the usual effect on the willingness of those in the trade to hold inventories as carrying charges vary.

Energy shortages which might well occur from time to time can greatly affect prices because of shipping costs and the considerable fuel needed to bond plywood.

As open interest and volume have expanded, the opportunity to utilize intermarket spreads between plywood and lumber has grown apace.

CHAPTER NINETEEN

Frozen Pork Bellies and Live Hogs

FROZEN PORK BELLIES

INTRODUCTION

The term "pork belly" refers to uncured bacon which comes from the underside of the hog. Each hog has two "pork bellies" (not stomachs).

Futures trading in frozen pork bellies began in September 1961 on the Chicago Mercantile Exchange. The belly market became active in 1964, and, since the bull market of 1965, volume and open interest have become substantial. Contracts traded are February, March, May, July, and August. Trading typically begins 11 or 12 months before the delivery month of the contract.

The contract traded is a unit of 36,000 pounds of 12- to 14-pound pork bellies, delivered during the months indicated as contracts. Price is quoted in cents per pound, the minimum price fluctuation being .025 cents, or $2\frac{1}{2}$ points a pound, which represents $9.00 per contract. The maximum allowable daily range is 3.0 cents, with a maximum fluctuation of 1.5 cents, either up or down, from the preceding day's settlement price.

FACTORS WHICH INFLUENCE
PORK BELLY PRICES

Because pork bellies are the by-product of hogs, the supply of bellies is related to the size of the pig crop and to the pattern of hog slaughter. Hogs are farrowed (born) throughout the year and typically are slaughtered six to eight months after birth. Farrowings tend to be larger in the fall and spring. The hog's age at slaughter largely determines its weight and may affect the marketing pattern. To a large extent the hog's age at slaughter will depend on the hog-corn price ratio (the ratio of the price of a hog to that of the corn it takes to feed it) during the preceding six months; for example, a high ratio indicates that corn is cheap in relation to hogs; therefore farmers will continue to feed corn to the hogs and slaughter their hogs at an older age, perhaps at seven or eight months, and therefore at a heavier weight. Conversely, a low hog-corn ratio shows that the price of corn compared with that of hogs is high. Such a situation encourages the early slaughter of hogs—at about six months of age.

Storage stocks are determined by previous slaughter and consumption. As a result of the seasonal pattern of farrowings, slaughter generally exceeds demand during the period from November through April or May; therefore storage stocks accumulate during that period and reach a peak early in May. From May through September the slaughter rate diminishes and storage stocks decline until October.

Pork bellies are used primarily in the manufacture of bacon. Because the rate of bacon consumption changes relatively little as the price changes, consumption is typically not an important factor in determining price movements. However, for very high or very low prices important changes in the consumption rate do occur as the price changes.

SOURCES OF INFORMATION

The following U.S. Department of Agriculture publications constitute the primary sources of information for economic factors relating to pork belly prices:

The *Livestock and Meat Situation Reports* are released bimonthly, beginning on January 10, and include historical summaries of data and professional comment on general economic conditions affecting the various livestock and meat markets. Because the reports are primarily intended to provide information for farmers, they deal with economic conditions that, from the speculator's point of view, have long-term price implications.

The *Feed Situation Reports* are published five times a year, in February, April, May, August, and November, approximately at mid-month. They provide general information related to the various animal feed markets, including current and previous hog-corn (price) ratios for both Chicago and the United States.

The *Hogs and Pigs Reports,* formerly the *Pig Crop Reports,* are released quarterly, in approximately the third week in December, March, June,

CHART 19-1

PORK BELLIES WEEKLY HIGH, LOW & CLOSE OF NEAREST FUTURES CONTRACT—CHICAGO—IN CENTS PER POUND

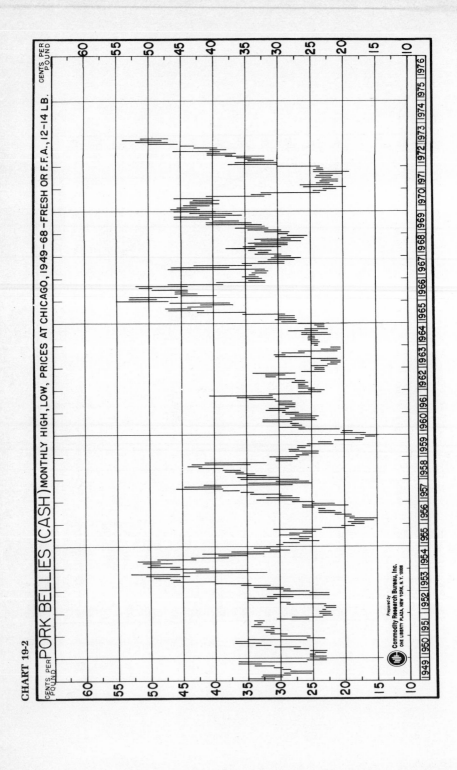

CHART 19-2

PORK BELLIES (CASH) MONTHLY HIGH, LOW, PRICES AT CHICAGO, 1949-68 —FRESH OR F.F.A., 12-14 LB.

CENTS PER POUND

Prepared by
Commodity Research Bureau, Inc.
ONE LIBERTY PLAZA, NEW YORK, N. Y. 10006

and September. The report shows sows' farrowings, pigs per litter, and the total pig crop by six-month periods. The six-month estimates of sow farrowings are separated into quarterly farrowings — December–February, March–May, June–August, and September–November. Estimates are made of the number of animals being kept for breeding and the number intended for market. The latter category is reported in five weight groups: under 60 pounds, 60 to 119 pounds, 120 to 179 pounds, 180 to 219 pounds, and 220 pounds and over.

The number of hogs on farms and the last six months' actual farrowings are useful data in estimating the number of marketable hogs to be available in the coming six months. Obviously, the farrowing intentions have longer term significance. The number of hogs and pigs on farms can be anticipated by utilizing private surveys of gilt retentions during preceding months and, to some extent, by predictions based on the hog-corn (price) ratio. The December and June reports cover all 50 states, whereas the March and September reports cover only the 10 most important states.

The *Monthly Cold Storage Reports*, released about mid-month, analyze the cold-storage holdings as of the first of the month. These reports sometimes have a violent but short-lived effect on belly prices. The monthly storage figures can be anticipated by using daily and/or weekly storage data (for products in Chicago and other warehouses) released by the Chicago Mercantile Exchange. Although these data do not include storage in "nonapproved" warehouses, which are usually largest during November and December, they can be used to estimate total pork bellies stored or withdrawn during the month.

The *Livestock Commercial Slaughter and Meat Production Report* produced at the end of each month gives the slaughter data by numbers and by weights for the preceding month.

The *Livestock, Meat, and Wool Markets News* is published weekly. It constitutes a current source of information for weekly and monthly slaughter, for weekly bacon slicings, and for the hog-corn (price) ratio.

The following nongovernment publications are also important sources of data:

The *Chicago Mercantile Exchange Year Book* contains daily prices, volume, and open interest of each contract, as well as daily cash prices. It also includes most of the important statistical information relating to the supply of and demand for bellies.

The *Drovers Journal* is a daily newspaper that carries trade and legislative news of interest to those engaged in the cattle, hog, and sheep trade. It also contains wholesale price information and comments on price trends.

The *National Provisioner* distributes two publications. Its weekly magazine for the meat-packing and allied industries has information similar to that given by the *Drovers Journal*. It also shows the weekly bacon slicings as reported by the USDA. Its *Daily Market and News Service*, "The Yellow

Sheet," gives daily hog market quotations, slaughter figures, and prices of the different cuts of meat.

The sources listed above will provide current and historical information about the more important economic factors affecting pork belly prices:

Size of the pig crop.
Monthly and weekly cold-storage data.
Monthly and weekly slaughter.
Farrowing intentions.
Weekly bacon slicings.
Hog-corn (price) ratios.
Average weight of hogs slaughtered.

Exhibits 19-1 and 19-2 provide two forms for summarizing some of the important information.

EXHIBIT 19-1

Month	Slaughter (Commercial 48 states, F.I.S. and other thousand head)		Slaughter weight (live average weight, pounds)		Frozen storage stocks (beginning of month, thousand pounds)		Hog /corn ratio (monthly average)
	Original	Revised	Original	Revised	Original	Revised	
Jan.							
Feb.							
Mar.							
Apr.							
May							
June							
July							
Aug.							
Sept.							
Oct.							
Nov.							
Dec.							

EXHIBIT 19-2

	June Report		December Report		
	Prior year	Current year	Prior year	Current year	Next year
December–May (spring)					
Sow farrowing					
Pig crop					
June–November (fall)					
Sow farrowing					
Pig crop					
December–November					
Total pig crop					

SUPPLY

Because pork bellies are a by-product of the hog and on the average constitute a relatively fixed proportion (approximately 11 percent, or 25 to 26 pounds per hog) of its total weight, production is usually analyzed in terms of total weight of hogs slaughtered, typically on a per capita basis.

Total pork production, including hams, bellies, and loins, can be estimated by multiplying the number of hogs slaughtered by the average weight. Hog production has a consistent seasonal pattern. The spring pig crop, those born in December through May, typically constitutes more than 55 percent of the yearly production. Most of this crop is slaughtered in the fall, and marketings reach their peak between October and January.

Monthly estimates of production can be made by using the hog farrowing data of the preceding six- to eight-month period. Changes in farrowings cause seasonal fluctuation in hog production and therefore in pork belly production, which reaches a maximum in late fall and early winter— October to December—and a minimum during the summer—June to August. Because of this seasonal production pattern, storage stocks typically accumulate from November to May and decline from June to September.

Forecasting total pork belly supplies requires adding the weight of the cold storage supplies to that calculated from an estimate of the number of hogs available for slaughter. The latter calculation is made by utilizing the farrowings reported six to eight months before and then converting this number into pounds of pork bellies by multiplying the hog-slaughter estimate by the 25- to 26-pound average weight of bellies per hog as related to the total weight of hogs, which in turn depends on the hog's age at slaughter. As indicated in a preceding section of this chapter, the hog-corn price ratio is a major determinant of the average age at slaughters. The absolute price of hogs is also a factor.

It is important also to know whether the amount of wet corn in any harvesting is larger or smaller than usual, for when it is large growers may elect to delay marketing and feed their hogs to heavier weights.

In estimating the number of hogs to be marketed, one should be aware that farmers, by increasing or decreasing their breeding stock of sows (mature female hogs), can increase or decrease supplies by as much as 2 percent in the immediate marketing period. In periods of relatively high hog prices farmers tend to increase the size of their breeding stocks. This is accomplished when the number of gilts (young female hogs) retained for addition to the breeding stock exceeds the number of slaughtered sows from the present breeding stock. Similarly, during periods of low prices the number of gilts retained is typically smaller than the number of sows slaughtered, and the breeding stock is thereby decreased.

Because slaughter and consumption are approximately equal in a given "freeze year," the amount of bellies stored and the changes in storage become important indicators of price changes. Whenever a packer slaughters

TABLE 19-1 FEDERALLY INSPECTED HOG SLAUGHTER IN THE
UNITED STATES (IN MILLION HEAD)

Year	Jan.	Feb.	Mar.	Apr.	May	June	July	Aug.	Sept.	Oct.	Nov.	Dec.	Total
1953	6.27	4.55	4.96	4.33	3.64	3.61	3.28	3.40	4.06	4.99	5.54	5.19	53.81
1954	4.71	3.88	4.55	3.85	3.38	3.45	3.33	3.85	4.74	5.18	5.84	6.12	52.89
1955	5.52	4.64	5.49	4.47	4.16	3.71	3.43	4.48	5.14	6.14	6.86	7.32	61.37
1956	6.71	5.92	6.33	5.25	4.88	4.33	4.20	4.56	4.98	6.35	6.56	5.70	65.75
1957	5.66	5.00	5.38	5.00	4.88	3.99	4.19	4.42	5.06	6.09	5.51	5.52	60.68
1958	5.53	4.45	4.82	4.96	4.44	4.21	4.33	4.52	5.22	5.91	5.26	5.81	59.46
1959	5.89	5.69	5.73	5.65	4.97	4.90	5.18	4.98	5.77	6.65	6.34	6.97	68.71
1960	6.52	5.84	6.12	5.57	5.48	5.09	4.30	5.20	5.17	5.41	5.71	5.75	66.15
1961	5.74	5.08	6.11	5.05	5.60	5.09	4.32	5.11	5.24	6.22	6.33	5.74	65.63
1962	6.09	5.31	6.23	5.67	5.80	5.04	4.70	5.21	4.74	6.64	6.38	5.95	67.77
1963	6.33	5.67	6.56	6.34	5.91	4.88	5.00	5.17	5.87	6.78	6.38	6.70	71.58
1964	6.96	5.90	6.42	6.48	5.48	5.04	4.93	4.84	5.63	6.80	6.55	6.65	71.67
1965	6.05	5.30	6.53	5.80	4.72	4.72	4.43	4.75	5.48	5.42	5.50	5.01	63.71
1966	4.72	4.65	5.81	5.30	4.91	4.67	4.23	5.09	5.89	6.05	6.20	6.22	63.74
1967	6.18	5.65	6.60	5.87	5.31	5.18	4.74	5.81	6.11	6.68	6.43	6.10	70.76
1968	6.50	5.70	6.24	6.48	6.41	5.13	5.45	5.94	6.35	7.41	6.57	6.62	74.79
1969	6.81	6.24	6.81	6.85	6.05	5.60	5.74	5.71	6.61	7.10	5.83	6.34	75.69
1970	6.17	5.51	6.42	6.68	5.88	5.64	5.77	6.05	7.03	7.66	7.35	7.99	78.15
1971	7.49	6.38	8.27	7.79	6.93	6.98	6.22	6.92	7.38	7.19	7.57	7.55	86.67
1972	6.40	6.28	7.80	6.73	6.79	6.31	5.27	6.51	6.42	7.05	6.99	6.20	78.75
1973	6.64	5.71	6.65	5.99	6.64	5.71	5.00	5.57	5.35	6.61	6.53	5.86	72.26

a hog, he either sells or freezes it. The more bellies stored at a given time, the higher the immediate price level and the lower the price when the bellies come out of storage. Frozen-storage stocks are relatively unimportant for several months, beginning in October, because of annual clearings before the larger amounts of fresh production become available. Storage becomes most important late in the contract year (approximately in May and June) when consumption exceeds production. Tables 19-1 and 19-2 show the federally inspected hog slaughter and the frozen-storage stocks, respectively.

One approach to identifying the strong relationship between change in price and change in supply is illustrated by Gallacher.[1] He related the change in average price to the change in supplies for the nine years 1963 to 1972. The results are shown in Table 19-3 and Figure 19-1.

DEMAND

The only readily available measure of pork belly consumption is given by the figures in the U.S. Department of Agriculture's "Weekly Sliced Bacon Production." Slicings tend to increase during the summer months when production is relatively low and to decrease when production is high. This phenomenon causes a pronounced pork belly seasonal price fluctuation.

Currently only 65 percent of the bacon slicings are federally inspected

[1] William Gallacher, "'73 Bellies—Priced to Clear," *Commodities* (March 1973).

TABLE 19-2 U.S. FROZEN PORK BELLY STORAGE STOCKS (IN THOUSAND POUNDS, AS OF FIRST OF THE MONTH)

Year	Jan.	Feb.	Mar.	Apr.	May	June	July	Aug.	Sept.	Oct.	Nov.	Dec.
1960	73,023	92,488	108,393	115,771	131,992	130,720	113,278	75,580	44,691	18,813	15,828	20,732
1961	33,510	43,038	58,880	74,812	78,095	79,984	64,811	33,787	11,710	5,553	7,153	22,825
1962	39,352	44,445	60,956	84,599	99,428	109,525	91,355	61,623	34,493	12,482	15,863	35,107
1963	57,822	64,240	73,277	103,411	119,888	112,447	94,813	65,919	36,842	22,142	23,146	38,455
1964	60,800	84,180	113,713	139,494	156,572	154,758	133,160	86,272	46,487	22,238	33,649	54,195
1965	74,589	84,859	97,900	113,770	120,908	103,142	73,520	40,867	21,607	8,768	8,958	16,164
1966	25,318	29,472	36,053	48,768	62,688	65,838	47,659	27,019	12,495	7,034	9,310	19,847
1967	44,921	50,191	67,803	91,284	108,506	100,453	88,993	60,577	33,275	20,796	32,098	48,756
1968	68,882	66,810	77,182	92,099	115,682	129,377	102,949	59,462	27,393	15,809	20,437	33,774
1969	49,076	46,699	56,173	76,035	96,249	96,670	84,284	46,755	21,719	12,167	19,565	26,074
1970	38,697	37,017	47,094	61,068	74,004	82,061	67,250	39,300	20,393	9,823	21,043	42,054
1971	76,437	81,561	83,004	111,579	131,262	146,093	140,778	105,015	70,504	50,654	53,057	68,004
1972*	86,065	84,092	84,243	87,894	107,540	130,856	105,598	69,826	35,689	16,584	22,061	34,225
1973*	39,278	31,433	30,015	45,992	49,782	54,870	48,106	26,106	10,122	9,139	15,736	31,912
1974*	48,453											

*Preliminary.
SOURCE: Crop Reporting Board, USDA.

**TABLE 19-3 SUPPLY/PRICE RELATIONSHIP DURING PERIOD
DECEMBER 1 TO SEPTEMBER 30**

Year	Commercial slaughter Dec.–Sept. (000 head)	Supplies from slaughter	Cold storage stocks (in millions of pounds)	Total supplies Dec.–Sept.	Change from preceding year (%)	Average cash price Dec.–Sept.	Change from preceding year
1963	67,800	1,695.0*	35.1	1,730.1		24.4¢	
1964	67,400	1,685.0	38.4	1,723.4	− 0.4	24.7	0.3¢
1965	63,140	1,578.5	54.2	1,623.7	− 5.3	34.3	9.6
1966	58,450	1,461.2	16.2	1,477.4	− 9.5	47.0	12.7
1967	67,090	1,677.2	19.8	1,679.0	14.9	35.0	−12.0
1968	69,020	1,725.5	48.8	1,774.3	4.6	31.6	− 3.4
1969	70,070	1,751.8	33.8	1,785.6	0.6	35.6	4.0
1970	67,620	1,690.5	26.1	1,716.6	− 3.9	40.7	5.1
1971	79,090	1,977.2	42.1	2,019.3	17.7	23.1	−17.6
1972	71,280	1,782.0	70.2	1,852.2	− 8.3	35.1	12.0

* Assuming 25 pounds of belly per hog.

FIG. 19-1 Frozen pork bellies: price change (P) as a function of supply change (S).

and reported. The other 35 percent represents (a) slab bacon, (b) bacon used in pork and beans, and (c) bacon from hogs not slaughtered under federal inspection and not available for sale in interstate commerce. It should be noted that the percentage of federally inspected bacon slicings is slowly increasing.

Pork belly prices as high as 45 to 50 cents or as low as 30 cents a pound may cause consumption changes of 15 to 20 percent, but for prices between these figures the consumption rate changes little with changes in price. Pork bellies cannot be stored for long periods of time. The maximum is eight months, with penalties assessed for deliveries of seven- or eight-month-old bellies. Economic analyses are therefore made under the assumption that all the production is consumed; large amounts are not carried over to affect the supply of a subsequent period. Using a year beginning October 1, carry-over stocks remain very small—less than one week's consumption at the end of each year. The frozen pork belly inventory in October is relatively unimportant to the storage situation because of annual clearings. Packers do not want bellies that have been frozen when they can get their supplies from fresh production.

SEASONAL INFORMATION

That pork belly supply and demand exhibit pronounced seasonal patterns has already been mentioned. This regularity is caused primarily by the seasonal hog-slaughter pattern and is reinforced by the consumption pattern. Because of these patterns, prices should drop to a fall or winter low price, then rise seasonally. The tendency is to reach a peak sometime between July and September. However, because the pork belly market is large and fairly efficient, speculators have all but eliminated the intrayear repetitive patterns.

Table 19-4 shows the monthly midrange prices of August pork bellies from 1961–62 to 1972–73. It also shows each midrange as a percentage of the average price for the season. Figure 19-2 is a graph of these percentages for the last 10 years. The latter represents a seasonal pattern for pork belly price futures. There seems to be no repetitive seasonal variation in pork belly futures prices.

CYCLICAL VARIATIONS IN PRICE

Stoken[2] describes in detail a four-year cycle in the pig crop and relates it to a similar cycle in pork belly cash prices. He points out that during the period 1952 to 1966, whenever hog supplies, as given by the number of hogs and pigs on farms as of January 1, and predicted by earlier breeding intentions reports, end their expansion and begin to contract, a two-year cyclical price rise occurs; then as hog production begins to increase because

[2] D. Stoken, "Forecasting Pork Belly Futures Prices," *Commodity Year Book*, Commodity Research Bureau, New York, 1966, pp. 17–27.

Year	Sept.	Oct.	Nov.	Dec.	Jan.	Feb.	Mar.	Apr.	May	June	July	Aug.	Monthly average price and %
1961–1962	.....	.....	.....	.....	.....	.....	29.40	29.75	29.37	30.37	31.12	30.55	30.10
	.....	.....	.....	.....	.....	.....	97.67	98.83	97.57	100.89	103.38	101.49	100.00
1962–63	.....	.....	.....	.....	.....	25.25	24.72	25.12	25.22	28.10	27.80	26.75	26.12
	.....	.....	.....	.....	.....	96.67	94.64	96.17	96.55	107.58	106.43	102.41	100.00
1963–64	.....	.....	26.02	26.67	27.65	27.87	27.85	28.70	27.25	23.92	22.85	25.40	26.42
	.....	.....	98.48	100.94	104.65	105.48	105.37	108.62	103.14	90.53	86.48	96.13	100.00
1964–65	.....	28.80	28.60	29.75	32.77	31.92	31.57	31.47	33.50	38.07	42.57	44.87	33.97
	.....	84.78	84.19	87.57	96.46	93.96	92.93	92.64	98.61	112.06	125.31	132.08	100.00
1965–66	.....	38.97	41.85	46.52	44.55	43.57	39.60	41.87	40.80	39.65	43.62	46.10	42.47
	.....	91.75	98.54	109.53	104.89	102.59	93.24	98.58	96.06	93.36	102.70	108.54	100.00
1966–67	36.37	34.60	34.77	35.72	35.65	34.72	35.02	34.97	35.15	40.20	34.85	31.07	35.25
	103.17	98.15	98.63	101.33	101.13	98.49	99.34	99.20	99.71	114.04	96.79	88.14	100.00
1967–68	32.25	32.90	32.70	32.77	32.27	32.90	34.55	37.92	33.90	29.12	28.60	27.00	32.25
	100.00	102.02	102.01	102.01	100.00	102.02	107.13	114.49	105.12	90.31	88.68	83.72	100.00
1968–69	33.85	32.57	31.80	31.87	32.30	34.62	37.07	36.05	38.05	36.72	33.65	38.07	34.72
	97.48	93.79	91.58	91.78	93.02	99.70	106.75	103.82	109.58	105.75	96.90	109.63	100.00
1969–70	37.67	38.85	41.05	41.67	41.77	43.05	42.20	40.90	38.72	35.90	38.12	35.52	39.62
	95.07	98.04	103.60	105.16	105.41	108.64	106.50	103.22	97.72	90.60	96.20	89.64	100.00
1970–71	34.50	32.52	31.05	28.37	25.25	26.50	27.55	26.17	26.00	24.87	21.52	21.85	27.17
	126.98	119.69	114.28	104.42	92.93	97.53	101.40	96.32	95.69	91.53	79.21	80.42	100.00
1971–72	30.05	31.20	31.02	33.67	37.92	35.75	37.12	39.25	37.72	35.32	37.65	37.30	35.35
	85.01	88.26	87.75	95.25	107.27	101.13	105.01	111.03	106.70	99.92	106.51	105.52	100.00
1972–73	40.27	40.47	42.07	43.05	46.12	48.87	53.12	51.32	55.42	56.90	65.45	*	49.37
	81.56	81.96	85.21	87.19	93.41	98.98	107.58	103.94	112.24	115.24	132.56	*	100.00

* No trading

of higher prices, pork belly prices decline from their cyclical top for approximately two years to a cyclical low. See Table 19-5 and Chart 19-2.

Many analysts think that this hog-production (and hog-slaughter) cycle and the cycles in the hog-corn price ratio are the principal factors in the big swings in pork belly prices. Many feel that it is reasonably possible to predict the direction and potential impact of these cycles.

As useful as a knowledge of the seasonal and cyclical factors may be in providing a point of reference, their limitations should be understood; for example, in the fall of 1964, because of the substantial decline in farrowings, speculators bought early and heavily, anticipating a significant seasonal advance. This buying caused futures prices to rise early, whereas

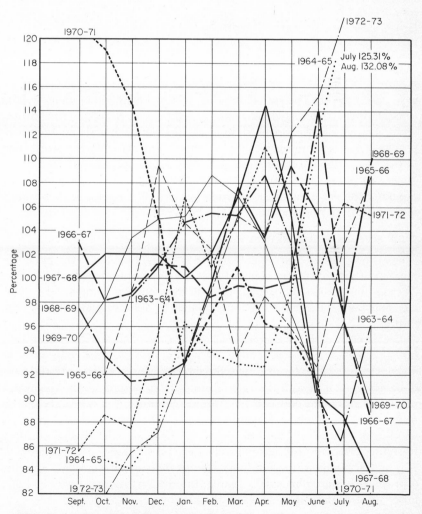

FIG. 19-2   August pork bellies, seasonal: monthly midrange price of August pork bellies as a percentage of average yearly price.

TABLE 19-5   HOGS AND PIGS
ON UNITED STATES FARMS
ON DECEMBER 1 (JANUARY 1
OF NEXT YEAR FOR 1966
AND PRECEDING YEARS)
1952–1973 (IN THOUSAND
HEAD)

Year	Total	Year	Total
1952	62,117	1963	57,993
1953	51,755	1964	56,757
1954	45,114	1965	50,792
1955	50,474	1966	47,414
1956	55,354	1967	58,777
1957	51,897	1968	60,632
1958	51,517	1969	56,655
1959	58,045	1970	67,449
1960	59,026	1971	62,972
1961	55,560	1972	59,180
1962	56,619	1973	61,022

cash prices lagged. The spread in price, which remained inordinately large through April, encouraged heavy hedge selling, which stopped the advance and eventually broke prices sharply as speculators liquidated their long positions. By mid-June prices had declined 7 cents from the April high. In this case, although the immediate supply was ample, as reflected by the lower cash price, speculators had bid the futures prices to a level that could not be sustained. As with the seasonal pattern, it is becoming increasingly more difficult to find and trade on the basis of known cyclical patterns.

PRICE SPREADS AND CARRYING CHARGES

There is no "normal" carrying charge in commodities; but if the price premium of a distant futures contract over a nearby one exceeds the costs of carrying the commodity, speculators will buy the near futures, take delivery, and hold the commodity long enough to deliver against the distant futures.

The monthly carrying charges, including storage, interest, and insurance, for pork bellies is approximately 70 points, or $252 per contract. This amount is not stable; for example, the interest charge varies with the price of bellies as well as with the rate of interest. To determine the theoretical maximum premium between two futures contracts it is necessary merely to multiply the number of months between the contracts by 70 points a month; for example, if belly supplies are adequate, the August contract, reflecting relatively full carrying charges, might trade at a premium of 350 to 420 points to the February futures delivery. If, however, supplies of fresh bellies are abnormally scarce, the distant contract might sell at a lower price or discount relative to the nearby.

When comparing a futures contract price to the cash price, rather than to that of another futures contract, an additional charge must be considered: another 150 points must be added to cover costs such as handling and inspection and of putting the bellies into and taking them out of storage. Bellies stored before December are ineligible for delivery against any futures contract.

Price spreads between futures contracts or between that of a futures contract and cash sometimes change in a predictable manner over time; for example, in the month of February the August contract tends to maintain approximately a 300-point premium over the cash or spot price. As time passes this premium diminishes and typically disappears by May or June. Between June and the end of the contract the price relationship customarily reverses, with the August futures contract selling at a discount to the spot price. The latter phenomenon is related to two factors:

1. After May the hog slaughter diminishes and fresh bellies become relatively scarce, a fact that tends to keep the cash price firm.

2. Storage bellies must be delivered before the beginning of the new season; therefore, if frozen stocks are large, the price of storage bellies on which the futures contracts prices are based declines. With large storage stocks the futures price might go to a discount of 2 cents under the spot price; smaller stocks generally lead to discounts of approximately ½ to 1 cent.

LIVE HOGS

INTRODUCTION

Futures trading in live hogs began in February 1966 on the Chicago Mercantile Exchange. Trading has continued to expand each year since that time and by 1973 equaled that of pork bellies. Contracts are traded for delivery in February, April, June, July, August, October, and December. Trading typically begins 11 or 12 months before the delivery month.

The contract traded is a unit of 30,000 pounds. Price is quoted in cents per pound, the minimum price fluctuation being .025 cents, or 2½ points a pound, which represents $7.50 per contract. The maximum allowable daily fluctuation is 1½ cents (150 points) a pound upward or downward from the preceding day's settlement price.

Definitions of some common terms may be helpful in reading the following tables and discussion.

Boars are male hogs used for breeding purposes.

Stags are boars castrated after sexual maturity.

Barrows are male hogs castrated (as are steers in the beef cattle business) before maturity. Barrows supply much of the pork and gain weight more rapidly than boars.

Farrowing is the act of giving birth. The litter size typically ranges from 5 to 15 pigs.

CHART 19-3

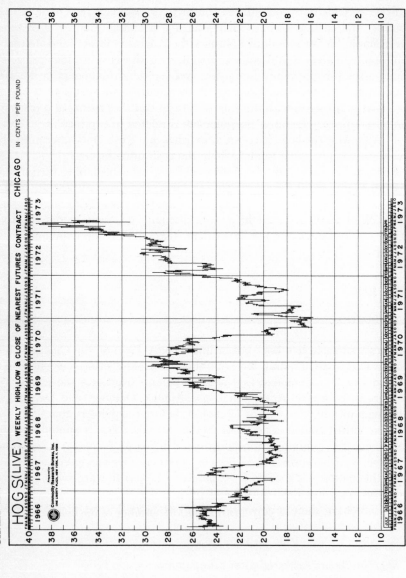

HOGS(LIVE) WEEKLY HIGH-LOW & CLOSE OF NEAREST FUTURES CONTRACT CHICAGO IN CENTS PER POUND

Prepared by
Commodity Research Bureau, Inc.
ONE LIBERTY PLAZA, NEW YORK, N. Y. 10006

Gilts are female swine which have not yet farrowed. They may be young hogs not yet bred or they may have been bred but not yet farrowed.

Sows are female hogs that have already given birth to a litter. Sows typically farrow twice a year and have a gestation period that is said to be three months, three weeks, and three days, or approximately 114 days.

FACTORS WHICH INFLUENCE HOG PRICES

As with other commodities, short-term (but sometimes significant) price changes will often depend on short-term changes in supply and demand relations. The longer run supply-demand relationships depend on the number of hogs raised on farms, the number slaughtered, and the amount of pork in storage. The demand is mainly influenced by consumer requirements for pork and pork products and the supply, demand, and price of competing products.

SUPPLY

Four Corn Belt states, Iowa, Illinois, Indiana, and Missouri, produce approximately one-half the hogs raised in the United States. The other six Corn Belt states shown in the USDA quarterly *Hogs and Pigs Reports* account for another 25 percent of the total. Other states are rapidly increasing their hog production and will probably increase their market share.

The number of hogs reaching market at any given time depends on the producer's decisions made 9 to 11 months earlier. Given the gestation period of almost 4 months, up to a month for breeding, and 5 to 7 months for the hogs to reach marketable weight, the producer must make relatively early decisions concerning future market prices. Because these decisions are often made on the basis of current market conditions, rather than those that will exist 9 to 11 months later, they tend to lag behind the market and thus cause a hog cycle (in both production and prices).

The sources of information and most of the supply and demand factors affecting hogs are discussed in the pork bellies section of this chapter. Table 19-6 lists some salient statistics on hog production and slaughter, and more detailed slaughter information is given in Table 19-1. Table 19-7 shows the cold storage holdings, an important supply factor.

Table 19-8 charts the hog-corn price ratio, the number of bushels of corn required to buy 100 pounds of (live) hogs, from 1960 to 1973. If this ratio is unusually high or low, it becomes a factor in production and slaughter decisions.

DEMAND

An estimate of the demand for pork and pork products typically begins with a consideration of the quantity consumed per year per person, and the relation of this quantity to its price as well as those of beef, poultry, lamb, fish, and other competitive foods.

TABLE 19-6 PIGS AND HOGS SALIENT STATISTICS IN THE UNITED STATES

Year	Pig crop Spring[b] Sows farrowed	Pig crop Spring[b] Pigs saved	Pig crop Fall[c] Sows farrowed	Pig crop Fall[c] Pigs saved	Total pig crop	Value of hogs on farms, Dec. 1[e] Dollars per head	Value of hogs on farms, Dec. 1[e] Total (million $)	Hog marketings (thousand head)	Quantity produced (live weight) (million lb)	Value of production (million $)	Hogs slaughtered Commercial Federally inspected	Hogs slaughtered Commercial Other	Hogs slaughtered Commercial Total	Hogs slaughtered Farm	Hogs slaughtered Total
	(thousand head)														
1960	6,782	47,228	5,839	40,988	88,216	18.50	1,092	79,831	19,203	2,946	66,153	12,883	79,036	5,114	84,150
1961	7,018	50,366	5,918	42,347	92,713	27.20	1,541	80,326	20,167	3,355	65,632	11,702	77,335	4,639	81,974
1962	6,996	49,535	6,098	44,073	93,608	27.50	1,556	81,743	20,275	3,312	67,770	11,564	79,334	4,090	83,424
1963	7,099	50,749	5,987	43,307	94,056	27.50	1,596	86,163	20,960	3,128	71,577	11,747	83,324	3,793	87,117
1964	6,596	47,682	5,525	39,862	87,544	23.40	1,328	86,086	20,217	2,989	71,667	11,352	83,018	3,266	86,284
1965	5,890	42,525	5,006	36,415	78,940	24.50	1,244	76,079	18,055	3,716	63,708	10,076	73,784	2,610	76,394
1966	6,201	45,422	5,811	42,811	87,563	45.20	2,144	76,504	19,107	4,354	63,729	10,282	74,011	1,314	75,325
1967	6,559	48,117	5,901	43,551	91,668	28.30	1,663	84,995	20,634	3,896	70,915	11,209	82,124	1,297	83,421
1968	6,659	49,099	6,130	45,078	94,155	30.50	1,857	87,907	21,102	3,910	74,789	10,371	85,160	1,241	86,401
1969	6,323	46,521	5,745	42,155	88,676	39.00	2,225	88,335	20,489	4,537	75,682	8,156	83,838	1,120	84,958
1970	7,134	52,292	6,882	49,629	101,921	23.50	1,584	87,143	21,861	4,963	78,187	7,630	85,817	1,145	86,962
1971[a]	7,303	52,589	5,967	43,174	98,436	28.50	1,781	99,586	23,062	4,025	86,667	7,771	94,438	1,093	95,531
1972[d]	6,512	47,654	5,856	41,942	93,720	42.00	2,484	91,514	21,585	5,412	78,738	5,949	84,687	966	85,653
1973[d]	6,459	46,103				60.00	3,686								
1974[a]	6,491	46,735													

[a] Preliminary.
[b] December–May.
[c] June–November.
[d] Breeding intentions.
[e] Data before 1967 are for January 1 of the following year.
SOURCE: Statistical Reporting Service, USDA.

TABLE 19-7   COLD STORAGE HOLDINGS OF PORK* IN THE UNITED STATES ON FIRST OF MONTH (IN MILLIONS OF POUNDS)

Year	Jan.	Feb.	Mar.	Apr.	May	June	July	Aug.	Sept.	Oct.	Nov.	Dec.
1962	200.0	209.1	235.5	279.7	315.9	338.5	295.1	233.6	181.8	138.5	161.3	211.8
1963	229.5	249.0	275.4	332.6	374.5	356.3	322.5	274.0	220.0	210.4	208.9	250.2
1964	276.7	332.8	382.3	411.2	473.6	468.8	412.9	321.4	229.1	184.0	221.7	275.0
1965	283.6	309.2	318.9	334.8	334.4	292.0	223.5	176.1	134.8	126.3	128.4	141.5
1966	151.9	155.4	183.5	217.1	272.3	268.3	214.1	178.5	140.0	151.0	171.2	205.7
1967	234.2	256.2	290.3	331.2	387.5	336.0	293.1	238.7	198.6	202.6	250.5	278.6
1968	285.9	289.1	291.8	305.5	354.9	387.3	326.0	245.0	196.4	197.1	222.4	236.9
1969	256.3	249.3	264.3	270.2	324.0	298.7	245.7	196.2	168.3	173.9	201.5	220.6
1970	210.9	210.4	237.4	268.5	329.0	350.5	304.3	254.7	217.5	210.0	246.2	303.5
1971	336.1	351.1	338.8	387.0	463.6	494.8	477.3	402.3	330.0	306.9	310.4	325.3
1972	330.0	301.1	289.5	331.1	395.2	381.4	318.8	253.6	204.3	192.1	208.5	242.5
1973	214.2	206.8	201.0	241.6	248.5	259.0	252.8	202.4	179.6	198.3	223.5	276.5

* Includes dry salt pork and pickled pork, cured and in process of cure, and frozen pork. Excludes lard.

SOURCE: Statistical Reporting Service, USDA.

Some general relationships can be inferred from the following 1971 data presented by Lessiter.[3]

In 1971 per capita consumption of pork in the United States was 73 pounds. During the same year it was 113 pounds of beef, 3 pounds of veal, and 3 pounds of lamb.

[3] Frank Lessiter, "Forecasting Hog Futures Prices," *Commodity Year Book*, Commodity Research Bureau, New York, 1972, pp. 8–9.

TABLE 19-8   HOG-CORN PRICE RATIO* AT OMAHA†

Year	Jan.	Feb.	Mar.	Apr.	May	June	July	Aug.	Sept.	Oct.	Nov.	Dec.	Average
1960	10.9	12.0	13.5	13.4	13.3	14.1	14.8	14.3	14.3	16.7	18.4	17.2	14.4
1961	15.8	16.1	15.9	15.9	14.7	15.0	15.7	16.2	16.6	15.7	14.9	15.7	15.7
1962	16.0	15.5	14.7	14.4	13.6	14.9	16.4	17.0	17.1	15.5	15.6	14.6	15.4
1963	13.3	12.8	11.9	11.7	12.6	13.7	14.5	13.5	11.9	13.3	12.9	12.2	12.7
1964	12.2	12.4	12.0	11.6	11.8	12.9	14.3	13.9	13.5	13.0	12.5	12.8	12.7
1965	12.5	13.5	13.3	13.5	15.6	18.5	19.4	21.0	19.3	20.0	21.1	23.0	17.6
1966	21.7	21.9	20.6	17.7	18.6	20.1	18.6	18.6	17.1	15.9	15.0	14.5	18.4
1967	14.8	14.9	14.2	13.8	16.8	17.1	17.7	18.0	16.7	16.1	16.0	15.6	16.0
1968	16.1	17.1	16.4	16.5	15.8	17.6	19.0	18.4	18.4	16.5	15.3	16.6	17.0
1969	16.4	17.5	17.8	16.5	18.5	20.2	21.6	22.1	22.8	22.5	22.8	23.6	20.2
1970	22.8	23.5	21.7	19.6	18.8	18.8	19.5	16.3	14.5	13.2	11.5	10.8	17.6
1971	11.0	13.2	11.6	11.3	11.8	12.2	13.9	15.1	16.3	17.2	16.7	16.6	13.9
1972	19.7	20.6	19.0	18.2	19.7	21.5	22.8	23.5	22.6	21.8	20.6	20.5	20.9
1973	21.4	23.3											

* Ratio computed by dividing average price packer and shipper purchases of barrows and gilts by average price No. 2 yellow corn both at Chicago. This ratio represents the number of bushels of corn required to buy 100 pounds of live hogs.

†Prices before 1970 are at Chicago.

SOURCE: USDA.

For each 1 percent decrease in the price of pork the quantity demanded increased by 0.75 percent. Also, each 1 percent increase in personal income raised the demand for pork by 0.32 percent.

As the prices of substitute products (beef, poultry, and fish) increase in relation to that of pork, consumers buy more pork; for example, a 1 percent increase in the price of beef causes a 0.13 percent increase in the quantity of pork demanded. Similarly, each 1 percent increase in the price of chicken causes a 0.06 percent increase in the quantity of pork demanded.

NOTES FROM A TRADER

Pork bellies provide a favorite vehicle for day traders in that the typical day's range can easily cover the reduced commission granted for day trades and provide a good profit. Of course, this is not to say that day trading as a general practice is a wise idea. Day traders should not expect to get filled at their specified stop prices if they use stop orders in this volatile market. Market-on-close orders are often the wrong way to liquidate a position, whether they are buy or sell orders, because many day traders in this market use alternative orders; that is, they instruct their brokers to liquidate at a given price or, if this proves impossible, at the market on the close. This makes prices during the last minutes of trading quite volatile, and execution prices are often disappointing.

The belly market lends itself well to spreads such as February–July or February–August. Nearby contracts usually gain enough on the distant in bull markets and lose enough in bear markets to make these spreads attractive, especially considering the lower margin and reduction in risk.

The market opening may respond to the news of the day out of proportion to its significance, particularly the morning hog run, storage movement, or hog prices. It also tends to anticipate important reports, such as the pig-crop or cold-storage supply, more accurately than other markets, such as grains.

Because the market is so much better oriented to changes in supply than in demand, it is easier for traders to determine meaningful relationships than in more two-sided markets. In utilizing the *Weekly Sliced Bacon Production Report* as a guide to demand, the trader should keep in mind that this report is at least three weeks old in addition to its other shortcoming, that of indicating only about 65 percent of demand to begin with.

If one is stubborn and willing to fight markets, it is advisable to choose markets other than pork bellies or hogs.

CHAPTER TWENTY

Cattle

INTRODUCTION

The United States raises about 10 percent of all the cattle in the world on farms normally exceeding 100 million animals. Only India has a significantly greater cattle population, many of which are not commercial. The world cattle and buffalo population is listed in Table 20-1. The breakdown of cattle and calves in the United States is given in Table 20-2. The production of beef in the United States utilizes more land and creates more market value than any other livestock or grain crop produced in the country. As the largest single segment of American agriculture, it accounts for about one-fourth of all farm income. Except in unusual years, the cattle and calves sold for beef produce as much income to its producers as wheat, corn, soybeans, and cotton combined. Beef production also accounts for the greatest single use of feed consumption.

In 1964 the Chicago Mercantile Exchange announced that it was about to begin trading in live cattle. Such an idea could hardly have been more revolutionary. Over a period exceeding 100 years futures trading had been considered necessarily confined to inanimate products which had certain rigid characteristics. It had been believed that products traded on a futures

TABLE 20-1 WORLD CATTLE AND BUFFALO NUMBERS (IN MILLION HEAD)

Year	Argentina	Australia	Brazil	Canada	China	Colombia	France	W. Germany	Turkey*	Mexico	South Africa	USSR	United Kingdom	United States	World Total†
1960	43.4	16.5	72.8	10.5	65.4	15.1	18.7	12.5	1961-65	21.0		74.2	11.5	96.2	1,007
1961	43.2	17.3	74.0	10.9		15.4	19.4	12.9	Avg.	21.1		75.8	11.7	97.7	1,041
1962	43.3	18.0	76.2	10.9		15.6	20.3	13.3	(13.8)	22.5		82.1	11.6	100.4	1,060
1963	40.1	18.5	79.1	11.2		15.6	20.3	13.4		25.4		87.0	11.6	104.5	1,057
1964	40.5	19.1	79.9	11.6		15.6	20.1	13.0		21.6		85.4	11.4	107.9	1,070
1965	45.0	18.8	84.1	11.9		16.5	20.2	13.1		23.0	12.4	87.2	11.7	109.0	1,100
1966		17.9	90.6	11.6		17.1	20.6	13.7		23.3	12.2	93.4	12.0	108.9	1,129
1967	51.2	18.3	90.1	11.7		17.9	21.2	14.0		23.3	11.9	97.1	12.2	108.8	1,166
1968	51.5	19.2	90.0	11.8		18.8	21.7	14.0	15.4	23.6	12.1	97.2	12.0	109.4	1,182
1969	48.3	20.6	92.8	11.5		19.6	22.1	14.1	15.0	24.9	11.8	95.7	12.1	110.0	1,190
1970	48.4	22.2	95.3	11.8		20.4	21.7	14.3	14.4	25.1	11.7	95.2	12.3	112.4	1,199
1971‡	40.8	24.4	96.6	12.2		21.2	21.7	14.0	13.9	26.1	12.6	99.2	12.4	114.6	1,215
1972†		26.5		12.6		21.8	21.8	13.6	13.6	26.8		102.5	12.9	117.9	1,230
1973†									13.6					122.0	

*Data includes buffaloes.
†Estimate.
‡Preliminary.
SOURCE: Foreign Agricultural Service, USDA

TABLE 20-2 NUMBER OF CATTLE AND CALVES ON U.S. FARMS AND RANCHES ON JANUARY 1, BY CLASSES (IN THOUSAND HEAD)

Year	Total cattle and calves	Cows and Heifers that have calved			Heifers 500 lb and over				Steers 500 lbs and over	Bulls 500 lbs and over	Heifers, steers and bulls under 500 lbs
		Beef cows	Milk cows	Total	For beef cow replacement	For milk cow replacement	Other heifers	Total			
1965	109,000	33,400	15,380	48,780	5,700	4,780	5,980	16,460	14,050	2,180	27,530
1966	108,862	33,500	14,490	47,990	5,760	4,450	5,990	16,200	14,770	2,150	27,752
1967	108,783	33,770	13,725	47,495	5,900	4,215	6,100	16,215	14,780	2,155	28,138
1968	109,371	34,570	13,115	47,685	6,110	4,080	6,020	16,210	14,820	2,195	28,461
1969	110,015	35,490	12,550	48,040	6,150	3,990	5,930	16,070	14,905	2,220	28,780
1970	112,369	36,689	12,091	48,780	6,431	3,880	6,132	16,443	15,265	2,272	29,609
1971	114,578	37,877	11,909	49,786	6,664	3,843	6,113	16,620	15,610	2,327	30,235
1972	117,862	38,807	11,778	50,585	6,987	3,828	6,399	17,214	15,999	2,376	31,688
1973*	121,990	41,102	11,651	52,753	7,470	3,875	6,430	17,775	16,655	2,465	32,342

*Preliminary.

SOURCE: Crop Reporting Board, USDA.

market must have more precise and generally accepted grade standards than those for cattle, in order to be delivered and accepted successfully against futures contracts. Interchangeability of contract units seemed to require something more homogeneous than live steers, which vary so much in weight and quality. Trading was usually confined to products that were storable over quite long periods of time, which obviously was not possible for live steers. Even beef is not extensively stored because the limited storage facilities are expensive and many consumers do not like frozen beef. Most important of all, a successful futures market must be supported by the trade or those engaged in the production or processing of the product. Any number of new futures markets have been started which appeared logical to an exchange and which appeared to have a potential speculative following. New markets that did not receive the support of the trade failed to survive. Much of the nation's packing industry not only did not encourage the formation of a futures market in live beef cattle but opposed it vehemently. The Board of Directors of the American Meat Institute, which represents the great majority of United States meat packers, voted unanimously in opposition to the establishment of a futures market for live beef cattle. They may have had some concern that futures trading might become a vehicle for expanding governmental controls over the livestock and meat industry. The Chicago Mercantile Exchange was not dissuaded, especially after the outstanding success enjoyed by the pork bellies futures market it had started in 1961. Trading in live beef cattle began in November 1964. Enough interest was expressed almost from the beginning by speculators, cattlemen, and even some packers to make the new trading medium a success from the start.

The trading unit established in the beef futures market on the Chicago Mercantile Exchange is 40,000 pounds of steers, live-weight basis. Standards, tolerances, and substitution provisions are all outlined in the futures contract which was developed with the help of the U.S. Department of Agriculture. Contracts typically call for delivery in February, April, June, August, October, and December. The basic delivery point specified is Chicago, although Omaha is an alternative at a differential of 75 cents per hundredweight below the Chicago basis and Kansas City, Mo., was added as another alternative delivery point at $1 per hundredweight allowable. Price is quoted in cents per pound, with the minimum fluctuation $2\frac{1}{2}/100$ cents ($2\frac{1}{2}$ points) a pound and the maximum price change per day (daily limit), 100 points. This is 1 cent a pound ($1.00 per hundredweight) upward or downward from the preceding day's settlement price. The maximum range per day is 2 cents (200 points) a pound. The delivery unit of 40,000 pounds consists of choice-grade or better live steers. Steers within the weight range of 1,000 to 1,150 pounds must have estimated yields of 61 percent; those within the weight range of 1,151 to 1,300 pounds require yields of 62 percent. Minor changes in contract specifications are made by the Exchange from time to time.

CHART 20-1

CATTLE (LIVE BEEF) WEEKLY HIGH, LOW & CLOSE OF NEAREST FUTURES CONTRACT CHICAGO MERC. EXCH. IN CENTS PER POUND

Prepared by
Commodity Research Bureau, Inc.
One Liberty Plaza, New York, N.Y. 10006

FACTORS WHICH INFLUENCE CATTLE PRICES

As with most farm products, the demand side of the beef price equation is dominated by a few buyers, whereas there is a large number of suppliers. The demand for beef by the public depends on such factors as the size of the population, its purchasing power, the prices of competitive products, such as pork, lamb, poultry, and fish, unexplainable changes in the public's taste that occur from time to time, and government purchases for schools, institutions, and welfare programs. Public demand is expressed to an important degree by the buyers for large packing houses and grocery chains. All beef produced will be consumed quickly at some price because of the limited storage facilities. Because demand is less volatile than supply in the short run, current market price depends heavily on available supplies of beef in relation to those of competitive meats. Variations in supply (slaughter) are indicated in Tables 20-3 and 20-4. In the longer run the demand for beef per capita has been in an uptrend that will probably continue. A summary of the supply and distribution is shown in Table 20-5.

In ultimate response to the public's demand for beef, ranchers buy breeding stock, grain farmers buy feeders, packing houses buy fat cattle, and retailers buy sides of beef. The available supplies depend on such factors as the size of calf crops and inventories of cattle on feed, and the weight to which they are carried before slaughter depends partly on the cost of feed and the condition of grazing land. Good grazing conditions will encourage

TABLE 20-3   COMMERCIAL SLAUGHTER OF CATTLE AND CALVES IN THE UNITED STATES† (IN THOUSAND HEAD)

	Cattle		Calves		Total[2] cattle and calves
Year	Federally inspected	Total†	Federally inspected	Total†	
1958	17,642	23,555	5,672	9,315	32,870
1959	17,458	22,930	4,875	7,683	30,613
1960	19,394	25,224	5,260	8,225	33,449
1961	19,968	25,635	5,005	7,701	33,336
1962	20,339	26,083	4,980	7,494	33,577
1963	21,662	27,232	4,535	6,833	34,065
1964	25,133	30,818	4,820	7,254	38,072
1965	26,614	32,347	5,076	7,420	39,767
1966	27,319	33,727	4,432	6,647	40,374
1967	27,780	33,869	4,002	5,919	39,788
1968	29,592	35,026	3,876	5,443	40,469
1969	30,536	35,237	3,637	4,863	40,100
1970	30,793	35,025	3,024	4,072	39,097
1971°	31,419	35,585	2,806	3,689	39,274
1972°	32,251	35,774	2,420	3,051	38,825

°Preliminary.
†Includes other wholesale and retail slaughter.
SOURCE: Crop Reporting Board, USDA.

TABLE 20-4 FEDERALLY INSPECTED SLAUGHTER OF CATTLE IN THE UNITED STATES (IN THOUSANDS)

Year	Jan.	Feb.	Mar.	Apr.	May	June	July	Aug.	Sept.	Oct.	Nov.	Dec.	Total
1960	1,564	1,437	1,577	1,412	1,606	1,692	1,592	1,787	1,782	1,746	1,625	1,576	19,394
1961	1,632	1,435	1,627	1,502	1,754	1,785	1,628	1,803	1,712	1,817	1,683	1,589	19,968
1962	1,781	1,467	1,649	1,522	1,766	1,718	1,765	1,870	1,654	1,898	1,686	1,562	20,339
1963	1,795	1,559	1,694	1,727	1,875	1,752	1,838	1,900	1,829	2,092	1,793	1,808	21,662
1964	2,013	1,710	1,877	2,045	2,070	2,207	2,162	2,125	2,199	2,359	2,111	2,254	25,133
1965	2,166	1,919	2,226	2,021	2,043	2,219	2,238	2,337	2,406	2,390	2,334	2,314	26,614
1966	2,305	2,037	2,232	2,103	2,249	2,397	2,236	2,469	2,416	2,335	2,285	2,257	27,319
1967	2,368	2,107	2,339	2,185	2,428	2,423	2,238	2,461	2,330	2,433	2,254	2,214	27,780
1968	2,493	2,258	2,241	2,286	2,541	2,367	2,609	2,648	2,540	2,813	2,416	2,380	29,592
1969	2,676	2,356	2,423	2,414	2,466	2,434	2,611	2,608	2,724	2,887	2,424	2,568	30,536
1970	2,653	2,318	2,477	2,545	2,493	2,615	2,642	2,538	2,723	2,752	2,564	2,611	30,793
1971	2,569	2,299	2,681	2,544	2,536	2,797	2,725	2,720	2,788	2,667	2,564	2,528	31,419
1972	2,556	2,457	2,698	2,471	2,807	2,833	2,488	2,923	2,789	2,909	2,705	2,615	32,250
1973	2,807	2,422	2,618	2,167	2,692	2,560	2,441	2,363	2,360	2,863			

SOURCE: USDA.

TABLE 20-5   CATTLE SUPPLY AND DISTRIBUTION IN THE UNITED STATES (IN THOUSAND HEAD)

Year	Cattle and calves on Farms Jan. 1	Calves born	Total supply	Livestock slaughter—cattle and calves					Deaths on farms	Total slaughter and deaths
				Commercial			Farm	Total slaughter		
				Federally inspected	Other†	All commercial				
1960	96,236	39,416	135,752	24,654	8,795	33,449	1,195	34,637	4,100	38,735
1961	97,700	40,180	137,880	24,973	8,363	33,336	1,218	34,550	4,018	38,571
1962	100,369	41,441	141,810	25,319	8,258	33,577	1,194	34,762	4,125	38,885
1963	104,488	42,268	146,756	26,197	7,867	34,064	1,213	35,277	4,040	39,317
1964	107,903	43,809	151,712	29,953	8,119	38,072	1,242	39,314	4,232	43,546
1965	109,000	43,922	154,822	31,690	8,077	39,767	1,196	40,963	4,248	45,211
1966	108,862	43,537	152,399	31,751	8,623	40,374	661‡	41,035	4,038	45,073
1967	108,783	43,803	152,586	31,782	8,006	39,788	617	40,405	4,038	44,443
1968	109,371	44,315	153,686	33,468	7,001	40,469	558	41,027	3,986	45,013
1969	110,015	45,177	155,192	34,173	5,927	40,100	486	40,586	4,150	44,734
1970	112,369	45,871	158,240	33,817	5,280	39,097	462	39,559	4,328	43,887
1971*	114,578	46,739	161,317	34,225	5,049	39,274	446	39,720	4,464	44,183
1972*	117,862	47,889	165,751	34,671	4,154	38,825	425	39,250	4,809	44,059
1973*	121,990									

*Preliminary.

†Wholesale and retail.

‡Data beginning 1966 not comparable with previous year due to change in definition.

SOURCE: Economic Research Service, USDA.

more demand for range cattle and make the supply of feeder cattle relatively scarce. A drought in range areas could force grass cattle to market earlier and depress prices. Drought in the Corn Belt can raise the cost of feed enough to discourage feeding. The supply side of the beef price equation is concerned with two important concepts that are treated in more detail later in this chapter. One is the cattle cycle and the other is the seasonal cycle.

Exports and imports are of relatively little importance in the analysis of cattle prices. Imports of beef are comparatively small because of shipping costs, although the United States does import some beef from countries such as Australia, New Zealand, Argentina, Ireland, Mexico, and Canada. Some live cattle are imported from Canada and Mexico. The United States is a net exporter of beef products such as tallow, grease, and hides. It also exports a small amount of beef, primarily to Canada.

SOURCES OF INFORMATION

The cattle trader who seeks basic current information will rely primarily on many of the same government and nongovernment publications discussed in the preceding chapter in connection with pork bellies. Some of them, particularly the *Monthly Cold Storage Reports,* have less effect on prices in the cattle futures markets than on prices in the more volatile pork bellies market.

Reports pertaining more particularly to cattle, not mentioned in Chapter 19, include the *Cattle and Calves Report,* published monthly, the *Livestock and Poultry Inventory Report* as of January 1, published about the middle of February, *Meat Animals Annual Summary,* published early each year, and *Shipments of Stocker and Feeder Cattle and Sheep,* published in January. Every five years a census of agriculture is taken which provides a complete count of livestock and poultry on farms. It is considerably more accurate than the annual estimates, which are based on sample and can be quite unreliable. When the census figures become available, the annual estimates of livestock numbers are revised to conform with the numbers revealed in the census.

The *Special Range Reports* may also be useful. *Cattle on Pastures* is published in June, the *Western Range and Livestock Report* is published during the second week of each month, and the *Special Wheat Pasture Report* is issued near the last part of each month from September through December. All are U.S. government reports that can be ordered directly from the Department of Agriculture.[1] Those interested in less detail can learn the high points of the reports from news wires, financial journals, or the commodity departments of brokerage houses.

[1] The Agricultural Marketing Service, USDA, also publishes a source booklet under the title, "Reports and Publications of USDA's Agricultural Marketing Service." A more complete list of government data may be obtained from the Division of Information, Office of Management Services, U.S. Department of Agriculture, Washington, D.C., 20250.

The sources listed will provide the trader interested in fundamentals with such data as

size of the calf crops,
cattle on feed,
pasture conditions,
steer and heifer slaughter figures,
average weight of cattle slaughtered,
cold-storage stocks,
supplies of pork, lamb, and poultry,
cash live-steer and carcass prices.

THE CATTLE CYCLE

The production of cattle, hence beef, differs from most other farm products because of the existence of a distinct long-term cyclical variation in cattle numbers. There are many reasons for the cycle. One is the lifespan of the cattle themselves. It is about 3 years from the time a cow is bred until a consumer can obtain his choice steak from the steer offspring. Another cause is the heavy investment required to enter most phases of the cattle business. Changes in the demand for beef and changes in availability and cost of feed also influence the cycle; for example, a severe drought is almost certain to cause reduction in herds, whereas abundant feed supplies coupled with low herd numbers will encourage an increase. Good grazing conditions encourage feeder producers to hold back their stock. The producer will be willing to pay more for the heavier yearling he receives if feed grains such as corn are abundant enough to ensure reasonably low feed prices. The fundamentalist wishing to analyze the factors affecting the cattle cycle might apply some ratio between the price of cattle and that of feed. The cattle price could be the average farm selling price of choice steers. It might be necessary to consider both corn- and range-fed cattle by combining a cattle-corn ratio and a cattle-hay ratio, assuming that the price of hay measures pasture conditions.

The upswing phase of the typical cattle cycle begins when producers decide to expand their breeding stock in response to rising prices or expectations that they will rise and prices of breeding stock accordingly begin to rise because the latter are being held back. Cows, heifers, and heifer calves are withheld to use for herd expansion. Calves, yearlings, and steers are withheld to be fed (finished) to an older age and heavier weight. Rising prices further encourage withholding, especially of cows, heifers, and heifer calves to be used to produce still more calves. When the larger number of new calves from the expanded herds mature, slaughter begins to increase because fully finished steers must be marketed regardless of the stage of the cycle. Prices begin to fall and marketing becomes still heavier. Prices begin to break, the liquidation phase of the cycle has been entered, and prices fall even more, most for breeding stock and least for high-grade fed cattle. Slaughter of cows and calves is increased because herd expansion is no longer considered desirable, a fact that depresses cattle prices even more. Finally, herds become so thin that prices begin to firm, cattle producers realize that the bottom of the cycle has been reached, and the expansion of numbers of cattle is ready to begin again with the rise in steer prices coupled with the increasing scarcity of cow beef as cows are again held back for breeding. Both the expansion and liquidation phases may last for years, with the buildup typically requiring considerably longer than the liquidation. A complete cycle has frequently lasted for 10 years or considerably more, although the recent trend has been for shorter cycles, especially with respect to the liquidation phase.

One of the early signs of an impending buildup in cattle numbers is the withholding of cows, calves, and heifers from slaughter to be used for rebuilding herds. This creates an interesting problem for packers and housewives. Cow prices fluctuate more than steer prices, and cow meat is used for supposedly low-priced products such as hamburger and sausage meat. Just when the consumer is ready to switch to such low-cost substitutes from higher priced cuts of beef she finds that their prices are proportionately up more than the high-priced cuts.

There are consistent relations between the phase of the cattle cycle and both the slaughter weights of steers and the cost of feeding expressed by the beef-steer corn-price ratio. When cattle feeders become optimistic enough to begin accumulating cattle, the average live weight of steers begins to rise because they are withheld to be finished to heavier weights. The rise in cattle prices usually tends to be more rapid than the accompanying rise in feed costs, and feeding to heavier weights remains profitable even though the most economical weight gains take place in young animals and the conversion efficiency ratio declines sharply as animals become heavier. Feeders who wait too long find themselves withholding their cattle and seeking higher prices only to find that the cycle is in its liquidation phase and may have difficulty recovering even the cost of production. At this point selling may assume almost panic proportions.

The cattle trader interested in the cycle might note the price relationship of the varying grades of cattle. When marketings are light, the price premium for high grades tends to be highest because cattle are coming out of feedlots at lighter weights. When prices begin to fall in response to increasing supplies, feeders extend the feeding period of more of their cattle to heavier weights, and the early stage of liquidation may be indicated. This retention of some of the lighter cattle to be fed to heavier weights reduces the relative scarcity of the heavier higher grades of beef and the premium narrows. When marketings become heavy, feeders may have to market their heavy cattle at low prices and lose money.

SEASONAL INFORMATION

There is no planting or harvest season for cattle, as there is for other crops, but there is a period of high production. Most calves are born within 45 days of April 1 and weaned within 45 days of October 1. The 350- to

450-pound calf is then usually "rough wintered" on a Southwestern range for about six months, during which period he gains about 100 pounds. Then he is "summered" for another 6 months, perhaps in Kansas or Nebraska, and gains about another 225 pounds. Then he goes to a feedlot, quite likely in Iowa, where he eats corn instead of grass, and gains weight at the rate of about two pounds a day for about 210 days. The distribution of cattle on farms is indicated in Table 20-6 and of those in feedlots in Table 20-7. After a typical young steer has eaten his corn for the 210 days he is about 26 months old, weighs about 1,150 pounds, if he is a medium choice steer, and is ready to go to a stockyard for slaughter in Chicago, Kansas City, Omaha, or Sioux City, among other cities. The rate of slaughter tends to be fairly level throughout the year, but there is some tendency to reach its maximum in October and its minimum in February. Feeding operations make cattle that were taken off grass in the fall available for slaughter in the spring. In the fall the cattle slaughtered tend to be grass-fed, hence of a lower grade than the better finished cattle available in greater abundance in the spring and summer. Prices of cattle sold off grass grazing land, including stocker and feeder cattle and cows as well as the lower grade slaughter steers, are lowest about October. These same classes reach their highest price levels in the spring when the grazing season begins and demand is strong for stocker cattle.

In the Midwest Corn Belt the prices of fed cattle take a different course from those of cattle coming off the grass. Cattle go to the feedlots in greatest volume from September to November and remain there from 3 to 12 months, depending on the degree of finish desired and their age when they entered. Prices are relatively lowest for each grade of cattle as it becomes available in greatest supply. "Commercial"-grade cattle are priced lowest in the fall when prices of better grades are near their highs. "Good"-grade cattle are cheapest in winter when they are ready for marketing after their relatively short feeding period. The higher "choice" grade is most plentiful in the spring, and the highest grade, "prime," which requires the longest feeding period, is ready for the market in its greatest quantity in summer.

Cattle on feed may be owned by packers, chain retailers, speculators, farmer feeders, commercial feeders, or ranchers. Farmer and commercial feeders dominate by a wide margin. Many cattle in custom feedlots are fed for absentee owners under contract. The cattle drives so popular in movie westerns have been replaced by less romantic assembly-line tactics. The range cowboy, the small cattle ranch, and the small feedlot have all declined drastically because of the effort to produce tender steaks at reasonable prices. The stockyards in the big cities have also felt the changing times. Because of the spiraling costs of transportation and feed, as well as the decreasing supply of grassland, the trend has been toward large, mechanized feedlots in order to achieve such benefits of size as volume buying. In warm areas cattle may be kept in shaded pens provided with sprinkler systems to reduce temperatures and settle the dust. Special diets have

TABLE 20-6 CATTLE AND CALVES ON U.S. FARMS ON JANUARY 1, BY LEADING STATES (IN THOUSAND HEAD)

Jan.1	California	Colorado	Illinois	Iowa	Kansas	Minnesota	Mississippi	Missouri	Montana	Nebraska	Ohio	Oklahoma	South Dakota	Texas	Wisconsin
1960	4,121	2,267	3,981	6,660	4,429	3,975	2,107	3,980	2,245	5,072	2,250	3,378	3,262	9,106	4,253
1961	4,207	2,282	3,901	6,460	4,562	4,094	2,149	4,099	2,155	5,134	2,272	3,513	3,327	9,379	4,296
1962	4,238	2,394	3,862	6,654	4,973	4,258	2,213	4,263	2,133	5,434	2,272	3,654	3,493	9,660	4,339
1963	4,562	2,590	3,978	7,053	5,222	4,386	2,257	4,306	2,325	5,773	2,295	3,837	3,738	10,240	4,382
1964	4,682	2,616	3,938	7,194	5,431	4,518	2,370	4,478	2,627	6,048	2,272	4,106	4,074	10,342	4,470
1965	4,670	2,600	3,859	7,482	5,214	4,518	2,465	4,657	2,758	6,077	2,204	4,352	4,196	10,239	4,515
1966	4,826	2,889	3,782	7,332	5,735	4,292	2,465	4,564	2,841	6,259	2,094	4,396	4,238	10,546	4,244
1967	4,837	3,017	3,555	7,405	5,620	4,163	2,370	4,655	2,869	6,377	2,052	4,308	4,323	11,000	4,159
1968	4,808	3,060	3,413	7,331	5,564	4,080	2,290	4,748	2,984	6,394	2,011	4,480	4,280	11,425	4,117
1969	4,778	3,035	3,345	7,404	5,675	3,958	2,190	4,748	2,984	6,330	2,011	4,659	4,237	12,200	4,076
1970	4,730	3,212	3,325	7,478	6,016	3,958	2,210	4,940	3,014	6,330	2,031	4,985	4,237	12,830	4,076
1971	4,680	3,414	3,300	7,403	6,497	3,998	2,254	4,989	3,165	6,457	2,072	5,085	4,322	13,200	4,158
1972	4,662	3,610	3,400	7,773	6,757	3,998	2,322	5,238	3,165	6,780	2,113	5,441	4,408	13,464	4,241
1973*	4,710	3,756	3,330	7,770	6,850	4,038	2,415	5,550	3,197	6,915	2,134	5,660	4,496	15,350	4,283
1974															

*Preliminary.

SOURCE: Crop Reporting Board, USDA.

TABLE 20-7 NUMBER OF CATTLE AND CALVES ON FEED† ON JANUARY 1 IN THE UNITED STATES (IN THOUSAND HEAD)

Jan.1	Arizona	California	Colorado	Illinois	Indiana	Iowa	Kansas	Minnesota	Missouri	Nebraska	Ohio	South Dakota	Texas	Wisconsin	Total U.S.
1960	265	665	404	688	210	1,510	275	416	292	665	209	247	248	121	7,574
1961	293	716	414	729	220	1,540	337	478	318	699	236	294	254	121	8,048
1962	310	782	397	780	231	1,571	383	440	299	845	248	325	323	121	8,520
1963	377	1,000	525	858	263	744	443	497	329	898	298	332	450	133	9,702
1964	324	946	508	815	302	1,796	447	487	316	1,022	313	329	478	137	9,845
1965	348	915	534	791	272	1,850	451	506	348	1,027	307	322	488	137	9,979
1966	364	952	596	807	321	1,776	480	536	435	1,227	328	348	538	138	10,582
1967	373	984	609	791	311	2,025	586	557	398	1,308	341	390	674	149	11,268
1968	385	902	628	721	336	1,924	610	585	426	1,354	341	406	810	143	11,417
1969	442	968	711	786	349	2,213	766	556	442	1,430	324	361	1,075	154	12,534
1970	510	1,031	795	755	349	2,213	892	589	402	1,477	318	361	1,417	146	13,190
1971	524	1,001	888	649	314	1,992	916	548	342	1,422	308	339	1,480	150	12,209
1972	539	1,045	983	662	327	2,112	1,100	537	373	1,550	320	363	1,781	144	13,330
1973*	655	1,181	1,050	585	276	1,981	1,250	494	310	1,581	300	378	2,245	143	13,920
1974															

*Preliminary.

†Cattle and calves being fattened for slaughter market on grain or other concentrates and are expected to produce a carcass that will grade good or better.

SOURCE: Crop Reporting Board, USDA.

been developed for hot regions. Large lots maintain their own feed-mixing mills and many have developed their own formulas, each believing its recipe is best. Many feedlots, especially in the Far West, are geared toward producing the popular "choice" grade of beef. The "prime" grade, preferred by high-priced restaurants, is becoming increasingly scarce. Iowa and California are the top feedlot states, although in Iowa the typical lot is considerably smaller than that in California. Many farmers in Iowa still maintain a few cattle on feed grown by the farmers themselves. Texas has traditionally been the largest source of feeder cattle but has lagged in the development of feedlots. Although consumption of beef is heavy in the Northeastern states, beef supplies continue to be imported from the Corn Belt, partly because of the cold weather in the consuming area and partly because it is so far from the source of feeder cattle and feed.

Much of the risk in the cattle business is absorbed by the owner of cattle on feedlots. Once he is committed to feeding calves or yearlings he has little choice but to bring his animals to a marketable weight, regardless of the fluctuations of cattle or feed. In addition to the costs of inventory and feed, he must pay for transportation, marketing, taxes, administration, shrinkage, labor, insurance, repairs, veterinary services, and interest. To reduce the risk some lots sell their cattle some months in advance of their being finished with provisions for a price adjustment in accordance with the actual condition of the cattle when delivery time arrives. This is called selling by "private treaty" and is still carried on, although futures trading has provided an alternative.

MARKETING

There are many ways of marketing cattle, but the most common is the country auction in which cattle lots are auctioned in a local sales barn on a fee basis. Auctions now number in the thousands and account for most cattle sales by far. Buyers include feeders, packers, and traders. Some large feeders contract for stock months in advance and avoid the auctions. This method of direct marketing is most common in the Far West. As a result of the auctions, terminal marketing has declined. The large cattle movements that used to come into these cities by rail have lost considerable business to the smaller, more economical markets that have been able to operate efficiently with low-cost trucking. Country auctions have become important enough even to attract buyers from large packers. The cattle feeder usually buys range cattle, transports them to his feedlot, keeps them for at least 150 days, and finally sells them directly or indirectly to a packer, hopefully at a profit.

Because of the weather, the marketing of cattle in the Far West differs somewhat in timing. Fall rains result in the best grass conditions in winter, so cows are bred to have calves born in September and it is hoped to sell the yearlings by June.

NOTES FROM A TRADER

In most years the cattle futures market is a good trading medium. Except for unusually surprising reports, the market is one of the less volatile. The length of time required for significant changes in the cattle cycle makes for long trends in the futures market. There may be long periods of narrow ranges which might try the patience of more aggressive traders.

The analysis of this market may prove easier than that of some others because of the dominance of the supply side and the relative availability of figures. Some, however, such as cattle-on-feed figures, may prove inaccurate sometimes. There is less reliance on government programs than in the case of many other commodities. Primarily, there is the beef-buying program to consider as well as the feed-grain programs.

Intramarket spreads in the live-cattle market may prove attractive even though there is no normal carrying charge because there are no frozen live cattle stored to be carried.

CHAPTER TWENTY-ONE

Fresh Eggs and Iced Broilers

FRESH EGGS

INTRODUCTION

Although the practice of maintaining flocks of hens may be traced back some 3,000 years to China and other parts of Asia, the egg industry as it is known today in the United States has commercial roots dating back about 100 years. In the 1860s the growth of cities and mass producers was facilitated by the dynamic westward growth of the railroad industry.

The dual problems of large seasonal production and egg perishability were met initially around the 1870s by basement storage and the use of limewater or oil to seal the egg pores. About this time icehouses were built for egg storage and the 30-dozen case was substituted for the 70-dozen barrel.

In the early 1900s backyard flocks were prevalent and the cobweb theory was fully operative. In a year when egg prices were high, more chicks were purchased. The following year more eggs were produced and the increased supplies drove prices down. No new birds would be added and prices the following year would be high. Geographic shifts in production areas, the tendency toward larger farms, and scientific methods have helped ease volatility in the egg-production cycle.

The United States, whose production tops 71 billion, is by far the world's largest producer of eggs. The USSR is next with approximately 45 billion. The egg business is mainly domestic. The gross income received averaged more than $1.9 billion in the last decade.

Shell eggs are traded on the Chicago Mercantile Exchange and the Pacific Commodities Exchange, Monday through Friday, from 9:15 A.M. to 12:45 P.M. (CST). The shell contract was established in 1919 in Chicago and in 1973 on the West Coast. Contracts on both exchanges are traded for delivery in every month of the year.

Both exchanges require delivery to be made in units of 750 cases of 30 dozen each (22,500 dozen), commonly known as "one carload." The minimum price fluctuation is 5/100 cent a dozen (5 points), which equals $11.25 per contract. The maximum daily price range is 400 points per contract (4 cents), of which 200 points may be above and 200 points below the preceding day's settlement price.

Delivery under the terms of the Chicago Mercantile contract requires quality eggs graded large A. Delivery is basis the Chicago area in qualified packing plants with delivery permissible throughout the continental United States and set allowances against "out of town" plants. The buyer, after receiving Notice of Tender and learning the position of delivery, must remove the eggs from the delivering plant within three business days.

The Western Slope contract specifies that delivery can be demanded only in the 11 states between the Rocky Mountains and the Pacific Coast and calls for delivery of nest run eggs rather than graded eggs.[1]

The most important difference between the contracts is the provision in the Western egg contract for delivery. The "long" who receives notice of delivery will get it by the receipt of a certificate, which is, in a sense, negotiable. If he does not want delivery, he can establish a short position in the market and retender the certificate to the exchange. If the buyer wants to accept delivery after receiving the certificate, he issues shipping instructions to the seller stating where in the Western Slope and when during the delivery month he wants delivery. The USDA inspection takes place at destination. Because the "long" determines when and where the eggs will be delivered and can be assured of the quality of the product at the delivery point, some of the problems normally associated with accepting delivery under a futures egg contract are mitigated.

---

[1] Nest run eggs are those eggs that are at the beginning phase of movement through marketing channels and have not yet been washed, graded, or sized. The contract calls for U.S. Nest Run 20% AA Quality with an average net weight per case of 48 to 52 pounds. Eggs weighing 43 to 48 pounds per case are acceptable with a discount of $\frac{1}{4}$ cent a dozen for each $\frac{1}{2}$ pound by which the average weight per case falls below 48 pounds.

CHART 21-1

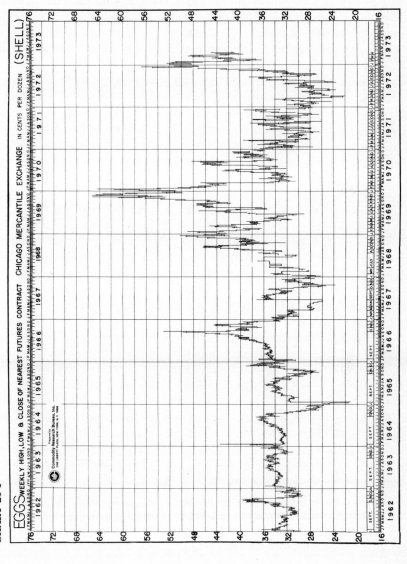

EGGS WEEKLY HIGH,LOW & CLOSE OF NEAREST FUTURES CONTRACT   CHICAGO MERCANTILE EXCHANGE   IN CENTS PER DOZEN   (SHELL)

Prepared for
Commodity Research Bureau, Inc.
ONE LIBERTY PLAZA, NEW YORK, N. Y. 10006

FACTORS WHICH INFLUENCE EGG PRICES

In the short run a producer's cost of production are largely fixed, except for the cost of feed, which is variable. A producer will generally tend to operate as long as he covers his variable costs of production, even if, in the short run, he does not cover all his fixed costs. The egg-feed price ratio becomes an important variable that affects the short-run supply of eggs. Historically, the egg-feed ratio and the monthly price of eggs in Chicago tend to move in unison.

A recent study by Larsen[2] indicates a long-run cycle in cash egg prices and an opposed one in production of about 30 months. This period is four times the 7- to 8-month interval required for a fertile egg to produce a laying pullet. In studying the years 1955 to 1965, Larsen noted that the cycle was quite flattened from 1961 to 1963 and has recently begun to reemerge. In superimposing a 12-month seasonal on a 30-month cycle, it was found that the cycle contributes almost as much to cash egg price changes as the seasonal.

The basic features of the egg cycle are that producers use current prices to base future price expectations and seem to expect that present prices will continue through the period for which they make plans; that producers use the current rate of profitability of production to expand or contract future production by a given percentage factor; and that a fixed lag in production delays realization of changes in the level of production so that when the changes eventually appear they are no longer appropriate.[3]

Supply factors are extremely important because the demand for eggs is quite inelastic. Therefore a small change in the factors that regulate production can have a significant impact on prices. One study estimated the price elasticity of eggs at 0.30[4]; that is, a 1 percent change, plus or minus, in the quantity of eggs demanded results in a 3 percent change in the price of eggs.

There is generally no strong relationship between the demand for eggs and the price of other foods, which indicates that the substitutability factor for eggs is low. There is some relation, however, between beef and egg consumption. Historically, as the demand for beef decreases because of high prices the demand for eggs has increased.

Another short-term factor affecting the price of eggs may be the demand of "breakers"; that is, those who buy eggs for processing purposes. Breakers try to anticipate their needs so that purchases may be timed to coincide with low prices; however, to the extent to which they are not successful,

[2] Arnold B. Larsen, "Price Prediction on the Egg Futures Market," *Proceedings of a Symposium on Price Effects of Speculation in Organized Commodity Markets, Food Research Institute Studies,* 7 (1967), 49–64.

[3] *Ibid.*

[4] G. E. Brandon, *Interrelations Among Demand for Farm Products and Implications for Control of Market Supply,* Pennsylvania State Agricultural Experiment Station Bulletin 680, 1961, p. 17.

their activities may cause significant short-run increases or decreases in demand.

A recent economic analysis of egg prices[5] determined that the average Chicago monthly egg price (Y) was tied closely to the number of layers on farms by months (X_1), the monthly egg-feed ratio (X_2), and the average monthly retail beef price (X_3). The regression analysis below indicated that $r^2 = 0.85$; that is, approximately 85 percent of all variation in Chicago egg prices during 1969 was explained by the three variables

$$Y = 0.0019(X_1) + 3.52(X_2) + 0.55(X_3)$$

SOURCES OF INFORMATION

The major sources of information for the egg trader are as follows:

1. The *Poultry and Egg Situation* is issued four or five times a year by the USDA and presents statistics relating to supply.

2. The *Crop Production Report* is issued monthly by the USDA and provides monthly statistics on

(a) hatching production of egg-type chicks,
(b) average number of laying hens on farms,
(c) pullets not of laying age on farms,
(d) potential layers, layers plus pullets not of laying age,
(e) egg production, average number laid per 100 layers per month,
(f) commercial poultry slaughter report for egg-type fowl.

3. *Producers' Price—Current* is published daily by Urner-Barry Publications, 92 Warren St., New York, N.Y.

4. *Dairy and Poultry News* is published daily by the USDA at 536 South Clark St., Chicago, Ill.

5. The *Chicago Mercantile Exchange Year Book* is published each April for the preceding year by the Exchange, 444 W. Jackson Boulevard, Chicago, Ill. This valuable booklet covers daily egg prices for all contracts, as well as production and stock figures.

NATURE OF PRODUCTION

The specialized poultry farm (10,000 to 1 million hens) sells to breakers (manufacturers of dried, liquid, or frozen eggs), wholesalers, and brokers or directly to supermarkets. Poultry farmers buy egg-type chicks from commercial hatcheries, and birds begin to lay at the age of 20 to 22 weeks. Because of improvements in the breed, some hens are capable of laying more than 350 eggs a year. After one year a hen's laying efficiency declines significantly. At this point the hen is culled (sold for slaughter) or put into forced molting.

During the latter stage the hen is starved into a state of shock in which

[5] Tom Danis, "An Economic Analysis of Egg Prices in 1969," The Chicago Mercantile Exchange, Research Report #1, April 1970.

it loses feathers and stops laying altogether, following which it is fed heavily. When it begins to lay again, egg production recovers as high as 95 percent of its preceding peak. Through two or three molts a bird's productive life may be extended until the hen is 24 to 36 months old.

There are several factors affecting the supply of eggs, but the principal determinants are the size of the laying flock and the output per layer.

The size of the laying flock. The number of layers in any period being analyzed is equal to the present number, plus birds coming into production, minus birds culled. Table 21-1 presents the number of million birds of laying age on farms in the United States on the first of each month for a number of years. The summer period traditionally reflects a decline in layers. Pullets started in the spring begin to lay small eggs in the fall and reach peak production late the following winter or spring. Their output then declines into fall. After a year of producing many hens are culled to make room for the new pullets.

Reduction in the number of layers throughout the year results from mortality and the sale of layers. The mortality rate reflects the quality of disease control and sanitation practices. The number of layers sold is determined largely by poultry feed prices and farm egg prices.

Feed is by far the largest item of expense on a poultry farm. Assuming average feed costs, a large, efficient producer has a cost between 25 and 27 cents per dozen eggs. Of this amount between 16 and 19 cents per dozen reflects feed. The egg-feed ratio represents the number of pounds of poultry feed equal in value to one dozen eggs. If the ratio is low, feeding is more expensive. The higher the ratio, the more favorable the feed prices. Table 21-2 summarizes the egg-feed ratio in the United States for a number of years. High feed costs relative to egg prices encourage culling of flocks and restricting feed allowances per bird. For this reason culling statistics will generally move contrary to the trend in cash egg prices. Low feed prices tend to encourage orders from hatcheries for new chicks. A high cash return for poultry usually results in the marketing of layers.

Output per layer. The output of eggs per layer in a given year largely mirrors previous trends in breeding and production practices. Table 21-3 summarizes the average number of eggs laid per 100 layers in the United States for several years. From 1954 to 1973 the average rate of lay per hen during the month of January rose from 14.8 to 19.0 eggs, an increase of more than 22 percent. The most significant gain in the rate of lay occurred in fall production.

Seasonal variation in egg production. There are definite seasonal patterns in egg production. The variations are not so pronounced today as they were a few years ago, primarily because of environmental housing, such as keeping lights on at night, scientific feeding, better breeding stock, spraying of eggs with fine oil for better shelf life, and forced molting. Table 21-3 indicates that egg production in 1954 decreased 25.6 percent from spring highs to late-summer lows. The comparable figure 18 years

TABLE 21-1 HENS AND PULLETS OF LAYING AGE ON FARMS IN THE UNITED STATES, FIRST OF MONTH, 1954-1973 (IN MILLIONS)

Year	Jan. 1	Feb. 1	Mar. 1	Apr. 1	May 1	June 1	July 1	Aug. 1	Sept. 1	Oct. 1	Nov. 1	Dec. 1
1954	347.1	339.2	328.5	316.2	301.4	289.1	276.6	274.5	291.2	322.7	338.9	345.7
1955	344.1	332.2	324.8	312.4	300.1	287.1	278.3	274.1	285.0	313.8	327.7	334.7
1956	332.9	328.7	321.0	309.5	299.7	288.8	280.5	281.3	294.5	317.1	329.1	334.4
1957	336.6	327.5	319.9	308.5	398.2	287.3	277.2	277.4	289.2	306.9	314.8	321.3
1958	321.3	314.5	307.4	300.5	290.2	283.1	278.3	280.3	288.7	306.4	317.0	325.8
1959	330.0	323.8	318.8	312.5	302.6	291.3	281.4	281.6	291.4	306.4	315.5	318.7
1960	319.5	312.6	305.9	298.7	291.7	284.3	277.9	274.6	278.9	291.0	299.3	307.1
1961	308.3	301.8	298.0	294.4	287.7	282.1	278.3	277.3	284.5	297.6	305.0	309.5
1962	312.4	307.6	305.2	300.6	293.8	287.1	282.0	283.0	289.2	300.2	306.1	308.6
1963	307.4	303.3	300.7	298.4	294.2	288.5	284.1	285.7	290.8	299.1	303.0	307.0
1964	306.8	301.7	301.0	297.8	293.3	289.9	286.1	287.3	292.7	301.4	304.7	311.3
1965	312.9	307.2	304.3	301.2	297.8	295.6	294.0	292.1	296.2	302.4	305.2	307.9
1966	308.1	305.5	303.9	301.5	298.1	295.0	293.0	293.0	300.2	310.0	316.1	321.0
1967	322.1	320.3	317.0	315.8	311.4	309.3	306.7	305.4	309.8	317.5	321.7	323.4
1968	325.3	324.1	321.7	320.0	314.5	309.6	306.4	301.4	302.3	307.2	309.8	310.8
1969	309.7	316.3	313.3	313.5	311.5	310.2	307.9	295.2	303.7	307.2	310.1	313.5
1970	317.5	324.0	322.9	320.8	318.7	314.9	314.6	314.5	317.8	324.8	328.4	331.1
1971	327	322	317.7	323.1	318.8	316.3	312.6	313.6	315.7	318.7	324.7	321.0
1972*	321	320	315.3	312	304	301	298	300	299	301	302	302
1973*	301	299	296.5	297	292	388	282	281	283	287	290	296

* Preliminary.

SOURCE: Crop Reporting Board, USDA.

TABLE 21-2   EGG-FEED RATIO*, IN THE UNITED STATES, 1954–1973

Year	Jan.	Feb.	Mar.	Apr.	May	June	July	Aug.	Sept.	Oct.	Nov.	Dec.	Average
1954	12.1	11.9	9.9	8.9	8.3	8.5	8.9	9.6	8.7	8.5	9.0	8.7	9.4
1955	8.5	10.4	10.6	9.6	9.1	9.2	9.7	11.2	12.6	12.5	12.9	13.9	10.8
1956	13.7	11.8	11.6	11.0	10.4	10.0	10.0	10.1	10.6	10.8	10.5	10.4	10.9
1957	9.3	9.4	8.8	8.8	8.4	8.5	9.5	10.6	11.9	13.0	13.8	13.4	10.5
1958	11.9	11.3	12.2	11.1	10.5	10.1	10.6	10.9	12.2	11.6	11.8	11.1	11.3
1959	10.9	10.5	10.0	8.2	7.3	7.4	8.9	9.1	9.9	9.6	9.6	9.5	9.2
1960	9.1	8.9	9.8	10.7	9.7	9.3	9.6	10.4	11.7	13.4	14.3	13.8	10.9
1961	12.0	11.8	10.9	10.0	9.5	9.1	10.1	10.3	10.5	11.1	10.8	10.5	10.6
1962	10.6	10.8	9.9	9.3	8.5	8.3	8.6	9.6	10.6	10.7	10.8	10.6	9.9
1963†	8.6	8.8	8.6	7.7	7.0	7.0	7.3	7.7	8.5	8.4	8.6	8.4	8.0
1964	8.9	8.2	8.1	7.5	7.1	7.3	7.6	8.3	8.4	8.3	8.2	7.9	8.2
1965	7.4	7.4	7.4	7.9	7.1	7.2	7.5	8.1	8.7	8.9	9.1	9.9	7.6
1966	8.9	9.8	9.9	9.2	7.9	7.8	8.1	9.0	9.6	9.3	9.5	9.3	9.5
1967	8.6	7.5	7.9	6.9	6.7	6.3	7.0	7.0	7.5	6.8	7.2	7.7	7.9
1968	7.9	7.5	7.6	7.2	6.8	7.6	8.2	8.7	10.9	9.6	9.9	10.7	7.4
1969	10.9	9.9	10.1	9.3	7.6	7.8	9.4	8.9	10.0	10.1	12.3	13.5	9.9
1970	13.0	11.4	10.2	8.5	7.3	7.3	8.7	7.9	9.0	7.6	8.5	8.8	10.9
1971	8.2	7.4	7.2	7.2	6.7	6.4	6.4	7.1	7.1	6.9	7.2	8.2	7.6
1972	7.1	6.9	7.6	6.4	6.4	6.4	7.0	6.9	7.7	6.9	8.0	8.5	7.2
1973	8.9	7.3	7.7	7.9	6.9	6.4	7.0	8.4	8.7	8.3			

* Pounds of laying feed equivalent in value to one dozen eggs.
† New Series. Comparable earlier data not available.
SOURCE: USDA.

later was only 7 percent. Egg production still varies significantly, however. Production usually peaks in the spring, declines through the summer, and gradually builds through the winter to the peak spring levels. Hatching and culling also respond to seasonal factors. Hatching peaks in the spring and culling is generally heaviest in the fall as the new birds hatched the preceding spring come on line.

NATURE OF CONSUMPTION

Eggs are probably the least expensive source of protein available for human consumption. This characteristic, plus the breakfast-habit factor, influences the relatively inelastic demand picture for egg consumption. Per capita disappearance of eggs for a number of years in the United States is listed in Table 21-4. Since 1954 per capita consumption has declined substantially, even though the tendency has been for processed-egg demand to rise. Distribution channels in the U.S. egg market may be visualized by referring to Figure 21-1. A high percentage (90 percent) move directly to the consumer in shell form. Approximately 10 percent of production is taken by breakers, who convert shell eggs into liquid, frozen, and dried eggs. Although there is a normal export of small eggs to the Caribbean area, the trader may generally disregard the import and export of eggs as

TABLE 21-3 EGG PRODUCTION: AVERAGE NUMBER OF EGGS LAID PER 100 LAYERS IN THE UNITED STATES, 1954–1973

Year	Jan.	Feb.	Mar.	Apr.	May	June	July	Aug.	Sept.	Oct.	Nov.	Dec.	Total
1954	1,484	1,498	1,837	1,819	1,847	1,672	1,579	1,475	1,366	1,384	1,376	1,482	18,819
1955	1,548	1,491	1,800	1,844	1,900	1,751	1,672	1,537	1,418	1,444	1,411	1,491	19,307
1956	1,561	1,585	1,832	1,839	1,891	1,746	1,695	1,589	1,457	1,497	1,466	1,566	19,724
1957	1,606	1,543	1,862	1,872	1,919	1,772	1,718	1,621	1,491	1,489	1,459	1,588	19,940
1958	1,664	1,537	1,806	1,861	1,933	1,796	1,757	1,660	1,530	1,564	1,548	1,632	20,288
1959	1,676	1,612	1,908	1,911	1,963	1,828	1,798	1,701	1,565	1,570	1,542	1,661	20,745
1960	1,719	1,667	1,851	1,873	1,969	1,850	1,816	1,736	1,601	1,600	1,561	1,649	20,892
1961	1,699	1,634	1,923	1,903	1,952	1,833	1,815	1,739	1,616	1,645	1,617	1,697	21,073
1962	1,713	1,618	1,902	1,901	1,972	1,859	1,840	1,756	1,646	1,680	1,637	1,706	21,205
1963	1,699	1,594	1,896	1,907	1,965	1,855	1,846	1,777	1,665	1,703	1,669	1,726	21,287
1964	1,757	1,727	1,924	1,910	1,973	1,870	1,859	1,789	1,692	1,731	1,680	1,763	21,652
1965	1,815	1,684	1,912	1,896	1,973	1,874	1,873	1,811	1,712	1,755	1,705	1,776	21,775
1966	1,792	1,650	1,901	1,894	1,964	1,871	1,868	1,817	1,738	1,781	1,731	1,801	21,788
1967	1,832	1,696	1,931	1,908	1,971	1,883	1,904	1,858	1,764	1,805	1,748	1,811	22,094
1968	1,830	1,746	1,915	1,886	1,946	1,858	1,953	1,839	1,749	1,804	1,742	1,797	21,994
1969	1,807	1,680	1,918	1,885	1,962	1,868	1,887	1,853	1,768	1,819	1,755	1,814	21,994
1970	1,814	1,653	1,881	1,857	1,921	1,832	1,868	1,843	1,759	1,809	1,762	1,834	21,821
1971	1,854	1,702	1,913	1,873	1,947	1,879	1,910	1,880	1,802	1,863	1,813	1,880	22,316
1972*	1,895	1,799	1,962	1,915	1,974	1,900	1,944	1,918	1,837	1,886	1,825	1,900	22,316
1973*	1,901	1,741	1,952	1,913	1,990	1,906	1,939	1,907	1,835	1,896			22,700

* Preliminary.

SOURCE: Crop Reporting Board, USDA.

TABLE 21-4 EGGS: CIVILIAN PER CAPITA DISAPPEARANCE IN THE UNITED STATES, 1954–1973 (NUMBER OF EGGS)

Year	Jan.	Feb.	Mar.	Apr.	May	June	July	Aug.	Sept.	Oct.	Nov.	Dec.	Total* (Shell)	Pro-cessed†	Total
1954	31.3	28.2	31.2	30.4	30.1	26.7	27.4	27.1	26.8	29.3	30.5	32.4	351	25	376
1955	31.2	27.9	30.9	29.0	28.4	26.8	27.3	27.4	27.2	29.3	29.8	31.2	346	25	371
1956	30.8	28.8	31.1	28.6	27.6	25.9	27.7	27.1	27.2	29.0	29.3	31.4	345	24	369
1957	30.5	27.2	30.2	28.2	27.6	25.7	26.7	26.9	26.4	27.7	27.8	30.0	335	27	362
1958	29.4	25.5	29.6	27.6	26.8	25.0	26.4	26.6	26.1	27.8	28.2	29.2	328	26	354
1959	29.0	25.5	29.0	26.4	26.2	24.4	25.6	25.6	25.1	26.7	26.6	28.4	319	33	352
1960	27.5	24.7	27.7	26.6	24.9	23.1	24.9	24.4	24.0	25.3	25.6	26.9	306	29	335
1961	26.2	23.3	26.3	25.3	24.4	22.5	24.4	24.3	23.9	25.3	25.2	26.7	298	30	328
1962	26.3	23.5	26.5	25.3	24.4	22.4	23.6	24.0	23.6	24.9	25.0	26.4	296	31	327
1963	25.5	22.5	25.8	24.2	23.9	22.5	23.6	23.8	23.3	24.5	24.5	25.5	290	28	318
1964	25.2	23.4	25.4	23.5	23.7	22.1	23.3	23.9	23.1	24.3	23.9	25.3	287	30	318
1965	25.3	22.1	24.5	24.1	24.1	22.1	23.6	23.6	22.9	24.4	23.7	24.7	285	28	314
1966	24.5	22.0	24.6	23.4	23.6	21.8	23.3	23.4	22.8	24.6	24.2	25.1	283	30	314
1967	25.0	22.1	25.2	23.8	23.9	22.2	24.0	24.0	23.4	24.6	24.5	25.8	289	35	324
1968	25.7	23.5	25.4	24.2	24.2	22.5	23.7	23.5	23.0	24.1	23.7	24.8	288	32	321
1969	24.8	22.2	25.6	23.9	24.4	22.5	23.6	23.9	23.2	23.9	23.7	24.8	287	31	318
1970	24.9	21.9	24.9	23.7	24.0	22.2	23.6	23.9	22.9	24.1	24.0	25.4	286	33	319
1971‡	25.4	22.2	24.6	23.8	24.4	22.7	23.5	23.7	21.3	23.8	23.8	24.8	285	37	322
1972‡	24.5	22.3	24.1	22.8	22.6	21.1	22.5	22.2	21.5	22.2	21.7	23.7	271	41	312
1973	23.4	20.5	23.0	22.4	22.5	20.6	21.3	21.2							

*Monthly totals do not necessarily add to yearly figures due to rounding.
† Liquid, frozen, and dried egg (eggs solids) converted to shell egg equivalent.
‡ Preliminary.
SOURCE: Economic Research Service, USDA.

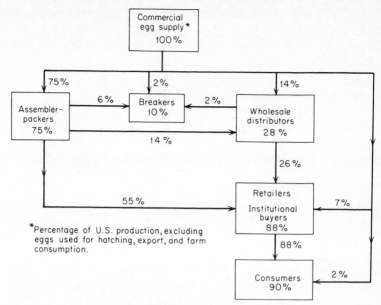

FIG. 21-1   Distribution channels in the U.S. egg market.

significant price-making influences. Consumer demand for eggs generally increases sharply during the two weeks before the Easter, Christmas, and Thanksgiving holidays. During the summer egg consumption tends to lag because of fear of spoilage and because hot weather acts as an appetite deterrent.

Breakers, until recently, followed a seasonal pattern of their own, operating near capacity in the spring and tailing off during the remainder of the year. The appearance of modern pasteurization equipment enables breakers to pack quality eggs during the summer. Many companies that also use egg products have the capacity to purchase one year's requirements at a time. For these reasons breaker demand may peak during the seasonally lower spring egg-price levels.

The egg futures market responds quickly to another source of demand —U.S. government purchases. In recent years the government has purchased dried eggs in periods of low prices to help put a floor under prices. Besides the regular military demand, distribution of eggs by the USDA is effected in school-lunch programs and surplus-food programs in depressed areas. Government egg purchases originate from two sources: daily and special purchases by the Defense Subsistence Supply Center (army purchases) and the aforementioned special purchases by the USDA. Because delivery of "army" eggs takes place approximately two weeks after the opening of sealed bids, "army" prices are watched closely for indications of egg-dealer estimates of near-future market conditions. Since army purchases are loose eggs packed 30 dozen to the case, army prices may be compared with major cash egg markets in Los Angeles, Chicago, or New York for clues to future price changes. Special purchases of dried eggs from the same source can affect the egg market substantially because they are announced without warning.

Prices, production, and consumption, then, have a complex relation in the egg industry that stems from the fact that production affects the retail price, the price received by farmers, and, to a certain degree, the level of consumption. The farm price, in turn, influences egg production by its effect on the number of pullets raised and on the sales of layers. Such interaction makes a meaningful measurement of demand a formidable problem.

SEASONAL INFORMATION

In 1954 egg production in the spring quarter (March, April, and May) was 29.2 percent of the annual total. In 1972 the same quarter represented only 25.5 percent of the year's egg production. This leveling tendency is reflected in the lack of a high-probability recurrent seasonal price pattern in egg futures. Figure 21-2, however, shows the average seasonal open-interest and volume figures for a number of years to assist the trader in determining the quality of price moves as they occur.

ICED BROILERS

INTRODUCTION

It is said that a Roman Emperor, concerned with excessive chicken consumption, issued an order that hens and roosters be consumed in moderation. To circumvent the order the rooster was desexed, thus producing the capon and the ability to keep consumption high by allowing resourceful Romans to maintain that a capon was neither a hen nor a rooster. Later, a special dish was produced for Napoleon who celebrated a victory during the Italian Campaign in 1801—Chicken Marengo. When Herbert Hoover promised the American people "a chicken in every pot," broilers, still a rare delicacy, totaled less than 30 million birds a year. By post-World War II production had increased tenfold, and by the 1970s chicken production in the United States topped 3 billion birds.

The production of commercial broilers exceeded that of farm chickens in 1952. From that date forward chicken meat became a product rather than a by-product of the egg industry. More than 90 percent of the broiler output derives from operations that are integrated vertically, that is, in which all phases of production, processing, and marketing are under centralized management. The economics of the modern integrated broiler industry has led to such concentration that the National Commission on Food Marketing estimates that fewer than 20 firms may account for 50 percent of the total output.

FIG. 21-2 Fresh eggs: monthly open interest and volume as a percentage of average monthly open interest and volume for the years 1962–1971 at the Chicago Mercantile Exchange. (Commodity Exchange Authority, USDA.)

Futures trading in iced broilers began in August 1968 on the Chicago Board of Trade. The contract traded is a unit of 25,000 pounds consisting of whole, eviscerated broiler-fryer chickens. Contracts are traded for delivery in January, March, May, July, September, and November. Individual birds must be in the 2½ to 3½-pound range and must be ice-packed, ready to cook, and graded USDA Grade A. Price is quoted in dollars and cents per hundred pounds, the minimum price fluctuation being 0.025 cents, or 2½ points, a pound, which represents $6.25 per contract. The maximum allowable daily fluctuation is $2.00 per 100 pounds (200 points) above or below the preceding day's settlement price.

CHART 21-2

BROILERS (ICED) CHICAGO (WEEKLY HIGH, LOW & CLOSE OF NEAREST FUTURES) IN CENTS PER POUND

FACTORS WHICH INFLUENCE
ICED BROILER PRICES

The economics of the iced broiler industry is unique among agricultural commodities. Perhaps nowhere else do the factors that influence supply and demand react so swiftly in prices. From the incubator to the skillet requires a passage of only 9 weeks. Perhaps the most important catalyst in the incredibly short production cycle is scientifically produced feed. In 1941 4½ pounds of feed were required to produce one pound of edible poultry meat. In the 1970s the amount had been reduced to 2¼ pounds. Efficiency in feeding is credited with reducing the time to raise a chicken to market weight from an average of about 14 weeks to the present 9 to 10 weeks.

As a result, price changes can be swift and sharp. As one study indicated, "Within the 44 weeks ending in mid-June, 1968, weekly average broiler prices in Chicago have ranged from a low of 21.65 cents to a high of 29.25 cents, nearly a 38 percent change. Equally impressive is the fact that these prices have not held at the same level for more than 3 weeks. In fact, they held steady for 3 weeks on only 3 occasions, steady for 2 weeks on 7 occasions, and the rest of the time they changed from week to week."[6]

The uniqueness of the supply information in the broiler industry lies in the high predictability of forthcoming supplies. In the short run these supplies are influenced by the number of chicks placed on feed as reported by the USDA. Production forecasts can be lengthened still another 3 weeks by observing the number of eggs set in incubators. Efforts to project prices further into the future turn to such indicators as the size and age of the hatchery supply flock—those birds that produce eggs for incubators and eventual feeding as broilers. Longer run supply factors such as the number of breeder hens placed, the number tested, and the number slaughtered provide clues to changes in the size of the laying age (7 to 15 months) breeding flock.

Whether or not capacity is translated into actual production depends on the level of demand in the short run. Because broilers are perishable, they must be consumed within a short time after they are packed. If demand lags for a given week, prices must drop to clear the available supplies. In the short run broiler production must equal consumption, a fact that frequently explains market volatility.

Demand is generally measured on a per capita basis and is influenced by changes in disposable income and consumer preferences as well as by the supply and price of competing products such as pork, lamb, turkey, beef, and eggs. Seasonal considerations indicate that peak demand occurs during the summer months in response to barbeque popularity and demand

[6] Max E. Brunk and Lawrence B. Darrah, *The Futures Market: A Broiler Marketing Tool,* Chicago Board of Trade, Chicago Ill., 1968, p. 18.

is weakest during the traditional turkey holidays of Thanksgiving and Christmas.

SOURCES OF INFORMATION

The major source of information for the broiler trader is the USDA. Reports are generally issued from two services—The Economic Research Service and The Statistical Reporting Service. To be put on the subscription list, usually at no charge, the trader may write to the service listed below, U.S. Department of Agriculture, Washington, D.C., 20250.

Reports published by the Economic Research Service are the following:

1. *The Poultry and Egg Situation,* issued four or five times a year, presents statistics relating to supply.
2. *The Livestock and Meat Situation,* published six times a year, discusses the outlook for broilers and provides statistical information.
3. *The Feed Situation,* published five times a year, discusses the outlook and also contains statistical information.

Monthly reports published by the Statistical Reporting Service are the following:

1. *Eggs, Chickens and Turkeys*
2. *The Poultry Slaughter and Processing Report*
3. The *Hatchery Production Report*
4. *Pullet Chicks for Broiler Hatchery Supply Flocks*
5. *Turkeys and Chickens Tested*
6. *Livestock Slaughter and Meat Production*
7. *Cold Storage Report*

The *Statistical Annual,* published by the Chicago Board of Trade, 141 West Jackson Blvd., Chicago, Illinois, 60604, contains information on fundamentals as well as daily prices.

NATURE OF PRODUCTION

Southern states dominate broiler supply figures with Georgia, Arkansas, and Alabama accounting for more than 40 percent of all U.S. broiler production. Figure 21-3 shows the geographical distribution and Table 21-5 lists salient production statistics.

The short run supply of broilers is dominated by three factors: egg sets, chick placements, and pullet placements.

Egg sets. Even before the 9-week race to market automation dominates the life of the broiler-to-be. Eggs from hatchery egg farms are shipped to hatcheries where incubation takes place in a rigidly controlled environment. Temperature is kept at 98° F and humidity at 97 percent. Eggs are tilted every hour to prevent the embryro from sticking to the eggshell. After approximately 3 weeks eggs are transferred to a hatching unit for 3 days.

TABLE 21-5 BROILER SALIENT STATISTICS IN THE
UNITED STATES

Year	Commercial production		Average			Consumption per capita—by quarters				
	Number (millions)	Live-weight (million lb)	Live-weight per bird (lb)	Farm price (cents/lb)	Value of production (million $)	1st	2nd	3rd	4th	Total
								(In pounds)		
1960	1,795	6,017	3.35	16.9	1,014	5.1	6.2	6.6	5.5	23.4
1961	1,991	6,832	3.43	13.9	947	5.4	7.4	7.3	5.7	25.8
1962	2,023	6,907	3.41	15.2	1,049	5.6	7.0	6.8	6.3	25.7
1963	2,102	7,276	3,46	14.6	1,063	6.1	7.1	7.4	6.4	27.0
1964	2,161	7,521	3.48	14.2	1,070	6.4	7.4	7.4	6.4	27.6
1965	2,334	8,115	3.48	15.0	1,218	6.6	7.7	8.1	7.1	29.5
1966	2,572	8,993	3.50	15.3	1,372	7.2	8.3	8.8	8.0	32.3
1967	2,593	9,187	3.55	13.3	1,223	7.6	8.7	8.7	7.8	32.8
1968	2,621	9,332	3.50	14.2	1,326	7.7	8.4	8.9	8.1	33.1
1969	2,788	10,046	3.60	15.2	1,531	8.0	9.1	9.3	8.8	35.2
1970	2,987	10,821	3.62	13.6	1,475	8.8	9.9	9.8	8.8	37.3
1971*	2,945	10,818	3.67	13.7	1,487	8.8	9.4	9.8	9.1	37.1
1972*	3,075	11,478	3.73	14.1	1,622	9.3	10.2	10.0	9.3	38.8

* Preliminary.
SOURCE: Economic Research Service, USDA.

Chick placements. When the chicks are born, they are vaccinated and debeaked and then are placed with individual growers for 9 weeks of feeding. After approximately 9 weeks they grow to the desirable slaughter weight and are trucked to a processing plant.

Pullet placements. To forecast the changes in egg sets the number of birds in the nation's breeding flock must be analyzed. This number can change because of changes in the number of pullets added to breeder re-

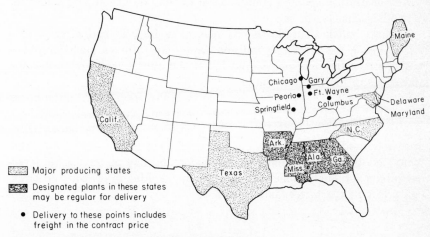

FIG. 21-3 Broiler production in the United States.

placement flocks, the number of breeders tested, and the number slaughtered. The laying age of the breeding flock consists of hens 7 to 15 months old.

A recent analysis[7] indicates that the dominant force behind the expansion or contraction of broiler supplies is the relation between revenues received, and feed and chick costs in any given year.

NATURE OF DEMAND

Demand for broilers, as measured on a per capita basis, has been increasing almost annually, as indicated by Table 21-5. For many years increased demand seemed to be accomplished primarily by lower average prices. Recent years, however, have witnessed continued per capita increases in consumption while average prices remain in a relatively narrow range. The willingness of the broiler industry to provide such increases probably stems from increases in volume per firm as economies of scale take effect and the ability to produce one pound of meat with much less feed.

Demand for broilers in general is a function of disposable income, prices of competing products, and seasonal factors.

NOTES FROM A TRADER—EGGS AND BROILERS

The complexity of interaction among all the factors that may effect supply and demand for egg and broiler futures at any given moment have been well documented.

For these reasons the trader should leave the assumption of heavy commitments to the trade.

Futures prices may respond to cash prices, which in turn are thin and quickly changeable. Futures prices may trade in wide swings with no immediately apparent changes in the basic supply-demand situation.

Facing, as he does, a relatively inelastic demand schedule, the trader is well advised to spend a good amount of time on developing a feel for impending changes in supply.

Because hatchery production is seasonally high in spring, prevailing prices during the preceding fall and winter are often a good forecaster of the size of the following spring hatch and subsequently of production and prices in the fall and winter.

Future supply of eggs may be affected by the relation between the prices of large eggs and smaller eggs. Large eggs come from larger birds and smaller eggs come from birds just beginning to produce. If large-egg prices are strong and smaller egg prices are weak, the trader should note that many new birds are presently in production and that an increase in large-egg production might come shortly, thereby resulting in pressure on large-egg prices in the foreseeable future.

---

[7] Fred Bailey, "Understanding the Iced Broiler Futures Market," *Commodity Year Book*, Commodity Research Bureau, New York, 1969, p. 40.

CHAPTER TWENTY-TWO

Currencies

INTRODUCTION

A massive market has existed for years in which foreign currencies are bought and sold for delivery in the future, frequently with no cash required until the transaction date. This is the "forward market" maintained by large banks in such world money centers as New York, London, Tokyo, Zurich, and Paris, in which hundreds of billions of dollars are exchanged annually over an elaborate telephone and wire network.

The market caters mainly to international companies, which use it to hedge their business operations against the risk of adverse swings in exchange rates. For instance, a concern owing a future payment coming due in a foreign currency can buy that currency at a set price in the forward market and thereby protect itself from the risk of the currency's rising in value before the payment date. Companies also sometimes speculate in the forward market under the guise of hedging.

Private citizens wanting to speculate in currencies generally are barred from the forward market, although banks occasionally will make exceptions for influential individuals. Although no laws prohibit private speculation, bankers say the Federal Reserve Board and central banks they deal with overseas exert informal pressure to prevent this sort of activity because of its potentially disruptive impact on exchange rates.

Futures contracts in foreign currencies began trading on the International Monetary Market (IMM) of the Chicago Mercantile Exchange in May 1972. The British pound, Mexican peso, Canadian dollar, German deutsche mark, Swiss franc, Italian lira, Japanese yen, and Dutch guilder are currently traded on that exchange.

HISTORY

A brief history and discussion of the world monetary environment should be helpful before discussing the specific contracts, the mechanics of trading, and factors that influence exchange rates. The following quote is excerpted from an address by Paul A. Samuelson, delivered at the IMM Monetary Conference in Chicago on February 24, 1972.

If the world were willing to play the rules of the game of the pre-1914 gold standard, there would still be need for dealers and banks engaged in foreign-exchange operations. Even with exchange rates free to fluctuate only within the narrow gold points set by the cost of transportation of gold, a middleman's function would be worthwhile. However, the extent of this function would be quite limited and there is no reason to expect that informal dealings between and among the public and the banks would not suffice. But the automatic gold standard died, if not in 1914, then sometime after 1929.

After World War II, the Bretton Woods system envisaged exchange rate fluctuations limited just about as severely as in the automatic gold standard case. The Bretton Woods system served the world well in the decades after 1944. However, economists are now agreed that *this system lacked sufficient exchange-rate flexibility.* Modern mixed economies simply will not enslave themselves to the dictates of the external balance of payments. Countries running a chronic surplus will not contrive domestic inflation at home in whatever excess is needed to restore balance-of-payments equilibrium. Nor will they deflate themselves at home by whatever degree is needed to restore equilibrium. What the authorities at Bretton Woods did not realize was how often and great would be the requirements for intermittent parity readjustments in a world of mixed economies subject to (1) differential rates of change of productivities, demands and tastes, and (2) differential degrees of internal cost-push or sellers' inflation. For some odd reason, the Bretton Woods founders thought that the exchange rates that happened to prevail after the war would somehow remain very near to the equilibrium pattern forever and ever. They did not realize that when their . . . pre-supposition would be demonstrating its own falsehood, the result would be massive one-way . . . avalanches of successful speculation that would have a self-fulfilling character in toppling pegged parities.

Actually, the first exchange rates under Bretton Woods were set in the wake of a war that was destructive to our allies and our former enemies. Hence in the last part of the 1940s the dollar was probably seriously under-valued. The sizable and widespread currency devaluations of 1949, coupled with Marshall Plan and other American aid programs and with our German and Japanese occupation programs, succeeded in gradually curing this under-valuation of the dollar. So miraculous was the sprint of advanced nations, just less affluent than the United States, and so extensive have been the Cold War security and aid expenditures of the United States and the direct foreign investments of our corporations, that gradually *the dollar became severely over-valued.* Since the escalation of the Viet Nam War in the mid-1960s, with its ensuing demand-pull and subsequent cost-push inflations, the degree of the dollar over-valuation sharply accelerated. By the late 1960s dollar over-valuation became obvious to everyone. Stopgap measures such as the tying of aid, controls on capital, interest-rate-equalization taxes, tariffs and quotas could not put off the *de facto* suspension of American gold payments (March 1967, when the two-tier gold system was finally established) or *de jure* suspension of gold convertibility by President Nixon on August 15, 1971.

The December 1971 agreement among the group of 10 finance ministers at the Smithsonian in Washington set central rates and widened the band within which currencies are free to fluctuate against the dollar or against official gold and paper gold (SDRs of the International Monetary Fund) to 2¼ percent (the previous rate was 1 percent) on each side.

Permitting exchange rates to fluctuate 2¼ percent above or below the official exchange rate—a total of 4½ percent, compared with the IMM cash margin requirement of approximately 2 percent of the value of the currency contract traded—has created a situation in which considerable gains or losses are possible. Even within the official currency fluctuation band the speculator can make a profit of more than 200 percent. Conversely, he can lose more than twice his cash margin. With the ever-present possibility of a currency revaluation gains or losses can be much greater.

Nearly 100 of these revaluations have occurred since World War II, some of them major. In 1972, for example, the Japanese yen rose 17 percent in value against the dollar, whereas the German deutsche mark climbed nearly 14 percent. With the recent moves toward greater exchange-rate flexibility many foreign-exchange experts foresee even more frequent changes in official currency parities.

MECHANICS

The mechanics of speculating on the IMM are best illustrated by a hypothetical trade. Assume that a speculator thinks the British pound is likely to rise in price in relation to the U.S. dollar before the end of the year. He could buy a contract for December delivery (on the IMM traders are able to choose from contracts maturing 1 to 18 months in the future) at $2.40 a pound, roughly the assumed official central rate. Although the full 25,000-pound contract would be worth $60,000, the speculator would be required to put up a cash margin of $2,000. Assume that by November the price of the pound has risen to $2.44 and the speculator sells the contract. His contract would then have risen in value to $61,000 from $60,000 giving him a gross profit of $1,000. After subtracting brokerage commissions of $45 he would have a net gain of $955 on an investment of $2,000. Had the price of the pound dropped instead to, say, $2.36, his contract would have de-

TABLE 22-1 SUMMARY OF MONETARY CONTRACTS

Ticker symbol	Currency	Contract size	Approximate U.S. dollars of one contract	Minimum fluctuations		Daily limit from previous close	
				Dollars per unit of currency	Dollars per contract	Dollars per unit of currency	Dollars per contract
BP	British pound	25,000 pounds	$ 60,000	$0.0005 (5 pts)	$12.50	$0.03	$750.00
MP	Mexican peso	1,000,000 pesos	$ 80,000	$0.00001 (1 pt)	$10.00	$0.00075	$750.000
CD	Canadian dollar	100,000 dollars	$100,000	$0.0001 (10 pts)	$10.00	$0.0075	$750.00
DM	German deutsche mark	250,000 deutsche marks	$100,000	$0.00005 (5 pts)	$12.50	$0.003	$750.00
SF	Swiss franc	250,000 francs	$ 82,000	$0.00005 (5 pts)	$12.50	$0.003	$750.00
IL	Italian lira	25,000,000 lire	$ 43,375	$0.0000004 (4 pts)	$10.00	$0.00000003	$750.00
JY	Japanese yen	12,500,000 yen	$ 47,375	$0.000001 (10 pts)	$12.50	$0.00006	$750.00
DG	Dutch guilder	125,000 guilders	$ 46,000	$0.00004 (4 pts)	$ 5.00	$0.006	$750.00

clined in value to $59,000, leaving him with a net loss of $1,045 after commission costs.

The relevant contract information for the eight currencies now traded is given in Table 22-1.

FACTORS WHICH INFLUENCE
MONETARY EXCHANGE RATES

The most important factor affecting sizable fluctuation in a country's exchange rates is the balance of payments—that is, the net inflow or outflow of its total currency transactions with other countries. These transactions alter the supply and demand for a specific currency. For the United States they include exports and imports of goods and services, investment by foreigners in this country or by U.S. citizens abroad, government transactions, aid, and grants. Table 22-2 shows these transactions in balance-sheet form.

The following example illustrates how exchange rates fluctuate whenever one currency is in greater demand than another. The currency's exchange rate rises or falls to encourage new supplies or encourage new demand for specific currency. Currency, however, has value only in terms of its buying power of goods and services; for example, Americans may buy pounds with their dollars to pay for a hotel room, a bicycle, or a computer. Britons may buy dollars with their pounds for some of the same reasons, because hotel rooms, bicycles, and computers can exist simultaneously in both countries. If the number of pounds wanted for dollars is equivalent to the dollars wanted for pounds, then buying and selling pressure are in balance and the exchange rate remains stable. If more pounds are wanted for dollars than dollars for pounds, then the pound will rise in relation to the dollar; that is, it will take more dollars to buy pounds. As the exchange rate increases in terms of dollars, American goods become cheaper to anybody holding pounds because they need fewer pounds to buy the same number of dollars. When the American goods become cheap enough in terms of pounds, pound holders will buy dollars with their pounds to buy

TABLE 22-2   U.S. BALANCE OF PAYMENTS

Claims by the United States against foreigners (increases demand for dollars by foreigners and tends to *increase* exchange rate of dollar vis-à-vis other currency)	Claims by foreigners against the United States (increases demand for other currency and tends to *decrease* exchange rate of dollar vis-à-vis other currency)
Exports of goods and services	Imports of goods and services
Foreign investment in the United States	Investments by U.S. citizens abroad
Net amounts received through U.S. official transactions	Foreign aid, grants, and expenditures by U.S. travelers abroad
Other amounts received from foreigners, including gifts, loans, or foreign travelers' expenditures in the United States	

the "cheaper" American goods. At that point pounds are being offered for dollars and the exchange rate for pounds sterling in terms of dollars declines.

The net of all transactions as described above and as shown in Table 22-2 is the balance of payments. Its two main components are the balance of trade and the flow of capital.

The balance of trade measures the difference between exports and imports of goods and services. It measures the relative balance between any two or more economies. A continued balance of trade deficit by one country with respect to one or more other countries is a signal that that country is operating inefficiently compared with the other countries. Its exports are hindered by high prices and its imports are buoyed by the relatively low prices of the other countries. This situation can become critical because valuable foreign exchange is lost and because demand for internal goods is tempered by imports thus slowing down production and economic growth. If this is allowed to continue in any country, its economy will tend to slow down as inventories build up and production drops. The usual remedy is to devalue its currency in terms of the currencies of other countries to make its exports more attractive and its imports more expensive.

The other part of the balance of payments is the capital flow which measures the movement of money for investment purposes. Americans buy pounds to buy English bonds or stocks; Germans buy dollars to buy American bonds or stocks. Sometimes the balance of trade and the capital flow accounts move in opposite directions. Until the fourth quarter of 1972 the net inflow of funds of other nations into the United States almost offset the continued balance of trade deficit. Changes in the capital flow statistics are quicker and more pronounced than changes in the balance of trade statistics. This has led to the term "hot" money as corporate treasurers, traders, and speculators move staggering sums of money around the world in search of the highest returns available.

One of the key indicators for anticipating shifts in capital flow and thus in the total balance of payments is the interest rate differential between countries. An interest rate differential between countries is an economic signal that funds are not being utilized efficiently. Tight funds in one country cause higher interest rates which indicate that additional funds are required there. This causes currencies to move between countries. As this happens the exchange rate rises in the higher interest rate country and declines in the lower interest rate country. Now, fewer funds are required in the higher interest rate country as its higher exchange rate causes exports to become more expensive. Therefore production will slow down, fewer funds will be needed, and interest rates will drop. Meanwhile, in the lower interest rate country more funds will be required as its exports, becoming cheaper, encourage a production increase. Therefore its interest rates will rise. Thus it can be seen that interest rates have a *long-term* tendency to approach "0" difference between any two countries. It can also be seen that the movement of funds between countries should not necessarily be given the negative connotation usually associated with such "hot" money. Artifically controlled interest rates (with which governmental authorities keep a country's interest artifically below where it would be, given free market conditions) can produce tremendous ripples in the currency exchange markets as an interest differential between any two countries continues to draw funds from the low interest rate country into the higher interest rate country.

Inflation can also be a key factor in the fluctuation of exchange rates. Basically, inflation is a rise in the price of goods and services with no associated rise in quality. It can be caused by a variety of factors, such as a rapidly increasing money supply, a lack of production capacity with the price of the factors of production being bid up, or by higher wage increases than productivity indicates. In any case, inflation usually places a country's currency in a soft position vis-à-vis other currencies as investment funds search for stronger markets and as its exports rise in price, all of which, of course, has a negative effect on the balance of payments.

Exchange rates are also influenced (especially in the short run) by political actions, seasonal change expectations, International Monetary Fund, central bank, or other international actions or agreements, and the relation between spot and forward exchange rates.

SOURCES OF INFORMATION

Some of the more important items carried on news wires and in newspapers, federal reserve bulletins, and economic newsletters, are balance of payments data, interest rates, economic news, and the forward and spot rates quoted by the world's financial centers.

Balance of payments data usually run 2 to 6 months behind actual events. Although they do indicate long-term trends, their value in short-term forecasting is limited. Trade balances, which are compiled only 1 to 2 weeks after the fact, are only the flow of *goods*. The figure does not include services or capital flows.

Interest rates are an up-to-date indicator of short-term trends in foreign exchange rates. Treasury bill rates are carried on the money wire and banks can also give quotes. Treasury bills of England, Germany, Italy, Switzerland, and Japan are not available to nonresidents but are an excellent indicator of the general level of short-term interest rates. Certificates of deposit are, as a rule, available to nonresidents. They, too, are good indicators of general interest rate levels.

An interest rate that has had increasing influence on exchange rates in recent years is that on Eurocurrencies. This relatively new term applies to currency held outside the country in which it was issued; for example, Eurodollars are U.S. dollars held in Europe by foreigners and foreign banks. Eurofrancs are French francs held outside France by other Europeans. Because these currencies are held outside a country, they do not come under various governmental restrictions on currency and are unaffected by monetary policy. They are relatively unrestricted deposits of money that anyone may borrow at the going interest rate.

Because the dollar is the base currency for international settlements, Eurodollars may be borrowed by anyone and in turn used to buy any currency. Lately they have been the source of funds for international speculators and arbitrageurs.

Eurodollars are a supply of dollars out of reach of the U.S. government but nevertheless have an effect on exchange rates via the laws of supply and demand. If the supply of Eurodollars is high, exchange rates for the dollar will be low and interest rates will be low. If demand for Eurodollars is high, interest rates will be high. Wire services carry the current interest rates for Eurodollars.

This rate on Eurodollars gives the trader an indication of the relative supply of dollars held by foreigners and may also reveal the demand for Eurodollars; for example, if interest rates on Eurodollars are up, this would indicate that either the supply was down or demand was up. Eurocurrencies have grown to the size at which forward rates may be at interest rate parity, basis the Eurocurrency interest rates, rather than the interest rates *inside* various countries.

Of a longer term nature are prime rates which are the interest rates banks charge their best customers. These rates can be determined by calling any bank that deals in foreign exchange.

News affecting the economy of a country can create short-term swings in exchange rates; for example, the Chancellor of the Exchequer of the United Kingdom in his 1972 budget speech announed a tax cut for British citizens totaling $3.0 billion. Naturally any announcement so bullish for a nation's economy was bound to be bullish for its exchange rate. Such was precisely the case. The British pound was nervous in anticipation of the Chancellor's speech and subsequently jumped significantly, both in the forward and spot markets.

Even less important news events can cause short-term swings. Well known and respected people in the field of international finance often cause minor fluctuations when they make public speeches.

The most up-to-the-minute source of trend information is carried on 24-hour-a-day news wires in the form of forward and spot rate quotes.

NOTES FROM A TRADER

Actions of governments affect the currency markets more than any others. These actions may be inconsistent and apparently illogical at times. They also often happen with little warning in order to give speculators as little chance as possible to profit by them (and perhaps because some decisions are made and implemented hastily). The most drastic moves involve devaluations or revaluations of currency, but there may also be important changes of interest rates or surprising announcements of policies that may affect trade balances. In addition, there can be a change in government itself which can cause a considerable rise or fall in confidence in a country's economic stability.

The volume of trading in most currencies seems to build quickly after periods of dullness and may then revert to dullness just as suddenly. Traders will turn their attention from one currency to another in accordance with real or anticipated financial news.

Traders, as usual, tend to concentrate their interest in the nearby months, but apparently many people take long-term positions in some of the currency markets that lead to an unusual difference in these markets compared with most others. Although volume is heavy in the nearby months, open interest is almost invariably concentrated in the distant months.

Spreading in currencies provides traders who believe that the economic fortunes of one country will gain or lose on those of another with interesting opportunities.

CHAPTER TWENTY-THREE

Metals: Copper, Silver, the Platinum Group, and Mercury

I shoot the hippopotamus with
bullets made of platinum,
For if I use leaded ones,
His hide would surely flatinum.

COPPER

INTRODUCTION

In the United States, futures trading in copper takes place on the Commodity Exchange, Inc., (COMEX) in New York from 10:15 A.M. to 2:10 P.M. (EST), except on Saturdays and Sundays and other times designated by the exchange. Contracts traded are January, March, May, July, September, October, and December.

The contract unit is currently 25,000 pounds with prices quoted in cents per pound, and the minimum price fluctuation is $5/100$ of a cent per pound ($12.50 per contract). The maximum daily fluctuation is 5 cents ($1,250 per contract) above or below the preceding day's close, with the exception of the spot month, in which there is no limit after the first notice day.

Copper has the reputation of reflecting relatively unstable prices over the short term when compared with most major metals, thereby offering the nimble trader good opportunities for profit.

FACTORS WHICH INFLUENCE COPPER PRICES

Copper is a world commodity and no single nation has a monopoly on its sources or production. However, labor negotiations involving major pro-

CHART 23-1

COPPER

WEEKLY HIGH, LOW & CLOSE OF NEAREST FUTURES CONTRACT — NEW YORK   IN CENTS PER POUND

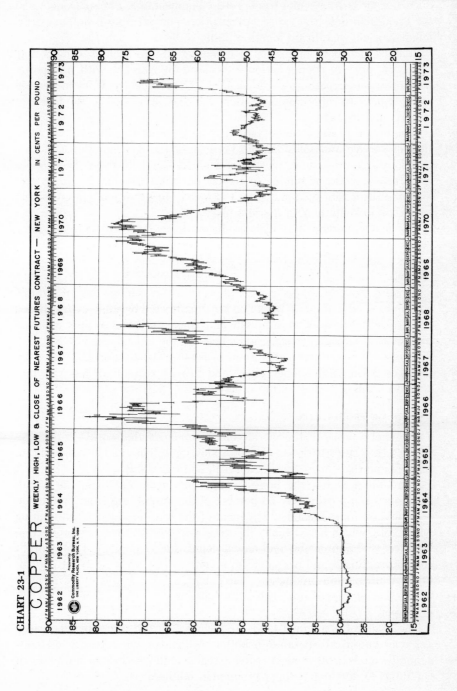

Prepared by
Commodity Research Bureau, Inc.
ONE LIBERTY PLAZA, NEW YORK, N.Y. 10006

ducers, such as Anaconda, Kennecott, Chuquicamata, Phelps Dodge, and the Rhodesian Selection Trust, affect prices considerably if output is curtailed over any significant length of time.

Political and social upheavals in emerging nations such as Zambia may affect the price of copper seriously because interference with transportation interrupts exports to world markets. Government policies in general affect copper consumption and price stabilization as well as the levels of imports and exports.

Copper companies compete largely among themselves in nonprice areas such as service and salesmanship because of the constant threat of substitutions from the steel, plastic, and aluminum industries. The copper industry has found by bitter experience that wildly fluctuating prices produce real user reticence and that it is much harder to win old customers back than to keep them in the first place.

The major method by which producers have been able to gain some control over prices is to increase production so that temporary demand bulges result in drawing from well-padded stockpiles rather than in panic bidding.

Because much of copper consumption is in the manufacture of durable consumer goods, copper tends to be greatly affected by trade cycles. Based on historical averages, the growth and consumption of copper will approximate 2 percent a year, or about one-half the annual rise in GNP. The difference in growth is related to an increasing substitution of other commodities during high copper prices and to requirements of less raw material to fulfill the needs of the economy.

NATURE OF PRODUCTION

Four general areas in the world contain much of the world's copper reserves—the western slopes of the Andes mountains in Chile and Peru, Zambia and the Congo, North America, and the USSR.

The United States, the largest copper-producing nation in the world, accounts for approximately 23 percent of the output. Zambian production accounts for approximately 12 percent of the total production, alternating with Chile, which has virtually the same percentage. Canada's production has increased appreciably and now accounts for 11 percent of the world's copper ore. Russia and her satellites account for approximately 14 percent of the world's mine production. See Table 23-1 for details of world mine production of copper ore. Table 23-2 lists the world smelter production of copper.

The grade of ore mined tends to decline over the years, but increased per man output attributable to better technology and recovery methods generally tends to offset higher ore-tonnage handling costs. Open-pit mining continues to dominate copper production methods.

TABLE 23-1 WORLD MINE PRODUCTION OF COPPER (CONTENT OF ORE) (IN THOUSANDS OF SHORT TONS)

Year	Australia	Canada‡	Chile	Finland	Japan	Mexico	Peru	Zambia	Norway	Sweden	South Africa	Philippines	United States‡	World Total*
1960	122.4	439.3	586.6	31.0	98.3	66.5	200.3‡	635.3	17.0	18.4	50.8	48.5	1,080	4,640
1961	107.1	439.1	607.2	37.5	106.3	54.4	218.3‡	633.5	15.4	20.0	58.0	57.2	1,165	4,850
1962	119.8	457.4	653.6	38.7	114.2	51.9	183.9‡	619.9	17.1	21.0	51.1	60.3	1,228	5,085
1963	126.5	452.6	660.0	37.4	118.2	60.7	198.5‡	648.2	15.7	18.4	60.8	70.2	1,213	5,088
1964	116.5	486.9	689.1	35.9	117.0	57.3	194.5‡	697.0	16.5	17.8	65.6	66.6	1,247	5,297
1965	101.2	507.9	667.9	33.2	118.0	60.9	198.8‡	766.9	16.3	17.4	66.6	69.2	1,352	5,549
1966	122.6	507.9	731.2	29.4	123.1	62.3	194.4	687.2	16.3	16.8	137.4	81.3	1,429	5,800
1967	102.7	613.3	731.8	32.2	130.9	61.7	212.4	729.8	15.9	16.8	165.4	94.2	954	5,552
1968	120.4	633.3	734.9	33.1	132.2	67.4	234.3	732.9	18.5	20.1	141.4	121.6	1,205	5,641
1969	144.5	573.2	770.6	36.5	133.5	72.9	219.1	824.7	23.3	27.7	139.1	144.9	1,545	6,224
1970	173.9	672.7	783.4	34.1	131.7	67.3	242.8	754.1	22.0	29.0	164.5	176.7	1,720	6,633
1971†	195.1	719.9	790.9	31.4	133.4	69.6	234.7	718.3	24.8	30.3	173.6	229.6	1,522	6,664
1972*		770	800				240	850					1,643	7,100
1973														

* Estimate.
† Preliminary.
‡ Recoverable.
SOURCE: Bureau of Mines.

TABLE 23-2 WORLD SMELTER PRODUCTION OF COPPER (IN THOUSANDS OF SHORT TONS)

Year	Australia	Zaire (Congo)	Canada	Chile	W. Germany	Japan	Mexico	Zambia	Peru	Sweden	USSR	South Africa	United States	World Total
1960	79.1	333.2	417.0	556.6	340.7	206.5	64.9	625.9	181.6	23.9	510	50.8	1,234	4,950
1961	70.0	325.4	406.4	578.1	335.5	232.7	52.7	627.1	200.7	22.8	610	57.6	1,207	5,120
1962	97.8	327.4	382.9	614.2	339.8	298.1	50.2	602.3	164.9	25.1	720	50.9	1,323	5,410
1963	99.1	299.1	380.1	614.4	333.8	325.4	59.2	635.9	173.6	50.1	660	60.1	1,297	5,447
1964	90.3	304.9	407.9	645.8	370.7	376.7	55.4	708.6	167.6	50.3	715	60.1	1,338	5,792
1965	82.2	318.1	434.1	633.4	393.9	403.1	59.5	755.0	174.9	55.7	770	60.0	1,434	6,105
1966	101.3	348.0	433.9	696.2	413.8	446.3	60.9	421.7	166.5	56.4	825	137.4	1,466	6,124
1967	79.3	351.5	499.8	695.4	392.1	518.0	60.0	679.8	177.7	52.6	880	140.5	862	5,923
1968	103.5	359.9	524.4	691.6	105.5†	604.5	61.5	733.2	205.2	51.5	570	150.7	1,265	6,051
1969	128.1	401.0	450.2	729.5	102.3	552.4	71.5	766.0	185.6	43.1	610.0	140.3	1,585	6,414
1970	123.1	425.0	538.7	725.5	93.0	668.1	65.7	753.1	195.0	40.4	630.0	159.5	1,641	6,731
1971*	157.9	444.7	526.5	705.3	91.1	728.9	68.3	698.2	183.8	38.0	680.0	167.9	1,500	6,736
1972*													1,710	

* Preliminary.

† Data beginning in 1968 consists only of blister and anode copper. Previously included refined metal.

SOURCE: Bureau of Mines.

NATURE OF UTILIZATION

The properties of copper that ensure its widespread consumption are its excellent electrical and heat conductivity, corrosion resistance, strength, ductility, and malleability. Copper may be alloyed readily with nickel and silver. Approximately one-half of all copper consumed is in electrical applications.

The United States is also the world's largest copper-consuming country. Although no data on copper consumption by end uses are available, Table 23-3 gives the utilization of refined copper in the United States for a number of years. Traditional markets for copper consume large tonnages, but there are exciting new uses developing as an outgrowth of industry-sponsored research. One of the most promising is in the desalinization of water, in which a plant of 1-million gallons' daily capacity using the flash evaporation method will require as much as 20 million pounds of copper or cupro-nickel tubing. Table 23-4 lists salient statistics related to production and utilization.

SEASONAL INFORMATION

The only relevant observation a trader can make regarding a seasonal price analysis in copper is the tendency for softness to appear sometime in June, which may carry into the July–August period. These periods of weakness may be sharp, as in 1966, when copper futures declined more than 20 cents a pound in this period.

NOTES FROM A TRADER

Copper futures can be extremely volatile. Such volatility is related to the international flavor of events that affect prices as well as the relatively thin open interest that marks the futures market for the red metal. Because of the thin market, orders should be placed each day before the opening if they are within range because frequently only a few trades take place at the extreme prices of the day. When copper is fluctuating wildly, it is a good day-trading vehicle because commissions are only approximately 15 points.

SILVER

INTRODUCTION

Demands from industry, particularly the electrical, electronics, and photo-film industries, have priced silver out of the market for use as coin of the realm. The fact that silver has neared the end of its considerable history as money in the United States has opened a relatively inactive market into an extremely volatile one.

For many years silver was a surplus commodity supported by the United States Treasury purchases of all domestic output at a price above market

TABLE 23-3 CONSUMPTION OF REFINED COPPER† IN THE UNITED STATES (IN THOUSANDS OF SHORT TONS)

Year	By-products						By class of consumer					Total consumption
	Cathodes	Wire bars	Ingot and ingot bars	Cakes and slabs	Billets	Other	Wire mills	Brass mills	Chemical plants	Secondary smelters	Foundries and misc.	
1960	90.7	859.4	108.6	137.9	145.6	7.7	828.8	486.5	1.0	8.2	25.4	1,349.9
1961	135.2	854.6	122.7	153.1	190.6	6.7	823.8	599.8	1.3	9.5	28.5	1,462.8
1962	127.6	956.0	124.4	184.3	199.6	7.8	922.9	636.1	1.5	9.5	29.7	1,599.6
1963	151.9	1,068.5	118.3	186.9	210.6	8.2	1,036.2	673.9	1.2	3.7	29.3	1,744.3
1964	137.1	1,131.1	143.1	184.4	220.7	9.0	1,097.5	690.4	2.2	4.7	30.5	1,825.3
1965	129.5	1,247.6	189.6	195.7	232.0	10.2	1,223.4	739.9	2.4	6.5	32.4	2,004.6
1966	196.0	1,396.0	259.0	234.3	264.0	10.6	1,370.8	928.5	2.3	19.7	38.6	2,360.0
1967	166.8	1,254.6	149.1	153.1	202.0	9.8	1,240.2	650.4	2.4	9.0	33.6	1,935.6
1968	164.5	1,191.7	169.6	122.4	221.6	10.5	1,189.3	652.5	1.6	6.4	30.6	1,880.3
1969	241.1	1,270.8	179.8	172.5	258.4	19.6	1,296.3	797.1	3.1	7.0	38.7	2,142.2
1970	247.0	1,275.8	145.7	157.1	202.0	15.7	1,338.7	660.6	2.2	7.0	34.7	2,043.3
1971*	309.4	1,236.9	118.3	154.8	182.3	17.7	1,324.9	655.8	1.5	6.9	30.4	2,019.5
1972‡	416.3	1,329.6	122.7	159.7	161.0	6.8	1,523.1	666.0	N.A.	6.9	N.A.	2,220.1
1973												

*Preliminary.

†Primary and secondary.

‡Estimate of 24,000 tons included in total.

SOURCE: Bureau of Mines.

TABLE 23-4 U.S. SALIENT STATISTICS OF COPPER (IN THOUSANDS OF SHORT TONS)

| | New copper produced | | | | | | Imports[c] | | Exports | | Stocks – Dec. 31 | | | Apparent consumption[f] | |
| | From domestic ores | | | From foreign ores[b] | Total new | Secondary recovered[g] | | | | | | | | | |
Year	Mines	Smelters	Refineries				Un-mfg.	Re-fined	Metal-lic[d]	Re-fined[e]	At producers	Re-fined	Blister and materials in solution	Primary refined	Primary and old copper[h]
1960	1,080	1,143	1,121	398	1,519	429	524	143	510	434	359	98	261	1,148	1,577
1961	1,165	1,162	1,181	369	1,550	411	458	67	483	429	285	49	236	1,237	1,648
1962	1,228	1,282	1,214	398	1,612	416	479	99	367	337	317	71	246	1,352	1,768
1963	1,213	1,258	1,219	377	1,596	422	539	119	345	311	304	52	252	1,423	1,845
1964	1,247	1,301	1,260	397	1,656	474	586	140	381	316	283	37	246	1,495	1,969
1965	1,352	1,403	1,336	376	1,712	513	523	137	379	325	281	35	246	1,526	2,039
1966	1,429	1,430	1,353	358	1,711	535	595	164	319	273	313	43	270	1,594	2,128
1967	954	841	847	286	1,133	483	649	331	221	159	247	27	220	1,320	1,803
1968	1,205	1,235	1,161	276	1,437	521	710	400	314	241	320	48	272	1,576	2,097
1969	1,545	1,547	1,469	274	1,743	575	414	131	241	200	320	39	291	1,683	2,258
1970	1,720	1,605	1,521	244	1,765	504	392	132	274	221	470	130	340	1,585	2,089
1971	1,522	1,471	1,411	181	1,592	445	359	164	263	188	378	75	303	1,623	2,068
1972[a]	1,643	1,669	1,616	193	1,809	478	416	192	238	181	339	57	282	1,838	2,068
1973															

[a] Preliminary.

[b] Also from matte, etc., refinery reports.

[c] Data are "general" imports; that is, they include copper imported for immediate consumption plus material entering country under bond.

[d] Total exports of copper, exclusive of ore, concentrates, composition metal, and unrefined copper. Exclusive also of "other manufacturers of copper."

[e] Ingots, bars, etc.

[f] Withdrawals from total supply on domestic account.

[g] From old scrap only.

[h] Old scrap only.

SOURCE: Bureau of Mines.

CHART 23-2

SILVER WEEKLY HIGH, LOW & CLOSE OF NEAREST FUTURES CONTRACT   NEW YORK

value. The Treasury bought approximately 3 billion ounces from 1934 to 1959 at an average price below 60 cents an ounce. The Coinage Act of 1965 eliminated the use of silver in dimes and quarters and reduced the silver content in half dollars from 90 to 40 percent. The results of this move lowered the use of silver in coinage to 54 million ounces in 1966 from 320 million ounces in 1965. On July 14, 1967, the Treasury halted its sales of silver at $1.2929 per fine ounce begun in 1963, and the white metal immediately soared to $1.87 an ounce in New York.

To prevent melting down old silver coins, which became profitable at $1.3824, a ban was issued. In addition, the Treasury minted more than 8 billion of the "clad" dimes and quarters between 1965 and 1967, which is almost two-thirds of the supply of the preceding 25 years.

In the middle of 1967 Congress authorized the Secretary of the Treasury to rule that an estimated $150 million of outstanding silver certificates were either destroyed, lost, or privately held and would not be presented for redemption. After June 24, 1968, any remaining certificates were no longer redeemable in silver.

In spite of these actions, the unexpectedly high demand for coinage and industrial needs led to inventory accumulation and hoarding. The gold crisis of 1968 exacerbated an already explosive demand, and prices for silver exceeded $2.50 per ounce. The gold crisis and devaluation of 1973 was much more explosive and drove the price of silver up to new highs.

Futures trading in silver in the United States takes place from Monday through Friday on the Commodity Exchange, Inc., (COMEX) in New York. Contracts traded are January, March, May, July, September, and December.

The contract unit is 10,000 troy ounces (10 bars), with price quoted in cents per pound and with a minimum price fluctuation of $1\%_{100}$ cent (10 points) an ounce ($10 per contract). The maximum daily fluctuation is 20 cents an ounce (2,000 points) above or below the preceding closing price, except during the spot month from the first notice day forward. However, the maximum permissible range between the high and low price of any one trading session is also 4,000 points. This constraint is removed only in the spot month on the last trading day.

Futures trading in silver in the United States also takes place on the Chicago Board of Trade. Contracts traded on that exchange include February, April, June, August, and October. The contract unit is 5,000 troy ounces (5 bars), one-half the size of the New York contract, and therefore the dollar value *per contract* of each tick or of the maximum daily fluctuation is also one-half that of the other contract. The minimum price fluctuation and the daily maximum price fluctuation *per ounce* are the same as that described above.

FACTORS WHICH INFLUENCE SILVER PRICES

Silver has been found in most countries of the world, and wide fluctuation in demand and price has marked its use and value. Before World War II world production comfortably exceeded consumption, but in the postwar years demand for silver outstripped production. The supply deficiency has been filled by drawing down stocks.

Even though the price of silver has risen substantially, dramatic increases in production are not expected. The rich silver ores which have yielded most of the world's silver are largely depleted, and today's reserves are contained in ores mined chiefly for other metals, principally copper, lead, zinc, and tin.

The discontinuance of silver coinage in such countries as Britain, Australia, and Canada will help fill the supply gap, but the most accessible source is the silver content in old United States coins, which contains an estimated 1.6 to 1.8 billion ounces of silver.

Apart from the singular supply-and-demand considerations relating to

TABLE 23-5 WORLD PRODUCTION OF SILVER, BY SELECTED COUNTRIES (IN MILLIONS OF FINE OUNCES (TROY OUNCES)

Year	Argentina	Australia	Zaire (Congo)	Bolivia*	Canada	Morocco	W. Germany	Honduras	USSR†	Japan	Mexico	Peru	United States	Yugoslavia	World Total†
1960	1.7	15.2	4.0	4.9	34.0	1.1	1.8	2.9	25.0	6.9	44.5	30.8	36.8	3.0	241.3
1961	1.4	13.1	3.5	3.9	31.4	0.9	1.9	3.5	25.0	8.0	40.3	34.2	34.8	3.5	236.9
1962	2.1	17.6	1.6	3.8	30.7	0.8	1.9	3.2	27.0	8.7	41.2	33.1	36.8	3.8	245.8
1963	1.94	19.64	1.10	4.87	29.84	0.77	2.07	3.16	28.0	8.81	42.76	35.20	35.24	3.79	250.0
1964	1.94	18.43	1.48	4.81	29.90	0.60	2.06	3.22	29.0	8.71	41.72	34.42	36.33	4.04	248.5
1965	2.29	17.28	1.54	4.11	32.27	0.60	2.02	3.67	31.0	9.99	40.33	36.47	39.81	4.15	257.4
1966	2.21	18.89	1.85	5.12	32.83	0.71	2.02	3.73	33.0	10.32	41.98	32.84	43.67	3.65	266.7
1967	2.58	19.84	1.84	4.52	37.21	0.77	2.04	4.01	35.0	10.80	38.27	32.11	32.12	3.08	258.2
1968	2.42	21.39	2.14	5.18	45.01	0.92	1.77	4.40	35.0	10.69	40.03	36.36	32.73	3.02	275.3
1969	3.11	24.46	1.90	6.01	43.53	0.86	1.68	3.91	37.0	10.81	42.90	35.89	41.91	3.82	295.7
1970	2.05	25.99	1.71	6.82	44.25	0.68	1.77	3.82	38.0	10.80	42.84	39.84	45.01	3.42	303.9
1971‡	2.05	21.62	1.80	5.37	46.02	0.81	1.80	3.64	39.0	11.29	36.66	38.40	41.56	3.35	298.8
1972†	2.12		1.80	5.66	47.00			3.80	40.0	10.00	32.48	40.00	37.23	3.58	301.1

* Exports
† Estimate.
‡ Preliminary.
SOURCE: Bureau of Mines; Handy & Harman.

silver, the policies of the United States in regard to its international balance of payments affect the prices of all the metal group, and silver prices react wildly to the varying level of the confidence the world has in the stability of the United States dollar.

NATURE OF PRODUCTION

Table 23-5 records world production of silver for a number of years. Canada, the United States, Peru, Mexico, and the USSR produce most of the world's silver. Because silver in recent years had been assigned the role of by-product of ores mined primarily for copper, lead, and zinc, labor unrest in any of the primary metal industries can lead to a disruption of silver production. Such was the case during the 1967 copper strike, when the United States Treasury sold approximately 2 million ounces of silver per week through the GSA.

There are substantial stocks of silver throughout the world, which have been estimated at more than 2 billion ounces. These sources include more than 1 billion ounces in the existing subsidiary coinage of the United States, an estimated 500 million in private hoards in India and Asia, and United States Treasury stocks and overseas subsidiary coinage. Figure 23-1 illustrates the sharp decline in the United States Treasury stocks in the post-

FIG. 23-1   U.S. Treasury silver stocks at close of year since 1945. (Daily statements of the U.S. Treasury.)

World War II years which has resulted in the halting of unrestricted sales at $1.2929 and a cutoff date for certificate redemptions.

NATURE OF UTILIZATION

Table 23-6 relates the recent history of world consumption of silver by country. The drastic decrease in world coinage consumption helped ease the tremendous production-consumption gap of 1965; however, the basic long-run problem remains. Comparison of Tables 23-5 and 23-6 shows that consumption of silver continues to outstrip production by a wide margin.

The United States is the largest user of silver. Table 23-7 shows the total U.S. consumption of silver by end use. Although use for coinage has declined, both industrial use and total consumption are increasing dramatically.

NOTES FROM A TRADER

The tone early in the trading session may be set by overnight events in the monetary field and the price action on the London exchange. Because of the changing international price system for gold and the inability of U.S. citizens legally to hold gold, trading in the metals, especially silver, has expanded tremendously, and prices tend to reflect changes in the price of gold in the free world. The market is marked by high volatility and relatively high margins. Limit-price moves are not unusual.

Of critical importance is a ruling affecting the trader long silver in a delivery month. The trader may not re-tender a notice of intention to deliver silver and is obligated to accept delivery.

PLATINUM GROUP

INTRODUCTION

The platinum group of metals also includes palladium, iridium, osmium, rhodium, and ruthenium. In addition to their decorative features and their resistance to tarnish, the platinum-group metals are efficient catalysts and enjoy numerous electrical applications. Smaller amounts are used for dental, medical, and jewelry purposes.

In the platinum group the trader may trade platinum futures and palladium futures. Platinum futures are traded on the New York Mercantile Exchange. Delivery months are January, April, July, and October. The unit of trading is a contract of 50 troy ounces (1 sheet or bar) with price quoted in dollars per ounce. The minimum price fluctuation is 10 cents an ounce (10 points), which equals $5 per contract. The maximum daily price range is $20 an ounce (2,000 points), of which 1,000 points may be above and 1,000 points below the preceding day's close. These limits are removed from the spot month on the last trading day.

Palladium futures are also traded on the New York Mercantile Exchange with delivery in March, May, June, August, September, November, and

TABLE 23-6 WORLD SILVER CONSUMPTION (IN MILLIONS OF OUNCES)

	Industrial uses								Coinage						
Year	Canada	France	W. Germany	India	Japan	United Kingdom	United States	World† Total	Canada	France	W. Germany	Japan	United States	World Total	World† Total
1960	4.3	13.0	40.2	1.5	21.6	16.5	100.0	224.6	7.5	12.2		4.6	46.0	103.9	328.5
1961	4.5	14.0	43.5	1.5	19.1	20.0	105.0	239.5	6.2	23.8		1.4	55.9	137.1	376.6
1962	4.8	13.5	41.8	1.5	19.6	20.0	110.0	258.5	10.9	13.7		1.4	77.4	127.6	386.1
1963	4.6	13.9	40.5	2.5	20.0	20.0	110.0	260.7	13.0	12.2		4.2	111.5	166.4	427.1
1964	5.0	14.8	46.3	12.0	20.0	23.0	123.0	299.2	13.7	10.7		17.3	203.0	267.1	566.3
1965	5.3	14.0	54.6	16.0	25.0	25.0	137.0	336.6	20.4	7.2		5.8	320.3	381.1	717.7
1966	5.8	14.7	48.2	16.0	31.5	25.0	150.0	355.1	14.4	8.7		9.0	53.8	129.5	484.6
1967	5.4	14.7	48.2	15.0	33.2	24.0	145.0	348.7	14.5	7.5		—	43.9	105.3	454.0
1968	5.1	18.0	50.0	16.0	36.2	23.0	145.0	350.8	9.9	2.9	4.3	—	37.0	89.3	440.1
1969	5.7	18.0	50.0	16.0	41.5	25.0	142.0	366.5	—	0.6	5.0	0.7	19.4	40.0	406.5
1970	6.0	16.0	48.2	16.0	46.0	25.0	128.5	357.1	—	3.7	14.0	—	0.7	33.6	390.7
1971	6.0	19.0	48.2	16.0	46.5	25.0	129.0	359.8	0.2	0.6	13.0	—	2.5	27.3	387.1
1972*	7.5	20.0	49.0	13.0	49.0	27.5	142.0	382.0	0.1	0.8	24.0	—	2.3	40.5	422.5

* Preliminary.

† Non-communist areas only.

SOURCE: Handy & Harman.

TABLE 23-7 U.S. CONSUMPTION OF SILVER BY END USE (IN THOUSANDS OF TROY OUNCES)

Year	Bear-ings	Brazing alloys and solders	Cata-lysts	Dental and medical	Electro-plated ware	Electrical and electronic products		Jewelry	Mirrors	Photo-graphic materials	Sterling ware	Misc.†	Total net industrial consump-tion	Coinage	Total consump-tion
						Batteries	Contacts and con-ductors								
1966	569	18,419	2,638	2,457	21,486	12,517	33,676	6,349	2,946	48,435	30,894	2,564	183,696	53,852	237,548
1967	600	15,391	5,847	2,690	17,897	11,405	26,777	5,751	2,174	50,306	30,269	1,925	171,032	43,851	214,883
1968	451	15,124	2,310	3,094	15,279	5,764	25,805	4,538	1,744	41,607	28,349	1,228	145,293	36,833	182,126
1969	481	16,549	4,081	1,591	12,706	3,799	34,555	3,011	1,510	41,380	20,291	1,592	141,546	19,408	160,594
1970	383	14,035	1,999	1,804	11,437	6,342	25,183	5,119	1,386	38,044	19,115	3,556	128,404	709	129,113
1971	355	12,085	1,730	1,485	10,909	5,631	27,954	3,447	1,112	36,073	22,729	5,636	129,146	2,474	131,620
1972*	346	11,951	3,430	1,984	12,566	5,594	32,941	4,871	1,226	38,251	27,163	6,379	146,701	2,284	148,985

* Preliminary.
†Includes silver-bearing copper, silver-bearing lead anodes, and ceramic paints.
SOURCE: Bureau of Mines.

CHART 23-3

PLATINUM WEEKLY HIGH, LOW & CLOSE OF NEAREST FUTURES CONTRACTS— N.Y. MERCANTILE EXCH. IN DOLLARS PER OUNCE

CHART 23-4

PALLADIUM   NEW YORK (WEEKLY HIGH, LOW & CLOSE OF NEAREST FUTURES)   IN DOLLARS PER OUNCE

December. The unit of trading is a contract of 100 troy ounces (4 sheets or ingots) with price quoted in dollars per ounce. The minimum price fluctuation is 5 cents an ounce (5 points), which equals $5 per contract. The maximum daily price range is $8 an ounce (800 points), of which 400 points may be above and 400 below the preceding day's close. These limits are removed from the spot month on the last trading day.

FACTORS WHICH INFLUENCE PLATINUM AND PALLADIUM PRICE LEVELS

Because an ample supply of the platinum-group metals is considered vital to the country's defense capabilities, government stockpiling activity is a potential price-making influence. Stockpiling is necessary because the United States produces only a small fraction of the supply of platinum-group metals it consumes and relies heavily on imports and secondary sources to satisfy its needs.

TABLE 23-8 WORLD PRODUCTION OF PLATINUM-GROUP METALS (IN TROY OUNCES)

Year	Philippines	Finland	Canada	Colombia‡	Ethiopia‡	Japan	South Africa	USSR	United States	World Total*
1962	–	–	470,787	14,100	180	3,244	305,600	800,000	28,742	1,625,000
1963	–	–	357,651	22,983	180	3,040	305,185	1,300,000	49,750	2,038,805
1964	–	–	376,238	20,647	180	4,074	604,135	1,500,000	40,487	2,545,761
1965	–	–	463,127	11,141	353	5,418	753,820	1,700,000	35,026	2,968,885
1966	–	–	396,059	15,671	318	8,227	783,400	1,800,000	51,423	3,055,098
1967	–	–	401,263	19,000	282	6,399	832,000	1,900,000	16,365	3,175,309
1968	–	–	485,891	22,280	349	6,436	864,000	2,000,000	14,793	3,393,749
1969	–	–	310,404	27,805	343	7,017	964,000	2,100,000	21,586	3,431,155
1970	1,230	645	482,428	26,358	273	7,906	1,502,800	2,200,000	17,316	4,238,956
1971†	2,459	600	475,169	25,610	217	8,826	1,253,200	2,300,000	18,029	4,084,110
1972*	7,522	650	399,000	26,000	248	9,899	1,803,000	2,350,000	17,112	4,613,431

* Estimate.
† Preliminary.
‡ Placer platinum.
SOURCE: Bureau of Mines.

Though consumption is small, the functions of the platinum group are critical in industry; hence, even at high prices, consumption continues to increase at a rapid rate.

In addition to the increase in consumption, precious metals have moved into the limelight as hedges against untoward international monetary developments. The devaluation of the British pound in November 1967 resulted in a steep price rise in platinum. Rising gold prices overseas and threats of dollar devaluation resulted in significant increases in both platinum and palladium in early 1968. Following the adoption of the two-tier gold-pricing system, both metals slumped. The 1973 sharp price rise in gold and the dollar devaluation again brought some large price increases. It appears that future price movements will continue to reflect the forces of supply and demand as well as world currency developments.

NATURE OF PRODUCTION

There has been a decided uptrend in world production of the platinum-group metals for a number of years, as shown in Table 23-8. The USSR accounts for more than half the world's production. South Africa is second with about a third of the total, and Canada completes the top three producers with more than 10 percent. Reserves in major producing countries are large and of good grade.

The United States accounts for less than 1 percent of the world's production, virtually all of which is obtained as a by-product of gold and copper refining.

NATURE OF UTILIZATION

The United States is the largest consumer of the platinum-group metals. In fact, consumption of platinum and palladium has been increasing rapidly in recent years. As Table 23-9 indicates, usage from 1960 to 1965 of both platinum and palladium increased dramatically to levels which have not been exceeded since that date.

In both platinum and palladium the United States produces only a small fraction of what it consumes. Therefore imports and secondary sources are relied on to satisfy needs. Table 23-10 shows some salient U.S. statistics of the platinum group.

Palladium is the lowest-priced of the platinum group, despite the fact that the United States consumes more palladium than platinum. Besides the fact that domestic supplies of palladium are larger, the price spread between platinum and palladium is caused by the fact that platinum acts as a more efficient catalyst. Substitution between the two metals is growing; however, in the petroleum industry, three times as much palladium as platinum is required to do a catalytic job.

The chief use (60 percent) of palladium is in the field of communications, where it is used to face electrical contacts. Platinum and palladium are

TABLE 23-9 PLATINUM-GROUP METALS SOLD TO CONSUMING INDUSTRIES IN THE UNITED STATES (IN THOUSANDS OF TROY OUNCES)

Year	Chemical Platinum	Chemical Others†	Electrical Platinum	Electrical Others†	Dental and medical Platinum	Dental and medical Others†	Jewelry and decorative Platinum	Jewelry and decorative Others†	Glass Platinum	Glass Others†	All platinum-group metals Platinum	All platinum-group metals Palladium	All platinum-group metals Other† metals	All platinum-group metals Total
1960	71.3	84.4	106.9	278.5	15.9	39.5	32.7	31.4	59.4	8.3	324.6	414.2	36.4	775.2
1961	72.0	100.4	87.4	359.0	16.5	49.0	30.2	23.3	35.2	2.5	283.1	508.0	32.1	823.2
1962	87.8	122.5	100.6	338.5	22.6	56.2	28.6	23.2	45.5	5.3	304.3	519.9	42.3	866.5
1963	156.4	134.2	110.6	341.8	18.9	43.5	33.0	24.7	57.9	13.3	424.3	526.5	52.4	1,003.2
1964	137.2	136.7	103.6	361.9	19.4	51.0	29.6	34.3	49.7	24.0	451.4	591.4	74.9	1,117.7
1965	131.6	176.9	106.8	444.4	26.5	50.8	35.4	29.2	19.8	11.7	411.4	717.1	58.2	1,186.7
1966	191.4	244.1	117.2	543.6	24.3	69.9	40.5	44.4	90.6	35.5	690.8	894.2	90.8	1,675.8
1967	159.4	220.2	99.7	340.4	24.6	55.6	33.3	31.6	45.2	11.7	633.9	621.1	79.3	1,334.3
1968	157.7	248.8	117.3	343.2	24.9	63.0	40.2	31.5	47.9	7.5	580.2	721.5	66.2	1,367.9
1969	175.4	248.3	112.6	445.3	22.3	54.1	36.2	32.3	63.4	14.9	516.7	758.7	83.1	1,358.5
1970	148.3	231.4	103.3	442.9	18.3	49.2	29.2	27.5	46.7	28.7	566.4	739.3	82.8	1,388.5
1971*	135.1	253.8	51.9	447.6	23.1	63.1	18.6	30.6	40.7	4.2	431.1	760.1	74.5	1,265.7
1972‡											542.9	876.0	140.9	1,559.8

* Preliminary.

† Iridium, osmium, rhodium, and ruthenium.

‡ Estimate.

SOURCE: Bureau of Mines.

Year	Production Crude[e]	Refinery New metal	Refinery Secondary metal	Stocks as of Dec. 31[a] Platinum	Stocks as of Dec. 31[a] Palladium	Stocks as of Dec. 31[a] Other	Stocks as of Dec. 31[a] Total	Imports for consumption	Value of imports (million $)	Exports Platinum[f]	Exports Other groups[c]	Exports Manufacturing[d] (thousand $)
1960	23,609	51,243	76,857	260,916	204,345	50,489	515,750	680,646	34.1	49,497	15,652	2,978
1961	43,248	79,453	85,971	255,654	244,910	54,881	555,445	884,463	36.8	41,385	20,460	2,983
1962	28,472	54,775	132,102	256,755	285,173	56,174	598,102	720,352	32.7	49,651	10,940	4,106
1963	49,750	80,208	117,099	320,601	315,756	63,218	699,575	1,003,608	50.4	51,236	11,776	2,256
1964	40,487	71,090	120,147	378,896	317,691	70,677	767,264	882,705	50.5	125,139	21,167	5,083
1965	35,026	61,723	108,525	422,804	427,450	76,119	926,373	1,172,643	69.0	72,925	30,172	2,515
1966	51,423	73,615	103,321	459,669	574,651	95,284	1,129,604	1,352,256	83.5	102,031	103,425	3,794
1967	16,365	29,663	365,799	327,919	460,624	80,668	869,211	1,321,278	92.1	161,585	118,267	2,378
1968	14,793	12,305	329,455	322,932	393,882	85,897	802,711	1,773,984	125.7	222,998	172,159	
1969	21,586	17,875	371,659	370,675	608,716	98,087	1,077,478	1,225,851	93.9	223,569	277,495	
1970	17,316	21,395	350,176	346,852	332,726	85,745	765,332	1,410,786	104.8	270,584	143,182	
1971[b]	18,029	32,102	278,175	445,821	316,126	94,837	856,784	1,302,740	93.7	320,842	83,768	
1972[g]		22,000	265,000	379,358	346,571	86,721	812,650	1,675,000		223,935	52,708	

[a] In hands of refiners, importers, and dealers.
[b] Preliminary.
[c] Palladium, rhodium, iridium, osmium ruthenium, and osmium metals and alloys, including scrap.
[d] Except jewelry.
[e] From crude platinum placers and byproduct platinum-group metals.
[f] Ore, concentrates. Bars, ingots, sheets, wire, sponge, and other forms, including scrap.
[g] Estimate.
SOURCE: Bureau of Mines.

heavily used in the chemical industry. Table 23-9 lists the consumption by industry of the platinum-group metals.

SEASONAL INFORMATION

Because prices of the platinum-group metals respond violently to international considerations not associated solely with supply and demand, seasonal price analysis is not relevant. The supply side is controlled by the USSR and South Africa; therefore the sources of production are beyond the control of the United States. The additions and deletions to and from strategic stockpiles is a highly variable market factor not related to seasonal considerations.

NOTES FROM A TRADER

Platinum and palladium sometimes take price cues from silver over the short run. The open interest in silver is many times larger than the combined open interest in platinum and palladium. Open interest in saladium eroded after an early flurry.

MERCURY

INTRODUCTION

Mercury prices are extremely volatile. Like the other metals discussed earlier, sudden changes in demand are a primary price-making influence. The history of futures trading in mercury, like that in palladium, is recent. A market was established in January 1967 on the Commodity Exchange, Inc., (COMEX) in New York. Contracts traded are March, May, July, September, and December.

The contract unit is 10 flasks of mercury weighing 76 pounds each, and the minimum price fluctuation is $1 a flask ($10 per contract), or 1 point. The maximum daily fluctuation is $50 (50 points) above or below the preceding day's closing price, and the maximum range allowed between the high and low prices of any day is $100 a flask (100 points).

FACTORS WHICH INFLUENCE MERCURY PRICES

In addition to its well-known applications in thermometers and coating for mirrors, mercury abounds in agricultural and industrial uses. Its compounds are employed extensively in insecticides, fungicides, and bactericides, pharmaceuticals, the control of slime in pulp and paper mills, protective paints, precision casting, and batteries. Because of the broad demand base, mercury consumption has a tendency to correlate well with general business conditions (gross national product) in the United States.

Data coverage is lacking for much of the mercury world and revisions of facts available are common. The market may be influenced by buying for or selling from government stockpiles or by setting price floors by Spain and Italy, the major world producers.

CHART 23-5

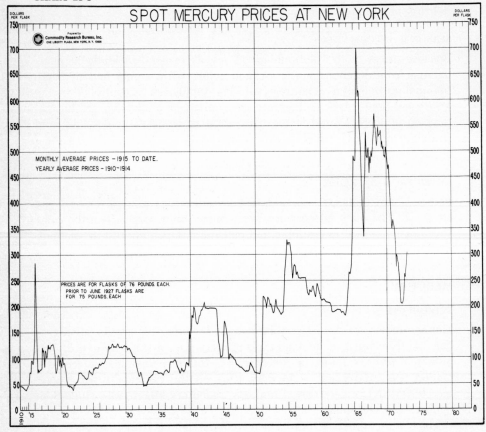

SPOT MERCURY PRICES AT NEW YORK

MONTHLY AVERAGE PRICES – 1915 TO DATE.
YEARLY AVERAGE PRICES – 1910–1914

PRICES ARE FOR FLASKS OF 76 POUNDS. EACH.
PRIOR TO JUNE 1927 FLASKS ARE
FOR 75 POUNDS. EACH

Demand must be strong and prices kept high over a lengthy period to influence a significant increase in supply. Rapid rises over the short run do not bring out rapid supply increases.

Table 23-11 shows some salient statistics for mercury in the United States.

NATURE OF PRODUCTION

Mercury is produced from cinnabar, the red sulfide, whose important deposits are limited to a few areas in the world, as shown in Table 23-12. The largest mercury mine in the world is located in Spain, which has produced more than 7 million flasks since the seventeenth century.

Mercury is mined by both underground and surface methods. About 90 percent of the United States production is underground. The metal is separated from the ore by furnace heating and condensation of the vapor. Handling the vapor, which is poisonous, requires safety precautions, so that high fuel and labor costs make the treatment of low-grade ores uneconomical.

TABLE 23-11 SALIENT STATISTICS OF MERCURY IN THE UNITED STATES [IN FLASKS (76 POUNDS EACH)]

Year	Ore treated (1,000 short tons)	Mercury produced† Flasks	Mercury produced† Pounds per ton of ore	Production Mine	Production Secondary	Stocks, Dec. 31 Producers	Stocks, Dec. 31 Consumers and dealers	Stocks, Dec. 31 Total	Exports	Total	U.S. imports (for consumption) from Canada	Italy	Mexico	Spain	Yugoslavia
1960	258.1	33,106	9.7	33,223	5,350	2,561	17,200	19,761	357	19,488	20	3,420	2,419	12,464	900
1961	262.1	31,633	9.2	31,662	8,360	2,033	15,500	17,533	285	12,326	24	2,073	3,023	6,544	355
1962	146.5	26,228	13.6	26,277	5,800	1,224	13,700	14,924	224	31,552	61	10,501	7,618	9,826	3,276
1963	113.5	19,101	12.8	19,117	10,520	1,581	10,600	12,181	187	42,872	150	8,474	4,292	19,950	4,459
1964	149.9	14,115	7.2	14,142	24,519	708	16,654	17,362	188	41,153	538	5,236	1,230	24,344	3,953
1965	339.1	19,353	4.3	19,582	46,670	1,432	18,954	20,386	7,543	16,238	32	1,203	1,290	10,995	1,101
1966	321.1	21,993	5.2	22,008	16,400	1,976	18,100	20,076	357	31,364	349	13,942	6,030	6,115	3,277
1967	439.8	23,767	4.1	23,784	22,150	757	17,520	18,277	2,627	24,348	391	4,091	1,234	13,470	3,085
1968	434.2	28,857	5.1	28,874	34,380	1,059	21,848	22,907	7,496	23,246	5,626	252	1,928	12,900	1,171
1969	432.6	28,552	5.0	29,640	13,650	2,920	19,772	22,692	507	31,924	15,546	5,041	7,398	2,602	831
1970	424.5	26,795	4.8	27,296	8,051	3,861	12,693	16,554	4,653	21,972	17,872	1,101	920	2,002	—
1971*	261.7	17,188	5.0	17,627	16,666	4,867	12,133	17,000	7,232	28,449	18,198	250	4,786	2,152	420
1972‡				6,296	12,598	3,824	10,025	13,849	400	29,100	13,800	—	5,400	1,100	1,400

*Preliminary.

†Excludes mercury produced from placer operation and from clean-up activity at furnaces and other plants.

‡Estimate.

SOURCE: Bureau of Mines.

TABLE 23-12 WORLD PRODUCTION OF MERCURY [IN FLASKS OF 34.5 KILOGRAMS (76 POUNDS)]

Year	Yugo-slavia	Peru	Philip-pines	Chile	China*	Canada	Turkey	Italy	Japan	Mexico	Spain	Tunisia	United States	USSR*	World Total
1960	14,069	3,034	3,041	2,876	23,000	—	1,339	55,492	5,791	20,114	53,369	166	33,223	25,000	242,000
1961	15,954	3,001	3,167	1,509	26,000	—	1,881	55,376	5,437	18,101	51,202	54	31,662	25,000	240,000
1962	16,273	3,481	2,767	791	26,000	—	2,687	54,506	4,199	18,855	52,798	—	26,277	35,000	245,000
1963	15,838	3,092	2,651	613	26,000	—	3,042	54,448	4,668	17,202	56,954	—	19,117	35,000	239,652
1964	17,318	3,275	2,496	267	26,000	—	2,615	57,001	4,972	12,561	78,322	87	14,142	35,000	255,133
1965	16,419	3,117	2,384	435	26,000	—	2,755	57,320	4,689	19,203	74,661	714	19,582	35,000	267,873
1966	15,896	3,166	2,443	96	26,000	—	3,420	53,549	4,846	22,104	70,054	254	22,008	40,000	264,994
1967	15,890	3,135	2,611	184	20,000	—	4,147	48,066	4,617	14,417	49,227	292	23,784	40,000	232,073
1968	14,794	3,132	3,544	513	20,000	5,700	4,670	53,317	5,084	17,202	56,943	309	28,874	45,000	259,694
1969	14,330	3,592	3,478	286	20,000	21,200	6,544	48,733	5,613	22,500	64,862	244	29,640	45,000	289,267
1970	15,461	3,125	4,648	388	20,000	24,400	8,592	44,382	5,170	30,265	45,543	100	27,296	47,000	283,816
1971†	16,593	3,066	5,020	502	26,000	18,500	10,460	42,613	5,564	35,390	50,851	340	17,883	48,000	298,552
1972*	16,419	3,066	3,341	500	26,000	14,600	11,000	42,120	5,172	22,510	60,500		7,286	50,000	279,508

* Estimate.
† Preliminary.
SOURCE: Bureau of Mines.

The high cost of production in the United States is evident in the fact that the supply of mercury could be significantly expanded at the $1,000-per-flask level. It is estimated that there would be a 2- to 4-year lag from increased prices to subsequent increased supply. In Spain, where much production is of the lower cost open-pit variety, reaction to increased demand is swift.

The United States is not self-sustaining in mercury production, in spite of efforts by the Office of Minerals Exploration to grant loans as high as 50 percent on exploration costs. Therefore secondary mercury production is a significant percentage of the domestic supply (Table 23-11). Almost all mercury can be reclaimed from cells, boilers, and electrical apparatus.

Mercury has been designated a critical material for stockpiling. Imports are derived from Italy, Spain, and Mexico.

NATURE OF UTILIZATION

Mercury is the only metal that is liquid at ordinary temperatures. The use of mercury electrolytic cells for the production of chlorine and caustic soda has been a vital expansive force in consumption. Table 23-13 details the domestic uses of mercury for selected years.

Large start-up quantities of mercury (as many as 1,000 flasks per 100 tons per day of chlorine capacity) are required for each new chlorine plant (now 70 in the United States), and it is estimated that replacement demand amounts to 5 to 10 percent of the initial installation. If the additions to chlorine capacity in the United States continue in this decade as they did in the last, the 6½ percent annual increase will result in a high demand for mercury cells. However, the chemical industry is sensitive to general business conditions, and any general slowdown could affect capital expenditures significantly.

SEASONAL INFORMATION

Sudden supply or demand changes follow no seasonal price patterns, and the major sources of supply are nondomestic, hence beyond U.S. government control.

NOTES FROM A TRADER

Apart from the usual warning of volatility, the mercury futures trader must beware of wide differences between the bid and ask, both of which might prove to be nominal.

More than in other markets, the trader must sell on rallies and buy on declines because the open-interest and volume averages are not high.

SOURCES OF INFORMATION—METALS

The basic source of information for the metal trader is the Federal Bureau of Mines, which operates within the U.S. Department of the Interior.

Copper information includes monthly and annual data on mine produc-

TABLE 23-13 MERCURY CONSUMED IN THE UNITED STATES (IN FLASKS)

Year	Agri-culture	Amal-gama-tion	Catal-ysts	Dental prepara-tion	Elec-trical apparatus	Electro-lytic prepara-tions	General labora-tory use	Industrial and control instru-ments	Paint Anti-fouling	Paint Mildew proofing	Paper and pulp manufac-turing	Pharm-aceut-icals	Other	Grand Total
1966	2,374	248	1,932	2,133	17,638	11,541	2,217	7,294	140	8,789	612	232	16,359	71,509
1967	3,732	219	2,489	2,386	16,223	14,306	1,940	7,459	152	7,026	446	283	12,856	69,517
1968	3,430	267	1,914	3,079	19,630	17,453	1,989	7,978	392	10,174	417	424	8,275	75,422
1969	2,689	195	2,958	2,880	18,490	20,720	1,936	6,655	244	9,486	558	712	9,134	77,372
1970	1,811	219	2,238	2,286	15,952	15,011	1,806	4,832	198	10,149	226	690	5,858	61,503
1971*	1,477	N.A.	1,141	2,387	16,938	12,262	1,809	4,871	414	8,191	2	682	2,300	52,475
1972†	1,835			2,550	14,630	11,491		5,874		8,188			5,107	53,200

* Preliminary.
† Estimate.
SOURCE: Bureau of Mines.

tion of recoverable copper and on stocks, production, consumption, and shipments of copper sulfate. Consumption of refined copper and scrap by major industry classes is reported monthly. Data on consumption by geographic locations as well as by end uses are not available. Imports and exports of copper are obtained by the Bureau of the Census. World production figures are published by the American Bureau of Metal Statistics and the British Bureau of Non-Ferrous Metal Statistics.

Silver statistics on refinery production and on domestic and foreign consumption are compiled by the Bureau of the Mint, and data on foreign trade in silver are supplied by the U.S. Department of Commerce. The U.S. Treasury Department publishes data on monetary silver stocks and coinage silver in circulation in monthly bulletins. The Bureau of the Mint gives "Transaction Statements" on stocks, acquisitions, sales, and withdrawals of silver for coinage.

Platinum-group information, which is gathered and compiled by the Bureau of Mines, includes domestic mine production, recovery of refined metals from both new and secondary sources, sales to consuming industries by metals and uses, and dealers' stocks. Data on imports and exports are supplied to the Bureau by the Department of Commerce.

Mercury information on production, shipments, and stocks is supplied to the Bureau of Mines on a monthly and annual basis by domestic producers. Quarterly data on consumption are obtained from consumers by the Bureau, as are data on the stocks of mercury at plants and in transit. Brokers, dealers, and importers furnish quarterly reports that show receipts of mercury from abroad and purchases of domestic mercury. United States imports and exports of mercury are obtained by the Bureau of the Census and by the Department of Commerce.

Other extremely useful general information includes the following:

1. The *Minerals Yearbook,* published by the U.S. Bureau of Mines, Washington, D.C. 20240.

2. *Mineral Industry Surveys,* published monthly by the U.S. Bureau of Mines.

3. The *Engineering and Mining Journal,* published monthly by the McGraw-Hill Book Company, 1221 Avenue of the Americas, New York, N.Y., 10020.

CHAPTER TWENTY-FOUR

Sugar, World and Domestic, and Coffee

SUGAR, WORLD AND DOMESTIC

INTRODUCTION

A century and half ago sugarcane was king of commerce. To England, its holdings in the Antilles represented more wealth than its 13 colonies, and sugar was the most important trade commodity. In France, where Napoleon ruled, frustration over the English blockade of sugarcane imports resulted in the Emperor's decree that 70,000 acres of sugar beets be planted to help make that country self-sufficient.

Only a few years before Napoleon's decree a process was developed for extracting sugar from the white beet. The use of this previously unknown sugar source spread quickly, and by 1840 beet production overtook cane production and remained in the lead during most years until World War I. Destruction caused by both World War I and II cut back beet planting severely, but later increases in the price of world sugar encouraged replanting. The resurgence of beet production, superimposed on high cane output, ushered in years of depressed prices.

The competition between beet and cane sugar has resulted in the division of the sugar world into sheltered trading areas. About two-thirds of the

CHART 24-1

WORLD SUGAR   WEEKLY HIGH, LOW & CLOSE OF NEAREST FUTURES CONTRACT   N.Y. COFFEE & SUGAR EXCH.   IN CENTS PER POUND

Prepared by
Commodity Research Bureau, Inc.
ONE LIBERTY PLAZA, NEW YORK, N.Y. 10006

world's trade in sugar takes place under arrangements that tend to minimize price fluctuations. In the United States, for example, sugar imports are controlled under the "Sugar Act." England has a "Preferential Commonwealth System," and the French equivalent is labeled an "Arrangement with Associated Territories." Controls within these various systems are administered by way of import quotas, export quotas, preferential markets, sliding-tax systems, guaranteed prices, and other contrivances.

The unprotected, or free, sugar market accounts for the remaining third of the total world supply and is known as "world sugar." Prices for such "free" market sugar show much more variation than prices in the controlled markets.

Sugar futures are actively traded on the New York Coffee and Sugar Exchange. Two contracts are traded; the #11 contract is concerned with world sugar, and the #10 contract, with domestic sugar. World sugar trading contracts are September, October, March, May, and July. Domestic sugar trades the same contracts plus November. The contract traded for both world and domestic sugar is 50 long tons, or 112,000 pounds. Price

CHART 24-2

DOMESTIC SUGAR WEEKLY HIGH, LOW & CLOSE OF NEAREST FUTURES CONTRACT N.Y. COFFEE & SUGAR EXCH. IN CENTS PER POUND

is quoted in cents and hundredths of a cent a pound, with the minimum fluctuation being $\frac{1}{100}$ (0.01) cent a pound (1 point), or $11.20 per contract. The maximum allowable daily range is 200 points (2 cents) a pound, with a maximum fluctuation of 100 points (1 cent) above or below the preceding day's close. Both limits are removed from the spot month on the last trading day.

World sugar is also traded actively in London at the United Terminal Sugar Market Association. Because London quotes are available before the U.S. sugar markets are open, the price equivalents in Table 24-1 may be used by the trader as a convenient reference.

FACTORS WHICH INFLUENCE PRICES

The price level of sugar is affected by many factors, one of the most important of which is the level of income in a given country. Although sugar is a relatively cheap and highly concentrated form of food energy, it has traditionally been considered a luxury. Millions of people still consume only

TABLE 24-1 LONDON—NEW YORK SUGAR PRICE
EQUIVALENTS (AT 1 POUND STERLING =$2.40
EXCHANGE RATE)

London* (pounds sterling per long ton)	New York,† (cents per pound)	London (pounds sterling per long ton)	New York (cents per pound)
10	1.07	135	14.46
15	1.61	140	15.00
20	2.14	145	15.54
25	2.68	150	16.07
30	3.21	155	16.61
35	3.75	160	17.14
40	4.29	165	17.68
45	4.82	170	18.21
50	5.36	175	18.75
55	5.89	180	19.29
60	6.43	185	19.82
65	6.96	190	20.36
70	7.50	195	20.89
75	8.04	200	21.43
80	8.57	205	21.96
85	9.11	210	22.50
90	9.64	215	23.04
95	10.18	220	23.57
100	10.71	225	24.11
105	11.25	230	24.64
110	11.79	235	25.18
115	12.32	240	25.71
120	12.86	245	26.25
125	13.39	250	26.79
130	13.93	255	27.32
		260	27.86

* Basis Commonwealth sugar, CIF United Kingdom.
† Basis selected raws, port of origin, FOB and stowed or in suitable port warehouses.

Converting London Prices to New York Equivalents
Two possible London
  quotes in pounds sterling
  per long ton . . . . 25.00 and 25.10
1. Multiply by $2.40. . . . . . $60.00   and $60.24/ton
2. Divide by 2240 lb . . . . . $0.02678 and $0.02689/lb
3. Round to approximate
  New York equivalent . . . 2.68 and 2.69¢/lb

1. 1 pound sterling = $2.40
   (approximately)
2. 1 long ton = 2,240 lb

a fraction of the approximately 100 pounds per capita consumption of wealthier countries like the United States.

Another dominant factor in world prices is the size of world sugar stocks. An increase in stocks of world sugar, as recorded on September 1 of each year (the beginning of the season), indicates that supplies are more than adequate to offset demand at a given price level. Frequently a significant reduction in world sugar stocks leads to subsequent price increases. Production and demand for a given year play important roles, too; it is significant, however, that reductions in September 1 stocks tend to precede dynamic bull markets.

Increased demand for sugar is ordinarily a gradual affair, averaging about 3 percent annually. The U.S.-Cuban schism in 1961 led to the shift to Soviet bloc destinations of millions of tons of sugar, only a small portion of which was reexported. Excess capacity in the Soviet refining industry was used to process most of the sugar for domestic consumption, thereby resulting in a major net addition to world absorption.

The effect on world demand of a change in the wholesale price of raw sugar is likely to be small because retail prices reflect raw-sugar price changes only slightly, owing to the high tax element in the price structure. Demand, then, is fairly inelastic to changes in wholesale raw-sugar prices.

An assessment of the policies and practices of various regulatory agencies is basic to an understanding of the sugar market. Because of the high percentage of world sugar supply that is insulated from the free market, there is a tendency for world production to outrun world demand. Such a situation leads inevitably to the effort to cope with subsequent marketing problems by international agreement. One agreement was initiated by the International Sugar Council but lapsed in 1961 when participating countries were unable to come to terms, particularly on the size of the Cuban quota. The termination of international quotas does not seriously affect approximately two-thirds of the world's sugar trade, which is focused in the sheltered areas mentioned earlier.

Finally, several economic variables affect sugar prices, some of which are the indicated acreage, yields, and weather in key sugar-producing countries. Futures may also influence the bargaining position of major buyers and sellers.

SOURCES OF INFORMATION

1. *Sugar Reports. Sugar Reports* is issued monthly by the Agricultural Stabilization and Conservation Service of the Department of Agriculture. Market reviews, world statistics, and United States statistics are presented.

2. *Foreign Agricultural Circular.* This is issued by the Foreign Agricultural Service of the U.S. Department of Agriculture and contains statistics and general comment on world production and stocks.

3. *F. O. Licht's International Sugar Report.* This authoritative report covers daily and bimonthly statistics on the world sugar economy. Published by F. O. Licht, K. G. 2418 Ratzeburg/Schleswig-Holstein, P. O. Box 90, West Germany.

4. *International Sugar Council Statistical Bulletin.* This statistical bulletin is published by the International Sugar Council, 28 Haymarket, London, S. W. I., England.

5. *Crop Production.* Published monthly by the U.S. Department of Agriculture, this report contains current estimates on beet and cane production.

6. *New York Coffee and Sugar Exchange, Inc., Weekly Review.* The weekly review contains daily data on futures trading and the latest domestic statistics.

NATURE OF PRODUCTION

Any discussion of sugar must deal with the end product of two different plants—sugarcane and the sugar beet. Sugarcane is a tall, bamboolike grass which is grown in tropical and semitropical regions. It is harvested approximately 18 months after planting and proceeds to issue new shoots yearly for perhaps a decade. In the United States the growing season for sugarcane varies from as short as 12 months in Louisiana to as long as two years in Hawaii. Sugarcane's rival is the white sugar beet, which is generally sown in the spring and harvested in the fall. Both cane and beets are subject to disease and a total of more than 40 insect pests. The leafhopper in Hawaii has caused a decrease in cane yields as high as 80 percent over three successive crops.

Cane harvesting occurs at different times of the year in different areas of the world. An unusual amount of rain at harvest time may reduce the cane sugar yield. Cane accumulates the greatest percentage of its sugar in its last period of growth, and once mature it must be quickly harvested to ensure maximum yield.

A good sugarcane harvest will result in an average of 20 tons per planted acre. If the average sugar content is 14 percent, 2.8 tons of raw sugar will be harvested per acre. Comparable figures for beets are 12 tons of topped beets per acre with a 15 percent sugar content, from which 1.8 tons of raw sugar per acre are produced.

The harvested beets and cane must submit to a great deal of complicated processing before becoming raw sugar and an article of commerce. The main steps are extraction, purification, evaporation, crystallization, and centrifuging. Raw sugar is further refined by means of a long series of processes. The growing, processing, and refining of both beet and cane sugars require significant capital expenditures.

Sugar is being planted or harvested continuously somewhere in the world, but there are significant seasonal variations. In the spring season, the time of world beet plantings, preliminary estimates are made of the size of the sugar crop. As the year progresses cane plantings and harvestings become known and the picture becomes more complete. Weather is a factor as the growing season progresses.

Table 24-2 lists world production of centrifugal sugar for a number of years. The trader should center his attention on centrifugal sugar, because it accounts for more than 85 percent of world production and virtually all the world's trade. "Noncentrifugal" sugars are produced by another process and are consumed where they are grown.

The United States grows both sugar beets and sugarcane. Because the climate is chiefly temperate, beet planting predominates, and only in the southernmost states and Hawaii is sugarcane planted in any quantity. Sugarcane does well on the coasts of Louisiana, where there is a moist sea breeze and tropical temperatures, and beets thrive in Colorado, where there are moderate temperatures and a definite annual spring-fall cycle.

NATURE OF UTILIZATION

The world demand for sugar has been increasing at the rate of about 3 percent a year. The largest sugar consumers are not the largest producers. Table 24-3 summarizes centrifugal sugar imports by country for a number of years. The United States, the USSR, England, and Japan account for about 60 percent of the sugar imported annually.

Because two-thirds of the world demand for sugar takes place under arrangements that tend to minimize price fluctuations, internal controls are important price-making influences. The U.S. Domestic Market is an excellent example of such regulation. As Table 24-3 indicates, the United States, apart from trade with its territories, imports just under 5 million metric tons of sugar each year. Under the "Sugar Act," the Secretary of Agriculture is empowered to set import quotas for selected countries. In most years the price offered is a substantial premium over the current world price. In years of limited supplies and high prices, then, the United States is assured of an ample supply of sugar at the established price. In general, countries that have been granted quotas are content with this arrangement, knowing that when sugar prices decline they will have access to a stable market at a reasonable price. The proof of the efficacy of this arrangement lies in the relative stability of domestic sugar prices in years like 1963 and early 1964, when the sixfold increase in the price of world sugar resulted in a doubling of the domestic price.

Long-term Food and Agricultural Organization (FAO) projections indicate a slight decline in the consumption growth rate in the long run as more countries approach a stable "saturation" level. In countries of low to modest per capita consumption rapid growth in usage will continue, but it will be met largely by local production.

ECONOMIC RELATIONSHIPS

Price action in world sugar futures is extremely difficult to predict because of the repercussions of international tensions, structural changes in the pattern of international tade, and threats to currency stability. A good starting point, however, invariably revolves around total supply and demand figures for a number of years. These figures are presented in Table 24-4, beginning with the crop year 1961–62. Stocks of sugar each year, plus production, provide the total supply. Figure 24-1 shows the relationship between total supply as a ratio of the preceding year's disappearance in thousands of short tons (x axis) to the weekly Wednesday high price reached by the September futures contract of world sugar from April 1 to the end of the contract. The scatter which is considerable indicates a low correlation

TABLE 24-2 WORLD PRODUCTION OF SUGAR (CENTRIFUGAL SUGAR—RAW VALUE) (IN THOUSANDS OF SHORT TONS)

Crop Year	Australia cane	Brazil cane	Cuba cane	Hawaii cane	India cane	Indonesia cane	Philippines cane	Poland beet	Puerto Rico cane	United States Beet	United States Cane	USSR beet	Mexico	France	World total all
1960–61	1,504	3,791	7,459	1,092	4,042	745	1,451	1,650	1,110	2,450	630	6,600	N.A.	N.A.	60,050
1961–62	1,512	3,934	5,308	1,120	3,693	709	1,618	1,808	1,009	2,404	858	7,170	1961–65	1961–65	56,989
1962–63	2,000	3,576	4,211	1,101	2,979	648	1,714	1,464	990	2,598	853	6,600	Av.	Av.	54,895
1963–64	1,883	3,620	4,400	1,179	3,470	725	1,856	1,570	989	3,086	1,184	6,475			59,919
1964–65	2,132	4,152	6,600	1,218	4,285	715	1,767	1,975	897	3,332	1,147	11,270	(2,043)	(2,225)	72,567
1965–66	2,187	5,324	4,950	1,234	4,514	671	1,590	1,620	883	2,820	1,104	10,700	2,320	2,585	69,293
1966–67	2,564	4,807	6,200	1,191	3,039	661	1,718	1,856	818	2,860	1,215	10,304	2,679	1,967	71,112
1967–68	2,686	4,922	5,500	1,232	3,092	716	1,759	2,109	645	2,694	1,457	11,531	2,575	1,905	73,007
1968–69	3,052	4,804	5,200	1,180	4,640	775	1,760	1,880	483	3,510	1,214	10,922	2,826	2,623	74,537
1969–70	2,440	5,063	9,400	1,162	5,523	835	2,124	1,683	460	3,325	1,071	9,570	2,648	2,974	78,941
1970–71†	2,771	5,642	6,500	1,286	4,963	800	2,270	1,659	321	3,322	1,253	9,975	2,729	2,972	77,628
1971–72†	2,920	5,939	4,837	1,124	4,222	750	2,003	1,887	298	3,531	1,206	8,813	2,778	3,530	77,501
1972–73*	3,015	6,909	6,063	1,125	4,915	772	2,435	2,043	265	3,684	1,615	8,793	3,145	3,285	83,441

* Estimated.

† Preliminary.

SOURCE Foreign Agricultural Service, USDA.

TABLE 24-3 CENTRIFUGAL SUGAR (RAW VALUE) IMPORTED INTO SELECTED COUNTRIES (IN THOUSANDS OF METRIC‡ TONS)

Year	Algeria	Canada	Chile	France	W. Germany	Israel	Japan	Malaysia	Morocco	Netherlands	United Kingdom	U.S. trade with territories	United States	USSR	World total†
1963	246	830	292	425	339	Av.	1,628	311	411	247	2,817	1,933	4,486	1,255	19,113
1964	236	845	166	566	71	(71)	1,701	273	447	288	2,547	1,923	3,596	2,082	18,777
1965	287	924	230	480	268		1,902	343	411	162	2,398	1,974	3,856	2,528	20,175
1966‡	241	782	202	509	315	75	1,739	280	340	139	2,227	1,743	3,846	1,843	19,003
1967	330	893	158	489	320	93	1,817	418	301	156	2,138	1,774	4,252	2,483	19,940
1968	283	863	180	377	285	146	2,054	344	281	199	2,074	1,542	4,654	1,755	19,609
1969	200	946	294	106	181	118	2,228	361	253	183	2,149	1,363	4,432	1,335	18,569
1970	207	949	100	60	193	118	2,600	380	273	180	1,839	1,360	4,711	3,005	21,372
1971*	261	899	195	108	177	139	2,427	330	246	15	2,134	1,117	4,821	1,536	20,708
1972*	207	907	305	125	125	101	2,777	259	222	39	2,163	1,144	4,750	1,924	20,573

* Preliminary,
† Excludes U.S. trade with territories
‡ Data before 1966 are in thousands of short tons.
SOURCE *Foreign Agricultural Service, USDA.*

**FIG. 24-1   World sugar: stocks plus production as percentage of previous
year's usage related to the weekly Wednesday high price in the September
contract from April 1 to the end of the contract, 1962/63–1971/72.**

coefficient. However, in the years in which x equaled less than 1.15 prices
had to ration usage severely.

COFFEE

INTRODUCTION

The early history of coffee is so confused by myth, conjecture, and romance
that its real beginnings as a beverage must be considered lost. There is no
record of its having been known to the ancient Greeks, Romans, or Egyp-
tians, but there is little doubt not only that the Ethiopians used coffee from
the most ancient times but that they were the first to use it. From Ethiopia
it apparently spread throughout the various Arabian countries, Egypt and
Turkey and in the early 1600s, into Europe by way of Italy. By 1650 coffee

TABLE 24-4   WORLD SUGAR SUPPLY AND
DISAPPEARANCE FOR THE YEARS 1961–1962
THROUGH 1972–1973 (IN THOUSANDS OF
SHORT TONS)

Sugar-making season	Stocks	Production	Total supply	Disappearance
1961–62	9.0	57.0	66.0	58.3
1962–63	7.7	54.9	62.6	57.3
1963–64	5.3	59.9	65.2	59.2
1964–65	6.0	72.6	78.6	68.3
1965–66	10.3	69.3	79.6	68.0
1966–67	11.6	71.1	82.7	70.8
1967–68	11.9	73.0	84.9	72.1
1968–69	12.8	74.5	87.3	74.0
1969–70	13.3	78.9	92.2	78.2
1970–71	14.0	77.6	91.6	79.4
1971–72*	12.2	77.8	90.0	77.9
1972–73†	12.1	82.0	94.1	

* Preliminary.
† Estimated.

houses in England had become numerous and popular. Coffee houses were
also common in the United States quite early in the country's history and
coffee consumption quickly exceeded even that of the producing countries.
Although tea is generally more widely consumed, coffee is commercially
the most important beverage, surpassing both tea and cocoa.

After the Civil War the U.S. Coffee Trade, which had by then been centered in the New York City area, was in a chaotic condition. Increasingly
heavy supplies which had become available during the 1870s caused the
price to crash below 8 cents a pound. The result was ruin for some importers. In an effort to prevent a repetition of the disaster some of the coffee
merchants who survived the debacle founded the New York Coffee Exchange which opened for business in 1882. Futures trading in sugar was
added in 1916 and the name of the exchange was changed to the New York
Coffee and Sugar Exchange.

The New York market provides for the trading of three types of coffee
designated as "B", "C", and "U". The "B" and "U" trade in units of 32,500
pounds and the "C," in 37,500 pounds, all in approximately 250 bags.
Prices are quoted in dollars and cents with a minimum fluctuation of $\frac{1}{100}$
cent a pound equal to $3.25 per contract for types "B" and "U" and $3.75
for type "C." Trading is conducted for delivery during the current month
and 12 succeeding months. Type "B" is Brazilian coffee. Type "C" comes
from Mexico, El Salvador, Guatemala, and Colombia. Type "U" is Robusta
or Aribica coffee. Sources of coffee imports into the United States are listed
in Table 24-5.

Coffee also trades on the London Coffee Terminal Market Associations
in contracts of 5 long tons. Prices are quoted in pound sterling per long ton.
This market trades on a morning call followed by free trading and a mid-

CHART 24-3

COFFEE WEEKLY HIGH, LOW & CLOSE OF NEAREST FUTURES CONTRACT NEW YORK COFFEE & SUGAR EXCH. IN CENTS PER POUND

SANTOS "B" THRU MAY 1968
"U" THRU JAN. 1972
"C" TO DATE

Prepared by
Commodity Research Bureau, Inc.
ONE LIBERTY PLAZA, NEW YORK, N.Y. 10006

TABLE 24-5 TOTAL COFFEE* IMPORTS INTO THE UNITED STATES (IN THOUSANDS OF BAGS OF 132.276 POUNDS EACH OR 60 KILOGRAMS)

Year	Ethiopia	Brazil	Colombia	Costa-Rica	Dominican Republic	Ecuador	Guate-mala	Haiti	Mexico	Nica-ragua	Portu-guese Africa	Sal-vador	Vene-zuela	Grand Total
1961	679	8,633	4,087	369	266	202	950	76	1,316	225	1,031	583	344	22,464
1962	661	9,094	4,332	385	418	369	967	154	1,408	190	1,480	847	272	24,549
1963	816	9,278	3,952	287	368	294	1,080	122	841	224	1,124	763	313	23,893
1964	924	7,213	3,712	293	532	230	789	122	1,480	170	1,246	683	262	22,892
1965	1,158	5,744	3,324	305	310	502	904	100	1,160	251	1,285	714	236	21,347
1966	792	6,731	2,710	231	353	432	1,110	89	1,035	135	1,212	593	271	22,062
1967	1,059	6,069	3,063	324	254	467	706	88	990	174	1,481	853	283	21,312
1968	963	8,318	3,050	294	329	417	718	90	1,293	216	1,759	579	159	25,378
1969	943	5,780	2,480	271	326	377	825	61	1,125	153	1,296	596	283	20,233
1970	1,071	4,717	2,497	375	352	600	716	60	982	128	1,385	539	253	19,732
1971†	1,130	6,536	2,642	350	338	404	813	138	1,286	192	1,590	645	246	22,686
1972†	965	7,112	2,711	294	460	491	714	139	1,212	111	1,297	413	243	22,321
1973														

* For consumption.
† Preliminary.
SOURCE: Department of Commerce.

day call. In the afternoon there is a P.M. call followed by another period of free trading and a closing call. If the market moves its daily limit of 20 pounds, there is a 30-minute recess followed by a special call. The market then trades without limits until the close. As in most other commodities that trade in both London and New York, many traders like to use London prices as a guide to an expectation of the opening of the New York market. The data in Table 24-6 may prove helpful, but it should be remembered that London coffee contract prices will differ from New York coffee contract prices because of the differences in deliverable types and grades of coffee and because of freight considerations. The bulk of London trading is in the Robusta contract most comparable to the New York "U" contract.

About 80 percent of the world's coffee comes from Central and South America where wide commercial production began in the 1700s. The largest producer is Brazil which accounts for about half the world crop. Colombia produces 25 percent or more. The popular mild types of coffee which generally command the highest prices come from Colombia, Mexico,

TABLE 24-6 COFFEE: LONDON–NEW YORK PRICE EQUIVALENTS (AT 1 POUND STERLING = $2.40 EXCHANGE RATE)

London (pounds sterling per long ton)	New York (cents per pound)	London (pounds sterling per long ton)	New York (cents per pound)	London (pounds sterling per long ton)	New York (cents per pound)
400.0	42.86	535.0	57.32	670.0	71.79
405.0	43.40	540.0	57.86	675.0	72.32
410.0	43.93	545.0	58.39	680.0	72.86
415.0	44.46	550.0	58.93	685.0	73.39
420.0	45.00	555.0	59.46	690.0	73.93
425.0	45.54	560.0	60.00	695.0	74.46
430.0	46.07	565.0	60.54	700.0	75.00
435.0	46.61	570.0	61.07	705.0	75.54
440.0	47.14	575.0	61.61	710.0	76.07
445.0	47.68	580.0	62.14	715.0	76.61
450.0	48.21	585.0	62.68	720.0	77.14
455.0	48.75	590.0	63.21	725.0	77.68
460.0	49.29	595.0	63.75	730.0	78.21
465.0	49.82	600.0	64.29	735.0	78.75
470.0	50.36	605.0	64.82	740.0	79.29
475.0	50.89	610.0	65.36	745.0	79.82
480.0	51.43	615.0	65.89	750.0	80.36
485.0	51.96	620.0	66.43	755.0	80.89
490.0	52.50	625.0	66.96	760.0	81.43
495.0	53.04	630.0	67.50	765.0	81.96
500.0	53.57	635.0	68.04	770.0	82.50
505.0	54.11	640.0	68.47	775.0	83.04
510.0	54.64	645.0	69.11	780.0	83.57
515.0	55.18	650.0	69.64	785.0	84.11
520.0	55.71	655.0	70.18	790.0	84.64
525.0	56.25	660.0	70.71	795.0	85.18
530.0	56.79	665.0	71.25	800.0	85.71

El Salvador, Guatemala, and other Central American countries. African production has been increasing for some years, but its popularity, particularly in the United States, which consumes half the world supply, is not so great as the varieties originating in the Western Hemisphere. African coffee is grown primarily in the Ivory Coast, Angola, Uganda, and Ethiopia and is chiefly of the Robusta variety. Major sources of coffee are noted in Table 24-7.

FACTORS WHICH INFLUENCE PRICES

Like any crop, the supply of coffee depends to a considerable degree on natural conditions, although the range of considerations adequate for satisfactory coffee production is wide. The trees require at least 40 inches of rain each year and considerable moisture before the berries mature. Dry weather is preferable during the harvest.[1] Temperatures should be in the high 60s, although somewhat warmer temperatures are tolerable. Frost and wind, however, are mortal enemies of the coffee tree. Many types of soil are acceptable, but the differences in the coffee produced because of the nature of the soil may be quite material. It is widely believed that coffee grown where it is shaded from the full heat of the sun is to be preferred. Coffee, of course, is also affected by diseases, insects, and fungi. In addition, large scale wars have affected prices considerably because so much of what is grown must be shipped long distances to consuming countries. Spot prices in New York, for example, rose from 10 cents a pound before World War I to 20 to 25 cents by 1919. About the same range was covered between 1940 and 1946.

One of the most extraordinary price rises in the history of any commodity occurred in early 1954 when the price rose almost vertically to more than 95 cents a pound in the spot and futures markets and more than $1.35 at retail. Starting on the night of July 5, 1953, huge blasts of frigid air had swept over the entire southern regions of South America, enveloping the coffee-growing areas of Brazil in freezing weather for 2 days and 3 nights. Because damage to coffee trees from cold is not immediately apparent, the scope of the disaster was not readily understood at first. By September and October, however, it was becoming obvious that what had happened was one of the greatest calamities ever to strike a crop. According to Brazilian coffee officials, more than 904,000,000 coffee trees were destroyed or damaged. The result was a huge speculation in both cash and futures. Panicked housewives stood in line to buy coffee at ever-increasing prices while those who had coffee to sell withheld it anticipating even higher prices. Almost two dozen federal and state agencies in the United States engaged in investigations because of the fury of the buyers who blamed speculators for the rise.[2]

[1] L. V. D. Wickizer, *Coffee, Tea, and Cocoa,* Stanford University Press, Stanford, Calif., 1951, pp. 42–44.

[2] Andres Uribe C., *Brown Gold,* Random House, New York, 1954, p. 73.

TABLE 24-7 WORLD GREEN COFFEE (EXPORTABLE)‡ PRODUCTION [IN THOUSANDS OF BAGS (60 KILOGRAMS EACH)]

Crop Year†	Angola	Brazil	Cam-eroom	Colombia	Costa Rica	Ethiopia	Guate-mala	Indo-nesia	Ivory Coast	Kenya	Mexico	Sal-vador	Uganda	Zaire (Congo, K)	World Total
1960–65 av	2,859	18,840	780	6,800	937	1,152	1,500	1,756	3,135	605	1,521	1,702	2,416	940	51,453
1965–66	2,740	30,200	1,170	7,000	895	1,170	1,835	1,850	4,500	855	1,800	1,690	2,585	925	66,244
1966–67	3,240	12,000	970	6,350	1,080	1,385	1,450	1,490	2,145	915	1,350	1,825	2,435	850	44,483
1967–68	3,340	14,475	1,070	6,700	1,210	1,380	1,625	1,650	4,445	630	1,500	2,260	2,685	950	51,726
1968–69	3,040	8,000	1,070	6,570	1,115	1,420	1,505	1,500	3,350	780	1,400	1,755	3,320	950	43,410
1969–70	3,200	10,250	1,170	7,080	1,250	1,375	1,510	1,500	4,535	880	1,575	2,350	3,335	1,025	48,078
1970–71	3,200	1,500	1,125	6,390	1,095	1,450	1,590	1,450	3,950	988	1,680	2,015	2,985	1,150	40,110
1971–72	3,300	14,850	1,220	5,750	1,190	1,490	1,845	1,320	4,000	973	1,835	2,440	2,830	1,200	53,051
1972–73*	3,450	16,500	1,320	7,100	1,165	1,630	1,990	1,650	4,975	1,172	2,100	1,935	2,830	1,265	57,903
1973–74*	3,500	6,003	1,095	7,950	1,285	1,520	1,930	1,625	3,425	1,000	1,800	1,830	2,880	1,200	45,748

* Preliminary.

† Coffee marketing year begins in July in some countries and in others about October.

‡ Exportable production represents total harvested production minus estimated domestic consumption.

SOURCE: Foreign Agricultural Service, USDA.

A most dynamic price influence has been provided by the International Coffee Agreement which went into effect in 1964. Following its implementation, spot coffee prices rose from a general level of 30–35 cents to 45–50 cents. Some of the credit given to the agreement, however, perhaps should have been given to an unusual period of severe weather damage to the Brazilian crops which was followed by widespread fires that destroyed some of the crop that had survived the preceding drought. The damage was severe enough to result in Brazil's drawing down some of the surplus built during the period of high production beginning in 1954 and ending in 1963. Unlike many commodity agreements often entered into by a group by producers hoping to increase price levels of a commodity, the coffee agreement involved 62 countries, including most major producers and consumers as well. It was also supported by a number of trade associations in the consuming countries. The large number of participants among consuming countries would seem to reduce the problems faced by other commodity agreements which historically broke down because of noncompliance of the signers and competition from the nonsigners. The agreement covering the September 1973 to September 1975 period eliminated the import quotas and limitations, indicator prices, and import-export control mechanisms that had been provided for in agreements in the preceding years. The effect of the change was a major reduction in restraint of the coffee market.

SOURCES OF INFORMATION

1. International Coffee Organization, General Statistical Documents. 22 Berners St., London, WIP 4DD, England.

2. Annual Coffee Statistical Pan-American Coffee Bureau, New York, N.Y.

3. Foreign Agricultural Circular, *Coffee*, published by the Foreign Agricultural Service, USDA, Washington, D.C.

NATURE OF PRODUCTION

In order to grow coffee on an important commercial scale, the trees must have intense sunlight, rich soil, and warm rains. Coffee thrives in most tropical and subtropical areas; 80 percent of its production is concentrated in the Western Hemisphere, about 15 percent in Africa, and the remainder in Asia and Oceania. A botanical oddity is that the best coffees grow in areas in which the coffeeplant does not grow wild.[3] It is odd, too, to note that coffee does not grow in or around Mocha.

Most of the world's coffee comes from a tree known as the Aribica, which apparently originated in Ethiopia but now grows in most coffee-producing regions. The trees produce small white flowers which fall off and are soon replaced by small clusters of cherries that grow along the limbs of the trees

---

[3] *Ibid.*

for a period of 6 or 7 months. They change in color as they mature from green to deep red. Aribica takes about 5 years to mature enough to bear fruit, unlike the Robusta variety which requires only 2 or 3 years. Robusta, which has become commercially important only during about the last 75 years, is popular among producers partly because of its rapid growth to maturity and its resistance to disease. It has succeeded, however, in capturing only a relatively small amount of the world's consumption because of the less popular aroma and flavor of the coffee produced from it.

Most coffee trees produce the first full crop in about their fifth year. Each tree produces about 1 pound of marketable coffee each year until the tree is 25 or 30 years old, although some are productive much longer. The beans ripen at various times in different countries and are harvested, usually by hand, over a period of 4 to 6 weeks. The cherries which are picked consist of a sweet pulpy fruit usually covering two flat beans. This pulp must be removed by one of two methods. (Surprisingly, no commercial use has yet been discovered for the pulp, despite long efforts to find one.) One is the "wet" or "washed" method in which the cherries are first washed and depulped and then fermented in tanks for several hours, washed again, and dried either in the sun or by machine. The washed method, used for most of the higher priced mild coffees, produces higher prices than the "dry" or "natural" method.

The dry method simply utilizes the sun to bake the coverings away from the coffee beans, after which the beans are cleaned before being readied for shipment to consuming countries. The originating countries also perform two other functions before shipping the beans. One is classification by size and the other is grading. When these steps have been completed, the coffee is packed in heavy bags for storage or shipment to market. Green coffee can be stored for long periods with little change in quality.[4]

In addition to the usual requirements such as proper soil, labor, adequate financing, and assured markets, coffee presents some special problems. The investment required is far beyond normal. The trees are subject to a wide variety of highly destructive insects, fungi, and disease. Worst of all, the yield from even the best trees is wildly unpredictable. The maximum crop from a given tree can vary 10 times from its minimum to its maximum and it can produce bumper crops for several years in a row followed by sparse yields for the next several years with no apparent pattern. With so much land available for coffee growing in countries that can produce it and the ever growing demand for it the probability of wide variations in supply, both long- and short-term, is high.

NATURE OF UTILIZATION

Coffee is enormously popular in many parts of the world and is used almost entirely as a beverage. Major coffee importing countries are indicated in

[4] *Ibid.*, pp. 45–72; describes the productive process of coffee in great detail.

Table 24-8. Less than 1 percent is used for other purposes such as flavoring candies and desserts. Coffee is not in demand because of its capacity to quench thirst nor has it any nutritive value whatsoever unless the user adds cream or milk and sugar. The popularity of coffee, like tea, which has the same characteristics, is almost certainly due to its being a stimulant because it contains caffeine. Yet it has an unpleasant or harmful effect on almost no one, if used in moderation, despite its being habit forming. Unlike alcoholic beverages, coffee and tea do not cause secondary states of depression after the initial stimulation and, unlike soft drinks containing caffeine, do not interfere with nutrition because they have no sugar.[5] Unlike its supply, the demand for coffee varies little over the years and responds little even to reasonable changes in price or purchasing power. Coffee has only one purpose. It has no substitute acceptable to most of its consumers and is regarded as a necessity by most of them up to a number of cups per day. A further stabilizing effect is the fact that green coffee is storable at relatively low cost for long periods which evens out to some degree the effects of sometimes violent changes in supply. It is this highly inelastic, short-term demand, coupled with great changes in supply, that has led over many years to control of supply and marketing of crops, burning of supplies, and demands for subsidies to growers and exporters.

The marketing process of coffee is relatively simple. The export of green coffee is handled by a small number of firms who deliver the coffee into jobbers' or roasters' warehouses in a number of ports among which the most important are New York, New Orleans, San Francisco, Le Havre, and Antwerp. It is then blended, roasted, and packaged for sale to the consumer. Blending is a highly skilled secret process done to get the best possible combination of aroma, flavor, appearance, and price to encourage maximum market demand with a favorable dollar return to the seller. A major problem to sellers is caused when there is any deviation in the supply of milds because the total supply is relatively small to begin with and milds are essential to the flavor and aroma of blended coffees, particularly blends.

SEASONAL INFORMATION

Although coffee grows only in tropical and semitropical areas, it thrives in so many areas of the world that no seasonal is evident. Further, crops come in irregularly and in some areas there are several harvests a year. Coffee plants can endure greater extremes of climate and soil variations than any other variety of tropical plant.[6] In addition, the ease of storage tends to even out seasonal influences. The coffee year is assumed to start July 1st, although that date has little real significance.

[5] Wickizer, *op cit.*, p. 6.

[6] Joseph M. Walsh, *Coffee, Its History, Classification and Description*, Henry T. Coates & Co., Philadelphia, 1894, p. 20.

TABLE 24-8 TOTAL WORLD GREEN COFFEE IMPORTS BY COUNTRIES OF DESTINATION [IN THOUSANDS OF BAGS (60 KILOGRAMS OR 132.276 POUNDS EACH)]

Year	United States	Other Western Hemisphere†	Canada	Africa	Europe									Asia and Oceania	Total world imports
					Belgium and Luxembourg	Denmark	France	West Germany	United Kingdom	Italy	Netherlands	Sweden	Total Europe		
1960	22,104	607	995	1,146	1,109	698	3,477	3,323	920	1,653	917	1,222	17,018	736	42,593
1961	22,464	720	1,119	1,096	1,036	727	3,454	3,540	978	1,753	1,147	1,295	17,807	742	43,917
1962	24,549	600	1,230	1,084	923	761	3,472	3,899	1,155	1,865	1,063	1,397	18,563	889	46,915
1963	23,893	595	1,288	1,213	922	883	3,645	3,958	1,275	1,935	1,257	1,467	19,994	1,018	48,001
1964	22,892	600	1,247	1,211	1,049	805	3,842	4,276	1,303	1,993	1,380	1,552	21,347	1,336	48,633
1965	21,347	665	1,258	853	1,129	824	3,617	4,597	973	2,006	1,378	1,532	21,604	1,486	47,213
1966	22,063	833	1,164	1,012	905	886	3,794	4,663	1,360	2,058	1,417	1,615	22,736	1,953	49,761
1967	21,312	722	1,344	928	1,038	892	3,659	4,594	1,344	2,420	1,572	1,691	23,631	1,824	49,743
1968	25,378	735	1,394	1,144	1,091	934	4,091	5,009	1,529	2,536	1,701	1,769	25,462	1,936	56,049
1969	20,233	889	1,363	1,100	1,165	998	3,969	5,141	1,701	2,597	1,969	1,764	27,165	2,534	53,284
1970	19,732	748	1,256	1,179	989	970	3,984	5,169	1,539	2,741	1,838	1,768	27,527	2,798	53,019
1971*	21,655	783	1,412	1,210	1,121	954	4,213	5,393	1,789	2,957	2,053	1,697	26,951	2,360	54,366
1972‡	20,769	865	1,317	1,214	1,118	1,014	4,308	5,688	1,711	2,959	2,191	1,788	29,278	2,955	56,398
1973															

* Preliminary.
† Except Canada.
‡ Estimated.
SOURCE: Pan-American Coffee Bureau.

NOTES FROM A TRADER—SUGAR AND COFFEE

World sugar is one of the few commodities that can be readily spread between the United States and European (London) markets. Those who utilize the international spread in sugar are often more interested in possible changes in the relative values in currency than in the sugar itself, although this motivation for trading spreads is declining as the markets in currencies themselves become better established. The trader who is speculating on money market changes must beware of the possibility of changes in the price of the commodity that will cause profits to be more than offset by losses in purchasing power.

World sugar contracts in the United States provide a better trading vehicle than domestic sugar contracts because fluctuations in the latter are tempered so much by the quota system. Spreaders of world versus domestic sugar should make certain that open interest and activity in the selected domestic sugar contract are adequate to provide liquidity.

Charts that seem to be relatively flat can be quite deceiving in world sugar. The contract of 112,000 pounds which results in an unusually high move per point of $11.20 can represent surprisingly high leverage during periods when margins are low. Sugar markets sometimes erupt suddenly after quiet periods of months or even years and may catch both the trader and his margin clerk unawares.

Many traders who rely most heavily on fundamentals tend to overemphasize sugarcane because of the influence of such headline news as tropical hurricanes and political upheaval, whereas the beet sugar crops provide newsworthy items much less often. The sugar produced from the beets, however, is identical with that produced from the cane. A high percentage of beet sugar is raised in European nations, from many of which accurate crop news is difficult to obtain.

The sugar market is quite efficient. If the board seems to be telling its own story, it probably should not be ignored.

For the "fundamentalist" coffee analysis is simpler than most. Its sources and areas of demand are well defined. The United States is the prime consumer and there are few signs of any change in the consuming habits of coffee drinkers in this country. About 80 percent of all citizens over the age of 16 consume a total of more than 100 billion cups of coffee each year, regardless of price and with little consideration of current purchasing power. Warnings of hazards to health to date have concerned only consumption in quite large amounts or those who have health problems such as heart trouble. The International Coffee Agreement, unlike most such agreements, has a history of working reasonably well.

The greatest hazard to a trader would appear to be any violence done to sources of supply, but even it is easy to define. It usually involves severe growing problems in Brazil or interference with shipping such as a war or long strike. Such factors can be of special influence on coffee prices because of the enormous influence of U.S. consumers who have no domestic supply except Hawaii, which produces only relatively small amounts.

The only great change in coffee patterns in many years is that made by instant, or soluble, coffee, which is becoming ever more popular because of its simplicity of preparation despite its inadequacies in aroma and flavor.

The coffee market tends to be thin, and this condition, combined with the risk of materially great and unexpected supply changes, may cause extended violent moves. It is no place for the underfinanced or the timid. Inverted markets are unusually frequent and therefore popular with those who like to buy the discounts on the theory that the price level is probably underestimated and they will make money sooner or later. Surprisingly, this practice has proved to be profitable quite often, and hedgers continue to use the market even though they must absorb an obvious bias.

CHAPTER TWENTY-FIVE

Cocoa

INTRODUCTION

Futures trading in cocoa takes place primarily on the London Cocoa Terminal Market and the New York Cocoa Exchange. Traders can note price action on the London market before the New York opening each day. Because London prices are quoted in shillings per hundredweight, Table 25-1 presents a price-conversion schedule for the convenience of the trader.

The New York Cocoa Exchange is open for trading daily from 10 A.M. to 3 P.M. (EST) except on Saturdays and Sundays and holidays designated by the Exchange. Contracts traded are December, March, May, July, and September.

The contract unit is 30,000 pounds, and there is no provision for trading in "job lots." The minimum fluctuation is 0.01 cent a pound ($3 per contract), which is known as a "point." The maximum daily fluctuation is 200 points above or below the preceding day's close, with the exception of the spot month, in which there is no limit after the first transferable notice day.

Cocoa has been attractive over the years for full-move trades because it occasionally tends to have wide price moves whose directions are relatively difficult to reverse.

TABLE 25-1 COCOA: LONDON—NEW YORK PRICE EQUIVALENTS (AT 1 POUND STERLING = $2.40 EXCHANGE RATE)

London* (pounds sterling per metric ton)	New York† (cents per pound)	London (pounds sterling per metric ton)	New York (cents per pound)
200	21.77	490	53.34
210	22.86	500	54.43
220	23.95	510	55.52
230	25.04	520	56.61
240	26.13	530	57.70
250	27.22	540	58.79
260	28.30	550	59.87
270	29.39	560	60.96
280	30.48	570	62.05
290	31.57	580	63.14
300	32.66	590	64.23
310	33.75	600	65.32
320	34.84	610	66.41
330	35.92	620	67.49
340	37.01	630	68.58
350	38.10	640	69.67
360	39.19	650	70.76
370	40.28	660	71.85
380	41.37	670	72.94
390	42.46	680	74.03
400	43.54	690	75.11
410	44.63	700	76.20
420	45.72	710	77.29
430	46.81	720	78.38
440	47.90	730	79.47
450	48.99	740	80.56
460	50.08	750	81.65
470	51.17	760	82.74
480	52.25	770	83.82

*Basic good fermented main crop Ghana in bond ex-store London.

†Basic standard growths, exchange licensed warehouse in New York or Philadelphia.

Converting London Cocoa Prices to New York Equivalents

Two possible London quotes in pounds sterling per metric ton	£580.00 and £580.48	
1. Multiply by 240 to get cents per metric ton	139,200 and 139,813 cents/ metric ton	1 pound sterling = $2.40 (approximately) = 240 cents
2. Divide by 2204.62 to get cents per pound	63.14 and 63.42 cents/lb	2204.62 lb/metric ton

CHART 25-1

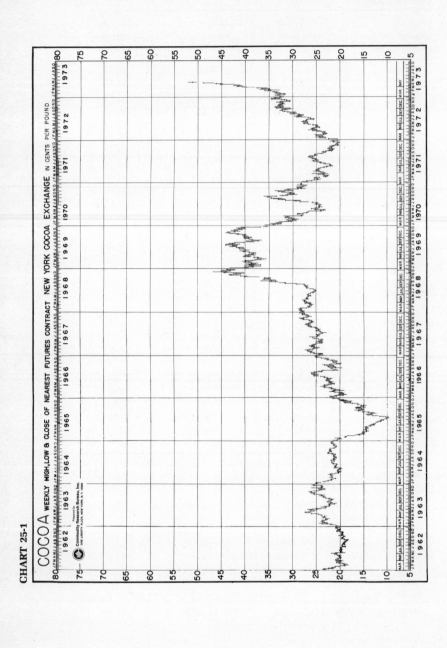

COCOA WEEKLY HIGH, LOW & CLOSE OF NEAREST FUTURES CONTRACT NEW YORK COCOA EXCHANGE IN CENTS PER POUND

FACTORS WHICH INFLUENCE COCOA PRICES

Wild price swings are the result of the lag in the adjustment of supply and demand factors; 4 or 5 years elapse from the planting of the cocoa tree until it bears on a commercial scale. Therefore cocoa production (supply) in any given year cannot respond to increased or decreased grindings (demand), leaving price alone to ration existing supply. The level of cocoa grindings does not react quickly to price changes either. It may be generally stated that in the short run the demand and supply for cocoa are relatively inelastic.

After living on a hand-to-mouth basis in cocoa from 1945 to 1958 the manufacturers' position changed significantly as the gain in production outpaced the increase in world grindings. From 1958 to 1965 stocks increased significantly. From 1965 to 1969 and also from 1972 to 1974 deficits again appeared in the relation between the net world crop and calendar-year grindings. These changes are highlighted in Table 25-2.

As a result of producer concern with low prices in the early 1960s (21-cent average) the Cocoa Producers' Alliance (CPA) was formed in September 1963. Six countries (Ghana, Nigeria, Brazil, Ivory Coast, Cameroon, and Togo), which controlled 80 percent of the world's cocoa production, devised a system of annual and quarterly quotas to limit member ex-

TABLE 25-2   WORLD COCOA SUPPLY AND DEMAND (IN THOUSANDS OF LONG TONS)

(1) Crop year*	(2) Stocks Oct. 1	(3) Net world crop†	(4) Total availability	(5) Calendar year grindings	(6) Closing stocks	(7) Stock change
1960–61	346	1,161	1,507	1,018	418	+168
1961–62	514	1,113	1,627	1,109	422	+ 29
1962–63	422	1,146	1,568	1,144	424	+ 2
1963–64	424	1,204	1,629	1,180	449	+ 25
1964–65	449	1,467	1,916	1,320	590	+141
1965–66	590	1,193	1,783	1,370	411	−179
1966–67	411	1,320	1,731	1,366	367	− 44
1967–68	367	1,320	1,690	1,392	299	− 68
1968–69	299	1,208	1,509	1,333	176	−123
1969–70	352	1,404	1,581	1,336	244	+ 69
1970–71	448	1,464	1,912	1,398	514	+ 66
1971–72‡	512	1,533	2,060	1,496	564	+ 50
1972–73§	564	1,350	1,914	1,568	346	−218
1973–74 est.	346	1,432	1,778	1,472	306	− 40

*Crop year season is Oct.–Sept.
†The net world crop is obtained by adjusting the gross world crop for percent loss in weight.
‡Preliminary.
§Forecast.
SOURCE: Gill and Duffus, Ltd.

ports. The alliance broke down in 1965 and chaotic marketing conditions followed.

Market intervention by governments complicates the analysis of cocoa. The natural outgrowth of industrialization programs is a tendency for the cocoa-producing countries to take a larger part in the processing of cocoa beans. Whether such attempts are economically feasible remains to be seen. The large buyers of cocoa can also affect prices by their decisions regarding inventory levels.[1]

As the specific supply and demand components of cocoa are analyzed in the following sections, it will be well to remember that a statistical approximation formulated early in the season is likely to differ considerably from actual figures late in the season. Because the absolute figures are uncertain, the *trend* of production and that of consumption become ever more important. Changes, and the direction of those changes, are more important than comparison of the levels of supply and demand.

To quantify these changes the comparison of demand and supply in Table 25-2 is useful. If "supply" is defined as stocks on October 1 plus production (column 4) and "demand" is synonymous with grindings (column 5), Table 25-3 relates the ratio of demand-supply to spot cocoa-bean average monthly prices in New York.[2] Figure 25-1 illustrates the two variable relationships in Table 25-3. Although the "scatter" about the straight line which represents the average forecasting relationship is considerable, it can be stated that a high ratio is associated with higher cocoa prices in New York and that a low ratio generally accompanies lower prices. It re-

[1] It will be helpful at this point for the reader to refer to Chapter 6 in which the effects of inventory and inventory expectations are discussed in detail.

[2] A simple model of this type was computed by Irwin Shisko, "How to Forecast Cocoa Prices," *Commodity Year Book,* Commodity Research Bureau, Inc., New York, 1959, pp. 26–33.

TABLE 25-3   COCOA DEMAND-SUPPLY RATIO COMPARED
WITH SPOT COCOA AVERAGE MONTHLY PRICES IN
NEW YORK, 1960–61, TO 1972–73.

Year	Demand/Supply	Spot cocoa average monthly prices (Accra) in New York in cents per pound
1960–61	0.68	22.7
1961–62	0.68	20.8
1962–63	0.73	25.4
1963–64	0.72	23.4
1964–65	0.69	17.2
1965–66	0.77	24.6
1966–67	0.79	28.8
1967–68	0.82	24.4
1968–69	0.88	45.8
1969–70	0.85	34.1
1970–71	0.75	26.8
1971–72	0.76	32.3
1972–73	0.77	

FIG. 25-1 Relationship between cocoa demand/supply yearly (October–September) and spot cocoa average monthly prices (Accra) in New York.

mains to isolate and analyze the production (supply) and consumption (grindings) figures that constitute the relationships noted in Figure 25-1.

SOURCES OF INFORMATION

In any analysis of the production-consumption outlook for cocoa the following sources of information will prove useful:

1. The weekly main-crop purchases by the market boards of Ghana and Nigeria beginning in October of each year.

2. The *Census Bureau Monthly Reports* which cover the *United States Confectionery Store Reports* on poundage and dollar sales of chocolate items.

3. The New York Cocoa Exchange reports on stocks of cocoa available for delivery as well as daily open-interest and volume figures.

4. The United Nations Food and Agricultural Organization and the Producers' Alliance release periodic figures on production forecasts.

5. Private sources, such as Gill and Duffus, Ltd., of London, constantly issue statistical and analytical information about current supply and demand.

NATURE OF PRODUCTION

Cocoa trees are grown in tropical climates and thrive within 20 degrees of the equator. The cocoa bean is found in pods, about the size of small cantaloupes, which grow along the bark of the tree and extend up into the foliage. The beans, after being picked, dried, and allowed to ferment for six days or more, are shipped to the consumer country, where they are segregated and cleaned. After roasting in air heated to more than 400° F, they are shattered into fragments ("nibs") and separated from their brittle husks by forced air. Following a milling process, the mass becomes a liquid (half of which is cocoa butter) known as "chocolate liquor." The liquor is then allowed to cool and harden into "cake," which is unsweetened chocolate used primarily for baking purposes.

In the manufacture of cocoa, however, more than half the cocoa butter is removed from the liquor and is available for inclusion in the manufacture of semisweet and milk chocolate.

In processing milk chocolate, the moisture is removed from a creamy paste consisting of milk and sugar blended with chocolate liquor. As a result of this operation the mass emerges as a powder and is blended with cocoa butter. Flavor refinement is accomplished by the conching process. Conches are machines in which the chocolate is rubbed across granite by heavy rollers of the same material.

The most important cocoa-growing country is Ghana, West Africa, which produces almost 40 percent of the total world crop. It is followed by Nigeria, with about 20 percent. Brazil and the Ivory Coast rank third with 15 percent, followed by Cameroon, Dominican Republic, and others.

The crop year in cocoa runs from October through September. This period covers a "main" crop (October to March), which is the major source of production, and a similar second crop or "midcrop" (May to June). The only exception is Brazil, where the midcrop is usually greater than the main crop. About 80 percent of the world's output is harvested from September through March and only 20 percent from April through August.

The Ghana authorities usually release the first estimate of the coming main crop in late September. Sometime in October a series of world production estimates are issued by the USDA, the Food and Agricultural Organization of the United Nations, and private sources. Because of their importance as top cocoa producers, the development of the crop in Ghana and Nigeria is watched closely. At the beginning of the crop year the rate at which the crop moves into the hands of the government marketing boards is a clue to the size of the forthcoming total crop. These boards in both countries purchase all the cocoa from individual farmers at a set price and in turn sell it to the world. Marketing-board purchases reflect the major supply of cocoa available for export to the consuming countries.

Some traders plot end-of-October purchases in both Ghana and Nigeria to anticipate the final main-crop figures. The results of these forecasts are questionable, and the resulting correlation coefficients are not statistically significant. The rate of marketings may not be evenly distributed. Too, the boards have been known to withhold figures or to report main-crop purchases later with midcrop figures. It is not known whether this is deliberate, but it is known that a bullish bias helps increase the profit of the marketing boards which represent an important part of their countries' economies.

Systematic analysis of weekly purchase figures as they are released assist the trader in deciding whether cocoa production is significantly ahead of or behind the forecast level. A sample of two crop-year purchases is presented in Figure 25-2. In analyzing the two years, the trader is struck by the tendency of October purchases of the 1965–1966 season to lag considerably behind those of the preceding year. The October 29 purchase figure

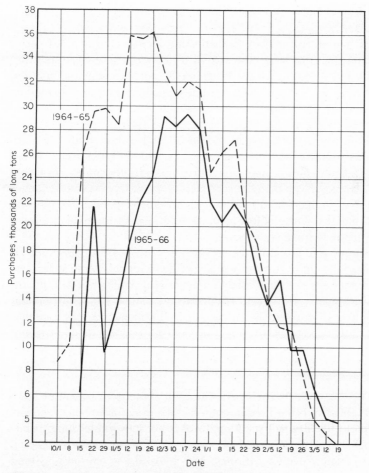

FIG. 25-2   Weekly purchases: Ghana main crop.

of 9,857 tons fueled a four-week advance in the December 1965 cocoa contract, which carried from 14.50 to more than 19.00 cents before any reaction occurred. Such obvious divergences may help the trader substantially in his efforts to be aware of the trend in world cocoa production.

Prospects in smaller producing countries may be important for technical reasons that have to do with the types of delivery that can be made on expiring futures contracts. If these producers of lower priced cocoas have poor years, some tightness in expiring contracts could be experienced. It should be remembered, however, that this is a short-run phenomenon and that in the long run market action is highly correlated with broad supply-demand factors.

NATURE OF UTILIZATION

The elasticity of demand for cocoa beans is approximately 0.25. In other words, if cocoa production were 25 percent less in any one year, all other things being equal, prices would have to rise 100 percent to ration usage. Similarly, if cocoa doubled in price, consumption would decrease by only one-quarter.

The candy manufacturer does the adjusting for the consumer. If cocoa appreciably increases in price, the size of a chocolate candy bar may be reduced, chocolate coatings may be thinned, box assortments may be changed to favor nonchocolate lines, or some cocoa butter may be deleted in favor of dairy butter. Because these changes are costly for the manufacturers, there is a wide area of what may be called "price indifference."

Each quarter the Association of Cocoa and Chocolate Manufacturers issues grindings reports that cover all but 10 percent of the industry. These figures are studied, together with price, to give the trader some clue to the direction of changes. Even though usage is not very elastic, eventual changes play a major part in determining future equilibrium levels. It is not unusual to see 6 to 8 months elapse before manufacturers adapt their consumption response to price or quantity changes.

The consumption of cocoa is also a function of disposable consumer income. In high per capita income countries, however, a rise in consumer income does not have the same effect on usage as a similar rise in a poorer country; for example, a 10 percent rise in income in a poorer country might be reflected in a 10 percent rise in cocoa consumption, whereas a similar income rise in the United States might account for only a 1 percent rise in chocolate usage.

SEASONAL INFORMATION

When cocoa prices over a year's period are not flattened because of large carry-over supplies or other fundamental factors, prices may tend to follow a seasonal pattern. Although such a pattern is not inexorable, some recurring tendencies may be observed in Figure 25-3. After heavy main-crop shipments from late November through March–April, the market may tend

FIG. 25-3 Cocoa seasonal price index.

to be sluggish as manufacturer pipelines are filled. In summer demand quickens to discount expected heavier fall grindings. Main crops have been sold out by this time, and only Brazil's midcrop is a serious supply factor. Yearly October-November comparisons between weekly African main-crop purchases or simply uncertainty over the size of the main crop can lend strength in the November-December period.

Table 25-4 shows the 21-year outcome of trading March cocoa to take advantage of recurring fall seasonal strength. If a trader buys March cocoa on September 25 and sells on November 30, he will average 1.69 cents per pound per year for the first 20 years. However, the first 10-year average return was 2.77 cents, whereas the second 10-year average slipped to 0.62 cents because of generally larger carry-overs into the main-crop marketing season. Price action in 1973 was without precedent.

Table 25-5 illustrates a plan for exploiting recurring seasonal price strength in the spring of the year. If a trader buys September cocoa on March 15 and sells on May 15 each year, his results will be those appearing in columns 4 and 5. Through 1963 the results were excellent; however, since 1964 the trend toward longer harvest periods and larger midcrops in Ghana has caused marketing pressures to extend into summer.

It is evident that the overall supply-demand situation for each season must be examined before the trader attempts to exploit the timing device of the seasonal price pattern.

TABLE 25-4   SEASONAL COCOA PRICES: MARCH COCOA NET
PRICE GAIN FROM SEPTEMBER 25 TO NOVEMBER 30, 1953–1973
(IN CENTS PER POUND)

Year	Closing prices 9/25	Closing prices 11/30	Net gain 9/25–11/30	Highest price reached 9/25–11/30 Date	Highest price reached 9/25–11/30 Price	Maximum possible gain from 9/25
1953	29.75	36.20	6.45	11/30/53	37.03	7.28
1954	44.65	46.50	1.85	11/12/54	50.70	6.05
1955	30.78	31.11	0.33	10/17/55	33.30	2.52
1956	26.17	26.48	0.31	11/22/56	26.80	0.63
1957	31.20	37.93	6.73	11/18/57	40.08	8.88
1958	32.20	37.21	5.01	11/17/58	40.18	7.98
1959	29.85	30.38	0.53	10/27/59	31.94	2.09
1960	26.49	24.50	—(1.99)	10/21/60	26.82	0.33
1961	19.86	26.98	7.12	11/30/61	27.08	7.22
1962	19.96	21.28	1.32	11/30/62	21.45	1.49
1963	24.96	25.52	0.56	10/31/63	27.49	2.53
1964	22.96	22.16	—(0.80)	9/28/64	23.19	0.23
1965	15.98	19.70	3.72	11/29/65	19.80	3.82
1966	22.16	22.42	0.26	10/19/66	24.34	2.18
1967	27.92	27.35	—(0.57)	11/16/67	29.43	1.51
1968	36.08	42.75	6.67	11/18/68	44.40	8.32
1969	39.45	39.53	0.08	11/03/69	43.70	4.25
1970	30.70	28.67	—(2.03)	10/26/70	33.15	2.45
1971	23.36	21.22	—(2.14)	9/28/71	23.44	0.08
1972	31.07	31.55	.48	10/3/72	33.80	2.25
1973	61.95	50.45	—(11.50)	9/26/73	63.95	2.00

TABLE 25-5   SEASONAL COCOA PRICES: SEPTEMBER CÓCOA
NET CHANGE FROM MARCH 15 TO MAY 15, 1957–1973
(IN CENTS PER POUND)

(1) Year	(2) Close, 3/15	(3) Close, 5/15	(4) Net change	(5) Percent change
1957	21.54	23.27	+1.73	+8.0
1958	39.85	42.70	+2.85	+7.2
1959	32.90	34.64	+1.74	+5.3
1960	25.68	26.44	+0.76	+3.0
1961	20.60	22.12	+1.52	+7.4
1962	21.50	22.10	+0.60	+2.8
1963	24.20	27.16	+2.96	+12.2
1964	22.98	21.00	−1.98	−8.6
1965	17.70	15.62	−2.08	−11.8
1966	22.04	22.52	+0.48	+2.2
1967	27.17	24.92	−2.25	−8.3
1968	27.74	26.99	−0.75	−2.7
1969	38.94	37.60	−1.34	−3.4
1970	30.31	25.25	−5.06	−16.7
1971	25.32	22.48	−2.84	−11.2
1972	26.39	27.39	+1.02	+3.8
1973	37.00	51.30	+14.30	+38.6

NOTES FROM A TRADER

Trading cocoa presents special problems for the fundamentalist and the technician. The fundamentalist must rely on supply figures which are notoriously unreliable to make up his price model. The technician often faces a relatively wide bid and ask, commission and margin requirements that are higher than average, and the price movement that represents only $3.00 per point.

There is no forecasting value in comparing the size of a given midcrop with the size of the subsequent main crop. There is, however, a high correlation between a late main crop and substandard production. The trend in production and consumption is more important than the respective supply-demand levels.

Seasonal studies bear watching in conjunction with fundamentals. If November cocoa prices surpass the highest prices achieved in October, the probabilities favor still higher prices. If the upward penetration of the highs in cocoa prices in the last half of July occurs during the first two weeks in August, the market generally carries higher by an average of more than 100 points.

CHAPTER TWENTY-SIX

Cotton, Wool, and Orange Juice

COTTON

INTRODUCTION

During the last century world cotton (and other textile) trade utilized the futures markets located in New York, New Orleans, and Liverpool in order to hedge inventory risks and to schedule forward transactions. In the early 1920s cotton futures trading volume reached its peak, and even in the late 1940s the dollar volume traded in cotton futures equaled the trade in all other commodities combined and exceeded, by several times, the dollar volume of stocks traded on the New York Stock Exchange.

The government price and production control programs, which started during the depression of the 1930s, progressively supplanted the influence of the free market. Government programs which attempted to maintain the historical positions of growers came into conflict with changes that would have resulted from the rapid technological progress in the production and use of cotton had the free market been permitted to function. The government continued to pay for and store relatively undesirable short-staple cotton as well as long-fiber cotton with undesirable Micronaire. The United

CHART 26-1

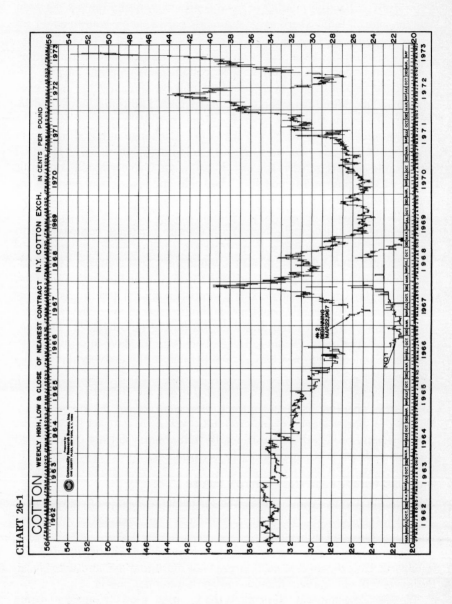

COTTON WEEKLY HIGH, LOW & CLOSE OF NEAREST CONTRACT N.Y. COTTON EXCH. IN CENTS PER POUND

States has been progressively losing its once-dominant position in the world cotton market.

Cotton was still traded actively during the seasons 1947–1948 through 1956–1957, when the number of open contracts typically ranged between 20,000 and 35,000. Then, as government participation continued to increase (at times the CCC has held as much as 73 percent of the total carry-over), the trade lost its incentive to hedge inventories. Interest in trading cotton futures declined rapidly and the cotton futures market became virtually dormant until 1967. In recent years, however, much of the carry-over inventory has shifted from the government back into trade hands and interest in the cotton futures market has been revived.

On March 22, 1967, the New York Cotton Exchange initiated trading in a new cotton futures contract (No. 2), middling-grade 1 $\frac{1}{16}$-inch cotton deliverable at ports in New Orleans, Houston, and Galveston and at interior points in Memphis and Greenville. The trade and speculators have shown high interest in the new contract. Both volume and open interest have grown substantially.

A futures contract on the New York Cotton Exchange consists of 100 bales, or 50,000 pounds, of cotton. Price is quoted in cents per pound and the minimum fluctuation is $\frac{1}{100}$ cent a pound, or $5 per contract. The maximum allowable daily range is 4 cents and the maximum fluctuation from the preceding day's settlement price is 2 cents a pound. These limits are removed from the deliverable contract on the first day of the delivery month.

The crop year for United States cotton begins on August 1. Delivery months are currently October, December, March, May, and July, with trading commencing as much as 17 months before the delivery date of the contract.

In mid-1968 the exchange converted the old middling 1-inch contract into a new middling $\frac{15}{16}$-inch contract (new contract No. 1) to cover principally the shorter staples in the crop not covered by contract No. 2. However, because of lack of interest, a sufficient volume did not develop and trading of the new No. 1 contract has ceased.

FACTORS WHICH INFLUENCE COTTON PRICES

As with many other commodities, the major determinants of cotton prices within the constraints set by the government loan program are the free-market supply and demand.

Early analysis of the cotton supply should include both the quantity and quality of the free-market carry-over. Planting intentions and acreage allotments will give early indications of the production levels.

Weather developments throughout the planting, growing, and harvesting seasons can sometimes materially affect both the quantity and quality of production. In general, too little rainfall tends to retard germination and plant growth, whereas too much moisture reduces fruiting and causes late maturity. Temperature extremes also reduce the quality and quantity of the crop; for example, rain and cold weather may delay planting, and, if there is any great amount of late cotton as a result, early frosts may kill it before it can attain maturity. A wet and cool fall can result in heavy boll rot. Insect pests—boll weevil, bollworms, and thrips—abound, but they can be successfully held down by poisoning if rain does not wash the poison off the plants.

In general, the growing season is an exciting affair in the cotton futures market. Traders often react vigorously to the official weekly weather reports and other information on crop developments. These reactions effected by the supply of cotton typically have an immediate but short-term influence on futures prices.

The important demand factors usually require more time than the supply factors to influence futures prices, but their impact is typically greater and longer lasting. The demand for cotton is related in an important but complicated way to factors such as (a) cloth inventories and sales potential of major cloth manufacturers, (b) the quantity and quality of raw-cotton inventories held by mills, (c) competition, both domestic and foreign, from other fibers and cloths, (d) mill margins, and (e) foreign inventories and prices of raw cotton. It is extremely difficult, except when major shifts occur, to relate these factors in a manner that will allow meaningful price prediction to be made.

The adoption of the 1 $\frac{1}{16}$-inch or medium-long staple contract was designed to meet changed conditions in the cotton textile industry. Although the 1 $\frac{1}{16}$-inch cotton is more expensive than shorter cotton, it usually is cheaper in the long run, for the textile machinery can be run more rapidly with a minimum of costly breakages and less consequent necessity of shutting down machinery while breakages are repaired than when the shorter and less strong cotton is used.

To some extent the supply-and-demand situation for the medium-staple cotton is unrelated to the supply-and-demand situation for all cotton; for example, a few seasons ago, when the total United States supply of cotton was huge and burdensome, tightness in medium-staple cotton began to develop as a result of improved mill technology.

Accordingly, in analyzing price prospects for medium-long staple cotton, separate treatment is necessary. The trader needs to know how much of this cotton is in the carry-over and how much in the new crop; he must know how much the demand may be for this cotton and how high the price may go before mills turn to blends of cotton and synthetic fibers or to the shorter cottons, despite the increased likelihood of costly breakages.

Tables 26-1 and 26-2 summarize the supply and distribution data for cotton in the United States for recent years.

SOURCES OF INFORMATION

The *Cotton Production Reports* by the USDA's Crop Reporting Board releases monthly reports from July through December on the eighth, or the

TABLE 26-1 SUPPLY AND DISTRIBUTION OF ALL COTTONS IN THE UNITED STATES
(IN THOUSANDS OF RUNNING BALES)

| Year beginning Aug. 1 | Carryover—August 1 | | | Produc-tion† | City Crop§ | Imports | Total supply | Con-sumption | Exports | De-stroyed§ | Total distri-bution |
	Free	Govern-ment	Total								
1960	2,504	5,055	7,559	14,353	120	157	22,189	8,279	6,632	50	14,961
1961	5,725	1,503	7,228	14,384	64	158	21,834	8,954	4,915	134	14,003
1962	3,124	4,707	7,831	14,822	246	137	23,036	8,419	3,351	50	11,820
1963	2,986	8,230	11,216	15,197	173	113	26,699	8,609	5,662	50	14,321
1964-65	1,941	10,437	12,378	15,177	69	89	27,713	9,171	4,060	191	13,422
1965-66	2,602	11,689	14,291	14,763	193	104	29,351	9,497	2,942	50	12,489
1966-67	4,506	12,356	16,862	9,809	50	76	26,797	9,485	4,669	110	14,264
1967-68	6,704	5,829	12,533	7,188	30	145	19,896	8,981	4,206	261	13,448
1968-69	6,241	207	6,448	10,991	39	66	17,544	8,242	2,731	50	11,023
1969-70	3,610	2,911	6,521	9,863	134	52	16,570	7,991	2,768	50	10,809
1970-71	2,726	3,035	5,761	10,233	77	37	16,108	8,068	3,738	50	11,856
1971-72*	3,938	314	4,252	10,147	152	71	14,622	8,039	3,229	50	11,318
1972-73‡	3,035	269	3,304	13,282	51	71	16,750	7,800	4,500	50	12,350
1973-74‡			4,400								

*Preliminary.
†Includes in-season ginnings.
‡Estimated.
§Adjustments, if any.
SOURCE: New York Cotton Exchange.

TABLE 26-2 SUPPLY AND DISTRIBUTION OF AMERICAN COTTON IN THE UNITED STATES (IN THOUSANDS OF RUNNING BALES)

Crop year	Carryover on August 1						Produc-tion*	Season supply	Con-sumption	De-stroyed‡	Net exports	Total season distri-bution
	At mills	Public ware-houses	Farms and in transit	Total Carry-over	Govern-ment stock	"Free" stock						
1960	1,390	5,919	215	7,523	5,055	2,468	14,532	22,055	8,186	50	6,632	14,868
1961	1,886	4,754	490	7,187	1,503	5,684	14,495	21,682	8,844	134	4,915	13,893
1962	1,504	6,095	190	7,789	4,707	3,082	15,051	22,840	8,316	50	3,351	11,717
1963	1,196	9,647	280	11,123	8,230	2,893	15,404	26,527	8,509	50	5,662	14,221
1964–65	1,120	10,916	270	12,306	10,437	1,869	15,249	27,555	9,081	191	4,060	13,332
1965–66	1,472	12,521	230	14,223	11,689	2,534	14,975	29,198	9,405	50	2,942	12,397
1966–67	1,339	15,274	188	16,801	12,356	4,445	9,851	26,652	9,398	110	4,669	14,177
1967–68	1,757	10,318	400	12,475	5,829	6,646	7,280	19,755	8,886	261	4,206	13,353
1968–69	1,825	4,277	300	6,402	207	6,195	11,035	17,437	8,167	50	2,731	10,948
1969–70	1,623	4,466	400	6,489	2,911	3,578	10,013	16,502	7,950	50	2,768	10,769
1970–71	1,411	3,962	360	5,733	3,035	2,698	10,329	16,062	8,037	50	3,738	11,825
1971–72†	1,630	2,207	400	4,237	314	3,923	10,324	14,561	8,002	50	3,229	11,281
1972–73§	1,523	1,607	150	3,280	269	3,011	13,390	16,670	7,700	50	4,500	12,250
1973–74§				1,140								

*Includes city crop.

†Preliminary.

‡Includes adjustment items, if any.

§Estimate.

SOURCE: New York Cotton Exchange.

first business day thereafter, at 11 A.M. The July report shows planted acreage by states on July 1. The other monthly reports show planted acreage, yield per harvested acre, and production, all by states, as of the first of the respective months. Trade sources typically make private estimates before each report.

The *Cotton Situation Report,* issued by the Economic Research Service of the USDA in January, March, May, July, September, and October, is perhaps the most useful source of information for the trader. It summarizes historical data and includes a broad assessment of the cotton market. This furnishes an excellent base on which continuous current analysis can be made by utilizing daily and weekly information from other sources. Some analysts express the opinion that the USDA consistently overstates the prospects for domestic mill use and exports, thereby reflecting a bias toward growers. Since revisions and corrections typically are belatedly issued, the trader should watch carefully for indications of changing trends in demand.

Several important cotton reports are issued by the U.S. Census Bureau:

1. Ginnings reports are issued semimonthly from the beginning (August 1) of the crop year through January.

2. Cotton quality reports are also issued at irregular intervals.

3. On approximately the twentieth of each month the bureau reports cotton consumption as well as stocks at mills and in storage. The New York Cotton Exchange makes public estimates of these figures each month before the report.

4. Reports showing production of certain cotton goods inventories and unfilled orders are issued monthly.

5. Monthly reports of raw-cotton exports are issued by country of destination.

The New York Cotton Exchange issues weekly reports on the cotton market and on data such as certified stocks of cotton, loan entries, and withdrawals. It also reports useful daily information, such as cotton exports and spot prices.

SUPPLY

Most of the cotton in the United States is planted by May 31 and harvested by October. The various crop-production and situation reports referred to earlier will give the most authoritative information about quantity, quality, and timing of production. Cotton grows best in hot weather with adequate, uniformly spaced applications of moisture. Variations from these requirements can cause substantial reductions in the size and quality of the crop.

Descriptions of the major production areas will give the trader a point of reference when he is evaluating such price-influencing factors as the timing of shipments, relative production by area, and effects of unusual weather at different times and in different areas.

The South Central area, including Mississippi (the second largest producer) and the nearby states of Arkansas, Tennessee, Louisiana, and Missouri, produces more than 30 percent of the cotton grown in the United States. Most of the planting in this area is completed in May and harvested from late September to the middle of November.

The Southwest area, including Texas, the leading producer, and Oklahoma, also produces more than 30 percent of the total cotton. In the Rio Grande Valley cotton is typically planted in early March and harvested throughout July and August. In the Corpus Christi, Austin, and Dallas region the planting season extends into April and harvesting continues through September. Near Lubbock and eastward both the plantings and the harvest are about a month behind those in the Corpus Christi area.

Approximately 20 percent of the crop is grown in the West—California (the third largest producer), Arizona, and New Mexico; a large portion of it is grown on irrigated land with high per-acre yields. Cotton grown in the Western areas (San Joaquin Valley, Imperial Valley, Tucson, and Phoenix) tends to be high grade and long staple.

The Southeast (including the Carolinas, Georgia, and Alabama) produces slightly less than 15 percent of the United States crop. Most of the planting in this area is completed by the end of April. Harvesting occurs from October to early November.

DEMAND

After cotton is harvested various interests (ginners, brokers, mill buyers, and shippers) begin to accumulate it from the growers and from each other for marketing purposes. As they accumulate the cotton, or as they make commitments to sell it, they also expose themselves to the price risk. Hedging in the cotton futures market can transfer some of this price risk to the speculator.

Figure 26-1 shows the physical flow of cotton, whereas Figure 26-2 shows the ownership changes. Examination of these figures can be helpful in understanding the distribution process and the various information discussed in the "Sources of Information" section. Figure 26-3 shows the ownership changes for cotton products, and Figure 26-4 generally describes the stages used in converting raw cotton to end products.

The mill, which links Figure 26-2 to Figure 26-3, represents the final step in the merchandising of raw cotton and the first step in getting the final product to the ultimate consumer. The different demand factors, for both raw cotton and finished products, exert their influence with different time schedules, and their total influence is complex and difficult to predict.

Much of the raw cotton is acquired by vertically integrated companies that buy raw cotton, spin cotton into yarn, weave yarn into cloth, and finish the cloth. Most plants, integrated or not, are located along the Atlantic seaboard. In order of importance, some of the end uses for cotton are trousers, bedding, shirts, towels, men's underwear, fabrics, and dresses. Unless

FIG. 26-1   Physical flow of U.S. cotton. (Economic Research Service, USDA.)

significant shifts occur in the demand for these products or unless significant substitutions of other materials occur, it is difficult to determine the net impact of changes in demand for them. Cotton's share of the textile market has decreased to less than 50 percent of the total in recent years, as it has given way to inroads made by man-made fibers.

Traders typically equate short-term demand with the daily rate of mill use. This figure is regularly estimated by the New York Cotton Exchange

FIG. 26-2   Flow of ownership documents for merchandising U.S. cotton (warehouse receipts and bills of lading). (Economic Research Service, USDA.)

1. Reflects demand for fabrics
2. Reflects industrial production
3. Reflects consumer demand for mill-made products
4. Reflects consumer demand for piece goods
5. Reflects consumer demand for garments
6. Consumer expenditures

FIG. 26-3   Major flow of ownership changes for cotton textile and apparel products. (Economic Research Service, USDA.)

and reported by the U.S. Census Bureau. Data are provided that show mill usage and mill and warehouse inventories. When interpreting these data, the seasonal pattern of mill usage should be considered. October–November and February–March are periods of heavy mill consumption. Cotton exports in the United States, which recently averaged more than 4 million

FIG. 26-4   Distribution of a bale of U.S. cotton. (Economic Research Service, USDA.)

bales (approximately 30 percent of U.S. production), represent an important though steadily declining market. Japan, by far our largest customer, buys approximately 25 percent of our total exports. Exports are also made under the government Public Law 480 program. Such exports total less than 1 million bales a year.

The level of cotton exports depends on the level of foreign production, usage, and relative prices. However, varying time lags make intraseason price forecasting difficult. Exports are heaviest in the post-U.S. harvest December–January period, when foreign stocks are small; they tend to be smallest in July, August, and September, before the availability of the new U.S. crop.

Typically, traders compare cumulative (August) exports with the same date for the preceding year. It might be better to compare them with former years. A more important comparison is that made between the aforementioned cumulative exports and the latest USDA total-season estimates. Discrepancies in these figures tend to cause proportionately larger changes in the carry-over estimates which can have sizable price consequences; for example, a high speculative, long open interest might build up in anticipation of inadequate supplies. Such speculative interest will push the price to a higher level. However, if cumulative export shipments are lower than anticipated and not consistent with the expected short supply, liquidation of long positions can cause a sharp market-price break.

It is usually impossible to ascertain, at the time, the reason for discrepancies, even large ones, between the estimated and actual export shipments. It may be that foreign buyers are merely delaying purchases while hoping for lower prices, or it may be that there are reduced-consumption or increased supplies abroad. Trading positions based on anticipation of such factors are hazardous, even if based on reliable and objective information.

GOVERNMENT PROGRAMS

The government loan and disposal programs have significant influence on the total supply and demand of cotton, and they therefore exert significant influence on prices. The extent of this influence has been large in recent years; at times more than 40 percent of the crop has been under loan and therefore removed from the free market. Also, during this period, the Commodity Credit Corporation has held more than 70 percent of total carry-over. When such conditions prevail, the effects of government action can overwhelm other price-affecting factors.

The primary purpose of the current government cotton program is to influence production by direct support payments and acreage-division payments and to maintain a relatively low support price that will not discourage domestic and export demand; for example, the 1973 average loan rate for middling or 1-inch upland cotton was 19.50 cents a pound and was available to farmers who diverted a specified acreage of their cotton allotment into soil-conversion uses.

The price support loan is available to any grower who complies with the government acreage allotment. As with similar loans for other crops, the grower may terminate his cotton loan (a) by repaying the loan, in which case he will sell his cotton on the open market; (b) by selling his cotton subject to the loan to a third party (in which case the third party will have these three options available to him); or (c) by defaulting on the loan, that is, by not repaying it and thereby allowing the Commodity Credit Corporation to take title to the cotton at maturity. The amount of cotton placed under loan and the amount redeemed will depend, of course, on the relation between the free-market price and the loan price, as well as on premiums and discounts for various grades of cotton, all at particular dates during the season.

Most cotton that moves from government hands to the commercial market does so under a program in which the CCC sells cotton in the free market at the same price it sells it for export. This price cannot be less than the loan price plus 120 points. In many circumstances, then, the government can set an effective ceiling on the price of cotton.

A discussion dealing with the government loan and selling prices and their relations to three important market price levels is included in the Corn and Oats chapter. The same general principles apply equally to cotton.

SEASONAL INFORMATION AND CARRYING CHARGES

As with other commodities, the price of cotton in a free market will usually reach its lowest price during and immediately after the harvest, then rise to a high price later in the season when supplies become relatively scarce. As described in other chapters of this book, speculators' actions tend to overcome this seasonal tendency. Government action may also have a contraseasonal effect at times.

Carrying charges, which determine the maximum premium of distant futures over the nearby, are mainly a function of price and interest rates. A typical example is shown in the following computation for monthly cotton carrying charges.

	Approximate equivalent "points" in futures market (1 pt. = 500 cents per contract)
1. Storage for 1 month at 1.5 cents a bale or 150 cents per contract. (150 cents a day per contract × 31 days = 4,650 cents per contract)	9 pts.
2. Interest on one contract at, for example, 10% on 50-cent cotton, for 31 days (50 cents a lb × 50,000 lb per contract × ⅚% per month) = 20,800 cents per contract per month...................................	42 pts.
3. Insurance for 1 month at 4 cents per $100 per contract (4 cents per $100 × $25,000 per contract = 1000 cents)...	2 pts.
Total	53 pts.

WOOL

INTRODUCTION

The wool industry, including all activities from the production of raw fiber to the manufacture and sale of wool fiber for clothing and other uses, consists of two major divisions, apparel and carpet. These uses are quite separate from one another, requiring markedly different fineness or diameter of the individual fiber.

Futures markets dealing in wool (grease wool) and wool tops are concerned with the finer apparel wool—the only kind produced in the United States. Grease wool futures are actively traded in the exchange created by The Wool Associates of the New York Cotton Exchange. In recent years the wool top futures market on the same exchange has become relatively inactive. Grease wool (or wool) futures traded on the New York Cotton Exchange are therefore emphasized. It should be mentioned, however, that wool is also actively traded on numerous world exchanges, including a London wool top market and a grease wool futures market in Sydney.

A grease wool futures contract on the New York Cotton Exchange consists of 6,000 pounds of clean weight. Price is quoted in cents and $\frac{10}{100}$ of a cent a pound delivered in NYCE-licensed warehouses located in Boston, Massachusetts. The minimum price fluctuation is $\frac{10}{100}$ of 1 cent a pound, which corresponds to $6 per contract of grease wool. No trade may be made at more than 10 cents a pound (100 points or $600 per contract) above or below the preceding day's settlement price, and the range in any one day cannot exceed 20 cents (200 points). These limits are removed on and after the eighth day of the delivery month.

The most actively traded contract months for grease wool futures on the New York Cotton Exchange are March, May, July, and October. Trading sometimes commences 18 months before the expiration of a contract. The season for wool is assumed to coincide with the calendar year. It therefore begins on January 1.

FACTORS WHICH INFLUENCE WOOL PRICES

Wool is produced and consumed in almost every country and traded freely in world commerce. Arbitrage transactions, which tend to equalize differences between local areas, are common in most world markets. Therefore price changes in wool are caused largely by worldwide conditions, with local bullish or bearish factors sometimes having little or no effect.

The freedom with which wool is traded in world commerce and with which wool prices immediately reflect world conditions in all local markets imparts to wool many of the characteristics of a world currency. Wool prices are affected by changes, and anticipated changes, in the relative value of currencies and interest rates in the major consuming countries; for example, if devaluation of currency is anticipated in a particular country, speculators in that country will buy wool instead of holding cur-

CHART 26-2

GREASE WOOL WEEKLY HIGH, LOW & CLOSE OF NEAREST FUTURES CONTRACT WOOL ASSOCIATION-N.Y.C.E. IN CENTS PER POUND rency, thereby increasing the price of wool in that country; for example, from late 1971 to early 1973 wool futures prices rose from approximately 50¢ a pound to approximately $5.00 a pound.

Historically, war and the threat of war have caused rapid wool stock-piling and dramatic price increases. The last such example was the Korean War, when futures prices in New York rose from $1.25 a pound to almost $3.50. The price quickly fell back, however, and it failed to rise dramatically during subsequent conflicts and threats. Probably the availability of synthetic fibers has reduced the need for wool as a war commodity.

In estimating wool bullish price moves, it should be kept in mind that the decreasing price and increasing availability and substitutability are probably placing a ceiling on the price of wool, above which it would be difficult to maintain a price for any length of time.

Table 26-3 lists some salient statistics relating to apparel wool in the United States. When considering these distribution data, note the flow chart and comments in the "Demand" section of this chapter relating to the measurement of demand.

SOURCES OF INFORMATION

The *Wool Situation Report* is published four times a year—in February, May, August, and October (the Outlook issue)—by the Economic Research Service of the USDA. The report summarizes the broad economic wool situation and furnishes an excellent base for further current analysis.

More current information is found in the *Livestock, Meat, and Wool Market News: Weekly Summary and Statistics.* These weekly reports are issued by the Consumer and Marketing Service of the USDA. The USDA's Statistical Reporting Service also publishes the report, *Wool and Mohair: Production, Price, and Value,* which summarizes those data for the year, showing comparisons with the preceding year.

The New York Cotton Exchange publishes three services: (1) *Daily Market Report,* (2) *Weekly Trade Report,* and (3) *Basic Data Service.*

The Wool Bureau at 360 Lexington Avenue in New York also compiles extensive data on wool and wool products. These data are available on request.

SUPPLY

There are two broad categories of apparel wool: worsted and woolen types. In manufacturing worsted cloth, the raw wool is combed into continuous strands of parallel fibers called "wool tops." This combing process removes the short fibers, leaving only the more expensive longer ones. The wool top is then cut into slivers and spun into yarn. Because the fibers are parallel, it is a hard yarn. This worsted yarn is eventually woven into a (hard) *worsted cloth.* The short fibers, or noils, which were combed out in the process, are pressed together and become felt cloth.

TABLE 26-3 SALIENT STATISTICS OF WOOL IN THE UNITED STATES

Year	Stock sheep Jan. 1 (thousands)	Sheep and lambs shorn† (thousands)	Weight per fleece (lb)	Shorn wool production (thousand lb)	Price per pound‡ (cents)	Value of production (thousand $)	Pulled wool production (thousand lb)	Total wool production — As reported (thousand lb)	Total wool production — Clean fiber content (million lb)
1964	23,455	25,455	8.34	212,333	53.2	112,877	25,100	237,433	119.6
1965	21,843	23,756	8.48	201,463	47.1	94,999	23,300	224,763	113.1
1966	21,456	22,923	8.51	195,053	52.1	101,204	24,100	219,153	110.6
1967	20,677	22,022	8.58	188,919	39.8	75,163	22,400	211,319	106.4
1968	19,108	20,761	8.55	177,591	40.5	71,867	20,500	198,091	99.7
1969	18,355	19,554	8.47	165,655	41.8	69,485	17,100	182,755	91.5
1970	17,433	19,163	8.43	161,587	35.5	57,162	15,200	176,787	87.9
1971	16,946	19,036	8.41	160,157	19.4	31,416	12,000	172,157	85.3
1972*	15,835	18,778	8.41	157,881	35.0	55,287	9,700	167,581	82.0
1973*	14,853								

*Preliminary.
†Includes sheep shorn at commercial feeding yards.
‡Average price is for the marketing season April thru March.
SOURCE: Economic Research Service, USDA.

In the manufacture of woolen cloth, the raw wool is not combed. Therefore the fibers, both long and short, are not made parallel but stay in random directions. When spun and woven, the resulting cloth is a soft cloth with nonparallel fibers.

The worsted-type wools, at least those of a particular fineness (grade or quality), are traded on the various futures exchanges, either grease wool, wool top, or yarn; for example, the New York Cotton Exchange requires delivered wool to be of grade 64 or finer and at least 2½ inches in length. For purposes of perspective the U.S. grade classifications of wool (including the coarser carpet wools) are shown in Table 26-4.

Over a period of several months prices of both the worsted and the woolen type of wool will tend to move together, as will prices for fine and coarse grades. During a shorter period of time, however, prices for different types and grades often diverge significantly. Because only fine-grade worsted wool is traded on the futures market, the trader should not be misled by changing prices for woolens and coarse grades.

Australia, the principal wool-producing country, accounts for approximately 60 percent of the supply of fine (worsted) wool. Australian wool is sold at auction, and reports from these auctions are important indications of what world wool buyers are willing to pay based on total world supply and demand. They are not reflections of Australian wool production. The amount of world wool production, although increasing slowly, is relatively constant from year to year. The price and the production level are almost independent of each other. One reason for this unusual phenomenon is that wool is extracted from animals that continue to live. Flocks are raised in numerous farflung places. Sheep are hardy animals not much affected by weather, and worldwide, the number of animals remains relatively constant.

TABLE 26-4   UNITED STATES GRADE CLASSIFICATION OF WOOL

Blood grade	Count grade
Fine (merino)	80's
	70's
	64's—Standard of futures
½ blood	60's—Minimum deliverable grade
⅜ blood	58's
	56's
¼ blood	54's
	50's Woolen wools or nondeliverable worsted wools
Low ¼ blood	48's
	46's
Common	44's
Braid	40's Carpet wools
	36's

By appropriate crossbreeding, say of a ram with fine wool and an ewe with coarse wool, any type of grade characteristic can be achieved. There are several thousand commercial grades of wool, ranging from fine worsteds (the grade and type traded in the futures markets) to coarse carpet grades. Table 26-5 shows the world production of wool for recent years.

DEMAND

Interpretation of the measurements of the production and distribution processes for wool requires some appreciation of the relationships among certain of the data, especially in the distribution or consumption portions. Figure 26-5, a flow chart of this process, contains the various important inventories of wool.

The first inventory shown in Figure 26-5, inventories of raw wool, can be measured with good accuracy because these inventories are all at the same stage of development (raw) and, as indicated in the preceding section, the total production of wool is relatively constant from year to year. All of the later inventory levels are extremely difficult to measure.

The only reliable consumption data that can be gathered are those that occur during the various processing operations. As shown in the diagram, these data do not reflect actual consumption. In fact, after the point at which consumption is measured, the wool fiber continues to exist in the pipeline as wool top, yarn, cloth, or clothing. Therefore price projections made on the basis of measured production and consumption, but ignoring this huge inventory and the actual rate of usage, can lead to extreme errors.

Table 26-6 shows worldwide "consumption" of wool.

UNITED STATES GOVERNMENT PROGRAMS

Because of the worldwide nature of wool price-determining factors, the U.S. government in 1954 wisely abandoned its price support program for domestic wool. It agreed to allow the domestic price to be determined in the free-world market place. The USDA, however, substituted a direct subsidy system, which in effect pays each producer the difference between the price he received for wool on the free market and an arbitrarily set "incentive price" determined by the USDA. This system insulates domestic wool producers from having to compete in the world market. It does not materially affect the world price.

SEASONAL INFORMATION

Most of the domestic raw wool is shorn and available for sale during the short period of April, May, and June. Unless there is a holding movement on the part of producers, there is a small tendency for the domestic price to be depressed during this season.

Other countries also exhibit seasonal variations in supply and price. These slight seasonals are superimposed on what many analysts believe to be a longer term worldwide wool cycle. Past cyclical and seasonal patterns

TABLE 26-5 WORLD PRODUCTION OF WOOL [IN MILLIONS OF POUNDS (GREASY BASIS)]

Year	Brazil	Argentina	Australia	China	France	Morocco	India	New Zealand	Spain	Turkey	South Africa	United Kingdom	United States	Uruguay	USSR	World† Total
1963	60.7	434.7	1,785	145.0	54.0	34.0	75.0	617.0	81.3	92.6	322.8	130.6	281.4	194.0	821.7	5,837
1964	70.2	447.7	1,784	147.0	52.8	34.0	78.0	623.0	80.7	94.8	315.1	126.7	255.0	189.6	751.1	5,766
1965	78.2	445.3	1,663	164.0	56.0	30.9	77.2	699.0	79.8	94.8	350.1	129.3	241.1	183.0	787.0	5,836
1966	59.4	462.4	1,762	168.7	52.5	30.9	80.0	709.0	79.4	97.0	311.2	131.3	236.0	189.6	817.8	5,958
1967	69.3	450.7	1,770	173.6	48.3	28.7	81.6	728.3	79.0	101.4	321.4	127.0	227.0	178.6	869.7	6,040
1968	88.9	436.8	1,948	179.6	45.1	33.1	81.6	731.7	76.1	104.7	334.6	119.0	212.4	176.4	915.1	6,271
1969	82.5	445.3	2,036	183.2	44.4	37.5	77.2	723.1	73.7	105.8	340.6	104.0	194.7	165.3	860.0	6,247
1970	88.2	423.1	1,935	187.8	44.9	34.2	79.4	736.1	74.5	104.7	278.0	98.0	186.8	172.0	914.5	6,123
1971†	75.7	416.2	1,930	192.0	46.3	29.8	81.6	710.5	70.7	104.8	267.2	96.1	180.6	136.7	945.3	6,027
1972*	81.8	412.7	1,666		46.8	44.1	80.5	680.8	55.1	105.8	245.8	103.2	174.4	134.5	923.7	5,706
1973*	84.9	438.7	1,626		47.3	39.7	79.4	650.4	63.9	105.8	226.0	109.0	159.3	136.7	956.8	5,660

* Estimated.
† Preliminary.
SOURCE: Foreign Agricultural Service, USDA.

FIG. 26-5   Flow chart of wool production and consumption.

are difficult to use for predictive purposes and may be of little value to the futures market trader.

NOTES FROM A TRADER—COTTON AND WOOL

The trader cannot learn so much about cotton from the past as he can about some other commodities. Conditions affecting cotton changed materially during the early 1960s, when futures trading was virtually nonexistent. The New Orleans Cotton Exchange, with its popular 50-bale contract, abandoned trading, leaving the trader a choice of using the New York Cotton Exchange or of doing business on one of the foreign exchanges. In addition, the rapid growth of artificial fibers has continued.

For many years traders of both cotton and wool have been concerned about the obvious competition of man-made fibers and have tended to overestimate their effects. In addition to the increasing overall demand for fibers, there is still a preference among many consumers for the natural types, which tends to keep prices firm. Furthermore, many new materials use blends of natural and artificial fibers. Other factors that keep prices of natural fibers buoyant include world population growth and competition for arable land by other crops.

There are many types of cotton and even more of wool. In evaluating supply-and-demand conditions, the trader should make certain that the conditions that he is considering affect the type of cotton or wool that is represented by his contracts on the futures exchange. It is disconcerting to consider increasing demand for short-staple cotton as favorable to one's

TABLE 26-6 WORLD CONSUMPTION OF WOOL [IN MILLIONS OF POUNDS (CLEAN BASIS)]

Year	Argentina	Australia	Belgium	Canada	France	W. Germany	Italy	Japan	Netherlands	New Zealand	South Africa	United Kingdom	United States‡	Uruguay	World total
1963	30	82	97	18	276	153	196	302	23		24	458	412	46	3,324
1964	53	77	95	18	245	142	185	310	22		27	418	357	49	3,203
1965	52	78	98	18	237	146	189	326	21		28	403	387	40	3,281
1966	46	72	96	17	263	151	242	367	22	14	25	388	370	48	3,405
1967	47	76	80	16	217	123	218	354	21	16	28	360	313	48	3,249
1968	48	73	88	17	239	149	211	371	18	16	28	391	330	50	3,451
1969	55	77	93	14	268	158	236	395	19	15	31	385	313	46	3,537
1970*	60	81	89	11	293	150	205	433	18	19	28	337	240	48	3,464
1971†	74	77	67		318	163	195	402	19	20	26	311	192	45	3,410
1972†		80	65		322	170	213	430	19	28		336	219		3,523

* Preliminary.
† Estimate.
‡ Consumption on woolen and worsted systems only.
SOURCES: Bureau of the Census; Commonwealth Economic Committee.

long position only to find that the demand for long-staple is declining or to buy wool because demand for wool carpets is increasing and then discover that one is trading apparel wool.

For the wool trader conditions in Australia are important. Droughts affecting sheep-grazing land can cause significant reduction in the number of sheep available. This, of course, can produce tightness until flocks are replaced, with an attendant rise in Australian wool prices, and could affect wool futures prices.

Neither cotton nor wool lends itself well to intercommodity or to intermarket spreads. The wool market is too thin to spread on any important scale against cotton, against wool tops, or against positions on foreign exchanges. The cotton spreader is largely limited to intramarket spreads. When the No. 2 cotton market is active, it is one of the more popular day-trading vehicles.

ORANGE JUICE

INTRODUCTION

The popularity of frozen juice, especially since World War II, has caused expansion of the production of oranges in Florida and the orange concentrate industry to their present capacity of a hundred and fifty million gallons a year. About one-fourth of the total world supply of oranges are grown in Florida and approximately three-quarters of all Florida oranges end up as frozen concentrated orange juice (FCOJ).

Frozen concentrated orange juice was conceived by Dr. L. G. MacDowell of the Florida Citrus Commission and two colleagues. Several scientists had previously concentrated orange juice but had found that the orange flavor disappeared with the water. Dr. MacDowell's innovation was to over-concentrate the juice by reducing it to a thick, syrupy liquid, and then adding fresh orange juice and other favorings to restore the natural taste and appearance lost during the evaporation process.

Sugar is the important ingredient in FCOJ. When processors buy fruit for concentrate they are concerned with "pounds solids," not oranges. In other words, they want solids dissolved in the juices. These solids, which remain as concentrate after the water is evaporated, consist primarily of sugar. Oranges get sweeter as the crop year progresses. Valencias provide the best juice because they have the greatest number of pounds solids per box.

Ownership of the huge amounts of concentrate has caused substantial business risk for growers, processors, and canners. Accordingly, a frozen orange juice contract was inaugurated by the Citrus Associates of the New York Cotton Exchange in 1966 to supply a futures market to provide for a hedging of these risks. The market proved immediately successful. Open interest surpassed 5,000 contracts within 18 months, and the volume of trading was heavy. The volume and open interest has remained substantial since that time.

CHART 26-3

ORANGE JUICE WEEKLY HIGH, LOW & CLOSE OF NEAREST FUTURES CONTRACT NEW YORK IN CENTS PER POUND

The contract unit established was 15,000 pounds (44 55-gallon drums) of frozen orange juice concentrate with price quoted in cents per pound. The minimum price fluctuation is $\frac{5}{100}$ cents a pound; hence a price of 54.55 would indicate $54\frac{55}{100}$ cents a pound. A minimum rise to 54.60 or a minimum decline to 54.50 would represent a change per contract of five points, or a dollar value change of $7.50. The permissible daily limit is 3 cents (300 points or $450 per contract) a pound up or down from the close of the preceding day. The maximum permissible range during a trading session is also 3 cents, which means that, having risen by the daily limit, the price may no longer fall below the close of the day before or, having fallen the daily limit, may not rise above the close of the day before. This varies from the rules governing most other futures markets, for which the daily allowable range is usually twice the daily limit. On and after the eighth day of the current delivery month there is no limit on fluctuations for that contract.

Trading in frozen orange juice futures is regularly conducted for deliveries in January, March, May, July, September, and November. Deliveries must be made in Florida warehouses licensed by the exchange. The marketing year for oranges is considered to be December 1 to November 30, which corresponds to the crop year for oranges.

FACTORS WHICH INFLUENCE ORANGE JUICE PRICES

The market demand for orange juice depends to a degree on the size of the population and its purchasing power, but it also responds to industry promotion and price because the demand is somewhat more elastic than the demand for many other commodities. Processors attempt to increase consumer demand when supplies are large and try to avoid excessive price increases when supplies are low to avoid curbing the demand.

The price of orange juice at a given time depends more on supply than on demand conditions. Current supply is affected by the amount of frozen orange juice concentrate produced (the pack), movement to retail outlets, and stocks on hand. Juice available for concentrates is affected by such variables as the number of trees, fruit per tree, size of the oranges, and drop. Highly accurate mathematical models involving these factors have been developed to compute probable production. The volatility of stocks is indicated in Table 26-7. Weather affects many commodities, but few more than oranges. Trees are sensitive to cold and to sudden heat. If the temperature falls to 25°, both the fruit and the trees may be damaged. At 20° injury may be quite severe. During cold waves trees must be kept warm by artificial means if they are to survive. Effects of severe damage may be long lasting because it usually takes about five years for new trees to produce a good crop, should replacements be necessary.

In addition to warmth, an orange tree requires considerable moisture, and in some areas irrigation is required. Drought during blooming is especially serious. Trees might also suffer from inadequately drained soil, too much irrigation, and insects. Sudden heat waves can cause young fruit to fall off the trees. Strong winds may also prove dangerous.

In extremely warm areas oranges may ripen during the fall and winter months, but in cooler climates they ripen in the spring or summer a year after blooming. Some ripen early, some in midseason, and some late. In California they ripen throughout the year.

SOURCES OF INFORMATION

The U.S. Department of Agriculture (USDA) publishes several reports of interest to the trader in orange juice. The *Fruit Situation Report* is released four times each year: early in February, July, September, and November. This report summarizes the available supply and consumption figures and provides some analysis in an attempt to project the outlook for prices of the fruit and income for the producers. An annual *Summary of the Citrus Fruit Industry* is issued, usually in early October. The orange crop estimate for the approaching season is also issued in October.

TABLE 26-7 U.S. COLD STORAGE STOCKS OF ORANGE JUICE (IN MILLIONS OF POUNDS)

Year	Jan. 1	Feb. 1	Mar. 1	Apr. 1	May 1	June 1	July 1	Aug. 1	Sept. 1	Oct. 1	Nov. 1	Dec. 1
1961	137.0	228.8	352.7	336.2	369.3	468.5	495.8	421.9	363.9	296.5	222.7	165.4
1962	182.8	297.3	410.4	387.3	421.2	601.0	664.2	631.8	553.9	503.0	418.8	351.1
1963	389.5	474.9	459.0	466.7	483.9	470.3	422.7	362.1	320.5	272.5	223.5	189.0
1964	194.5	260.2	278.9	283.7	354.6	419.3	385.3	341.4	295.9	246.6	183.1	137.5
1965	173.8	282.9	401.8	410.8	559.2	616.9	575.0	523.4	451.5	380.5	294.8	242.2
1966	214.8	251.2	338.9	355.2	393.7	514.1	534.9	470.7	391.2	310.5	242.9	187.4
1967	184.7	251.9	370.9	449.7	500.5	631.9	803.2	753.3	637.4	499.2	394.8	343.0
1968	340.3	407.4	434.6	348.8	349.2	457.2	488.3	444.2	356.4	285.3	216.7	159.9
1969	188.8	256.4	331.2	373.0	410.6	505.7	601.6	547.2	478.2	383.6	293.7	239.4
1970	281.2	401.6	505.0	482.5	538.1	711.1	783.1	677.7	579.8	473.3	355.7	284.7
1971	323.7	462.8	573.3	581.6	574.5	642.9	684.3	603.1	535.4	450.5	347.3	262.2
1972	289.4	414.6	505.4	512.3	598.4	718.1	816.3	807.2	733.6	606.2	515.4	429.6
1973*	423.1	526.4	654.4	775.0	830.3	910.0	1,068	1,116	1,054.3	910.8	792.4	667.7

*Preliminary.

SOURCE: Statistical Reporting Service, USDA.

The *Crop Production Report*, issued six times yearly, summarizes conditions of the orange, grapefruit, lemon, lime, tangelo, and tangerine crops and compares them with previous crops. (May, June and July reports apply to the old crop and October, November, and December reports, to the new crop.)

The *Monthly Cold Storage Reports*, released about the middle of each month, indicate frozen orange juice stocks on the first of each month. Government estimates break Florida production into its various important types of crop, such as Temples, Early, Midseason, Navel, and Late (Valencias). For futures market traders the prospects for the Valenica crop are especially important because they provide the main ingredient for the production of frozen concentrate.

The Florida Canners Association, Winter Haven, Florida, publishes weekly industry statistical reports stating carry-over, pack, movement, goods on hand, and utilization for important Florida fruits and fruit juices. The Florida Citrus Mutual publishes some current information in its regular publication, *Triangle*. It also publishes a weekly summary of citrus statistics, including usage of the crop, shipments, gallons of concentrate packed, gallons moved, price data, and similar information concerning chilled juices and sections.

Detailed statistical information concerning all Florida citrus crops is available from the Florida Crop and Livestock Reporting Service of the Florida Department of Agriculture. Their annual publication *Citrus Summary*, contains detailed figures concerning acreage, production, utilization, prices, and shipments of citrus fruits from all states. The figures are obtained from the Florida and the U.S. Departments of Agriculture, Florida Canners Association, National Canners Association, producers, shippers, canners, and transportation firms.

NATURE OF PRODUCTION AND UTILIZATION

The largest single producer of oranges is the United States, which grows about one-third of all the world's oranges. It is followed in importance by Japan, Spain, Brazil, and Italy. World production is shown in Table 26-8.

About 90 percent of the oranges grown in the United States are produced in Florida and California. Florida is the leader by a wide margin. Its dominance results from its more abundant rainfall, lower cost resulting from less need to cultivate the soil, and less alternative competition for the land. During recent years Florida added substantially to the land it uses for orange production, and it now accounts for about 75 percent of the United States citrus production on about 70 percent of the nation's citrus fruit acreage. The importance of Florida in relation to other states is shown in Table 26-9, Salient Statistics of Oranges in the United States.

Oranges have been grown in Florida since the 1500s and in California since the 1700s. Most of the 10 percent production outside Florida and

TABLE 26-8 WORLD PRODUCTION OF ORANGES (INCLUDING TANGARINES) (IN MILLIONS OF BOXES ‡)

Season	Algeria	Argentina	Brazil	Australia	Greece	Israel	Italy	Japan	Mexico	Morocco	Spain	Turkey	South Africa	United States	World total
1960	6.7	22.6	25.0	1960–	6.7	12.6	27.2	35.2	21.5	14.1	48.2	7.5	8.5	121.5	389.6
1961	8.0	21.5	25.0	64	7.2	12.1	29.2	35.0	14.0	14.2	52.1	7.6	12.7	142.1	413.5
1962	13.2	21.8	26.0	Av.	7.2	17.3	26.1	34.1	24.8	13.9	48.0	7.8	11.3	106.9	394.5
1963	11.0	22.5	24.0	(6.3)	7.0	19.4	33.6	38.8	25.2	19.2	58.3	10.7	16.0	96.3	420.3
1964	12.4	22.5	25.7		10.1	21.3	37.3	48.4	27.1	16.1	54.9	9.0	16.3	125.2	265.7
1965	12.0	16.4	40.4	6.6	10.0	20.8	37.0	52.0	27.2	18.8	58.9	10.5	16.7	177.9	523.0
1966–67	12.0	23.8	49.2	7.3	12.8	25.1	43.1	65.6	27.7	21.3	73.9	11.6	15.8	241.5	650.1
1967–68	13.0	25.7	49.8	8.7	6.6	29.9	45.3	61.7	27.8	24.4	65.4	14.0	16.4	165.7	573.7
1968–69	14.8	32.7	51.1	7.7	11.2	26.6	52.8	89.2	28.3	22.7	54.5	16.8	14.7	237.0	681.1
1969–70	13.9	34.4	63.1	10.8	14.6	28.6	52.6	76.3	29.5	25.8	67.2	14.9	15.5	241.2	708.8
1970–71*	14.0	39.5	65.1	9.3	13.3	34.4	50.4	94.5	32.1	23.7	69.4	15.7	15.1	248.8	750.0
1971–72†	14.5	39.5	67.2	9.9	11.8	34.0	54.8	89.8		25.7	68.6	17.4	13.3	246.2	641.1
1972–73		30.7	86.9										16.2		

* Preliminary.

† Estimate.

‡ The net content per box of oranges varies. Approximate averages are 75 pounds in California and Arizona and 90 pounds in Florida and other states.

SOURCE: Foreign Agricultural Service, USDA.

TABLE 26-9 SALIENT STATISTICS OF ORANGES IN THE UNITED STATES

Season	Production† (million boxes) Arizona	California	Florida	Texas	Total	Farm price ($ per box)	Farm value (million $)	Foreign trade‡ (million boxes) domestic exports	imports	Quantities processed	Florida crop processed Frozen concentrates	Chilled Pdt's juice and salads (million boxes)	sections	Other processed	Total processed
1960-61	1.2	25.0	86.7	3.5	112.3	3.60	404.3	5.2	0.4	74.0		Not available			
1961-62	1.4	20.7	113.4	2.3	133.0	2.68	356.9	5.0	0.2	95.7		Not available			
1962-63	1.6	28.8	74.5	0.1	102.4	3.46	354.0	4.4	0.8	71.7	47.2	5.6	0.5	9.2	62.5
1963-64	2.2	32.0	58.3	0.2	88.5	4.67	413.6	5.1	1.7	52.3	34.2	4.9	0.6	5.7	45.5
1964-65	2.4	31.6	86.2	0.9	116.4	3.15	367.0	5.6	1.1	74.6	54.5	7.3	0.5	7.3	69.6
1965-66	2.6	36.9	100.4	1.3	135.5	2.48	335.9	6.7	0.7	92.1	61.8	12.3	0.8	8.0	82.9
1966-67	3.9	36.8	139.5	2.7	182.9	1.85	337.5	7.9	0.3	134.1	96.8	16.5	0.8	10.2	124.3
1967-68	3.1	19.2	100.5	1.8	124.6	3.08	384.1	3.6	1.7	91.7	62.0	16.0	0.8	6.8	85.5
1968-69	5.4	44.3	129.7	4.5	183.9	2.60	479.4	7.1	1.1	138.7	92.1	17.8	0.8	9.4	120.1
1969-70	4.6	39.0	137.7	4.2	185.5	2.43	450.8	6.8	0.9	141.0	100.7	18.6	0.8	8.2	128.4
1970-71	3.6	37.5	142.3	6.2	189.6	2.09	388.0	6.2	1.1	145.4	103.5	19.8	0.7	8.8	132.8
1971-72*	4.9	43.3	137.0	5.8	191.0	2.45	465.1			147.0	104.4	19.5	0.5	7.7	132.2
1972-73*	5.1	42.1	169.7	7.4	224.3	2.88	549.4								
1973-74	3.5	36.0	151.0	7.2	203.7										

* Preliminary.

† Fruit ripened on trees, but destroyed before picking is not included.

‡ Year beginning Nov. 1.

SOURCE: Economic Research Service, USDA.

California occurs in Texas, Arizona, Louisiana, and Mississippi. The Florida orange differs from the California orange because of the variation in the climate of the two states. The Florida orange is juicier, contains less acid, and is paler in color and thinner skinned.

Most oranges were once shipped fresh and squeezed into juice by the housewife. Now important parts of the crop are converted into concentrates which can be frozen and stored. Although the primary use of the orange is still its juice, there are useful by-products. These include the peel, which can be candied, dried, or made into marmalade, pectin, or orange oil, which is used for flavoring or perfumes. The pulp can be used for livestock feed.

The fundamentalist attempting to arrive at an economic value for frozen orange juice concentrate will start with beginning (12/1) stocks (inventory). He will try to arrive at total supply by adding the current season's pack plus imports to the beginning stocks. The current year's estimated usage (movement) subtracted from the total supply will indicate the carry-out. In determining whether the movement is likely to vary from its current rate, current price levels must be considered. If the movement (purchases) is unusually high or low in relation to apparent supplies, price must rise to perform a rationing function or fall to prevent an unusually high carry-out. Aside from price, the figures that are probably watched most closely by short-term traders are the weekly concentrate movement figures.

NOTES FROM A TRADER

Trading the frozen orange juice contract is attractive for those who find wide sudden movement of price appealing. For those whose pocketbooks or nerve cannot stand sudden adversity, possibly of considerable magnitude, other markets may provide better trading vehicles.

With all the factors affecting orange juice prices, one dominates; that is, Florida weather. Reports of cold waves, drought, or timely rainfall can affect prices drastically. The short history of the orange juice futures market, lack of comparable futures markets, and the relatively recent history of the orange juice concentrate industry do not present the fundamentalist with nearly so much basic information as is available in other commodities.

The trader should beware of judging demand by the size of the concentrate movement immediately after price increases. Chain stores and other major buyers are normally offered a brief period of price protection during which they can build stocks—which they naturally do whenever a significant price increase is announced.

CHAPTER TWENTY-SEVEN

Potatoes

INTRODUCTION

Maine potatoes. Futures trading in Maine potatoes on the New York Mercantile Exchange has accounted for most of the potato futures trading since the end of World War II. Accordingly, this is the major contract which will be discussed. Contracts traded are November, January, March, April, and May. Trading typically begins 10 to 12 months before the delivery month for the contract. The contract unit traded is a carlot of 50,000 pounds with price quoted in dollars per hundredweight (cwt). The minimum price fluctuation is 1 cent per hundredweight ($5 per contract), with a maximum allowable daily range of $1 and a maximum fluctuation of 50 cents from the preceding day's closing price. On the last day of trading in a contract month there is no limit on price fluctuations.

Idaho potatoes. In recent years Idaho potatoes have been traded on the Chicago Mercantile Exchange. Since 1968 considerable trading has taken place at times in the May contract. Trading in that contract begins in June

CHART 27-1

POTATOES (MAINE) WEEKLY HIGH,LOW & CLOSE OF NEAREST FUTURES CONTRACT N.Y. MERC.EXCH. IN CENTS PER POUND

of the year before. As with the Maine contract, the unit traded is 50,000 pounds with price quoted in dollars per hundredweight and a minimum fluctuation of 1 cent per hundredweight ($5 per contract). The maximum fluctuation is 50 cents from the preceding day's settlement price.

FACTORS WHICH INFLUENCE POTATO PRICES

Price changes in the potato futures market have been relatively volatile, responding rapidly, though not always consistently, to government reports, weather developments, and other information.

Following are some of the principal factors to which potato futures prices respond. Relevant information is available from the U.S. Department of Agriculture reports and forecasts, from the Commodity News Service (CNS), and from brokers generally.

1. Estimates of and actual planted acreage and comparisons with USDA forecasts.

CHART 27-2

POTATOES (IDAHO) CHICAGO **(Weekly High, Low & Close of Nearest Futures)** CENTS PER POUND

2. Weather conditions and forecasts during the growing and harvesting seasons in the important producing areas: Maine, New York, Idaho, Minnesota, and North Dakota, for the late summer and fall crops, Florida, for the winter and early spring crops, California and Alabama, for the late spring crops.

3. Monthly crop production estimates and storage stocks reports (changes in the latter give the potato disappearance rate) by the USDA.

4. Cash price at terminal markets and shipping points and their relation to futures prices.

5. Government programs and growers' participation therein, including potato movements into existing diversion programs.

6. Canadian crop reports, released regularly; in general they do not exert a major influence on the futures price of Maine potatoes.

SOURCES OF INFORMATION

The U.S. Department of Agriculture is the primary source of information relating to the supply of and demand for potatoes. Following are the principal production reports:

1. The *Prospective Plantings Report* is released approximately March 15. The *Crop Reports,* released monthly July 10 through November 10, indicate production and yield estimates at the first of each month. (From the preceding December through August the USDA makes monthly estimates of segments of the winter and spring crops, but the July 10 release is the first estimate of the total crop.)

2. The *Annual Crop Summary,* released in mid-December, is the end-of-the-season estimate for the total crop. By this date approximately half the United States crop will have been marketed.

3. Monthly, from December through March, the USDA releases reports that give total storage stocks of potatoes held by growers on the first of each month in the fall-producing areas. In recent years approximately 70 percent of the fall crop has been in storage on December 1. Approximately 15 percent of this amount is then taken from storage (disappearance) each month.

NATURE OF PRODUCTION

Potatoes are grown in all seasons of the year and in virtually every state (Figure 27-1). Most of the production is concentrated in a few widely scat-

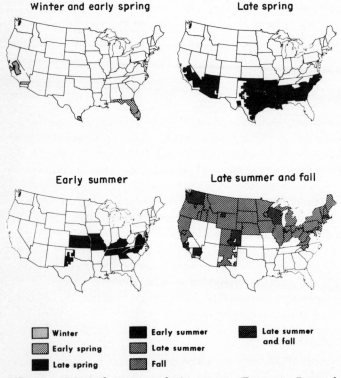

FIG. 27-1 Principal potato-producing areas. (Economic Research Service, USDA.)

tered regions: Aroostook County, Maine, the Snake River area in Idaho, Kern County, California, and certain counties in New York, Minnesota, and North Dakota. In recent years the states noted here have accounted for approximately 70 percent of total domestic production.

Seasonal crops. The USDA Statistical Reporting Service classifies the various seasonal crops according to the customary harvest dates (Table 27-1), although some crops can be harvested "early" or "late," according to the producers' evaluation of the potential price structure.

Except for the fall crop, a portion of which is stored for more than half a year beyond the harvest season, the marketing periods directly follow the harvest.

1. Early crops: The "early crops," constituting the first four categories in Table 27-1, account for 15 to 20 percent of total United States production. For these crops the marketing season generally follows the harvest, with very little going into storage.

A. The winter and early spring crops: These potatoes (Florida 65 percent, California 30 percent, and Texas) account for only about 3 percent of total United States production but provide 13 percent of the potato consumption during January through April.

B. The late spring crop: These potatoes (California 65 percent, Alabama, North Carolina, Arizona, and seven other Southern states) account for about 10 percent of total production but constitute more than half the supply available for food during May and June. The size of the late spring crop therefore has a dominant influence on prices received by growers. On the average, a 1 percent change in crop size is associated with an opposite change of approximately 4 percent in the prices received by growers.

C. The early summer crop: These potatoes (Virginia, California, Delaware, Texas, and others) provide for approximately half the total consumption during the early summer. They constitute 5 percent of total production and exert little influence on prices.

2. Late summer and fall crops: These crops make up at least 80 percent of the total United States production. Because portions of the late summer and fall crops are stored for more than six months, they exert a dominant influence on prices during a major portion of the year. They are the sole

TABLE 27-1   SEASONAL CATEGOR-
IES OF POTATO CROPS

Seasonal crop	Approximate time of harvest
Winter	January through March
Early spring	April 1 to May 15
Late spring	May 16 to June 30
Early summer	July 1 to August 15
Late summer	August 15 to September 30
Fall	October through December

market influence from August through December and remain a dominant force from January through April (when they compete with early potatoes). They have less influence in late spring. Because of the relatively inelastic demand (a change in price is accompanied by a less than proportional change in demand) for potatoes and the importance of the late crop in determining total available supplies, during the last decade a 1 percent change in late-crop production has been associated with an opposite average change of 5 percent in the price received by growers.

Maine and Idaho together produce about 40 percent of the late summer and fall crops. Minnesota and North Dakota contribute another 10 percent, and most of the balance comes from New York, Washington, Colorado, Wisconsin, Oregon, California, Michigan, and Pennsylvania, in that order.

A. The Eastern region produces about one-third of the late summer and fall crops, half the Eastern potatoes coming from Maine. New Jersey marketings peak in August, New York (Long Island) in October, and Pennsylvania in December. Maine marketings tend to be heaviest in the March to June period for potatoes sold out of storage.

B. The Central region (Minnesota, North Dakota, Wisconsin, and Michigan) produces about one-fourth of the total late summer and fall crops. Marketings of Minnesota and North Dakota potatoes range from January through April; Wisconsin and Michigan, from August to October.

C. The Western region (Idaho, Washington, Colorado, Oregon, and California) produces approximately two-fifths of the late summer and fall crop, with Idaho producing more than half the region's total. Throughout the September to June period Idaho potatoes compete heavily with Eastern and Central region potatoes in many Eastern and Midwestern cities.

Table 27-2 shows U.S. production by seasonal groups, as described above, for the years 1960 to 1973.

Table 27-3 summarizes some salient potato statistics in the United States for the years 1960 to 1973.

NATURE OF UTILIZATION

Potatoes are utilized primarily for domestic consumption as food. Per capita consumption of potatoes declined steadily during the first half of the present century, from 198 pounds in 1910 to 106 pounds in 1950. Although per capita consumption of fresh unprocessed potatoes has continued to decline, the consumption of processed potatoes since 1950 (potato chips, frozen French fries, dehydrated potatoes) has expanded dramatically so that it now utilizes approximately one-half the total crop. Table 27-4 indicates that total utilization of potatoes has shown no significant trend in recent years. In the short run the demand for potatoes for human food consumption has been relatively inelastic; that is, relatively large price changes do not cause consumption to change significantly.

TABLE 27-2 UNITED STATES POTATO PRODUCTION BY SEASONAL GROUPS [IN MILLIONS OF HUNDREDWEIGHT (CWT)]

| Year | Winter | Early Spring | Late Spring | | Early summer | Late summer | Fall | | | | | | | | Total United States |
| | | | California | Total | | | 8 Eastern | | 8 Central | | | 9 Western | | Total fall | |
							Maine	Total	Minnesota	North Dakota	Total	Idaho	Total		
1960	3.3	3.5	16.9	26.5	14.6	34.6	33.7	62.4	12.4	14.3	45.5	40.8	67.2	175.0	257.1
1961	5.0	4.6	19.0	27.8	15.5	36.1	37.0	67.6	13.1	14.0	48.4	55.0	88.6	204.6	293.2
1962	4.2	3.4	13.9	21.7	12.7	33.7	39.0	68.7	11.4	14.6	46.1	43.6	76.2	191.0	264.8
1963	3.9	5.1	15.2	23.8	12.6	28.9	37.6	65.6	13.1	13.3	44.3	53.5	87.4	197.3	271.2
1964	3.7	4.2	13.4	19.7	11.7	27.3	38.4	64.9	10.0	11.0	40.6	39.7	69.0	174.5	241.1
1965	3.7	4.9	17.1	24.2	12.0	29.6	35.7	63.7	12.9	15.4	51.5	61.7	101.6	216.8	291.1
1966	5.1	4.9	17.2	25.9	13.7	29.4	37.9	65.0	10.8	14.3	47.5	70.2	115.3	227.8	307.2
1967	4.9	2.9	15.9	23.7	14.0	28.6	37.6	67.2	11.8	14.3	49.4	63.9	114.6	231.2	305.8
1968	3.9	5.0	14.1	20.5	14.0	29.9	36.4	63.8	12.2	15.7	49.6	59.5	107.4	220.8	295.4
1969	3.8	5.7	14.6	21.3	13.5	29.1	35.1	62.0	13.5	16.2	51.2	69.9	125.3	238.5	312.4
1970	3.6	4.8	14.5	21.2	12.9	29.8	35.7	62.6	11.4	17.8	53.2	74.7	137.8	253.5	325.8
1971	3.1	3.7	13.4	19.9	11.3	27.5	37.7	64.2	14.9	20.0	62.5	77.3	132.8	266.7	319.4
1972*	2.3	3.5	11.1	17.5	10.6	26.4	33.3	51.4	13.3	17.4	55.0	77.3	134.5	248.8	296.0
1973*	2.9	3.5	11.7				28.9	50.4	13.1	19.5	57.0	77.5		252.0	297.5

* Preliminary, December estimate.

SOURCE: Crop Reporting Board, USDA.

TABLE 27-3 SALIENT STATISTICS OF POTATOES IN THE UNITED STATES

Year	Acreage		Yield per harvested acre (cwt.)	Farm disposition				Farm price ($ cwt.)	Value of		Stocks on Jan. 1[d] (1,000 cwt.)	Foreign trade[e]		Civilian consumption per capita (lb.)
	Planted	Harvested		Used where grown					Prod.[f]	Sales		Domestic exports	Imports	
	(1,000 acres)			Seed	Feed[b]	Household use	Sold[c]		(million $)			(1,000 cwt.)		
				(million cwt.)										
1960	1,400	1,386	185	7.6	15.9	5.3	228.3	2.00	513	457	98,640	2,307	715	108
1961	1,511	1,480	198	7.2	20.9	4.8	260.3	1.36	400	354	103,595	2,347	871	109
1962	1,378	1,347	197	6.0	17.0	4.0	237.9	1.67	441	398	122,215	3,359	912	107
1963	1,337	1,323	205	5.9	16.6	3.4	245.2	1.78	483	435	115,770	1,699	298	111
1964	1,311	1,272	190	7.4	12.2	2.8	218.7	3.50	846	756	115,000	1,617	348	111
1965	1,418	1,383	210	6.5	19.6	2.6	263.2	2.52	731	665	94,205	2,855	113	107.8
1966	1,498	1,463	210	8.1	31.4	2.4	265.0	2.04	620	543	124,170	2,247	274	113.6
1967	1,499	1,460	209	7.4	25.3	2.3	270.3	1.86	566	503	128,050	3,592	128	108.0
1968	1,415	1,383	214	6.9	20.9	2.1	264.2	2.23	653	589	139,170	2,569	264	115.8
1969	1,458	1,416	221	6.9	24.2	1.5	279.8	2.23	694	623	130,350	2,971	185	116.8
1970	1,450	1,421	229	6.9	25.4	1.4	292.1	2.21	720	644	138,140	2,928	130	117.7
1971[a]	1,432	1,391	230	5.6	30.0	1.4	282.5	1.90	606	537	150,030			118.9
1972[a]	1,305	1,254	236				268.1	2.36	894	808	151,400			120.2
1973[a]	1,320	1,303									134,320			

Note: 60 pounds equals one bushel.

[a] Preliminary.

[b] Also shrinkage and loss.

[c] For all purposes, including food, seed, processing livestock feed.

[d] Merchantable stocks held by growers and local dealers.

[e] Year beginning July.

[f] Farm weight basis. Excludes canned and frozen potatoes.

SOURCE: Economic Research Service, USDA.

TABLE 27-4 UTILIZATION OF POTATOES IN THE UNITED STATES (IN MILLIONS OF CWT)

Year	Table stock	Chips, shoe-strings	For dehy-dration	Frozen french fries	Other frozen products	Canned potatoes	Other canned products†	Starch and flour	Live-stock feed	Seed	Total sales	Used on farms where grown	Total
				For processing					Other sales				
1960	149.2	21.0	10.1	13.4	1.7	1.6	1.2	10.2	5.3	14.8	228.5	28.9	257.4
1961	153.3	22.6	8.5	15.9	2.2	1.5	1.3	20.5	20.3	13.8	260.1	33.5	293.6
1962	150.9	24.1	9.3	16.0	2.4	1.7	1.3	11.3	7.9	14.3	239.1	27.6	266.7
1963	146.5	26.7	9.9	19.8	2.6	1.8	1.4	11.7	10.1	14.2	244.8	26.9	271.7
1964	127.0	28.8	10.8	20.5	3.2	1.7	1.5	3.0	5.6	14.2	216.2	23.2	239.4
1965	139.5	31.3	20.2	32.3	5.0	1.7	1.6	8.1	5.8	16.9	262.5	28.7	291.2
1966	133.9	32.7	19.8	34.0	5.6	2.0	1.4	11.0	8.4	16.2	265.0	41.9	306.9
1967	131.2	32.4	19.1	34.6	5.0	1.8	1.5	12.0	16.8	15.8	270.3	35.0	305.3
1968	124.5	34.0	22.8	37.8	6.8	2.2	1.8	7.8	8.9	17.4	264.0	30.0	294.9
1969	127.4	35.5	25.5	44.7	6.9	2.1	1.8	8.8	9.6	17.6	279.8	32.6	312.4
1970*	129.8	35.9	26.1	54.5	7.4	2.4	1.9	8.6	8.3	17.4	292.1	33.7	325.8
1971*	120.2	35.4	27.0	54.7	8.9	2.6	2.0	7.8	7.2	16.8	282.5	36.9	319.4
1972	111.2	34.9	22.7	56.8	7.2	2.1	2.2	3.1	5.0	17.8	268.1	27.9	296.0

*Preliminary.

† Hash, stews, soups.

SOURCE: Crop Reporting Board, USDA.

Starch plants constitute an important outlet for poor quality and surplus potatoes. Government programs are sometimes designed to aid the industry in times of oversupply by offering an incentive payment to growers to encourage diversion into starch. Regular and modified potato starches are used in paper manufacture, textile sizing, and food processing.

Potatoes are also used for livestock feed, seed requirements, and exports. Year-to-year variations in seed utilization are slight, and exports and imports (Canada is the primary source of trade) generally have only minor influence on prices. Year-to-year variation does occur in the utilization for livestock-feed purposes, but this generally is not a substantial price-determining influence.

Government programs since 1950 have been relatively small in scope; they have been concerned primarily with reducing the available supply to the market "requirements." These programs have included (1) acreage marketing guides to encourage adjustments in production, (2) federal and state marketing agreements to regulate the quality and volume of potatoes shipped to market, and (3) Section 32 diversion or purchase programs to stimulate utilization of lower grade potatoes and to buy surplus potatoes for distribution to schools and institutions.

SEASONAL INFORMATION

Although erratic, the price of potatoes does exhibit some seasonal characteristics. Since the harvesting of a major portion of the crop takes place in the fall, a substantial quantity is stored at that time to supplement the small winter and spring crops produced in the South and West. Potato prices tend to decline as the fall harvest expands, contract lows frequently occurring before the year end. Prices may then become firmer as storage supplies are reduced. Because the demand for potatoes is relatively inelastic, the size of storage stocks, especially late in the storage season, has a strong effect on prices; tight supplies can bring a sharp price advance in the spring, whereas a relatively large supply, or one of poor quality, frequently results in pronounced weakness.

Table 27-5 shows the monthly midrange prices of the May potato contract each year from 1960–1961 to 1972–1973. The average of these prices is shown in the last column. Under each midrange price is the percentage of that price to the average for the year. These percentages for several past years are plotted in Figure 27-2, where any tendency for a repetitive seasonal variation would appear.

Although the averages of these percentages show no such seasonal pattern, an interesting phenomenon is apparent. Examination of Figure 27-2 shows that after the month of February potato prices usually move significantly in one direction without much reversal. This has obvious implications as to the time when a position should be taken. Figure 27-3 shows the open-interest and volume seasonal patterns for potato futures contracts traded on the New York Mercantile Exchange.

TABLE 27-5 MONTHLY MIDRANGE PRICE OF MAINE MAY POTATOES AND PERCENT OF AVERAGE YEARLY PRICE

Year	June	July	Aug.	Sept.	Oct.	Nov.	Dec.	Jan.	Feb.	Mar.	Apr.	May	Monthly average price and %
1960-61	2.75	2.62	2.78	3.12	3.21	3.13	2.94	2.65	2.96	2.69	2.29	2.15	2.77
	99.27	94.58	100.36	112.63	115.88	112.99	106.13	95.66	106.86	97.11	82.67	77.61	100.00
1961-62	3.05	3.02	2.74	2.50	2.36	2.20	2.08	2.11	2.25	2.33	2.36	2.33	2.44
	125.00	123.76	100.00	102.46	96.72	90.16	85.24	86.47	92.21	95.49	96.72	95.49	100.00
1962-63	2.92	2.82	2.82	2.83	2.64	2.61	2.65	2.75	2.85	2.44	2.01	1.89	2.60
	112.31	108.46	108.46	108.84	101.54	100.38	101.92	105.77	109.61	93.84	77.30	72.69	100.00
1963-64	2.88	2.82	2.84	2.81	2.64	2.62	2.65	2.71	2.85	2.43	2.01	2.89	2.68
	107.46	105.22	105.97	104.85	98.50	97.76	98.88	101.11	106.34	90.67	75.00	107.83	100.00
1964-65	2.61	2.62	2.59	2.64	2.59	2.56	2.59	2.80	2.93	3.07	3.23	3.83	2.84
	91.90	92.25	91.20	92.96	91.20	90.14	91.20	98.59	103.17	108.09	113.73	134.85	100.00
1965-66	3.23	3.18	2.75	2.95	3.15	2.90	3.10	3.36	3.43	4.02	4.69	4.32	3.42
	94.44	92.98	80.40	86.25	92.10	84.79	90.64	98.24	100.29	117.54	137.13	126.31	100.00
1966-67	2.88	3.30	3.92	4.19	3.77	4.03	4.45	4.21	3.48	2.91	2.17	2.51	3.48
	82.76	94.83	112.64	120.40	108.33	115.80	127.87	120.97	100.00	83.62	62.35	72.18	100.00
1967-68	3.16	3.05	3.00	3.38	3.54	3.16	2.80	2.43	2.24	2.31	2.88	2.73	2.85
	110.87	106.81	105.26	118.59	124.21	110.87	98.24	85.26	78.59	81.05	83.51	95.79	100.00
1968-69	3.17	3.06	3.00	3.39	3.53	3.16	2.80	2.42	2.24	2.31	2.88	2.73	2.89
	109.69	105.88	103.81	117.30	122.15	109.34	96.89	83.74	77.51	79.93	99.65	94.46	100.00
1969-70	3.30	3.40	3.69	4.05	3.79	3.92	3.56	3.39	3.39	3.50	3.09	2.66	3.48
	94.83	97.70	106.03	116.38	108.91	112.64	102.30	97.41	97.41	100.57	88.79	76.44	100.00
1970-71	3.38	3.33	3.24	3.15	3.28	3.46	3.78	4.33	4.44	4.32	4.12	4.10	3.74
	90.37	89.04	86.63	84.22	87.70	92.51	101.07	115.78	118.72	115.51	110.16	109.63	100.00
1971-72	3.73	3.84	3.80	3.79	3.58	3.59	3.71	3.94	3.78	3.33	2.99	2.39	3.54
	105.36	108.48	107.35	107.06	101.13	101.41	104.80	111.30	106.78	94.07	84.46	67.51	100.00
1972-73	4.17	4.89	5.22	5.13	5.38	5.71	6.41	6.65	7.64	8.41	8.28	8.31	6.35
	65.67	77.01	82.20	80.79	84.72	89.92	100.94	104.72	120.31	132.44	130.39	130.87	100.00

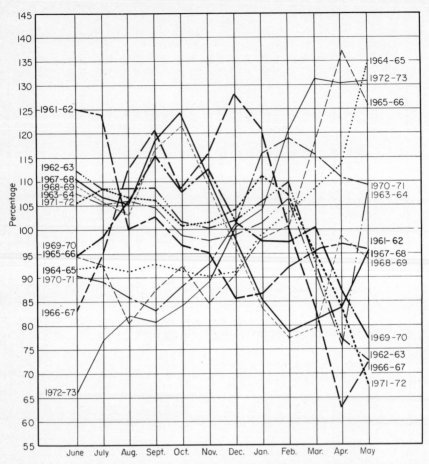

FIG. 27-2   Maine May potatoes, seasonal: monthly midrange price of May potatoes as a percentage of average yearly rate.

ECONOMIC RELATIONSHIPS

Some of the major economic factors that influence potato production and utilization for the late summer and fall crop are shown in Figures 27-4 and 27-5, where the arrows indicate direction of influence.

Production. Potato production depends on both acreage and yield per acre—the former, influenced mainly by earlier prices and by weather, being the more important factor in the short run. Growers, however, respond to prices not only by varying planted acreage but also by changing such inputs as fertilizers that affect the yield per acre.[1] Analysis of the total late summer and fall crop, 1952–1960,[2] shows that the elasticity of acreage with respect

[1] Olman Hee, "The Effect of Price on Acreage and Yield of Potatoes," *Agricultural Economic Research,* 10:131–141, 1958.

[2] "An Economic Study of the U.S. Potato Industry," *Agricultural Economic Report No. 6,* USDA Economic Research Service, 1962.

FIG. 27-3 Potatoes: monthly open interest and volume as a percentage of average monthly open interest and volume for the years 1962–1971 at the New York Mercantile Exchange (10-year, 1955–1964, average). (Commodity Exchange Authority, USDA.)

to the preceding year's (average) price (received by farmers) is 0.13; that is, the relative change in planted acreage averaged 13 percent of the relative change in the average price of the year before. The elasticity of yield per acre for the same crop was slightly lower.

Estimates of the economic relations affecting production can be made by

FIG. 27-4   Potato production.

using various techniques, such as regression analysis; for example, a USDA[3] estimate of planted acreage A_t of the late summer and fall crop (based on 1952–1960 data) for year t is given by the following linear regression equation:

$$A_t = 118.183 + 69.321 P_{t-1} + 0.688 A_{t-1} + 0.970 T_{t-1}$$

where P_t is the average price received by farmers in year t and T_t is an index of technology (calculated by the USDA[4]) for the same period.

Utilization and price. As indicated in Figures 27-4 and 27-5, production, price, and utilization for food, livestock feed, and starch are interrelated in a changing and fairly complex manner. Estimates of the more important relationships for the various potato crops are available from government reports and other sources,[5] as are estimates of the various elasticities; for

[3] *Ibid.*
[4] *Ibid.*
[5] See, for example, USDA Technical Bulletin No. 1380, July 1967. See also Nos. 12, 16, 22, 23, 65, etc., in the bibliography of Bulletin No. 1380.

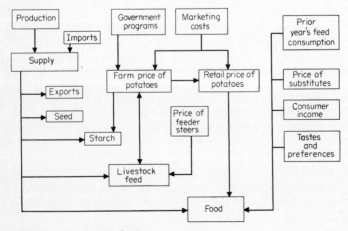

FIG. 27-5   Potato marketing.

example, the following linear relationship[6] relates the average price of the fall crop to prior price and to consumption data:

$$P_f = 9.351 - 0.188\,C_f + 0.698\,P_s - 0.00257\,D - 0.013\,M + 0.96_t$$

where P_f is the average price (divided by the BLS consumer price index) received by farmers for fall storage potatoes, C_f is the apparent per capita consumption (January to April) of fall storage potatoes for food in pounds, P_s is the comparable amount for winter and early spring storage potatoes, D is the per capita disposable income (first quarter) divided by the BLS consumer price index, M is an index of the cost of marketing potatoes, and t is the year (1947 = 1).

It should be pointed out that the relationships described by the above regression equations represent estimates based on past years and that these relationships may change in the future. New estimating equations should be regularly derived by using the most recent data.

NOTES FROM A TRADER

More than most other commodities, potatoes tend to move ahead of the news which ultimately proves to cause the move. Therefore they often appear to be going contrary to present news.

They seem to reflect values inconsistent with the cash market. Some growers maintain that the futures market does more to warp potato price relationships than to smooth them. The market is somewhat less popular with the trade than are other markets. Much of the agitation to eliminate potato trading has actually come from members of the trade who maintain that the market does more harm than good.

Spreaders should beware of the March–May spread when March is at a big discount to May and a bull market occurs. More often than not the spread does not improve but may get wider even as the price rises. The May–November spread seems to work considerably better. The dominant position of the May contract (which usually has by far the greatest open interest) is probably a major reason for this phenomenon.

Potatoes can usually be traded on a small margin, a fact that makes them popular with small traders, who fail to realize the volatility of this market. When trading becomes active, the day-trade commission can be overcome rather easily, which makes potatoes a popular vehicle for scalpers.

[6] *Ibid.*

CHAPTER TWENTY-EIGHT

Flaxseed, Rapeseed, and Rye

FLAXSEED

INTRODUCTION

Flaxseed futures are traded on the Winnipeg Commodity Exchange for delivery in May, July, October, November, and December. On the Winnipeg Commodity Exchange the contract traded, or board lot, consists of 5,000 bushels (1,000 bushel job lots are also traded) to be delivered during the months indicated. Flaxseed is quoted in cents and eighths of a cent a bushel, the minimum fluctuation being $\frac{1}{8}$¢ $\times$ 5,000 = $6.25 per contract.

The daily trading limits are 30 cents up or down from the preceding clearing close and, on the opening day of trading in a futures contract from the middle of the opening range.

FACTORS WHICH INFLUENCE CANADIAN
FLAXSEED PRICES —SUPPLY AND DEMAND

Canadian flax is generally sown in May and June and harvested in September and October. Production during the years 1962 to 1971 averaged about 22 million bushels. In 1970 a crop of nearly 49 million bushels was harvested. Although small amounts are grown in Eastern Canada, the main acreage is in the three Prairie Provinces, particularly in the southern areas.

The standard weight of flaxseed, for contract delivery, is 56 pounds a

CHART 28-1

FLAXSEED WEEKLY HIGH, LOW & CLOSE OF NEAREST FUTURES CONTRACT WINNIPEG GRAIN EXCH. IN CENTS PER BUSHEL

bushel. The seed, when crushed, yields an average of 42 percent linseed oil plus a by-product of oilcake or linseed meal, which normally has a protein content of more than 42 percent.

Linseed oil is used in outside paints, varnishes, printing inks, linoleum, and other industrial products. A new use for linseed oil is the protection of concrete surfaces against winter damage. Researchers have developed new linseed oil emulsion paints to help meet the competition of synthetics and other vegetable oils used in paint manufacture. Linseed meal, with its high protein content, is a valuable supplement in livestock and poultry feeding.

Canada, the United States, Argentina, the Soviet Union, and India are the world's principal flaxseed producers.

Canada is the world's largest exporter of flaxseed and surpasses its competitors by a wide margin. Argentina, although a large producer, exports most of the crop in the form of linseed oil. Europe, Japan, and the United Kingdom are Canada's best customers. More than 50 percent of the export movement is via Thunder Bay and Eastern ports, and the balance is shipped via Vancouver.

Canadian crushers process 2½ to 3 million bushels annually. The total domestic disappearance, including seed requirements, averages about 6 million bushels.

Tables 28-1 and 28-2 show world production and exports of flaxseed.

SOURCES OF INFORMATION

Statistics. Canadian Grain Commission, Statistics Branch, 280 Grain Exchange Building, Winnipeg, Manitoba, R3B 0T6

The Winnipeg Commodity Exchange, *Quarterly Summary,* 678 Grain Exchange Building, Winnipeg, Manitoba, R3B 0V7

Sanford Evans Services Limited, *Annual Summary,* P.O. Box 6900, Winnipeg, Manitoba, R3C 3B1

Crop reports and estimates. Dominion Bureau of Statistics, Ottawa, Canada.

General. Agriculture, Fisheries and Food Products Branch, Department of Industry, Trade and Commerce, Ottawa, Canada.

RAPESEED

INTRODUCTION

Rapeseed contracts for future delivery are traded primarily on the Winnipeg Commodity Exchange with delivery months as follows: Vancouver rapeseed futures, September, November, January, March, and June. Thunder Bay rapeseed futures, October, November, December, May, and July. The trading unit or broad lot is 5,000 bushels (1000 bushel job lots are also traded).

Rapeseed is quoted in cents and eighths of a cent a bushel, with the minimum fluctuation ⅛ cent a bushel representing ⅛¢ × 5,000 = $6.25 per contract. The maximum daily trading limits are 20 cents up and down from the preceding clearing house close and on the opening day of trading in a contract from the middle of the opening range.

The Winnipeg Commodity Exchange is used extensively by those who market Canadian rapeseed. The primary sellers are country elevator operators who buy rapeseed from producers and hedge these purchases by selling varying quantities for future delivery. The primary buyers are the merchandisers, crushers, and exporters who use the futures both to hedge their inventories and to cover sales they have made for immediate or future shipment. Futures trading by members of the public permits the primary sellers and buyers to complete their operations with a minimum of market movement.

FACTORS WHICH INFLUENCE CANADIAN
RAPESEED PRICES—SUPPLY AND DEMAND

The main acreage of rapeseed production is in the three Prairie Provinces; originally sown in the northern areas, this crop is rapidly increasing

TABLE 28-1 WORLD PRODUCTION OF FLAXSEED (IN THOUSANDS OF METRIC TONS)†

Crop Year	Argentina	Australia	Brazil	Canada	Ethiopia	France	India	Mexico	Poland	Romania	Turkey	Uruguay	United States	USSR	World total
1960-61	22,124	543	1,188	23,020	1955-9 Av (1,497)	1955-9 Av (1,592)	17,239	970	1955-9 Av (2,113)	1955-9 Av (380)	878	2,632	30,402	13,600	124,325
1961-62	32,203	504	1,098	14,318			15,558	787			709	3,770	22,178	18,500	121,562
1962-63	30,014	1,030	1,717	16,042			17,960	737			748	3,324	32,230	N.A.	133,650
1963-64	30,353	1,181	802	21,116	2,047	2,104	17,038	737	2,401	709	709	2,444	31,041	17,900	136,583
1964-65	32,085	1,864	2,114	20,313	2,165	1,972	14,920	748	1,378	937	689	2,808	24,401	17,600	131,231
1965-66	22,440	244	1,659	29,254	2,205	1,094	19,806	787	3,031	1,374	551	1,482	35,402	22,835	147,735
1966-67†	597	14	36	559	57	39	335	14	72	38	11	40	594	607	3,111
1967-68	385	11	28	238	60	33	260	15	73	39	12	27	509	519	2,319
1968-69	510	20	28	500	60	24	438	10	65	30	12	56	685	485	3,035
1969-70	640	37	31	700	62	27	329	10	57	38	12	105	887	451	3,508
1970-71	680	27	22	1,243	64	16	469	30	65	42	7	64	751	471	4,055
1971-72	316	13	22	567	70	20	474	40	75	58	7	25	462	470	2,746
1972-73*	345	9	25	483		17	510	10			7	22	353		2,564

*Preliminary.

†Data before 1966-1967 are in thousands of bushels.

SOURCE: Foreign Agricultural Service, USDA.

TABLE 28-2 WORLD EXPORTS OF FLAXSEED FROM SPECIFIED COUNTRIES (IN THOUSANDS OF METRIC TONS)†

Year	Argentina	Belgium and Luxembourg	Canada	China	Ethiopia	Brazil	Iraq	France	Morocco	Netherlands	Tunisia	W. Germany	United States	Uruguay	World total
1960	2,195	594	14,508	373	741	55	191	—	400	473	—	—	4,149	—	23,727
1961	3,511	797	13,854	146	646	177	195	—	86	470	—	—	4,527	216	24,709
1962	1	729	11,515	160	1,020	274	271	—	92	351	—	—	3,942	1,078	19,464
1963	815	1,002	11,537	200	1,463	965	72	—	72	551	23	—	3,408	65	20,213
1964†	—	29.3	377.1	1.0	31.1	—	9.7	—	0.9	10.1	0.7	—	176.5	0	638.3
1965	—	37.2	408.9	0	19.3	6.1	4.9	—	2.0	14.7	0.1	0.4	99.7	0	595.4
1966	0	29.8	513.1	0	10.5	1.0	7.1	—	1.9	8.2	—	0.1	169.2	0	742.0
1967	—	31.0	353.6	—	9.7	0	7.5	—	1.5	7.3	0.4	1.0	153.2	—	565.8
1968	—	25.1	278.4	N.A.	3.7	0	10.0	—	0.8	6.6	0.4	0.3	231.2	—	556.8
1969	0	24.3	404.0	N.A.	0.3	0	0	0.1	1.8	3.2	0.4	0.3	207.5	—	641.7
1970	0	22.6	494.2	N.A.	—	4.5	0	2.7	2.5	2.9	0.4	13.3	74.3	—	617.5
1971*	0	25.2	626.1		1.0	0	0	5.6	1.5	2.5	0.2	0.1	10.7	—	673.0
1972															

*Preliminary.

†Data before 1964 are in thousands of bushels.

SOURCE: Foreign Agricultural Service, USDA.

CHART 28-2

RAPESEED WEEKLY HIGH, LOW & CLOSE OF NEAREST FUTURES CONTRACT WINNIPEG IN CENTS PER BUSHEL

(VANCOUVER)

in acreage throughout the southern prairies. It is generally sown in May and early June and harvested between August and October.

The standard weight of rapeseed for contract delivery is 50 pounds a bushel. The traditional high erucic acid varieties (Polish, Arlo, Echo, and Target) yielded an average of 43.9 percent oil. The new low erucic varieties (Span, Zephyr, and Oro) now yield about 40 percent oil, but a definite increase is expected by further selective breeding. In 1971 the high erucic varieties exported yielded 40 to 41 percent oil, with low erucic varieties giving 2 to 3 percent less.

The oil is used for margarine, shortening, cooking and salad oil, and to some extent as an industrial lubricant. Rapeseed meal has a protein content of about 40.5 percent and is a valuable supplement in livestock and poultry feeding. In Japan, where the meal was originally used only as a fertilizer, addition to animal feed formulas has increased during recent years.

Rapeseed competes in world markets directly with 12 other vegetable oils, and its price is influenced significantly by these and another six animal or marine oil sources, ranging down in volume from soybean, peanut and sunflower through tallow, fish, and whale.

More and more farmers are finding rapeseed a valuable cash crop. Canadian production increased from less than 6 million bushels in 1962 to nearly 100 million bushels in 1971. Canadian crushers now process more than 10 million bushels a year. Canada, the world's largest exporter, ships more than all the other exporting countries combined. Principal importers of Canadian seed have been Japan, The Netherlands, Italy, West Germany, Pakistan, India, and France.

Canada, also the world's largest producer of rapeseed, is followed by India, Pakistan, and China. Rapeseed is also grown in Japan, Sweden, France, Denmark, Germany, and Poland; these countries consume most of their supplies at home, but at times some of them are substantial exporters.

Table 28-3 shows the world production of rapeseed.

SOURCES OF INFORMATION

The sources of information relating to Canadian rapeseed are shown in the flaxseed section of this chapter.

NOTES FROM A TRADER—
FLAXSEED AND RAPESEED

Those who trade flax and rapeseed for the first time after some experience in corn and wheat may have to revise their ideas about price movement and range. The great price volatility in these commodities sometimes makes close stops almost meaningless. Those utilizing a large part of their trading capital in these markets should consider their risk carefully. Spreaders between old and new crops may find one or even both sides of their spreads in unusually thin markets, which can lead to disorderly execution of market or stop orders. Partial rather than complete fills of limit orders are not uncommon.

Both flax and rapeseed are sometimes, but not always, responsive to European oil prices. In the case of both commodities oil is usually a more important end product than solids or fibers. Flax tends to be quite responsive to weather conditions in Saskatchewan, Manitoba, and Alberta, particularly to dryness in July.

Trends, particularly in flax, are long and strong. Those who like to probe against markets for tops or bottoms may do well to try elsewhere.

RYE

INTRODUCTION

Rye futures are traded on the Winnipeg Commodity Exchange. That exchange is used extensively by those who market Canadian rye. The primary sellers are country elevator operators who buy rye from producers and hedge these purchases by selling varying quantities for future delivery. The primary buyers are exporters, processors, and distillers who purchase con-

TABLE 28-3 WORLD PRODUCTION OF RAPESEED (IN THOUSANDS OF METRIC‡ TONS)

Year†	Canada	China	Czecho-slovakia	Denmark	France	E. Germany	W. Germany	India	Japan	Netherlands	Pakistan	Poland	Sweden	Chile	World total
1961	280.5	645.0	92.6	29.1	117.4	191.0	82.0	1,485	301.5	10.8	351.1	283.3	130.0	*1960–4*	4,189
1962	146.5	575.0	52.9	57.4	176.3	182.2	127.1	1,484	272.0	11.3	341.6	397.9	160.8	(45.9)	4,130
1963	209.0	625.0	45.2	29.1	148.8	141.3	105.6	1,426	120.0	11.0	399.8	250.2	113.4	55.9	3,778
1964‡	300.1	660.0	46.0	52.3	246.6	175.7	108.7	903	134.6	10.3	301.8	267.0	181.1	50.9	3,557
1965	512.6	700.0	74.0	49.9	337.8	213.8	106.5	1,466	125.5	10.9	306.8	504.0	216.5	60.0	4,802
1966	585.1	735.0	78.0	33.1	317.1	210.8	98.7	1,276	94.6	13.1	278.4	448.0	95.0	77.0	4,455
1967	560.2	800.0	85.0	39.2	432.5	272.6	124.6	1,228	79.2	15.2	306.8	651.0	245.7	60.7	5,043
1968	440.0	786.0	73.0	29.9	457.3	265.4	169.9	1,568	68.4	18.0	396.3	712.0	262.9	47.9	5,435
1969	757.5	688.0	48.0	21.1	512.5	163.6	158.1	1,347	48.0	12.2	358.0	204.0	208.0	63.6	4,737
1970	1,638	780.0	63.0	22.2	567.1	181.0	185.0	1,564	30.1	21.8	378.0	566.0	191.0	69.9	6,431
1971	2,155	830.0	100.6	51.0	668.0	197.0	228.2	1,975	22.8	32.7	296.4	595.0	253.0	52.0	7,849
1972*	1,300	996.0	101.0	45.0	722.0	234.0	248.7	1,433	16.0	45.2	315.9	430.0	323.0	77.9	6,596
1973	1,207	1,000.0	100.0	90.0	636.0	250.0	222.3	1,853	13.0	40.6	324.1	645.0	350.0	39.7	7,086

*Preliminary.

† Harvest generally occurs in the first half of the calendar year given in all major producing countries except Canada.

‡ Data before 1964 are in thousands of short tons.

SOURCE: Foreign Agricultural Service, USDA.

CHART 28-3

RYE   WEEKLY HIGH,LOW & CLOSE OF NEAREST FUTURES CONTRACT   WINNIPEG GRAIN EXCHANGE   IN CENTS PER BUSHEL

tracts in order to cover sales they have made for immediate or future shipment or to assure themselves of a supply at a known price. Trading by the
public permits the primary sellers and buyers to complete their operations
with a minimum of market movement.

Rye futures are traded for delivery in October, December, May, and
July. As with other grains, the futures contract in rye consists of 5,000
bushels (1000 bushel job lots are also traded), with the price quoted in
cents per bushel and a minimum fluctuation of $\frac{1}{8}$ cent a bushel, or $\frac{1}{8}$¢ $\times$
5,000 = \$6.25 per contract. The maximum allowable daily range is 20
cents, with a maximum fluctuation of 10 cents either up or down from the
preceding day's close.

FACTORS WHICH INFLUENCE RYE PRICES—
SUPPLY AND DEMAND

Rye is grown on all continents except Africa. Extensive production occurs
in Eastern and Northern Europe, Asia, and North America. Russia, by far
the world's largest producer of rye, is followed by Poland and Germany.
Canada accounts for only a small part of world production. In parts of
Northern Europe and Soviet Russia rye is still an important cereal used for
human food and is a staple part of the diet.

TABLE 28-4 WORLD PRODUCTION OF RYE (IN THOUSANDS OF METRIC TONS‡)

Crop year	Argentina	Austria	Canada	Czecho-slovakia	Denmark	France	Germany West	Germany East	Hungary	Nether-lands	Poland	Spain	Turkey	USSR	United States	World total
1960	20	14	10	35	18	16	149	78	14	18	310	15	24	520	33	1,330
1961	20.9	18.6	6.5	37.8	20.2	13.7	98.9	59.2	11.7	11.9	238.5	13.8	24.0	600	27	1,340
1962	6.5	18.4	12.0	36.1	20.2	14.0	116.6	63.9	9.2	13.4	263.2	17.8	24.6	540	41	1,246
1963	21.2	12.7	12.8	34.6	12.6	14.1	127.5	62.0	8.5	12.3	280.5	16.7	33.5	460	29	1,182
1964	25.6	15.3	12.2	34.3	11.5	15.3	142.1	74.4	10.4	14.0	275.0	13.8	26.6	504	32	1,256
1965–66	9.6	12.4	16.7	32.4	10.4	15.2	111.2	75.2	11.3	9.8	326.3	13.4	27.6	571	33	1,327
1966–67	10.6	14.3	17.2	30.9	5.5	14.0	106.1	64.6	9.5	7.5	306.7	14.1	30.7	472	28	1,170
1967–68‡	352	377	304	689	118	365	3,218	1,986	225	239	7,645	336	825	11,900	608	30,280
1968–69	360	413	331	769	127	351	3,247	1,936	238	239	8,438	364	780	12,700	583	31,879
1969–70	377	440	419	687	126	330	2,928	1,544	235	207	8,166	348	770	9,800	767	28,057
1970–71	181	363	570	454	134	306	2,701	1,483	155	172	5,433	256	680	10,800	936	25,596
1971–72*	256	448	557	496	150	308	3,093	1,754	180	209	7,827	269	900	10,600	1,252	29,334
1972–73†	500	402	344	633	155	331	3,045	1,900	170	151	8,203	259	755	9,900	750	28,581
1973–74	432	426	366	650	129	315	2,700	1,764	180	150	7,820	250	700	8,500	648	25,974

*Preliminary.
†Estimate.
‡Data before 1967–1968 are in millions of bushels.
SOURCE: Foreign Agricultural Service, USDA.

Rye production in Canada is centered in the three Prairie Provinces. It is bought and sold on the open market. The domestic disposition of rye falls into four categories: human food, industrial use, seed, and feed. Rye is not an especially desirable feed for livestock nor, in this country, is it extensively used for bread. For these reasons the market for rye is limited and the production small. A portion of the crop is used in the distilling industry. The greater part of Canada's rye crop is available for export.

The bulk of Canada's rye crop, sown in September and October, lies dormant throughout the winter and is harvested in late July and August. Production during the years of 1961 to 1970 has averaged 12½ million bushels. The standard weight of rye for contract delivery is 56 pounds.

Canada, the United States, and Turkey are the leading rye exporters. The largest importer by far is Holland, followed by Sweden, Western Germany, Denmark, and Belgium.

Table 28-4 shows the world production of rye.

SOURCES OF INFORMATION

The sources of information relating to Canadian rye are shown in the flax-seed section of this chapter.

NOTES FROM A TRADER

Those who trade rye should realize that this is basically a European crop and that the smaller Canadian market is quite thin and dominated by a few traders. This might produce problems where liquidity is important, especially in the case of liquidation under adverse conditions. Those who think that they can trade rye, or even a rye spread, with a 1-cent stop had better review their charts.

There are three important reasons for the volatility of the rye market: (a) The crop is small and a relatively small change in the supply-demand balance will often have significant price consequences. (b) There is a smaller amount of hedging pressure and trade buying than in most other grains. (c) Because the rye market is relatively "thin," prices often fluctuate more than prices of the other grains.

CHAPTER TWENTY-NINE

Coconut Oil

INTRODUCTION

Copra (the dried meat of coconut) and coconut oil are among the world's major source of fats and oils. Coconut oil is one of the six major vegetable oils moving in world trade, along with soybean, cottonseed, sunflower, peanut, and rapeseed oils. In terms of physical volume it is second only to soybean oil. Until 1972 there was no viable futures market for coconut oil, even though it appears to be an ideal commodity for futures trading, subject to little government control, and completely fungible, reflecting a world market and a history of volatile price movement. Attempts have been made to establish futures markets in Rotterdam and London, but were unsuccessful, possibly because of the structures of the markets themselves or because of foreign exchange problems. In 1972 the Pacific Commodities Exchange, located in San Francisco, was authorized to trade coconut oil futures as a regulated commodity.

Trading in coconut oil began late in 1972 and was successful enough to encourage the exchange to plan to begin trading other commodities such as eggs, cattle, white wheat, and, perhaps, wine. A gradually increasing open interest attracted various large wire houses that bought memberships in the exchange, which appears to have a good chance of becoming established as the first West Coast exchange whose commodities are authorized for trading by the Commodity Exchange Authority. Coconut oil futures are traded in the months of January, March, May, July, September, November, and December of each year. Trading typically begins 12 months before the delivery month of the contract. The contract is for 60,000 pounds of crude coconut oil for delivery in store at U.S. Pacific or Atlantic Coast ports during the month of the contract. The 60,000 pound quantity is equivalent to one standard tank car or two standard tank wagons of coconut oil, as in the case of the soybean oil contract on the Chicago Board of Trade. Buyers taking delivery are given the option of accumulative receipts to enable them to ship in jumbo tank cars that hold 150,000 pounds, equivalent to 2½ contracts. The price is quoted in cents per pound with a minimum fluctuation of 1/100 cent a pound which represents $6.00 per contract. The maximum allowable daily range is 2 cents a pound with a maximum fluctuation of 1 cent a pound or $600 per contract, either up or down from the preceding day's settlement price. These limits do not apply to trading in the spot month after the first notice day. Trading hours are from 7:30 to 11:15 A.M. Pacific time in order that the trading hours will coincide with the trading hours for soybean oil on the Chicago Board of Trade.

FACTORS WHICH INFLUENCE PRICES—
SUPPLY AND DEMAND

Coconut oil is a commodity that is marketed internationally at prices determined exclusively by the influences of supply and demand in a free market, without direct benefits or hindrances of government support prices or international marketing agreements. The highly volatile price of coconut oil attracts a demand for hedging by segments of related industries and by speculators.

Initial trading in coconut oil was helped by the fact that 1972 copra production in the Philippines increased spectacularly and exports rose 42 percent over those of 1971, which had, in turn, been 40 percent over 1970. As a consequence, coconut oil prices in 1972 reached a 25-year low of about 9 cents a pound duty paid, f.o.b. San Francisco or Los Angeles. The production and exports of copra and coconut oil for calendar years 1964 to 1972 are given in Table 29-1.

Year-to-year changes in world exports of copra and coconut oil are the most critical factor that influences the pricing of coconut oil; for example, the 180,000-ton decline in exports in 1967 was associated with a rise in price of about 10 cents a pound. The increase in exports during 1971 and 1972 was associated with a decline in price of about 6 cents a pound. These yearly changes can be attributed almost entirely to fluctuations in exports of copra and coconut oil from the Philippines.

An important reason for the export-price relationship is that copra production is insensitive to changes in price (price inelastic). Because it takes five years for a coconut palm to begin bearing coconuts and another year from the blossoming to the harvesting of the nuts, it is not possible for a

TABLE 29-1   PRODUCTION AND EXPORTS OF COPRA AND
COCONUT OIL (1000 METRIC TONS OF OIL OR OIL
EQUIVALENT)

	Calendar years—1964–1972								
	1964	1965	1966	1967	1968	1969	1970	1971	1972
Production									
Philippines:	930	933	1040	930	870	755	800	1080	1350
Others:	1340	1207	1220	1230	1280	1285	1310	1290	1300
Total world	2270	2140	2260	2160	2150	2040	2110	2370	2650
Exports									
Philippines:	746	783	904	758	688	576	602	840	1068
Others:	574	477	471	437	547	484	483	500	500
Total World	1320	1260	1375	1195	1235	1060	1085	1340	1568

E = estimated.
SOURCE: Pacific Commodities Exchange.

high price to stimulate a production increase in the short run nor for a
lower price to stimulate a reduction. This marks a vital point of difference
between the production of copra and other oilseeds that are directly affected by year-to-year price changes.

Starting in the fall of 1962, the major copra producing areas of the world
experienced a drought. Philippine production leveled off in the latter part
of 1972 and in 1973 was running materially below the 1972 levels. Declines in copra production in Ceylon and Indonesia resulted in a complete
ban of exports from those countries. Prices of coconut oil advanced from
9 cents a pound between the end of 1972 to a five-year high of more than
20 cents early in 1973, which provides an example of the volatility possible
in this commodity. This spectacular advance in price was well beyond that
occasioned by the accompanying poor sunflower, peanut, and fish oil
production, probably because of the unusually low level from which the
price of coconut oil began its advance and the fact that the demand for
coconut oil is less elastic than the demand for other fats and oils.

Coconut oil prices are strongly influenced by the prices of other edible
oils, particularly when coconut oil supplies are abundant. Coconut oil has
specific advantages for certain uses, for which buyers will pay a substantial
premium if supplies are short. Coconut oil's lathering qualities make it
especially useful in soaps and detergents. Its distinctive flavor characterizes
certain edible products. These qualities tend to exclude competition to a
point, but when the quantities available exceed the demand for such
special purposes coconut oil must compete with other oils on a price basis.
This competition occurs primarily in the Rotterdam markets, but its impact
is also felt quickly in markets in the United States and the Philippines.

The three major markets for coconut oil are the producing countries, the
United States, and Western Europe. Coconut oil is consumed primarily as
an edible oil, and secondly as a raw material in the manufacture of soap,
synthetic detergents, cosmetics, and industrial products.

In producing countries coconut oil is a principal edible oil with little competition from other vegetable oils. Consequently, in these countries the demand is relatively insensitive to changes in price because only small quantities of other edible oils are available as substitutes. The low level of income in these countries has precluded increases in per capita consumption. Thus their consumption tends to increase in direct proportion to their population growths.

Most coconut oil in the United States is used as an industrial raw material and as such is classified by the U.S. Census Bureau and by the Department of Agriculture as a "soap oil." Although increasing quantities are being consumed in the United States as an edible oil in imitation milk products, cookies, pastries, margarine, and shortening, it is usually higher priced than competitive oils and tends to be used only when its particular qualities make price relatively unimportant. For this reason the demand for coconut oil in the United States, as in the producing countries, is relatively insensitive to price changes.

In the European markets coconut oil is used primarily as an edible oil and also for industrial products. In these markets coconut oil and other edible oils are more interchangeable than in the United States and producing country markets and therefore there is more active price competition. Consequently, when the world supply of coconut oil changes materially, most of the adjustment in consumption needed to bring world supply and demand into equilibrium takes place in Western Europe. Because of the inelasticity in the other two markets, price fluctuations related to changes in world supply can be extreme.

Although prices of coconut oil vary in different markets of the world, price changes in terminal markets are closely related. Thus changes in one market, reflected quickly in the others, result in a sensitive international market price structure for this commodity.

As in the case of soybean oil, crushing margins and the value of the by-product meal affect the cost of production of coconut oil. However, changes in the price of copra meal are much less significant for coconut oil than changes in soybean meal prices for soybean oil. Copra yields 63 to 64 percent oil and 33 to 34 percent meal compared with soybean yields of about 18 percent oil and 80 percent meal. Copra has the highest oil-bearing yield of any known material. A one dollar per short ton fluctuation in the price of copra meal changes the cost of coconut oil by less than 3 points (0.03 cents a pound), whereas a fluctuation of one dollar per ton on soybean meal is equivalent to about 22 points (0.22 cents a pound) on soybean oil.[1] Therefore copra and coconut oil prices are more closely related to one another than are soybean and soybean oil prices.

Freight and insurance costs are usually quite stable, but at times they too can have a pronounced influence on coconut oil prices. An increase of

---

[1] For conversion factors from pounds to short tons, long tons, and metric tons see Table 29-4.

$14 per long ton in the freight rate on copra will increase the cost of coconut oil 1 cent a pound, and such an increase can occur, especially during periods of international crisis. Part of the 1967 rise in coconut oil prices was caused by the rising costs of freight and war-risk insurance resulting from the six-day war and the coincident closing of the Suez Canal.

Copra is duty free, but import duties on coconut oil are a market factor. Crude coconut oil of all origins bears the same 5 percent rate of duty in the European Common Market. The U.S. rate on oil from the Philippines was designated as 1 cent a pound and from other origins 3 cents a pound until 1974, when all coconut oil of any origin was accorded equal treatment. The import duty was set at 1 cent a pound to be collected from 1974 on.

SOURCES OF INFORMATION

Various government reports deal with coconut oil specifically and some provide comparative data with other oils.

Current Industrial Reports Fats and Oils, Production, Consumption and Stocks, Series M20K, U.S. Bureau of the Census.

Fats and Oils Situation, Economic Research Service, USDA.

Foreign Agriculture Circular, FFO, Foreign Agricultural Service, USDA.

U.S. Fats and Oils Statistics 1909–1965, Statistical Bulletin No. 376, Economic Research Service, USDA.

U.S. Fats and Oils Statistics 1950–1971, Statistical Bulletin No. 489, Economic Research Service, USDA.

World Agricultural Production and Trade, Statistical Report, Foreign Agricultural Service, USDA.

PRODUCTION FACTORS

The tables that follow (Tables 29-2 and 29-3) list world copra production and world copra and coconut oil exports from 1950 to 1972. About 80 percent of the world's production of copra is derived from the Philippines, Indonesia, India, and Ceylon, where coconut palms thrive in tropical climates. By far the most prolific source, the Philippines produces about one-third of the total world supply, some two-thirds of all world exports, and nearly 100 percent of the U.S. supply. Indonesia, the second largest producer, consumes most of its copra production in domestic markets, and India consumes its entire output. Although Ceylon exports a large portion of its production, that country's exports are dwarfed by those of the Philippines.

From 1961 to 1970 total world production of copra was essentially "flat" at approximately 3.4 million tons (2.2 million tons of oil equivalent). Starting in the late 1950s, the Philippines conducted a major program to expand its acreages of coconut palms. From 1960 to 1970 more than 100 million new trees were planted, principally in the southern islands, where

TABLE 29-2   WORLD COPRA AND COCONUT OIL EXPORTS, 1950–1971*

| Calendar year | Copra exports | | | | Coconut oil exports | | Copra and coconut oil exports, oil equivalent† |
| | Copra | | Oil equivalent† | | | | |
	1000 long tons	1000 metric tons	1000 long tons	1000 metric tons	1000 long tons	1000 metric tons	1000 metric tons
1950	1395.0	1417.4	892.8	907.1	238.0	241.8	1148.9
1951	1646.0	1672.4	1053.4	1070.3	327.0	332.2	1402.6
1952	1348.0	1369.6	862.7	876.5	348.0	353.5	1230.1
1953	1218.0	1237.5	779.5	792.0	268.0	272.3	1064.3
1954	1414.0	1436.7	905.0	919.5	279.0	283.4	1202.9
1955	1425.0	1447.8	912.0	926.6	301.1	305.9	1232.5
1956	1593.0	1618.5	1019.5	1035.8	347.1	352.6	1388.5
1957	1712.0	1739.4	1095.7	1113.2	300.9	305.7	1419.0
1958	1334.0	1355.4	853.8	867.5	261.8	266.0	1133.4
1959	1219.0	1238.5	780.2	792.6	221.1	224.6	1017.3
1960	1520.0	1544.4	972.8	988.4	197.8	200.9	1189.3
1961	1598.0	1623.6	1022.7	1039.1	271.2	275.5	1314.7
1962	1397.0	1419.4	894.1	908.4	328.8	334.0	1242.5
1963	1431.0	1453.9	915.8	930.5	384.7	390.8	1321.4
1964	1383.0	1405.2	885.1	899.3	421.5	428.2	1327.6
1965	1334.0	1355.4	853.8	867.5	388.6	394.8	1262.3
1966	1398.0	1420.4	894.7	909.1	466.9	474.3	1383.4
1967	1238.0	1257.8	792.3	805.0	390.0	396.2	1201.3
1968	1164.0	1182.6	745.0	756.9	480.6	488.3	1245.2
1969	1024.0	1040.4	655.4	665.9	389.8	396.0	1061.9
1970	868.0	882.0	555.5	564.5	519.7	528.0	1092.4
1971	1176.0	1195.0	753.0	765.0	592.0	601.0	1366.0

*Figures for 1971 are estimates.
† Based on a 64 percent oil yield.
SOURCE: Pacific Commodities Exchange.

damage by typhoons is less likely than in other areas. Because weather factors have a far more significant effect on production in the short run than the number of producing trees, the consequences of serious typhoons and drought from 1967 to 1969 delayed increased production from the new plantings until 1971. In 1971 and 1972, however, the planned increase in production amounting to about 850,000 tons (550,000 tons of oil equivalent) finally occurred.

The quantities of copra crushed in producing countries are increasing annually. Substantial copra crushing operations are also conducted in Western Europe, Japan, and the United States, where crushing plants are located at San Francisco and Los Angeles. Because most other countries of origin consume the greater part of their production, forecasts of copra production are made by government and trade sources based on rainfall and the size of nuts on producing trees in the Philippines.

TABLE 29-3   WORLD COPRA PRODUC-
TION, 1950–1972

	Copra		Oil equivalent (based on 64 percent yield)
Calendar year	1000 long tons	1000 metric tons	1000 metric tons
1950	2755.0	2800.0	1791.7
1951	3132.0	3182.0	2036.6
1952	2881.0	2927.0	1873.3
1953	2783.0	2828.0	1809.8
1954	3020.0	3069.0	1964.0
1955	3111.0	3161.0	2023.0
1956	3418.0	3473.0	2222.6
1957	3467.0	3522.0	2254.3
1958	3027.0	3076.0	1968.6
1959	2839.0	2885.0	1846.1
1960	3015.0	3063.0	1960.3
1961	3378.0	3432.0	2196.4
1962	3129.0	3179.0	2034.5
1963	3278.0	3331.0	2131.8
1964	3489.0	3545.0	2268.8
1965	3286.0	3339.0	2136.9
1966	3473.0	3529.0	2258.5
1967	3327.0	3380.0	2163.2
1968	3310.0	3363.0	2152.3
1969	3137.0	3187.0	2039.6
1970	3243.0	3295.0	2108.8
1971	3792.0	3853.0	2466.0
1972	4035.0	4100.0	2624.0

SOURCE: Pacific Commodities Exchange.

NOTES FROM A TRADER

Those trading coconut oil, like most commodities relatively newly traded, should keep in mind the usual trade-off of a major opportunity with a major limitation. The opportunity comes from some inefficiency in the market, hence a warping that provides the opportunity for a speculative profit when

TABLE 29-4   CONVERSION FACTORS.
(To convert from the units on the left to the units along the top, multiply by the factors given)

Unit	Factors for obtaining			
	metric tons	long tons	short tons	pounds
Metric tons	1.0	0.984196	1.1023	2,204.6
Long tons	1.016057	1.0	1.12	2,240.0
Short tons	0.907194	0.892857	1.0	2,000.0
Pounds	0.0004536	0.00044643	0.005	1.0

SOURCE: Pacific Commodities Exchange.

EXHIBIT 29-1   Comparison of Coconut Oil and Soybean Oil Prices. In most years from 1960 to 1972, coconut oil prices exceeded soybean oil prices by several cents a pound. The few exceptions occurred when coconut oil production increased abnormally. To balance supply and demand during these periods, coconut oil had to buy its way into new markets. (Pacific Commodities Exchange, San Francisco.)

the warping is corrected. On the other hand, lack of futures market history makes historical data less valuable than for longer established markets. Cash market information is available, of course, but there are often substantial differences in the way cash market prices and futures market prices move.

One of the more interesting opportunities opened up by the coconut oil futures market is the possibility of spreading coconut oil against soybean oil as was done for so many years between soybean oil and cottonseed oil. Coconut oil and soybean oil prices tend to parallel each other at times, but at other times they deviate substantially. Coconut oil even trades considerably below soybean oil instead of at its more usual premium of 2 or 3 cents. (The premium results from the import duty, shipping costs, and unique qualities.) Generally speaking, the two markets will tend to move in the same direction when coconut oil is in relatively abundant supply, but coconut oil will go its own way when it is in short supply as it was in 1967 and 1968 (see Exhibit 29-1).

Bibliography [1]

The following list of sources does not include all applicable government reports; they may be found in each chapter of Section 5 under "Sources of Information." A complete list may be obtained from the USDA.

I. FUTURES TRADING AND COMMODITY EXCHANGES

Arthur, Henry B. "Economic Risk, Uncertainty and the Futures Market," in *Futures Trading Seminar,* vol. 3, Mimir, Madison, Wis., 1966.

Baer, J. B., and O. G. Saxon, *Commodity Exchanges and Futures Trading: Principles and Operating Methods,* Harper, New York, 1949.

Bailey, Fred, Jr. "What Every Banker Should Know About Commodity Futures Markets," reprint of the following articles from *Banking:* "What a Futures Market Is and How It Works (October 1967); "Hedging for Country Grain Elevators" (November 1967); "How Farmers Can Use the Futures Markets" (December 1967); "The Cattle Feeder and the Futures Market" (January 1968).

Bakken, H. H. *Theory of Markets and Marketing,* Mimir, Madison, Wis., 1953.

Blau, G. "Some Aspects of the Theory of Futures Trading," *Review of Economic Studies,* 7 (1), No. 31 (1944–1945) 1-3a.

Boyle, J. E. *Speculation and the Chicago Board of Trade,* Macmillan, New York, 1920.

Campbell, D. A. "Trading in Futures Under the Commodity Exchange Act," *George Washington Law Review,* **26,** No. 2 (January 1958), 215–254.

Chicago Board of Trade. Futures Trading Seminar, Commodity Marketing Forum for College Teachers of Economics, Chicago, April 28–30, 1965, *Proceedings,* Erwin A. Gaumnitz, ed., Chicago Board of Trade, Mimir, Madison, Wis., 1966.

---

[1] Although individual works may encompass more than one subject classification, they are listed only under the *dominant* category.

Chicago Board of Trade. Futures Trading Seminar, Influence of Environmental Factors, Chicago, September 5–6, 1962, *Proceedings,* Chicago Board of Trade, Mimir, Madison, Wis., 1963.

Chicago Board of Trade, Symposium Proceedings, 1948 to date.

Commodity Trading Manual, Chicago Board of Trade, Chicago, Ill., 1973.

Cootner, Paul H. "Common Elements in Futures Markets for Commodities and Bonds," *Proceedings of the American Economic Association,* 51 (May 1961), 173–183.

Corbett, Caroline Louise (Phillips). *Economic Phases of Futures Trading: A Selected List of References,* Commodity Exchange Administration, Washington, D.C., 1937.

Dewey, T. H. *A Treatise on Contracts for Future Delivery and Commercial Wagers Including "Options," "Futures," and "Short Sales,"* Baker, Voorhis, New York, 1886.

Dow, J. C. R. "A Symposium on the Theory of the Forward Market. II. Addenda to Mr. Kaldor's Note," *Review of Economic Studies,* 7 (1939–1940), 201–202.

Dow, J. C. R. "A Theoretical Account of Futures Markets," *Review of Economic Studies,* 7 (1939–1940), 185–195.

The Economist (London). The London Metal Exchange, Whitefriars Press, Tonbridge, England, 1958.

Geiger, H. Dwight. "The Grain Futures and Cash Markets (and Some of Their Accounting Implications)," *The Arthur Young Journal* (Winter 1969).

Gold, G. *Modern Commodity Futures Trading,* Commodity Research Bureau, New York, 1966.

Gray, R. W. "Search for a Risk Premium," *Journal of Political Economy,* 69, No. 3 (June 1961), 250–260.

Gray, R. W. "Some Current Development in Futures Trading," *Journal of Farm Economics,* 40, No. 2 (May 1958), 344–351.

Gunnelson, J. A. *A Study of the Impact of Organizational Changes in Agricultural Commodity Markets,* Ph.D. Dissertation, Purdue University, 1970.

Harlow, C. V., and R. J. Teweles. "Commodities and Securities Compared," *Financial Analysts Journal* (September–October 1972).

Hawtrey, R. G. "Mr. Kaldor on the Forward Market," *Review of Economic Studies,* 7 (1939–1940), 202–205.

Heater, Nancy L. *Commodity Futures Trading, A Bibliography,* Department of Agricultural Economics, University of Illinois College of Agriculture, December 1966.

Hieronymus, T. A. "Should Margins in Futures Trading be Regulated?," *Commercial and Financial Chronicle,* 173 (5004) (April 19, 1951), 1648–1685.

Hoffman, G. W. *Future Trading upon Organized Commodity Markets in the United States,* University of Pennsylvania Press, Philadelphia, 1932.

Hoffman, G. W. "Past and Present Theory Regarding Futures Trading," *Journal of Farm Economics,* 19 (1937), 300–309.

Hoos, Sidney. "Future Trading in Perishable Agricultural Commodities, *Journal of Marketing,* 6 (1942), 358–365.

Houthakker, H. S. "The Scope and Limits of Futures Trading," in Moses Abramovitz et al., *The Allocation of Economic Resources,* Stanford University Press, Stanford, Calif., 1959.

How to Buy and Sell Commodities, a booklet published by Merrill Lynch, Pierce, Fenner and Smith, New York, January 1969.

Kaldor, Nickolas, "A Note on the Theory of the Forward Market," *Review of Economic Studies,* 7 (1939–1940), 196–201.

Larson, Arnold B. "Estimation of Hedging and Speculative Positions in Futures Markets," *Food Research Institute Studies,* 2, No. 3 (1961), 203–212.

Lindley, A. F. "Essentials of an Effective Futures Market," *Journal of Farm Economics,* 19 (1937), 321–330.

Mehl, J. M. *The Development and Operation of the Commodity Exchange Act,* Commodity Exchange Authority, Washington, 1953.

Mehl, Paul. *A Rapid Method of Calculating Profits Made or Losses Sustained in Privilege Trad-*

ing on the Chicago Board of Trade, U.S. Grain Futures Administration, Washington, D.C., 1931.

Mehl, Paul. *Trading in Privileges on the Chicago Board of Trade,* USDA Circular 323, 1934.

Miller, Katherine D. *Futures Trading and Investor Returns; An Investigation of Commodity Market Risk Premiums,* Thesis, University of Chicago, 1971.

New York Coffee and Sugar Exchange. *History and Operation of the New York Coffee and Sugar Exchange, Inc., 1882-1947,* New York, 1947.

Phillips, J. "The Theory and Practice of Futures Trading," *Review of Marketing and Agricultural Economics* (June 1966).

Powers, M. J. "Effects of Contract Provisions on the Success of a Futures Contract," *Journal of Farm Economics,* **49,** No. 4 (November 1967) 833-843.

Teweles, Richard J., and Charles V. Harlow: "The Commodity Futures Game: Who Wins? Who Loses? Why?" A two-part series in *The Journal of Commodity Trading,* **5,** No. 1 (January-February 1970), 5, No. 2 (March-April 1970).

Teweles, Richard J., Charles V. Harlow, and Herbert L. Stone, *The Commodity Futures Trading Guide,* McGraw-Hill, New York, 1969.

U.S., 56th Congress, 2nd Session, House, *U.S. Industrial Commission Report* (1900-1901), House Doc. 94.

U.S., 85th Congress, 1st Session, House, *Hearings* before the Committee on Agriculture and Forestry, May 1-3, 1957.

U.S., 85th Congress, 1st Session, Senate, *Hearings* before a Subcommittee of the Committee on Agriculture and Forestry, August 12, 1957.

U.S., 85th Congress, 2nd Session, Senate, *Hearings* before the Committee on Agriculture and Forestry, March 22-26, 1958.

U.S., 88th Congress, 1st Session, House, *Hearings* on H.R. 904, April 8-10, 1963.

U.S., 89th Congress, 2nd Session, House, *Hearings* before the Subcommittee on Domestic Marketing and Consumer Relations of the Committee on Agriculture on H.R. 11788, April 4-6, 1966.

Venkataramanan, L. S. *The Theory of Futures Trading,* Asia Publishing, New York, 1965.

Working, Holbrook. "Tests of a Theory Concerning Floor Trading on Commodity Exchanges", *Food Research Institute Studies,* Supplement, 7 (1967), 5-48.

Working, Holbrook, "Western Needs for Futures Markets," *Proceedings of the Western Farm Economics Association* (1952), 95-98.

Working, Holbrook. "Whose Markets? Evidence on Some Aspects of Futures Trading," *Journal of Marketing,* **19,** No. 1 (July 1954), 1-11.

II. HISTORY AND EVOLUTION OF FUTURES TRADING

Anderson, M. A. "Ninety Years Development: Fundamental and Technicalities of Futures Trading Explained," *Cotton Digest,* **21,** No. 27 (March 26, 1949), 18-19, 42-43, 46-47.

Boyle, J. E. *Cotton and the New Orleans Cotton Exchange; a Century of Commercial Evolution,* Country Life, New York, 1934.

Cowing, Cedric B. *Populists, Plungers and Progressives: A Social History of Stock and Commodity Speculation, 1860-1936,* Princeton University Press, Princeton, N.J., 1965.

Dies, E. J. *The Plunger; A Tale of the Wheat Pit,* Covici, New York.

Dies, E. J. *The Wheat Pit,* Argyle, Chicago, 1925.

Irwin, H. S. *Evolution of Futures Trading,* Mimir, Madison, Wis., 1954.

Killough, H. B. "Effects of Governmental Regulation of Commodity Exchanges in the United States," *Harvard Business Review,* **11** (1933), 307-315.

Lermer, G. "The Futures Market and Farm Programs," *Canadian Journal of Agricultural Economics,* **16,** No. 2 (June 1968), 27-30.

Miller, Norman C. *The Great Salad Oil Swindle,* Coward-McCann, New York, 1965.

Nimrod, Vance L. and Richard S. Bower. "Commodities and Computers," *Journal of Financial and Quantitative Analysis,* **2,** No. 1 (March 1967).

Norris, Frank. *The Pit*, Doubleday, Page, New York, 1903.

Pine, L. G. "London: A Commercial History Since the Roman Occupation," Supplement to *The Public Ledger*, London, January 1960.

Robinson, H. G. *History and Evolution of Trading in Futures in Potatoes, 1930–1956*, Ph.D. Dissertation, Ohio State University, 1957.

Sowards, J. K. *Western Civilization to 1660*, St. Martin's, New York, 1965.

Taylor, C. H. *History of the Board of Trade of the City of Chicago*, Robert O. Law Co., Chicago, 1917.

Tomek, W. G. "A Note on Historical Wheat Prices and Futures Trading," *Food Research Institute Studies*, **10** (1971).

Working, Holbrook. "Review of H. S. Irwin, 'Evolution of Futures Trading,'" *Journal of Farm Economics*, **37** (1950), 377–380.

III. ECONOMIC THEORY AND EVIDENCE

Boulding, Kenneth. *The Skills of the Economist*, Clarke, Irwin, Toronto, Canada, 1958.

Brandow, G. E. *Interrelations Among Demand for Farm Products and Implications for Control of Market Supply*, Penn State Agricultural Experiment Station Bulletin 680, 1961.

Chamberlin, E. H. *The Theory of Monopolistic Competition*, Harvard, Cambridge, Mass., 1938.

Fama, Eugene F. "Efficient Capital Markets: A Review of Theory and Empirical Works," *Journal of Finance*, **25** (1970), 383–423.

Fama, Eugene F. "Mandelbrot and the Stable Paretian Hypothesis," *Journal of Business*, **36**, No. 4 (October 1963), 420–429.

Fishman, G. S. *Spectral Methods in Econometrics*, Harvard, Cambridge, Mass., 1969.

Foote, Richard J. *Analytical Tools for Studying Demand and Price Structure*, USDA Handbook 146, 1958.

Foote, Richard J., and Karl A. Fox. *Analytical Tools for Measuring Demand*, USDA Handbook 64, 1954.

Friedman, M. *Essays in Positive Economics*, University of Chicago Press, Chicago, 1953.

Gordon, D. F. "A Statistical Contribution to Price Theory: Discussion," *American Economic Review*, Papers and Proceedings, **48** (1958), 201–203.

Granger, C. W. J. and M. Hatanaka. *Spectral Analysis of Economic Time Series*, Princeton University Press, Princeton, N.J., 1964.

Gray, Roger W., and David J. S. Rutledge. "The Economics of Commodity Futures Markets: A Survey," *Review of Marketing and Agricultural Economics*, **39**, No. 4.

Houthakker, H. S. *Economic Policy for the Farm Sector*, American Enterprise Institute for Public Policy Research, Washington, D.C., 1967.

Johnson, D. G. *Forward Prices for Agriculture*, University of Chicago Press, Chicago, 1947.

Keynes, J. M. *The General Theory of Employment, Interest, and Money*, Harcourt, Brace, and World, New York, 1964.

Keynes, J. M. *A Treatise on Money*, Vol. 2, Harcourt, Brace, and World, New York, 1930.

Kogiker, K. C. "A Model of the Raw Materials Markets," *International Economic Review*, No. 8 (February 1967).

Nerlove, Marc. *Distributed Lags and Demand Analysis for Agricultural and Other Commodities*, USDA Handbook 141, 1958.

Nerlove, Marc. "On the Nerlove Estimate of Supply Elasticity," *Journal of Farm Economics*, **40** (August 1958), 723–728.

Nerlove, Marc, and William Addison. "Statistical Estimation of Long-Run Elasticities of Supply and Demand," *Journal of Farm Economics*, **40** (November 1958), 861–880.

Perrin, R. K. *Analysis and Prediction of Crop Yields for Agricultural Policy Purposes*, Ph.D. Dissertation, Iowa State University, 1968.

Schultz, H. *The Theory of Measurement of Demand.*, University of Chicago Press, Chicago, 1938 (reprinted 1957).

Selvestre, Helios. *Demand Analysis: An Attempt to Develop A Methodology for Detecting the*

Point in Time Where Structural Changes Took Place, Ph.D. Dissertation, Cornell University, 1969.

Taylor, F. M. *Principles of Economics*, 2nd ed., University of Michigan Press, Ann Arbor, 1913.

Watson, Donald. *Price Theory and Its Uses*, Houghton Mifflin, Boston, 1963.

Waugh, Fredrick V. *Demand and Price Analysis: Some Examples from Agriculture*, USDA Technical Bulletin 1316, 1964.

Weymar, F. Helmut: "The Supply of Storage Revisited," *American Economic Review*, 56 (December 1966), 1226–1234.

World, H., and L. Jureen. *Demand Analysis: A Study in Econometrics*, Wiley, New York, 1953.

Working, Holbrook. "The Investigation of Economic Expectations," *American Economic Review*, 39, No. 3 (May 1949), 150–166.

Working, Holbrook. "Theory of Price of Storage," *American Economic Review*, 39, No. 6 (December 1949), 1254–1262.

IV. TRADERS: BEHAVIOR AND RETURNS

Baruch, Barnard. *My Own Story*, Holt, New York, 1957.

Cantril, Hadley. *The Invasion From Mars*, Harper and Row, New York, 1966.

Cootner, P. H. "Returns to Speculators: Telser versus Keynes," *Journal of Political Economy*, 68, No. 4 (August 1960), 396–414, followed by L. G. Telser, "Reply," pp. 404–415 and P. H. Cootner, "Rejoinder," pp. 415–418.

Glick, Ira O. *A Social Psychological Study of Futures Trading*, Ph.D. Dissertation, Department of Sociology, University of Chicago, 1957.

Harris, Thomas A. *I'm OK—You're OK*, Harper and Row, 1967.

Houthakker, H. S., and L. G. Telser. *Commodity Futures II: Gains and Losses of Hedgers and Future Speculators*, Cowles Commission Discussion Paper, Economics No. 2090, December 1952.

Le Bon, Gustave. *The Crowd*, Viking, New York, 1960.

Lefevre, Edwin. *Reminiscences of a Stock Operator*, American Research Council, New York, 1923.

Longstreet, Roy W. *Viewpoints of a Commodity Trader*, Frederick Fell, New York, 1968.

MacKay, Charles. *Extraordinary Popular Delusions and the Madness of Crowds*, Page, London, 1932.

Market Vane Commodity Letter, Pasadena, Calif.

Matuszewski, T. I. "Trader's Behaviour—An Alternative Explanation," *Review of Economic Studies*, 25 (1958), 126–130.

Neill, Humphrey. *The Art of Contrary Thinking*, Caxton, Caldwell, Ohio, 1960.

Reisman, David. *The Lonely Crowd*, Yale, New Haven, Conn., 1950.

Rockwell, C. S. "Normal Backwardation Forecasting, and the Returns to Speculators," *Food Research Institute Studies*, Supplement, 7 (1967), 107–130.

Schwed, Fred, Jr. *Where are the Customer's Yachts*, John Magee, Springfield, Mass., 1955.

Smidt, Seymour. *Amateur Speculators: A Survey of Trading Styles, Information Sources, and Patterns of Entry into and Exit from Commodity-Futures Markets by Non-professional Speculators*, Cornell University Graduate School of Business and Public Administration, Ithaca, N.Y., 1965.

V. EFFECTS OF SPECULATION

Baumol, W. J. "Speculation, Profitability and Stability," *Review of Economics and Statistics*, 39 (August 1957), 263–271.

Emery, H. C. "Legislation Against Futures," *Political Science Quarterly*, 10, (1886), 62–68.

Emery, H. C. "Speculation on the Stock and Produce Exchanges of the United States," in the Faculty of Political Science of Columbia University, (Eds), *Studies in History and Economics*, Vol. 7, New York, 1896.

Emerson, P. M. and W. G. Tomek. "Did Futures Trading Influence Potato Prices?" *American Journal of Agricultural Economics*, 51, No. 3 (August 1969), 666–672.

Gray, Roger W. "The Attack Upon Potato Futures Trading in the United States," *Food Research Institute Studies*, 4, No. 2 (1964), 97–121.

Gray, Roger W. "Onions Revisited," *Journal of Farm Economics*, 45, No. 2 (May 1963), 273–276.

Gray, Roger W. "Price Effects of a Lack of Speculation," *Food Research Institute Studies*, Supplement, 7 (1967), 177–194.

Gray, Roger W. "Speculation Helps the Onion Grower," *Minnesota Farm Business Notes*, University of Minnesota, Institute of Agriculture, March–April, 1959.

Hieronymus, T. A. *Appropriate Speculative Limits for Soybean Oil and Lard,* Chicago Board of Trade, 1953.

Hieronymus, T. A. *Effects of Future Trading on Grain Prices,* Illinois Farm Economics No. 190–191, 1951, pp. 1150-1155.

Hooker, R. H. "The Suspension of the Berlin Produce Exchange and Its Effect Upon Corn Prices," *Royal Statistical Society Journal,* 64 (1901), 574–604.

Kaldor, N. "Speculation and Economic Stability," *Review of Economic Studies,* 7 (1939–40), 1–27.

Kemp, M. C., "Speculation, Profitability, and Price Stability," *Review of Economics and Statistics,* 45, No. 2 (May 1962), 185–189.

Marine, C. L. "Effects of Futures Trading on Price Variation," M.S. thesis, University of Illinois, Urbana, 1959.

Meade, J. E. "Degrees of Competitive Speculation," *Review of Economic Studies,* 17 (1950), 159–167.

Naik, A. S. *Effects of Futures Trading on Prices,* K. R. Samat for Somaiya Publications Pty., Ltd., Bombay, India, 1970.

Pavaskar, M. G. *Marketing of Cash Crops: Efficiency of Futures Trading,* Economics and Political Weekly, Bombay, India, 1971.

Powers, M. J. "Does Futures Trading Reduce Price Fluctuations in the Cash Markets?" *American Economic Review,* 60, No. 3 (June 1970), 460–464.

Stewart, Blair. *An Analysis of Speculative Trading in Grain Futures,* USDA Technical Bulletin 1001, October 1949.

Taylor, A. E. "Speculation, Short Selling, and the Price of Wheat," *Food Research Institute Wheat Studies,* (1931), 231–266.

Telser, L. G. "A Theory of Speculation Relating Profitability and Stability," *Review of Economics and Statistics,* 41 (1959), 295–301.

USDA, Commodity Exchange Authority. *Speculation in Onion Futures,* Washington, D.C., March 1957.

USDA, Economic Research Service. *Margins, Speculation and Prices in Grains Futures Markets,* Washington, D.C., December 1967.

Usher, A. P. "The Influence of Speculative Marketing Upon Prices," *American Economic Review,* 6 (1916), 49–60.

Vaile, R. S. "Speculation and the Price of Grain," *Journal of Marketing,* 12 (1947), 497–498.

Wesson, William T. *The Economic Importance of Futures Trading in Potatoes,* U.S.D.A., Marketing Research Report No. 241, Washington, D.C. June, 1958.

Williams, J. B. "Speculation and the Carryover," *Quarterly Journal of Economics,* 51 (May 1936), 436–455.

Working, Holbrook. "Futures Markets Under Renewed Attack," *Food Research Institute Studies,* 4, No. 1 (1963), 13–24.

Working, Holbrook. "Price Effect on Futures Trading," *Food Research Institute Studies,* 1, No. 1. (February 1960), 3–31.

Working Holbrook. "Price Effects of Scalping and Day Trading," *Proceedings of the Seventh Annual Symposium: Commodity Markets and the Public Interest,* Chicago Board of Trade, 1954.

Working, Holbrook. "Spoiling the Broth; Congress Acted Unwisely When It Banned Trading in Onion Futures," *Barron's*, **43**, No. 5 (February 4, 1963), 11, 22.

Yamey, Basil S. "Speculation and Price Stability: A Note," and Robert Z. Aliber, "Speculation and Price Stability: A Reply," *Journal of Political Economy*, **74** (April 1966), 206–208.

VI. INDIVIDUAL COMMODITY STUDIES

Armore, S. J. *The Demand and Price Structure for Food Fats and Oils*, USDA Technical Bulletin 1068, June 1953.

Aronson, J. R. *The Soybean Crushing Margin, 1953–62: An Economic Analysis of the Futures Market, for Soybeans, Soybean Oil and Soybean Meal*, Clark University, Worcester, Mass., 1964.

Atwood, E. C., Jr. *Theory and Practice in the Coffee Futures Market*, Princeton University Press, Princeton, N.J., 1959.

Bakken, H., (Ed.) *Futures Trading in Livestock—Origins and Concepts*, Mimir, Madison, Wis., 1970.

Brand, Simon S. "The Decline in the Cotton Futures Market," *Food Research Institute Studies*, **4**, No. 3, (1964).

Breimyer, Harold F. *Demand and Prices for Meat*, USDA Technical Bulletin 1253, 1961.

Brown, C. A. "Future Trading in Butter and Eggs," *Journal of Farm Economics*, **15** (1933), 670–75, followed by E. A. Duddy, "Discussion," 675–76.

Burrows, J. C., W. Hughes, and J. Valette. *An Economic Analysis of the Silver Industry*, Heath, Lexington, Mass., 1974.

Chapman, S. J., and Douglas Knoop. "Dealings in Futures on the Cotton Market," *Royal Statistical Journal*, **69** (1906), 321–364.

Danis, Tom. "An Economic Analysis of Egg Prices in 1969," The Chicago Mercantile Exchange, Research Report #1, April 1970.

Dominick, B. A., Jr., and F. W. Williams. *Future Trading and the Florida Orange Industry*, Florida Agricultural Experiment Stations, December 1965.

Drake, A. F., and V. I. West. *Econometric Analysis of the Edible Fats and Oils Economy*, Agricultural Experiment Station Bulletin 695, University of Illinois, Urbana, 1963.

"An Economic Study of the U.S. Potato Industry," *Agricultural Economic Report* No. 6, Economic Research Service, USDA, 1962.

Ehrich, Rollo. "The Impact of Government Programs on Wheat Futures Markets: 1953–63, *Food Research Institute Studies*, **6**, No. 3 (1966).

Ertek, Tumay. *World Demand for Copper, 1948–1963: An Econometric Study*, Ph.D. Dissertation, University of Wisconsin, 1967.

Evans, W. S. "Canadian Wheat Stabilization Operations, 1929–35," *Wheat Studies*, **12**, No. 7 (March 1926), 249–272.

Foote, R. J., John A. Craven, and Robert R. Williams, Jr. "Pork Bellies: Quarterly 3-Equation Models Designed to Predict Cash Prices," Texas Tech. University, 1971. Mimeographed.

Foote, R. J., J. W. Klein, and M. Clough. *The Demand and Price Structure for Corn and Total Feed Concentrates*, USDA Technical Bulletin 1061, October 1952.

Gallacher, William. "1973 Bellies–Priced to Clear," *Commodities* (March 1973).

Gerra, M. J. *The Demand, Supply and Price Structure for Eggs*, Technical Bulletin 1204, USDA, 1959.

Gray, Roger W. "The Futures Market of Maine Potatoes: An Appraisal," *Food Research Institute Studies*, **11**, No. 3 (1972).

Gray, Roger W. "The Prospects for Wool Price Stability," *Proceedings: International Wool Textile Organization Conference*, Brussels, Belgium (June 1967).

Gray, Roger W. *Wool Futures Trading in Australia—Further Prospects*, University of Sydney, Department of Agricultural Economics, Research Bulletin No. 5, 1967.

Green, Leslie. "Understanding the Frozen Orange Juice Market," in Harry Jiler (Ed.), *Commodity Year Book*, Commodity Research Bureau, New York, 1968.

Gutman, G. O. and B. R. Duffin. "The London Wool Top Futures Market," *Quarterly Review of Agricultural Economics,* **8**, No. 4, Bureau of Agricultural Economics, Canberra (October 1955), 185–192.

Harlow, Arthur. *Factors Affecting the Price and Supply of Hogs,* USDA Technical Bulletin 1247, 1964.

Hee, Olman. "The Effect of Price on Acreage and Yield of Potatoes," *Agricultural Economic Research,* **10** (1958), 131–141.

Hieronymus, T. A. *The Economics of Risk in the Marketing of Soybeans and Soybean Products,* Ph.D. Dissertation, University of Illinois, Urbana, 1949.

Hieronymus, T. A. *Farm Speculation in Soybeans,* University of Illinois Department of Agricultural Economics AERR 9, Urbana, 1965.

Hieronymus, T. A. *Futures Trading and Speculation in Soybeans,* University of Illinois Agricultural Extension Service AE-2777, 1951.

Hieronymus, T. A. "Futures Trading and Speculation in Soybeans by Country Elevators," *Grain and Feed Review,* **40**, No. 7 (March 1951), 20, 22, 56, 57.

Honhon, Georges L. J. *An Econometric Analysis of the Corn Market in an Open Economy,* Ph.D. Dissertation, University of Illinois, 1970.

Houck, James P. *Demand and Price Analysis of the U.S. Soybean Market,* Agricultural Experiment Station Bulletin 244, Minnesota, 1963.

Houck, James P. "A Statistical Model of the Demand for Soybeans," *Journal of Farm Economics,* **46** (May 1964), 366–374.

Houck, James P. and J. S. Mann. *Domestic and Foreign Demand for U.S. Soybeans and Soybean Products,* Agricultural Experiment Station Technical Bulletin 256, University of Minnesota, Minneapolis, 1968.

Houck, J. P., M. E. Ryan, and A. Subotnik. *Soybeans and their Products: Markets, Models and Policy,* University of Minnesota Press, Minneapolis, 1972.

Johnson, A. C. Jr. "Whose Markets? The Case for Maine Potato Futures," *Food Research Institute Studies,* **11**, No. 3 (1972).

Kofi, T. A. *Feasibility Analysis of International Commodity Agreements on Cocoa,* Ph.D. Dissertation, University of California, Berkeley, 1970.

Kohls, R. L. "A Technique for Anticipating Change in the Volume of Eggs Shortage," *Journal of Farm Economics,* **32**, No. 4 (November 1950), 663–666.

Koudele, J. W. *An Economic Analysis of Trading in Egg Futures, 1934–1954,* Ph.D. Dissertation, Michigan State University, 1956.

Labys, Walter C. *Dynamic Commodity Models: Specification, Estimation, and Simulation,* Heath, Lexington, Mass., 1973.

Langemeier, L., and R. G. Thompson. "Study of Demand, Supply, and Price Relationships on the Beef Sector, Post World War II Period," *Journal of Farm Economics,* **49** (February 1967), 169–183.

Leuthold, R. M., A. J. A. MacCormick, A. Schmitz, and D. G. Watts. "Forecasting Daily Hog Prices and Quantities: A Study of Alternative Forecasting Techniques," *Journal of the American Statistical Association* **65** (March 1970).

Lowell, Fred R. *The Wheat Market,* Keltner Statistical Service, Kansas City, Mo., 1968.

Meinken, K. W. *The Demand and Price Structure for Wheat,* USDA Technical Bulletin 1136, November 1955.

Miracle, Diane S., "The Egg Futures Market: 1940 to 1966," *Food Research Institute Studies,* **11**, No. 3 (1972).

Myers, L. H. *Economic Analysis of the Monthly Structure of the Hog Pork Sector of the U.S.,* Ph.D. Dissertation, Purdue University, 1968.

Peery, J. S. *Theory and Practice in the Forward Market for Shell Eggs,* Ph.D. Dissertation, Northwestern University, 1964.

Powers, Mark J. *An Economic Analysis of the Futures Market for Pork Bellies,* Thesis, University of Wisconsin, 1966.

Rourke, B. E. *Causes and Predictability of Annual Changes in Supplies and Prices of Coffee,* Ph.D. Dissertation, Stanford University, 1969.

Roy, Sujit. "Econometric Models for Predicting Short Run Egg Prices," Pennsylvania State University, University Park, Pa., 1971. Mimeographed.

Skadberg, J. M., and G. A. Futrell. "An Economic Appraisal of Futures Trading in Livestock," *Journal of Farm Economics*, 48, No. 5 (December 1966), 1485–1489.

Smith, J. G. *Organized Produce Markets*, Longmans, London, 1922.

Snape, R. H. *Protection and Stabilization in the World Sugar Industry*, Ph.D. Dissertation, University of London, 1962.

Sohn, H. K. *A Spatial Equilibrium Model of the Beef Industry in the United States*, Ph.D. Dissertation, University of Hawaii, 1970.

Telser, L. G. "Futures Trading and the Storage of Cotton and Wheat," *Journal of Political Economy*, 66, No. 3 (June 1958), 233–255.

Telser, L. G. "The Supply of Speculative Services in Wheat, Corn and Soybeans," *Food Research Institute Studies*, Supplement, 7 (1967), 131–176.

Telser, L. G. *The Supply of Stocks: Cotton and Wheat*, Ph.D. Dissertation, University of Chicago, 1956.

Tewes, T. "Sugar: A Short-Term Forecasting Model for the World Market, with a Forecast of the World Market Price for Sugar in 1972–1973," *The Business Economist*, 4 (Summer 1972), 89–97.

USDA, Agricultural Marketing Service. *Possibilities for Futures Trading in Florida Citrus Fruit and Products*, Marketing Research Report No. 156, Washington, D.C., February 1959.

USDA, Commodity Exchange Authority. *Trading in Frozen Pork Bellies*, Washington, D.C., October 1967.

USDA, Consumer and Marketing Service. *Fats and Oils Situations*, Washington, D.C.

USDA, Economic Research Service. *Demand and Price Analysis for Potatoes*, USDA Technical Bulletin 1380, July 1967.

USDA, Economic Research Service. "An Economic Study of the U.S. Potato Industry," *Agricultural Economic Report*, No. 6, 1962.

U.S. Federal Trade Commission, *Economic Report of the Investigation of Coffee Prices*, Washington, D.C.

U.S. Federal Trade Commission, *Report on the Grain Trade*, 7 vols., Washington, D.C., 1920–1926.

Uribe C., Andres. *Brown Gold*, Random House, New York, 1954.

Vandenborre, Roger J. "Demand Analysis of the Markets for Soybean Oil and Soybean Meal," *Journal of Farm Economics*, 28 (November 1946), 920–934.

Walsh, Joseph M. *Coffee, Its History Classification and Description*, Henry T. Coates and Co., Philadelphia, 1894.

Weiss, J. S. "A Spectral Analysis of World Cocoa Prices," *American Journal of Agricultural Economics*, 52 (February 1970), 122–126.

Weisser, M. *The Sydney Wool Futures Market*, Bureau of Agricultural Economics, Wool Economic Research Report No. 4, Canberra, June 1963.

Weymar, F. Helmut. *The Dynamics of the World Cocoa Market*, M.I.T., Cambridge, Mass., 1968.

Wickizer, L. V. D. *Coffee, Tea, and Cocoa*, Stanford University Press, Stanford, Calif., 1951.

Witherall, W. H. *Dynamics of the International Wool Market: An Econometric Analysis*, Econometric Research Program Memorandum 91, Princeton University Press, Princeton, N.J., September 1967.

Working, Holbrook. Economic Functions of Futures Markets, in H. Bakken, ed., *Futures Trading in Livestock—Origins and Concepts*, Mimir, Madison, Wis., 1970.

Working Holbrook. "Financial Results of Speculative Holding of Wheat," *Food Research Institute Wheat Studies*, 7, No. 81 (July 1931).

Working, Holbrook, "Futures Trading and Hedging as Applied to the Wine Industry," *Food Research Institute Studies*, (1953).

Yamey, B. S. "Cotton Futures Trading in Liverpool," *Three Banks Review*, No. 41, (March 1959), 21–38.

VII. PRICE BEHAVIOR

Alexander, Sidney. "Price Movements in Speculative Markets: Trends or Random Walks," No. 2, as reprinted in Paul Cootner, (Ed.), *The Random Character of Stock Market Prices,* M.I.T., Cambridge, Mass., 1964, pp. 338–372.

Armstrong, Charles E. "Testing Cycles for Statistical Significance," *Journal of Cycle Research* (October 1961).

Arnold, David B. *An Econometric Study on the Weekly Behavior of the Cash Basis for Corn at Chicago,* Thesis, University of Illinois, 1969.

Bachelier, Louis. "Theory of Speculation," reprinted in Paul Cootner, ed., *The Random Character of Stock Market Prices,* M.I.T., Cambridge, Mass., 1964.

Bear, R. M. *Martingale Movements in Commodity Futures,* Ph.D. Dissertation, University of Iowa, 1970.

Beckmann, M. J. "On the Determination of Prices in Futures Markets," reprinted in M. J. Brennan, (Ed.), *Patterns of Market Behavior,* Brown University Press, Providence, R.I., 1965.

Brinegar, C. S. *A Statistical Analysis of Speculative Price Behavior,* Ph.D. Dissertation, Stanford University, 1954.

Brinegar, C. S. "A Statistical Analysis of Speculative Price Behavior," *Food Research Institute Studies,* Supplement, 9 (1970).

Clough, Malcolm. "Relation between Corn and Wheat Futures," *Journal of Farm Economics,* 21 (1939), 500–502.

Cootner, Paul H., (Ed.) *The Random Character of Stock Market Prices,* M.I.T., Cambridge, Mass., 1964.

Cootner, P. H. "Stock Prices: Random vs Systematic Changes," *Industrial Management Review,* 3, No. 2 (Spring 1962).

Cowles, Alfred, and H. E. Jones. "Some A Posteriori Probabilities in Stock Market Action," *Econometrica,* 5 (1937), 280–294.

Dow, J. C. R. "The Inaccuracy of Expectations; a Statistical Study of the Liverpool Cotton Futures Market 1921/22–1937/38," *Economica,* n.s., 8 (1941), 162–175.

Ehrich, R. L. "Cash-Futures Price Relationships for Live Beef Cattle," *American Journal of Agricultural Economics,* 51, No. 1 (February 1969), 26–40.

Fama, Eugene. "The Behavior of Stock Market Price," *Journal of Business,* (January 1965).

Fama, E. F., L. Fisher, M. C. Jensen, and R. Roll. "The Adjustment of Stock Prices to New Information," *International Economic Review,* 10, (February 1969), 1–21.

Fielitz, B. D. "Stationarity of Random Data: Some Implications for the Distribution of Stock Price Changes," *Journal of Financial and Quantitative Analysis,* 6 (June 1971), 1025–1034.

Godfrey, M. D., C. W. J. Granger, and O. Morgenstern. "The Random Walk Hypothesis of Stock Market Behaviour," *Kyklos,* 17 (1964), 1–30.

Graham, R. W. *Cash-Future Price Relationships in Corn,* M. S. Thesis, University of Illinois, Urbana, 1954.

Granger, C. W. J. "What the Random Walk Model Does Not Say," *Financial Analysts Journal* (May–June 1970), 91–93.

Granger, C. W. J. "Some Aspects of the Random Walk Model of Stock Prices,'" *International Economic Review,* 9 (1968), 283–287.

Granger, C. W. J. and O. Morgenstern. "Spectral Analysis of New York Stock Market Prices," *Kyklos,* 16 (1963), 1–27.

Gray, Roger W. "The Characteristic Bias in Some Thin Futures Markets," *Food Research Institute Studies,* 1, No. 3 (November 1960).

Gray, Roger W. "Fundamental Price Behavior Characteristics in Commodity Futures," *Futures Trading Seminar,* Vol. 3, Madison, Wis., 1966.

Gray, Roger W. "The Relationship among Three Futures Markets," *Food Research Institute Studies,* 2, No. 1 (February 1961).

Gray, Roger W. "The Seasonal Pattern of Wheat Futures Under the Loan Program," *Food Research Institute Studies*, **3**, No. 1 (February 1962).

Gray, Roger W. and S. T. Nielsen. "Rediscovery of Some Fundamental Price Behavior Characteristics," paper presented at meeting of Econometric Society, Cleveland, Ohio, September, 1963.

Gray, Roger W., and W. G. Tomek. "Temporal Relationships Among Futures Prices: Reply," *American Journal of Agricultural Economics* (May 1971).

Gusler, G. "Price Discovery II. How Egg Futures Affect Prices," *Egg Producer*, **91**, No. 3 (March 1960), 8–9.

Heifner, R. G. "Temporal Relationships Among Futures Prices: Comment," *American Journal of Agricultural Economics* (May 1971).

Hendel, J., "Price Making in Organized Commodity Markets," Western Agricultural Economics Research Council, *Marketing Research Commission Report*, **5** (1963) 71–98.

Hoffman, G. W. *Future Trading and the Cash Grain Markets*, USDA Circular 201, 1932.

Hoffman, G. W. *Grain Prices and the Futures Markets*, USDA Technical Bulletin 747, January 1941.

Hoos, Sidney, and Holbrook Working. "Price Relations of Liverpool Wheat Futures with Special Reference to the December-March Spread," *Food Research Institute Wheat Studies*, **17** (1940), 101–143.

Houthakker, H. S. *Commodity Futures IV: An Empirical Test of the Theory of Normal Backwardation*, Cowles Commission Discussion Paper; Economics No. 2124, June 1955.

Houthakker, H. S. *Restatement of the Theory of Normal Backwardation*, Foundation Discussion Paper, Economics No. 44, December 1957.

Houthakker, Hendrik. "Systematic and Random Elements in Short-term Price Movements," *American Economic Review*, **51** (1961).

Irwin, H. S. "Seasonal Cycles in Aggregates of Wheat-Futures Contracts," *Journal of Political Economy*, **43** (1935), 34–49.

Irwin, H. S. *Seasonal Tendencies in Wheat Futures Prices*, Grain Futures Administration, Washington, D.C., 1938.

Jensen, Michael. "Comment," *Financial Analysts Journal* (November–December 1967), 77–85.

Jensen, Michael C., and George A. Benington. "Random Walks and Technical Theories: Some Additional Evidence," *Journal of Finance*, **25** (1970), 469–481.

Kassouf, S. T. "Stock Price Random Walks: Some Supporting Evidence," *Review of Economic Statistics* (May 1968).

Kendall, M. G. "The Analysis of Economic Times Series—Part I: Prices," *Journal of the Royal Statistical Society*, Series A (General), **116**, No. 1 (1953), 11–25.

Keynes, J. M. "Some Aspects of Commodity Markets," *Manchester Guardian Commercial*, European Reconstruction Series, Section 13, March 29, 1923, pp. 784–786.

Labys, Walter C. *Commodity Price Fluctuations: A Short Term Explanation for Selected Commodities on the American Market*, Ph.D. Dissertation, University of Nottingham, 1968.

Larson, A. B. *Evidence on the Temporal Dispersion of Price Effects of New Market Information*, Ph.D. Dissertation, Stanford University, 1960.

Larson, A. B. "Measurement of a Random Process in Futures Prices," *Food Research Institute Studies*, **1**, No. 3 (1960).

Larson, A. B. "The Quiddity of the Cobweb Theorem," *Food Research Institute Studies*, **7**, No. 2 (1967).

Levy, R. A. "Random Walks: Reality or Myth?" *Fianancial Analysts Journal*, (November–December, 1967), 69–77.

Malkiel, B. G., and J. G. Cragg. "Expectation and the Structure of Share Prices," *American Economic Review*, **60** (1970), 601–617.

Mandelbrot, Benoit. "The Variation of Certain Speculative Prices," *Journal of Business*, **36**, No. 4 (1963), 394–419.

Manderscheid, L. V. *Influence of Price Support Program on Seasonal Corn Prices*, Ph.D. Dissertation, Stanford University, 1961.

Margins, Speculation and Prices in Grains Futures Markets, Economic Research Service, USDA, December 1967.

McCain, Wesley G. *Price Effects of Margin Changes in Commodity Future Markets,* Ph.D. Dissertation, Stanford University, 1969.

Mehl, Paul. "Relationship Between Daily Price Range and Net Price Change, Opening to Close of the Dominant Corn Future and the Daily Volume of Trading in Corn Futures on the Chicago Board of Trade," U.S. Grain Futures Administration, Washington, D.C., 1938.

Mehl, Paul. "Trading in Futures and Price Fluctuations," *Journal of Farm Economics,* **16,** (1934), 481–495.

Mehl, Paul. "Trading in Wheat and Corn Futures in Relation to Price Movements," *Journal of Farm Economics,* **22** (1940), 601–612.

Moore, Arnold. *A Statistical Analysis of Common Stock Prices,* Ph.D Dissertation, Graduate School of Business, University of Chicago, 1962.

Muth, John F. "Rational Expectations and the Theory of Price Movements," *Econometrica,* **29** (July 1961), 315–335.

Osborne, M. F. M. "Brownian Motion in the Stock Market," *Operations Research,* **7,** No. 2 (March–April 1959), 145-173.

Osborne, M. F. M. "Some Quantitative Tests for Stock Price Generating Models and Trading Folklore," *Journal of the American Statistical Association* (June 1967), 321–340.

Parzen, E. *Time Series Analysis Papers,* Holden Day, San Francisco, 1968.

Peston, M. H., and B. S. Yamey. "Inter-temporal Price Relationships with Forward Markets: A Method of Analysis," *Economica,* n.s., **27** (1960), 355–367.

Pinches, George E., and William R. Kinney, Jr. "The Measurement of the Volatility of Common Stock Prices," *Journal of Finance,* **26** (1971), 119–125.

Praetz, P. D. "The Distribution of Share Price Changes," *Journal of Business,* **45** (January 1972), 49–55.

Roberts, Harry. "Stock Market 'Patterns' and Financial Analysis: Methodological Suggestions," *Journal of Finance* (March 1959), 4–5.

Rocca, L. H. *Time Series Analysis of Commodity Futures Prices,* Ph.D. Dissertation, University of California, Berkeley, 1969.

Samuelson, Paul A. "Intertemporal Price Equilibrium: A Prologue to the Theory of Speculation," *Welwirtschaftliches Archiv,* **79** (December 1957) 181–221.

Samuelson, Paul A. "Proof that Properly Anticipated Prices Fluctuate Randomly," *Industrial Management Review,* **6,** No. 2 (Spring 1965), 41–49.

Samuelson, Paul A. "A Random Theory of Futures Prices," *Industrial Management Review,* **6** (June 1965).

Sargent, T. J. "Commodity Price Expectations and the Interest Rate," *Quarterly Journal of Economics,* **83** (February 1969), 126–140.

Shelton, J. P. "The Value Line Contest: A Test of the Predictability of Stock Market Changes," *Journal of Business* (July 1967).

Smidt, Seymour. "A New Look at the Random Walk Hypothesis," *Journal of Financial and Quantitative Analysis,* **3,** No. 3 (1968), 235–261.

Smidt, Seymour. "A Test of the Serial Independence of Price Changes in Soybean Futures," *Food Research Institute Studies,* **5,** No. 2 (1965).

Snape, R. H. "Price Relationships on the Sydney Wool Futures Market," *Economica,* n.s., **35,** No. 138 (May 1968), 169–178.

Sobel, Eugene. "Approximate Best Linear Prediction of a Certain Class of Stationary and Non-Stationary Noise Distorted Signals," *Journal of the American Statistical Association,* **66,** No. 334 (June 1971), 363–370.

Stein, J. L. "The Simultaneous Determination of Spot and Futures Prices," *American Economic Review,"* 51, No. 5 (December 1961), 1012–1025.

Stevenson, Richard, and Robert M. Bear. "Commodity Futures: Trends or Random Walks?" *Journal of Finance,* **25,** No. 1 (March 1970), 65–81.

Taussig, F. W. "Is Market Price Determinate?" *Quarterly Journal of Economics*, 35 (May 1921), 394–411.

Telser, Lester G. "Price Relations between May and New Crop Wheat Futures at Chicago Since 1885," *Wheat Studies*, 10 (February 1934), 183–228.

Teweles, Richard J., and Charles V. Harlow. "An Inquiry into Non-Random Elements of the Commodity Futures Markets," *Journal of Commodity Trading*, 4, (July–August 1969).

Tomek, W. G. and Roger W. Gray. "Temporal Relationships Among Prices on Commodity Futures Markets: Their Allocative and Stabilizing Roles," *American Journal of Agricultural Economics*, 52. No. 3 (August 1970), 372–380.

Turnowsky, Stephen J. "Stochastic Stability of Short-Run Market Equilibrium," *Quarterly Journal of Economics*, 82, (November 1968), 666–681.

12 Years of Achievement under Public Law 480, Economic Research Service, USDA, 1967.

Vaile, R. S. "Inverse Carrying Charges in Futures Markets," *Journal of Farm Economics*, 30, No. 3 (August 1948), 574–575.

Vaile, Roland. "Cash and Futures Price of Corn," *Journal of Marketing*, 9 (July 1944).

Vance, Lawrence. "Grain Market Forces in the Light of Inverse Carrying Charges," *Journal of Farm Economics*, 28 (November 1946), 1036–1040.

Weiss, Moshe. *Quantitative Analysis of Egg Price Quotations*, Ph.D. Dissertation, Cornell University, 1969.

White, G. R., "Some Statistical Aspects of Future Trading on a Commodity Exchange," *Royal Statistical Society Journal*, n.s., 99 (1936), 297–329.

Working, Holbrook. "The Post Harvest Depression of Wheat Prices," *Food Research Institute Wheat Studies*, 5 (November 1929).

Working, Holbrook. "Frontiers in Uncertainty Theory: The Evidence of Futures Markets; New Concepts Concerning Futures Markets and Prices," *American Economic Review Papers and Proceedings*, 51, No. 2 (May 1961), 160–163.

Working, Holbrook. "Memorandum on Measurement of Cycles in Speculative Prices," *Food Research Institute Studies*, (1949).

Working, Holbrook, "New Concepts Concerning Futures Markets and Prices," *American Economic Review*, 52, No. 3 (June 1962), 431–459.

Working, Holbrook. "New Ideas and Methods for Price Research," *Journal of Farm Economics*, 38, No. 5 (December 1956), 1427–1436.

Working, Holbrook. "A Note on Mr. Meade's Theory of Competitive Speculation," *Review of Economic Studies*, 18 (1951), 188–189.

Working, Holbrook. "Note on the Correlation of First Differences of Averages in a Random Chain," *Econometrica*, 28 (1960), 916–918.

Working, Holbrook. "Price Relations Between May and New-Crop Wheat Futures at Chicago since 1885" *Food Research Institute Wheat Studies*, 10 (1934), 183–228.

Working, Holbrook. "Price Relations Between July and September Wheat Futures at Chicago Since 1885," *Food Research Institute Wheat Studies*, 9 (1933), 187–238.

Working, Holbrook. "Professor Vaile and the Theory of Inverse Carrying Charges," *Journal of Farm Economics*, 31, No. 1 (February 1949), 168–172.

Working, Holbrook. "A Random-Difference Series for Use in the Analysis of Time Series," *Journal of the American Statistical Association*, 29, No. 185 (March 1934), 11–24.

Working, Holbrook. "Theory of the Inverse Carrying Charge in Futures Markets," *Journal of Farm Economics*, 30, No. 1 (February 1948), 1–28.

VIII. PRICE FORECASTING

Ainsworth, R. M. *Profitable Grain Trading*, Ainsworth Financial Service, Mason City, Ill., 1933.

Ashby, Andrew W. "On Forecasting Commodity Prices by the Balance Sheet Approach," *Journal of Farm Economics*, 46 (August, 1964), 633–643.

Ashby, R. B. "Cotton Futures as Forecasters of Cotton Spot Prices," *Journal of the American Statistical Association*, 24, No. 168 (December 1929), 412–419.

Bates, J., and C. W. J. Granger. "Combining Forecasts," *Operations Research Quarterly,* **20** (1969), 451–467.

Belveal, L. D. *Commodity Speculation,* Commodities Press, Wilmette, Ill., 1967.

Belveal, Lee Dee. *Commodity Speculation: With Profits in Mind,* Commodities Press, Wilmette, Ill., 1968.

Benner, Samuel. *Benner's Prophecies of Ups and Downs In Prices,* privately printed, Cincinnati, Ohio, 1875.

Bernstein, L. A. "How Commodity Price Charts Disclose Supply-Demand Shifts," *Commodity Year Book,* Commodity Research Bureau, New York, 1958, pp. 33–42.

Bolton, Hamilton. *The Elliot Wave Principle—A Critical Appraisal,* Bolton, Tremblay and Co., Montreal, 1960.

Bostian, David. *Intra-Day Intensity Index,* privately printed, Fort Benjamin Harrison, Indiana, 1967.

Brown, Robert. *Smoothing, Forecasting and Prediction of Discrete Time Series,* Prentice-Hall, Englewood Cliffs, N.J., 1963.

Busby, William T. *A Model for Speculation in Pork Belly Futures,* Ph.D. Dissertation, University of Southern California, May 1971.

Christian, Roy E. *New Methods for Long Term Stock Market Forecasting,* Physicians Market Letter, Aptos, Calif., 1966.

Cohen, A. *The Chartcraft Method of Point and Figure Trading,* Chartcraft, Larchmont, N.Y., 1960.

Collins, Charles. "The Elliott Wave Principle—1966 Supplement," *The Bank Credit Analyst,* Quebec, Canada.

Collins, Charles. "Market Ebb Tide," *Barron's* (March 1970).

Cowles, Alfred W. "Can Stock Market Forecasters Forecast?" *Econometrica,* **1** (1933).

Cox, H. *A Common Sense Approach to Commodity Futures Trading,* Reynolds, New York, 1968.

Dahl, Curtiss. *Consistent Profits in the Commodity Futures Market,* Tri-state Offset Co., Cincinnati, Ohio, 1960.

Devillers, Victor. *The Point and Figure Method of Anticipating Stock Price Movements,* Tender Press, New York, 1972.

Dewey, Edward R. *Cycles, The Science of Prediction,* Holt, New York, 1949.

Dewey, Edward R. "The 5½ Year Cycle in Corn Prices," *Cycles Magazine* (February 1955).

Dewey, Edward R. "Kick in the Pants Cycles," *Cycles Magazine* (August 1961).

Dewey, Edward R. "Samuel Turner Benner," *Cycles Magazine* (March, 1955).

Dewey, Edward R., and O. G. Mandino. *Cycles: Mysterious Forces that Trigger Events,* Hawthorne, New York, 1971.

Dines, James. *How the Average Investor Can Use Technical Analysis for Stock Profits,* Dines Chart Corp., New York, 1972.

Donchian, R. D. "High Finance in Copper," *Financial Analysts Journal,* **16**, No. 6 (November-December 1960), 133–142.

Donchian, Richard. "Trend Following Methods in Commodity Price Analysis," *Guide to Commodity Price Forecasting,* Commodity Research Bureau, New York, 1965, pp. 48–60.

Drew, Garfield. "A Clarification of the Odd-Lot Theory," *Financial Analysts Journal,* (September–October 1967).

Dunnigan, William. *New Blueprints for Gains in Stocks and Grains,* privately published, San Francisco, Calif., 1956.

Edwards, Robert D., and John Magee. *Technical Analysis of Stock Trends,* John Magee, Springfield, Mass., 1961.

The Egg-spread Method, Market Research Associates, Pasadena, Calif., 1966.

Elliott, R. N. *Nature's Law—The Secret of the Universe,* privately published, New York, 1946.

Elliott, R. N. "The Wave Principle," *Financial World* (1939).

Farrell, M. J. "Profitable Speculation," *Economica,* n.s., **33**, No. 130 (May 1966), 183–193.

"The Fibonacci Numbers," *TIME* (April 1969).

Floss, Carl W. *Market Rhythm,* Investors Publishing, Detroit, 1955.

Gann, W. D., and J. L. Gann. *How to Make Profits Trading in Commodities; A Study of the Commodity Market, with Charts and Rules for Successful Trading and Investing,* W. D. Gann and Sons, New York, 1941; rev. ed., 1951.

Gardner, Robert L. *How to Make Money in the Commodity Market,* Prentice-Hall, Englewood Cliffs, N.J., 1961.

Gartley, H. M. *Profits in the Stock Market,* H. M. Gartley, New York, 1935.

Gotthelf, Edward B. *The Commodex System,* Commodity Futures Forecast, New York,

Granger, C. W. J., and O. Morgenstern. *Predictability of Stock Market Prices,* Heath, Lexington, Mass., 1970.

Granville, Joseph. *Granville's New Key to Stock Market Profits,* Prentice-Hall, Englewood Cliffs, N.J., 1963.

Hamilton, William Peter. *The Stock Market Barometer,* Harper, New York, 1922.

Harlow, Charles V. *An Analysis of the Predictive Value of Stock Market "Breadth' Measurements,* Investor's Intelligence, Larchmont, N.Y., 1968.

Hart, John K. *Commodity Trend Service,* Columbus, Ga.

Heiby, Walter. *Stock Market Profits Through Dynamic Synthesis,* Institute of Dynamic Synthesis, Chicago, Ill., 1965.

Hieronymus, T. A. *Economics of Futures Trading for Commercial and Personal Profit,* Commodity Research Bureau, New York, 1971.

Hieronymus, T. A. "Forecasting Soybean and Soybean Product Prices," in H. Jiler, (Ed.), *Guide to Commodity Price Forecasting,* Commodity Research Bureau, New York, 1965.

Hill, John R. *Technical and Mathematical Analysis of the Commodity and Stock Markets,* Commodity Research Institute, Chicago, Ill.

Hingorani, G. G. "Forecasting Economic Time Series Generated by Random Processes," *Proceedings of the Business and Economic Statistics Section of the Annual Meeting of the American Statistical Association,* 1966.

Houthakker, H. S. "Can Speculators Forecast Prices?" *Review of Economics and Statistics,* 39, No. 2 (May 1959), 143–151.

Irwin, H. S. "Technical Conditions are Important Factors in Short-Time Movements of Wheat Prices," *Journal of Farm Economics,* 18 (1936), 736–742.

Jarrett, F. G. "Short Term Forecasting of Australian Wool Prices," *Australian Economic Papers,* 4. (June–December 1965), 93–102.

Jevons, William Stanley. *The Periodicity of Commercial Crises and Physical Explanation,* University of Manchester, 1875.

Jevons, William Stanley. *The Solar Period and the Price of Corn,* University of Manchester, 1875.

Jiler, William (Ed.) *Guide to Commodity Price Forecasting,* Commodity Research Bureau, New York, 1965.

Jiler, William. *How Charts Can Help You in the Stock Market,* Commodity Research Publishing Corporation, New York, 1961.

Kaish, Stanley. "Odd Lot Profit and Loss Performance," *Financial Analysts Journal* (September–October 1969).

Keltner, Chester. *How to Make Money in Commodities,* Keltner Statistical Service, Kansas City, Mo., 1960.

Kewley, Thomas J., and R. A. Stevenson. "The Odd Lot Theory—A Reply," *Financial Analysts Journal,* (January–February 1969).

Labys, W. C., and C. W. J. Granger. *Speculation, Hedging and Commodity Price Forecasts,* Heath, Lexington, Mass., 1970.

Larson, Arnold B. "Price Prediction on the Egg Futures Market," *Proceedings of a Symposium on Price Effects of Speculation in Organized Commodity Markets,* Food Research Institute Studies, 7 (1967), 49–64.

Leslie, Conrad. *Guide for Successful Speculation,* Darnell Press, Chicago, 1970.

Levine, Irving. *Successful Commodity Speculation,* Levro Press, Newark, N.J., 1965.

Levy, Robert A. *The Relative Strength Concept of Common Stock Price Forecasting,* Investor's Intelligence, Larchmont, N.Y., 1967.

Lindsay, George. "A Timing Method for Traders," *The Encyclopedia of Stock Market Techniques,* Investor's Intelligence, 1965.

Lowell, Fred R. *Profits in Soybeans,* Keltner Statistical Service, Kansas City, Mo., 1966.

Mandelbrot, B. "Forecasts of Future Prices, Unbiased Markets and Martingale Models," *Journal of Business,* **39,** Part 2 (January 1966), 242–255.

Markstein, David L. *How to Chart Your Way to Stock Market Profits,* Parker Publishing, West Nyack, N.Y., 1966.

Martel. R. F. *Charting Supply and Demand for Stock Analysis,* Martel., Reading, Pa., 1961.

Neill, Humphrey. *Tape Reading and Market Tactics.* Fraser, Burlington, Vt., 1960.

O'Connor, William. *Stocks, Wheat and Pharoahs,* Werner Books, New York, 1961.

Relative Volume Index, Trend Way Advisory Service, Louisville, Ky.

Rhea, Robert. *The Dow Theory,* Vail-Ballou, Binghamton, N.Y., 1932.

Rockwell, C. S. *Profits, Normal Backwardation, and Forecasting in Commodity Futures,* Ph.D. Dissertation, University of California, Berkeley, 1964.

Runner, Tim Jon. "Pit-falls of Computer Simulations," *Commodity Journal,* **6,** No. 4 (July–August 1971).

Schabacker, Richard W. *Stock Market Profits,* Fraser, Burlington, Vt., 1967.

Schabacker, Richard W. *Technical Analysis and Stock Market Profits,* B. C. Forbes Publishing Company, New York, 1934.

Scheinman, William X. *Why Most Investors are Mostly Wrong Most of the Time,* Lancer, New York, 1970.

Schultz, John. *The Intelligent Chartist,* WRSM Financial Service, New York, 1962.

Seligman, Daniel. "The Mystique of Point and Figure," *Fortune,* March 1962.

Stoken, D. "Forecasting Pork Belly Futures," *Commodity Year Book,* Commodity Research Bureau, New York, 1966.

Shishko, Irwin, "Forecasting Sugar Prices," in H. Jiler, (Ed.), *Guide to Commodity Price Forecasting,* Commodity Research Bureau, New York, 1965.

Shishko, Irwin. "How to Forecast Cocoa Prices," in H. Jiler, (Ed.), *Guide to Commodity Price Forecasting,* Commodity Research Bureau, New York, 1965.

Shishko, Irwin. "Techniques of Forecasting Commodity Prices," *Commodity Year Book,* Commodity Research Bureau, New York, 1965, pp. 30–36.

Taylor, Robert Joel. "The Major Price Trend Directional Indicator," *Commodities Magazine* (April 1972).

Tomkins, Edwin H. *Systematic Stock Trading,* The Moore Guide, Riverside, Ill., 1969.

Unacek, Edward, Jr. *An Econometric Analysis and Forecasting Model for Pork Bellies.* Ph.D. Dissertation, Texas A. and M., 1967.

Van Horne, James, and G. Parker. "Technical Trading Rules: A Comment," *Financial Analysts Journal* (July–August 1968), 128–132.

Walters, James, and Larry Williams. "Measuring Market Momentum," *Commodities Magazine* (October 1972).

Weymar, F. H., "Cocoa, the Effects of Inventories on Price Forecasting," *Commodity Year Book,* Commodity Research Bureau, New York, 1969.

Wheelan, Alexander. "Point and Figure Procedure in Commodity Market Analysis," *Guide to Commodity Price Forecasting,* Commodity Research Bureau, New York, 1965.

Wheelan, Alexander. *Study Helps in Point and Figure Technique,* Morgan, Rogers and Roberts, New York, 1962.

Williams, Larry. *Accumulation—Distribution Studies,* Williams Reports, Carmel, Calif.

Williams, Larry. *The Secret of Selective Stocks for Immediate and Substantial Gains,* Conceptual Management, Carmel, Calif., 1973.

Working, Holbrook. "Quotations on Commodity Futures as Price Forecasts," *Econometrica,* **10** (1942), 39–52.

Working, Holbrook. "A Theory of Anticipatory Prices," *American Economic Review,* **48**, No. 2 (May 1958), 188–199.

Wyckoff, Richard. *Studies in Tape Reading,* Traders Press, New York, 1972.

IX. MONEY MANAGEMENT AND RISK CONTROL

Barger, Harold. "Speculation and the Risk-Preference," *Journal of Political Economy,* **46** (1938), 396–408.

Barnes, Robert M. "A Statistical Method for Setting Stops in Stock Trading," *Operation Research,* 18 (July 1970), 665–688.

Blume, Marshall E. "On the Assessment of Risk," *Journal of Finance,* **26** (1971), 1–10.

Briloff, A. J. "Income Tax Aspects of Commodity Futures Transactions," in H. Jiler, ed., *Guide to Commodity Price Forecasting,* Commodity Research Bureau, New York, 1965.

Dalrymple, Brent B. *Risk Analysis Applied to Commodity Speculation,* Ph.D. Dissertation, Louisiana State University, 1970.

Epstein, R. A. *The Theory of Gambling and Statistical Logic,* Academic, New York, 1969.

Feller, W. *An Introduction to Probability Theory and Its Applications,* Vol. 2, Wiley, New York, 1966.

Goldberg, Samuel. *Probability: An Introduction,* Prentice-Hall, Englewood Cliffs, N.J., 1960.

Goldfein, Lawrence, and Lester Houchberg. "Use of Commodity Straddles Can Effect Impressive Tax Savings," *The Journal of Taxation,* **29**, No. 6 (December 1968).

Hadley, G. *Introduction to Business Statistics,* Holden-Day, San Francisco, Calif., 1968.

Hardy, C. O. *Risk and Risk Bearing,* University of Chicago Press, Chicago, 1923.

Helmuth, J. W. *Futures Trading Under Conditions of Uncertainty,* Ph.D. Dissertation, University of Missouri, Columbia, 1970.

Hieronymus, T. A. *Principles of Inventory and Risk Management,* University of Illinois Agricultural Extension Service AE 2831, 1951.

Irwin, H. S. "The Nature of Risk Assumption in the Trading of Organized Exchanges" *American Economic Review,* **27** (1937), 267–278.

Knight, Frank H. *Risk, Uncertainty and Profit,* Houghton Mifflin, Boston, 1921 (reprinted 1957).

Markowitz, H. M. *Portfolio Selections: Efficient Diversification of Investments,* Wiley, New York, 1959.

Rinfret, P. A. "Investment Managers are Worth Their Keep," *Financial Analysts Journal* (March–April 1968).

Sandor, Richard L., and James E. Rhodes. "The Development of a Trading Strategy," *Commodities Magazine,* (July 1972), 22–28.

Schwartz, Marvin. "Scientific Money Management," *Commodity Journal,* **6**, No. 3 (May–June, 1971).

Shackle, G. L. S. "An Analysis of Speculative Choice," *Economica,* n.s., **12** (1945), 10–21.

Sowders, A. G., Jr. "The Commodity Markets and Taxes," *Arthur Young Journal* (July 1960).

Standard Federal Tax Reporter, Code Volume, Commerce Clearing House, New York, 1969.

Thorpe, Edward O. *Beat the Dealer,* Random House, New York, 1962.

Von Neumann, John, and Oskar Morgenstern. *The Theory of Games and Economic Behavior,* Princeton University Press, Princeton, N.J., 1947.

Wilson, Allen N. *The Casino Gambler's Guide,* Harper and Row, New York, 1970.

Zweig, M. E. *An Analysis of Risk and Return on Put and Call Option Strategies,* Ph.D. Dissertation, Michigan State University, 1969.

X. HEDGING

Arthur, Henry B. "Inventory Profits in the Business Cycle," *American Economic Review,* **28**, No. 1 (March 1938).

Arthur, Henry B. "The Nature of Commodity Futures as an Economic and Business Instrument," *Food Research Institute Studies,* **9**, No. 3 (1972).

Brennan, M. J. "A Model of Seasonal Inventories," *Econometrica*, 27 (April 1959), 228–244.

Brennan, M. J. "The Supply of Storage," *American Economic Review*, 48, No. 1 (March 1958), 50–72.

Cootner, P. H. "Speculation and Hedging," *Food Research Institute Studies*, Supplement, 7 (1967), 65–106.

English, E. D. "The Use of Commodity Exchanges by Millers," *Proceedings of Fifth Annual Symposium, Chicago Board of Trade* (September 11–12, 1952).

Farmer Use of Futures Markets, Illinois Agricultural Experiment Station AE 3760, 1962.

Graf, T. F. "Hedging—How Effective Is It?" *Journal of Farm Economics*, 35, No. 3 (August 1953), 398–413.

Gray, R. W. "The Importance of Hedging in Futures Trading; and the Effectiveness of Futures Trading for Hedging," *Futures Trading Seminar*, Madison, Wis., Vol. 1, 1960.

Gruen, F. H. "The Pros and Cons of Futures Trading for Woolgrowers," *Review of Marketing and Agricultural Economics*, 28, No. 3 (September 1960), 1–12.

Hardy, C. O., and L. S. Lyon. "The Theory of Hedging," *Journal of Political Economy*, 31, No. 2 (April, 1923), 276–287.

The Hedger's Handbook: A Businessman's Guide to the Commodity Futures Market, a booklet published by Merrill Lynch, Pierce, Fenner and Smith, New York, 1970.

Heifner, R. G. "The Gains from Basing Grain Storage Decisions on Cash-Future Spreads," *Journal of Farm Economics*, 48, No. 5, (December 1966), 1490–1495.

Heironymus, T. A. "Four Ways to Make a Profit on Futures," *Better Farming Methods*, 35, No. 1 (January 1963), 22–25.

Hieronymus, T. A. *Hedging for Country Elevators*, Agricultural Economics Research Report 91, University of Illinois, March 1968.

Hieronymus, T. A. "How You Can Use the Futures Market," *Successful Farming*, 60, No. 4 (April 1972), 51, 70–71.

Hieronymus, T. A. *Making Use of Basis Changes to Earn Income*, University of Illinois Department of Agricultural Economics AE 3537, Urbana, 1959.

Hieronymus, T. A. *Uses of Grain Futures Markets in the Farm Business*, University of Illinois Agricultural Experiment Station Bulletin 696, 1963.

Hieronymus, T. A., F. S. Scott and W. J. Wills. "Hedging Cattle Feeding Operations," *Illinois Farm Economics*, No. 200 (January, 1952), 1272–1276.

Hobson, Karl. *Wheat Prices in 1964—How to Forecast Them, How to Insure Them*, Washington State University, Agricultural Extension Service E.M. 2332, 1963.

Hoffmann, G. W. *Hedging by Dealing in Grain Futures*, Ph.D. Dissertation, University of Pennsylvania, Philadelphia, 1925.

Howell, L. D. *Analysis of Hedging and Other Operations in Grain Futures*, USDA Technical Bulletin 971, August 1948.

Howell, L. D. *Analysis of Hedging and Other Operations in Wool and Wool Top Futures*, USDA Technical Bulletin 1260, January 1962.

Howell, L. D. *Influence of Certificated Stocks on Spot-Futures Price Relationships for Cotton*, USDA Technical Bulletin 1119, 1955.

Howell, L. D., and L. J. Watson. *Relation of Spot Cotton Prices to Futures Contracts and Protection Afforded by Trading in Futures*, USDA Technical Bulletin 602, January 1938.

Huebner, S. S. "The Insurance Service of Commodity Exchanges," in *Annals of the American Academy of Political and Social Science*, 155, Part 1 (May 1931), 1–6.

Irwin, H. S. *Speculation versus Hedging in Country Elevator Operation*, Commodity Exchange Administration, Washington, D.C., 1938.

Johnson, L. L. "Price Instability, Hedging, and Trade Volume in the Coffee Market," *Journal of Political Economy*, 45 (1957), 306–321.

Johnson, L. L. "The Theory of Hedging and Speculation in Commodity Futures," *Review of Economic Studies*, 27 (3), No. 74 (June, 1960), 139–151.

Johnson, Leland L. *Hedging, Speculation and Futures Trading in the Coffee Market Since World War II*, Ph.D. Dissertation, Yale University, 1957.

McKinnon, R. I. "Futures Markets, Buffer Stocks and Income Stability for Primary Producers," *Journal of Political Economy*, 75, No. 6 (December 1967). 844–861.

Paul, Allen B. "The Pricing of Binspace—A Contribution to the Theory of Storage," *American Journal of Agricultural Economics*, 52, No. 1 (February 1970), 1.

Rutledge, David J. S. "Hedgers' Demand for Futures Contracts: A Theoretical Framework with Applications to the United States Soybean Complex," *Food Research Institute Studies*, 10, No. 3 (1972).

Rutledge, D. J. S. *The Relationship between Prices and Hedging Patterns in the United States Soybean Complex*, Ph.D. Dissertation, Stanford University, 1970.

Schrock, Nicholas W. *A Portfolio Analysis of Straddle Operations in the Futures Markets*, Thesis, University of Oregon, 1967.

Schultz, Theodore W. "Spot and Futures Prices as Production Guides," *American Economic Review*, 39 (May 1949).

Snape, R. H., and B. S. Yamey. "Test of the Effectiveness of Hedging," *Journal of Political Economy*, 73, No. 5 (October 1965), 540–544.

Stevens, W. H. S. "The Relation of the Cash-Future Spread to Hedging Transactions," *Journal of Business*, 2, No. 1 (January 1929), 28–49.

Telser, L. G. "Safety First and Hedging," *Review of Economic Studies*, 23 (1), No. 60 (1955–1956), 1–16.

Working, Holbrook. "Futures Trading and Hedging," *American Economic Review*, 43, No. 3 (June 1953), 314–343.

Working, Holbrook. "Hedging Reconsidered," *Journal of Farm Economics*, 35, No. 4 (November 1953), 544–561.

Working, Holbrook. "Price Support and the Effectiveness of Hedging," *Journal of Farm Economics*, 35 (1953), 811–818.

Working, Holbrook. "Speculation on Hedging Markets," *Food Research Institute Studies*, 1, No. 2 (1960).

Yamey, B. S. "Addendum" to "An Investigation of Hedging on an Organized Produce Exchange," in P. T. Bauer and B. S. Yamey, *Markets, Market Control and Marketing Reform*, Weidenfeld and Nicolson, London, 1969.

Yamey, B. S. "An Investigation of Hedging on an Organized Produce Exchange," *The Manchester School of Economics and Social Studies*, 19 (September 1951), 305–319.

XI. PRICES AND RELATED STATISTICAL DATA

Boyle, J. E. *Chicago Wheat Prices for Eighty-One Years*, unpublished manuscript, 1922.

Chicago Board of Trade Annual Report, 1858 to date.

Chicago Board of Trade Year Book, Chicago Board of Trade, 141 West Jackson Boulevard, Chicago, Ill.

Chicago Mercantile Exchange Year Book, Chicago Mercantile Exchange, 444 West Jackson Boulevard, Chicago, Ill. 1923 to date.

Commodity Year Book, Commodity Research Bureau, New York (annual), 1929 to date.

Hoffman, G. W., and J. W. T. Duvel, *Grain Prices and the Futures Market: A 15 Year Survey*, USDA Technical Bulletin 747, January 1941.

New York Mercantile Exchange Year Book, New York Mercantile Exchange, New York.

Thomsen, F. L., and R. J. Foote. *Agricultural Prices*, McGraw-Hill, New York, 1952.

USDA, Commodity Exchange Authority. *Commodity Futures Statistics*, Washington, D.C., annual from 1947.

USDA, Commodity Exchange Authority. *Grain Futures Statistics 1921–1951*, Statistical Bulletin No. 131, Washington, D.C., 1952.

USDA, Consumer and Marketing Service. *Cotton Price Statistics*, Washington, D.C.

USDA, Consumer and Marketing Service. *Grain and Feed Statistics,* Washington, D.C.

USDA, Economic Research Service. *Statistics on Cotton and Related Data, 1925–62,* Statistical Bulletin No. 329, Washington, D.C., 1963.

Working, Holbrook. "Prices of Cash Wheat and Futures at Chicago since 1883," *Food Research Institute Wheat Studies,* 10 (November 1934), 103–117.

Working, Holbrook, and Sidney Hoos. "Wheat Futures Prices and Trading at Liverpool since 1886," *Food Research Institute Wheat Studies,* 15 (November 1938).

Index

Index

51310